A FIRST DICTIONARY OF
LINGUISTICS AND PHONETICS

THE LANGUAGE LIBRARY

EDITED BY DAVID CRYSTAL

A FIRST DICTIONARY OF
LINGUISTICS AND PHONETICS

꧁꧁꧁꧁꧁

David Crystal

WESTVIEW PRESS
BOULDER, COLORADO

Published in 1980 in the United States of America by
Westview Press
5500 Central Avenue
Boulder, Colorado 80301

Frederick A. Praeger, Publisher

hardcover ISBN 0-86531-051-3
paperback ISBN 0-86531-050-5
Library of Congress Catalog Card Number 80-51338

First published 1980 by
André Deutsch Limited
105 Great Russell Street London WC1

Printed in Great Britain at the
University Press, Cambridge

PREFACE

🝔🝔🝔🝔🝔

When I took the first survey of my undertaking, I found our speech copious without order, and energetick without rules: wherever I turned my view, there was perplexity to be disentangled, and confusion to be regulated; choice was to be made out of boundless variety, without any established principle of selection; adulterations were to be detected, without a settled test of purity; and modes of expression to be rejected or received, without the suffrages of any writers of classical reputation or acknowledged authority.

SAMUEL JOHNSON
Preface to *A Dictionary of the English Language*

One sign of immaturity [in a science] is the endless flow of terminology. The critical reader begins to wonder if some strange naming taboo attaches to the terms that a linguist uses, whereby when he dies they must be buried with him. DWIGHT BOLINGER

Aspects of Language, p. 554

What is needed, of course, is a comprehensive lexicographical survey, on historical principles, of twentieth-century terminology in linguistics and phonetics. One could use the techniques, well-established, which have provided dictionaries of excellence, such as the O.E.D. and Webster's. The painstaking scrutiny of texts from a range of contexts, the recording of new words and senses on slips, and the systematic correlation of these as a preliminary to representing patterns of usage: such steps are routine for major surveys of general vocabulary, and could as readily be applied for a specialised vocabulary, such as the present undertaking. Needless to say, it would be a massive task – and one which, for linguistics and phonetics, has frequently been initiated, but never completed. I am aware of several attempts to work along these lines, in Canada, Great Britain, Japan and the United States, sometimes by individuals, sometimes by committees. All seem to have foundered, presumably for a mixture of organisational and financial reasons. I tried to initiate such a project myself, twice, but these both failed, for the same reasons. The need for a proper linguistics dictionary is thus as urgent now as it ever was; but to be fulfilled, it requires a combination of academic expertise, time, physical resources and finance which so far have proved impossible to attain.

But how to cope, in the meantime, with the apparently 'endless flow of terminology' which Bolinger, amongst many others, laments? And how to deal with the enquiries from the *two* kinds of consumer of linguistic and phonetic terms? For this surely is the peculiar difficulty which linguists nowadays have to face – that their subject, despite its immaturity, carries immense popular as well as academic appeal. Not only, therefore, is terminology a problem for the academic linguist and phonetician; these days, such people are far outnumbered by those who, for private or professional reasons, have developed more than an incidental interest in the subject. It is of little use intimating that the interest of the outside world is premature, as has sometimes been suggested. The interest exists, in a genuine, responsible and critical form, and requires a comparably responsible academic reaction. The present dictionary is, in the first instance, an attempt to meet the popular demand for information about linguistic terms, pending the fuller, academic evaluation of the subject's terminology, which one day may come.

The demand has come mainly from those for whom a conscious awareness of language is an integral part of the exercise of a profession, and upon whom the influence of linguistics has been making itself increasingly felt in recent years. This characterisation includes two main groups: the range of teaching and remedial language professions, such as foreign language teaching and speech therapy; and the range of academic fields which study language as part of their concerns, such as psychology, sociology, literary criticism and philosophy. It also includes an increasing number of students of linguistics – especially those who are taking introductory courses in the subject at postgraduate or in-service levels. In addition, there are the many categories of first-year undergraduate students of linguistics and phonetics. My aim, accordingly, was to provide a tool which would assist these groups in their initial coming to grips with linguistic terminology, and it is this which has motivated my title: a *first* dictionary...

COVERAGE

Once a decision about readership had been made, the problem of selecting items and senses for inclusion simplified considerably. It is not the case that the whole of linguistic terminology, and all schools of thought, have proved equally attractive or useful to the above groups. Some terms have been used (and abused) far more than others. For example, COMPETENCE, LEXIS, GENERATE, STRUCTURALISM, MORPHOLOGY and PROSODY are a handful which turn up so often in these students' early experience of the subject that their exclusion would have been unthinkable. On the other hand, *anthropophonics*, *allolog*, *bahuvrihi*, *hyperplexon* and *paraphonology* are unlikely to cause any problems for my intended readership, as they will not encounter them in their initial contact with linguistic ideas. Likewise, some linguistic theories and descriptions have achieved far more popularity than others – generative grammar, most obviously, and (in Great Britain) Hallidayan linguistics and the Quirk reference grammar, for example (cf. references, p. 390). The terminology of phonetics, also, is so pervasive that it is a priority for special attention. On the other hand, despite their considerable relevance to the formation of ideas in linguistic theory, the detailed terminology of, say, glossematics, or stratificational grammar, has not made so direct an impact on the general consciousness of the above groups. While I have included several of the more important theoretical terms from these less widely-used approaches, therefore, I have not presented their terminology in any detail. Similarly, theoretical terminology which has developed since the mid-1970s will not be found. The biases of this dictionary, I hope, will be seen to be those already present in the applied and introductory literature – with a certain amount of systematisation and filling-out in places, to avoid gaps in the presentation of a topic (for example, whereas many introductory texts selectively illustrate DISTINCTIVE FEATURES, this topic has been systematically covered in the present book).

Bearing in mind the background of the above groups helped to simplify the selection of material for inclusion in a second main way: only terms or senses which have arisen because of the influence of twentieth-century linguistics and phonetics have been included. This dictionary is therefore in contrast with several which have appeared in recent years, where the aim seems to have been to cover the whole field of language, languages and communication, as well as linguistics and phonetics. My attitude here is readily summarised: one does not need to include such terms as *alphabet*, *abbreviation* and *acronym*, because these are terms whose general sense any good dictionary would handle routinely; *as terms*, they owe nothing to the development of ideas in linguistics. Similarly, while such terms as *reinforcement*, *rhyme-scheme* and *runic* are more obviously technical, their special ranges of application derive from conceptual frameworks other than linguistics. None of these terms therefore has any place in the present dictionary. Likewise, proper names of languages and language families (such as *Chinese*, *Indo-European*) and any associated fields of study (e.g. *Chinese linguistics*) have been excluded. On the other hand, I devote a great deal of space to the many 'harmless looking' terms which are used by linguists, where an apparently everyday word has developed a special sense, often after many years of linguistic debate, e.g. FORM, FUNCTION, FEATURE, ACCENT, WORD, SENTENCE. These are terms which, perhaps on account of their less technical appearance, cause especial difficulty at an introductory level. Particular attention is paid to them in this dictionary, therefore, alongside the more obvious technical terms, such as PHONEME, BILABIAL, ADJUNCTION, MORPHO-PHONEMIC and HYPONYMY.

Several other constraints on coverage have been introduced, to preserve the dictionary's coherence. In particular, four categories of terminology have been excluded:

(a) The technical terms of traditional language studies (i.e. pre-twentieth century), unless they have been the focus of attention in linguistics and phonetics. For example, classical rhetorical terms are not included, such as *anaptyxis, prosiopesis* and *alliteration*. Similarly, most of the *detailed* terms of traditional grammatical description have been excluded as separate entries (though many of them are referred to as part of some larger entry), e.g. *masculine, feminine, neuter* (but cf. GENDER), *definite, indefinite* (but cf. ARTICLE).

(b) The technical terms that properly belong to other disciplines, unless linguistics or phonetics have introduced a special sense, or a fresh dimension to their use. Acoustic phonetics, for example, uses many terms from physics (*spectrum, amplitude*, etc.), but as no special sense is involved, these terms have been excluded. A similar principle applied in relation to the terms of information theory (e.g. *noise*), audiology (e.g. *audiogram*), and the detailed terminology belonging to logical and philosophical analysis of language. On the other hand, the formalisation of linguistic ideas initiated by Chomsky has introduced several terms from philosophy, logic and mathematics which have become fundamental to thinking in grammar and semantics (AXIOM, ALGORITHM, PROPOSITION, CALCULUS, etc.), and thus the more important of these have been included.

(c) Terms which relate primarily to the various fields of applied language studies, such as foreign language teaching (e.g. *transfer*) and language pathology (e.g. *aphasia*).

(d) The classical terminology of comparative philology (e.g. *umlaut, ablaut*).

There are no proper names in the dictionary, save in a few cases where major schools of thought have developed, e.g. CHOMSKYAN, BLOOM-FIELDIAN, PRAGUE SCHOOL.

On this basis, the dictionary will be seen to contain just over 1000 entries (boldface headwords). Within an entry, technical phrases involving the headword may also appear, and these account for a further 1000 boldface items.

I remain doubtful even now whether the most appropriate title for this book is 'dictionary'. The definitional parts of the entries, by themselves, were less illuminating than one might have expected; and consequently it proved necessary to introduce in addition a more discursive approach, with several illustrations, to capture the significance of a term. Most entries accordingly contain encyclopedic information, about such matters as the historical context in which a term was used, or the relationship between a term and others from associated fields. At times, due to the absence of authoritative studies of terminological development in linguistics, I have had to introduce a personal interpretation in discussing a term; but I hope this has been balanced by the further context provided through bibliographical references at the end of every entry – a chapter from one of a small number of basic text-books (listed on p. 390). I have used several well-established introductory texts, as well as a few more advanced ones. These references do not usually constitute the original sources of terms, but act as a convenient locus where one may obtain further information about the framework of ideas from which the terms derive their significance. That is why the references are to chapters and not to pages.

Each entry is self-contained: that is, there are no obligatory cross-references to other entries to complete the exposition of a sense. Nor have I made use of the convention 'See Y' after looking up a term. Given the interdependence of so much terminology (COMPETENCE–PERFORM-ANCE, DEEP STRUCTURE–SURFACE STRUCTURE, etc.), to put all the information under one of these terms, with a mere 'See...' under the other, involves an arbitrariness of organisation that can cause a reader much frustration. I have preferred to work on the principle that, as most dictionary-users open a dictionary with a *single* problematic term in mind, they should be given a satisfactory account of that term as immediately as possible. I therefore explain *competence* under COMPETENCE, *performance* under PERFORMANCE, and so on. As a consequence of the interdependence of these terms, however, this procedure means that there must be some repetition: at least the salient characteristics of the term *performance* must be incorporated into the entry for COMPETENCE, and vice versa. This repetition would be a weakness, if the book were read from cover to cover; but a dictionary should not be used as a text-book, and while the result has been a somewhat longer volume than would have been the case if the 'See...' convention had been used, I remain convinced of the greater benefits of look-up convenience and entry coherence.

Preface

Within an entry, the main terms being defined are printed in boldface (along with their main inflectional variants). Any other terms and phrases, less central to the exposition of the headword, are printed in quotation marks. Terms defined elsewhere in this dictionary are printed in small capitals – but only on their *first* appearance within an entry, and only where their technical status is important for an appreciation of the sense of the entry.

ACKNOWLEDGEMENTS

I have been fortunate in having several colleagues in my department who have given generously of their time to read the text of this dictionary, in whole or in part, advised me on how to proceed in relation to several of the above problems, and pointed out places where my own biases were intruding too markedly. I have benefited enormously from their comments, and I wish only that there had been more time to go into the large number of points of interpretation which emerged in the process. Such discussions have confirmed me in my view that there is an urgent need for the job to be done properly. In the meantime, I thank them all for their perseverance, and apologise if I have not done their comments justice in my revisions. I would dearly like to have had all my errors eliminated in this way: the responsibility for those that may be left is mine, and I would welcome comments from readers about weaknesses which might be taken account of in any future edition. I am most grateful, accordingly, to Ron Brasington, Paul Fletcher, Michael Garman, Arthur Hughes, Frank Palmer and Irene Warburton, for all their help. And to my wife, lastly, who typed the entire manuscript (much of it, more than once), and who still claims she enjoyed it: her support and encouragement have been crucial.

David Crystal
Reading, December 1978

A

🙾🙾🙾🙾🙾🙾

ablative In languages which express GRAMMATICAL relationships by means of INFLECTIONS, this term refers to the FORM taken by a WORD, usually a NOUN or PRONOUN, typically used in the expression of a range of LOCATIVE or INSTRUMENTAL meanings. English does not have an 'ablative CASE', as did Latin, but uses other means (the PREPOSITIONS *with*, *from* and *by* in particular) to express these notions, e.g. *He did it **with** his hands*. See Lyons 1968: Ch. 7.

abrupt A term sometimes used in the DISTINCTIVE FEATURE theory of PHONOLOGY, as part of the phrase **abrupt release**; it refers to a sound released suddenly, without the acoustic turbulence of a FRICATIVE, as in PLOSIVE CONSONANTS. Its opposite is DELAYED release, used to characterise AFFRICATES. See Hyman 1975: Ch. 2.

accent (1) The cumulative auditory effect of those features of a person's pronunciation which identify where he is from, regionally or socially. The LINGUISTICS literature emphasises that the term refers to pronunciation only, and is thus distinct from DIALECT, which refers to GRAMMAR and VOCABULARY as well. **Regional accents** can relate to any locale, including both rural and urban communities within a country (e.g. 'West Country', 'Liverpool') as well as national groups speaking the same language (e.g. 'American', 'Australian'), and our impression of other languages ('foreign accent', 'Slavic accent'). **Social accents** relate to the cultural and educational background of the speaker. Countries with a well-defined traditional social class system, such as India and Japan, reflect these divisions in language, and accent is often a marker of class. In Britain, the best example is the regionally neutral accent associated with a public school education, and of the related professional domains, such as the Civil Service, the law courts, the Court and the BBC – hence the labels 'Queen's English', 'BBC English', and the like. RECEIVED PRONUNCIATION (RP) is the name given to this accent, and because of its regional neutrality, RP speakers are sometimes thought of as having 'no accent'. This is a misleading way of putting it, however: linguistics stresses that everyone must have an accent, though it may not indicate regional origin. The popular label 'broad' accent refers to those accents that are markedly different from RP. See Trudgill 1974: Ch. 1.

(2) (**-ed, -ual, -uation**) The emphasis which makes a particular WORD or SYLLABLE stand out in a stream of speech – one talks especially of an **accented** sound/word/syllable, or the 'accent(ual) pattern' of a PHRASE/SENTENCE. The term is usually found in a discussion of metre (METRICS), where it refers to the 'beats' in a line of poetry – the accented syllables, as opposed to the **unaccented** ones. But any style of spoken language could be described with reference to the relative weight (**accentuation**) of its syllables: one might talk of the 'strongly accented' speech of a politician, for instance.

Technically, accent is not solely a matter of LOUDNESS, but also of PITCH and DURATION, especially pitch: comparing the VERB *record* (as in *I'm going to record the tune*) and the NOUN (*I've got a record*), the contrast in **word accent** between *record* and *record* is made by the syllables differing in loudness, length and pitch movement. A similar use of these variables is found in the notion of **sentence accent** (also called 'contrastive accent'). This is an important aspect of linguistic analysis, especially of INTONATION, because it can affect the ACCEPTABILITY, the MEANING, or the PRESUPPOSITIONS of a sentence, e.g. *he was wearing a red **hat*** could be heard as a response to *was he wearing a red coat?*, whereas *he was wearing a **red** hat* would respond to *was he wearing a green hat?* The term STRESS, however, is often used for contrasts of this kind (as in the phrases 'word stress' and 'contrastive stress').

The total SYSTEM of accents in a language is sometimes called the **accentual system**, and would be part of the study of PHONOLOGY. The coinage 'accentology' for the study of accents is not usually found in linguistics. See Bolinger 1975: Ch. 3; Gimson 1970: Ch. 9.

acceptability (acceptable) The extent to which linguistic DATA would be judged by NATIVE-SPEAKERS to be possible in their language. An 'acceptable UTTERANCE' is one whose use would be considered permissible or normal. In practice, deciding on the acceptability of an utterance may be full of difficulties. Native-speakers often disagree as to whether an utterance is normal, or even possible. One reason for this is that INTUITIONS differ because of variations in regional and social backgrounds, age, personal preferences, and so on. An utterance may be normal in one DIALECT, but unacceptable in another, e.g. *I ain't, I be, I am*. Much also depends on the extent to which people have been brought up to believe that certain forms of LANGUAGE are 'correct' and others are 'wrong': many do not accept as desirable those sentences which the PRESCRIPTIVE approach to GRAMMAR would criticise, such as *I will go tomorrow* (for *I shall go...*), or *this is the man I spoke to* (for *...to whom I spoke*). To a LINGUIST, all such utterances are acceptable, insofar as a section of the community uses them consistently in speech or writing. The analytic problem is to determine which sections of the community use which utterances on which occasions. Within a DIALECT, an utterance may be acceptable in one CONTEXT, but unacceptable in another, cf. the contrast between colloquial and FORMAL speech, between spoken and written language, between legal, religious, scientific and other VARIETIES of language.

Linguistics has devised several techniques for investigating the acceptability of linguistic data. These usually take the form of experiments in which native speakers are asked to evaluate sets of utterances containing those language features over whose acceptability there is some doubt (**acceptability tests**). It is necessary to have some such agreed techniques for judging acceptability as, especially in speech, very many utterances are produced whose status as sentences is open to question. In one sample of data, someone said, *I think it's the money they're charging is one thing*. The job of the linguist is to determine whether this was a mistake on the speaker's part, or whether this is a regular feature of his speech SYSTEM; if the latter, then whether this feature is idiosyncratic, or characteristic of some social group; and so on. Such investigations by their nature are inevitably large-scale, involving many INFORMANTS and sentence-patterns; they are therefore very time-consuming, and are not often carried out.

An utterance which is considered unacceptable is marked by an asterisk; if 'marginally acceptable', usually by a question-mark, as follows:

*the wall was arrived before
?the wall was arrived before by the army sent by the king

These conventions are also used to indicate ungrammatical or marginally grammatical sentences. In linguistic theory, though, the difference between the acceptability and the GRAMMATICALITY of a sentence is important. A sentence may be grammatically correct, according to the RULES of the grammar of a language, but nonetheless unacceptable, for a variety of other reasons. For example, due to the repeated application of a rule, the internal structure of a sentence may become too complex, exceeding the processing abilities of the speaker: these PERFORMANCE limitations are illustrated in such cases of multiple EMBEDDING as *this is the malt that the rat that the cat killed ate*, which is much less acceptable than *this is the malt that the rat ate*, despite the fact that the same grammatical operations have been used. In

GENERATIVE linguistic theory, variations in acceptability are analysed in terms of performance; grammaticality, by contrast, is a matter of COMPETENCE. See Lyons 1968: Ch. 4; Huddleston 1976: Ch. 1.

accessibility (1) A term derived from psychology, and used in PSYCHO-LINGUISTICS to refer to the extent to which a speaker can retrieve a linguistic unit from memory. Problems of accessibility are evident in 'tip-of-the-tongue' and TONGUE-SLIP phenomena, as well as in the varying times it takes someone to react to STRUCTURES involving different degrees of COMPLEXITY. See Clark & Clark 1977: Ch. 12.

(2) In RELATIONAL GRAMMAR, the term is used as part of the phrase **accessibility hierarchy**, to refer to a postulated LINEAR series of DEPENDENCIES between NOMINAL entities, which controls the applicability of SYNTACTIC RULES. In the hierarchy, each entity in the series more freely undergoes syntactic rules than the items to the right. For example, the nominal operating as a SUBJECT is said to be 'more accessible' than that operating as DIRECT OBJECT; the direct object is more accessible than the INDIRECT object; and so on. The notion has been applied to several grammatical areas (e.g. RELATIVE CLAUSE formation, the use of REFLEXIVES, and QUANTIFIERS), but the full application of this principle remains to be explored. See Radford 1981: Ch. 4.

accidence Most TRADITIONAL GRAMMARS recognise accidence as one of their main sub-divisions, along with GRAMMAR. It refers to the variations in WORD STRUCTURE which express grammatical MEANINGS, such as CASE, TENSE, NUMBER and GENDER. In English for example, the reason for the difference between *walk, walks, walking* and *walked*, or between *boy, boys, boy's* and *boys'* would be described as part of the accidence section of a grammar. In LINGUISTICS, this term is rarely used, as these phenomena are handled under the heading of MORPHO-LOGY, where they are seen as one process of WORD-FORMATION alongside several others. See Matthews 1974: Ch. 4.

accusative In languages which express GRAMMATICAL relationships by means of INFLECTIONS, this term refers to the FORM taken by a WORD, usually a NOUN or PRONOUN, when it is the OBJECT of a VERB. In Latin, for example, *I see the man* would be *video hominem* and not **video homo*, and *hominem* would be referred to as being 'in the accusative CASE'. LINGUISTS emphasise that it is not clear to use terms such as 'accusative' in languages which do not inflect words in this way. In English, for instance, whether a word is the object of the verb or not usually depends on word ORDER, as in *Dog bites postman,* where the recipient of the action is plainly the postman. Some traditional grammars would say here that postman is therefore 'accusative', but as there is no formal change between this word's use as object and its use as SUBJECT (*Postman bites dog*), linguists argue that this is a misleading use of the term, and avoid using it in such contexts. The only instance of a genuine accusative form of a word in English is in some PRONOUNS, e.g. *he hit **him**, she saw **her**, the man **whom** I saw*, and even here many linguists would prefer to use a neutral term, such as 'OBJECTIVE CASE', to avoid the connotations of TRADITIONAL GRAMMARS. See Lyons 1968: Ch. 7; Quirk *et al* 1972: Ch. 4.

acoustic feature/cue A characteristic of a speech sound when analysed in physical terms, e.g. FUNDAMENTAL frequency, amplitude, harmonic structure. Such analyses are provided by ACOUSTIC PHONETICS, and it is possible to make acoustic classifications of speech sounds based upon such features, as when one classifies VOWELS in terms of their FORMANT structure. The acoustic properties of a sound which aid its identification in speech are known as **acoustic cues**. In the DISTINCTIVE FEATURE theory of PHONOLOGY of JAKOBSON & Halle, acoustic features are the primary means of defining the BINARY oppositions that constitute the phonological SYSTEM of a language. See Ladefoged 1975: Ch. 8; Catford 1977: Ch. 4.

acoustic phonetics (acoustic(s)) The branch of PHONETICS, also known as **acoustics**, which studies the physical properties of speech sound, as transmitted between mouth and ear. It is wholly dependent on the use of instrumental techniques of investigation, particularly electronics, and some grounding in physics and mathematics is a prerequisite for advanced study of this subject. Its importance to the phonetician is that acoustic analysis can provide a clear, objective datum for investigation of speech – the physical 'facts' of utterance. In this way, acoustic evidence is often referred to when one wants to support an analysis being made in ARTICULATORY or AUDITORY PHONETIC terms. On the other hand, it is important not to become too reliant on acoustic analyses, which are subject to mechanical limitations (e.g. the need to calibrate measuring devices accurately), and which are often themselves open to multiple interpretations. Sometimes, indeed, acoustic and auditory analysis of a sound conflict – for example, in INTONATION studies, one may hear a speech melody as RISING, whereas the acoustic facts show the FUNDAMENTAL frequency of the sound to be steady. In such cases, it is for the phonetician to decide which evidence he will pay more attention to; there has been a long-standing debate concerning the respective merits of physical (i.e.

acoustic) as opposed to psychological (i.e. auditory) solutions to such problems, and how apparent conflicts of this kind can be resolved. See Ladefoged 1975: Ch. 8; Catford 1977: Ch. 4.

acquisition In the study of the growth of LANGUAGE in children, the term refers to the process or result of learning a particular aspect of a language, and ultimately the language as a whole. **Child language acquisition** is the label usually given to the field of studies involved. The subject has involved the postulation of 'stages' of acquisition, defined chronologically, or in relation to other aspects of behaviour, which it is suggested apply generally to children; and there has been considerable discussion of the nature of the learning strategies which are used in the process of acquiring language, and of the criteria which can decide when a STRUCTURE has been acquired. Some theorists make a distinction between 'acquisition' and 'development', the former referring to the learning of a linguistic RULE (of GRAMMAR, PHONOLOGY, SEMANTICS), the latter to the further use of this rule in an increasingly wide range of linguistic and social situations. Others see no clear distinction between these two facets of language learning, and use the terms interchangeably. In GENERATIVE linguistics, the term **language acquisition device** (LAD) is used to refer to a model of language learning in which the infant is credited with an INNATE predisposition to acquire linguistic structure. This view is usually opposed to those where language acquisition is seen as a process of imitation-learning or as a reflex of cognitive development.

'Acquisition' is also used in the context of learning a foreign language: 'foreign' or 'second language' acquisition is thus distinguished from 'first language' or 'mother-tongue' acquisition. See Bolinger 1975: Ch. 1; Clark & Clark 1977: Chs. 8–10.

active A term used in the GRAMMATICAL analysis of VOICE, referring to a SENTENCE, CLAUSE, or VERB FORM where, from a SEMANTIC point of view, the grammatical SUBJECT is typically the actor, in relation to the verb, e.g. *The boy wrote a letter*. It is contrasted with PASSIVE, and sometimes with other forms of the verb, e.g. the 'middle voice' in Greek. See Quirk *et al* 1972: Ch. 12; Lyons 1968: Ch. 8.

actor–action–goal A phrase used in the GRAMMATICAL and SEMANTIC analysis of SENTENCE patterns, to characterise the typical sequence of FUNCTIONS within STATEMENTS in many languages. In the sentence *John saw a duck*, for example, *John* is the actor, *saw* the action, and a *duck* the goal. On the other hand, languages display several other 'favourite' sequences, such as Welsh, where UNMARKED sequence is action–actor–goal. The phrase is widely used, but not without criticism, as the semantic implications of terms such as 'actor' do not always coincide with the grammatical facts, e.g. in *The stone moved*, the SUBJECT of the sentence is hardly an 'actor' in the same sense as *John* is above. See Lyons 1968: Ch. 8.

actualisation (actualise) A term used by some linguists to refer to the physical EXPRESSION of an abstract LINGUISTIC unit, e.g. PHONEMES are 'actualised' in PHONIC SUBSTANCE as PHONES, MORPHEMES as MORPHS. Any UNDERLYING form may be seen as having a corresponding actualisation in substance. REALISATION is a more widely-used term. See Lyons 1968: Ch. 2.

acute One of the features of sound set up by JAKOBSON & Halle in their DISTINCTIVE FEATURE theory of PHONOLOGY, to handle variations in PLACE OF ARTICULATION; its opposite being GRAVE. Acute sounds are defined articulatorily and ACOUSTICALLY as those involving a medial articulation in the VOCAL TRACT, and a concentration of acoustic energy in the higher frequencies; examples of [+acute] sounds are FRONT VOWELS, and DENTAL, ALVEOLAR and PALATAL CONSONANTS. See Hyman 1975: Ch. 2.

address The general use of this term, in the sense of 'the manner of referring to someone in direct linguistic interaction', has provided SOCIOLINGUISTICS with a major field of study. **Forms of address** have been analysed between different types of participant in different social situations, and RULES proposed to explain the speaker's choice of terms, e.g. governing the use of first names, titles, intimate PRONOUNS, etc. Social psychological concepts, such as power and solidarity, have been suggested as particularly significant factors in understanding 'address systems', i.e. the SYSTEM of RULES used by a speaker or group, governing their use of such forms as *tu* and *vous* (T FORMS and V FORMS). See Gumperz & Hymes 1971: Ch. 7.

adequacy (adequate) A term used in LINGUISTIC theory as part of the evaluation of levels of success in the writing of GRAMMARS. Several sets of distinctions based on this notion have been made. **External adequacy** judges a grammar in terms of how well it corresponds to the DATA (which are 'external' to the grammar); **internal adequacy** is a judgement based on the 'internal' characteristics of the grammar, such as its SIMPLICITY, elegance, etc. From a different point of view, grammars are said to be **weakly adequate** if they GENERATE some desired set of SENTENCES; they are **strongly adequate** if they not only do this, but also assign to each sentence the correct STRUCTURAL DESCRIPTION. An alternative formulation recognises three levels of achievement in grammars: **observational adequacy** is achieved when a grammar generates all of a particular sample (CORPUS) of data; **descriptive adequacy**, when a grammar goes beyond this, and describes the INTUITIONS (COMPETENCE) of the language's speakers; **explanatory adequacy** is achieved when a principled basis is established for deciding between alternative grammars, all of which are descriptively adequate. See Huddleston 1976: Ch. 1; Lyons 1968: Ch. 6.

adjacency pair A term used in SOCIOLINGUISTIC analyses of conversational interaction to refer to a single stimulus-plus-response sequence by the participants. Adjacency pairs have been analysed in terms of their role in initiating, maintaining and closing conversations (e.g. the various conventions of greeting, leave-taking, topic-changing), and constitute, it has been suggested, an important methodological concept in investigating the ETHNOGRAPHY OF COMMUNICATION. See Clark & Clark 1977: Ch. 6; Gumperz & Hymes 1971: Ch. 12.

adjective (adjectival) A term used in the GRAMMATICAL classification of WORDS to refer to the main set of items which specify the attributes of NOUNS. From a FORMAL point of view, four criteria are generally invoked to define the class in English: they can occur within the noun PHRASE, i.e. they function in the 'attributive' position, e.g. *the big man*; they can occur in a post-verbal or 'predicative' position, e.g. *the man is big, he called it stupid*; they can be PREMODIFIED by an INTENSIFIER, such as *very*, e.g. *the very big man*; and they can be used in a COMPARATIVE and SUPERLATIVE form, either by INFLECTION (e.g. *big, bigger, biggest*) or PERIPHRASTICally (e.g. *interesting, more interesting, most interesting*). However, not all adjectives satisfy all these criteria (e.g. *major*, as in *A major question*, does not occur predicatively – cf. **The question is major*), and the sub-classification of adjectives has proved quite complex. Both narrow and broad applications of the term 'adjective' will be found in grammars. In its broadest sense, it could include everything between the DETERMINER and the noun, in such a phrase as *the vicar's fine old English garden chair*; but many linguists prefer to restrict it to the items which satisfy most or all of the above criteria (to include only *fine* and *old*, in this example), the other items being called 'adjective-like', or 'adjectivals'. Adjectives may also be the HEADS of phrases ('adjective phrases', such as *that's very important*) and an adjectival function is sometimes recognised for certain types of CLAUSE (e.g. *he's the man I saw*). See Quirk *et al* 1972: Ch. 5.

adjunct A term used in GRAMMATICAL theory to refer to an optional or secondary element in a CONSTRUCTION: an adjunct may be removed without the STRUCTURAL identity of the rest of the construction being affected. The clearest examples at SENTENCE level are ADVERBIALS, e.g. *John kicked the ball* **yesterday** vs. *John kicked the ball*, but not **John kicked yesterday*, etc.; but other elements have been classed as 'adjunctival', in various descriptions, such as VOCATIVES and ADJECTIVES. Many adjuncts can also be analysed as MODIFIERS, attached to the HEAD of a phrase (as with adjectives, and some adverbs). The term may also be given a highly restricted sense, as when it is used by Quirk *et al* to refer to a sub-class of adverbials. See Quirk *et al* 1972: Ch. 8; Lyons 1968: Ch. 8.

adjunction (adjoin) A basic SYNTACTIC operation in recent TRANSFORMATIONAL GRAMMAR referring to a RULE which places certain ELEMENTS of STRUCTURE in adjacent positions, with the aim of specifying how these structures fit together in larger UNITS. Two main types of adjunction are recognised. In **sister-adjunction**, two elements are formally adjoined *under* a particular NODE and thus become sister CONSTITUENTS of that node. For example, in one formulation of the VERB PHRASE, the NEGATIVE PARTICLE is 'sister-adjoined' to the elements MODAL and TENSE, as follows:

(Some linguists talk alternatively of 'daughter-adjunction' here.) **Chomsky-adjunction** provides an alternative way of handling this situation. This suggestion involves adjoining an element to a node, and not to another element; a copy of this node is then made immediately above it, and it is this which DOMINATES the adjoined elements. Under this analysis, the negative particle could be handled as follows:

adnominal

```
                        Aux
            ┌────────────┼──────────────┐
          Tense        Modal             \
            │            │                \
            │          Modal               \
            │            │                   \
            │            │                     \
         Present        will                   not
```

This ensures that whatever happens to modal will also happen to *not* – for instance, CONTRACTED *not* (*n't*) needs to stay with the modal if the latter is moved, as in *won't he, can't he,* etc. It is thus claimed that this operation allows LINGUISTICALLY SIGNIFICANT GENERALISATIONS to be made which might otherwise be missed, or which would be handled less ECONOMICALLY. However, the relative status of these transformations has remained controversial. See Akmajian & Heny 1975: Ch. 5; Huddleston 1976: Ch. 12.

adnominal A term used by some GRAMMARIANS to refer to the elements in a NOUN PHRASE which MODIFY a noun (an analogy with ADVERBIAL), e.g. ADJECTIVES, PREPOSITIONAL phrases, and 'possessive' nouns, e.g. *the **big** hat, the **vicar's** hat, the hat **in the box***. See Lyons 1968: Ch. 7.

adultomorphic (adultocentric) Labels sometimes used in language ACQUISITION studies to characterise an analysis of children's speech in terms which were originally devised for the study of the adult language, e.g. referring to *allgone* as an ELLIPTICAL SENTENCE, or describing babbling using the INTERNATIONAL PHONETIC ALPHABET. It is of course difficult to devise a terminology or NOTATION for child speech which is largely or totally free of adult values, but, it is argued, caution is nonetheless needed to avoid introducing too many adult assumptions, and as a consequence attributing to the child a knowledge of language which he does not possess. See Clark & Clark 1977: Ch. 8.

adverb(ial) A term used in the GRAMMATICAL classification of WORDS to refer to a heterogeneous group of items whose most frequent function is to specify the mode of action of the VERB. In English, many (by no means all) adverbs are signalled by the use of the *-ly* ending, e.g. *quickly*, but cf. *soon*. SYNTACTICALLY, one can relate adverbs to such QUESTIONS as *how, where, when,* and *why,* and classify them accordingly, as adverbs of 'manner', 'place', 'time', etc.; but as soon as this is done the functional equivalence of adverbs, **adverb phrases** and **adverb clauses** becomes apparent, e.g. A: *When is he going?* B: *Now/In five minutes/When the bell rings.* The term **adverbial** is widely used as a general term which subsumes all three categories. 'Adverb' is thus a word-CLASS (along with NOUN, ADJECTIVE, etc.), whereas 'adverbial' is an ELEMENT of CLAUSE structure (along with SUBJECT, OBJECT, etc.). Within adverbials, many syntactic roles have been identified, of which verb MODIFICATION has traditionally been seen as central. A function of adverbials as SENTENCE modifiers or sentence CONNECTORS has been emphasised in linguistic studies, e.g. *However/Moreover/Actually/ Frankly...I think he was right.* Several other classes of items, very different in DISTRIBUTION and FUNCTION, have also been brought under the heading of adverb(ial), such as INTENSIFIERS (e.g. *very, awfully*), and negative PARTICLES (e.g. *not*); but often linguistic studies set these up as distinct word-classes. See Quirk *et al* 1972: Chs. 5, 8, 11.

affect(ive) A term sometimes used in SEMANTICS as part of a classification of types of MEANING: it refers to the attitudinal element in meaning, as in the differing emotional associations (or CONNOTATIONS) of LEXICAL items (e.g. *a youth/youngster stood on the corner*) or the expression of attitude (or 'affect') in INTONATION. **Affective meaning** is usually opposed to COGNITIVE meaning. Alternative terms include EMOTIVE and ATTITUDINAL. See Lyons 1977b: Ch. 7.

affirmative A term used in GRAMMATICAL description to refer to a type of SENTENCE or VERB which has no marker of NEGATION, i.e. it is expressing an assertion. The affirmative, or positive 'pole' of this contrast is opposed to negative, and the grammatical SYSTEM involved is often referred to under the heading of POLARITY. See Quirk *et al* 1972: Ch. 2.

affix(-ation, -ing) The collective term for the types of FORMATIVE that can be used only when added to another MORPHEME (the ROOT or STEM), i.e. affixes are a type of 'bound' morpheme. Affixes are limited in number in a language, and are generally classified into three types, depending on their position with reference to the root or stem of the WORD: those which are added to the beginning of a root/stem (PREFIXES), e.g. *unhappy*; those which follow (SUFFIXES), e.g. *happiness*; and those which occur within a root/stem (INFIXES). The morphological process whereby GRAMMATICAL or LEXICAL information is added to a stem is known as **affixation** ('prefixation', 'suffixation', 'infixation'). From an alternative point of view, affixes may be divided affricate

into INFLECTIONAL and DERIVATIONAL types. The number of affixes in a word has been suggested as one of the criteria for classifying languages into types (the **affix(ing) index**). Languages which express grammatical relationships primarily through the use of affixes are known as **affixing languages**, e.g. a 'prefixing' language (as in Bantu), or a 'suffixing' language (as in Latin or Greek).

In GENERATIVE grammar, the term 'affix' applies to such notions as 'present' and 'past', as well as *-ing, be, have*, etc., in the formulation of RULES. **Affix-hopping**, in this approach, is an OBLIGATORY TRANS-FORMATIONAL rule which attaches an affix to the appropriate formative in a STRING: the affix 'hops' over the VERB, which is adjacent to it, e.g. *-ing+go* becoming *go+-ing*. See Matthews 1974: Ch. 7; Robins 1971: Ch. 5; Akmajian & Heny 1975: Ch. 4.

affricate (-d, affrication) A term used in the classification of CONSONANT sounds on the basis of their MANNER OF ARTICULATION: it refers to a sound made when the air-pressure behind a complete CLOSURE in the VOCAL TRACT is gradually released; the initial RELEASE produces a PLOSIVE, but the separation which follows is sufficiently slow to produce audible friction, and there is thus a FRICATIVE element in the sound also. However, the DURATION of the friction is usually not as long as would be the case for an independent fricative sound. If it is very brief indeed, the term 'affrication' is used: in some English DIALECTS, such as Cockney, 'affricated' plosives may be heard, such as [tˢ] and [dᶻ], the auditory brevity of the friction element being indicated in the TRANSCRIPTION by the small symbols. It is, then, the combination of plosion and friction which identifies an affricate. In English, only [t] and [d] are released in this way, as in ch- [tʃ] of *chip* and j- [dʒ] of *just*. German examples are [pf-] *pfennig*, 'penny' and [ts] *zu*, 'to'. While affricates are PHONETICALLY easy to define, it is often a problem for PHONOLOGICAL analysis to decide whether a sequence of plosive and fricative elements constitute a single functional unit, or are best analysed as two separate units. English [tʃ], for example, occurs initially, medially and finally in a word, readily contrasting with other PHONEMES, e.g. *chip/sip, richer/ripper, patch/pat*. On the other hand [tr], while occurring initially and medially (*trip/sip, petrol/petal*), does not occur finally. Further, [tθ] only occurs finally (*eighth/eight*). Phonetically, all could be considered affricates; but phonologically, there would be difference of opinion as to whether those with a restricted DISTRIBUTION could usefully be identified in this way. See Gimson 1970: Ch. 8; Catford 1977: Ch. 11.

agentive (agent) A term used in GRAMMATICAL description to refer to a FORM or CONSTRUCTION whose typical FUNCTION in a SENTENCE is to specify the 'agent' or means whereby a particular action came about. In some languages, the term is used as one of the CASES for NOUNS, along with ACCUSATIVE, etc. In English, the term has especial relevance with reference to the PASSIVE construction, where the agent may be expressed or unexpressed (e.g. *the man was bitten* [*by a snake*]). In active constructions in English, the agent is usually the grammatical SUBJECT, but in some sentences (and often in some other languages) a more complex statement of agentive function is required (as in such sentences as *the window broke* (cf. ERGATIVE) and *we ran the car out of petrol*). The term has a special status in CASE grammar, where it is defined similarly to the above, but it is seen as one of a fixed set of SEMANTIC cases, along with OBJECTIVE, DATIVE, etc. See Lyons 1968: Chs. 7, 8; Bolinger 1975: Ch. 15.

agglutinative (agglutinat-ing, -ion) A type of language established by COMPARATIVE LINGUISTICS using STRUCTURAL (as opposed to HISTORICAL) criteria, and focusing on the characteristics of the WORD: in **agglutinative** or **agglutinating languages**, words typically contain a linear sequence of MORPHS – as seen in English /*dis*/*establish*/*ment* – and thus contrast with ISOLATING and INFLECTIONAL languages. As always in such classifications, the categories are not clear-cut: different languages will display the characteristic of 'agglutination' to a greater or lesser degree. Languages which display agglutination to a major extent include Turkish and Japanese. See Robins 1971: Ch. 8; Lyons 1968: Ch. 5.

agreement A traditional term used in GRAMMATICAL theory and description to refer to a formal relationship between ELEMENTS, whereby a FORM of one WORD requires a corresponding form of another. In Latin, for example, agreement between elements is of central importance, being one of the main means of expressing grammatical relationships, in the absence of fixed patterns of WORD ORDER. The term CONCORD is more widely used in linguistic studies. See Lyons 1968: Ch. 6; Robins 1971: Ch. 6.

air-stream mechanism Any physiological process which provides a source of energy capable of being used in SPEECH sound PRODUCTION. Air is moved inwards or outwards by the movement of this mechanism, producing respectively an INGRESSIVE and an EGRESSIVE air-flow. The main initiator of air movement is the lungs (the PULMONIC air-stream), which underlies the majority of human speech sounds. The 'glottalic' air-stream mechanism, as its name suggests, uses the movement of the glottis (the aperture between the VOCAL CORDS) as the source of energy (cf. GLOTTAL). The 'velaric' air-stream mechanism, also as its name suggests, involves an air flow produced by a movement of the BACK of the TONGUE against the velum (cf. VELAR). It is also possible to start air vibrating using other movable parts of the vocal tract, such as the cheeks or the oesophagus, but these are not methods used in normal speech production. The use of the cheeks produces a 'buccal' voice (the basis for the Donald Duck effect); the 'oesophageal' voice is characteristic of the speech taught to people who have had their larnyx surgically removed. See Gimson 1970: Chs. 2, 4; Catford 1977: Ch. 5.

alethic A term derived from modal logic and used by some LINGUISTS as part of a theoretical framework for the analysis of MODAL VERBS and related STRUCTURES in LANGUAGE. **Alethic modality** is concerned with the necessary or contingent truth of propositions, e.g. the use of the modals in sentences such as *the car must be ready*, i.e. 'it follows from what is known (e.g. that the car is outside) that it is ready'. It contrasts with EPISTEMIC and DEONTIC modality, which would interpret this sentence respectively as 'it is surely the case that the car is ready' and 'I oblige you to ensure that the car is ready'. See Lyons 1977b: Ch. 17.

algorithm An application in LINGUISTICS and PHONETICS of the general use of this term in cybernetics, computing, etc., referring to a procedure devised to carry out a complicated operation by breaking it down into a precisely specified sequence of simpler operations, as in the flow-chart of a computer program. The main use of this reasoning in linguistics is found in the analytic statements of a GENERATIVE GRAMMAR. See Lyons 1977a: Ch. 4.

alienable A term used in GRAMMATICAL analysis to refer to a type of possessive relationship formally MARKED in some languages (e.g. Chinese). If a possessed item is seen as having only a temporary or non-essential dependence on a possessor, it is said to be 'alienable', whereas if its relationship to the possessor is a permanent or necessary one, it is **inalienable**. Distinctions of **alienable possession** are not MORPHOLOGICALLY marked in English, but SEMANTICALLY the contrast can be seen in *the boy's book* (alienable) and the *boy's leg* (inalienable). See Lyons 1968: Ch. 7; 1977b: Ch. 9.

allo- A prefix used generally in LINGUISTICS to refer to any noticeable variation in the FORM of a linguistic UNIT which does not affect that unit's FUNCTIONAL identity in the language. The formal variation noted is not linguistically distinctive, i.e. no change of MEANING is involved. The written language, for example, consists of a series of letters, or GRAPHEMES, but each of these graphemes can be written in several different ways, depending on such matters as linguistic CONTEXT, choice of type, handwriting variation, and so on, e.g. 'a letter A' may appear as *A*, *a*, *a*, *a*, etc. Each of these possibilities is a graphic VARIANT of the abstract grapheme ⟨A⟩: they are all **allographs** of the grapheme ⟨A⟩. The identity of the word *cat* stays the same, regardless of whether it is written *cat*, *cAt*, *cat*, etc. (though not all of these would be equally acceptable).

The first relationship of this kind to be established was in PHONO-LOGY., *viz* the relationship of **allophones** to PHONEMES. The phonemes of a language are abstractions, and the particular phonetic shape they take depends on many factors, especially their position in relation to other sounds in a sentence (cf. COMPLEMENTARY DISTRIBUTION). The English phoneme /t/, for example, is usually articulated in ALVEOLAR position (as in *eight*), but it may occur in DENTAL position, as in *eighth*, where it has been influenced by the place of articulation of the *th* sound following. We would thus talk of the alveolar and dental allophones of /t/, in this example. Many allophones are always in principle possible for any phoneme, given the wide range of idiosyncratic pronunciations which exist in a speech community (cf. FREE variation). Textbooks provide information about the major variants, *viz* those clearly conditioned by linguistic or social (e.g. ACCENT) contexts. From a terminological point of view, one may also refer to the above phenomenon as an **allophonic variant** of a phoneme (sometimes simply a 'phonetic variant' or a 'sub-phonemic variant'). The relationship between allophones and phonemes is one of REALISATION: a phoneme is 'realised' by its allophones. The differences between allophones can be stated using phonological RULES.

Later, the notion of variant units in GRAMMAR was established, on analogy with the allophone/phoneme distinction. Many of the MORPHEMES of the language appear in different forms, depending on the context in which they appear. The morpheme which expresses plurality in English, for instance, appears in several variants: *cap – caps*, *log – logs*, *force – forces*, *mouse – mice*, *sheep – sheep*, etc. Each of these variant forms – the voiceless [s] of *caps*, the voiced [z] of *logs*, the irregular shape of *mice*, and so on – would be said to be an **allomorph** of the plural morpheme. They have also been referred to as **morpheme** (or **morphemic**) **alternants**.

These are the main allo- terms which have been introduced, all opposed to an -EMIC term, and the suggestion has been made that this relationship, of allo- to -eme, is an important explanatory principle in linguistic analysis. Certainly many other such allo- relationships have been postulated since the terminology was first introduced in the 1930s. Some are **allochrone** (non-distinctive variant of a minimal unit of length, or CHRONEME), **allokine** (non-distinctive variant of a KINEME, i.e. a minimal unit of body movement, such as a gesture or facial expression) and **alloseme** (non-distinctive variant of a minimal unit of meaning, or SEMEME). None have proved to be as useful as allophone or allomorph, however, and the extent to which this terminology is helpful when applied to such other areas of linguistic analysis – and to behavioural analysis generally, as in the classification of units of dance, song, taste, movement – is disputed. See Bolinger 1975: Chs. 3, 4; Robins 1971: Chs. 4, 5; Lyons 1968: Chs. 3, 5.

alpha notation A TRANSCRIPTIONAL convention in GENERATIVE LINGUISTICS which makes it possible to simplify the statement of a RULE by introducing a variable. In generative PHONOLOGY, for example, it is used in cases where there is a mutual predictability between sets of FEATURES, and avoids the necessity of having to make separate statements for the conditions of occurrence of each feature. For example, in order to state that a VOICED PLOSIVE in a language is always ROUNDED whereas a voiceless plosive is always unrounded, one can conflate the two rules by using the variable α to stand for the two possible correlations [+voice] $\sim$ [+round] and [−voice] $\sim$ [−round], viz [α voice] $\Rightarrow$ [α round]. Several developments of this convention will be encountered in this approach to phonology, including the use of other variables. See Hyman 1975: Ch. 4.

alternation (alternant) A term used in LINGUISTICS to refer to the relationship which exists between the alternative FORMS, or VARIANTS, of a linguistic UNIT. The usual symbol for alternation is $\sim$. In PHONOLOGY, for example, the related VOWEL QUALITIES of such words as *telegraph* $\sim$ *telegraphic*, *receive* $\sim$ *reception* are sometimes described as alternants, as are the various ALLOphones of a PHONEME. The term has had particular currency in MORPHOLOGY, however, where 'morphemic/morpheme alternant' is another term for allomorph, and where various sub-types have been distinguished. For example, 'phonologically conditioned alternants' are illustrated in the various forms of the plural MORPHEME (/-s/, /-z/, /-ɪz/), which are predictable from the preceding phonological context ('MORPHOPHONEMIC alternants'). 'Grammatically conditioned alternants' are cases where there is no such rationale, the occurrence of an alternant depending entirely on the particular morphemes which occur in its environment, as in the various forms of the past participle in English (*frozen, jumped*, etc.). SUPPLETION is another category of alternation, referring to a morpheme lacking *any* regular phonological correspondence with other forms in a PARADIGM, as in *go* ~ *went*. In SYNTAX, examples of sets of alternants can be seen in the various grammatical CATEGORIES, such as TENSE (e.g. present ~ past ~ future). See Matthews 1974: Ch. 5; Hyman 1975: Ch. 1.

alveolar A term in the classification of CONSONANT sounds on the basis of their PLACE OF ARTICULATION: it refers to a sound made by the BLADE of the TONGUE (or the TIP and blade together) in contact against the **alveolar ridge** (or 'alveolum'), which is the bony prominence immediately behind the upper teeth. A number of sounds are given an alveolar articulation in English – [t], [d], [l], [n], [s] and [z]. If the sound is articulated towards the back of the alveolar ridge, near where the palate begins, the term **post-alveolar** can be used. In English the *r* in *red*, *trip*, *drill* is articulated in POST-alveolar position. See Gimson 1970: Ch. 4; Catford 1977: Ch. 8.

alveo(lo)-palatal A term used in the PHONETIC classification of speech sounds on the basis of their PLACE OF ARTICULATION: it refers to a sound made by the FRONT of the TONGUE a little in advance of the PALATAL articulatory area, i.e. in the direction of ALVEOLAR articulations. Only two such sounds are distinguished in the INTERNATIONAL PHONETIC Alphabet, the FRICATIVES [ɕ] and [ʑ], which occur for example in Polish. See Catford 1977: Ch. 8.

ambiguity (ambiguous) The general sense of this term, referring to a WORD or SENTENCE which expresses more than one MEANING, is found in LINGUISTICS, but several types of ambiguity are recognised. The most widely discussed type in recent years is **grammatical** (or **structural**) **ambiguity**. In PHRASE-STRUCTURE ambiguity, alternative CONSTITUENT STRUCTURES can be assigned to a CONSTRUCTION, as in *new houses and shops*, which could be analysed either as *new [houses and shops]* (i.e. both are new) or *[new houses] and shops* (i.e. only the houses are new). In TRANSFORMATIONAL ambiguity, the alternative SEMANTIC representations can be shown only by relating the ambiguous sentence to different structures. For example, *visiting speakers can be awful* is relatable to either *it is awful to visit speakers* or *speakers who visit are awful*. A sentence with more than two structural interpretations is said to be **multiply ambiguous**. An analysis which demonstrates the ambiguity in a sentence is said to DISAMBIGUATE the sentence. Ambiguity which does not arise from the grammatical analysis of a sentence, but is due solely to the alternative meanings of an individual LEXICAL ITEM, is referred to as **lexical ambiguity**, e.g. *I found the table fascinating* (='object of furniture' or 'table of figures' – cf. POLYSEMY). In recent semantic discussion, a distinction is sometimes drawn between 'ambiguity' and 'vagueness': an ambiguous sentence is formulated as having more than one distinct structure; a vague sentence, on the other hand, permits an unspecifiable range of possible interpretations (i.e. is unstateable in syntactic or PHONOLOGICAL terms). For example, deciding on the implications of a NEGATIVE sentence such as *He didn't hit the dog* is a matter of vagueness, in this view, in that it is not possible to state specifically a fixed number of different underlying structures involved in its interpretation (*What **did** he hit? Did he do something else to the dog?*). See Lyons 1968: Ch. 6; 1977b: Ch. 10.

anacoluthon A traditional rhetorical term, sometimes encountered in LINGUISTIC studies of conversational speech. It refers to a SYNTACTIC break in the expected GRAMMATICAL sequence within a SENTENCE, as when a sentence begins with one CONSTRUCTION and remains unfinished, e.g. *The man came and – are you listening?* 'Anacolutha' have come to be especially noticed in recent linguistic studies as an area of PERFORMANCE features which a grammar of a language would aim to exclude. See Quirk *et al* 1972: App. 3.

analogy A term used in HISTORICAL and COMPARATIVE LINGUISTICS, and language ACQUISITION, referring to a process of regularisation which affects the exceptional forms in the GRAMMAR of a language. The influence of the REGULAR pattern of plural formation in English, for example, can be heard in the treatment of irregular forms in the early UTTERANCES of children, e.g. *mens, mans, mouses*: the children are producing these forms 'on analogy with' the regular pattern. DIALECTS also often illustrate analogical processes at work, which the STANDARD language has so far resisted, e.g. *goed/seed/knowed* for *went/saw/know*, etc., and this process is of course common in the ERRORS of foreign learners of the language. Processes of 'analogical creation' are one of the main tendencies in the history of languages, as when VERBS which had an irregular past TENSE form in Old English came to be produced with the regular *-ed* ending, e.g. *help* becoming *helped*. See Robins 1971: Ch. 8; Lyons 1968: Ch. 1.

analysable A term used in GENERATIVE GRAMMAR to refer to the characteristic of a STRING in relation to a TRANSFORMATION. If the string meets the STRUCTURAL DESCRIPTION (SD) of the transformational RULE, it is said to be 'analysable', and the rule is thereby applicable. For example, for the PASSIVE rule to operate (in one formulation), the following SD is required: NP – Aux – V – NP. A string such as *the boy is kicking the ball* would thus be 'analysable', with respect to this rule; *the boy has gone*, on the other hand, would not meet the SD of the rule, and would thereby be 'unanalysable'. See Akmajian & Heny 1975; Ch. 5.

analysis-by-synthesis A theory of SPEECH PERCEPTION which credits listeners with an internal, language-specific mechanism that responds to incoming speech by selecting certain ACOUSTIC cues, and then attempting to synthesise a replica of the input. When this is achieved, the synthesis has, in effect, carried out an analysis of the input. Such a procedure, it is argued, has the merit of being able to explain how listeners resolve the acoustic variability in signals, stemming from the differences between speakers, contexts, etc. See Clark & Clark 1977: Ch. 5.

analytic(ity) (1) A type of language established by COMPARATIVE LINGUISTICS using STRUCTURAL (as opposed to HISTORICAL) criteria, and focusing on the characteristics of the WORD: in 'isolating' languages, all the words are invariable (and SYNTACTIC relationships are shown primarily by WORD-ORDER). The term is seen in opposition to SYNTHETIC (and sometimes also POLYSYNTHETIC) languages (which include AGGLUTINATIVE and INFLECTING types), where words typically contain more than one MORPHEME. Several languages of South-East Asia illustrate analyticity in their word structure. As always in such classifications, the categories are not clear-cut: different languages will display the characteristic of analyticity to a greater or lesser degree. See Robins 1971: Ch. 8; Lyons 1968: Ch. 5.

(2) Considerable use is made in SEMANTICS of the sense of 'analytic' found in logic and philosophy, where an **analytic proposition/sentence** is one whose GRAMMATICAL FORM and LEXICAL MEANING make it necessarily true, e.g. *spinsters are unmarried women*. The term contrasts with SYNTHETIC, where the truth of the proposition is established using empirical criteria. See Lyons 1977b: Ch. 6.

anaphora (anaphoric) A term used in GRAMMATICAL description for the process or result of a linguistic UNIT referring back to some previously expressed unit or meaning. 'Anaphoric reference' is one way of marking the identity between what is being expressed and what has already been expressed. In such a sentence as *he did that there*, each word has an anaphoric reference (i.e. they are 'anaphoric substitutes', or simply 'anaphoric words'): the previous sentence might have been *John painted this picture in Bermuda*, for instance, and each word in the response would be anaphorically related to a corresponding unit in the preceding CONTEXT. Anaphora is often contrasted with CATAPHORA (where the words refer forward), and sometimes with EXOPHORA (where the words refer directly to the extra-linguistic SITUATION). It may however also be found subsuming both forwards- and backwards-referring functions. See Quirk *et al* 1972: Ch. 10; Lyons 1977b: Ch. 15.

animate (in-, -ness) A term used in the GRAMMATICAL classification of words (especially NOUNS) to refer to a subclass whose REFERENCE is to persons and animals, as opposed to inanimate entities and concepts. In some languages, distinctions of 'animateness' are made MORPHO-LOGICALLY, as a contrast in GENDER. In English, the distinction can be made only on SEMANTIC grounds, apart from a certain correspondence with personal and relative PRONOUNS (*he/she/who* vs. *it/which*). In adjectives expressing the concept 'old', for example, *elderly* is animate, *antique* inanimate; *old* is neutral, being applicable to either category. See Bolinger 1975: Ch. 6; Lyons 1968: Ch. 4.

antecedent A term taken over from TRADITIONAL GRAMMAR by some grammarians, and used for a linguistic UNIT to which a later unit in the SENTENCE refers (ANAPHORIC REFERENCE). In particular, personal and relative PRONOUNS are said to refer back to their antecedents, as in *The car **which** was parked...It was...* See Lyons 1977b: Ch. 15.

anterior One of the features of sound set up by CHOMSKY & Halle in their DISTINCTIVE FEATURE theory of PHONOLOGY, to handle variations in PLACE OF ARTICULATION (CAVITY features). Anterior sounds are defined articulatorily as those produced with a STRICTURE in front of the PALATO-ALVEOLAR area in the mouth. LABIAL and DENTAL consonants are [+anterior] (abbreviated as [+ant]). Its opposite is **non-anterior**, referring to sounds produced without such a stricture, as in VELAR, GLOTTAL and VOWEL sounds, which are [−anterior] ([−ant]). See Ladefoged 1975: Ch. 11; Hyman 1975: Ch. 2.

anthropological linguistics A branch of LINGUISTICS which studies language variation and use in relation to the cultural patterns and beliefs of man, as investigated using the theories and methods of anthropology. For example, it studies the way in which linguistic features may identify a member of a (usually primitive) community with a social, religious, occupational or kinship group. The term overlaps to some degree with ETHNOLINGUISTICS and SOCIOLINGUIS-

TICS, reflecting the overlapping interests of the correlative disciplines involved – anthropology, ethnology and sociology. It is also known as **linguistic anthropology.** See Robins 1971: Ch. 9.

anticipation A term used by some PSYCHOLINGUISTS to refer to a type of TONGUE-SLIP where a later LINGUISTIC UNIT is anticipated, as when *catch the ball* might become *batch the call*. See Clark & Clark 1977: Ch. 7; Bolinger 1975: Ch. 12.

anticipatory (1) A term used in PHONETICS and PHONOLOGY as part of the classification of types of ASSIMILATION. In **anticipatory** (or 'regressive') **assimilation,** a sound changes because of the influence of the preceding sound, as when [t] becomes [k] in *hot cakes*. It is opposed to PROGRESSIVE and COALESCENT assimilations. See Gimson 1970: Ch. 11.

(2) The term is also used with reference to the commonest type of COARTICULATION (**anticipatory coarticulation**), wherein an ARTICULATOR not involved in a particular sound begins to move in the direction of a TARGET articulation needed for a later sound in the UTTERANCE. An example is the NASALISATION which can be heard on VOWELS followed by a nasal CONSONANT, due to the soft PALATE beginning to lower in anticipation of the consonant during the articulation of the vowel. See Catford 1977: Ch. 10.

antonym(y) A term used in SEMANTICS as part of the study of oppositeness of MEANING. 'Antonymy' is one of a set of SENSE relations recognised in some analyses of meaning, along with SYNONYMY, HYPONYMY, INCOMPATIBILITY and others. In its most general sense, it refers collectively to all types of semantic oppositeness, with various sub-divisions then being made (e.g. between **graded antonyms,** such as *big ~ small*, where there are degrees of difference, and **ungraded antonyms,** such as *single ~ married*, where there is an either/or contrast). Some linguists (e.g. the British linguist John Lyons (b. 1932)) have reserved the term for a particular type of oppositeness: graded antonyms are referred to as 'antonyms', the other type just illustrated being referred to as COMPLEMENTARIES. It is a matter of controversy how many types of opposites one should usefully recognise in semantic analysis, and the use of the term 'antonym' must always be viewed with caution. See Lyons 1977b: Ch. 9; Bolinger 1975: Ch. 7.

A-over-A A term introduced by Noam CHOMSKY (see *Language and Mind*, 1968) to characterise a CONDITION imposed on the operation of certain

GRAMMATICAL TRANSFORMATIONS. The **A-over-A principle** (or **condition**) states that if a transformation applies to a STRUCTURE of the form [s...[A...]A...]s, then for any category A, it must be interpreted as applying to the maximal PHRASE of the type A. For example, the SENTENCE *John kept the car in the garage* is AMBIGUOUS: it can mean either 'It was in the garage that he kept the car' or 'The car in the garage was kept by John' (cf. 'the car in the street by Mary', etc.). The sentence can be DISAMBIGUATED by such INTERROGATIVES as *How much did the car in the garage cost?*, which relates only to the second of these, i.e. to the sentence where the phrase *in the garage* is part of the larger NOUN phrase. The A-over-A principle ensures that any transformational operation applying to *car* will also apply to *garage*. The reference given above illustrates several other types of construction which evidence the need for a condition of this sort. Its precise formalisation and range of application has, however, provoked considerable discussion.

apex (apic-al, -o) A term used in PHONETICS for the end point of the TONGUE (also known as the TIP), used in the ARTICULATION of a few speech sounds, such as the TRILLED [r], or some varieties of DENTAL (sc. 'apico-dental') sounds. Such sounds could then be classified as 'apical'. See Catford 1977: Ch. 8.

application (applicab-le, -ility) (1) A term used by some LINGUISTS to refer to the overall relationship which exists between LANGUAGE and non-linguistic entities, situations, etc. The 'application' of a linguistic UNIT is its use in a specific CONTEXT; a unit is said to be 'applicable' to that context. For example, a LEXICAL ITEM may be applied to a range of situations (none of which would constitute part of its normal DENOTATION or REFERENCE), e.g. *heap* being applied to a car, a house, a sculpture. The term is particularly useful in the context of translation, where pairs of apparently equivalent terms turn out to have different ranges of application, e.g. the use of *merci* in French differs from the use of *thank you* in English. If items from different languages totally correspond in the range of situations where they may be used, they are said to have the same application. See Lyons 1977b: Ch. 7; 1968: Ch. 9.

(2) **Applicational grammar** is the name given to a type of GENERATIVE linguistic theory proposed by the Soviet linguist S. K. Šaumjan (b. 1916). See Lyons 1977a: Ch. 8.

applied linguistics A branch of LINGUISTICS where the primary concern is the application of linguistic theories, methods and findings to the elucidation of LANGUAGE problems which have arisen in other areas of experience. The most well-developed branch of applied linguistics is the teaching and learning of foreign languages, and sometimes the term is used as if this were the only field involved. But several other fields of application have emerged in recent years, including the linguistic analysis of language disorders (CLINICAL LINGUISTICS), the use of language in mother-tongue education, and developments in LEXICOGRAPHY, translation and STYLISTICS. There is an uncertain boundary between applied linguistics and the various interdisciplinary branches of linguistics, such as SOCIOLINGUISTICS and PSYCHOLIN-GUISTICS, especially as several of the latter's concerns involve practical outcomes of a plainly 'applied' kind (e.g. planning a national language policy). On the other hand, as these branches develop their own theoretical foundations, the distinction between 'pure' and 'applied' is becoming more apparent, and the characterisation of research as being in 'applied psycholinguistics', etc. is now more regularly encountered. See Corder 1973: Ch. 7.

apposition(al) A traditional term retained in some models of GRAM-MATICAL description for a sequence of units which are CONSTITUENTS at the same grammatical LEVEL, and which have an identity or similarity of REFERENCE. In *John Smith, the butcher, came in*, for example, there are two NOUN PHRASES; they have identity of reference; and they have the same SYNTACTIC function (as indicated by the omissibility of either, without this affecting the sentence's ACCEPTABILITY, e.g. *John Smith came in / The butcher came in*). There are however many theoretical and methodological problems in defining the notion of apposition, because of the existence of several constructions which satisfy only some of these criteria, and where other SEMANTIC or syntactic issues are involved, as in titles and other designations (*the number six, my friend John,* etc.). See Quirk *et al* 1972: Ch. 9.

appropriate(ness) An application of the general sense of this term in LINGUISTICS, and especially in SOCIOLINGUISTICS and STYLISTICS, to refer to a linguistic VARIETY or FORM which is considered suitable or possible in a given social situation. For example, ELLIPTICAL and CONTRACTED forms (e.g. *I'll, isn't, going to lunch?,* etc.) are appropriate for relatively informal conversational situations; forms such as *thou, vouchsafe,* etc. are appropriate for some kinds of religious situations. The point of the term is to provide an alternative to the absolute implications of CORRECTNESS encountered in PRESCRIPTIVE approaches to language, where linguistic forms are held to be either right or wrong, no reference being paid to the different expectations of different situations. See Bolinger 1975: Ch. 8; Palmer 1971: Ch. 1.

approximant A general term used by some PHONETICIANS in the classification of speech sounds on the basis of their MANNER OF ARTICULATION, and corresponding to what in other approaches would be called FRICTIONLESS CONTINUANTS, i.e. [w], [j], [r], [l], and all VOWELS. The term is based on the ARTICULATIONS involved, in that one articulator approaches another, but the degree of narrowing involved does not produce audible friction. In some analyses, [h] would also be considered an approximant (i.e. the voiceless equivalent of the VOWEL following). See Ladefoged 1975: Chs. 1, 3.

arbitrariness (arbitrary) A suggested defining property of human LANGUAGE (contrasting with the properties of other SEMIOTIC systems) whereby LINGUISTIC FORMS are said to lack any physical correspondence with the entities in the world to which they refer. For example, there is nothing in the word *table* which reflects the shape, etc. of the thing. The relationship between sound and meaning is said to be 'arbitrary' – or 'conventional', as classical tradition put it. By contrast, some words in a language may be partly or wholly ICONIC, i.e. they do reflect properties of the non-linguistic world, e.g. onomatopoeic expressions, such as *splash, murmur, mumble*. See Lyons 1977b: Chs. 3, 4; 1968: Ch. 1.

arc A convention used in RELATIONAL GRAMMAR to represent a directional relation of DEPENDENCE between a SYNTACTIC UNIT (or 'governor') and the entities which constitute the relational STRUCTURE of that unit. The 'arcs' in a 'relational network' are represented by arrows, e.g.

CLAUSE

NOM	V	NOM
The man	saw	the cat

Relationships are postulated between pairs of arcs, and these pairs of arcs can then in turn be inter-related in 'pair-networks' (as is found in **arc pair grammar**, a development of relational grammar proposed in the mid-1970s). See Radford 1981: Ch. 4.

archiphoneme A term used in PHONOLOGY referring to a way of handling the problem of NEUTRALISATION (i.e. when the CONTRAST between PHONEMES is lost in certain positions in a WORD). In such cases as PLOSIVES following initial /s-/, where there is no OPPOSITION (e.g.

there is no *sgin to contrast with *skin*), the problem for the phonologist is how to analyse the second element of these words. To choose either the voiceless TRANSCRIPTION /skɪn/ or the voiced one /sgɪn/ would be to attribute the element with a contrastive status it does not possess. The solution suggested by the PRAGUE SCHOOL phonologist, Nikolai Trubetskoy (1890–1939) was to set up a new category for such cases, which he called an archiphoneme, and to transcribe it with a different symbol. A capital letter is sometimes used, e.g. /sKɪn/. Alternative ways of analysing the problem have been suggested, as in MORPHO-PHONEMIC approaches. See Lyons 1968: Ch. 3; Hyman 1975: Ch. 3.

area(-1) A term used in DIALECTOLOGY for any geographical region isolated on the basis of its LINGUISTIC characteristics. The study of the linguistic properties of 'areas' – the analysis of the divergent FORMS they contain, and their historical antecedents – is known as **areal linguistics**. An **areal classification** would establish **areal types** (or **groups**), such as the Scandinavian languages, or the London-influenced dialects – cases where it is possible to show certain linguistic features in common as a result of the proximity of the SPEECH communities. Such a classification often cuts across that made on purely historical grounds. It is often possible to identify a **focal area** – the region from which these linguistic characteristics have spread to the area as a whole (as in the case of London) – and several other significant parts of an area have been terminologically distinguished, e.g. the **transitional areas** which occur between adjacent areas, the **relic areas** which preserve linguistic features of an earlier stage of development. Areal linguistics is contrasted with **non-areal** differences in language use, e.g. contrasts between male and female speech, and between some social VARIETIES. See Bolinger 1975: Ch. 11.

argument A term used in PREDICATE calculus, and often found in the discussion of SEMANTIC theory, to refer to the relationship of a name to the simple PROPOSITION of which it is a part. For example, in the proposition, *the boy is naughty*, *the boy* is an 'argument' of the proposition. In CASE GRAMMAR, each underlying proposition is analysed in terms of a predicate word and an unordered set of argument slots, each of which is labelled according to its semantic ('case') relationship with the predicate word. See Lyons 1977b: Ch. 6; Bolinger 1975: Ch. 15.

arrangement A term used in LINGUISTICS to refer to any SEQUENCE of linguistic ELEMENTS in terms of their relative position, or DISTRIBU-TION, e.g. the possible combinations of PHONEMES within SYLLABLES and WORDS, or of MORPHEMES within words and SENTENCES. This

article

notion is fundamental to the ITEM-AND-ARRANGEMENT model of linguistic description. See Lyons 1968: Ch. 2.

article A term used in the GRAMMATICAL classification of WORDS, referring to a sub-class of DETERMINERS which display a primary role in differentiating the uses of NOUNS, e.g. *the/a* in English. Many languages have no article system (e.g. Russian). Of those which do, a distinction is usually made into **definite** and **indefinite** (or 'non-definite') types, partly on SEMANTIC and partly on grammatical grounds. Articles may appear before the noun (as in English), or after (as in Swedish). See Quirk *et al* 1968: Ch. 4; Lyons 1968: Ch. 7.

articulation (articulat-e, -or) (1) The general term in PHONETICS for the physiological movements involved in modifying an air flow to produce the various types of speech sounds, using the VOCAL TRACT above the LARYNX. Sounds are classified in terms of their PLACE and MANNER OF ARTICULATION in the vocal apparatus. Reference is usually made to the nature of the AIR-STREAM MECHANISM, the action of the VOCAL CORDS, the position of the soft PALATE, and the other organs in the mouth – TONGUE and lips in particular. Any specific part of the vocal apparatus involved in the production of a sound is called an **articulator**. Two kinds of articulators are distinguished: 'active' articulators are the movable parts of the vocal apparatus, such as the lips, tongue and lower jaw; 'passive' articulators are those parts of the vocal tract which cannot move, but which provide the active articulators with points of reference, e.g. the roof of the mouth, the upper teeth.

In recent years, the study of articulation using instrumental techniques has emphasised the importance of seeing articulation not as a sequence of independently articulated sounds, but as a continuum of sound production. This principle is obscured through the use of phonetic TRANSCRIPTION. The transcription [kæt] suggests the existence of three DISCRETE segments: what it obscures is the existence of the TRANSITIONS between segments, as the several articulators, working simultaneously, gradually move from one articulatory position to the next. Forms of transcription which draw attention to these continuously varying (DYNAMIC) parameters are devisable, but they are complex, and lack the immediate readability of the SEGMENTAL transcription.

Several types of articulation can be distinguished. Most sounds are produced with a single point of articulation. Sounds may however be produced involving two points of articulation (COARTICULATION), in which case two articulatory possibilities emerge: the two points of articulation both contribute equally to the identity of the sound ('double articulation' or 'co-ordinate coarticulation'); or one point of articulation may be the dominant one (the 'primary (co-)articulation') the other having a lesser degree of stricture (the 'secondary (co-)articulation'). Examples of secondary articulation are palatalisation (cf. PALATAL), velarisation (cf. VELAR), pharyngealisation (cf. PHARYNX) and labialisation (cf. LABIAL). See Catford 1977: Chs. 8, 10; Ladefoged 1975: Chs. 1, 7, 9.

(2) There is a second use of the phrase **double articulation**, within the linguistic theory associated with the French linguist, André Martinet (b. 1908). He used the term to refer to the two LEVELS of STRUCTURE in which LANGUAGE is organised: speech can be analysed into the meaningful FORMS of language (i.e. MORPHEMES, WORDS, etc.), and this constitutes a 'first' articulation; these units are then capable of further analysis into the meaningless sound-units of language (i.e. PHONEMES), and this constitutes a 'second' articulation. A corresponding term in more widespread use is DUALITY OF STRUCTURE. See Lyons 1968: Ch. 2.

articulatory phonetics The branch of PHONETICS which studies the way in which speech sounds are made ('articulated') by the VOCAL ORGANS. It derives much of its descriptive terminology from the fields of anatomy and physiology, and is sometimes referred to as 'physiological phonetics'. This area has traditionally held central place in the training of phoneticians, the movements involved being reasonably accessible to observation and, in principle, under the control of the investigator. The classification of sounds used in the INTERNATIONAL PHONETIC alphabet, for example, is based on articulatory variables. In recent years, there has been much progress in the development of instrumental techniques for observing and measuring such factors as TONGUE, lip, PALATE and VOCAL CORD movement, such as the palatograph, which displays tongue contact with the palate, the electro-aerometer, which measures the relative flow of air from mouth and nose, and ELECTROMYOGRAPHY, for the measurement of muscular movement while speaking. Using such techniques, a far more detailed understanding of articulation is possible than using traditional visual and kinaesthetic methods. See Ladefoged 1975: Ch. 1; Catford 1977: Chs. 2, 7, 8, 12.

articulatory setting The general position of all the ARTICULATORS in relation to each other, which one adopts and maintains during speech. This accounts for some of the broad qualitative differences between LANGUAGES and DIALECTS, e.g. a characteristic NASAL twang, or marked degree of lip ROUNDING. It is however an aspect of articulation which

ascriptive

has received little study in PHONETICS. See Abercrombie 1967: Ch. 6.

ascriptive A term used in GRAMMATICAL analysis to refer to a SENTENCE of the type *The cat is angry*, where there is an attributive identity between the pre- and post-verbal ELEMENTS, but no permutability (unlike the otherwise similar EQUATIVE sentence – cf. **angry is the cat*, but *Fred is the leader/The leader is Fred*). Sentences of the type *Fred is a doctor* are also sometimes called ascriptive, but are more problematic to analyse. See Lyons 1977b: Ch. 12.

aspect(ual) A category used in the GRAMMATICAL description of VERBS (along with TENSE and MOOD), referring primarily to the way the grammar marks the duration or type of activity denoted by the verb. A well-studied 'aspectual' CONTRAST, between 'perfective' and 'imperfective', is found in many Slavonic languages: in Russian, for example, there is a perfective/imperfective contrast – the former referring to the completion of an action, the latter expressing duration without specifying completion. The English verb PHRASE makes a formal distinction which is usually analysed as aspectual: the contrast between PROGRESSIVE (or 'continuous') and 'non-progressive' (or SIMPLE) duration of action. The contrast between *I was living* and *I have been living*, and other uses of the *have* auxiliary, are also often analysed in aspectual terms, but this analysis is more controversial. Other English constructions have sometimes been analysed in terms of aspect, e.g. involving 'habitual' contrasts (as in *used to*); and in other languages, further aspectual distinctions may be found, e.g. 'iterative' or 'frequentative' (referring to a regularly occurring action), 'inchoative' or 'inceptive' (referring to the beginning of an action). See Quirk *et al* 1972: Ch. 3; Lyons 1968: Ch. 7.

Aspects model/theory A commonly used abbreviation for the approach to GENERATIVE GRAMMAR expounded in Noam CHOMSKY's 1965 book, *Aspects of the Theory of Syntax*; also known as the 'STANDARD THEORY'. MODELS similar in principle to this one are 'Aspects-type' models. See Lyons 1977a: Ch. 8.

aspiration (aspirated) A term in PHONETICS for the audible breath which may accompany a sound's ARTICULATION, as when PLOSIVE CONSONANTS are released. It is usually symbolised by a small raised [ʰ] following the main symbol. In examples such as English *pin* [pʰɪn], the aspiration may be felt by holding the back of the hand close to the mouth while saying the word; the contrast with *bin*, where there is no aspiration, is noticeable. Some languages, such as Hindi, have contrasts of aspiration applying to both voiceless and VOICED STOPS, *viz* a four-way contrast of [p-], [pʰ-], [b-], and [bʰ-]. In some phonetic environments the aspiration effect varies, as when in English the PLOSIVES are followed by /l, r, w, j/: here the aspiration devoices these consonants, as in *please, twice, queue*. Following initial /s/, the aspiration contrast is lost altogether, as in [spɪn]. Other sounds than plosives may be aspirated, but they are less commonly encountered. See Ladefoged 1975: Chs. 3, 12.

assign A term used in GENERATIVE linguistics to refer to the action of RULES: rules attribute, or 'assign' structure to SENTENCES. By the use of REWRITING rules, a STRING of ELEMENTS is introduced as a series of stages, each stage being associated with a pair of LABELLED BRACKETS, e.g.

$$S \rightarrow NP + VP \qquad (NP + VP)_S$$
$$VP \rightarrow V + NP \qquad (NP + (V + NP)_{VP})_S$$
$$NP \rightarrow D + N \qquad ((D + N)_{NP} + (V + (D + N)_{NP})_{VP})_S$$

In such a way, the structure of Noun Phrase, Verb Phrase, etc. can be assigned to any sentence to which these rules apply, e.g. ((the man)(saw (the dog))). See Lyons 1977a: Ch. 6.

assimilation A general term in PHONETICS which refers to the influence exercised by one sound segment upon the ARTICULATION of another, so that the sounds become more alike, or identical. The study of assimilation (and its opposite, DISSIMILATION) has been an important part of HISTORICAL LINGUISTIC study, but it has been a much neglected aspect of SYNCHRONIC speech analysis, owing to the traditional manner of viewing speech as a sequence of DISCRETE WORDS. If one imagines speech to be spoken 'word at a time', with PAUSES corresponding to the spaces of the written language, there is little chance that the assimilations and other features of CONNECTED SPEECH will be noticed. When passages of natural conversation came to be analysed, however, assimilation emerged as being one of the main means whereby fluency and RHYTHM are maintained.

Several types of assimilation can be recognised. It may be 'partial' or 'total'. In the phrase *ten bikes*, for example, the normal form in colloquial speech would be /tem baɪks/, not /ten baɪks/, which would sound somewhat 'careful'. In this case, the assimilation has been partial: the /n/ has fallen under the influence of the following /b/, and has adopted its BILABIALity, becoming /m/. It has not, however, adopted its PLOSIVENESS. The phrase /teb baɪks/ would only be likely

association

if one had a severe cold! The assimilation is total in *ten mice* /tem mais/, where the /n/ is now identical with the /m/ which influenced it.

Another classification is in terms of whether the change of sound involved is the result of the influence of an adjacent sound, or of one further away. The common type is the former, as illustrated above: this is known as 'contiguous' or 'contact' assimilation. An example of the opposite, 'non-contiguous' (or 'distance') assimilation, occurs in *turn up trumps*, where the /-n/ of *turn* may be articulated as /-m/, under the influence of later sounds. It also occurs in languages displaying VOWEL harmony, where a vowel in one part of a WORD may influence other vowels to be articulated similarly, even though there may be other sounds between them.

A further classification is in terms of the direction in which the assimilation works. There are three possibilities:

(1) **regressive** (or **anticipatory**) assimilation: the sound changes because of the influence of the following sound, e.g. *ten bikes* above: this is particularly common in English in ALVEOLAR consonants in word-FINAL position;

(2) **progressive** assimilation: the sound changes because of the influence of the preceding sound, e.g. *lunch score* articulated with the *s*- becoming /ʃ/, under the influence of the preceding -*ch*; but these assimilations are less common;

(3) **coalescent** (or **reciprocal**) assimilation: there is mutual influence, or FUSION, of the sounds upon each other, as when *don't you* is pronounced as /'dəʊntʃʊ/ – the *t* and the *y* have fused to produce an AFFRICATE.

See Gimson 1970: Ch. 11.

association (associative) The general senses of this term are often found in linguistic discussion – the non-linguistic feelings (cf. CONNOTATIONS) which a LEXICAL ITEM gives rise to, or the range of psychologically connected items which come to mind (i.e. the 'sense associations'). Some LINGUISTS have used the term with a more restricted definition, however. For example, the SAUSSUREAN conception of PARADIGMATIC relationships was referred to as 'associative relations'. Some linguists use the term 'associative field' (or 'association group') to refer to a set of lexical items which display a specific similarity of FORM or SENSE. See Bolinger 1975: Ch. 8; Lyons 1968: Ch. 9.

asterisk(ed) (1) In LINGUISTICS, a linguistic contruction that is unACCEPTABLE or unGRAMMATICAL is marked thus by the use of an initial asterisk, e.g. **the man do been go*. An **asterisked form** (or 'starred form') is a form which cannot occur in a language, e.g. *walkedn't. See Lyons 1968: Ch. 4.

(2) In HISTORICAL linguistics, asterisks are used to indicate a form which has been RECONSTRUCTED, there being no written evidence for its existence, as in the sounds and words postulated for Indo-European, e.g. *s, *penkʷe 'five'. See Robins 1971: Ch. 8.

attested A term used in LINGUISTICS to refer to a linguistic FORM for which there is evidence of present or past use. In HISTORICAL linguistics, for example, **attested forms** are those which appear in written texts, as opposed to the 'RECONSTRUCTED forms' arrived at by a process of deduction. In the studies of contemporary speech, the term is used to refer to actual recorded usage, compared with the hypothetical predictions of a GRAMMAR or the INTUITIVE (but otherwise unsupported) observations of the linguist. See Robins 1971: Ch. 8.

attitudinal A term sometimes used in SEMANTICS as part of a classification of types of MEANING: it refers to the emotional element in meaning, as in the different attitudes expressed by varying the INTONATION or loudness of a sentence, e.g. anger, sarcasm. In the context of PROSODY, 'attitudinal meaning' is usually distinguished from GRAMMATICAL. Alternative terms include AFFECTIVE and EMOTIVE; opposed terms include COGNITIVE and REFERENTIAL. See Lyons 1977b: Ch. 7.

attribute (attributive) (1) A term derived from auditory perception and used in AUDITORY PHONETICS to refer to an isolatable characteristic of sound sensation, e.g. the attributes of PITCH, LOUDNESS and TIMBRE. See Crystal 1969: Ch. 3.

(2) In GRAMMATICAL description, the term is normally used to refer to the role of ADJECTIVES and NOUNS when they occur as MODIFIERS of the HEAD of a noun PHRASE. For example, *red* has 'attributive' function in *the red chair*, as has *John's* in *John's hat*. The term contrasts with the PREDICATIVE function of these words, as in *the chair is red*, *the hat is John's*. Some MODELS of grammatical description have extended the use of this term to include such COMPLEMENT structures as *he is **my uncle**, I called him **a fool***, and this usage can include the adjectival use above (i.e. in *he is happy*, the adjective's SEMANTIC role in relation to *he* is one of 'attribution'). Ambiguity in this context is thus a real possibility. See Lyons 1968: Chs. 7, 8; Quirk *et al* 1972: Chs. 5, 7.

auditory phonetics The branch of PHONETICS which studies the perceptual response to speech sounds, as mediated by ear, auditory nerve and brain. It is a less well-studied area of phonetics, mainly because of the difficulties encountered as soon as one attempts to identify and measure psychological and neurological responses to speech sounds. Anatomical and physiological studies of the ear are well advanced, as are techniques for the measurement of hearing, and the clinical use of such study is now established under the headings of audiology and audiometry. But little pure research has been done into the attributes of speech sound sensation, seen as a phonetic SYSTEM, and the relationship between such phonetic analyses and PHONOLOGICAL studies remains obscure. See Robins 1971: Ch. 3; Gimson 1970: Ch. 3.

autonomous (1) An adjective often used in discussing the status of LINGUISTICS as a science: the implication is that the subject of language is now studied in its own terms, no longer being dependent on the incidental interest of scholars from other disciplines, such as logic, literary criticism, or history. See Robins 1971: Ch. 1.

(2) In PHONOLOGY, the term is used to characterise the notion of a PHONEME when no reference is made to its relationships with GRAMMATICAL (especially WORD) STRUCTURE. The **autonomous phoneme**, in this sense, is contrasted with the MORPHOPHONEME, or the SYSTEMATIC PHONEME of GENERATIVE linguistics, where other factors than the strictly phonemic are allowed into the analysis. See Hyman 1975: Ch. 3.

(3) **Autonomous syntax** is the view propounded by the STANDARD THEORY of generative grammar that the SYNTACTIC COMPONENT of the grammar is independent ('autonomous') of SEMANTICS, i.e. the factors which determine the GRAMMATICALITY of a SENTENCE operate without reference to those which determine the sentence's MEANING. This view is attacked in GENERATIVE SEMANTICS. See Lyons 1977a: Ch. 8.

aux The usual abbreviation for AUXILIARY.

auxiliary (1) A term used in the GRAMMATICAL description of the VERB PHRASE, to refer to the set of verbs, subordinate to the main LEXICAL verb, which help to make distinctions in MOOD, ASPECT, VOICE, etc. In English, the main auxiliaries are *do, be* and *have*, e.g. *he is coming*, ***does he know***, **he has taken**. The modal auxiliaries include *can/could, may/might, shall/should, will/would, must, ought to* and *used to*. The class of auxiliaries is distinguished grammatically from lexical verbs in several ways; for instance, they have a special NEGATIVE form (e.g. *isn't, hasn't, can't*, as opposed to **walkn't*), and they can be used with SUBJECT INVERSION (e.g. *is he, does he, will they*, as opposed to **walks he*). 'Marginal' or 'semi-auxiliaries', i.e. verbs which display some but not all of the properties of the auxiliary class, include *dare* and *need*. See Quirk *et al* 1972: Ch. 3; Palmer 1971: Ch. 4.

(2) In SOCIOLINGUISTICS, an **auxiliary language** is one which has been adopted by different SPEECH communities for purposes of communication, trade, education, etc., it being the native language of none of them. English and French are auxiliary languages for many communities in Africa for example; Swahili is used thus in parts of East Africa. This sense is unrelated to the use of the term 'auxiliary language' to mean an artificially constructed language, such as Esperanto. See Bolinger 1975: Ch. 16.

axiom(atic) An application in LINGUISTICS of the general use of this term in the branch of logic known as axiomatics. It refers to a set of initial propositions (or 'axioms') which a theory assumes to be true. Further propositions (or 'theorems') are then deduced from these by means of specific rules of inference (to which the term 'transformational rule' is sometimes applied). The full statement of an axiomatic system will contain a 'syntax', which determines the WELL-FORMEDNESS of its propositions, and a 'vocabulary', which lists the terms of the system. The application of these ideas in LINGUISTICS has come mainly from the influence of CHOMSKYAN ideas, concerning the FORMALISATION of LANGUAGE, and is central to MATHEMATICAL linguistics. In pre-GENERATIVE attempts at systematising ideas about language, the weaker term POSTULATES was usually used. See Lyons 1977a: App.

axis (1) A term sometimes used in LINGUISTICS to refer to intersecting dimensions of linguistic analysis, especially those introduced by the Swiss linguist Ferdinand de SAUSSURE. The distinction between SYNCHRONIC and DIACHRONIC is characterised as the 'axis of simultaneities' vs. the 'axis of successions'. Likewise the SYNTAGMATIC/PARADIGMATIC distinction may be referred to in terms of axes ('syntagmatic axis', 'axis of chain relationships', etc.). See Lyons 1968: Ch. 2.

(2) In some MODELS of GRAMMATICAL classification, the term refers to the second ELEMENT in an EXOCENTRIC CONSTRUCTION, the other being the DIRECTOR, e.g. *in the garden*, *see the man*. See Lyons 1968: Ch. 6.

B

⟨⟨⟨⟨⟨⟨

baby-talk (BT) An extension in LANGUAGE ACQUISITION studies of
the traditional sense of this term, to refer to the whole range of
DISTINCTIVE LINGUISTIC characteristics found in adult speech addressed
to young children. Baby-talk thus includes far more than the often
stereotyped use of endearing pronunciations and words (such as
doggie, /den/ for *then*, etc.) and is primarily characterised with reference
to the use of simplified SENTENCE STRUCTURES, and certain types of
linguistic interaction (such as the expansion of a child's sentence into
a full adult form, e.g. *dadda gone → yes, daddy's gone*). The study of
baby-talk, or 'language input' became a major focus of language
acquisition studies in the early 1970s, a particular stimulus coming
from SOCIOLINGUISTICS. See Bolinger 1975: Ch. 1.

back (sounds) Classification of back speech sounds are of two types: (a)
those articulated in the back part of the mouth; and (b) those
articulated with the back part of the TONGUE. In many cases, these two
criteria coincide: back VOWELS are 'back' in both senses, as in English
hard, talk, show, got, as are the back CONSONANTS heard at the beginning
of *go, car* and *way*. Consonants made in the LARYNX or PHARYNX,
however, such as [h], are 'back' in sense (a) only. Back vowels are
contrasted, in traditional PHONETIC classifications, with FRONT and
CENTRAL vowels.

In the traditional classifications, sounds made at the back of the
mouth are distinguished from those made at the front; and those made
by the back of the tongue are opposed to those made further forward,
by the TIP and BLADE (or front) of the tongue. In the DISTINCTIVE
FEATURE analysis of sounds proposed by CHOMSKY & Halle, the
equivalent of 'front' is ANTERIOR, and of 'tip/blade' is CORONAL. Back
sounds as a whole, in their terminology, are a type of CAVITY feature
(specifically, a TONGUE-BODY feature); they are contrasted with **non-
back** sounds, i.e. sounds produced without any retraction of the
tongue from the neutral position. Back vowels and consonants are
more difficult to control consciously, because of the relative lack of

feeling in that area of the mouth. See Gimson 1970: Ch. 2; Catford 1977: Chs. 8, 9.

back-formation A term used in historical studies of MORPHOLOGY to refer to an abnormal type of WORD-FORMATION where a shorter word is derived by deleting an imagined AFFIX from a longer form already present in the language. *Edit*, for example, comes from *editor*, and not the other way round. This DERIVATION presumably took place because NATIVE-SPEAKERS saw an ANALOGY between *editor* and other words where a normal derivational process had taken place, e.g. *credit/creditor*, *inspect/inspector*, *act/actor*, the NOUNS being in each case formed from the VERBS. The derivation of *edit* thus reverses the expected derivational pattern, hence the term 'back-formation'. See Quirk *et al* 1972: App. 1; Bolinger 1975: Ch. 12.

backlooping A term in TAGMEMIC GRAMMAR for the inclusion of higher LEVEL CONSTRUCTIONS within the SLOTS of a lower level construction, as in the use of RELATIVE CLAUSES within the NOUN PHRASE (e.g. *the lady who was talking*...); sometimes referred to as **loopback**. It is distinguished from LEVEL-SKIPPING and LAYERING. See Bolinger 1975: Ch. 15.

base (1) A term used in MORPHOLOGY as an alternative to ROOT or STEM: it refers to any part of a WORD seen as a UNIT to which an operation can be applied, as when one adds an AFFIX to a root or stem. For example, in *unhappy*, the **base form** is *happy*; if *-ness* is then added to *unhappy*, the whole of this item would be considered the base to which the new affix is attached. Some analysts, however, restrict the term 'base' to be equivalent to 'root', i.e. the part of a word remaining when all AFFIXES have been removed. In such an approach, *happy* would be the base form (the highest common factor) of all its DERIVATIONS – *happiness, unhappy, unhappiness*, etc. See Matthews 1974: Ch. 3.

(2) In a more abstract approach to GRAMMAR (SYNTAX as well as morphology), the term **basic form** is used to refer to any abstract unit which has been set up in order to allow a range of FORMS to be inter-related, i.e. seen as VARIANTS. In morphology, for example, the basic, or CANONICAL form of a MORPHEME might be identified as one of its ALTERNANTS (e.g. the **basic form** (or 'basic alternant') of the morpheme {*man*} is the morph *man*, with *men* being DERIVED from this in some way), or it might be a unit underlying both (e.g. a unit {m V n}, where both *man* and *men* are derived by some process of VOWEL (V) replacement). Similarly in syntax, a SENTENCE can be seen as having

a basic form from which other sentences are derived (e.g. ACTIVE underlying PASSIVE sentences, POSITIVES underlying NEGATIVES), or related structures can be seen as being derived from a common UNDERLYING form. GENERATIVE grammar is the approach which has exploited the potential of such analyses most fully. This sense of 'basic', it should be clear, is different from that used in language teaching or learning situations, where (possibly in addition to the above) the implication is that basic patterns of vocabulary are easier to learn, or are more useful for communication. See Matthews 1974: Ch. 3.

(3) As part of the STANDARD model of generative grammar, the term is used in the phrase **base component** (or 'sub-component'), which is one of the two main divisions of the grammar's syntactic COMPONENT, the other being the TRANSFORMATIONAL (sub-)component. In Noam CHOMSKY's *Syntactic Structures* (1957), the alternative term was 'phrase structure component', which specified the PHRASE-STRUCTURE RULES of the grammar. In *Aspects of the Theory of Syntax* (1965), the same distinction (between base and transformational sub-components) is made, but the roles of the two differ from the earlier version, in relation to the theory as a whole. In *Aspects*, the base now contains a 'categorial' component (specifying the CATEGORIES S, NP, VP, etc.) and a 'lexical' component (consisting of LEXICAL entries made up of such FEATURES as 'animate', 'human', etc.). Taken together, the information in these components specifies the DEEP STRUCTURE of sentences. In more recent versions of generative grammar, the role of the base component receives further modifications, as the relationship between syntax and SEMANTICS is investigated. See Akmajian & Heny 1975: Ch. 2; Lyons 1977a: Ch. 7.

basilect A term used by some SOCIOLINGUISTS, in the study of the development of CREOLE LANGUAGES, to refer to a linguistic VARIETY (or 'lect') most remote from the prestige language (the 'matrilect' or 'acrolect'). See Bolinger 1975: Ch. 11.

behaviourism In LINGUISTICS, the influence of this school of psychology (the study of observable and measurable behaviour) has been most marked in the work of the American linguist Leonard BLOOMFIELD. It can be seen in the Bloomfieldian insistence on rigorous DISCOVERY PROCEDURES, and most notably in his behaviourist account of MEANING in terms of observable stimuli and responses made by participants in specific situations. The limitations of behaviourist (or 'mechanistic') accounts of LANGUAGE (especially that associated with the work of the American psychologist Burrhus Frederic Skinner (b. 1904) were criticised by Noam CHOMSKY in the late 1950s, in writings which anticipate the development of MENTALISTIC ideas in linguistics. See Lyons 1977b: Ch. 5.

benefactive A term used in some GRAMMATICAL descriptions to refer to a CASE FORM or CONSTRUCTION whose FUNCTION in a SENTENCE is to express the notion 'on behalf of' or 'for the benefit of'. See Lyons 1968: Ch. 8.

bidialect(al)ism In its most general sense, the term refers to proficiency in the use by a person or a community of two DIALECTS of a language, whether regional or social. Several kinds of 'bidialectal' situation have been studied, one of the most well-known being the switching from a casual to a FORMAL VARIETY of speech (DIGLOSSIA). More specifically, it is a principle propounded in SOCIOLINGUISTICS and EDUCATIONAL LINGUISTICS wherein different dialects are attributed equal linguistic validity and recommended for use in their appropriate social settings. The principle is of particular importance in relation to educational policy in schools, where the differences between the non-standard and the STANDARD forms of a language can lead to considerable conflict. Bidialectalism recommends that both non-standard and standard dialects should be encouraged in the educational process, along with the fostering of children's abilities to use CODE-switching, thus developing a greater degree of understanding and control over the varieties of their language than would otherwise be the case. See Bolinger 1975: Ch. 12; Gumperz & Hymes 1971: Intro.

bilabial A term in the classification of CONSONANT sounds on the basis of their PLACE OF ARTICULATION: it refers to a sound made by the coming together of both lips. Examples are the initial sounds in *pin*, *bin*, *mat*; a non-English bilabial would be the initial sound in Welsh *mhen* 'my head'. The term is restricted to consonantal *articulation*; the active use of the lips in the articulation of VOWELS is discussed in terms of ROUNDING and SPREADING. The only common speech sounds in which a single lip is the primary articulator are known as LABIO-DENTALS. 'Monolabial' is not found as a technical term; 'quadrilabial' exists only in humour, as part of the PHONETICIAN's technical description of a kiss! See Gimson 1970: Ch. 4; Catford 1977: Ch. 8.

bilateral A type of OPPOSITION recognised in PRAGUE SCHOOL PHONO-LOGY, distinguished from MULTILATERAL. The opposition between English /t/ and /d/, for example, is bilateral, because these are the only UNITS in the SYSTEM which are ALVEOLAR/PLOSIVE, and they are

bilingual

differentiated by the single feature of VOICING; the opposition between, say, /t/ and /v/, however is multilateral, because there are other possibilities involving the same set of FEATURES, e.g. /d/ vs. /f/. See Hyman 1975: Ch. 2.

bilingual(ism) The general sense of this term – a person who can speak TWO LANGUAGES – provides a pre-theoretical frame of reference for linguistic study, especially by SOCIOLINGUISTS, and by APPLIED LINGUISTS involved in foreign or second language teaching. The focus of attention has been on the many kinds and degrees of 'bilingualism' and 'bilingual situations' which exist. Definitions of bilingualism reflect assumptions about the degree of proficiency a person must achieve before he qualifies as bilingual (whether comparable to a monolingual NATIVE-SPEAKER, or something less than this, even to the extent of minimal knowledge of a second language). Several technical distinctions have been introduced, e.g. between COMPOUND and CO-ORDINATE bilingualism (based on the extent to which the bilingual sees the two languages as SEMANTICALLY equivalent or non-equivalent), between the various methods of learning the two languages (e.g. simultaneously in childhood or through formal instruction), and between the various levels of abstraction at which the linguistic systems operate – bilingualism being distinguished from BIDIALECTISM, and DIGLOSSIA. Of particular importance is the way in which studies of bilingualism involve the analysis of social, psychological and national (e.g. in the case of Welsh and Flemish) concerns – such as the social status of the different languages, and their role in identifying speakers with particular ethnic groups. See Gumperz & Hymes 1971: Chs. 7, 15; Bolinger 1975: Ch. 12.

binary feature A property which can be used to classify linguistic UNITS in terms of two mutually exclusive possibilities, such as in PHONOLOGY the presence vs. the absence of VOCAL CORD vibration, or lip-ROUNDING. Binary features are a major organisational principle of DISTINCTIVE FEATURE theories of phonology, where it is conventional to mark the OPPOSITION using $+/-$ in square brackets, e.g. a sound is characterised as [+ voice] or [− voice]. Binary features are also established in GRAMMATICAL and SEMANTIC analyses of LEXICAL ITEMS, within GENERATIVE grammar, where the same TRANSCRIPTIONAL convention is used, e.g. NOUNS have such properties as [+ common], [− common].

Binarity, or **binarism**, in this sense is relatable to the principles of binary coding used in INFORMATION theory, but the status of such contrasts in language is often controversial, as it is not always clear whether the linguistic possibilities available in phonology, grammar and semantics are best seen as a series of 'binary choices'. In IMMEDIATE CONSTITUENT analysis, for example, which uses a binary technique for splitting SENTENCES into smaller parts, it is sometimes impossible to decide where a binary division should be made, as in the case of ADJECTIVE sequence (e.g. *nice old red chair* is not really divisible into *nice + old*, *red* or *nice*, *old + red*). In cases where binary features are used, it is sometimes possible to see one of the features as neutral, or unmarked, and the other as positive, or MARKED. See Lyons 1968: Ch. 2.

biolinguistics A developing branch of LINGUISTICS which studies the biological preconditions for language development and use in man, from the viewpoints of both the history of language in the race, and the development of language in the individual. It is also known as **biological linguistics**. Topics of common interest to the two subject-areas involved include the genetic transmission of language, neurophysiological models of language production, the anatomical parallels between human and other species, and the development of pathological forms of language behaviour (cf. CLINICAL LINGUISTICS). See Lyons 1977b: Ch. 3; Clark & Clark 1977: Ch. 13.

biuniqueness A principle in some approaches to PHONOLOGY which states that any sequence of PHONEMES will be represented by a unique sequence of PHONES, and vice versa – in other words, there is a one-to-one (or 'reversible') correspondence between phones and phonemes. For example, in the word *bin*, the relationship between the two LEVELS of analysis can be shown as

$$/b/ + /i/ + /n/$$
$$\updownarrow \qquad \updownarrow \qquad \updownarrow$$
$$[b] \qquad [i] \qquad [n]$$

There are, however, several cases where this straightforward correlation does not apply, and where the notion of a phoneme as a unique class of sounds consequently is invalid. In such cases (cf. OVERLAPPING), one phone is assigned to more than one phoneme, depending on the CONTEXT. The 'biuniqueness condition', along with the conditions of LINEARITY and INVARIANCE, on which it depends, has been particularly criticised in recent years by GENERATIVE phonologists, as part of their general attack on TAXONOMIC phonemics. See Hyman 1975: Ch. 3.

blade The part of the TONGUE between TIP and CENTRE, and which lies opposite the teeth and ALVEOLAR ridge when the tongue is in neutral position. Also known as the LAMINA, it is used in the articulation of several speech sounds, such as [t] and [s]. See Gimson 1970: Ch. 2; Catford 1977: Ch. 8.

bleeding A term used in GENERATIVE linguistic analysis of RULE-ordering, and originally introduced in the context of HISTORICAL PHONOLOGY, to refer to a type of FUNCTIONAL relationship between rules; opposed to FEEDING. A bleeding relationship is one where a rule (A) removes a STRUCTURAL REPRESENTATION to which another rule (B) would otherwise have applied. If rule B is of the form X → Y, then rule A must be of the form W → not X. In these circumstances, rule A is called a **bleeding rule** in relation to B, and the LINEAR ORDER of these rules is called a **bleeding order**. See Hyman 1975: Ch. 4.

blend(ing) A process found in the analysis of GRAMMATICAL and LEXICAL CONSTRUCTIONS, in which two ELEMENTS which do not normally co-occur, according to the RULES of the language, come together within a single LINGUISTIC UNIT. In GRAMMAR, the process is illustrated by such **syntactic blends** as *It's his job is the problem*, a combination of the SENTENCES *it's his job* and *his job is the problem*. In LEXIS, 'blending' is a common source of new WORDS (though not all become standard), e.g. *brunch, Interpol* and *Eurovision*. The term is also used by some PSYCHOLINGUISTS for a type of TONGUE-SLIP involving the FUSION of two target words, e.g. *swurse* for *swear + curse*. See Quirk *et al* 1972: App. 1; Bolinger 1975: Ch. 12.

block(-ed, -ing) A term used in TRANSFORMATIONAL grammar to refer to the non-application of a transformational RULE. A rule is said to be 'blocked' if it cannot be applied to a DERIVATION because of the occurrence of a specific property in the PHRASE-MARKER. See Akmajian & Heny 1975: Ch. 2; Huddleston 1976: Ch.12

Bloomfieldian(ism) Characteristic of, or a follower of the linguistic approach of the American linguist Leonard Bloomfield (1887–1949), as exemplified in his book *Language*, published in 1933. **Bloomfield-ianism** refers particularly to the school of thought which developed between the mid-1930s and 1950s, especially in America, and which was a formative influence on STRUCTURAL LINGUISTICS. It was especially characterised by its behaviouristic principles for the study of MEANING, its insistence on rigorous DISCOVERY PROCEDURES for establishing linguistic units, and a general concern to make LINGUISTICS AUTONOMOUS and scientific (in a BEHAVIOURIST sense). A reaction against Bloomfieldian tenets was a powerful force in producing GENERATIVE grammar. Though Bloomfieldianism is no longer fashionable, some of its methods are still widely used in field studies. See Lyons 1977a: Ch. 3; Bolinger 1975: Ch. 15.

borrow(ing) A term used in COMPARATIVE and HISTORICAL linguistics to refer to linguistic FORMS being taken over by one language or DIALECT from another; such 'borrowings' are usually known as 'loan words' (e.g. *restaurant, bonhomie, chagrin*, which have come into English from French) and several types have been recognised (cf. LOAN). Less commonly, sounds and GRAMMATICAL STRUCTURES may be borrowed, e.g. the pronunciation of the above loan words with a French or quasi-French accent, or the influence of English grammar often found in European languages, e.g. using an English plural *-s* for a noun, as in *drinks, ski-lifts, goals, girls*. See Bolinger 1975: Ch. 12.

bound A term used as part of the classification of MORPHEMES; opposed to FREE. A **bound morpheme** (or **bound form**) is one which cannot occur on its own as a separate WORD, e.g. the various AFFIXES *de-*, *-tion*, *-ise*, etc. See Matthews 1974: Ch. 5.

boundary-symbol/-marker Symbols used in TRANSFORMATIONAL GRAMMAR to indicate the boundaries between STRUCTURAL UNITS, e.g. the ELEMENTS of a STRING (+), or the boundaries of strings (#), e.g. # *the + man + pres + have + en + kick + the + ball* #. See Lyons 1968: Ch. 6; Huddleston 1976: Ch. 3.

bracketing (brackets) (1) A technique used in LINGUISTICS to display the internal (HIERARCHICAL) structure of a STRING of ELEMENTS, in a similar manner to that used in mathematics and symbolic logic. In the SENTENCE *the cat saw the king*, for example, the various intuitively-motivated divisions it is possible to make are each associated with the imposition of a pair of brackets onto the sentence, e.g. distinguishing *the cat* from *saw* from *the king* would lead to the representation (*the cat*) (*saw*) (*the king*). In a more sophisticated analysis, each pair of brackets would be associated with a label which indicated the grammatical reason for their presence (a 'labelled' bracketing), for example:

(the cat)$_{Subject}$ (saw)$_{Verb}$ (the king)$_{Object}$

In a more sophisticated analysis still, the order in which the pairs of brackets are applied is also made explicit, as in PHRASE-STRUCTURE grammar (here illustrated without labelling), for example:

branch

Sentence unit (the cat saw the king)
SUBJECT/PREDICATE (or NP + VP) ((the cat) (saw the king))
VERB/OBJECT (or V + NP) ((the cat) ((saw) (the king)))

It is plain that as sentences become more complex, the sets of brackets within brackets will become increasingly difficult to read. The TREE diagram display is the most widely-used convention to overcome this difficulty. See Lyons 1977a: Ch. 6; 1968: Ch. 6.

(2) Many of the abbreviating conventions used in writing a grammar involve brackets. In GENERATIVE grammar, the following kinds of brackets are widely used to conflate RULES:

(i) *parenthesis notation* (*round brackets*) ( ) enclose OPTIONAL elements, e.g. a rule involving D(Adj)N refers to the potential occurrence of two STRUCTURES, DN and D Adj N.

(ii) *brace notation* (*curly brackets*) { } enclose alternative elements, e.g. a rule involving $D \begin{Bmatrix} Adj \\ N \end{Bmatrix} N$ refers to the selection of only one of the two structures, *either* D Adj N *or* DNN. In other approaches these brackets are used to indicate MORPHEMES, or MORPHOPHONEMIC forms.

(iii) *bracket notation* [ ] requires that elements be matched along the same horizontal row, e.g. $\begin{bmatrix} A \\ B \end{bmatrix} \rightarrow \begin{bmatrix} C \\ D \end{bmatrix}$ reads that 'A becomes C' and 'B becomes D'.

(iv) *angled brackets notation* ⟨ ⟩ signals an interdependency between optional features in generative PHONOLOGY, e.g. $\begin{bmatrix} +A \\ \langle +B \rangle \end{bmatrix} \rightarrow \begin{bmatrix} +C \\ \langle +D \rangle \end{bmatrix}$ reads that 'feature A becomes feature C, and if feature B is present it becomes feature D'. In other approaches these brackets may be used to indicate GRAPHEMES.

(3) In PHONETICS, there are two main uses of brackets: square brackets enclose a SEGMENTAL phonetic TRANSCRIPTION or a DISTINCTIVE FEATURE notation (e.g. [+grave]); slashes / / enclose PHONEMIC transcription. See Gimson 1970: Ch. 5.

(4) Square brackets are also used to enclose FEATURES at a GRAMMATICAL or SEMANTIC LEVEL e.g. [+common], [−countable], [+male], [+female]. See Akmajian & Heny 1975: Ch. 2; Hyman 1975: Ch. 4.

branch(ing) A term used in LINGUISTICS to refer to the descending linear connections which constitute the identity of a TREE diagram, e.g.:

PHRASE-STRUCTURE RULES which generate such trees are sometimes called 'branching rules'. The NODES involved are referred to as 'branching nodes' (opposed to 'non-branching nodes'). See Akmajian & Heny 1975: Ch. 2.

breath group A stretch of UTTERANCE produced within a single expiration of breath. Where and how often one breathes while speaking can be of significance for the LINGUIST, in that the breathing pattern will impose a series of PAUSES on the utterance, and these will need to be related to PHONOLOGICAL, GRAMMATICAL and SEMANTIC structure. Within each breath group, also, it is possible that certain regularities exist, such as a predictable pattern of PROMINENCE, or RHYTHM, and some investigators have used this notion as part of their study of a language's PROSODY (though terms such as TONE UNIT are here more widely used). More recently, the term has been used as a means of identifying the earliest VOCALISATION units in infants. See Bolinger 1975: Chs. 3, 9.

breathy A term used in the PHONETIC classification of VOICE QUALITY, on the basis of ARTICULATORY and AUDITORY criteria. It refers to a vocal effect produced by allowing a great deal of air to pass through a slightly open GLOTTIS: this effect is also sometimes called 'murmur'. Some speakers do have an abnormally breathy voice quality, as a permanent feature of their speech. What is of particular significance for linguistic analysis is that breathy effects may be used with CONTRASTIVE force, communicating a PARALINGUISTIC meaning: the whole of an UTTERANCE may be thus affected, as in an extremely shocked pronunciation of *Oh really!* 'Breathy voice', or 'breathy phonation' is also sometimes encountered as a PHONOLOGICAL characteristic, as in Gujarati, where there is an opposition between breathy and non-breathy VOWELS. See Catford 1977: Ch. 6.

BT An abbreviation sometimes used in LANGUAGE ACQUISITION studies to refer to BABY-TALK.

buccal A term occasionally used in ARTICULATORY PHONETICS as an alternative to ORAL (as in 'buccal cavity'), but more often with reference to sounds made specifically within the cavity of the cheek. A well-known 'buccal voice' is that produced by Donald Duck. See Gimson 1970: Ch. 2.

bunching A term used in ARTICULATORY PHONETICS to refer to a TONGUE position in which the body of the tongue is held high and tense during the production of a sound, as in CLOSE VOWELS (e.g. [i], [u]), and FRICATIVES articulated in the PALATAL-ALVEOLAR area (e.g. [ʃ]). See Catford 1977: Ch. 7.

bundle A term used in PHONOLOGY to characterise one conception of the PHONEME: in the approach of the PRAGUE SCHOOL, the phoneme is seen as a 'bundle' of PHONETIC DISTINCTIVE FEATURES. The English phoneme /s/, for example, can be seen as the result of the combination of the features of ALVEOLARity, FRICTION, VOICELESSness, etc. See Dinneen 1967: Ch. 2.

burst A term used in ACOUSTIC PHONETICS, referring to a sudden, short peak of acoustic energy which occurs in the production of a sound, such as at the release stage of PLOSIVES, and in some FLAPS and TRILLS. See Ladefoged 1975: Ch. 8.

C

𝇐𝇐𝇐𝇐𝇐𝇐

calque (From French *calquer*, to trace.) A term used in COMPARATIVE and HISTORICAL linguistics to refer to a type of BORROWING where the morphemic constituents of the borrowed WORD or PHRASE are translated ITEM by item into equivalent MORPHEMES in the new language. Such 'loan translations' are illustrated in English *power politics* from German *Machtpolitik, Superman* from *Übermensch*. See Quirk *et al* 1972: App. 1.

canonical An application in LINGUISTICS and PHONETICS of the general sense of this term, to refer to a linguistic FORM cited as a NORM or standard for purposes of comparison. In PHONOLOGY, for example, the normal syllabic combinations of sounds in a LANGUAGE (or in language as a whole) are often referred to as 'canonical', e.g. a CONSONANT-VOWEL (CV) or CVC structure constitutes a 'canonical SYLLABLE' pattern. In MORPHOLOGY, the term is used sometimes to refer to the typical phonological shape of MORPHEMES in a language (e.g. CVCV in Polynesian), and sometimes for the basic form in which a MORPHEME is cited (e.g. *-s* for the plural morpheme in English). In SYNTAX, canonical STRUCTURES (such as WORD ORDER) have been postulated, e.g. SUBJECT–VERB–OBJECT, but this is an extended sense of the term. In some SOCIOLINGUISTIC and PSYCHOLINGUISTIC studies, the normal positions of human beings in relation to each other while conversing (i.e. face-to-face, etc.) is called a 'canonical encounter' or 'orientation'. See Lyons 1977b: Ch. 15; Bolinger 1975: Ch. 4.

capacity A term used in GENERATIVE linguistics to refer to the generative POWER of GRAMMARS. If a series of grammars generates an identical set of STRINGS (SENTENCES), they are said to have the same 'weak generative capacity'. If in addition they assign the same STRUCTURAL DESCRIPTIONS to these strings, then they have the same 'strong generative capacity'. See Lyons 1977a: Ch. 8.

cardinal A TRADITIONAL term retained in some models of GRAMMATICAL description, referring to the class of numerals *one, two*, etc., by contrast with the ORDINAL numbers *first, second*, etc. See Quirk *et al* 1972: Ch. 4.

cardinal vowels A set of standard reference points, devised by the British PHONETICIAN Daniel Jones (1881–1967), to provide a precise means of identifying the VOWEL sounds of a language. The cardinal vowel system is based on a combination of ARTICULATORY and AUDITORY judgments. Four theoretical levels of TONGUE height are recognised: (1) the highest position to which the tongue can be raised without producing audible FRICTION; (2) the lowest position the tongue is capable of achieving; (3) and (4), two intermediate levels, which divide up the intervening space into areas that are articulatorily and auditorily equidistant. Using the FRONT of the tongue, and without rounding the lips, four **primary** vowel types are produced, and these are given the symbols (from HIGH to LOW) [i], [e], [ɛ] and [a]. Using the BACK of the tongue, four more primary vowel types are recognised, symbolised as (from low to high) [ɑ], [ɔ], [o] and [u] – the last three involving lip ROUNDING. In addition, each of these primary values is coded numerically, from 1 to 8 respectively.

By reversing the lip position, a **secondary** series of vowel types is produced: rounding the lips for the front vowels produces (from high to low [y], [ø], [œ] and [Œ]; [ɒ] is the rounded equivalent of Cardinal 5, and [ʌ], [ɣ] and [ɯ] are the unrounded equivalents of Cardinals 6, 7 and 8 respectively. The numerical code for the secondary series runs from 9 to 16. Two further cardinal vowels represent the highest point the centre of the tongue can reach: these are symbolised by [ɨ] for the unrounded vowel and by [ʉ] for the rounded vowel, coded 17 and 18 respectively. The entire system is usually shown in the form of the 'cardinal vowel diagram', or 'cardinal vowel quadrilateral', in which

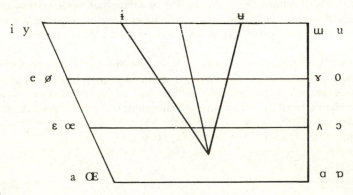

the aim is to give an approximate picture of the degree and direction of tongue movement involved. Additional lines help to delimit the area in which central vowel sounds are made. It should be emphasised that the cardinal vowels are not real vowels: they are invariable reference points (available on record), which have to be learned by rote. Once learned, phoneticians can use them in order to locate the position of the vowels of a LANGUAGE or to compare the vowels of different languages or DIALECTS. They can be sure that the vowels will all fall somewhere within the boundaries of the cardinal area. DIACRITIC marks can then be used to plot vowel positions more accurately, e.g. a hook beneath the vowel means that the articulation is more open than the cardinal value (as in [ǫ]), a dot beneath the vowel means that the articulation is closer (as in [e̩]).

Several other suggestions have been made concerning the best way of dividing up the vowel articulation area, but Daniel Jones's system is still the most widely used. See Gimson 1970: Ch. 4; Catford 1977: Ch. 9.

Cartesian linguistics A term used by some linguists to refer to any LINGUISTIC theories or methods which, it is claimed, illustrate the influence of the French philosopher René Descartes (1596–1650) and the GRAMMARIANS of PORT ROYAL. The discussion of UNIVERSALS in GENERATIVE linguistics, in particular, draws certain parallels with Cartesian views concerning the relationship between language and thought. This interpretation of the history of linguistic thought has remained controversial, since its initial statement by Noam CHOMSKY (cf. *Language and Mind* (1968)).

case (1) A GRAMMATICAL CATEGORY used in the analysis of WORD classes to identify the SYNTACTIC relationship between words in a SENTENCE, through such contrasts as NOMINATIVE, ACCUSATIVE, etc. The traditional CLASSIFICATION, such as is found in Latin GRAMMAR, is based on variations in the MORPHOLOGICAL forms of the word (a set of such forms constituting a PARADIGM, as in Latin *puella*, *puellam*, *puellae*, *puella*, the singular case forms of 'girl' – respectively nominative/ VOCATIVE, accusative, genitive/DATIVE and ABLATIVE). Each form is analysed in terms of a specific range of meaning, e.g. nominative is primarily the case of the grammatical SUBJECT of the sentence, genitive refers to such notions as possession, origin and so on. In languages which lack morphological variations of this kind, the term 'case', as traditionally used, does not apply. In English, for example, the only case-form which is so marked is the genitive (as in *boy's* or *boys'*); all other forms have no ending, the remaining case 'meanings' being expressed using PREPOSITIONS (as in *with a boy, to the boy*) or word order (as in the *cat chases mouse/mouse chases cat* contrast). A great deal of space in introductions to LINGUISTICS has been devoted to this point, in particular to criticism of TRADITIONAL grammars of English which insisted nonetheless on analysing the English noun in terms of cases. In some languages, highly complex morphological SYSTEMS are encountered – according to some, Finnish can be analysed as having sixteen cases, for example – along with a correspondingly complex descriptive terminology (using such terms as 'inessive' ('in' a place), 'elative' ('from inside' a place) and 'illative' ('into' a place)). See Lyons 1968: Ch. 7; Quirk *et al* 1972: Ch. 4.

(2) **Case grammar** refers to an approach to grammatical analysis devised by the American linguist Charles Fillmore (b. 1929) in the late 1960s, within the general orientation of GENERATIVE grammar. It is primarily a reaction against the STANDARD THEORY analysis of sentences, where notions such as SUBJECT, OBJECT, etc. are neglected in favour of analyses in terms of NP, VP, etc. By focusing on syntactic FUNCTIONS, however, it was felt that several important kinds of SEMANTIC relationship could be represented, which it would otherwise be difficult or impossible to capture. A set of sentences such as *The key opened the door, The door was opened by/with the key, The door opened, The man opened the door with a key*, etc. illustrate several 'stable' semantic roles, despite the varying SURFACE grammatical STRUCTURES. In each case the key is 'instrumental', the door is the entity affected by the action, and so on. Case grammar FORMALISES this insight using a MODEL which shows the influence of the PREDICATE calculus of formal logic: the DEEP STRUCTURE of a sentence has two CONSTITUENTS, MODALITY (features of TENSE, MOOD, ASPECT and NEGATION, relating to the sentence as a whole) and PROPOSITION (within which the VERB is considered central, and the various semantic roles that ELEMENTS of structure can have are listed with reference to it, and categorised as cases). The term 'case' is used because of the similarity with several of the traditional meanings covered by this term (cf. (1) above), but the deep structure cases recognised by the theory do not systematically correspond with anything in the surface morphology or syntax. The original proposal set up six cases (AGENTIVE, INSTRUMENTAL, DATIVE, FACTITIVE, LOCATIVE and OBJECTIVE) and suggested rules for their combination in defining the use of verbs, e.g. a verb like *open* can be used with an objective and instrumental case (e.g. *The key opened the door*), or with an additional agent (e.g. *The man opened the door with a key*). More recently, other cases have been suggested, some cases have been reinterpreted (and re-labelled), and certain cases have come to be given special study, it being claimed that they are more fundamental

(location and direction, in particular). In a locative or 'localist' case theory, for example, structures such as *there is a table, the table has legs, the table's legs*, and many more, could each be analysed as having an underlying locational feature. The problems in formalising this conception of linguistic structure remain very great, and case grammar came to attract somewhat less interest in the mid-1970s. See Lyons 1977a: Ch. 8; Huddleston 1976: Ch. 15.

cataphora (cataphoric) A term used by some GRAMMARIANS for the process or result of a LINGUISTIC UNIT referring forward to another unit. 'Cataphoric reference' is one way of marking the identity between what is being expressed and what is about to be expressed. For example, *I said this/the following...*, where the meaning of *this* and *the following* must be specified in the subsequent CONTEXT. *Here is the 9 o'clock news* shows the cataphoric function of *here*. 'Cataphoric words' (or 'substitutes') are usually contrasted with ANAPHORIC words (which refer backwards), and sometimes with EXOPHORIC words (which refer directly to the EXTRA-LINGUISTIC SITUATION). See Quirk *et al* 1972: Ch. 10.

category (categor-isation, -ial) A general term used in LINGUISTICS at varying levels of abstraction. At its most general level, **categorisation** refers to the whole process of organising human experience into general concepts with their associated linguistic labels; the linguistic study of this process (in SEMANTICS) overlaps with that of philosophers and psychologists. In the field of GRAMMAR, categorisation refers to the establishment of a set of classificatory UNITS or properties used in the description of language. The term **category** in some approaches refers to the CLASSES themselves, e.g. NOUN, VERB, SUBJECT, PREDICATE, noun PHRASE, verb phrase (any associated abbreviations being referred to as **category symbols**). More specifically, it refers to the defining properties of these general units: the categories of the noun, for example, include NUMBER, GENDER, CASE and COUNTABILITY; of the verb, TENSE, ASPECT, VOICE, etc. A distinction is often made between **grammatical categories**, in this second sense, and grammatical FUNCTIONS (or **functional categories**), such as SUBJECT, OBJECT, COMPLEMENT.

While both of these senses of 'category' are widespread, several specific applications of the term have developed within individual theories. Most distinctive of all, perhaps, is the special status given to the term in theories of **categorial grammar**, a type of FORMAL GRAMMAR, developed by several linguists and logicians in the 1950s (in particular, the linguist Yehoshua Bar Hillel (b. 1915)) the most developed of which operates in terms of two fundamental 'categories', SENTENCE and NOUN. All other categories are derived from these, the operations being based on an analysis of their SYNTACTIC DISTRIBUTION.

In SCALE-AND-CATEGORY grammar, the term is used primarily to refer to the notions of CLASS, SYSTEM, UNIT and STRUCTURE, which the theory recognised as basic. In recent GENERATIVE grammar, the set of PHRASE-STRUCTURE RULES in a grammar may be referred to as the **categorial component**, i.e. that part of the BASE component of the grammar which specifies such syntactic categories as S, NP, VP. Also, in some MODELS of generative grammar, the term **category feature** is used to refer to a type of CONTEXTUAL feature, i.e. a syntactic feature which specifies the conditions relating to where in a DEEP STRUCTURE a LEXICAL ITEM can occur. Category features specify which NODE will be the one to DOMINATE directly the lexical item, once it is introduced into the PHRASE-MARKER (replacing the corresponding EMPTY (DELTA) symbol), e.g. [+N], [+Det], [+V]. A related term in this model is **strict subcategorisation**, referring to features which specify further restrictions on the choice of lexical items in deep structure. See Lyons 1968: Chs. 6, 7; 1977a; Ch. 8; Palmer 1971: Ch. 2; Huddleston 1976: Ch. 10.

catenative A term used in some GRAMMATICAL descriptions of the VERB phrase to refer to a LEXICAL verb which governs another lexical verb, as in one possible analysis of *he **likes** to go, he **wants** to see*, etc. See Quirk *et al* 1972: Ch. 12.

causative A term used in GRAMMATICAL description to refer to the causal relationship between alternative versions of a SENTENCE. For example, the pair of sentences *the cat killed the mouse* and *the mouse died* are related, in that the transitive *kill* can be seen as a 'causative' version of the intransitive *die, viz* 'cause to die' (*the cat caused the mouse to die*); similarly, some AFFIXES have a causative role, e.g. *-ise*, as in *domesticise* (= 'cause to become domestic'). This is a relationship which is clearly established in the MORPHOLOGICAL STRUCTURE of some LANGUAGES (e.g. Japanese, Turkish), where an AFFIX can systematically distinguish between non-causative and causative uses of a VERB (e.g. 'he eats', 'he causes (someone) to eat', which is similar to English *he makes him eat*). Some linguists have also tried to apply the notion of causative systematically to English, seeing it as an abstract UNDERLYING category from which sets of 'surface' verbs (such as *kill* and *die*) can be derived. See Lyons 1968: Ch. 8; Bolinger 1975: Ch. 6.

cavity (1) In PHONETICS, this term refers to any of the anatomically defined chambers in the VOCAL TRACT which are the principal formative influences on the character of a sound. The main cavities are:

(i) the OESOPHAGEAL cavity, from oesophagus to stomach, which is only used in abnormal speech production, such as following a laryngectomy operation;

(ii) the PULMONIC cavity, made up of the lungs and trachea, which is the normal source of speech sounds;

(iii) the PHARYNGEAL cavity, from the LARYNX to the point where the soft PALATE makes contact with the back of the throat;

(iv) the ORAL cavity, made up of the whole of the mouth area, and the main means of modifying the RESONANCE of the sound produced at the larynx; sometimes referred to as BUCCAL;

(v) the NASAL cavity, made up of the nose and the part of the pharynx above the point of soft palate closure.

See Gimson 1970: Ch. 2.

(2) In CHOMSKY & Halle's DISTINCTIVE FEATURE theory of PHONOLOGY, 'cavity features' constitute one of the five main dimensions in terms of which speech sounds are analysed (the others being MAJOR CLASS FEATURES, MANNER OF ARTICULATION features, SOURCE FEATURES, and PROSODIC features). The features subsumed under this heading, all analysed as OPPOSITIONS, are CORONAL, ANTERIOR, TONGUE–BODY FEATURES (HIGH/LOW/BACK), ROUNDED, DISTRIBUTED, COVERED, GLOTTAL constrictions, and SECONDARY APERTURES (NASAL and LATERAL). See Ladefoged 1975: Ch. 11; Hyman 1975: Ch. 2.

ceneme (cene-matics, -tics) A term used in GLOSSEMATICS to refer to the minimal UNIT in a language's PHONOLOGICAL system. **Cenematics** and **cenetics** are the terms used to refer to the analysis of cenemes at LEVELS corresponding to those of phonology and PHONETICS respectively. See Dinneen 1967: Ch. 11.

centre (central-ise, -ation) (1) The top part of the TONGUE, between FRONT and BACK, and used especially in the production of 'central VOWELS' (also called 'neutral' vowels), such as the [ə] sound which opens the word *asleep* and closes the word *sofa*. In a sense, when compared with the theoretical extremes of vowel ARTICULATION which define the CARDINAL VOWELS in PHONETICS, *all* real LANGUAGE vowels are **centralised**; but the term is usually used to refer to cases where a vowel normally articulated in the periphery of the vowel area comes to be produced nearer the centre of the mouth, as when *bacon and* [= and] *eggs* becomes, in normal colloquial speech, *bacon* [ənd] *eggs*.

Several degrees of this process of **centralisation** can be heard. Markedly 'centralised vowels' are common in several urban British DIALECTS, for example. A DIPHTHONG which involves a GLIDE towards the centre of the mouth may be referred to as a 'centring' diphthong. See Gimson 1970: Chs. 4, 7; Catford 1977: Ch. 9.

(2) The most SONOROUS part of a SYLLABLE may be referred to as the 'centre' (or NUCLEUS), e.g. the [uː] in the word *boot* [buːt]. See Gimson 1970: Ch. 4.

(3) In those types of grammatical PHRASE where several words depend on one HEAD word (ENDOCENTRIC constructions), the head is often referred to as the 'centre' of the phrase. See Dinneen 1967: Ch. 3.

chain/choice.A pair of terms used by some LINGUISTS to refer to the two main AXES of linguistic organisation, corresponding to the distinction between SYNTAGMATIC ('chain') and PARADIGMATIC ('choice'). This sense of 'choice' is more restricted than that found in some discussions of SEMANTICS, where a widely-held conception of MEANINGfulness is based on the ability of the speaker/hearer to 'choose' from a selection of linguistic alternatives, which provide the information-carrying contrasts prerequisite for communication. See Lyons 1968: Ch. 9.

chart A term used in PHONETICS to refer to the INTERNATIONAL PHONETIC ASSOCIATION's classification of the sounds of LANGUAGE presented in matrix form: the 'IPA chart'. See Gimson 1971: App.

checked (1) One of the features of sound set up by JAKOBSON & Halle in their DISTINCTIVE FEATURE theory of PHONOLOGY, to handle SECONDARY ARTICULATIONS – in this case, glottalisation. Checked CONSONANTS are defined both articulatorily and acoustically, as those sounds produced with accompanying GLOTTAL activity, involving a rapid energy discharge in a short time interval. EJECTIVES and IMPLOSIVES, in this view, are [+checked]. The opposite term is **unchecked**, which applies to all non-glottalised sounds, signalled acoustically by a lower energy discharge over a larger time interval. See Hyman 1975: Ch. 2.

(2) The term is also found as an alternative to CLOSED, in the description of SYLLABLES: a **checked syllable** is one ending in a consonant, and a **checked vowel** is a vowel occurring in such a syllable. See. Abercrombie 1967: Ch. 3.

checking A term sometimes used in GRAMMATICAL description to refer to a sub-type of TAG-QUESTIONS: a **checking tag** is one which reverses the positive or negative value of the main CLAUSE VERB, and whose function is seen as one of confirmation, or 'checking', e.g. *he's coming, is he*. Other types of tag would be referred to as 'copy' tags. See Lyons 1977b: Ch. 16.

chest pulse A term used in PHONETICS to refer to a contraction of those muscles of the chest which are involved in the exhalation of air from the lungs. For the production of emphatic speech, these pulses are said to be 'reinforced' or 'stressed'. The chest pulse has been suggested as a central explanatory concept in one account of SYLLABLE production ('chest pulse theory'), but this view presents several problems. See Gimson 1970: Ch. 5; Ladefoged 1975: Ch. 10.

chômeur A term used in RELATIONAL GRAMMAR, derived from the French word meaning 'unemployed', to refer to a NOMINAL item which has its role in a CLAUSE taken over (or 'usurped') by another nominal; abbreviated as 'cho'. For example, in a PASSIVE SENTENCE, the UNDER-LYING SUBJECT is seen as having its subject FUNCTION usurped by the DIRECT OBJECT from the ACTIVE sentence; as a result, the subject of the active sentence becomes demoted into a 'chômeur'. By seeing such STRUCTURES in terms of RULES which alter relations (rather than in terms of a TRANSFORMATION of one PHRASE-MARKER into another), it is hoped that a more UNIVERSAL formulation of such rules will be obtained. See Radford 1981: Ch. 4.

Chomskyan Characteristic of, or a follower of, the linguistic principles of Avram Noam **Chomsky** (b. 1928), Professor of Modern Languages and Linguistics at the Massachusetts Institute of Technology. His theory of LANGUAGE STRUCTURE known as TRANSFORMATIONAL-generative grammar revolutionised work in LINGUISTICS in 1957, with the publication of his monograph *Syntactic Structures*. Later, major publications on technical linguistic topics included *Current Issues in Linguistic Theory* (1964) and *Aspects of the Theory of Syntax* (1965). The latter publication introduced a new direction into generative theory and became the orthodoxy for several years. His main publication on phonology was *The Sound Pattern of English* (1968), with Morris Halle; referred to in this dictionary as 'Chomsky & Halle'. More recent developments in his linguistic thinking in book form may be found in *Reflections on Language* (1976).

By the mid-1960s, Chomsky had come to stress the role of language as a key means to the investigation of the human mind. The view that linguistics can be profitably seen as a branch of cognitive psychology is argued especially in *Language and Mind* (1968), and it is this aspect of his thinking which has attracted a wide readership outside linguistics, especially amongst philosophers and psychologists.

Chomsky was also actively involved in politics during the period of the United States' involvement in Vietnam, and he has written widely on the issues raised, e.g. *American Power and the New Mandarins* (1964).

For an introduction to Chomsky's thinking, see Lyons 1977a.

chroneme (chrone) An abstract unit, used by some PHONOLOGISTS as a means of describing phonologically CONTRASTIVE differences in the LENGTH of speech sounds. Both VOWELS and CONSONANTS may display PHONEMIC contrasts in length: long and short vowels are found in German, long and short consonants in Lithuanian. The vowel length differences in English, such as in *bit* and *beat*, also involve differences of QUALITY, and the term chroneme is thus not applicable. Those who use this terminology would refer to the ETIC unit of duration as a **chrone**. See Gimson 1970: Chs. 3, 7.

citation form The FORM of a LINGUISTIC UNIT when it is cited in isolation, for purposes of discussion. More specifically, the term refers to the pronunciation given to a word when it is produced in isolation, and not in CONNECTED SPEECH.

The term 'citation' is also used in a general sense in LINGUISTICS, referring to the use of an UTTERANCE or piece of TEXT for quotation or reference purposes. In LEXICOGRAPHY, 'citation slips' are used to provide the evidence on which the dictionary's entries are selected and organised. See Lyons 1977b: Ch. 1.

class(ification, -ifier) (1) An application in LINGUISTICS and PHONETICS of the general use of this term, to refer to a set of entities sharing certain FORMAL or SEMANTIC properties. Its most widespread use is in relation to the classification of MORPHEMES into 'FORM classes' and WORDS into 'word classes' (other syntactic UNITS being less likely to be referred to in terms of classes). A major distinction is sometimes drawn between OPEN and CLOSED classes of words. The term 'class cleavage' is sometimes used where a word is analysable into different classes, e.g. *round* in *It's your round, round the corner*, etc. Some GRAMMARIANS refer to COUNTABLE NOUNS as 'class nouns'. 'Class' has a special status in HALLIDAYAN LINGUISTICS, where it is one of the four main CATEGORIES recognised by that theory (the others being STRUCTURE, UNIT and SYSTEM). Here, classes are any set of ITEMS having the same possibilities of operation in structure, e.g. the class of 'nominal groups' can operate as SUBJECT, OBJECT, etc. in CLAUSE structure.

Morphemes whose function is to indicate the formal or SEMANTIC class to which items belong are sometimes called **classifiers**, e.g. -*ly* is an ADVERB classifier, -*ess* is a 'femininity' classifier. The marking of LEXICAL items as belonging to the same semantic class is an important feature of many languages (e.g. Chinese, Vietnamese, Hopi), and sometimes quite unexpected bases of classifications are found, in terms of shape, size, colour, movability, animacy, status, and so on.

Classification is a feature of STRUCTURALIST linguistics, where PHONES were classified into PHONEMES, MORPHS into MORPHEMES, etc. The limitations of this TAXONOMIC approach to language provided a main argument for the development of GENERATIVE linguistics. See Bolinger 1975: Ch. 6; Clark & Clark 1977: Ch. 14.

(2) In SOCIOLINGUISTICS, the term **class dialects** is sometimes used to refer to VARIETIES of language which correlated with divisions of social class – alternatively known as 'social DIALECTS'. See Gumperz & Hymes 1971: Intro.

classeme A term used by some European LINGUISTS (e.g. Eugene Coseriu (b. 1921)), to refer to the relatively abstract SEMANTIC FEATURES shared by LEXICAL ITEMS belonging to different semantic FIELDS, e.g. ANIMATE/inanimate, adult/child. In this approach, the term contrasts with the irreducible semantic features (SEMES) which work, at a very particular level, within a particular semantic field, e.g. *table* being identified in terms of 'number of legs', 'shape', etc. See Lyons 1977b: Ch. 9.

clause A term used in some models of GRAMMAR to refer to a UNIT of grammatical organisation smaller than the SENTENCE, but larger than PHRASES, WORDS or MORPHEMES. The traditional classification is into 'main' and 'subordinate' (or 'dependent') CLAUSES, e.g. *The man arrived | after the rain started.* Some grammars distinguish FINITE and non-finite types of clause, depending on the FORM of the *verb* used, and further sub-divisions are sometimes made (e.g. a reduced 'verbless' clause, as in **when ripe**, *these apples will be lovely*). A more detailed sub-classification would take into account the FUNCTION of clauses within the sentence, e.g. as ADVERBIAL, NOUN or ADJECTIVE. It would also analyse clauses into formal ELEMENTS of structure, such as SUBJECT, VERB, OBJECT, COMPLEMENT and adverbial. Some grammars (such as GENERATIVE grammar) do not operate with the notion of clause, as COMPLEX sentence types are handled by the use of

clause-mate

TRANSFORMATIONS which EMBED one SIMPLE sentence within another. See Palmer 1971: Ch. 2; Quirk *et al* 1972: Chs. 2, 7, 11.

clause-mate A term used in recent GENERATIVE GRAMMAR to refer to a type of relationship between the ELEMENTS of a SENTENCE STRUCTURE within a PHRASE-MARKER. Elements are clause-mates if they are DOMINATED by the same S NODE. For example, in a tree partially illustrated by

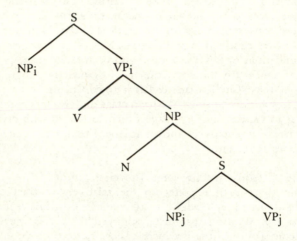

the elements NP_i and VP_i are clause-mates, as are the elements NP_j and VP_j; but NP_i is not a clause-mate of VP_j. The notion permits a certain economy of statement in discussing the properties of TRANS-FORMATIONAL rules: SELECTIONAL RESTRICTIONS, for example, apply only to clause-mates. See Huddleston 1976: Ch. 8.

clause-wall A term used in NONDISCRETE GRAMMAR, to refer to the different degrees of DEPENDENCY existing between CLAUSES. Clauses which have a relatively high 'clause-wall' between them are more independent than those which are separated by a relatively low clause-wall. See Radford 1981: Ch. 3.

clear 1 An impressionistic, but commonly used term for a variety of LATERAL sound, where the RESONANCE is that of a front VOWEL of an [i] quality, as in the standard pronunciation of /l/ before vowels and /j/ in English, e.g. *leap*, *lamp*. It is opposed to 'DARK L'. See Gimson 1970: Ch. 8.

cleft sentence A term used in GRAMMATICAL description to refer to a
CONSTRUCTION where a single CLAUSE has been divided into two
separate sections, each with its own VERB. For example, the sentence
Michael is driving a new car can be 'cleft' in various ways, e.g. *it's Michael
who is driving a new car, it's a new car that Michael is driving*. The VARIANTS
affect the distribution of emphasis within the SENTENCE, and correlate
closely with patterns of INTONATIONal PROMINENCE. Cleft sentences,
and the associated PSEUDO-CLEFT SENTENCES, have attracted particular
attention in TRANSFORMATIONAL grammar, because of the DERI-
VATIONAL problems they pose. See Quirk *et al* 1972: Ch. 14.

click (1) A term used in the classification of CONSONANT sounds on the
basis of their MANNER OF ARTICULATION: it is a shorthand way of
referring to the series of sounds produced by using the velaric
AIR-STREAM MECHANISM (cf. VELAR). In English, click sounds may be
heard in the 'tut tut' sound of disapproval, in some types of kiss, and
in the noise used to signal appreciation or to 'gee up' horses. In some
languages (e.g. Zulu, Hottentot, Xhosa), clicks have PHONEMIC status.
Generally, three categories of clicks are recognised: DENTAL [ǀ], LATERAL
[ǁ] and RETROFLEX [ǂ]. See Ladefoged 1975: Ch. 6.

(2) In PSYCHOLINGUISTIC experiments on SPEECH PERCEPTION and
COMPREHENSION, a 'click' refers to a BURST of ACOUSTIC noise
introduced extraneously into one ear while the listener attends to
speech in the other. For example, by varying the position of the click
in relation to the GRAMMATICAL STRUCTURE of the speech, information
can be gained concerning the way in which grammatical units are
perceived and organised by the brain. In one series of experiments,
when the click occurred at a grammatical boundary, it was recalled
as occurring there; but when it occurred within a CONSTITUENT, it was
recalled as occurring towards the constituent boundary ('click
displacement'). Such findings can then be interpreted in terms of the
perceptual or cognitive reality of constituent boundaries. See Clark &
Clark 1977: Ch. 2.

cline A term used in HALLIDAYAN LINGUISTICS to refer to a continuum
of potentially infinite gradation, e.g. the range of possible contrasts
between FALLING and RISING PITCH levels, or the degrees of contrast
capable of being drawn along a time scale. Since its original use in
SCALE-AND-CATEGORY GRAMMAR, the term has come to be used in other
fields than linguistics, often unnecessarily, as a synonym for
'continuum'. See Robins 1971: Ch. 7.

clinical linguistics A term sometimes used for the application of LINGUISTIC theories, methods and descriptive findings to the analysis of medical conditions or settings involving a disorder of language. This application involves the linguist working in collaboration with SPEECH pathologists/therapists, audiologists and others in helping to assess, diagnose and remediate disorders of the PRODUCTION and COMPREHENSION of spoken or written language – disorders which may of course occur in educational as well as clinical settings. The relevance of PSYCHOLINGUISTICS, NEUROLINGUISTICS and language ACQUISITION studies to this end is noteworthy. See Clark & Clark 1977: Ch. 14.

clitic A term used in GRAMMAR to refer to a FORM which resembles a WORD, but which cannot stand on its own as a normal UTTERANCE, being structurally dependent upon a neighbouring word in a CONSTRUCTION. (The term 'clitic' comes from the Greek word for 'leaning'.) Examples are the ARTICLES of English and French: a form like *the* cannot stand on its own in normal utterance, but it would be called a word nonetheless by NATIVE SPEAKERS. Such clitic words ('clitics') can be classified into **proclitics** (i.e. they depend upon a following word, as in the case of the articles above) and **enclitics** (i.e. they depend upon a preceding word, as in the attachment of some PRONOUNS to the end of a VERB form in Italian or Spanish). See Matthews 1974: Ch. 9.

close A term used in the four-level classification of vertical TONGUE movement in VOWEL sounds based on the CARDINAL VOWEL system, the others being 'half-close', 'half-open' and 'open'. It refers to a vowel made with the tongue in the highest position possible without causing audible FRICTION, as in the ARTICULATION of [i] and [u]: the closest vowels in English are in words like *seat* and *shoot*. The area of articulation immediately below 'close' is known as 'half-close' or 'mid-close', as in [e] and [o] (the nearest sounds in English are in words like *say* and *so* respectively). In a three-level classification of vowel sounds, the highest group are known as 'high' vowels (as opposed to 'low' and 'mid'). See Gimson 1970: Ch. 4.

closed (1) A term sometimes used in the GRAMMATICAL classification of WORDS to refer to one of two postulated major word CLASSES in language, the other being OPEN. A **closed class** is one whose membership is fixed or limited. New ITEMS are not regularly added, as is the case with 'open-class' items. PRONOUNS, PREPOSITIONS, CONJUNCTIONS, ARTICLES, etc. are all 'closed system' items, the term 'system' here reflecting the fact that the membership of such classes is finite, the members displaying an interdependence of MEANING and use. See Quirk *et al* 1972: Ch. 2; Robins 1971: Ch. 6.

(2) A term used in the two-way classification of SYLLABLE structure, referring to a syllable ending in a CONSONANT; its opposite is OPEN, where the syllable ends in a vowel. This feature is sometimes referred to as a CHECKED or blocked syllable. See Ladefoged 1975: Ch. 4.

closure A general term used in PHONETICS to refer to an ARTICULATION where the contact between active and passive articulators obstructs the air stream through the mouth and/or nose. A 'complete closure' exists in the case of PLOSIVES, AFFRICATES and NASALS, and in the glottalic and velaric AIR-STREAM MECHANISMS. An 'intermittent closure' exists in the case of ROLLS, FLAPS and TAPS. A 'partial closure' exists in the case of LATERALS. Some phoneticians would include FRICATIVES under the heading of 'partial' or 'incomplete' closure. A narrowing of the VOCAL TRACT where there is *no* articulatory contact is usually called a STRICTURE. See Catford 1977: Ch. 6; Gimson 1970: Ch. 4.

cluster A term used in the analysis of CONNECTED SPEECH to refer to any sequence of adjacent CONSONANTS occurring INITIALLY or FINALLY in a SYLLABLE, such as the initial [br-] of *bread*, or the final [-st] of *best*. Not all possible combinations of consonants occur in a LANGUAGE. Initially in syllables in English, for example, clusters are not possible with [ð], [tʃ], [dʒ] or [z]. Up to three consonants can occur initially, as in [spr-], [spl-], [skw-]; up to four can occur finally, as in *glimpsed* [-mpst] and *twelfths* [-lfθs]. See Gimson 1970: Ch. 9; Catford 1977: Ch. 11.

coalesce(nce) A term used in LINGUISTICS, especially in HISTORICAL studies, to refer to the coming together of linguistic UNITS which were originally distinguishable. ALLOphones of a PHONEME may coalesce, as may different phonemes and different MORPHEMES. Many CASES of Modern English /ʒ/, for example, are the result of coalescence of /z/ and /j/, e.g. *occasion*, *measure*; in WORDS like *formation*, one could analyse the AFFIX as a coalescence of the morphemes -*ate* + -*tion*. Analogous terms include SYNCRETISM, MERGER, FUSION and NEUTRAL-ISATION. See Gimson 1970: Part 2.

(2) (-**nt**) A term used in PHONETICS and PHONOLOGY as part of the classification of types of ASSIMILATION. in **coalescent** (or 'reciprocal') **assimilation**, each of two adjacent ARTICULATIONS influences the other. An example is the FUSION of [d] and [j] to produce [dʒ] in such phrases as *could you*. See Gimson 1970: Ch. 11.

coarticulation An ARTICULATION which takes place involving in a simultaneous or overlapping way more than one point in the VOCAL TRACT, as in the co-ordinate STOPS [pk], [bg], [pt] and [bd] often heard in West African languages. In 'anticipatory coarticulation', an articulator not involved in a particular sound begins to move in the direction of an articulation needed for a later sound in the UTTERANCE (its TARGET). An example is the *sh-* of *shoe*, which is normally pronounced with lip-ROUNDING, anticipating the influence of the following [u:]. Coarticulation may also be seen when a sound retains a characteristic deriving from an earlier articulation. See Catford 1977: Ch. 10.

cocktail party phenomenon An everyday effect studied scientifically in PSYCHOLINGUISTICS as part of a theory of SPEECH PERCEPTION. It refers to the process of SELECTIVE LISTENING, whereby people listening to several conversations at once are able to attend consciously to one of them, and to ignore the others. See Clark & Clark 1977: Ch. 5.

coda A term used in PHONETICS to refer to a SEGMENT of a SYLLABLE which may follow the syllabic NUCLEUS, e.g. the /p/ of /kʌp/. See Gimson 1970: Ch. 5.

code The general sense of this term – a set of conventions for converting one signalling system into another – enters into the subject-matter of SEMIOTICS and COMMUNICATION theory rather than LINGUISTICS. Such notions as 'encoding' and 'decoding' are sometimes encountered in PHONETICS and linguistics, but the view of language as a 'code' is not one which figures greatly in these subjects. The term has come to the fore mainly in SOCIOLINGUISTICS, where it is mainly used as a neutral label for any system of communication involving language – and which avoids the sociolinguist having to commit himself to such terms as DIALECT, LANGUAGE or VARIETY, which have a special status in his theories. The linguistic behaviour referred to as **code-switching**, for example, can be illustrated by the switch speakers may make (depending on who they are talking to, or where they are) between STANDARD and regional forms of English, between Welsh and English in parts of Wales, or between occupational and domestic varieties. On the other hand, several sociologists and sociolinguists have given 'code' a more restricted definition. For example, codes are sometimes defined in terms of mutual intelligibility (e.g. the language of a private or professional group). But the most widespread special use of the term is in the theory of communication codes propounded by the British sociologist, Basil Bernstein (b. 1924). His distinction between ELA-

BORATED and RESTRICTED codes is part of a theory of the nature of social systems, concerned in particular with the kinds of meanings people communicate, and how explicitly they do this, using the range of resources provided by the language. See Gumperz & Hymes 1971: Chs. 1, 17; Bolinger 1975: Chs. 8, 11; Lyons 1977b: Ch. 14.

cognate (1) A language or a LINGUISTIC FORM which is historically derived from the same source as another language/form, e.g. Spanish/Italian/French/Portuguese, are 'cognate languages' (or simply 'cognates'); *père* / *padre*, etc. ('father') are 'cognate words' or cognates.

(2) The term is also applied to the description of some kinds of SYNTACTIC RELATIONS: a 'cognate OBJECT' is one which has the same historical derivation as the VERB which governs it (or, more loosely, is SEMANTICALLY dependent upon the action of the verb), e.g. *to run a race, live a good life, ask a question*; a cognate SUBJECT–VERB–OBJECT sequence is illustrated by such sentences as *employers employ employees*. See Robins 1971: Ch. 8; Bolinger 1975: Ch. 7.

cognitive (meaning) A term sometimes used in SEMANTICS as part of a classification of types of MEANING. It refers to those aspects of meaning which relate directly to DENOTATIONS of LEXICAL items and the PROPOSITIONAL content of SENTENCES, and thus corresponds to an intellectually objective level of interpretation, as opposed to one where emotional or subjective interpretation is involved. Alternative terms include DENOTATIVE and REFERENTIAL; opposite terms include EMOTIVE and CONNOTATIVE. See Lyons 1977b: Ch. 7.

cohesion (cohesive(ness)) (1) A term often used in GRAMMAR to refer to a defining property of the WORD, seen as a grammatical UNIT. The criterion states that new ELEMENTS cannot usually be inserted into words in normal speech, but only at word boundaries. An alternative name for this criterion is 'uninterruptability'. The criterion works well for English (apart from such examples as *abso-blooming-lutely*), but has to be modified if applied to languages where INFIXES are used. See Matthews 1974: Ch. 9; Lyons 1968: Ch. 5.

(2) The term is used by some linguists to refer to the property of larger units than the MORPHEME to bind together in CONSTRUCTIONS, e.g. ARTICLE + NOUN. In this use, any group of words which acts as a CONSTITUENT of a larger unit can be said to be internally cohesive. In the HALLIDAYAN approach to grammatical analysis, cohesion is a major concept, referring to those features of an UTTERANCE or TEXT which link different parts of SENTENCES or larger units of DISCOURSE,

collapse

e.g. the cross-referencing function of PRONOUNS, ARTICLES and some types of ADVERB (as in *The man went to town. However, he did not stay long...*). See Robins 1971: Ch. 6; Lyons 1977b: Ch. 14.

collapse A term used in GENERATIVE GRAMMAR to refer to the notational conflation of two RULES into one, in the interests of a simpler and more general statement, e.g. NP → DN and NP → D Adj N, being replaced by NP → D(Adj)N, where the BRACKETS refer to the optional use of the adjective. See Akmajian & Heny 1975: Ch. 2.

collective A term used in GRAMMATICAL DESCRIPTION to refer to a NOUN which denotes a group of entities, and which is FORMALLY differentiated from other nouns by a distinct pattern of NUMBER contrast (and, in some languages, MORPHOLOGICALLY). **Collective nouns** (e.g. *government, army, club, jury, public*) fall into several grammatical sub-classes, but their distinctive characteristic is their ability to co-occur in the singular with either a singular or a plural VERB, this correlating with a difference of interpretation – the noun being seen as a single collective entity, or as a collection of individual entities (cf. *the committee is wrong* vs. *the committee are wrong*). See Quirk *et al* 1972: Ch. 4; Lyons 1977b: Ch. 9.

colligation (colligate) A term in FIRTHIAN LINGUISTICS for the process or result of grouping a set of WORDS on the basis of their similarity in entering into SYNTAGMATIC GRAMMATICAL RELATIONS. For example, a set of VERBS which take a certain kind of COMPLEMENT CONSTRUCTION would be said to be 'in colligation with' that construction, e.g. *agree, choose, decline, manage*, etc. **colligate** with *to* + infinitive constructions, as opposed to *-ing* forms, as in *I agree to go* vs. **I agree going*. Colligation is usually contrasted with COLLOCATION. See Robins 1971: Ch. 6.

collocation (colloc-ate, -ability) A term used in LEXICOLOGY by some (especially FIRTHIAN) LINGUISTS to refer to the habitual co-occurrence of individual LEXICAL ITEMS. For example, *auspicious* 'collocates' with *occasion, event, sign*, etc., and *letter* collocates with *alphabet, graphic*, etc., on the one hand, and *postman, pillar-box*, etc. on the other. Collocations are, then, a type of SYNTAGMATIC lexical relations. They are linguistically predictable to a greater or lesser extent (e.g. the bond between *spick* and *span* is stronger than that between *letter* and *pillar-box*), and this differentiates them from SENSE ASSOCIATIONS, which tend to include idiosyncratic connections (e.g. *mother-in-law* associating with *hippopotamus*). Some words have no specifiable **collocational restrictions** – grammatical words such as *the, of, after, in*. By contrast, there are many totally predictable restrictions, as in *eke + out*, *spick + span*, and these are usually analysed as IDIOMS, clichés, etc. Another important feature of collocations is that they are FORMAL (not SEMANTIC) statements of co-occurrence, e.g. *green* collocates with *jealousy* (as opposed to, say, *blue*, *red*), even though there is no REFERENTIAL basis for the link. Lexical items which are 'collocated' are said to be 'collocates' of each other; the potential of items to collocate is known as their 'collocability', or 'collocational range'. Collocational restrictions would be handled under the heading of SELECTIONAL RESTRICTIONS, in GENERATIVE GRAMMAR. See Robins 1971: Ch. 2; Bolinger 1975: Ch. 5.

combinatorial A fundamental function of LINGUISTIC UNITS to 'combine' with one another to produce more complex patterns. The 'combinatorial properties' or 'relations' of CONSONANTS and VOWELS, for example, can be used as a definition of SYLLABLE (vowel as NUCLEUS, consonants as MARGINS). Combination, in this sense, is a SYNTAGMATIC relation, and opposed to the PARADIGMATIC notion of CONTRAST. See Lyons 1968: Ch. 2.

command A term used in the classification of SENTENCE FUNCTIONS, and defined sometimes on GRAMMATICAL and sometimes on SEMANTIC or SOCIOLINGUISTIC grounds. SYNTACTICALLY, a command is a sentence which typically has no SUBJECT, and where the VERB is in the IMPERATIVE MOOD, e.g. *Come here!* Semantically it is primarily used to tell someone to do (or not do) something. From a SPEECH ACT point of view, the function of command may be expressed using other forms, e.g. *that boy will stand up*, or by a dominant intonation. The term is usually contrasted with three other major sentence functions: STATEMENT, QUESTION, EXCLAMATION. In grammatical discussion, commands are usually referred to as 'imperative' in form. See Quirk *et al* 1972: Ch. 7; Lyons 1977b: Ch. 1.

comment (1) A term used in SEMANTICS and GRAMMAR as part of an alternative binary characterisation of SENTENCE structure to that traditionally found in the SUBJECT/PREDICATE distinction; the opposite term is TOPIC. The topic of a sentence is the person or thing about which something is said, whereas the comment is that part of the sentence which says something further about the topic. In the sentence *The book was on the table*, *the book* is the topic, and the remainder of the sentence is the comment. English does not mark this distinction as clearly as in some languages, where grammatical PARTICLES, WORD order contrasts or INFLECTIONS may help to show the contrast. An

commissive

analogous distinction is made using the terms THEME and RHEME, by some linguists. See Lyons 1968: Ch. 8; Quirk *et al* 1972: Ch. 14.

(2) A type of CLAUSE recognised in some models of grammatical description, referring to an optional structure whose function is to add a parenthetic comment to another clause. There is a wide range of 'comment clauses' in English, e.g. *you know, to be honest, they say, generally speaking.* Several of these act as stereotyped conversation fillers, with several complex functions, e.g. *you see, mind you, I see.* See Quirk *et al* 1972: Ch. 11.

commissive A term used in the theory of SPEECH ACTS to refer to a type of UTTERANCE where the speaker commits himself to a future course of action, as in *I promise/I guarantee...* See Clark & Clark 1977: Ch. 3.

common (1) A term used in GRAMMATICAL description to refer to the unMARKED MORPHOLOGICAL form of a grammatical CATEGORY. In English, for example, the form of the NOUN other than the GENITIVE could be called the 'common CASE' form. Similarly, one might use 'common GENDER' in a language where only one contrast is made (e.g. feminine vs. masculine/neuter, etc.), or where sex is indeterminate out of context (as in French *enfant* 'child'). In TRADITIONAL grammar, 'common nouns' were a SEMANTICALLY defined sub-class of nouns (referring to 'general concepts') contrasted with PROPER nouns (names of individuals, etc.); LINGUISTIC approaches tend to emphasise the FORMAL distinctions that can be made between such sub-classes (e.g. different patterns of ARTICLE usage). See Quirk *et al* 1972: Ch. 4; Lyons 1968: Ch. 7.

(2) The phrase **common core** is used in some SOCIOLINGUISTIC and STYLISTIC studies, referring to the range of linguistic features common to all the VARIETIES, DIALECTS, etc. of a language. A usage such as *thou* in English, for example, would not be part of this common core, as it is restricted to religious CONTEXTS. See Lyons 1968: Ch. 4.

communication (communicat-e, -ive) A fundamental notion in the study of behaviour, which acts as a frame of reference for LINGUISTIC and PHONETIC studies. Communication refers to the transmission of INFORMATION (a 'message') between a source and receiver using a signalling system: in linguistic contexts, source and receiver are interpreted in human terms, the system involved is a LANGUAGE, and the notion of response to (or acknowledgement of) the message becomes of crucial importance. In theory, communication is said to have taken place if the information received is the same as that sent: in practice, one has to allow for all kinds of interfering factors, or 'noise', which reduce the efficiency of the transmission (e.g. unintelligibility of ARTICULATION, idiosyncratic ASSOCIATIONS of WORDS). One has also to allow for different levels of control in the transmission of the message: the speaker's purposive selection of signals will be accompanied by signals which communicate 'despite himself', as when the VOICE QUALITY in a person's speech signals the fact that he has a cold, is tired/old/male, etc.

Human communication may take place using any of the available sensory modes (hearing, sight, etc.), and the differential study of these modes, as used in communicative activity, is carried on by SEMIOTICS. A contrast which is often made, especially by psychologists, is between 'verbal' and 'non-verbal' communication, to refer to the linguistic vs. the non-linguistic features of communication (the latter including facial expressions, gestures, etc., both in man and animals). However, the ambiguity of the term 'verbal' here, implying that language is basically a matter of 'words', makes this term of limited value to linguists, and it is not usually used by them in this way.

The term 'communicative' is often used in a restricted sense. In the phrase **communicative competence**, for instance, it is in contrast with 'linguistic', a distinction being made between the NATIVE-SPEAKER'S awareness of the FORMAL patterning of his language, on the one hand (his 'linguistic competence'), and of the situational APPROPRIATENESS of his language, on the other. **Communicative dynamism** (or CD) is a fundamental concept of the modern PRAGUE SCHOOL theory of LINGUISTICS (cf. FUNCTIONAL SENTENCE PERSPECTIVE), whereby an UTTERANCE is seen as a process of gradually unfolding MEANING, each part of the utterance contributing variously ('dynamically') to the total communicative effect. Some parts of an utterance will contribute little to the meaning, because they reflect only what has already been communicated: these 'thematic' aspects would be considered to have the lowest degree of CD. By contrast, 'rhematic' aspects have the highest degree of CD, containing new information which advances the communicative process. Other aspects are also recognised. See Lyons 1977b: Chs. 2, 12; Robins 1971: Ch. 9; Bolinger 1975: Ch. 15.

commutation A term used by some PHONOLOGISTS to refer to a process of sound SUBSTITUTION to show CONTRASTIVITY. It is especially encountered in the phrase **commutation test**, which is a systematic use of the substitutability technique of MINIMAL PAIRS for establishing PHONEMES. Some LINGUISTIC theories have used the term in a more restricted sense: in GLOSSEMATICS, for example, it is contrasted with 'substitution', and refers only to one type of relationship between the compact

members of a PARADIGM. See Hyman 1975: Ch. 3; Dinneen 1967: Ch. 11.

compact One of the features of sound set up by JAKOBSON & Halle in their DISTINCTIVE FEATURE theory of PHONOLOGY, to handle variations in PLACE OF ARTICULATION; its opposite being DIFFUSE. Compact sounds are defined articulatorily and acoustically, as those which involve a STRICTURE relatively far forward in the mouth, and a relatively high concentration of ACOUSTIC energy in a narrow, central part of the sound spectrum. For example, OPEN VOWELS are [+compact] (abbreviated as [+comp]; HIGH or MID vowels are [−compact] ([−comp]). The feature is replaced by LOW in CHOMSKY & Halle's system. See Ladefoged 1975: Ch. 11; Hyman 1975: Ch. 2.

comparative (1) A term used to characterise a major branch of LINGUISTICS, in which the primary concern is to make statements comparing the characteristics of different LANGUAGES (DIALECTS, VARIETIES, etc.), or different historical states of a language. During the nineteenth century, the concern for comparative analysis was exclusively historical, as scholars investigated the relationships between such 'families' of languages as Sanskrit, Greek, Latin, their hypothetical antecedents (i.e. the 'proto' language from which such families developed), and the subsequent processes which led to the formation of the language groups of the present day. This study became known as **comparative philology** (or simply PHILOLOGY) – sometimes as **comparative grammar**. The phrase **comparative method** refers to the standard comparative philological technique of comparing a set of forms taken from COGNATE languages in order to determine whether a historical relationship connects them. If there were such a relationship, this analysis would then be used to deduce the characteristics of the ancestor language from which they were assumed to have derived (a process of 'comparative' or 'internal' RECONSTRUCTION).

Early twentieth-century linguistics switched from a DIACHRONIC to a SYNCHRONIC emphasis in language analysis, and while not excluding historical studies, comparative linguistics these days is generally taken up with the theoretical and practical analysis of the STRUCTURAL correspondences between living languages, regardless of their history, with the aim of establishing general types of language ('TYPOLOGICAL comparison', or 'typological linguistics') and ultimately the UNIVERSAL characteristics of human language. See Lyons 1968: Ch. 1; Robins 1971: Chs. 1, 8.

(2) A term used in the three-way GRAMMATICAL description of ADJECTIVES and ADVERBS into DEGREES, specifying the extent of their

application. The **comparative form** is used for a comparison between two entities, and contrasts with SUPERLATIVE, for more than two, and POSITIVE, where no comparison is implied. In English, there is both an INFLECTION (*-er*) and a PERIPHRASTIC construction (*more*) to express this notion (e.g. *nicer, more beautiful*). The construction which may follow the use of a comparative is called a 'comparative clause' or 'comparative sentence', e.g. *he is bigger **than I am***. See Quirk *et al* 1972: Chs. 5, 11.

competence A term used in LINGUISTIC theory, and especially in GENERATIVE GRAMMAR, to refer to a person's knowledge of his language, the SYSTEM OF RULES which he has mastered so that he is able to produce and understand an indefinite number of SENTENCES, and to recognise grammatical mistakes and AMBIGUITIES. It is an idealised conception of language, which is seen as in opposition to the notion of PERFORMANCE, the specific UTTERANCES of speech. According to CHOMSKY, linguistics before generative grammar had been preoccupied with performance in a CORPUS, instead of with the UNDERLYING competence involved. As a general conception, this distinction has been widely accepted, but increasing criticism has come from linguists who feel that the boundary between the two notions is not as clear-cut as their definitions would lead one to believe. There are problems, often in deciding whether a particular speech feature is a matter of competence or performance (e.g. a feature of INTONATION, or DISCOURSE).

A particularly strong line of criticism has emerged in the notion of **communicative competence**, which focuses on the NATIVE-SPEAKER'S ability to produce and understand sentences which are appropriate to the CONTEXT in which they occur – what he needs to know in order to communicate effectively in socially distinct settings. Communicative competence, then, subsumes the social determinants of linguistic behaviour, including such environmental matters as the relationship between speaker and hearer, and the pressures which stem from the time and place of speaking. If speakers have a tacit awareness of such communicative CONSTRAINTS, it is argued, then a linguistic theory ought to aim to provide an explicit account of these factors, insofar as these are systematic within a community, and not restrict itself to the analysis of STRUCTURE in purely FORMAL terms (as in the notion of 'linguistic' competence). This view has received a wide measure of acceptance, but to date relatively little progress has been made over the question of how to model this broader conception of competence in precise terms. See Palmer 1971: Ch. 4; Huddleston 1976: Ch. 1; Lyons 1977b: Ch. 14.

complement(-ation, -iser) A term used in the analysis of GRAMMATICAL FUNCTION, to refer to a major CONSTITUENT of SENTENCE or CLAUSE STRUCTURE, traditionally associated with 'completing' the action specified by the VERB. In its broadest sense, complement therefore is a very general notion, subsuming all obligatory features of the PREDICATE other than the verb, e.g. OBJECTS (e.g. *He kicked the ball*) and ADVERBIALS (e.g. *He was in the garden*). In some approaches, the complement is given a more restricted definition, e.g. to refer only to the 'completing' function of structures following the verb *to be* (or similar verbs) – in such an analysis, *He kicked the doctor* would be Subject-Verb-Object, whereas *He is a doctor* would be Subject-Verb-Complement. A further distinction is sometimes made between complements of the subject and those of the object, as in *He is a doctor* (**subject complement**) and *He called me a fool* (**object complement**). However, the domain of **complementation** remains an unclear area in linguistic analysis, and there are several unresolved issues, e.g. whether the PARTICLES in phrasal verbs (e.g. *come in*) should be subsumed under this heading. In GENERATIVE syntax, the term **complementiser** is used to refer to CONJUNCTIONS which mark an EMBEDDED sentence of a complement type, e.g. *that* in *I said that he's coming*. See Quirk *et al* 1972: Chs. 2, 12; Lyons 1968: Ch. 8; Huddleston 1976: Ch. 8.

complementary (complementarity) (1) A term used primarily in PHONOLOGY in the phrase **complementary distribution**, referring to the mutual exclusiveness of a pair of sounds in a certain PHONETIC ENVIRONMENT. In English, for example, the voiceless ALLOphone of the /l/ phoneme occurs after initial /s-/, as in *sleep*, and the VOICED allophone is excluded; conversely, [l] is used initially when no /s-/ precedes. [l] and [l̥] are thus said to be 'in complementary DISTRIBUTION' in this environment. The term is also used analogously in MORPHOLOGY, with reference to the distribution of pairs of FORMS in GRAMMATICAL environments (e.g. the selection of alternative forms of the plural MORPHEME in English). See Hyman 1975: Ch. 3.

(2) In SEMANTICS, the term is often used to refer to a category of SENSE relation between LEXICAL ITEMS. **Complementary terms** (or **complementaries**) display a type of oppositeness of MEANING, illustrated by such pairs as *single/married* and *boy/girl*. *Single* is said to be 'the complementary of' *married*, and vice versa. In such a relationship, the assertion of one of the items implies the denial of the other: an entity cannot be both at once. The relationship of 'complementarity' is characterised by the lack of any gradability between the items (there is no continuum of gradation between *boy* and *girl*, such that one can be **less boy*, **very boy*, and so on). In this

respect, the term contrasts with the technical sense of ANTONYMY, where gradations between the opposites are possible (cf. *big, bigger, very big*, etc. vs. *small, smaller*, etc.), and also with CONVERSENESS, where the opposites presuppose each other (e.g. *husband/wife*). The term CONTRADICTORY is an alternative preferred by some analysts. See Lyons 1977b: Ch. 9.

complex(ity) The general sense of this term is found in LINGUISTICS, with reference to both the FORMAL internal structuring of linguistic UNITS, and the psychological difficulty in using or learning them. The factors which contribute to the notion of complexity are a major topic in PSYCHOLINGUISTICS, both in studies of adult COMPREHENSION and PRODUCTION, and in child language ACQUISITION. A central theme is the nature of the interaction between levels of difficulty in cognitive and linguistic STRUCTURES, and especially the way this affects the order of emergence of language patterns in children. However, it has not yet proved feasible to establish independent measures of complexity defined in purely linguistic terms (such as the number of TRANSFOR-MATIONS in a SENTENCE DERIVATION, or the number of FEATURES in the specification of a linguistic unit, cf. SIMPLICITY METRIC), largely because of controversy over the nature of the linguistic measures used, and the interference stemming from other psychological factors, such as the language user's attention and motivation.

Several restricted senses are also used, e.g. 'complex SENTENCE' (in two senses: either a sentence consisting of more than one CLAUSE, or one consisting of a main clause and at least one SUBORDINATE clause), 'complex word' (i.e. one containing a free MORPHEME and at least one bound morpheme), 'complex tone' (an INTONATIONAL NUCLEUS with two distinct PITCH movements), 'complex stop' (a PLOSIVE with two points of ARTICULATION), 'complex nucleus' (a SYLLABIC peak with two distinct VOWEL qualities), and so on. See Lyons 1968: Ch. 6; Clark & Clark 1977: Ch. 9.

complex symbol A term used in some MODELS of GENERATIVE GRAMMAR (cf. ASPECTS) to refer to a symbol in a PHRASE-MARKER which has an internal structure of its own. It consists of an unordered set of SYNTACTIC FEATURES, e.g. [N], [+Abstract], [+Animate], and (in some accounts) the MORPHEME which the set of features specify, e.g.

$$\begin{bmatrix} +\text{N} \\ +\text{Human} \\ -\text{Proper} \\ \textit{man} \end{bmatrix}$$

See Huddleston 1976: Ch. 10.

component(ial) (1) A term used in GENERATIVE LINGUISTICS to refer to the main sections into which a generative GRAMMAR is organised. In Noam CHOMSKY's *Syntactic Structures* (1957), three components are recognised: the PHRASE-STRUCTURE component (which generates a set of underlying STRINGS), the TRANSFORMATIONAL component (which acts on these strings in various OPTIONAL and OBLIGATORY ways, introducing SEMANTIC changes), and the MORPHOPHONEMIC component (which converts each syntactic string into a string of PHONOLOGICAL UNITS). In *Aspects of the Theory of Syntax* (1965), the model is radically altered. The phrase-structure component is replaced by a **base component**, which generates the UNDERLYING PHRASE-MARKERS representing the DEEP STRUCTURE of SENTENCES, i.e. all semantically relevant grammatical notions. The base component contains the CATEGORIAL and LEXICAL components (or **sub-components**) of the grammar. Two things then happen to these markers: (i) they are semantically interpreted, using the rules of the **semantic component** (which has no equivalent in the *Syntactic Structures* model), and (ii) they are converted into SURFACE structures through the **transformational component** (which contains largely obligatory RULES, the optional ones now being handled by choices made in the base rules). Lastly, a **phonological component** operates on the surface structures, providing them with a PHONETIC interpretation. See Huddleston 1976: Ch. 10.

(2) In SEMANTICS, the term refers to an irreducible FEATURE in terms of which the SENSE of LEXICAL ITEMS can be analysed, e.g. *girl* can be analysed into the components 'human', 'female', 'child', etc. **Componential analysis** is a semantic theory which has developed from a technique for the analysis of kinship vocabulary devised by American anthropologists in the 1950s. It claims that all lexical items can be analysed using a finite set of components (or 'semantic features'), which may, it is felt, be UNIVERSAL. Certainly, several sets of lexical items exist to show the strengths of the approach (e.g. the correspondences between *boy/girl, man/woman, ram/ewe*, etc. can be stated in terms of [+male] vs. [−male] or [−female] vs. [+female]. There are several limitations to the componential models of analysis so far suggested, such as the extent to which BINARY analyses are possible for many lexical items, the claimed UNIVERSALITY of components, and the justification for selecting one value rather than the other for a possible component (e.g. whether the above example should be analysed in terms of [+male] or [−female]).

'Componential analysis' is also found in a general sense in linguistics, especially in Europe, referring to any approach which analyses linguistic units into components, whether in PHONOLOGY, grammar or semantics. In this view, PRAGUE SCHOOL phonological analysis is componential, as are the analysis of WORD-AND-PARADIGM MORPHO-LOGY. See Lyons 1977b: Ch. 9; Clark & Clark 1977: Ch. 11.

composition(-al, de-compos-ed, -ite) A term used in LINGUISTICS to refer to a HIERARCHICAL MODEL of linguistic STRUCTURE in which larger UNITS are seen as being 'composed' of smaller units. For example, in GRAMMATICAL analysis, the relationship between SEN-TENCE, CLAUSE, PHRASE, WORD and MORPHEME is sometimes described as one of 'composition' (CONSTITUENCY, or RANK), the units of higher rank being analysable ('decomposable') into units of lower rank. One might subsequently analyse such structures in terms of their 'compositional meaning'. Compositional models are to be found especially in SCALE-AND-CATEGORY, TAGMEMIC, STRATIFICATIONAL and PHRASE-STRUCTURE GRAMMARS. In relation to WORD-FORMATION, the term is used both in the general sense of 'processes of compounding', and sometimes in a restricted sense, referring to a particular type of compound. In TRANSFORMATIONAL grammar, PHRASAL VERBS (e.g. *switch on*, *take off*) may be referred to as 'composite verbs'. See Lyons 1968: Chs. 2, 5.

compound(ing) (1) A term used widely in DESCRIPTIVE LINGUISTIC studies to refer to a linguistic UNIT which is composed of ELEMENTS that function independently in other circumstances. Of particular currency are the notions of 'compounding' found in 'compound WORDS' (consisting of two or more free MORPHEMES, as in such 'compound NOUNS' as *bedroom*, *rainfall*, and *washing machine*) and 'compound SENTENCES' (consisting of two or more main CLAUSES); but other applications of the term exist, as in 'compound VERBS' (e.g. *come in*), 'compound TENSES' (*viz* consisting of an AUXILIARY + LEXICAL verb), 'compound SUBJECTS/OBJECTS', etc. (where the clause element consists of more than one noun PHRASE or PRONOUN, as in *the boys and the girls shouted*), and 'compound PREPOSITIONS' (e.g. *in accordance with*). See Quirk *et al* 1972: App. 1; Bolinger 1975: Ch. 5.

(2) The term is also used by some linguists in the classification of BILINGUALISM. **Compound bilinguals** are those who attribute identical MEANINGS to corresponding LEXICAL UNITS in the two languages – a distinction here being made with CO-ORDINATE bilingualism, where there is no such identity. See Trudgill 1974: Ch. 6.

comprehension The general sense of this term is found in LINGUISTICS, referring to the ability to understand and interpret spoken and written language; it is opposed to PRODUCTION. In PSYCHOLINGUISTICS, the analysis of the process of speech comprehension is a major theme, encompassing such topics as the strategies used by children in language ACQUISITION, the strategies adults use in interpreting different types of SENTENCE (e.g. AMBIGUITY, NEGATION, QUESTIONS), the role of the extra-linguistic SITUATION, and of cognitive factors (such as memory, attention and perception) in arriving at the interpretation of sentences and DISCOURSES. See Clark & Clark 1977: Ch. 2.

computational linguistics A branch of LINGUISTICS in which computational techniques and concepts are applied to the elucidation of linguistic and PHONETIC problems. Several research areas have developed, including SPEECH synthesis, speech recognition, automatic translation, the making of concordances, the testing of GRAMMARS and the many areas where statistical counts and analyses are required (e.g. in literary textual studies). See Bolinger 1975: Ch. 8; Catford 1977: Ch. 5.

conative A term used by some linguists to refer to a general type of LINGUISTIC FUNCTION – the use of language in order to achieve a result in an addressee, in accord with the speaker's wishes. Its use is illustrated by a range of 'directive' functions (e.g. COMMANDS, VOCATIVES), but its precise sense needs to take into account the range of other functions recognised by the theory in which it is used – in particular, the contrast which is often made between conative and EXPRESSIVE (personal) and REFERENTIAL (situational) functions. See Lyons 1977b: Ch. 2.

concatenation A term used in the FORMAL representation of LINGUISTIC STRUCTURES, and especially in GENERATIVE GRAMMAR, to refer to a process for forming STRINGS of ELEMENTS, the elements being seen in a relation of linear succession, e.g. $X + Y + Z$ or $X^\frown Y^\frown Z$ (i.e. X is 'concatenated with' or 'chained together with' Y, etc.). See Lyons 1968: Ch. 6; 1977a: App. 1.

concord A term used in GRAMMATICAL theory and description to refer to a formal relationship between ELEMENTS, whereby a FORM of one WORD requires a corresponding form of another. In English, for example, a singular SUBJECT co-occurs with a singular form of the VERB in the present TENSE, e.g. *he walks* (vs. *they walk*); in Latin, there is concord between the NUMBER, GENDER and CASE of ADJECTIVES and NOUNS. This formal correspondence was traditionally referred to as AGREEMENT (the adjective 'agrees' with the noun, etc.), and is usually contrasted in grammatical discussion with the notion of GOVERNMENT. See Robins 1971: Ch. 6; Quirk *et al* 1972: Ch. 7; Palmer 1971: Ch. 2.

condition A term used in LINGUISTICS to refer to any factors which, it might be argued, need to be taken into account in evaluating a theory, a GRAMMAR, or an individual analysis, e.g. such conditions as external ADEQUACY, GENERALITY, SIMPLICITY. More specifically, it refers to any criterion which must be met before a particular analysis may be carried out. In GENERATIVE grammar, for example, the STRUCTURAL DE-SCRIPTION which provides the input to a TRANSFORMATIONAL RULE specifies the conditions which must be met before the rule can operate. In SYSTEMIC grammar, the ENTRY conditions specify the structural criteria which must be satisfied in order for a particular grammatical system to become operative. See Dinneen 1967: Ch. 12.

conditional A term used in GRAMMATICAL DESCRIPTION to refer to CLAUSES whose SEMANTIC role is the expression of hypotheses or conditions. In English, these are introduced by *if, unless,* and a few other CONJUNCTIONS (e.g. *if John asks, tell him...*). The TRADITIONAL grammatical notion of 'conditional TENSE' (using *would, should*) is usually interpreted in terms of ASPECTUAL or MODAL VERB forms in analyses of English, though this is MORPHOLOGICALLY expressed in many languages (e.g. French). See Quirk *et al* 1972: Ch. 11.

conditioned/conditioning A term used in LINGUISTICS to refer to the FORM a linguistic UNIT takes when this is partly or wholly determined by the linguistic CONTEXT in which it occurs. For example, in English PHONOLOGY, the ALVEOLAR /t/ PHONEME predictably becomes DENTAL when followed by /θ/, as in *eighth*, i.e. [t̪] is a 'conditioned VARIANT' of /t/; in MORPHOPHONOLOGY, the indefinite ARTICLE *a* becomes *an* when followed by a VOWEL. The concept of ALLO- is the most succinct way of referring to phonological and GRAMMATICAL 'conditioning', and other terms are sometimes used for the same phenomenon, e.g. 'contextual/positional/combinatory/automatic' variants. The term 'conditioning' is also sometimes used with reference to the influence of the social/cultural situation on the choice of linguistic forms ('environmental conditioning'). See Lyons 1968: Ch. 2; Bolinger 1975: Ch. 4.

configuration (1) (**-al**) A term used to refer to the STANDARD MODEL of GENERATIVE GRAMMAR, seen in contrast with RELATIONAL theories of grammar. In the former, PHRASE-MARKERS are seen as clusters

congruence

('configurations') of SYNTACTIC CATEGORIES, arranged in LINEAR ORDER. See Akmajian & Heny 1975: Ch. 2.

(2) The term is also used generally in LINGUISTICS and PHONETICS for any formally identifiable ARRANGEMENT of ELEMENTS. It has been used, for example, with reference to the sequence of TONES which constitute an INTONATION CONTOUR (a 'tonal configuration') and to the set of SYNTACTIC FUNCTIONS which depend upon a particular VERB, as in CASE grammar (a 'configuration of cases'). See Bolinger 1975: Chs. 3, 15.

congruence A term used in LINGUISTICS to refer to a correspondence between the decisions made at one LEVEL of analysis (PHONOLOGY, GRAMMAR or SEMANTICS) and those made at another. The SENTENCE is the UNIT where there is maximum **congruence of levels**, in that criteria of identification at each level tend to coincide: certain classes of exception aside, a sentence is a grammatically, semantically and phonologically autonomous unit. The notion of WORD, by contrast, displays less congruence: phonological (and orthographic), MORPHO-LOGICAL, SYNTACTIC and semantic criteria often conflict in word-identification and CLASSIFICATION. See Lyons 1968: Ch. 5.

conjoin(-ing, -ed) A term used in GENERATIVE GRAMMAR to refer to a CONSTRUCTION where one SENTENCE is CO-ORDINATED ('conjoined') with another. Conjoining processes are distinct from EMBEDDING ones. The linking of CLAUSES using *and, but*, etc. would be carried out using conjoining (e.g. *The man fed the cat and the lady fed the dog*). See Lyons 1968: Ch. 6; Huddleston 1976: Ch. 7.

conjunction (conjunct) A term used in the GRAMMATICAL classification of WORDS to refer to an ITEM or a process whose primary function is to connect words or other CONSTRUCTIONS. The conventional sub-classification of these 'connective' items distinguishes CO-ORDINATING conjunctions (e.g. *and, or, but*) and SUBORDINATING conjunctions (e.g. *because, when, unless*) – also referred to as 'co-ordinators' and 'subordinators' respectively. Certain types of ADVERBIAL (those whose function is primarily connective) are also sometimes referred to as 'conjunctive', or simply as 'conjuncts', e.g. *however, moreover, indeed*. A process of conjunction is also recognised in TRANSFORMATIONAL accounts (as in formal logic), this normally being referred to as a CONJOINING transformation; the conjoined elements may also be referred to as 'conjuncts'. See Quirk *et al* 1972: Chs. 8, 11; Lyons 1968: Ch. 6; 1977b: Ch. 6.

conjunctive A term used in GENERATIVE PHONOLOGY to refer to a principle affecting the ORDERING OF RULES. **Conjunctive ordering** is found in the use of the brace NOTATION, which indicates an OBLIGATORY selection of one set of alternatives. If a SEQUENCE of rules is abbreviated using this notation (e.g. $X \begin{Bmatrix} Y \\ Z \\ W \end{Bmatrix} P$, which stands for (a) XYP, (b) XZP or (c) XWP), then this sequence forms a conjunctively ordered block, i.e. one or other of (a), (b), or (c) must apply. It is distinguished from DISJUNCTIVE ordering. See Lyons 1977b: Ch. 6; Hyman 1975: Ch. 4.

connected speech A term used in LINGUISTICS to refer to spoken language when analysed as a continuous sequence, as in normal UTTERANCES and conversations. Its significance lies in the contrast implied with studies of linguistic UNITS seen in isolation, such as an individual sound, WORD or PHRASE, which were the subject matter of much traditional linguistic enquiry. It is now realised that important changes happen to these units when they are used in connected speech, as demonstrated by such processes as ASSIMILATION and ELISION, e.g. *and* becoming /n/ in such phrases as *boys and girls*. See Gimson 1970: Ch. 11.

connection A term used by some FIRTHIAN linguists, as part of the phrase **renewal of connection**, referring to a way of validating an analysis predictively: an analysis made on the basis of a set of data (S_1) is applied again to a further sample (S_2) and is found to be adequate, in that in S_2 one meets again the EXPONENTS of the abstract UNITS originally postulated in S_1 (i.e. there has been a 'renewal of connection'). See Robins 1971: Ch. 2.

connective (connect-ivity, -or) A term used in the GRAMMATICAL classification of WORDS to characterise words or MORPHEMES whose function is primarily to link LINGUISTIC UNITS at any LEVEL. CONJUNCTIONS are the most obvious types (e.g. *and, or, while, because*), but several types of ADVERB can be seen as connective ('conjuncts' such as *therefore, however, nevertheless*), as can some VERBS (the COPULAS *be, seem,* etc.). One type of EXOCENTRIC construction is also referred to as 'connective', e.g. *was happy, stayed quiet*, where the first element is the connector, and the second a predicative ATTRIBUTE. See Quirk *et al* 1972: Ch. 10.

connotation (connotative) A term used in SEMANTICS as part of a classification of types of MEANING; opposed to DENOTATION. Its main application is with reference to the emotional associations (personal or communal) which are suggested by, or are part of the meaning of a LINGUISTIC UNIT, especially a LEXICAL ITEM. Denotation, by contrast, covers the relationship between a linguistic unit and the non-linguistic entities to which it refers. (The traditional philosophical use of 'connotation' and 'denotation' is quite different: here, the meanings involved largely correspond to the distinction between SENSE and REFERENCE, the former being concerned with the relationships of equivalence between terms and PROPOSITIONS, the latter with their external world status and truth-value.) For example, the connotations of the lexical item *December* might include 'bad weather', 'dark evenings', etc. (for north Europeans, at least), or 'parties', 'Christmas', etc. Alternative terms for 'connotative meaning' include AFFECTIVE and EMOTIVE. See Lyons 1977b: Ch. 7.

consonant(al) One of the two general CATEGORIES used for the classification of speech sounds, the other being VOWEL. Consonants can be defined in terms of both PHONETICS and PHONOLOGY. Phonetically, they are sounds made by a CLOSURE or narrowing in the VOCAL TRACT so that the air flow is either completely blocked, or so restricted that audible FRICTION is produced. Consonant ARTICULATIONS are relatively easy to feel, and as a result are most conveniently described in terms of PLACE and MANNER of articulation. In addition, a routine phonetic description of consonants would involve information about the mode of vibration of the VOCAL CORDS (see VOICING), and it is often necessary to specify the DURATION of the sound, the AIR-STREAM MECHANISM involved and the direction of air-flow (EGRESSIVE or INGRESSIVE). From a phonological point of view, consonants are those UNITS which function at the MARGINS of SYLLABLES, either singly or in CLUSTERS.

Usually, phonetic and phonological criteria coincide: [f], for example, is a consonant in that there is audible friction and the sound occurs marginally, as in *fat, leaf*. In sounds such as [l], [r], [w] and [j], however, there is a conflict between the two criteria. Phonologically, these sounds are consonants, because their role in syllables is the same as that taken by [f], [p], etc., e.g. *lip, rip, wet, yet*. But phonetically, they lack the friction required by the above definitions: they are vowel-like in character. Such sounds as a result are often called semi-vowels or **semi-consonants**.

The trouble arises from having only one term to do two jobs (phonetic and phonological descriptions). Several terminological solutions have been suggested, the most well-known one being the suggestion of the American linguist K. L. Pike (b. 1912) to reserve the term 'consonant' for the phonological level of analysis, and to introduce CONTOID for the phonetic level (as opposed to VOCOID). In this way, [p] would be consonant and contoid, and [l], etc. consonant and vocoid.

Consonantal is used both in a general adjectival sense, and also has separate technical status in the DISTINCTIVE FEATURE theory of phonology, where 'consonantal' and **non-consonantal** constitute one of the major class features in terms of which speech sounds are analysed. Consonantal sounds may be defined either articulatorily or acoustically in this approach: they are produced with a major obstruction in the middle of the vocal tract, and have low ACOUSTIC energy. Non-consonantal sounds lack this obstruction, and have high acoustic energy. Consonants in the above phonological sense would be analysed as having the feature [+consonantal]; vowels would be [−consonantal].

See Gimson 1970: Chs. 4, 5; Hyman 1975: Ch. 2.

conspiracy A term used in GENERATIVE PHONOLOGY to refer to any set of RULES which can be seen as acting together, or 'conspiring', to produce a specific result, which it would not be possible or economical to state as a single rule. See Hyman 1975: Ch. 4.

constant A type of OPPOSITION recognised in PRAGUE SCHOOL PHONOLOGY, distinguished from NEUTRALISABLE. A constant opposition exists when all its members can occur in all possible positions, e.g. wherever /p/ might be found in a LANGUAGE, a contrast with /b/ will also be found. A DISTINCTION such as English /t/vs./d/, however, is neutralisable because, in some positions, the CONTRAST disappears (as in /t/ following INITIAL /s/). See Hyman 1975: Ch. 2.

constative A basic term used in the theory of SPEECH-ACTS: it refers to UTTERANCES which are DESCRIPTIVE STATEMENTS, capable of being analysed in terms of truth values. 'Constative utterances' are contrasted with PERFORMATIVE utterances, where the function is one of 'doing' rather than 'saying'. See Lyons 1977b: Ch. 16.

constituent (constituency) A basic term in GRAMMATICAL analysis for a LINGUISTIC UNIT which is a component of a larger CONSTRUCTION. Based on a combination of intuitive and FORMAL (e.g. DISTRIBUTIONAL) criteria, a SENTENCE can be analysed into a series of constituents, such as SUBJECT + PREDICATE, or NP + VP, etc. These units thus produced can, in turn, be analysed into further constituents (e.g. a NOUN PHRASE might consist of a DETERMINER and a noun), and this **constituent analysis** process can be continued until no further sub-divisions are possible. The major divisions that can be made within a construction, at any level, are known as the **immediate constituents** (ICs) of that construction. The irreducible ELEMENTS resulting from such an analysis are known as the **ultimate constituents** (UCs) of the construction. So in analysing the sentence *The clock has stopped*, the ICs would be *the clock* and *has stopped* (how these constituents are to be LABELLED is a separate decision-making process). *The clock* has *the* and *clock* as its ICs. The ICs of *has stopped* are *has* and *stopped*. And *stopped* can be broken down further into *stop* and *-ed*. The process is often drawn in the form of a TREE diagram, as follows:

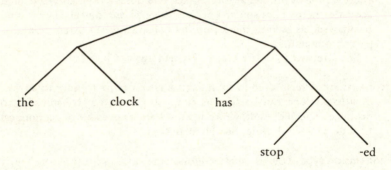

This **constituent structure** may also be represented using BRACKETS, each analytic decision being represented by the imposition of a pair of square brackets at the appropriate points in the construction, e.g. [[*the clock*] [*has stop*[*-ed*]]]. A grammar which analyses sentences wholly in this way, i.e. in terms of a HIERARCHY of structural layers, is sometimes called a 'constituent structure grammar'; in GENERATIVE linguistics, such an analysis is carried on by the PHRASE-STRUCTURE COMPONENT of the grammar. The term 'constituency grammar' will also be encountered.

The limitations of IC analysis have been much discussed in the linguistics literature, especially in relation to the greater POWER of TRANSFORMATIONAL grammars. IC analysis, for example, is unable to make explicit the relationships between formally connected sets of sentences (such as ACTIVE and PASSIVE), nor can it demonstrate the AMBIGUITY involved in several kinds of construction (a much-discussed example here being *it is too hot to eat*). But some kind of constituent analysis is an important feature of any grammatical system.

In generative grammar, the term 'constituent sentence' is also used to refer to an EMBEDDED sentence, i.e. one where an UNDERLYING sentence has been incorporated within another (MATRIX) sentence. For example, in the sentence *The cat sitting on the mat miaowed*, the CLAUSE *sitting on the mat* would be derived from an underlying sentence such as *the cat is sitting on the mat*, this would then be inserted into the matrix sentence *the cat miaowed* using an appropriate transformation, and would thereby become a constituent sentence. See Lyons 1968: Ch. 6; 1977a: Ch. 6; Robins 1971: Ch. 6.

constraint A term used in LINGUISTICS, and especially in GENERATIVE GRAMMAR, to refer to a CONDITION which restricts the application of a RULE. For example, in generative PHONOLOGY, a distinction can be made between 'simultaneous' and 'sequential' constraints: the former states the restrictions on the simultaneous occurrence of FEATURES, e.g. a SEGMENT cannot be at once [+high] and [+low]; the latter states the restrictions on sequences of features, e.g. whether a language permits CONSONANT CLUSTERS. In generative SYNTAX there are also several constraints which have to be imposed in order to prevent the DERIVATION of ILL-FORMED PHRASE-MARKERS, e.g. constraints on the ORDERING of rules. For example, 'surface structure' constraints (or 'output conditions') refer to conditions where a characteristic of SURFACE STRUCTURE decides which phrase-markers are well-formed, e.g. no phrase-marker containing an internal boundary symbol can qualify as a well-formed surface structure. See Huddleston 1976: Ch. 12; Hyman 1975: Ch. 1.

constriction (constricted) A general term used in ARTICULATORY PHONETICS to refer to a narrowing within the VOCAL TRACT. The different kinds and degrees of constriction are the basis of the articulatory classification of sound QUALITIES. The term 'constricted' is sometimes used in a restricted sense, referring to GLOTTALISED sounds. See Catford 1977: Chs. 6, 7.

construction (construct) (1) In its most general senses in LINGUISTICS, 'construction' refers to the overall process of internal organisation of a GRAMMATICAL UNIT – a SENTENCE, for example, being 'constructed' out of a set of MORPHEMES by the application of a set of RULES. More specifically, it refers to the SYNTAGMATIC result of such a process, a particular type of construction (a 'constructional type' or 'pattern') being defined as a sequence of units which has a FUNCTIONAL identity in the grammar of a LANGUAGE, such as SUBJECT + VERB + OBJECT (with reference to CLAUSES), or DETERMINER + NOUN (with reference to

PHRASES). Most specifically, it refers to a token of a constructional type, in the sense of STRING, e.g. *the + man + is + walking*. It is constructions of this last kind which are analysed into CONSTITUENTS, as in IMMEDIATE CONSTITUENT analysis. **Constructional homonymity** refers to a grammatical string with more than one interpretation in terms of the patterns of construction it contains (as defined, say, by a PHRASE-STRUCTURE grammar). In more traditional grammatical terms, the string would be said to be 'structurally ambiguous'. For example, *men and women in coats* could be analysed as *men and [women in coats]* (i.e. only the women have coats) or as *men and women [in coats]* (they all have coats). See Lyons 1968: Ch. 6; Palmer 1971: Ch. 3.

(2) In PSYCHOLINGUISTICS, the term is often used as part of a theory of COMPREHENSION, to refer to the psychological process of 'constructing' an interpretation of sentences, based on their ability to identify and interrelate the various ELEMENTS and LEVELS of MEANING involved. See Clark & Clark 1977: Ch. 2.

contact A term used in SOCIOLINGUISTICS to refer to a situation of geographical continuity or close social proximity (and thus of mutual influence) between LANGUAGES or DIALECTS. The result of 'contact situations' can be seen linguistically, in the growth of LOAN words, patterns of PHONOLOGICAL and GRAMMATICAL change, mixed forms of language (such as CREOLES and PIDGINS), and a general increase in BILINGUALISM, of various kinds. In a restricted sense, languages are said to be 'in contact' if they are used alternately by the same persons, i.e. bilinguals. The term 'contact language' is also sometimes used to refer to a pidgin. See Bolinger 1975: Ch. 11; Trudgill 1974: Ch. 7.

content The general sense of this term – referring to the MEANING of an expression – is found pre-theoretically in LINGUISTICS, but some linguists have given it a technical status, by analysing language into two major dimensions, distinguishing a 'content plane' from an 'expression plane' (analogous to the SAUSSUREAN distinction between the MEANING and FORM of linguistic SIGNS). More specifically, some approaches to WORD CLASSIFICATION recognise a class of 'content words', defined as words which have stateable LEXICAL meaning – the majority of words in the LANGUAGE, in fact, apart from the few FUNCTION words, whose role is primarily to express GRAMMATICAL relationships. Alternative terms include LEXICAL and FULL words. See Lyons 1968: Ch. 2; Bolinger 1975: Ch. 5.

context(-ual-isation) (1) A general term used in LINGUISTICS and PHONETICS to refer to specific parts of an UTTERANCE (or TEXT) near or adjacent to a UNIT which is the focus of attention. The occurrence of a unit (e.g. a sound, WORD) is partly or wholly determined by its context, which is specified in terms of the unit's relations, i.e. the other features with which it combines as a sequence. The everyday sense of the term is related to this, as when one 'puts a word in context', in order to clarify the MEANING intended, as in dictionary entries. Providing a context in this way is referred to as **contextualisation**. Words, it is suggested, have meaning only when seen in context.

The specification of FORMAL contexts is a particular characteristic of the formulation of rules in GENERATIVE linguistics, where forms can be classified in terms of whether they occur only within a specific context ('context-sensitive/restricted/dependent' rules) or are independent of context ('context-free' rules). A **context-free grammar** is one in which all the rules apply regardless of context, i.e. they would all be of the type 'Rewrite X as Y', no further conditions being specified. A **context-sensitive** grammar contains some rules of the type $A \rightarrow B/C—D$, where the oblique line means 'in the context of', and the horizontal line indicates the place in the structure where A is rewritten as B – in this case, between C and D. In some GENERATIVE MODELS (cf. ASPECTS), **contextual features** refer to one of the types of (BINARY) FEATURES which are contained in a LEXICAL entry (the others being INHERENT and RULE features); such features provide information as to where in a DEEP STRUCTURE REPRESENTATION a lexical item can occur. Three types of contextual features are recognised: CATEGORY features, STRICT SUBCATEGORISATION features, and SELECTIONAL features.

Variants of sound, GRAMMAR, etc. which are dependent on context for their occurrence are sometimes called 'contextual variants' (or 'conditioned variants'); an example is the allophone (cf. ALLO-). An analysis in these terms is sometimes called a 'contextual analysis'. Some scholars use the term CO-TEXT for context in sense (1), reserving the latter term for sense (2) below. See Lyons 1968: Chs. 6, 9; Huddleston 1976: Chs. 3, 10.

(2) The features of the non-linguistic world in relation to which linguistic units are systematically used. The term 'situation' is also used in this sense, as in the compound term **situational context**. In its broadest sense, situational context includes the *total* non-linguistic background to a text or utterance, including the immediate situation in which it is used, and the awareness by speaker and hearer of what has been said earlier and of any relevant external beliefs or PRESUPPOSITIONS. Others restrict the term to what is immediately observable in the co-occurring situation. Further distinctions are usually made in SEMANTICS and STYLISTICS, distinguishing, for example,

REFERENTIAL and EMOTIVE meaning from **contextual meaning,** i.e. information signalled about the kind of use a linguistic unit has in its social context, e.g. whether it has a 'restricted' use (as in social pleasantries, or religious settings), or how it relates to such factors as age, sex or class of the speakers.

(3) **Context of situation** is a specific term in FIRTHIAN linguistic theory, deriving from the work of the anthropologist Bronislaw Malinowski (1884–1942). In this theory, meaning is seen as a multiple phenomenon, its various facets being relatable on the one hand to features of the external world, and on the other hand to the different LEVELS of linguistic analysis, such as PHONETICS, grammar and semantics. Context of situation refers to the whole set of external world features considered to be relevant in the analysis of an utterance at these levels.

(4) Other related senses may be found. For example, the general term **context of utterance** is sometimes used to refer to all the factors which systematically determine the FORM, MEANING or appropriateness of UTTERANCES (i.e. including both sense (1) and sense (2) of this entry). 'Context' is also used in HALLIDAYAN linguistics, but in a restricted sense, as the name of an INTER-LEVEL of language organisation which relates linguistic form to extra-linguistic SITUATION – it is thus equivalent to SEMANTICS.

See Lyons 1968: Ch. 9; 1977b: Ch. 14; Robins 1971: Ch. 1.

continuant One of the features of sound set up by CHOMSKY & Halle in their DISTINCTIVE FEATURE theory of PHONOLOGY, to handle variations in MANNER OF ARTICULATION. Continuant sounds have been defined articulatorily and acoustically, as those produced with an incomplete CLOSURE of the VOCAL TRACT. All VOWELS and FRICATIVES are [+continuant] (abbreviated as [+cont]). The opposite term in JAKOBSON & Halle's approach is DISCONTINUOUS; in Chomsky & Halle's later system, it is **non-continuant** or STOP: these are sounds produced with a complete closure of the vocal tract, and thus characterised acoustically by a silence, as in PLOSIVES [−continuant] ([−cont]). The term INTERRUPTED is also sometimes used. See Ladefoged 1975: Ch. 11; Hyman 1975: Ch. 2.

continuous A term used in the GRAMMATICAL description of VERB FORMS, referring to a CONTRAST of a temporal or durative kind, and thus sometimes handled under the heading of TENSE and sometimes under ASPECT. The usual contrast recognised is between 'continuous' or PROGRESSIVE (e.g. *I am going*) and **non-continuous** SIMPLE, or 'non-progressive' (e.g. *I go*). Linguists prefer an aspectual analysis here, because of the complex interaction of durational, completive and temporal features of meaning involved; TRADITIONAL grammars, however, merely refer to 'continuous tense', etc., and thus imply a meaning which is to some degree an oversimplification. See Quirk *et al* 1972: Ch. 3; Lyons 1968: Ch. 7.

contoid A term invented by the American phonetician Kenneth Pike (b. 1912) to help distinguish between the PHONETIC and the PHONOLOGICAL notions of CONSONANT. Phonetically, a consonant is defined with reference to a complete CLOSURE in the VOCAL TRACT, or a narrowing sufficiently great to cause audible FRICTION. Phonologically, it is a unit which FUNCTIONS at the MARGINS of SYLLABLES. But there are cases where these criteria do not coincide, such as [l], [r], [w] and [j], which function as consonants in syllables, but which are phonetically VOWEL-like. To handle such cases, Pike proposed that separate terms be used for the phonetic and the phonological definitions of all sounds: contoid refers to the phonetic characterisation of a consonant, as defined above; consonant is reserved for the phonological sense. Its opposite is VOCOID. See Gimson 1970: Ch. 4.

contour A term used in SUPRASEGMENTAL PHONOLOGY, particularly by those phonologists working within the American tradition, to refer to a distinctive CONFIGURATION of PITCHES, TONES, or STRESSES in an UTTERANCE. Several types of contour are recognised, e.g. 'primary', 'secondary' and 'terminal' contours, which relate to major patterns in the analysis of INTONATION, or the notion of **stress contour** in GENERATIVE phonology, which refers to a sequence of stresses assigned through the application of the transformational CYCLE. See Hyman 1975: Ch. 6; Bolinger 1975: Ch. 3.

contraction (contracted) A term used in LINGUISTICS to refer to the process or result of PHONOLOGICALLY reducing a linguistic FORM so that it comes to be attached to an adjacent linguistic form, or FUSING a sequence of forms so that they appear as a single form. The first kind of 'contracted form' (or 'contraction') can be illustrated from *I've* from *I have*, *haven't* from *have not*. The second kind is seen in French *du*, *des* from **de le* and **de les* respectively. See Quirk *et al* 1972: Ch. 3.

contradictory A term sometimes used in SEMANTICS to refer to a SENSE relation between LEXICAL ITEMS. 'Contradictory terms' (or 'contra-dictories') display a type of oppositeness of MEANING, illustrated by such pairs as *male/female* and *single/married*. Because of the technical use of this term in logic (where it refers to a relationship between two propositions such that they cannot both be true or both false), some semanticists prefer to use COMPLEMENTARITY to refer to the LINGUISTIC relationship involved in such opposites. See Lyons 1977b: Ch. 9; Clark & Clark: Ch. 11.

contrary A term sometimes used in SEMANTICS to refer to a SENSE relation between LEXICAL ITEMS. 'Contrary terms' (or 'contraries') display a type of oppositeness of MEANING, illustrated by such pairs as *big/little*, *happy/sad*. Because of the technical use of this term in logic (where it refers to the relationship between two propositions such that they both cannot be true, though both can be false), some semanticists prefer to use ANTONYMY to refer to the LINGUISTIC relationship involved in such opposites. See Lyons 1977b: Ch. 9; Clark & Clark 1977: Ch. 11.

contrast(ive, -ity) (1) A term used in LINGUISTICS for a difference between units, especially one which serves to distinguish MEANINGS in a language. Such differences are also referred to as DISTINCTIVE, FUNCTIONAL or SIGNIFICANT. The principle of contrast is considered fundamental to linguistic analysis. It can be illustrated with reference to the notions of PHONEME (in particular), DISTINCTIVE FEATURE, MORPHEME, etc., which may all be defined as 'minimally contrastive units' at some LEVEL of analysis. Examples in PHONOLOGY are the contrast between English /p/ and /b/, or VOICED vs. voiceless; in GRAMMAR, between INFLECTIONAL endings, or the various possibilities of WORD ORDER. Many linguists use the term OPPOSITION in the same way, but in some approaches this term is given separate definition, referring only to the PARADIGMATIC differences between units ('contrast' being reserved for SYNTAGMATIC differences). See Bolinger 1975: Ch. 17; Robins 1971: Ch. 4; Lyons 1968: Ch. 2.

(2) The phrase **contrastive analysis** also identifies a general approach to the investigation of language, particularly as carried on in certain areas of APPLIED LINGUISTICS, such as foreign language teaching and translation. In a contrastive analysis of two languages, the points of STRUCTURAL difference are identified, and these are then studied as areas of potential difficulty in foreign language learning. Contrastive analyses are SYNCHRONIC; analogous 'contrastive' studies of two states in the history of a language would be grouped under a different heading, such as COMPARATIVE or HISTORICAL LINGUISTICS. See Corder 1973: Ch. 10.

convention(al) LINGUISTICS uses this term in its general sense – referring to any accepted practice in the use of LANGUAGE (e.g. the 'convention' of using certain formulae upon leave-taking), or in

developing a MODEL of language (e.g. it is 'conventional' to transcribe
PHONEMES using / / brackets). But there is also a restricted sense,
where it refers to the ARBITRARY nature of the relationship between
linguistic EXPRESSIONS and their MEANINGS: one says that the relationship between the LEXICAL ITEM *table* and the thing 'table' is 'conventional', the term here being used in a traditional philosophical
sense which dates from Plato. See Lyons 1968: Ch. 1.

convergence A term used in SOCIOLINGUISTICS to refer to a process of
DIALECT change in which the dialects become more like each other (or
'converge'). This usually happens when a non-standard dialect falls
under the influence of the STANDARD, but it may happen the other way
round – as in the current development of modified forms of RECEIVED
PRONUNCIATION in English. Geographically adjacent SPEECH communities are sometimes referred to as 'convergence areas'. The
opposite effect is known as DIVERGENCE. 'Convergence' also has a
currency in HISTORICAL linguistic studies, referring to the MERGING
of FORMS which at an earlier stage of a LANGUAGE were CONTRASTIVE.
See Gumperz & Hymes 1971: Intro.

converse(ness) A term often used in SEMANTICS to refer to a SENSE
relation between LEXICAL ITEMS. **Converse terms** display a type
of oppositeness of MEANING, illustrated by such pairs as *buy/sell*,
parent/child, *employer/employee*, and *above/below*. *Buy* is said to be
'the converse of' *sell*, and vice versa. In such a relationship, found
especially in the definition of reciprocal social roles, spatial relationships
and so on, there is an interdependence of meaning, such that one
member of the pair presupposes the other member. In this respect,
'converseness' contrasts with COMPLEMENTARITY, where there is no
such symmetry of dependence, and with the technical sense of
ANTONYMY, where there is a gradation between the opposites. See
Lyons 1977b: Ch. 9; Clark & Clark 1977: Ch. 11.

conversion A term used in the study of WORD-FORMATION to refer
to the DERIVATIONAL process whereby an ITEM comes to belong to
a new WORD CLASS without the addition of an AFFIX, e.g. VERBS/
NOUNS: *small/taste/hit/walk/bottle/brake*; ADJECTIVES/verbs: *dirty/
empty/lower*. Some GRAMMARS distinguish between 'full conversion'
and 'partial conversion' – the latter being cases where only some of
the characteristics of the new word class are adopted (e.g. *the rich*).
Other terms used for this phenomenon, which is very common in
English, include 'ZERO derivation' and 'FUNCTIONAL shift'. See Quirk
et al 1972: App. I.

co-occur(rence) A term used in LINGUISTICS and PHONETICS to refer to the permitted SYNTAGMATIC combination of UNITS, according to the GRAMMATICAL and LEXICAL RULES of a LANGUAGE. For example, *a* 'co-occurs' with *boy*, but not with *information*; *eke* co-occurs with *out*, but not with *in*. The CONSTRAINTS involved are known as 'co-occurrence relations' or 'restrictions', and are often specified in the form of CONTEXT-sensitive or TACTIC rules. The dependencies involved may be unidirectional (e.g. ADVERBS co-occurring with VERBS, but not necessarily the other way round), bidirectional (e.g. TRANSITIVE verbs and OBJECTS), and mutually exclusive (e.g. *a* cannot co-occur with *an* in the same NOUN PHRASE). See Robins 1971: Ch. 6.

co-operative principle A term derived from the work of the philosopher H. P. Grice and now frequently used in LINGUISTICS as part of the study of conversational structure. At its simplest, the principle states that speakers try to co-operate with each other when communicating; they will, in particular, attempt to be informative, truthful, relevant and clear (maxims of 'quantity', 'quality', 'relation' and 'manner' respectively). Listeners will normally assume that a speaker is following these criteria. Speakers may break these maxims (in lying, sarcasm, etc.), but conversation proceeds on the assumption that they do not. It is then possible to deduce implications from what *has* been said concerning what has *not* been said (conversational IMPLICATURES), though the extent to which this can be done consistently and generally is somewhat controversial. See Clark & Clark 1977: Ch. 3; Lyons 1977b: Ch. 14.

co-ordination (co-ordinat-(iv)e, -ing, -or) (1) A term in GRAMMATICAL analysis to refer to the process or result of linking LINGUISTIC UNITS of equivalent SYNTACTIC status, e.g. a series of CLAUSES, or PHRASES, or WORDS. (In this respect, it is usually distinguished from SUBORDINATE linkage, where the units are not equivalent.) **Co-ordinate clauses** are illustrated in the sentence *John came and Mary left*; the marker of linkage is *and*, a co-ordinating conjunction (or **co-ordinator**). Constructions may also be analysed as co-ordinate without any explicit marker (a phenomenon sometimes referred to as 'asyndetic co-ordination'), as in *There was an awkward, depressing silence*, where the 'co-ordinative' role of the two adjectives can be tested by the insertion of *and* between them. See Quirk *et al* 1972: Chs. 9, 11; Robins 1971: Ch. 6.

(2) **Co-ordinate** is also used by some linguists in the classification of BILINGUALISM. 'Co-ordinate bilinguals' are those who attribute partly or wholly different MEANINGS to corresponding LEXICAL units

in the two LANGUAGES – a distinction here being made with COM-POUND bilingualism, where the meanings are seen as identical. See Trudgill 1974: Ch. 6.

Copenhagen School A group of LINGUISTS who constituted the Copenhagen Linguistic Circle in the mid-1930s, and who developed an approach to linguistics known as GLOSSEMATICS. Largely through the work of their main theoretician, Louis Hjelmslev (1899–1965), the School developed a philosophical and logical basis for linguistic theory which was not to be surpassed until the FORMALISATION introduced by GENERATIVE grammar. See Bolinger 1975: Ch. 15.

copula(tive) A term used in GRAMMATICAL description to refer to a linking VERB, i.e. a verb which has little independent MEANING, and whose main function is to relate other elements of CLAUSE structure, especially SUBJECT and COMPLEMENT. In English, the main 'copulative' or 'equative' verb is *be*, e.g. *he is a doctor*, and the term is often restricted to this verb; but there are many others which have a similar function, e.g. *he feels angry, that looks nice, he fell ill*. See Lyons 1968: Ch. 7; Quirk *et al* 1972: Ch. 12.

copying (copy) A basic SYNTACTIC operation within the framework of TRANSFORMATIONAL GRAMMAR, which adds a copy of a CONSTITUENT in a PHRASE-MARKER to some other part of the phrase-marker. For example, to make a RULE deriving TAG QUESTIONS from such SENTENCES as *he is a doctor*, the VERB is taken and 'copied' to the right of the sentence (changing its status from POSITIVE TO NEGATIVE); the SUBJECT of the verb is then copied to the right of this verb. This would be one way of generating the sentence *he is a doctor, isn't he?* Outside GENERATIVE LINGUISTICS, some linguists use **copy tags** to refer to a sub-type of tag questions, *viz* only those which retain the same POSITIVE or NEGATIVE value as the main CLAUSE verb (the others being referred to as CHECKING tags), e.g. *he's coming, is he?* See Akmajian & Heny 1975: Chs, 1, 7; Lyons 1977b: Ch. 16.

co-referential(ity) A term used in LINGUISTICS, and especially in GENERATIVE GRAMMAR, to refer to CONSTITUENTS in a SENTENCE that have the same REFERENCE. For example, in the sentence *I said I would leave*, the two SUBJECTS are co-referential; in *he said he would come*, it is unclear whether co-referentiality applies, as the second *he* might refer to someone else. The distinction can be formulated using referentiality indices, e.g. *he$_i$ said he$_i$ would come* (co-referential) vs. *he$_i$ said he$_j$ would come* ('non co-referential'). See Huddleston 1976: Ch. 6.

coronal One of the features of sound set up by CHOMSKY & Halle in their DISTINCTIVE FEATURE theory of PHONOLOGY, to handle variations in PLACE OF ARTICULATION (CAVITY features). Coronal sounds are defined ARTICULATORILY, as those produced with the BLADE of the TONGUE raised from its neutral position. ALVEOLAR, DENTAL and PALATO-ALVEOLAR CONSONANTS are [+coronal] (abbreviated as [+cor]). Its opposite is **non-coronal**, referring to sounds produced with the tongue blade in neutral position, as in LABIAL and VELAR consonants [−coronal] ([−cor]). See Ladefoged 1975: Ch. 11; Hyman 1975: Ch. 2.

corpus (corpora) A collection of LINGUISTIC DATA, either written texts or a TRANSCRIPTION of recorded speech, which can be used as a starting-point of linguistic description or as a means of verifying hypotheses about a LANGUAGE. Linguistic DESCRIPTIONS which are 'corpus-restricted' have been the subject of criticism, especially by GENERATIVE GRAMMARIans, who point to the limitations of 'corpora' (e.g. that they are samples of PERFORMANCE only, and that one still needs a means of PROJECTING beyond the corpus to the language as a whole). In field-work on a new language, or in HISTORICAL study, it may be very difficult to get beyond one's corpus (i.e. it is a 'closed' as opposed to an 'extendable' corpus), but in languages where the linguist has regular access to NATIVE-SPEAKERS (and may be a native-speaker himself) his approach will invariably be 'corpus-based', rather than corpus-restricted. See Lyons 1968: Ch. 4.

correct(ness) A term usually encountered in LINGUISTICS in the context of criticism of PRESCRIPTIVE attitudes to LANGUAGE. The judgements of TRADITIONAL grammarians that usages were either 'right' or 'wrong' has been replaced by a concern to describe the observable facts of linguistic usage, without reference to value judgements, and to replace absolute notions of correctness by an emphasis on the relative APPROPRIATENESS of language to social settings. Similarly, the question of evaluating GRAMMAR in terms of correctness (as in a decision PROCEDURE) has given way to a concern over the relative merits of competing grammars, bearing in mind their purpose (as in an evaluation procedure). See Lyons 1968: Ch. 1; Trudgill 1974: Ch. 1.

correlation A term used in PRAGUE SCHOOL PHONOLOGY to refer to a systematic relationship between two SERIES of sounds. For example, the series of voiceless and voiced FRICATIVES in English are related by a 'correlation' of VOICE; voice is thereby the 'mark of correlation'. See Hyman 1975: Ch. 2.

correspond(ence) (1) A term used in LINGUISTICS to refer to any similarity of FORM between WORDS or STRUCTURES in related LAN-GUAGES. For example, there is a stateable relationship between the sound structure of such words as *fish* and *piscis* (Latin); /f/ and /p/, for example, can be shown to be in systematic correspondence, because of the nature of the sound changes which took place in the history of English. See Robins 1971: Ch. 8.

(2) The notion is often encountered in SEMANTIC discussion, deriving from the common philosophical view of truth, that a PROPOSITION is true only if it denotes an actual state of affairs which verifies it. The classical **correspondence theory** of MEANING argued that there is a direct relationship between a linguistic form and the entity it denotes, as shown, for example, by the existence of onomatopoeic words (such as *splash* and *murmur*). Because the vast majority of the words in a language demonstrate only the arbitrariness of the relationship between 'words' and 'things', however, this view is therefore often called the **correspondence fallacy**. See Lyons 1977b: Ch. 6.

(3) The **correspondence hypothesis** attracted considerable PSY-CHOLINGUISTIC interest in the 1960s, especially with reference to language ACQUISITION studies. It states that the sequence of RULES used in the GRAMMATICAL DERIVATION of a SENTENCE corresponds to the sequence of psychological processes that take place in SPEECH PRODUCTION and SPEECH PERCEPTION. Evidence in its favour came from several experiments which showed that the time it took for speakers to process sentences with more COMPLEX derivations was longer than their less complex counterparts (e.g. PASSIVES as opposed to ACTIVES, NEGATIVES as opposed to AFFIRMATIVES). Further experi-mental evidence, in the late 1960s, was less convincing, however, and methodological problems were raised (e.g. how one separates out effects due to length and meaning, as well as TRANSFORMATIONAL history); there have also been radical theoretical changes in the notions of transformation involved. As a result, the correspondence hypothesis is no longer influential as a research PARADIGM. See Clark & Clark 1977: Ch. 2.

cost A term used metaphorically in GENERATIVE PHONOLOGY in discussing the relative SIMPLICITY or NATURALNESS of phonological analyses. Increasing the complexity of an analysis (e.g. by adding FEATURES or RULES) is said to add to its cost, and vice versa. The principle involved here is a general one, sometimes discussed with reference to the notion of 'diminishing returns': as more CLASSES of LINGUISTIC UNIT are set up, each class comes to subsume less DATA, and while this permits an increase in the ability of the GRAMMAR to handle exceptions, there is a consequential drop in generality. There is thus plenty of room for controversy over where the least costly cut-off point in an analysis would be, in trying to reconcile generality with depth of descriptive detail. See Hyman 1975: Ch. 5; Lyons 1968: Ch. 4.

co-text A term used by some British LINGUISTS in an attempt to resolve the AMBIGUITY of the term CONTEXT, which can refer to both LINGUISTIC and SITUATIONAL ENVIRONMENTS. The practice is to reserve 'co-text' for the former, and 'context' for the latter. See Lyons 1977b: Ch. 14.

count(-able, -ability, un-) A term used in the GRAMMATICAL classification of NOUNS; opposed to 'uncountable' or MASS. This 'countability' distinction was often unrecognised in TRADITIONAL grammars, but it has been a focus of attention in LINGUISTIC analyses of the NOUN PHRASE, because of the way it can explain the DISTRIBUTION of nouns in relation to the use of such ITEMS as ARTICLES and QUANTIFIERS. **Countable** nouns are those which the LANGUAGE treats as separable entities, by using them with such forms as *a, many, two, three,* etc.; **uncountable** nouns are treated as continuous entities, having no natural bounds, by being used with such forms as *much, some.* The contrast can be seen in *a boy* vs. **much boy,* and *an information vs. *much information.* Many nouns can be used in both contexts, e.g. *a cake/many cakes/much cake.* See Quirk *et al* 1972: Ch. 4; Palmer 1971: App. B; Lyons 1968: Ch. 7.

counter-example LINGUISTICS and PHONETICS use this term in its general sense, referring to the process of constructing or encountering a piece of DATA which falsifies a hypothesis, and thus leads to revision in an analysis. As in other sciences, there is frequent discussion of whether a suggested counter-example is real or apparent, i.e. able to be analysed in such a way that one's analysis can be salvaged. See Akmajian & Heny 1975: Ch. 1.

counter-intuitive(ness) An implausible analysis, according to the INTUITION of the NATIVE-SPEAKER or the LINGUIST. For example, an analysis which derives STATEMENTS from QUESTIONS is felt to be less natural than one which derives questions from statements, and these feelings can be to some degree supported experimentally (e.g. by showing differences in reaction times). Obtaining intuitive reactions from native-speakers in a systematic, verifiable way is not easy, however, and is not often done, and the dangers of circularity are evident; especially when native-speaker and linguist are the same person (as is usually the case in much of the work done in theoretical linguistics), it is very easy to allow one's intuitions as a native-speaker to be swayed by the purpose of one's analysis, as a linguist. The problems inherent in the counter-intuitiveness criterion have been satirically summarised in one definition (by the British linguist, Angus MacIntosh (b. 1914)): 'going against everything that suits my theory or purpose, and don't ask me to explain why!'. See Palmer 1971: Ch. 4.

covered One of the features of sound set up by CHOMSKY & Halle in their DISTINCTIVE FEATURE theory of PHONOLOGY, to handle variations in PLACE OF ARTICULATION (CAVITY features). It is a tentative categorisation, referring to sounds produced with a narrowed, tensed PHARYNX and raised LARYNX, as may occur in some West African languages on tensed VOWELS. Its opposite is **non-covered**, where there is no such narrowing and tensing of the pharynx. See Ladefoged 1975: Ch. 11; Hyman 1975: Ch. 2.

covert A term used in LINGUISTIC analysis to refer to the relationships between linguistic FORMS which are not observable in the SURFACE STRUCTURE of a SENTENCE, but emerge only when sets of sentences are brought into relationship with each other. Examples of covert relations include SUBSTITUTABILITY (as in the notion of word CLASS) and TRANSFORMATIONAL equivalence. See Robins 1971: Ch. 6.

creak(y) A term used in the PHONETIC classification of VOICE QUALITY, on the basis of ARTICULATORY and AUDITORY PHONETIC criteria. It refers to a vocal effect produced by a very slow vibration of only one end of the VOCAL CORDS. Some speakers do have an abnormally creaky voice quality, as a permanent feature of their speech. What is of particular significance for linguistic analysis is that creaky effects may be used with contrastive force, communicating a PARALINGUISTIC MEANING: in RECEIVED PRONUNCIATION, for example, it is often heard to help to express disparagement, when a phrase such as *Oh I don't know* is pronounced at a very low PITCH level. 'Creaky voice', or simply 'creak', is also sometimes encountered as a phonological characteristic, as in Hausa, where there is an opposition between creaky and non-creaky PLOSIVES. Creaky sounds are also called 'laryngealised'. See Catford 1977: Ch. 6; Ladefoged 1975: Ch. 6.

creativity An application in LINGUISTICS of the usual sense of this term to refer to the capacity of LANGUAGE users to produce and understand an indefinitely large number of SENTENCES, most of which they will not have heard or used before. Seen as a property of language, it refers to the 'open-endedness' or 'PRODUCTIVITY' of patterns, whereby a finite set of sounds, STRUCTURES, etc. can be used to produce a potentially infinite number of sentences. In contrast with studies of animal communication, linguistic creativity is considered to be a species-specific property: the creation of new sentences is not a feature of animal communication systems. The notion of creativity has a long history in the discussion of language, but it has become a central feature of contemporary linguistics, since the emphasis placed upon it by CHOMSKY. One of the main aims of linguistic enquiry, it is felt, is to explain this creative ability, for which such constructs as GENERATIVE RULES have been suggested. Care must, however, be taken to avoid confusing this sense of 'creative' with that found in artistic or literary contexts, where notions such as imagination and originality are central. See Lyons 1977a: Ch. 2; 1977b: Ch. 3.

creole (creolise) A term used in SOCIOLINGUISTICS to refer to a PIDGIN LANGUAGE which has become the mother-tongue of a SPEECH community, as is the case in Jamaica, Haiti, Dominica, and in several other ex-colonial parts of the world. The process of **creolisation** expands the STRUCTURAL and STYLISTIC range of the pidginised language, such that the **creolised language** becomes comparable in FORMAL and FUNCTIONAL COMPLEXITY to other languages. See Trudgill 1974: Chs. 3, 7.

criteria In LINGUISTICS and PHONETICS, this term is used with reference to the FORMAL justification of an analysis or description – why one carries out a linguistic analysis in a particular way. The criteria may result from general considerations of the purpose of one's analysis (e.g. whether pure or applied, theoretical or descriptive, SYNCHRONIC or DIACHRONIC), or may relate to the range of specific factors felt to be relevant to a restricted problem. For example, in the setting up of WORD CLASSES, decisions must be made as to whether purely **linguistic criteria** will be used (e.g. PHONOLOGICAL, GRAMMATICAL, SEMANTIC), or whether reference will be made to **non-linguistic criteria** (e.g. logical, NOTIONAL, aesthetic). Linguistics has generally emphasised two principles: that criteria should always be made EXPLICIT, and should as far as possible be based on formal considerations, e.g. of grammar or phonology. See Lyons 1968: Ch. 1.

cross-over A term used in GENERATIVE GRAMMAR, referring to a principle restricting the operation of certain TRANSFORMATIONS which move a NOUN PHRASE (as in PASSIVES, REFLEXIVES, *TOUGH* MOVEMENT). In an early formulation, the principle states that a transformation cannot apply to a PHRASE-MARKER if it would result in one noun phrase crossing another with which it is CO-REFERENTIAL. The 'cross-over constraint' or 'principle' would be used, for example, to explain why passivisation cannot apply to structures of the type *John washed himself*: given an UNDERLYING STRUCTURE *John$_i$ washed John$_i$*, to derive a passive *John$_i$ was washed by John$_i$* would involve a violation of this principle. In later formulations, more specific constraints on the application of this principle are introduced. See Huddleston 1976: Ch. 15.

cultural transmission A suggested defining property of human LANGUAGE (contrasting with the properties of many other SEMIOTIC systems), whereby the ability to speak a language is transmitted from generation to generation by a process of learning, and not genetically. This is not to deny that children may be born with certain INNATE predispositions towards language, but it is to emphasise the difference between human language, where environmental learning has such a large role to play, and animal systems of communication, where instinct is more important. See Lyons 1977b: Ch. 3.

CV, CVC, etc. (1) Abbreviations for CONSONANT and VOWEL sequences, used especially in describing the types of SYLLABLE which exist in a LANGUAGE, e.g. in English, the statement of the PHONOTACTIC possibilities will include the information that it is possible to have CCCV-INITIALLY, as in *splice*, and -VCCCC FINALLY, as in *sixths*. See Gimson 1970: Ch. 9.
    (2) CV is also a commonly used abbreviation for CARDINAL VOWEL.

cycle (cyclic-al) (1) A principle in GENERATIVE LINGUISTICS that allows RULES to apply in a repeated ordered way to sections of a PHRASE-MARKER where a particular STRUCTURAL DESCRIPTION is met, instead of in a single scan to the phrase-structure as a whole. This application of the rules is referred to as 'cyclic', and the whole process is known as the **transformational cycle**. Its FORMALISATION requires that the rules apply first to the UNDERLYING SENTENCE most deeply EMBEDDED in a phrase-marker (the first cycle), and then to the next highest sentence (the second cycle), until the MATRIX sentence is arrived at. On each application, at a given level, in this view, the rules may not take into account information higher up the phrase-marker. This principle allows for a less complicated analysis to be assigned to sentences with 'repeated' elements, such as *The man seems to want to try a second time*. Various types of cyclic rules have been suggested, e.g. 'last-cyclic' rules, which apply only to main CLAUSES (i.e. the highest cyclic level in a DERIVATION), as might be suggested for handling the initial placement of QUESTION-words in English (e.g. *where did John say that he was going?*), or in TAG formation. It is also suggested that cyclic rules are 'structure preserving', whereas last-cyclic rules alter structure in a more fundamental manner.

In generative PHONOLOGY, the cyclic principle was established by CHOMSKY & Halle to account for the variations in STRESS contrast in relation to VOWEL QUALITY within WORDS and SENTENCES. It is argued that the place of a word's main stress, and the remaining stresses in a POLYSYLLABIC word, are explainable by referring to the SYNTACTIC and the SEGMENTAL phonological structure of an UTTERANCE. The SURFACE STRUCTURE of a sentence, in this view, is seen as a string of FORMATIVES which are bracketed together in various ways, the BRACKETS reflecting the grammatical structure assigned to the sentence, such as Sentence, NOUN PHRASE, VERB PHRASE, e.g. [[the [elephant]] [[kick[ed]] [the [ball]]]]. The cyclic principle makes the phonological rules apply first to the maximal STRINGS that contain no brackets; once applied, the brackets surrounding these strings are then erased. The phonological rules then apply again to the maximal strings without brackets produced by this first procedure, and again the innermost brackets are erased. The procedure continues until all brackets have been removed. Various types of rule have been devised to make this cyclical procedure work, such as the Compound Rule and the Nuclear Stress Rule, both of which are ways of assigning main degrees of stress to the various CONSTITUENTS of a sentence (the first in relation to compound items, the second to sequences of items in phrases). See Huddleston 1976: Ch. 7; Akmajian & Heny 1975: Ch. 7; Hyman 1975: Ch. 6.

(2) In SEMANTICS, the term is sometimes used to refer to a type of SENSE relationship between LEXICAL ITEMS (a sub-type of INCOMPATI-BILITY). **Lexical cycles** (or 'cyclical sets') are sets of items organised in terms of successivity, but lacking any fixed end-points, e.g. days of the week, months of the year. 'Serial' ordering, by contrast, displays fixed end-points, as in military ranks. See Lyons 1977b: Ch. 9.

D

⌘⌘⌘⌘⌘⌘

DAF The usual abbreviation for delayed auditory FEEDBACK.

dark l An impressionistic, but commonly used term for a variety of LATERAL sound, where the RESONANCE is that of a back vowel of an [u] quality, as in the standard English pronunciation of /l/ after VOWELS, before CONSONANTS, and as a SYLLABIC sound, e.g. *pull*, *altar*, *bottle*; it is opposed to CLEAR L. Alternatively, one might refer to this quality as a 'velarised' /l/ (cf. VELAR), transcribing it [ɫ]. See Gimson 1970: Ch. 8.

data The term is used in its general sense in LINGUISTICS, referring to the phenomena which constitute the subject-matter of enquiry (*viz* linguistic behaviour). There have, however, been two distinct views concerning the nature of this behaviour, which are usually seen in opposition to each other. The traditional conception of linguistic data is limited to the observable patterns of speech and writing, especially when recorded and gathered together in a CORPUS. GENERATIVE linguistic theory, on the other hand, goes beyond this, including as part of the raw data for analysis the language user's judgements (INTUITIONS) about his language. Much controversy has been generated by these opposed views (which are related to the more basic divergences between BEHAVIOURIST and MENTALIST philosophies), and the issue is still prominent, criticisms being made of the limited reliability and generality of observable data, and of the uncertain verifiability and objectivity of mentalistic data, as evidence of linguistic SYSTEM. In language ACQUISITION, the term 'primary linguistic data' refers to the language input to the child, deriving from parents, siblings, etc. See Huddleston 1976: Ch. 1.

dative One of the FORMS taken by a WORD, usually a NOUN or PRONOUN, in LANGUAGES which express GRAMMATICAL relationships by means of INFLECTIONS. The dative CASE typically expresses an INDIRECT OBJECT relationship, or a range of meaning similar to that covered by *to* or *for* in English; but there is a great deal of variation between languages in the way this case is used. English itself does not have a dative case form, but expresses the notion of indirect object using PREPOSITIONS and WORD ORDER, e.g. *he gave a book to the boy* or *he gave the boy a book*. The term is given special status in CASE grammar, where it refers to the case of the ANIMATE being affected by the VERB's state or action. See Lyons 1968: Ch. 7; Bolinger 1975: Ch. 15.

declaration A term used in the theory of SPEECH ACTS to refer to a type of UTTERANCE where the speaker's words bring about a new situation in the external world, as in *I name this ship/child...*, *I resign*. See Clark & Clark 1977: Ch. 3.

declarative A term used in the GRAMMATICAL classification of SENTENCE types, and usually seen in contrast to IMPERATIVE, INTERROGATIVE, etc. MOODS. It refers to VERB FORMS or sentence/CLAUSE types used in the expression of STATEMENTS, e.g. *the man is walking*. The term 'indicative' is also sometimes used in this sense. See Quirk *et al* 1972: Ch. 7; Lyons 1977b: Ch. 1.

deep structure/grammar A central theoretical term in GENERATIVE GRAMMAR; opposed to SURFACE STRUCTURE. 'Deep structure' (or 'deep grammar') is the abstract SYNTACTIC REPRESENTATION of a SENTENCE – an UNDERLYING LEVEL of structural organisation which specifies all the factors governing the way the sentence should be interpreted. This level provides information which enables us to distinguish between the alternative interpretations of sentences which have the same surface form (i.e. they are AMBIGUOUS), e.g. *Flying planes can be dangerous*, where *flying planes* can be related to two underlying sentences, *planes which fly...* and *to fly planes...* It is also a way of relating sentences which have different surface forms but the same underlying MEANING, as in the relationship between ACTIVE and PASSIVE structures, e.g. *the panda chased the man* vs. *the man was chased by the panda*. TRANSFORMA-TIONAL grammars would derive one of these alternatives from the other, or perhaps both from an even more abstract ('deeper') underlying structure. The various grammatical relations in such sentences can then be referred to as the 'deep SUBJECT', 'deep OBJECT', etc. (contrasted with 'surface subject', etc.). It is also possible to compute the 'depth' at which a transformation operates, by referring to the number of stages in a DERIVATION before it applies, and some attempt has been made to correlate this notion with the COMPLEXITY of a sentence.

In some recent generative studies, the role of deep structure has been called into question, it being suggested that a separate level of underlying syntactic organisation between surface structure and meaning is unnecessary and misleading (cf. GENERATIVE SEMANTICS). It is also possible to find the term used in the general sense of 'underlying structural interpretation', without commitment to a specific interpretation in terms of transformational grammar. Indeed, the original use of this term, by the American linguist Charles Hockett (b. 1916), antedates its CHOMSKYAN application. See Lyons 1968: Ch. 6; 1977a: Ch. 8; Huddleston 1976: Chs. 4, 6.

degree A GRAMMATICAL CATEGORY used to specify the extent of a comparison between ADJECTIVES or ADVERBS. A three-way contrast is usually recognised (POSITIVE vs. COMPARATIVE vs. SUPERLATIVE), but other possibilities are sometimes distinguished, e.g. an 'equative' degree (as in *as big as*). In English, both MORPHOLOGICAL and SYNTACTIC means are used in the expression of degree, e.g. *bigger/biggest* vs. *more fascinating/most fascinating*. See Quirk *et al* 1972: Ch. 5.

deixis (deictic) A term used in GRAMMATICAL theory to subsume those features of LANGUAGE which refer directly to the temporal or locational characteristics of the SITUATION within which an UTTERANCE takes place, whose MEANING is thus relative to that situation, e.g. *now/then*, *here/there, I/you, this/that* are 'deictics' ('deictic' or EXOPHORIC words). The term is also used for words which refer backwards or forwards in DISCOURSE (ANAPHORA and CATAPHORA respectively), e.g. *that, the following, the former*. The notion of deixis has proved to be fruitful in several areas of LINGUISTICS, especially in language ACQUISITION studies, where some investigators view the learning of these ITEMS by children as constituting a significant feature of early development. See Lyons 1968: Ch. 7.

delayed One of the features of sound set up by CHOMSKY & Halle in their DISTINCTIVE FEATURE theory of PHONOLOGY, as part of the phrase **delayed release**, to handle variations in MANNER OF ARTICULATION, specifying the nature of a sound's RELEASE. Delayed release sounds are defined both ARTICULATORILY and ACOUSTICALLY, as those sounds where a sound is produced with a gradual release sufficient to produce a sound similar to a FRICATIVE, as in AFFRICATES. Affricates are all [+delayed release] ([+del rel]). Its opposite is INSTANTANEOUS or ABRUPT release, referring to a sound released suddenly and without the ACOUSTIC turbulence of a fricative, as in PLOSIVES. See Ladefoged 1975: Ch. 11; Hyman 1976: Ch. 2.

deletion

deletion A basic operation within the framework of TRANSFORMATIONAL GRAMMAR, which eliminates a CONSTITUENT of an input PHRASE-MARKER. It is used in accounting for IMPERATIVE SENTENCES, for example (where the SUBJECT and AUXILIARY VERB of an UNDERLYING sentence is deleted, as in *kick the ball* from *you will kick the ball*). Other applications of the notion can be found in the transformational treatment of DUMMY symbols, and in several specific transformational operations (e.g. EQUI NP DELETION). Several formal CONSTRAINTS on the use of deletion transformations have been suggested, especially that the deleted elements must be recoverable, i.e. the deletion transformation must specify the elements to be deleted, and in the output phrase-marker the effects of the deletion must be clearly indicated. If this were not the case, there would be several unfortunate consequences, e.g. a single surface structure could be related to an indefinite number of deep structures, as in *He's been hit*, derivable from *Someone/John/a bullet...hit him*. See Akmajian & Heny 1975: Ch. 7; Huddleston 1976: Ch. 12.

delicacy (delicate) In HALLIDAYAN LINGUISTICS, this term is used to refer to one of the scales of analysis which interrelates the CATEGORIES of the theory, *viz* the dimension which recognises increasing depth of detail. An increasingly 'delicate' analysis of the notion of CLAUSE, for example, might recognise AFFIRMATIVE vs. INTERROGATIVE types; interrogative clauses could then be analysed into several QUESTION types; and so on. Other scales in this approach are labelled RANK and EXPONENCE. See Bolinger 1975: Ch. 15; Robins 1971: Ch. 7.

delta A symbol (Δ) used in some MODELS of TRANSFORMATIONAL GRAMMAR (cf. ASPECTS), which acts as a DUMMY element in the generation of DEEP STRUCTURES. The purpose of the **delta symbols** is to mark the places in an initial PHRASE-MARKER (a PRE-LEXICAL structure) where LEXICAL items are later to be inserted: lexical insertion RULES then replace each 'empty' delta by a COMPLEX SYMBOL containing the SYNTACTIC FEATURES which will be used to define the deep structures of the grammar. See Huddleston 1976: Ch. 10.

denotation (denotative) A term used in SEMANTICS as part of a classification of types of MEANING; opposed to CONNOTATION. 'Denotative meaning' involves the relationship between a LINGUISTIC UNIT (especially a LEXICAL ITEM) and the non-linguistic entities to which it refers – it is thus equivalent to REFERENTIAL meaning. For example, the denotation of *dog* is its dictionary definition of 'canine quadruped', etc.; its connotations might include 'friend', 'helper', 'competition', etc. See Lyons 1977b: Ch. 7.

dental A term in the PHONETIC classification of CONSONANT sounds on the basis of their PLACE OF ARTICULATION: it refers to a sound made by the tongue TIP and RIMS against the teeth. 'Apico-dental' is a more explicit, but less-used description of such sounds, 'apico-' being derived from APEX, an alternative term for tongue tip. Usually the upper teeth are the ones involved, as in the [d̪], [t̪] and [n̪] of some English DIALECTS, such as Irish English (this contrasts with the ALVEOLAR articulation of [d] and [t] in RECEIVED PRONUNCIATION); but both upper and lower teeth may be in contact with the tongue during the articulation, as in the *th-* sounds of *thin* [θ] and *this* [ð]. In [θ] and [ð], moreover, the tip of the tongue is usually slightly between the teeth, in which cases the more precise term INTERDENTAL can be used. If the sound is articulated towards the back of the upper teeth, close to the alveolar ridge, the term 'POST-dental' can be used. The phonetic symbol for 'dental articulation' is [̪], placed underneath the symbol for the consonant in question, as above. See Gimson 1970: Ch. 4; Catford 1977: Ch. 8.

deontic A term derived from modal logic and used by some LINGUISTS as part of a theoretical framework for the analysis of MODAL VERBS and related STRUCTURES in LANGUAGE. **Deontic modality** is concerned with the logic of obligation and permission, e.g. the use of the modals in SENTENCES such as *the car must be ready*, e.g. 'I oblige you to ensure that the car is ready'. It thus contrasts with ALETHIC and EPISTEMIC modality, which would interpret this sentence respectively as 'it follows that the car is ready' and 'it is surely the case that the car is ready'. See Lyons 1977b: Ch. 17.

dependency (grammar) A type of FORMAL GRAMMAR, developed by several LINGUISTS in the 1950s (in particular, the French linguist Lucien Tesnière (1893–1954)), which establishes types of dependencies between the ELEMENTS of a CONSTRUCTION as a means of explaining grammatical relationships. SYNTACTIC STRUCTURE is represented using **dependency trees** – sets of NODES whose inter-connections specify structural RELATIONS. Every tree contains a GOVERNOR, and a set of 'dependents', each of which bears a specific relation to the governor. For example, in a CLAUSE, the VERB is seen as governor, and the dependents are NOUN PHRASES, which are assigned numerical values, depending on the VALENCY attributed to the verb. See Lyons 1977a: Ch. 8; Radford 1981: Ch. 4.

dependent A general term used in GRAMMATICAL analysis as part of the classification of CLAUSE types: opposed to MAIN, and synonymous with SUBORDINATE. The term has a specific application in DEPENDENCY GRAMMAR. See Quirk *et al* 1972: Ch. 11.

depth hypothesis A hypothesis proposed by the American LINGUIST Victor Yngve (b. 1920) in the early 1960s as an explanation of the psychological differences between the two categories of linguistic CONSTRUCTION: LEFT-BRANCHING (e.g. *the man's hat*) and RIGHT-BRANCHING (e.g. *the hat of the man*). He argued that left-branching structures add more to the psychological COMPLEXITY (or transformational 'depth') of a SENTENCE, because the processing of such structures takes up more space in short-term memory than does the processing of right-branching structures. The hypothesis has been criticised on various grounds, particular reference being made to other important types of construction which complicate the issue, such as SELF-EMBEDDING. See Lyons 1977a: Ch. 9.

derivation(-al, derive(d)) (1) A term used in MORPHOLOGY to refer to one of the two main categories or processes of WORD-FORMATION, the other being INFLECTION(AL). These terms also apply to the two types of AFFIX involved in WORD-FORMATION. Basically, the result of a derivational process is a new word (e.g. *nation → national*), whereas the result of an inflectional process is a different form of the same word (e.g. *nations, nationals*). The distinction is not totally clear-cut, however (e.g. how best to analyse *-ly* in English). **Derivational affixes** change the grammatical CLASS of MORPHEMES to which they are attached (as in SUFFIXATION, e.g. *-tion* is a noun-forming derivational suffix); they also usually occur closer to the ROOT morpheme than do inflections, e.g. *nation-al-ise + -ing/-s/-d*. Often they have independently stateable LEXICAL MEANINGS (e.g. *mini-, sub-*), though these are not always easy to identify (e.g. *-er*). The combination of root and derivational affixes is usually referred to as the STEM of the word, i.e. the ELEMENT to which inflections are attached; several modes of classification are available in the literature on this subject. See Matthews 1974: Ch. 7; Robins 1971: Ch. 5.

(2) In GENERATIVE GRAMMAR, the term refers to the set of formally identifiable stages used in generating a SENTENCE from an INITIAL SYMBOL to a TERMINAL STRING, i.e. the whole set of PHRASE-STRUCTURE, TRANSFORMATIONAL, etc. RULES which have applied. In a more restricted context, a **derived structure** refers to the form of an output PHRASE-MARKER, after a transformational rule has applied. See Lyons 1977a: Ch. 6; Akmajian & Heny 1975: Ch. 2.

(3) In HISTORICAL LANGUAGE studies, the term is used to refer to the origins or historical development of a LANGUAGE or linguistic form. Sounds, words (cf. ETYMOLOGY) and structures are said to be 'derived' from corresponding FORMS in an earlier state of a language. See Robins 1971: Ch. 8.

description (descriptiv-e, -ism, -ist) The general sense of this term is found in LINGUISTICS, identifying one of the main aims of the subject – to give a comprehensive, systematic, objective and precise account of the patterns and use of a specific LANGUAGE or DIALECT, at a particular point in time. This definition suggests several respects in which 'descriptive' is in contrast with other conceptions of linguistic enquiry. The emphasis on objectivity, systematicness, etc. places it in contrast with the PRESCRIPTIVE aims of much TRADITIONAL grammar: the aim of **descriptive linguistics** is to describe the facts of linguistic usage as they are, and not how they ought to be, with reference to some real or imagined ideal state. The emphasis on a given time places it in contrast with HISTORICAL linguistics, where the aim is to demonstrate linguistic change: descriptive linguistics aims to describe a language SYNCHRONICALLY, at a particular time (not necessarily the present – one can describe the linguistic patterns of any period). The emphasis on 'a' language distinguishes the subject from COMPARATIVE linguistics, as its name suggests, and also from THEORETICAL linguistics, where the aim is to make general statements about language as a whole. It ought not to be forgotten, of course, that there is an interdependence between these various branches of the subject: a description is the result of an analysis, which must in turn be based on a set of theoretical assumptions. But in descriptive linguistics the theory is only a means to an end, *viz* the production of a **descriptive grammar** (or one of its subdivisions, e.g. PHONOLOGY, LEXICON, SYNTAX, MORPHOLOGY). An approach which is characterised by an almost exclusive concern with description, in the above sense, is known as **descriptivism**, and its proponents as **descriptivists**. In linguistics, the term is usually applied to American anthropological and STRUCTURALIST studies before the 'generativist' approach of the late 1950s. Within GENERATIVE grammar, also, the phrase **descriptive adequacy** adds a special dimension to the use of the term: it refers to an account of the NATIVE-SPEAKER'S linguistic COMPETENCE (and not merely to an account of a CORPUS of DATA, as would be intended by the earlier use of 'description'). See Lyons 1968: Ch. 11; Robins 1971: Ch. 1.

desiderative A term used in the GRAMMATICAL CLASSIFICATION of SENTENCE types, and usually seen in contrast to INDICATIVE, IMPERA-

TIVE, etc. MOODS. It refers to VERB FORMS or sentence/CLAUSE types used for the expression of wants and desires – approximately translatable by '*I want* + Sentence', but often LEXICALISED, e.g. *to want to eat → to hunger*. See Lyons 1977b: Ch. 17.

det The usual abbreviation for DETERMINER.

determiner A term used in some models of GRAMMATICAL description, referring to a class of ITEMS whose main role is to CO-OCCUR with NOUNS to express a wide range of SEMANTIC contrasts, such as QUANTITY or NUMBER. The ARTICLES, when they occur in a LANGUAGE, are the main sub-set of determiners (e.g. *the/a* in English); other WORDS which can have a determiner function in English include *each/every*, *this/that*, *some/any*, all of which have a DISTRIBUTION which includes the article position, e.g. *the/this/some...cake*. Some LINGUISTS extend the application of this term to include other types of word within the noun PHRASE (e.g. ADJECTIVES, PREdeterminers), and sometimes even to include MODIFIERS in other parts of the sentence. See Quirk *et al* 1972: Ch. 4.

developmental linguistics A branch of LINGUISTICS concerned with the study of the ACQUISITION of LANGUAGE in children. The subject involves the application of linguistic theories and techniques of analysis to child language DATA, in order to provide a precise description of patterns of development and an explanation of the norms and variations encountered, both within individual languages and UNIVERSALLY. In relation to the task of explanation, particular attention is paid to the role of non-linguistic factors, such as cognition, social background, the nature of the experimental task, and so on, and as a consequence there has been an increasingly multidisciplinary approach to the problem. Because of the particular relevance of psychological factors, the subject is sometimes referred to as **developmental psycholinguistics**. See Clark & Clark 1977: Chs. 8–10.

deviance (deviant) A term used in LINGUISTIC analysis to refer to a SENTENCE (or other UNIT) which does not conform to the RULES of a GRAMMAR (i.e. it is ILL-FORMED). Deviant sentences are conventionally marked with an initial ASTERISK, e.g. **Is they be going*. See Huddleston 1976: Ch. 1.

device A term derived from mathematics and used especially in GENERATIVE LINGUISTICS to refer to an abstract design specifically constructed to enable an analysis to be made. A GRAMMAR, in this sense, can be seen as a device for generating SENTENCES. The notion is sometimes encountered in child language studies, where, in the CHOMSKYAN view, children are credited with a 'language ACQUISITION device' (LAD) which enables them to work out the correct grammatical analysis of sentences on the basis of the speech DATA presented to them. See Lyons 1977a: Ch. 4.

dia- A commonly used PREFIX, derived from the term DIALECT, and used in LINGUISTIC studies whenever a dialectal frame of reference is required. **Dialinguistics** is sometimes used to refer to the study of the range of dialects and LANGUAGES used in a speech community. A **diatype** is a term used by some SOCIOLINGUISTS to refer to a VARIETY of language defined according to its use or purpose. It thus contrasts with **dialect**, which is a variety defined in terms of regional or social groups of users. Alternative terms include VARIETY and REGISTER. A **diasystem** is a network of FORMAL relationships which shows the common linguistic SYSTEM assumed to underlie two or more dialects, as a framework for displaying their STRUCTURAL differences. The notation used for this purpose includes formulae which display structural correspondence, e.g.

$$\frac{X}{Y} \frac{i \sim \mathfrak{i}}{i} \approx e \approx \frac{a}{a \sim e}$$

etc. where X and Y are the names of two areas, $\sim$ indicates a contrast which is relevant for one dialect only, $\approx$ for two (or more) dialects. Within such a framework, diasystemic UNITS can be identified: a **diaphone** is an abstract PHONOLOGICAL unit set up to identify an equivalence between the sound systems of different dialects, e.g. the diaphone /ei/, as in English *mate*, is realised as [ei], [ai], etc.; a **diamorph** displays equivalences between MORPHOLOGICAL units; and so on. See Gumperz & Hymes 1971: Intro.

diachronic One of the two main temporal dimensions of LINGUISTIC investigation introduced by the Swiss linguist, Ferdinand de SAUSSURE, the other being SYNCHRONIC. In 'diachronic linguistics', LANGUAGES are studied from the point of view of their historical development – for example, the changes which have taken place between Old and Modern English could be described in phonological, grammatical and semantic terms ('diachronic PHONOLOGY/SYNTAX/SEMANTICS'). An alternative term is 'HISTORICAL linguistics'. The earlier study of language in historical terms, known as COMPARATIVE PHILOLOGY, does not differ from diachronic linguistics in subject-matter, but in aims and method. More attention is paid in the latter to the use of synchronic description as a preliminary to historical study, and to the implications of historical work for linguistic theory in general. See Lyons 1968: Ch. 1; Robins 1971: Ch. 1.

diacritic In PHONETICS, a mark added to a symbol to alter its value, e.g. the various ACCENTS (´ ` ^ etc.), the signs of DEVOICING [₀] and NASALisation [~]. In GENERATIVE PHONOLOGY, **diacritic features** are introduced into the DERIVATION of FORMATIVES to account for the apparently exceptional behaviour of SEGMENTS. A readjustment RULE introduces the feature [D], e.g. to handle the exceptional STRESS pattern of words like *mómentary* (cf. the more regular *eleméntary*), [+D] would be inserted ad hoc at an early stage in their derivation. See Gimson 1970: App; Hyman 1975: Ch. 3.

dialect(al, -ology) A regionally or socially distinctive VARIETY of a language, identified by a particular set of WORDS and GRAMMATICAL STRUCTURES. Spoken dialects are usually also associated with a distinctive pronunciation, or ACCENT. Any LANGUAGE with a reasonably large number of speakers will develop dialects, especially if there are geographical barriers separating groups of people from each other, or if there are divisions of social class. One dialect may predominate as the official or STANDARD form of the language, and this is the variety which may come to be written down.

The distinction between 'dialect' and 'language' seems obvious: dialects are subdivisions of languages. What linguistics (and especially SOCIOLINGUISTICS) has done is to point to the complexity of the relationship between these notions. It is usually said that people speak different languages when they do not understand each other. But many of the so-called dialects of Chinese (Mandarin, Cantonese, Pekingese) are mutually unintelligible, in their spoken form. (They do however share the same written language, which is the main reason why one talks of them as 'dialects of Chinese'.) And the opposite situation occurs: Swedes, Norwegians and Danes are generally able to understand each other, but their separate histories, cultures, literatures and political structures warrant their being referred to as different languages.

The systematic study of all forms of dialect, but especially regional dialect, is called **dialectology**, also 'linguistic geography' or **dialect geography**. Traditional dialectology studies commenced in the late 19th century, and have taken the form of detailed surveys using questionnaires and (more recently) tape-recorded interviews. Regionally distinctive words (distinct in FORM, SENSE or pronunciation) were the centre of attention, and collections of such words were plotted on maps and compiled in a **dialect atlas** (or 'linguistic atlas'). If a number of DISTINCTIVE ITEMS all emerged as belonging to a particular area, then this would be the evidence for saying that a dialect existed. It was often possible to show where one dialect ended and the next began by plotting the use of such items, drawing lines around their limits of use (ISOGLOSSES), and where a 'bundle' of such isoglosses fell together, postulating the existence of a **dialect boundary**. On one side of the bundle of isoglosses, a large number of word forms, senses and pronunciations would be used which were systematically different from the equivalent items used on the other side. Dialect boundaries are not usually so clear-cut, but the principle works well enough. Traditional dialectological methods of this kind have more recently been supplemented by the methods of **structural dialectology**, which tries to show the patterns of relationship which link sets of forms from different dialects. The SYSTEMS of STRUCTURAL correspondence established by this approach are known as 'DIAsystems'.

Dialects which identify where a person is from are called **regional dialects**, though other terms are used, e.g. 'local', 'territorial', 'geographical'. It is sometimes thought that dialects of this type are dying out in Britain, but this is happening only in rural areas. Urban dialects are becoming more in evidence, especially with the growth of major conurbations. Within cities such as New York and London, it is possible to isolate local dialect areas, such as Brooklyn or the East End.

Dialects which identify where a person is in terms of a social scale are called **social dialects** or **class dialects**. More recently, the term SOCIOLECT has been used. Some languages are highly stratified in terms of social divisions, such as class, professional status, age and sex, and here major differences in social dialect are apparent. In English, the differences are not so basic, but it is possible to point to usages in vocabulary, grammar and pronunciation which are socially based, e.g. *ain't*, which has in its time identified both working class and upper class (e.g. Lord Peter Wimsey) types. Such variants were generally ignored in regional dialectology, and would these days tend to be studied under the heading of SOCIOLINGUISTICS.

'Dialect' is also sometimes applied to the linguistically distinct historical stages through which a language has passed, and here the term 'historical' or 'temporal dialect' might be used, e.g. Elizabethan English, 17th-century British English. 'Dialect' has further been used to refer to the distinctive language of a particular professional group ('occupational dialect'), but more recent terms have come to be used to refer to social variations of this kind (e.g. REGISTER, DIAtype,

diffuse

VARIETY). The popular application of the term to the unwritten languages of underdeveloped countries (cf. 'there are many dialects in Africa', and the like) is not a usage recommended in linguistics. See Trudgill 1975: Chs. 1, 4; Bolinger 1975: Ch. 11.

diffuse One of the features of sound set up by JAKOBSON & Halle in their DISTINCTIVE FEATURE theory of PHONOLOGY, to handle variations in PLACE OF ARTICULATION; its opposite is COMPACT. Diffuse sounds are defined ARTICULATORILY and ACOUSTICALLY, as those which involve a STRICTURE relatively far back in the mouth, and a relatively low concentration of acoustic energy in non-central parts of the sound spectrum. CLOSE VOWELS and FRONT CONSONANTS are [+diffuse] (abbreviated as [+diff]): MID or LOW vowels and PALATAL or VELAR consonants are [−diffuse] ([−diff]). This feature is replaced by HIGH in CHOMSKY & Halle's system. See Ladefoged 1975: Ch. 11; Hyman 1975: Ch. 2.

diglossia (diglossic) A term used in SOCIOLINGUISTICS to refer to a situation where two very different VARIETIES of a LANGUAGE CO-OCCUR throughout a SPEECH community, each with a distinct range of social function. Both varieties are STANDARDised to some degree, are felt to be alternatives by NATIVE-SPEAKERS and usually have special names. Sociolinguists usually talk in terms of a high (H) variety and a low (L) variety, corresponding broadly to a difference in FORMALITY: the high variety is learnt in school, tends to be used in church, on radio programmes, in serious literature, etc., and as a consequence has greater social prestige; the low variety in family conversations, and other relatively informal settings. Diglossic situations may be found in Greek (High: Katharevousa; Low: Dhimotiki), Arabic (High: classical; Low: colloquial), and some varieties of German (H: Hochdeutsch; L: Schweizerdeutsch, in Switzerland). See Trudgill 1974: Ch. 5.

digraph A term used in PHONETICS/PHONOLOGY and GRAPHETICS/GRAPHOLOGY to refer to a GRAPHic UNIT in which two symbols have combined to function as a single ELEMENT in a SYSTEM, e.g. [æ] for the vowel in RECEIVED PRONUNCIATION *cat*, or the linked *æ* in the classical spelling of some English words (e.g. *encyclopædia, onomatopœia*). See Gimson 1970: Ch. 4.

diminutive A term used in MORPHOLOGY to refer to an AFFIX with the general meaning of 'little', used literally or metaphorically (as a term of endearment). Examples include *-ino* in Italian, *-zinho* in Portuguese, and *-let* in English. See Quirk *et al* 1972: App. 1.

diphthong(-al, -isation, -ise) A term used in the PHONETIC classification of VOWEL sounds on the basis of their MANNER OF ARTICULATION: it refers to a vowel where there is a single (perceptual) noticeable change in quality during a SYLLABLE, as in English *beer, time, loud*. Related terms are MONOPHTHONG, where no qualitative change is heard, and TRIPHTHONG, where two such changes can be heard. Diphthongs, or 'gliding vowels', are usually classified into phonetic types, depending on which of the two elements is the more SONOROUS: 'falling' (or 'descending')' diphthongs have the first element STRESSED, as in the English examples: 'rising' (or 'ascending') diphthongs have the second element stressed, as in Portuguese *país* [pais] 'country'.

Other classifications of 'diphthongal' types exist, in terms of the extent of their movement (e.g. whether it is 'wide' or 'narrow') and their direction (whether the diphthong is 'centring' or not, i.e. ending with a CENTRAL vowel). **Diphthongisation** is the term used to describe a process where a monophthong has become a diphthong (has been 'diphthongised'), as in cases of historical or DIALECT change. Diphthongs are transcribed using symbols which represent the extremes of vowel movement between the two positions as in [ai] for the vowel in *fine*. See Gimson 1970: Chs. 4, 7; Catford 1977: Ch. 11.

direct (1) A term used in GRAMMATICAL description to refer to one of the two types of OBJECT ELEMENT which can function in CLAUSE STRUCTURE, the other being labelled INDIRECT. The relationship between the two is illustrated by such SENTENCES as *The man gave the boy a book*, where *a book* is the **direct object** (*What did the man give?*) and *the boy* is the **indirect object**. The direct object is the more central in clause structure, indirect objects requiring a direct object to relate to (cf. **The man gave the boy*). See Quirk *et al* 1972: Chs. 2, 11.

(2) The opposition between direct and indirect is also used to identify the two main ways of reflecting a person's speech: **direct speech** refers to the use of actual UTTERANCE, with no grammatical MODIFICATION, e.g. '*Is he coming?*', *John asked* is a **direct question**, whereas *John asked if he was coming* is an **indirect question**. See Quirk *et al* 1972: Ch. 11.

directive (1) In some classifications of SPEECH-ACTS, a 'directive' is an UTTERANCE whose purpose is to get other people to do something for the speaker. The LINGUISTIC means may be GRAMMATICAL (e.g. COMMANDS), SEMANTIC (appropriate vocabulary, e.g. *please*) or PHONOLOGICAL (e.g. persuasive INTONATION patterns). See Lyons 1977b: Ch. 16.

(2) (**director**) A term used in some MODELS of GRAMMATICAL CLASSIFICATION to refer to a type of EXOCENTRIC CONSTRUCTION in

which the initial ELEMENT is referred to as a 'director', and the 'directed element' as the AXIS. For example, in *kicked the ball*, *kicked* is the director, *the ball* the axis; in *in the box*, *in* is the director (or 'directive PARTICLE'), *the box* is the axis. See Robins 1971: Ch. 6.

disambiguate A term used in LINGUISTICS, and especially in TRANS-FORMATIONAL GRAMMAR, to refer to an analysis which demonstrates the alternative STRUCTURAL interpretations of an AMBIGUOUS SEN-TENCE, e.g. by ASSIGNING BRACKETS or specifying a transformational relationship. For example, the SENTENCE *it is too hot to eat* can be 'disambiguated' by showing how it can be related to such sentences as *the food is too hot to eat*, *the weather is too hot to allow eating*, and *the girl is too hot to eat anything*. See Lyons 1968: Ch. 6.

discontinuous (1) A term used by JAKOBSON & Halle in their DISTINC-TIVE FEATURE theory of PHONOLOGY to refer to sounds produced with a complete CLOSURE of the VOCAL TRACT, as in PLOSIVES. Its opposite is CONTINUANT, used to characterise FRICATIVES, VOWELS, etc. See Hyman 1975: Ch. 2.

(2) (**discontinuity**) In GRAMMATICAL analysis, discontinuity refers to the splitting of a CONSTRUCTION by the insertion of another grammatical UNIT. **Discontinuous constructions** or **constituents** are illustrated by the way the PARTICLE in some PHRASAL VERBS may be separated from the LEXICAL ELEMENT, e.g. *switch on* → **switch** the light **on**, by the double NEGATIVE system in some languages (French *ne...pas*, Welsh *nid...ddim*, etc.), or by the separation of AUXILIARY verb and main verb in QUESTION forms in English (e.g. *is he coming?*). Some analysts make use of the notion of a 'discontinuous morph(eme)', as when Arabic ROOT forms are identified by the CONSONANTS they contain, each of which is separated by a VOWEL (e.g. *k–t–b* 'write'). See Lyons 1968: Ch. 6; Matthews 1974: Ch. 7.

(3) In language ACQUISITION, the term refers to the view, primarily proposed by the American linguist Roman JAKOBSON, and now widely accepted, that the sounds of babbling bear no direct relationship to later PHONOLOGICAL development. It is opposed to a 'continuity' hypothesis, which argues that languages gradually select from the range of sounds used in babbling. Recent studies of babbling, however, suggest that elements of both hypotheses seem to play a part in accounting for the observed PHONETIC and phonological behaviour of young children. See Clark & Clark 1977: Ch. 10.

discourse A term used in LINGUISTICS to refer to a continuous stretch of (especially spoken) LANGUAGE larger than a SENTENCE – but within this broad notion, several different applications may be found. At its most general, a discourse is a behavioural UNIT which has a pre-theoretical status in linguistics: it is a set of UTTERANCES which constitute any recognisable SPEECH event (no reference being made to its linguistic STRUCTURING, if any), e.g. a conversation, a joke, a sermon, an interview. A classification of discourse functions, with particular reference to type of subject-matter, the situation, and the behaviour of the speaker, is often carried out in SOCIOLINGUISTIC studies (of primitive societies, in particular), e.g. distinguishing dialogues vs. monologues, or (more specifically), oratory, ritual, insults, narrative, and so on. In recent years, several linguists have attempted to discover linguistic regularities in discourses (**discourse analysis**), using GRAMMATICAL, PHONOLOGICAL and SEMANTIC criteria (e.g. COHESION, ANAPHORA, inter-sentence CONNECTIVITY). It is now plain that there exist important linguistic dependencies between sentences, but it is less clear how far these dependencies are sufficiently systematic to enable linguistic units higher than the sentence to be established.

In semantics, some use is made of the logical term **universe of discourse**, *viz* the range of entities, topics, situations, etc. within which a particular speech event makes reference. In this sense, the universe of discourse of sermons, for example, will be predictably different (usually) from the universe of discourse of commercial advertising. See Lyons 1977b: Ch. 15; Clark & Clark 1977: Ch. 6.

discovery A term used in LINGUISTICS to refer to a type of PROCEDURE used in carrying out an analysis. A **discovery procedure** is a set of techniques which can be automatically or 'mechanically' applied to a sample of LANGUAGE and which will produce a correct GRAMMATICAL analysis. Attempts to develop such procedures characterised the work of many BLOOMFIELDIAN linguists, and were strongly criticised in early formulations of GENERATIVE grammar. It is argued that it is never possible to identify with certainty all the factors which lead a linguist in the direction of a particular analysis. Nor is it desirable to seek such a procedure, as the analysis itself can be evaluated regardless of the means by which it was obtained. See Lyons 1977a: Ch. 4.

discrete(ness) A suggested defining property of human LANGUAGE (contrasting with the properties of other SEMIOTIC SYSTEMS), whereby the ELEMENTS of a signal can be analysed as having definable boundaries, with no gradation or continuity between them. A system lacking 'discreteness' is said to be 'continuous' or **non-discrete** (cf. NON-DISCRETE grammar). The term is especially used in PHONETICS and

disjunction

PHONOLOGY to refer to sounds which have relatively clear-cut boundaries, as defined in ACOUSTIC, ARTICULATORY or AUDITORY terms. It is evident that speech is a continuous stream of sound, but speakers of a language are able to SEGMENT this continuum into a finite number of discrete UNITS, these usually corresponding to the PHONEMES of the language. The boundaries of these units may correspond to identifiable acoustic or articulatory features, but often they do not. The minimal discrete units in phonetics are known as PHONES. See Lyons 1968: Ch. 2; 1977b: Ch. 3; Hyman 1975: Ch. 1.

disjunction (disjunct(-ive)) A term in formal logic now encountered as part of the theoretical framework of several areas in LINGUISTICS, especially SEMANTICS. It refers to the process or result of relating two PROPOSITIONS such that they are in 'either-or' relationship, e.g. (*Either*) *Mary is late or John is early*. With disjunction, it is usual to distinguish **inclusive** and **exclusive** interpretations: with the former, the disjunction is true if either, or both, of the propositions is true; with the latter, the disjunction is true only if one or other of the propositions is true (but not both). Under the exclusive interpretation, therefore, the above disjunction would be false, if both Mary was late and John was early; whereas under the inclusive interpretation, the disjunction would be true.

In some GRAMMATICAL descriptions, the term is adapted to refer to a process whose primary function is to mark a relationship of contrast or comparison between STRUCTURES, using such 'disjunctive' ITEMS as *or* and *but*. (Some grammarians, such as Quirk *et al* 1972: Ch. 8, have introduced the term **disjunct**, in a highly restricted sense, to refer to a sub-class of ADVERBIALS (such as *seriously, frankly, really*), which contrasts with CONJUNCTS and ADJUNCTS on SYNTACTIC and SEMANTIC grounds.) The two disjunctions above are often referred to as the 'exclusive *or*' and the 'inclusive *or*'. In GENERATIVE grammar, the notion is applied as a principle affecting the ordering of RULES. **Disjunctive ordering** is found in the use of the parenthesis NOTATION, which indicates OPTIONAL ELEMENTS. If a SEQUENCE of rules is abbreviated by using this notation (e.g. $X \rightarrow Y/Z(P)Q$, which stands for the sequence (a) $X \rightarrow Y/ZPQ$ and (b) $X \rightarrow Y/ZQ$), then this sequence forms a disjunctively ordered block, i.e. if (a) applies, (b) is not permitted to apply. It is distinguished from CONJUNCTIVE ordering. See Lyons 1977b: Ch. 6; Quirk *et al* 1972: Ch. 9; Hyman 1975: Ch. 4.

displacement (displaced) A suggested defining property of human LANGUAGE (contrasting with the properties of many other SEMIOTIC systems), whereby language can be used to refer to CONTEXTS removed from the immediate situation of the speaker (i.e. it can be 'displaced'). For example, if someone says *I was afraid*, it is not necessary that the speaker still is afraid; whereas animal calls seem generally tied to specific situations, such as danger or hunger, and have nothing comparable to **displaced speech** (unless this is artificially taught to them, as some recent experiments with chimpanzees have tried to do). See Lyons 1977b: Ch. 3.

dissimilation A general term in PHONETICS to refer to the influence exercised by one sound SEGMENT upon the ARTICULATION of another, so that the sounds become less alike, or different. Such changes have mainly been noticed in HISTORICAL LINGUISTIC studies, where the effects have manifested themselves over a long period of time (e.g. *pilgrim* from Latin *peregrinus*, with the first *r* dissimilating to *l*), but SYNCHRONIC dissimilations are also possible, as when we avoid a sequence of identical sounds (cf. the difficulty of tongue-twisters such as *Will will willingly...*). As with the opposite effect, ASSIMILATION, it is possible to classify dissimilations into types, based on the place, degree and direction of the changes involved. See Bolinger 1975: Ch. 12.

distinctive(ness) A term used in LINGUISTICS for any features of speech (or writing) which enable a CONTRAST to be made between PHONOLOGICAL, GRAMMATICAL or SEMANTIC UNITS. Such contrasts might also be labelled 'relevant', FUNCTIONAL or SIGNIFICANT. The main use of the term has been in phonology, as part of the phrase **distinctive feature**, where it refers to a minimal contrastive UNIT recognised by some linguists as a means of explaining how the sound SYSTEM of languages is organised. Distinctive features may be seen either as part of the definition of PHONEMES, or as an alternative to the notion of the phoneme. The first of these views is found in the approach of the PRAGUE SCHOOL, where the phoneme is seen as a BUNDLE of PHONETIC distinctive features: the English phoneme /p/, for example, can be seen as the result of the combination of the features of BILABIALity, VOICElessness, PLOSIVEness, etc. Other phonemes will differ from /p/ in respect of at least one of these features. In distinctive feature theories of phonology, however, the phoneme is not considered to be a relevant unit of explanation: symbols such as *p*, *b*, etc. are seen simply as convenient abbreviations for particular sets of FEATURES. It is the features which are the minimal units of phonological analysis, not the phonemes. It is argued that by substituting features for phonemes in this way, generalisations can be made about the relationships between sounds in a language, which would otherwise be missed. Moreover, because features are phonetic units, it should be possible to make inter-language (e.g. HISTORICAL and DIALECTAL) and cross-language comparisons, and ultimately statements about phonological UNIVERSALS, more readily than by using a phonemic model of phonology.

Distinctive feature analysts claim that there are several advantages over the traditional phonetic alphabet approach to phonological description, which describes UTTERANCES as a sequence of SEGMENTS. For example, it was originally suggested that a relatively small set of abstract feature OPPOSITIONS (a dozen or so) would account for all the phonological contrasts made in languages: it would not then be necessary to recognise so much phonetic classificatory detail, as exists on, say, the IPA chart, where the phonological status of the segments recognised is not indicated. In fact, it has turned out that far more features are required, as new languages come to be analysed. Another advantage, it is suggested, is that CONSONANTS and VOWELS can be characterised using the same set of phonetic features (unlike traditional descriptions, where the classificatory terminology for vowels – HIGH, LOW, etc. – is quite different from that used for consonants – LABIAL, PALATAL, etc.).

By using a system of this kind, some quite specific predictions can be made about the sound systems of languages. For example, using the JAKOBSON & Halle system below enables one to distinguish phonologically two degrees of FRONT/BACK contrast in the consonant system and three degrees of vowel height. But what follows from this is a universal claim, that no languages permit more than these numbers of contrasts in their phonological systems. These are empirical claims, of course, and in recent years much effort has been spent on investigating these claims and modifying the nature of the feature inventory required.

Two major statements concerning the distinctive feature approach have been made: one by Roman Jakobson & Morris Halle, in *Fundamentals of Language* (1956), the other by Noam CHOMSKY & Morris Halle, in *The Sound Pattern of English* (1968). The Jakobson & Halle approach set up features in pairs, defined primarily in ACOUSTIC terms (as could be detected on a SPECTROGRAM), but with some reference to ARTICULATORY criteria. Examples of their features include VOCALIC vs. non-vocalic, CONSONANTAL vs. non-consonantal, COMPACT vs. DIFFUSE, GRAVE vs. ACUTE, NASAL vs. ORAL, discontinuous vs. CONTINUANT, STRIDENT vs. MELLOW, FLAT vs. SHARP/PLAIN and VOICED vs. voiceless. The emphasis in this approach is firmly on the nature of the oppositions between the UNDERLYING features involved, rather than on the description of the range of phonetic REALISATIONS each feature represents. In the Chomsky & Halle approach, more attention is paid to the phonetic realisations of the underlying features recognised, and a different system of feature classification is set up. Some of the earlier features are retained (e.g. voice, consonantal, tense, continuant, nasal, strident), but many are modified, and new features added, some of which overlap with the earlier approach (e.g. SONORANT vs. OBSTRUENT, DELAYED vs. INSTANTANEOUS RELEASE, ANTERIOR vs. non-anterior, CORONAL vs. non-coronal, DISTRIBUTED vs. non-distributed, SYLLABIC vs. non-syllabic). The application of these features to languages is not without controversy, and in recent years further suggestions have been forthcoming as to the need for additional features, such as LABIALity. See Hyman 1975: Ch. 2; Bolinger 1975: Ch. 3; Lyons 1968: Ch. 3.

distinguisher A term used by some GENERATIVE LINGUISTS as part of a (controversial) two-way classification of the SEMANTIC COMPONENTS of LEXICAL ITEMS. 'Distinguishers' were said to be those components which are needed to keep apart the different meanings of HOMONYMS, but which are unsystematic in a LANGUAGE; that is, they have no general role to play in the statement of SELECTIONAL and other restrictions. For example, in one of the items originally analysed in this way, *bachelor*, one distinguisher is the component [having the academic degree conferred...]. Components which do operate systematically (e.g. [old], [male], [animate]) were known as MARKERS. See Lyons 1977b: Ch. 9.

distributed One of the features of sound set up by CHOMSKY & Halle in their DISTINCTIVE FEATURE theory of PHONOLOGY to handle variations in PLACE OF ARTICULATION (CAVITY features) in FRICATIVE sounds. Distributed sounds are defined ARTICULATORILY, as those produced with a STRICTURE which extends for a considerable distance along the direction of the air flow, as in BILABIAL, and PALATO-ALVEOLAR fricatives. Its opposite is **non-distributed**, referring to sounds produced with a relatively short stricture, as in DENTAL and RETROFLEX fricatives. See Ladefoged 1975: Ch. 11; Hyman 1975: Ch. 2.

distribution(al) A general term used in LINGUISTICS to refer to the total set of linguistic CONTEXTS, or ENVIRONMENTS, in which a UNIT (such as a PHONEME, a MORPHEME, or a WORD) can occur. Every linguistic unit, it is said, has a characteristic distribution. A **distributional analysis** would plot the places in larger linguistic units where smaller units occur, such as the distribution of phonemes within a SYLLABLE or word, or of words within a SENTENCE. Distributional ideas were originally developed in PHONOLOGY, but were later extended to other linguistic units. In some approaches, the notion of distribution became a major explanatory principle, being seen as a possible way of grouping sounds into phonemes without reference to the meaning or grammatical properties of the words in which they appear – or even, at times to the PHONETIC similarities existing between them. On this basis, for instance, [h] and [ŋ] in English might be considered members of the same phoneme, because they never share the same set of environments. In phonemic phonology, the most important continuing use of the term is in the phrase **complementary distribution**, which refers to the status of related sounds (or ALLOphones) when they are found in mutually exclusive environments, as in the use of a DENTAL vs. an ALVEOLAR allophone of /t/ in English, e.g. *eight* vs. *eighth*. (In GENERATIVE phonology, on the other hand, distributional statements of this kind are handled by a formulation in terms of phonological RULES.) See Hyman 1975: Ch. 3; Lyons 1968: Ch. 2.

disyllable (disyllabic) A term used in PHONETICS and PHONOLOGY to refer to a UNIT consisting of two SYLLABLES. A 'disyllabic' form is distinguished from MONOsyllabic, trisyllabic, etc. forms. See Gimson 1970: Ch. 9.

di-transitive A term used by some LINGUISTS to refer to a VERB which can take two OBJECTS, e.g. *give* (*I gave him a book*). It is usually distinguished from 'monotransitive' verbs, such as *kick*. See Quirk *et al* 1972: Ch. 2.

divergence A term used in SOCIOLINGUISTICS to refer to a process of DIALECT change in which the dialects become less like each other (or 'diverge'). This process (sometimes called 'dialectalisation') is only likely to happen in the absence of geographical and social links between populations within a SPEECH community, lines of communication thereby being few or difficult, and a STANDARD dialect probably being non-existent. The opposite effect is known as CONVERGENCE. 'Divergence' also has a currency in HISTORICAL linguistic studies, referring to the splitting of a FORM into two CONTRASTIVE UNITS. See Gumperz & Hymes 1971: Intro.

***do*-deletion/insertion/support** A set of RULES in GENERATIVE SYNTAX which determine the use of the EMPTY AUXILIARY VERB *do*. '*Do*-insertion' or '*do*-support' inserts the verb *do* into a place in a STRUCTURE, as part of the DERIVATION of a sentence. An example is in some types of TAG-QUESTIONS, where to form a tag from the sentence *he wants kicking*, a *do* needs to be introduced, *viz...doesn't he*. It is primarily used where a TENSE-marker has no verb FORMATIVE to attach to, as with tense variation in question forms (e.g. *did X happen*). 'Do-deletion' would apply if a *do* form previously generated by the rules for a given sentence were to be deleted. See Akmajian & Heny 1975: Chs. 1, 4.

domain (1) An extension of the general meaning of this WORD by some LINGUISTS to refer to the realm of application of any linguistic construct, e.g. the 'domain' of a RULE in a GRAMMAR would refer to the range of STRUCTURES to which that rule was applicable. In GENERATIVE linguistics, the term refers specifically to the parts of a TREE diagram deriving from any one NODE, i.e. the structure which the node DOMINATES. See Lyons 1968: Ch. 6; Matthews 1974: Ch. 5.

(2) A term used by some SEMANTICISTS to refer to the area of experience covered by the set of terms in a particular SEMANTIC FIELD, e.g. colour terms, kinship terms. See Lyons 1977b: Ch. 8.

(3) In SOCIOLINGUISTICS the term refers to a group of institutionalised social situations typically constrained by a common set of behavioural rules, e.g. the domain of the family is the house, of religion is the church, etc. The notion is seen as of particular importance in the analysis of MULTILINGUAL settings involving several participants, where it is used to relate variations in the individuals' choice and topic of language to broader sociocultural norms and expectations of interaction. See Gumperz & Hymes 1971: Ch. 15; Lyons 1977b: Ch. 14.

domination (domin-ate, -ance) A term in GENERATIVE LINGUISTICS for the relationship between NODES in a TREE diagram ('X dominates Y').

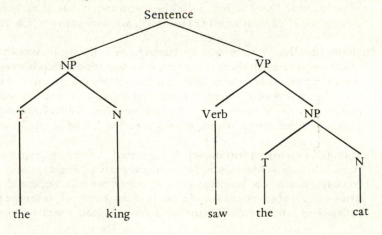

dorsal

If no nodes intervene between X and Y, one says that X is 'directly' or 'immediately' dominated by Y. For example, in the diagram of the sentence *the king saw the cat* the T and N are directly dominated by NP, the first NP is directly dominated by 'Sentence', and the second by the VP. It is by the use of this notion that distinctions such as SUBJECT and OBJECT can be made using this model, *viz* the Subject is that NP directly dominated by Sentence, the Object is that NP directly dominated by VP. See Lyons 1977a: Ch. 6; Akmajian & Heny 1975: Ch. 2.

dorsal (dorsum) A term sometimes used in the PHONETIC classification of speech sounds, referring to a sound made with the BACK, or dorsum of the TONGUE in contact with the roof of the mouth, as in VELAR (sc. 'dorso-velar'), or PALATAL (sc. 'dorso-palatal') sounds. Some authors include the BLADE of the tongue under this heading. See Catford 1977: Ch. 8; Abercrombie 1967: Ch. 4.

double-base A type of TRANSFORMATIONAL RULE recognised in early MODELS of GENERATIVE GRAMMAR, where the rule operates with an input of two or more TERMINAL STRINGS. Double-base transformations are also known as GENERALised transformations, and are opposed to 'single-base' types, where only one string is involved. See Lyons 1968: Ch. 6.

downgrading (downgraded) A term used by some LINGUISTS to refer to a GRAMMATICAL process in which a UNIT in the grammatical HIERARCHY is EMBEDDED within a unit from a lower LEVEL. For example, the clause *I don't care* is used as the equivalent of a WORD in the SENTENCE *That's a very I-don't-care attitude*; it has thus been 'downgraded' (cf. the notion of RANK-shift). See Bolinger 1975: Ch. 12.

dualism (dualist) A term used to characterise a theory of MEANING which postulates that there is a direct, two-way relationship between LINGUISTIC FORMS and the entities, states of affairs, etc. to which they refer (i.e. REFERENTS). Such theories are usually contrasted with TRIADIC theories of meaning, which postulate a three-fold relationship, namely between forms, referents and SENSE. See Lyons 1977b: Ch. 4.

duality (of patterning/structure) A suggested defining property of human LANGUAGE (contrasting with the properties of other SEMIOTIC SYSTEMS), which sees language as being STRUCTURALLY organised in terms of two abstract LEVELS. At the first, higher level, language is analysed in terms of combinations of (meaningful) UNITS (such as

MORPHEMES, WORDS); at another, lower level, it is seen as a sequence of SEGMENTS which lack any MEANING in themselves, but which combine to form units of meaning). These two levels are sometimes referred to as ARTICULATIONS – a 'primary' and 'secondary' articulation respectively. See Lyons 1977a: Ch. 2; 1977b: Ch. 3; Matthews 1975: Ch. 1.

dummy A term used in LINGUISTICS to refer to a FORMAL GRAMMATICAL ELEMENT introduced into a STRUCTURE or an analysis to ensure that a grammatical SENTENCE is produced. Apart from their formal role, 'dummy elements' have no meaning – they are SEMANTICALLY empty, e.g. *there* in *there were many people at the club*, *it* in *it's raining*. When this element acts as a locus for grammatical CONTRASTS, it is referred to as a 'dummy carrier', e.g. *do* in QUESTION forms is a 'dummy auxiliary', which carries the TENSE/NUMBER contrast for the VERB PHRASE (*do/did you know*, *do/does he know*). Notions involving ZERO (e.g. 'zero morpheme') could also be considered types of dummy. In TRANSFORMATIONAL grammar, 'dummy symbols' are sometimes introduced into the DEEP STRUCTURE of a sentence, to facilitate the DERIVATION of CLASSES of sentence, but which never appear in the sentence's surface structure, e.g. the S symbol which represents an EMBEDDED sentence in a PHRASE-MARKER, the various kinds of BOUNDARY symbol, or the DELTA (Δ) symbol which acts as a 'place-holder' for LEXICAL ITEMS (specified as COMPLEX SYMBOLS). See Lyons 1968: Ch. 7.

duration A term used in PHONETICS, to refer to the LENGTH of time involved in the ARTICULATION of a sound or SYLLABLE. Distinctions between relatively 'long' and relatively 'short' durations are measured in units of time, such as the millisecond (msec). In speech, the absolute duration of sounds is dependent to a considerable extent on the overall TEMPO of speaking. Issues which need reference to duration include the study of rhythm (cf. ISOCHRONY), CONSONANT articulation (cf. VOICE onset time, and JUNCTURE. See Catford 1977: Ch. 10.

dynamic (1) A term used in GRAMMATICAL classification, referring to one of the two main ASPECTUAL categories of VERB use; the other being STATIC. The distinguishing criteria are mainly SYNTACTIC; for example, dynamic verbs occur in the PROGRESSIVE form (e.g. *I'm running*, *He's playing*) and in the IMPERATIVE (e.g. *Run!*). The SEMANTICS of this class covers a wide range, including activity, process (e.g. *change*, *grow*), bodily sensation (e.g. *feel*, *hurt*), etc. See Quirk *et al* 1972: Ch. 3; Lyons 1968: Chs. 7, 8.

(2) A term used by some SOCIOLINGUISTICS to characterise a view

of LANGUAGE (**dynamic linguistics**) in which a temporal dimension is introduced into the study of language variation: SYNCHRONIC states are seen in terms of the processes ('waves') of change which produce and affect them, as defined in terms of such notions as relative rate and direction of change. A similar introduction of the temporal dimension into an otherwise 'static' view of a subject is found in parametric PHONETICS, and in several contemporary instrumental techniques for the study of ARTICULATION, as in myodynamic (muscular movement) and aerodynamic (air-flow) investigations. See Gumperz & Hymes 1972: Intro., Ch. 19.

E

𑁦𑁦𑁦𑁦𑁦𑁦

ear-training A technique used in PHONETICS whereby aspiring practitioners of the subject are trained to discriminate and identify the whole range of human speech sounds. The correlative technique of producing the sounds is known as PERFORMANCE. See Ladefoged 1975: Ch. 1.

echo A term used in some GRAMMATICAL descriptions to refer to a type of SENTENCE which repeats, in whole or in part, what has just been said by another speaker. Such 'echo utterances' include 'echo QUESTIONS' (e.g. A: *I saw a ghost.* B: *You saw what?*) and EXCLAMATIONS (e.g. A: *Have you been to the office?* B: *Have I been to the office!*). See Quirk *et al* 1972: Ch. 7.

eclectic(ism) The application of this general term in LINGUISTICS is found mainly in relation to MODELS of DESCRIPTION which have been built from a combination of features originating in more than one linguistic theory. For example, the descriptive handbook of English produced by Quirk *et al* is eclectic in that it makes use of concepts and procedures deriving from STRUCTURALIST, TRANSFORMATIONAL and other approaches. Eclectic accounts are justified by the multiple insights they can provide into an area of LANGUAGE. Their main weakness is the difficulty of developing a coherent theoretical framework within which the various descriptive components can be interrelated. See Bolinger 1975: Ch. 15.

economy A criterion in LINGUISTICS which requires that, other things being equal, an analysis should aim to be as short and use as few terms as possible. It is a measure which permits one to quantify the number of FORMAL constructs (symbols, RULES, etc.) used in arriving at a solution to a problem, and has been used, explicitly or implicitly, in most areas of linguistic investigation. This application of Occam's razor is a major feature of the proposals for evaluating analyses made by GENERATIVE GRAMMAR (cf. EXPLANATORY ADEQUACY). In generative PHONOLOGY, in particular, it has been claimed that the preferred analysis is one which is overall the simpler, i.e. it uses fewer FEATURES and RULES. On the other hand, it has been argued that it will not always be the case that the simpler solution, in this quantitative sense, will be the intuitively more ACCEPTABLE one, or the one which allows the most informative LINGUISTICALLY SIGNIFICANT GENERALISATIONS to be made.

Linguistic economy is a difficult criterion to work with: simplification made in one part of an analysis may cause difficulties elsewhere. And until a total description is made, any suggestions concerning economy are necessarily tentative. But generative theory argues that this notion is of major theoretical importance, and several attempts have been made to provide a formal account of what is involved in it, as in the notion of a SIMPLICITY METRIC.

An example of relative economy of statement can be found in the opening rules of a generative grammar, when these are seen to apply in a linear order:

$$(1) \ S \rightarrow NP + VP \quad (2) \ V \rightarrow V + NP \quad (3) \ NP \rightarrow Det + N$$

A reason for this particular ordering becomes clear when one considers what would have happened had rule (3) been used before rule (2): the NP in rule (3) would then REWRITE that introduced in rule (1), and the NP in rule (2) would still need to be expanded, thus requiring an additional rule (4), as follows (with subscripts added, for clarity):

$$(1) \ S \rightarrow NP_1 + VP \quad (2) \ NP_1 \rightarrow Det + N$$
$$(3) \ VP \rightarrow V + NP_2 \quad (4) \ NP_2 \rightarrow Det + N$$

The first ordering would thus seem to be superior, in terms of economy. See Hyman 1975: Chs. 3, 4; Lyons 1977a: Ch. 6.

-ed **form** A term used in English GRAMMATICAL description to refer to the simple past TENSE FORM of the VERB e.g. *I walked, He jumped*. It does not necessarily end in this form (e.g. *I ran, He saw*), which should be seen solely as a mnemonic device, useful mainly in writing RULES succinctly. The *-ed* ending is however also a common form of the past PARTICIPLE (e.g. *He has **walked***), and the potential AMBIGUITY has to be borne in mind. See Quirk *et al* 1972: Ch. 3.

educational linguistics A term sometimes used for the application of LINGUISTIC theories, methods and descriptive findings to the study of the teaching/learning of a mother-tongue in schools or other educational settings. Specific topics of interest include the study of reading and writing, ACCENT and DIALECT, oracy (cf. ORAL), language VARIETY across the curriculum, and the teaching of linguistics, GRAMMAR, etc. in schools. See Bolinger 1975: Chs. 14, 17.

egressive A term used in the PHONETIC classification of speech-sounds, referring to all sounds produced using an outwards-moving AIR-STREAM. The opposite category is INGRESSIVE, which is an uncommon mode for speech production. The vast majority of speech sounds are made with egressive air from the lungs (PULMONIC air). A few CONSONANTS are produced using an egressive air-flow originating at the LARYNX: these are known as EJECTIVE or 'glottalic' sounds (see GLOTTAL), such as [t', s', tʃ']. See Gimson 1970: Chs. 2, 4; Catford 1977: Chs. 3, 5.

ejective A term used in the PHONETIC classification of CONSONANT sounds on the basis of their MANNER OF ARTICULATION; it refers to the SERIES of sounds produced by using the glottalic AIR-STREAM MECHANISM. Air is compressed in the mouth or PHARYNX while the GLOTTIS remains closed, and then released. Ejective PLOSIVES are quite common in LANGUAGES (as in many languages of Africa and the Americas, e.g. Quechua, Amharic), and ejective FRICATIVES may also be found. These sounds are transcribed with a small raised GLOTTAL stop, or an apostrophe, following the segment involved, e.g. [p'], [s']. They are also referred to as 'glottalic' sounds, and occasionally as 'glottalised' sounds. See Ladefoged 1975: Ch. 6.

elaborated A term used by the sociologist, Basil Bernstein (b. 1924), to refer to one of two VARIETIES (or CODES) of LANGUAGE use, introduced as part of a general theory of the nature of social systems and social rules, the other being RESTRICTED. **Elaborated code** is used in relatively FORMAL, educated situations; it is not reliant for its meaningfulness on extra-linguistic CONTEXT (such as gestures or shared beliefs); and it permits the speaker to be individually creative in his expression, and to use a range of linguistic alternatives. It is said to be characterised linguistically by a relatively high proportion of such features as SUBORDINATE CLAUSES, ADJECTIVES, the PRONOUN *I*, and PASSIVES. Restricted code, by contrast, is said to lack these features. The correlation of elaborated code with certain types of social class background, and its role in educational settings (e.g. whether children used to a restricted code will succeed in schools where elaborated code is the norm – and what should be done in such cases) has brought this theory considerable publicity and controversy. See Gumperz & Hymes 1971: Ch. 17; Trudgill 1974: Ch. 2.

electrokymograph(-y, -ic) An instrument used in ARTICULATORY PHONETICS to enable a record to be made of the changes in ORAL and NASAL air-flow during speech. 'Electrokymography' involves the use of a face-mask which can differentiate the two kinds of flow, and associated equipment which can measure air volume and velocity, and record it visually (as an 'electrokymogram'). See Catford 1975: Ch. 12.

electromyograph(-y, -ic) (EMG) An instrument used in PHONETICS to observe and record muscular contractions during speech. 'Electromyography' involves the application of electrodes (surface pads or needles) to the muscles involved in the VOCAL TRACT, and the analysis of the 'electromyographic' traces produced visually ('electromyograms'). See Catford 1977: Ch. 12.

electropalatograph(-y, -ic) An instrument used in ARTICULATORY PHONETICS to enable a continuous record to be made of the contacts between TONGUE and PALATE during speech. 'Electropalatography' involves the use of an artifical palate containing several electrodes, which register the tongue-contacts as they are made; the results are presented visually as 'electropalatograms'. See Catford 1977: Ch. 12.

element A term used in LINGUISTICS, sometimes in the general sense of 'part', but often restricted, especially in GRAMMATICAL analysis, to refer to the IMMEDIATE CONSTITUENTS of a UNIT in a HIERARCHY. For example, SUBJECT/VERB, etc. are 'elements' of CLAUSE STRUCTURE; AFFIXES are 'elements' of WORD structure. See Quirk *et al* 1972: Ch. 2.

elicitation (elicit) A term used in LINGUISTICS and PHONETICS to refer to the method of obtaining reliable linguistic DATA from speakers (INFORMANTS) – either actual UTTERANCES, or judgements about utterances (e.g. their ACCEPTABILITY). Several ingenious 'elicitation techniques' have been suggested to obtain ('elicit') this information in an indirect and unselfconscious way, e.g. asking informants to perform linguistic tasks which, though apparently irrelevant to the purpose at hand, will bring to light features of direct interest to the analyst. See Gumperz & Hymes 1972: Intro.

elision A term used in PHONETICS and PHONOLOGY to refer to the omission of sounds in CONNECTED SPEECH. Both CONSONANTS and VOWELS may be affected, and sometimes whole SYLLABLES may be elided. UNSTRESSED GRAMMATICAL WORDS, such as *and* and *of* are particularly prone to be elided, as when the *f* is dropped in *cup of tea* (cf. *cuppa tea*), or the *a* and *d* are dropped in *boys 'n' girls*. Within POLYSYLLABIC words, the vowels and consonants in unstressed syllables regularly elide in conversational speech of normal speed, e.g. *camera* (/kamrə/), *probably* (/prɒblɪ/), *February* (/febrɪ/). Complex consonant CLUSTERS are also often reduced, e.g. *twelfths* becoming /twelθs/ or /twelfs/. Several intricate patterns of influence can be demonstrated.

Traditional rhetoric was much concerned with the phenomenon of elision, because of the implications for constructing well-formed metrical lines, which would scan well. In rhetorical terminology, an elision in word-initial position was known as *aphesis* or *prosiopesis*, in word-medial position as *syncope*, and in word-final position as *apocope*. A similar classification was made for the opposite of elision, INTRUSION. See Gimson 1970: Chs. 9, 11.

ellipsis (clide, ellipt-ed, -ical) A term used in GRAMMATICAL analysis to refer to a SENTENCE where, for reasons of economy, emphasis or style, a part of the STRUCTURE has been omitted, which is recoverable from a scrutiny of the CONTEXT. TRADITIONAL grammars talk here of an ELEMENT being 'understood', but LINGUISTIC analyses tend to constrain the notion more, emphasising the need for the 'elided' (or 'ellipted') parts of the sentence to be unambiguously specifiable. For example, in the sequence A: *Where are you going?* B: *To town*, the 'full' FORM of B's sentence is predictable from A's SENTENCE (I am going to town). But in such sentences as *Thanks*, *Yes*, etc., it is generally unclear what the full form of such sentences might be (e.g. 'Thanks is due to you'? 'I give you thanks'?), and in such circumstances the term 'ellipsis' would probably not be used. 'Elliptical' constructions are an essential feature of everyday conversation, but the rules governing their occurrence have received relatively little study. See Quirk *et al* 1972: Chs. 9, 10; Lyons 1968: Ch. 5.

embed(-ding, -ded) A term used in GENERATIVE GRAMMAR to refer to the process of CONSTRUCTION where one SENTENCE is included ('embedded') in another, i.e. in SYNTACTIC SUBORDINATION. 'Embedding' processes are distinct from CONJOINING (CO-ORDINATING) ones. The insertion of a RELATIVE CLAUSE within a NOUN PHRASE is an example of embedding, e.g. *The man **who has a suitcase** is in the bar* is derived from *the man has a suitcase*, which is embedded within the MATRIX sentence *The man is in the bar*. See Lyons 1968: Ch. 6; Huddleston 1976: Ch. 7.

emic/etic A pair of terms which characterise opposed approaches to the study of LINGUISTIC DATA. An 'etic' approach is one where the physical patterns of LANGUAGE are described with a minimum of reference to their function within the language SYSTEM. An 'emic' approach, by contrast, takes full account of FUNCTIONAL relationships, setting up a CLOSED system of abstract CONTRASTIVE UNITS as the basis of a DESCRIPTION. Emic is in fact derived from such terms as PHONEME and MORPHEME, where *-eme* refers to the minimal DISTINCTIVE units involved. An emic approach to INTONATION, for example, would describe only those features of the PITCH pattern which are used by a language to signal MEANINGS; an etic approach, on the other hand, would describe the UTTERANCE's pitch movements much more minutely, regardless of whether the features described were being used by the language to signal MEANINGS or not. The distinction is a central feature of the American linguist Kenneth Pike's (b. 1912) theory of language, known as TAGMEMICS. See Bolinger 1975: Ch. 15; Hyman 1975: Ch. 1.

emotive A term sometimes used in SEMANTICS as part of a CLASSIFICATION of types of MEANING. The 'emotive meaning' of an expression refers to its emotional effect on the listener, as in the 'emotive content' of propaganda speeches, advertising language, etc. Alternative terms include AFFECTIVE and CONNOTATIVE; opposed terms include COGNITIVE and REFERENTIAL. See Lyons 1977b: Ch. 7.

empty (1) A term used in some GRAMMATICAL descriptions to refer to a meaningless ELEMENT introduced into a structure to ensure its GRAMMATICALITY. There is an empty use of *it*, for example, in such sentences as *it's raining*, and EXISTENTIAL *there* is sometimes regarded in this way (e.g. *there are mice in the larder*). Such elements have also been called PROP words, or DUMMY elements. See Quirk *et al* 1972: Ch. 14.

(2) The term is also sometimes used in the grammatical CLASSIFICATION of WORDS to refer to one of two postulated major word classes in LANGUAGE, the other being FULL. **Empty words** are said to be words which have no LEXICAL MEANING, and whose function is solely to express grammatical relationships, e.g. *to, the, in, of*. The distinction has been criticised, on the grounds that there are degrees of meaning in most grammatical words, few (if any) being really devoid of CONTENT. The term is still used, however – though not as widely as some other terms (such as GRAMMATICAL WORD, FUNCTION WORD). See Palmer 1971: Ch. 2, Robins 1971: Ch. 7.

(3) A term used in MORPHOLOGY, in the phrase **empty morph**, to refer to a FORMAL FEATURE in a word which cannot be allocated to any MORPHEME. A well-discussed example in English is the word *children*, where a possible analysis is into ROOT *child* and plural SUFFIX *-en* (cf. *oxen*); the residual /r/ left by this analysis is then seen as an empty morph without which the word would not be exhaustively analysed at the morphemic LEVEL. See Palmer 1971: Ch. 3.

endocentric A term used in GRAMMATICAL analysis as part of a two-way classification of SYNTACTIC constructions using DISTRIBUTIONAL criteria: it refers to a group of syntactically related WORDS where one of the words is FUNCTIONALLY equivalent to the group as a whole (i.e. there is a definable 'centre' or HEAD inside the group, which has the same distribution as the whole); it is opposed to EXOCENTRIC. Endocentric constructions include NOUN PHRASES and VERB phrases (as traditionally defined), where the CONSTITUENT items are SUBORDINATE to the head, e.g. *the big man, the man in black, will be going*, and also some types of CO-ORDINATION, e.g. *boys and girls*. See Robins 1971: Ch. 6; Lyons 1968: Ch. 6.

-en form A term used in English GRAMMATICAL description to refer to the past PARTICIPLE FORM of the VERB, e.g. *I have **taken***. It does not necessarily have this ending, which should be seen solely as a mnemonic device, useful mainly in writing RULES succinctly. The *-ed* ending is also common in this function (e.g. *I have walked*), and may be seen as an alternative symbol. See Quirk *et al* 1972: Ch. 3; Akmajian & Heny 1975: Ch. 4.

entailment A term derived from formal logic and now often used as part of the study of SEMANTICS. It refers to a relation between a pair of SENTENCES such that the truth of the second sentence necessarily follows from the truth of the first, e.g. *I can see a dog – I can see an animal*. One cannot both assert the first and deny the second. In recent semantic discussion, entailment has come to be contrasted with PRESUPPOSITION, on the grounds that different consequences follow from either of the sentences being false. For example, if *I can see a dog* is false, then the notion of entailment requires that *I can see an animal* may be true or false; but the notion of presupposition requires that if the first of these is false, the second must be true. See Lyons 1977b: Ch. 6.

entry (1) A term used in SEMANTICS to refer to the accumulated STRUCTURAL information concerning a LEXICAL item as formally located in a LEXICON or dictionary. A dictionary is seen as a set of **lexical entries**. See Lyons 1977b: Ch. 13.

(2) In SYSTEMIC GRAMMAR, the phrase **entry condition** refers to the criterion which must be met in order for a particular grammatical system to become operative. For example, in order to operate the system which contains the choices DECLARATIVE ~ INTERROGATIVE ~ IMPERATIVE, the entry condition requires that the input be a main CLAUSE. The whole of LANGUAGE is viewed as a network of systems of this kind. See Bolinger 1975: Ch. 15.

environment (1) A general term used in LINGUISTICS and PHONETICS to refer to specific parts of an UTTERANCE (or TEXT) near or adjacent to a UNIT which is the focus of attention. Features of the linguistic environment may influence the selection of a particular unit, at a given place in an utterance, and thus restrict its occurrence, or DISTRIBUTION. For example, in PHONOLOGY, whether a CONSONANT PHONEME is lip-ROUNDED or not may depend on the presence of a rounded VOWEL in its phonetic environment. Sounds are referred to as being 'conditioned' by their environment. In GRAMMAR, the term is used similarly, e.g. the occurrence of one MORPHEME may depend on the prior use of another in its environment, as with *cran-*, which occurs only in the grammatical environment of *-berry*. In recent years, the term CONTEXT has come to be widely used in this sense. See Bolinger 1975: Ch. 4.

(2) Particularly in the phrase **linguistic environment**, the term refers to the SOCIOLINGUISTIC situation in relation to which a particular observation is being made. In language ACQUISITION, for example, a particular STRUCTURE might be said to appear at age two, 'regardless of the linguistic environment of the child', i.e. disregarding the kind of language he is used to hearing in his social situation. The term CONTEXT is sometimes used in this sense also. See Gumperz & Hymes 1972: Ch. 1.

epenthesis (epenthetic) A term used in PHONETICS and PHONOLOGY to refer to a type of INTRUSION, where an extra sound has been inserted medially in a WORD. The phenomenon is common both in HISTORICAL change and in CONNECTED SPEECH (e.g. *incredible* as /ɪŋkᵊredɪbl/). See Bolinger 1975: Ch. 12.

epistemic A term derived from modal logic and used by some LINGUISTS as part of a theoretical framework for the analysis of MODAL VERBS and related STRUCTURES in LANGUAGE. 'Epistemic logic' is concerned with the logical structure of statements which assert or imply that PROPOSITIONS are known or believed, e.g. the use of modals in SENTENCES such as *the car must be ready*, i.e. 'it is surely the case that the car is ready'. It contrasts with ALETHIC and DEONTIC modality, which would interpret this sentence respectively as 'it follows that the car is ready' and 'I oblige you to ensure that the car is ready'. See Lyons 1977b: Ch. 17.

equative (equational) (1) A term used in GRAMMATICAL analysis to refer to a type of SENTENCE where the REFERENTS of the pre-verbal and post-verbal NOUN PHRASES are in a relationship of identity, e.g. *Fred is the leader*. The VERB which links these ELEMENTS may be called an **equational verb** (or a verb with 'equative' function) – usually in English a form of the COPULA verb *be*. Some LANGUAGES (e.g. Russian) have equative sentences where the copula is not present – cf. the stereotyped language of film primitives (*him Tarzan*, etc.). See Lyons 1968: Ch. 8; 1977b: Ch. 12.

(2) Some grammatical descriptions recognise an 'equative' DEGREE, in analysing comparison between ADJECTIVES or ADVERBS, e.g. *as big as*. See Quirk *et al* 1972: Ch. 5.

equi NP deletion An OBLIGATORY RULE in TRANSFORMATIONAL SYNTAX, usually abbreviated to **Equi**, which deletes a NOUN PHRASE from a COMPLEMENT CLAUSE in a SENTENCE when it is identical in meaning (COREFERENTIAL) with another noun phrase in the main clause of the same sentence. An example is *John wants to see the film*, derivable in one analysis from *John wants something* and *John sees the film*. When these two UNDERLYING sentences are put together, a resultant structure such as *John wants for John to see the film* requires that the second *John* be deleted. See Akmajian & Heny 1975: Ch. 8; Huddleston 1976: Ch. 8.

equipollent A type of OPPOSITION recognised in PRAGUE SCHOOL PHONOLOGY, distinguished from PRIVATIVE and GRADUAL. An equipollent opposition is one where the members are seen as logically equivalent to each other, contrasted neither gradually nor by a BINARY FEATURE; e.g. the DISTINCTION between /p/ and /k/ cannot be analysed, according to Nikolai Trubetskoy, as a difference along a single PHONETIC continuum, nor can /p/ be seen as 'non-VELAR', or /k/ as 'non-BILABIAL'. See Hyman 1975: Ch. 2.

equivalence (equivalent) A relationship of equality of POWER between GRAMMARS. Grammars which GENERATE the same set of SENTENCES are said to be 'equivalent' or 'weakly equivalent'. Grammars which generate the same set of PHRASE-MARKERS are 'strongly equivalent', i.e. they generate not only the same sentences but assign the same STRUCTURAL DESCRIPTIONS to each. Grammars which display differences in the LABELLING or BRACKETING of structures, or which generate different sets of sentences, are said to be 'non-equivalent'. The term is also used in other SYNTACTIC and SEMANTIC contexts, e.g. 'DISTRIBUTIONAL equivalence' (between units with the same distribution), 'semantic equivalence' (i.e. SYNONYMY). See Lyons 1968: Ch. 6; 1977a: App.

ergative (ergativity) A term used in the GRAMMATICAL description of some languages, such as Eskimo and Basque, where a term is needed to handle CONSTRUCTIONS where there is a formal parallel between the OBJECT of a TRANSITIVE VERB and the SUBJECT of an intransitive one (i.e. they display the same CASE). The concept of 'ergativity' has also been applied to English and other languages by some LINGUISTS, though the formal markers of the relationships involved are less clear. In this approach, SENTENCES such as *the window broke* and *the man broke the window* would be analysed 'ergatively': the subject of the intransitive use of *broke* is the same as the object of its transitive use, and the AGENT of the action is thus said to appear as the 'ergative subject'. See Lyons 1968: Ch. 8.

error (1) A term used in PSYCHOLINGUISTICS referring to mistakes in spontaneous speaking or writing attributable to a malfunctioning of the neuromuscular commands from the brain. It is thus distinct from the traditional notion of error, which was based on the LANGUAGE user's ability to conform to a set of real or imagined standards of expression. Several types of psycholinguistic error have been recognised. 'Speaker's errors', involving difficulties with the timing or sequence of commands, will lead to the addition, deletion or substitution of sounds and MORPHEMES – and is most noticeable in the phenomenon labelled 'slips of the tongue' (re-labelled by some psycholinguists, 'slips of the brain'), and in the false starts, PAUSES, and other non-fluencies of everyday speech. 'Hearer's errors' are particularly noticeable in language ACQUISITION, as when a child mis-analyses an adult SENTENCE (e.g. A: *He's got his hat on* C: *Where's his hat on*), and in the history of language, where new forms have come from a re-analysis (or 'metanalysis') of older ones (e.g. *a napron → an apron*). The distinction between 'errors' of PRODUCTION and PERCEPTION is sometimes hard to draw, however – especially as often the only evidence for the latter is the former – and, generally, the term 'error' should be used with caution, especially in language acquisition studies, where it can be easily confused with the pedagogical notion of 'error' (in the context of essay marking, etc.). See Bolinger 1975: Ch. 12; Clark & Clark 1977: Ch. 7.

(2) In language teaching and learning, **error analysis** is a technique for identifying, classifying and systematically interpreting the mistakes made by someone learning a foreign language, using any of the principles and procedures provided by LINGUISTICS. See Corder 1973: Ch. 11.

état de langue A term introduced into LINGUISTICS by the Swiss linguist, Ferdinand de SAUSSURE, referring to a 'state of a language' seen as if at a particular point in time, regardless of its antecedents or subsequent history. An *état de langue* is therefore the primary subject-matter of SYNCHRONIC linguistic study. See Lyons 1968: Ch. 1.

ethnolinguistics (ethnography of communication) A branch of LINGUISTICS which studies LANGUAGE in relation to the investigation of ethnic types and behaviour. The term overlaps to some degree with ANTHROPOLOGICAL LINGUISTICS and SOCIOLINGUISTICS, reflecting the overlapping interests of the correlative disciplines involved – ethnology, anthropology and sociology. Recently, the phrase **ethnography of communication** has been applied by sociolinguists to the study of language in relation to the entire range of extra-linguistic variables which identify the social basis of communication, the emphasis being on the description of linguistic interaction. The student of such matters is known as an 'ethnolinguist'. See Gumperz & Hymes 1972: Ch. 1; Robins 1971: Ch. 9.

etymology (etymo-n, -logical) The term traditionally used for the study of the origins and history of the FORM and MEANING of WORDS. Insofar as etymology derives its methods from LINGUISTICS (especially SEMANTICS), it may be seen as a branch of HISTORICAL LINGUISTICS. The linguistic form from which a later form derives is known as its 'etymon'. A 'folk etymology' occurs when a word is assumed to come from a particular etymon, because of some association of form or meaning, whereas in fact the word has a different DERIVATION, e.g. *spit and image* becomes *spitting image*. The **etymological fallacy** is the view that an earlier (or the oldest) meaning of a word is the correct one (e.g. that *history* 'really' means 'investigation', because this was the meaning the etymon had in Classical Greek). This view is commonly held, but it contrasts with the attitude of the linguist, who emphasises the need to describe the meanings of modern words as they are now,

exclamation

and not as they once may have been in some earlier state of the language (the 'oldest' state, of course, being unknown). See Bolinger 1975: Ch. 12.

exclamation (exclamatory) A term used in the classification of SEN-TENCE FUNCTIONS, and defined sometimes on GRAMMATICAL and sometimes on SEMANTIC or SOCIOLINGUISTIC grounds. Traditionally, an exclamation referred to any emotional UTTERANCE, usually lacking the grammatical structure of a full SENTENCE, and marked by strong INTONATION, e.g. *Gosh!, Good grief!* In some grammars, 'exclamatory sentences' have a more restricted definition, referring to constructions which begin with *what* or *how* without a following INVERSION of SUBJECT and VERB, e.g. *What a fool he was!, How nice!* Semantically, the function is primarily the expression of the speaker's feelings – a function which may also be expressed using other grammatical means, e.g. *What on earth is he doing?* (when it is obvious what is being done). The term is usually contrasted with three other major sentence functions: STATEMENT, QUESTION and COMMAND. See Quirk *et al* 1972: Ch. 7.

exhaustiveness A principle of LINGUISTIC analysis whereby the aim is to specify totally the linguistic CONTRASTS in a set of DATA, and ultimately in the LANGUAGE as a whole. It is often cited as one of three scientific principles to be adhered to in linguistics, the others being logical self-consistency and ECONOMY. See Robins 1971: Ch. 1.

existential A term used in the GRAMMATICAL description of CLAUSE or SENTENCE types, referring to a type of STRUCTURE commencing with the unstressed word *there* followed by a form of the verb *be*, the notion of existence thereby being expressed, e.g. *there's plenty to do, there are three cats on the wall.* The relationship between such sentences and others (cf. *three cats are on the wall, the wall has three cats on it*, etc.) has attracted particular interest in LINGUISTICS, especially in TRANSFORMATIONAL grammar. Several types of existential sentences have been recognised (including some where other forms than *there* and *be* are involved, e.g. *she has a meal ready* and *there exist several such figures*), and the relationship between these and other SEMANTIC categories (such as location and possession) is considered to be an important aspect of the investigation of UNIVERSAL grammatical FUNCTIONS. See Quirk *et al* 1972: Ch. 4; Lyons 1968: Ch. 8.

exocentric A term used in GRAMMATICAL analysis as part of a two-way classification of SYNTACTIC CONSTRUCTIONS using DISTRIBUTIONAL criteria: it refers to a group of syntactically related WORDS where none of the words is FUNCTIONALLY equivalent to the group as a whole (i.e. there is no definable 'centre' or HEAD inside the group); it is opposed to ENDOCENTRIC. The English basic SENTENCE structure of SUBJECT + PREDICATE is exocentric, by this definition (a 'PREDICATIVE exocentric construction'), as neither part can substitute for the sentence structure as a whole, e.g. *the man fell* cannot be replaced by either *the man* or by *fell* alone. Other types include 'DIRECTIVE constructions', such as PREPOSITION + NOUN phrase sequences (e.g. *on the table*), where the ADVERBIAL function of the whole is not equivalent to any of its parts; VERB + OBJECT sequences (e.g. *kick the ball*); and 'CONNECTIVE constructions', where a connector ELEMENT is followed by an ATTRIBUTIVE element (e.g. *seemed angry*). See Robins 1971: Ch. 6; Lyons 1968: Ch. 6.

exophora (exophoric) A term used by some GRAMMARIANS to refer to the process or result of a LINGUISTIC UNIT referring directly (i.e. DEICTICALLY) to the extra-linguistic SITUATION accompanying an UTTERANCE, e.g. *there, that, him*. 'Exophoric reference' is usually contrasted with ANAPHORIC and CATAPHORIC reference. See Lyons 1977b: Ch. 15.

expansion A GRAMMATICAL process in which new ELEMENTS are added to a CONSTRUCTION without its basic STRUCTURE being affected, e.g. the addition of ADJECTIVES before a NOUN, or AUXILIARIES before a VERB. In GENERATIVE grammar, REWRITE RULES are sometimes called 'expansion rules', by virtue of the fact that a single symbol is 'expanded' into a STRING of symbols which represent its CONSTITUENT structure (e.g. VP → V + NP). The term is also found in broader senses, referring to any process whereby an initial LINGUISTIC STATE is enlarged, e.g. in historical SEMANTICS a WORD's earlier meaning may come to be 'expanded' to cover a wider range of REFERENTS (e.g. Modern English *gay*); in SOCIOLINGUISTICS, a LANGUAGE or VARIETY may come to be used in new situations, thus 'expanding' its influence (e.g. through LOAN words). See Lyons 1968: Ch. 6.

experiencer A term used in later versions of CASE GRAMMAR (cf. earlier use of DATIVE) to refer to the case of an entity or person affected by the action or state expressed by the VERB, as in **The man** *heard a bang*, *He kicked* **a ball**. See Clark & Clark 1977: Ch. 8.

explanatory A term used in GENERATIVE LINGUISTICS to refer to a level of achievement in the writing of GRAMMARS. **Explanatory adequacy**

explicit

is achieved when a principled basis is established for deciding the relative merits of alternative grammars, all of which are DESCRIPTIVELY ADEQUATE (i.e. they account for the NATIVE-SPEAKER'S COMPETENCE). Several criteria have been suggested for FORMALISING this notion, of which relative SIMPLICITY is the most investigated. See Huddleston 1976: Ch. 1.

explicit(ness) A characteristic of formulations in LINGUISTICS – and especially a primary goal of GENERATIVE analysis – whereby all the properties of a RULE and the conditions under which it operates are specified fully and precisely. In this sense, explicit descriptions contrast with several found in TRADITIONAL grammar, which were often ambiguous, or needed prior knowledge on the part of the NATIVE SPEAKER to be interpreted (as in the definition of NOUNS as names of persons, places and things, where it is up to the LANGUAGE user to decide whether a particular ITEM qualifies). See Lyons 1968: Ch. 4; 1977a: Ch. 4.

exponent (exponence) A concept in a HIERARCHICAL LINGUISTIC analysis, referring to the relationship of correspondence between an abstract linguistic UNIT at a higher LEVEL of analysis and the units occurring at a lower level. For example, WORDS can be said to have PHONOLOGICAL units (such as PHONEMES) as their 'exponents', and the exponents of the latter are PHONETIC features. The term REPRESENTATION is an equivalent. In this sense, abstract units are expounded by other abstract units or by physical units.

An alternative emphasis restricts the application of the term to the physical expression of any abstract unit (i.e. at any LEVEL), e.g. a MORPH being the exponent of a MORPHEME, a PHONE of a PHONEME, a particular FORMATIVE (such as -s) of a SYNTACTIC CATEGORY (such as 'plural'), the item *going* of the LEXEME *go*. There are plainly many possible types of exponence-relationships (e.g. to handle the 'fusion' or 'overlapping' of exponents). This sense of the term receives a specific technical status in HALLIDAYAN linguistic theory (cf. SYSTEMIC grammar), referring to one of the SCALES of analysis which interrelates the CATEGORIES of the theory, *viz* the relationship postulated between these categories and the raw DATA. For example, the LEXICAL item *boy* is an instance of (an 'exponent' of) the CLASS of NOUNS. Other scales in this approach are labelled RANK and DELICACY. See Robins 1971: Chs. 2, 7; Matthews 1974: Ch. 8.

expression (1) This term is used in a general sense in LINGUISTICS, referring to a STRING OF ELEMENTS treated as a UNIT for purposes of analysis and discussion: expressions have both a GRAMMATICAL and a LEXICAL character, and are definable in terms of both, e.g. the expression *so be it* can be analysed as a sequence both of FORM-CLASSES and of lexical ITEMS. Expressions can then be investigated in terms of their SEMANTIC properties, as is carried on in philosophical and logical discussion (through such notions as 'referring' and 'predicative expression'), and as is increasingly the case in linguistics. See Lyons 1977b: Chs. 1, 11.

(2) The term is also found in the SAUSSUREAN distinction between 'expression' (or NORM) and CONTENT (or MEANING): 'expression' here refers to all aspects of linguistic FORM, i.e. sounds and their grammatical SEQUENCES. A more restricted sense equates 'expression' solely with the LEVEL of linguistic organisation of SUBSTANCE, i.e. PHONOLOGY and GRAPHOLOGY. The abstract formal UNITS which are realised either in PHONIC or in GRAPHIC SUBSTANCE are sometimes referred to as 'expression-elements', e.g. the expression element /s/ is realised PHONETICALLY as [s] and GRAPHETICALLY as *s*, *ss*, etc. See Lyons 1968: Ch. 2.

expressive A term sometimes used in SEMANTICS as part of a classification of types of MEANING. The 'expressive meaning' of an EXPRESSION refers both to its emotional CONTENT and to any identity it might have in terms of the personality or individual creativity of the user (as in much poetic LANGUAGE). It is usually contrasted with DESCRIPTIVE and 'social' meaning. Other terms which overlap with 'expressive' include AFFECTIVE, CONNOTATIVE and EMOTIVE. The term is also used in the theory of SPEECH ACTS to refer to a type of UTTERANCE where the speaker expresses his feelings, e.g. *I apologise/sympathise/regret*. See Lyons 1977b: Ch. 2; Clark & Clark 1977: Ch. 3.

extended standard theory The name given to a MODEL of GENERATIVE GRAMMAR which developed in the early 1970s out of that expounded in Noam CHOMSKY's *Aspects of the Theory of Syntax* (1965) (the STANDARD THEORY). The 'extension' is primarily due to the range of the SEMANTIC RULES, some of which Chomsky suggested should now be allowed to operate with SURFACE STRUCTURE as input. Features of surface structure relevant to the semantics include various functions of STRESS and INTONATION, aspects of QUANTIFICATION, and the FOCUS in a sentence which provides information concerning the sentence's PRESUPPOSITIONS. In other words, it was no longer the case that only the DEEP STRUCTURE was the determinant of the semantic REPRESEN-TATION of a sentence. In a later development of this view, it is argued that perhaps the notion of deep structure can be dispensed with

extension

altogether, in relation to the semantics, this being determined by a developed notion of surface structure. See Lyons 1977a: Ch. 8; Huddleston 1976: Ch. 16.

extension(al) A term in philosophy and logic, and now often used as part of a theoretical framework for LINGUISTIC SEMANTICS, to refer to the class of entities to which a WORD is correctly applied. For example, the extension (or 'extensional meaning') of the term *flower* would be a list of all the entities referred to by the term, e.g. *daffodil*, *rose*, *fuchsia*... 'Extension' is opposed to 'intension', which includes only the defining properties of terms. See Lyons 1977b: Ch. 6.

extensive A term used in some GRAMMATICAL analyses to refer to structures where there is no close SEMANTIC relationship between elements of structure, such as SUBJECT and OBJECT (e.g. *he kicked the dog*) or DIRECT and INDIRECT object (e.g. *he gave me a letter*). **Extensive verbs** are either TRANSITIVE or intransitive, and are contrasted with INTENSIVE verbs, such as *be*. See Quirk *et al* 1972: Chs. 2, 7.

extralinguistic In its most general sense, this term refers to anything in the world (other than LANGUAGE) in relation to which language is used – the 'extralinguistic situation'. The term 'extralinguistic features' is used both generally, to refer to any properties of such situations, and also specifically, to refer to properties of communication which are not clearly analysable in LINGUISTIC terms, e.g. gestures, tones of voice. Some linguists refer to the former class of features as METALINGUISTIC: others refer to the latter class as PARALINGUISTIC. See Robins 1971: Ch. 1; Lyons 1977b: Ch. 3.

extraposition A term used in GRAMMATICAL analysis to refer to a process of moving (or 'extraposing') an ELEMENT from its normal position to a position at or near the end of the main SENTENCE, e.g. *that the boy came in late upset the teacher*, compared with *it upset the teacher that the boy came in late*. The *it* which is introduced in such sentences is known as 'extrapositive *it*'. See Quirk *et al* 1972: Ch. 14; Akmajian & Heny 1975: Ch. 8.

extrinsic A term used in GENERATIVE grammar referring to a type of constraint imposed on the ORDERING OF RULES (as opposed to a condition where such rules are allowed to apply in a random order). An extrinsic ordering is one where the SEQUENCE of rules is motivated solely by a consideration of the facts of a LANGUAGE and not by considerations of a logical kind: it is a specific ordering which is required to ensure that only GRAMMATICAL sentences are generated. Extrinsic rules are held by many to be of particular importance in organising the TRANSFORMATIONAL rules in a grammar, but the nature of these CONSTRAINTS is controversial, such as how much extrinsic ordering there ought to be, and how many times the rules in an ordered sequence should apply. See Akmajian & Heny 1975: Ch. 6; Huddleston 1975: Ch. 12; Hyman 1975: Ch. 4.

F

𑀟𑀟𑀟𑀟𑀟𑀟

factitive A term used in GRAMMATICAL description to refer to a CONSTRUCTION or FORM (usually a VERB) denoting an action in which a cause produces a result, e.g. *make, kill, choose, elect* could be called 'factitive verbs'. In CASE grammar, the term has special status, where it refers to the SEMANTIC case of the entity resulting from the verb's action, or understood as part of the verb's meaning, and is contrasted with AGENTIVE, DATIVE, etc. See Lyons 1977b: Ch. 12; Bolinger 1975: Ch. 15.

factive (factivity) A term used in the CLASSIFICATION of VERBS, referring to a verb which takes a COMPLEMENT CLAUSE, and where the speaker PRESUPPOSES the truth of the PROPOSITION expressed in that clause. For example, *know, agree, realise,* etc. are 'factive verbs': in *he knows that the cat is in the garden*, the speaker presupposes that the cat is in the garden. 'Factive predicators' may involve other clauses than verbs: ADJECTIVES and NOUN CONSTRUCTIONS, for example, may display 'factivity', as in *it's surprising that he came, it's a shame that he came*. By contrast, **non-factive** constructions do not commit the speaker to the truth of the proposition expressed in the complement-clause, e.g. *believe, think,* as in *he thinks that the cat is in the garden*. **Contra-factive** constructions presuppose the falsity of the proposition expressed in the complement clause, e.g. *wish, hope,* as in *I'd hoped the cat was in the garden*. See Lyons 1977b: Chs. 14, 17.

falling/fall (1) A term used in classifying the linguistic uses of PITCH, referring to a movement from relatively high to relatively low. Falling tones of various kinds (e.g. 'high/low falling', 'falling-rising') may be encountered in the study of INTONATION systems and of TONE LANGUAGES. See Bolinger 1975: Ch. 3.

(2) A term used in a two-way classification of DIPHTHONGS (opposed to RISING), referring to cases where the first ELEMENT of the diphthong receives the maximum PROMINENCE. See Gimson 1970: Ch. 7.

family A term used in HISTORICAL LINGUISTIC studies to characterise a genetic MODEL of the relationships between LANGUAGES. A 'family' of languages is the set of languages deriving from a common ancestor, or 'parent', e.g. the Indo-European family consists of the 'daughter' languages Sanskrit, Greek, Latin, etc. which all developed out of Proto-Indo-European. The **family tree** is a representation of these relationships devised by COMPARATIVE PHILOLOGISTS in the 19th century. See Bolinger 1975: Ch. 13; Robins 1971: Ch. 8.

favourite (non-) A term used by some LINGUISTS in the CLASSIFICATION of SENTENCE types to refer to the most PRODUCTIVE sentence pattern in a LANGUAGE. In English, the SUBJECT + PREDICATE (NP + VP) pattern is the favourite (or MAJOR) type, other types being referred to as **non-favourite** (or MINOR). See Quirk *et al* 1972: Ch. 2.

feature A term used in LINGUISTICS and PHONETICS to refer to any typical or noticeable property of spoken or written LANGUAGE. Features are classified in terms of the various LEVELS of linguistic analysis, e.g. 'PHONETIC/PHONOLOGICAL/GRAMMATICAL features' or in terms of a dimension of DESCRIPTION, e.g. 'ACOUSTIC/ARTICULATORY/AUDITORY features'. At the most general level, features may be classified as linguistic (or 'intralinguistic') as opposed to 'non-linguistic' (EXTRA-LINGUISTIC or METALINGUISTIC). At the most specific level, certain types of feature may be set up as the minimal UNITS of a theory, as in **distinctive feature** theories of phonology. In GENERATIVE grammatical analysis, the term has come to be associated with the way in which words are classified in the LEXICON in terms of their grammatical properties, such as [animate], [common], [masculine], [countable]. Such features are usually considered to be BINARY, as were phonological features, and analysed as [+ animate], [− animate], etc. SEMANTIC features, likewise, can be handled in binary terms, as in the analysis of *spinster* as [+ human], [+ adult], [+ never married] and [+ female] (or, perhaps, [− male]). Features are sometimes referred to as COMPONENTS, especially in semantic analysis. See Lyons 1968: Ch. 7; Hyman 1975: Ch. 2.

feedback An extension of the technical use of this term in COMMUNICATION theory, referring to the process whereby the sender of a message obtains a reaction from his receiver which enables him to check on the efficiency of his communication. More specifically, some LINGUISTS have suggested it as a defining property of human LANGUAGE (contrasting with the properties of other SEMIOTIC SYSTEMS), whereby speakers are able to monitor their own PERFORMANCE (both by self-observation, and by observing the response-signals of others). The term **complete feedback** is usually used for this property, when it is seen as a 'design feature' of language. In PHONETICS, the speaker's awareness of his own production of sounds is also referred to as feedback: this may be AUDITORY (via the ear), kinaesthetic (via the internal sensation of ARTICULATORY movement) or vibratory (via bone conduction). **Delayed auditory feedback** (DAF) takes place when a delay is artificially introduced into the transmission of speech between mouth and ear, so that the signal reaches the ear somewhat later than is normally the case. Certain periods of delay cause marked alteration in one's ability to speak with normal fluency; conversely, the speech of stammerers can often be improved by using this technique. See Lyons 1977b: Ch. 3.

feeding A term used in GENERATIVE LINGUISTIC analysis of RULE-ordering and originally introduced in the context of HISTORICAL PHONOLOGY, to refer to a type of FUNCTIONAL relationship between rules; opposed to BLEEDING. A feeding relationship is one where the application of one rule (A) creates a STRUCTURAL REPRESENTATION to which another rule (B) is applicable. If rule B is X → Y, then rule A must be of the form W → X. In these circumstances, rule A is called a **feeding rule** in relation to B, and the LINEAR ORDER of these rules is called a **feeding order**. See Hyman 1975: Ch. 4.

felicity conditions A term used in the theory of SPEECH-ACTS to refer to the criteria which must be satisfied if the speech act is to achieve its purpose. Several kinds of felicity conditions have been suggested. 'Preparatory conditions' relate to whether the person performing a speech act has the authority to do so (e.g. not everyone is qualified to fine, christen, arrest, etc.). 'Sincerity conditions' relate to whether the speech act is performed sincerely (e.g. the speaker is not lying). 'Essential conditions' relate to the way the speaker is committed to a certain kind of belief or behaviour, having performed a speech act (e.g. accepting an object that one has just requested). For example, felicity conditions which have been suggested for the analysis of indirect requests include the speaker believing that his hearer has the ability to carry out his request, and the existence of good reasons for making the request in the first place. An UTTERANCE which does not satisfy these conditions cannot function as a valid instance of the type of speech act to which they apply, e.g. *will you drive?* is inappropriate as a request if the speaker knows that his hearer has not learned to drive, and the mutual awareness of this inappropriateness would lead

to an interpretation of a different order (e.g. as a joke, as sarcasm, etc.).
See Lyons 1977b: Ch. 16; Clark & Clark 1977: Ch. 3.

field (1) A term used in SEMANTICS to refer to the vocabulary of a
LANGUAGE viewed as a SYSTEM of interrelated LEXICAL networks, and
not as an inventory of independent ITEMS. The theory of **semantic
fields** ('field theory') was developed in Europe in the 1930s (especially
by Jost Trier (b. 1894), and later Johann Weisgerber (b. 1899)).
Conceptual fields (e.g. colour, kinship) are isolated, and the lexical
items used to refer to the various features of these fields are analysed
in terms of a network of SENSE relations. This network constitutes the
lexical STRUCTURE of the semantic (or 'lexical') field. Several
interpretations of this notion can be found in the semantics literature
of the period. See Lyons 1977b: Ch. 8; Robins 1971: Ch. 2.

(2) In HALLIDAYAN linguistics, **field of discourse** (or simply,
'field') refers to a classification of REGISTERS in terms of subject matter,
e.g. the 'fields' of chemistry, religion, advertising. See Bolinger 1975:
Chs. 11, 15.

(3) The usual sense of the term **field-work** (or 'field study') is also
used in LINGUISTICS, referring to the principles and procedures of
obtaining linguistic DATA from INFORMANTS, especially in their home
environment. See Robins 1971: Ch. 9; Gumperz & Hymes 1971:
Intro.

(4) In TAGMEMICS, the term refers to the analysis of linguistic UNITS
in terms of their DISTRIBUTION – as distinct from their status as
PARTICLES (physically DISCRETE items) or WAVES (their VARIANT
forms). See Bolinger 1975: Ch. 15.

filled pause A term used by some LINGUISTS to refer to a non-silent
PAUSE, i.e. a hesitation which has been 'filled' by *er*, *erm*, or some such
VOCALISATION. See Clark & Clark 1977: Ch. 7.

filler A term used in some MODELS of LINGUISTIC analysis, especially
TAGMEMICS, to refer to a FORM which can be used at a given place, or
SLOT, in STRUCTURE. See Bolinger 1975: Ch. 15.

filter A process recognised in some MODELS of GENERATIVE GRAMMAR
(cf. ASPECTS), whereby in a DERIVATION only certain BASE PHRASE-
MARKERS are transformed into SURFACE STRUCTURES, others being
'filtered out' by the application of various CONSTRAINTS (specified, for
example, by the non-lexical TRANSFORMATIONS). See Huddleston 1976:
Ch. 12; Lyons 1977a: App.

final The usual way of referring to the last ELEMENT in a LINGUISTIC UNIT, especially in PHONOLOGY. For example, the PHONEME /t/ occurs 'in final position' (or 'finally') in the WORD *cat*; the MORPHEME of plurality occurs in final position in English words. Other positions are referred to as INITIAL and MEDIAL. See Gimson 1971: Ch. 5.

finite A term used in the GRAMMATICAL classification of types of VERBS and CLAUSES. A finite verb(-phrase) is a form that can occur on its own in an independent SENTENCE (or MAIN clause): it permits FORMAL CONTRASTS in TENSE and MOOD. **Non-finite** forms of the verb, on the other hand, occur on their own only in DEPENDENT clauses, and lack tense and mood contrasts. All forms except the INFINITIVES and PARTICIPLES (*-ing* and *-en* forms) are finite, e.g. *is walking, have walked, walks*. Clauses which contain a finite verb are 'finite clauses' (these always contain a SUBJECT, except in the case of COMMANDS); otherwise, they are non-finite clauses (e.g. *walking down the street, to kick the ball*). See Quirk *et al* 1972: Chs. 3, 11.

finite state grammar A type of GRAMMAR discussed by Noam CHOMSKY in his book *Syntactic Structures* (1957) as an illustration of a simple GENERATIVE DEVICE. Finite state grammars generate by working through a SENTENCE 'from left to right'; an INITIAL ELEMENT is selected, and thereafter the possibilities of occurrence of all other elements are wholly determined by the nature of the elements preceding them. For example, in the sentence *the cat saw the dog*, the grammar would start by specifying the first WORD (i.e. selecting one of the set of possible first words for a sentence in English), would proceed from this 'initial state' to specify the next word (i.e. one of the set of words which can follow *the*), and continue this process until the 'final state' of the sentence has been arrived at. Chomsky shows how this extremely simple kind of grammar is incapable of accounting for many important processes of sentence formation, as in DISCONTINUOUS CONSTRUCTIONS, e.g. *the boys who saw John are coming*, where the grammatical relationship of *boys* to *are* cannot be handled in a finite state grammar. Alternative grammars are discussed by Chomsky which improve on this MODEL in several respects (cf. PHRASE-STRUCTURE and TRANSFORMATIONAL grammars). See Lyons 1977a: Ch. 5.

Firthian Characteristic of, or a follower of, the LINGUISTIC principles of J. R. Firth (1890–1960), Professor of General Linguistics in the University of London (1944–1956), and the formative influence on the development of linguistics in Great Britain. A central notion is POLYSYSTEMICISM, an approach to linguistic analysis based on the view that LANGUAGE patterns cannot be accounted for in terms of a single system of analytic principles and categories (MONOsystemic linguistics), but that different SYSTEMS may need to be set up at different places within a given LEVEL of DESCRIPTION. Other central Firthian notions include his CONTEXTUAL theory of MEANING, with its strong emphasis on the social CONTEXT OF SITUATION; PROSODIC (as opposed to PHONEMIC) PHONOLOGY, and COLLOCATION. Relatively little of Firth's teaching was published, but many of his ideas have been developed by a **neo-Firthian** group of scholars, whose main theoretician is M. A. K. Halliday, Professor of General Linguistics in the University of London from 1965 to 1970 (cf. HALLIDAYAN). See Robins 1971: Ch. 1; Bolinger 1975: Ch. 15.

'fis' phenomenon A commonly used name for a behaviour recognised in language ACQUISITION, in which a child refuses to accept an adult's IMITATION of his own mispronunciation. The name derives from the first report of this behaviour in the early 1960s, since when, several other such names have been used (e.g. the 'wabbit' phenomenon). An investigator referred to a child's toy fish as his /fɪs/, imitating the child's form; the child refused to accept the adult's pronunciation of /fɪs/, despite the fact that his own version was identical. Such phenomena are interpreted as evidence for a more well-developed PERCEPTUAL than PRODUCTIVE LINGUISTIC ability in the young child, some investigators concluding that it is in fact the adult PHONOLOGICAL form which is stored in the child's brain. See Clark & Clark 1977: Ch. 10.

fixed A term used in LINGUISTICS and PHONETICS to refer to an unchanging aspect of the STRUCTURE of a linguistic UNIT; opposed to FREE. It occurs in such phrases as 'fixed STRESS' (i.e. the stress always falling on a particular SYLLABLE in a WORD, e.g. the penultimate syllable in Welsh) and 'fixed word ORDER' (i.e. languages with word order patterns that cannot be altered without a change of MEANING, e.g. English). See Hyman 1975: Ch. 6.

flap(ped) A term used in the PHONETIC classification of CONSONANT sounds on the basis of their MANNER OF ARTICULATION; it refers to any sound produced by a single rapid contact between two organs of articulation (excluding VOCAL CORD vibration). The usual occurrence of this is in the production of types of r sound, as when in English *very*, the r is produced by the TIP of the TONGUE in a 'flapped' articulation against the ALVEOLAR ridge (transcribed [ɾ]). The main PHONETIC contrast is between this sound and the TRILL, where several vibrations are involved. Some phoneticians distinguish systematically between flaps and TAPS, on the grounds that in the case of flaps, the articulator which makes the contact is returning to a position of rest, whereas in the case of taps, this is not so, and the contact resembles a very rapid STOP articulation. Such a distinction has been cited for Hausa and Tamil, but it is not common. See Gimson 1970: Chs. 4, 8; Ladefoged 1975: Ch. 7.

flat One of the features of sound set up by JAKOBSON & Halle in their DISTINCTIVE FEATURE theory of PHONOLOGY, to handle lip-ROUNDING, the opposite being PLAIN. Flat sounds are defined ARTICULATORILY and ACOUSTICALLY, as those involving a relatively narrow mouth opening with accompanying velarisation (cf. VELAR), and a weakening of the high frequency components of the sound spectrum. Lip-ROUNDED sounds all have the feature [+flat], as would RETROFLEX, velarised and pharyngealised (cf. PHARYNX) sounds; unrounded sounds are [−flat], as are all sounds lacking these SECONDARY ARTICULATIONS. See Hyman 1975: Ch. 2.

focus A term used by some LINGUISTS in a two-part analysis of SENTENCES which distinguishes between the INFORMATION assumed by the speaker, and that which is at the centre (or 'focus') of his communicative interest; 'focus' in this sense is opposed to PRESUPPOSITION. (The CONTRAST between GIVEN and NEW information makes an analogous distinction.) For example, in the sentence *It was Jòhn who came to tea*, *John* is the focus (as the INTONATION contour helps to signal). Taking such factors into account is an important aspect of inter-sentence relationships: it would not be possible to have the above sentence as the answer to the question *What did John do?*, but only to *Who came to tea?* See Lyons 1977b; Ch. 12.

foot A term used by some PHONETICIANS and PHONOLOGISTS to describe the UNIT of RHYTHM in LANGUAGES displaying ISOCHRONY, i.e. where the STRESSED SYLLABLES fall at approximately regular intervals throughout an UTTERANCE. It is an extension of the term used in traditional studies of metrical verse structure, where the many regular patterns of stressed/unstressed syllable sequence were given a detailed classification (e.g. 'iambic' for an unstressed + stressed (◡ /) pattern; 'trochaic' for a stressed + unstressed (/ ◡) pattern; 'spondaic' for a pattern of two stresses; 'dactylic' for / ◡ ◡; 'anapaestic' for ◡ ◡ /). In a more general phonological sense, the notion is applied to any utterance in a STRESS-TIMED language, not just verse. The rhythm of an utterance, in this approach, is analysed first in terms of INTONATION units, and these are analysed into feet, e.g. /the 'man is 'walking in the gàrden/ is a single TONE-UNIT consisting of three feet. See Catford 1977: Ch. 5; Abercrombie 1967: Ch. 6.

form(al) One of the most widely used terms in LINGUISTICS, with a correspondingly wide range of meanings. Its main areas of application are:

(1) **form** vs. **meaning/function**. In its most general sense, it refers to the abstract PHONOLOGICAL and/or GRAMMATICAL characterisation of LANGUAGE, as opposed to its MEANING, as in such phrases as 'linguistic form', 'grammatical form'. More specifically, it refers to the phonological/grammatical/LEXICAL characteristics of linguistic UNITS, such as SENTENCES, MORPHEMES, LEXEMES, NOUNS, etc., these being referred to as **linguistic forms**. The term here is often contrasted with FUNCTION: one can study a unit such as the noun PHRASE from both formal and functional points of view (e.g. its internal syntactic structure vs. its role as SUBJECT, OBJECT, etc. in a clause). More specifically still, it refers to a particular instance of a grammatical CATEGORY, as in such phrases as 'the analysis of the forms *be, seem, have...*' A set of forms displaying similar or identical grammatical FEATURES is said to constitute a **form-class**, e.g. *walk, come, see* are part of the form-CLASS of VERBS because they have similar MORPHOLOGICAL characteristics and SYNTACTIC DISTRIBUTION. Phonological/grammatical criteria which identify units and classes are known as **formal criteria**. 'Formal' here is also contrasted with the 'notional' approach of TRADITIONAL grammar, where attempts were made to characterise linguistic units in terms of UNIVERSAL notions, as in the definition of a sentence as 'the expression of a complete thought'.

(2) **form** vs. **substance**. Here, the term refers to the overall linguistic organisation, or STRUCTURE, of speech or writing, as opposed to the physical REALISATION of language in PHONIC or GRAPHIC SUBSTANCE. In this sense, SEMANTIC structure is included, along with grammar and phonology/GRAPHOLOGY, being part of the abstract language system.

(3) **form** vs. **substance** and **meaning**. HALLIDAYAN linguisitic theory models language in terms of three interdependent LEVELS: the level of 'form' (comprising the grammatical and lexical organisation of language) is distinguished from the levels of SUBSTANCE and CONTEXT.

(4) **forms** (*of a unit*). The variant realisations of a linguistic unit are referred to as 'forms' of the unit, i.e. the members of a set of PARADIGMATIC alternatives. For example, the forms of the verb *walk* are *walk, walking, walks*, etc.

(5) The critical characteristics of a linguistic theory, especially as

stated in the FORMALISED terms of logic or mathematics, are referred to as the 'form' of that theory. In GENERATIVE grammar, the formal characteristics of linguistic theory have received special attention, especially in the notion of 'formal UNIVERSALS'. **Formal semantics** refers to analysis (in terms of truth conditions, etc.) of a logical system, such as PROPOSITIONAL calculus – an approach which is beginning to be applied to the study of natural languages (cf. MONTAGUE GRAMMAR). See Lyons 1968: Chs. 2, 4, for all the meanings above.

(6) **(-ity)** in STYLISTIC and SOCIOLINGUISTIC studies, **formal** is opposed to such terms as **informal**, 'intimate', 'familiar', etc., as part of a system of 'formality' of expression, referring to a level of language considered APPROPRIATE to socially formal situations. See Bolinger 1975: Ch. 11.

formalise (formalis-m, -ation) A characteristic of formulations in LINGUISTICS – and especially a primary goal of GENERATIVE analyses – whereby the RULES governing an analysis are capable of being specified in a precise and rigorous way. Ultimately it ought to be possible, in any **formalisation**, for a linguistic analysis to be FORMALLY interpreted in logical or mathematical terms, and a calculus developed. A 'formalised' account of an area of LANGUAGE, in this sense, is opposed to an 'informal' one. A specific feature, or set of features, used as part of the process of formalisation, is known as a **formalism**. See Lyons 1968: Ch. 4; 1977a: App.

formant A term in ACOUSTIC PHONETICS of particular value in the classification of VOWELS and vowel-like sounds, and of TRANSITIONAL features between vowels and adjacent sounds. A formant is a concentration of acoustic energy, reflecting the way air from the lungs vibrates in the VOCAL TRACT, as it changes its shape. For any vowel, the air vibrates at many different frequencies all at once, and the most dominant frequencies combine to produce the distinctive VOWEL QUALITIES. Each dominant band of frequencies constitutes a formant, which shows up clearly on a sound SPECTROGRAPH as a thick black line. Three main formants provide the basis of vowel description: the 'first formant' is the lowest, and the 'second' and 'third formants' are respectively higher. Other formants are less significant for linguistic analysis. The formants can be related to the ARTICULATORY DESCRIPTIONS of vowels, as represented, say, by the CARDINAL VOWEL diagram. The first formant, for example, decreases in its frequency as one moves from low to high (e.g. *sat* → *set* → *seat*). In the case of CONSONANTS, similar correlations can be established; for example, in the transition from VELAR consonants, the second and third formants come very close together. See Ladefoged 1975: Ch. 8.

formation-rule A term used in relation to the GENERATIVE SEMANTICS MODEL of LINGUISTICS to refer to the initial set of RULES which generate the semantic REPRESENTATIONS of SENTENCES. See Lyons 1977a: Ch. 8.

formative A formally identifiable, irreduceable GRAMMATICAL ELEMENT which enters into the construction of larger LINGUISTIC UNITS, such as WORDS and SENTENCES. It has come to be used especially in GENERATIVE grammar, as an alternative to the term MORPHEME, for the TERMINAL elements in a SURFACE STRUCTURE REPRESENTATION of a sentence. Several types of formative can be distinguished, depending on their role in sentence structure, e.g. 'inflectional formatives' (*viz* INFLECTIONAL endings, etc.), 'lexical formatives' (*viz* forms which enable one LEXICAL item to be derived from another, e.g. *-tion*). See Matthews 1974: Ch. 1; Huddleston 1976: Ch. 10.

formulaic language A term used in some theoretical and DESCRIPTIVE studies of GRAMMAR to refer to UTTERANCES which lack normal SYNTACTIC or MORPHOLOGICAL characteristics. (It may also be used, literally, to mean 'language containing formulae', or special symbols, as in scientific writing.) Sentences such as *God save the Queen, the more the merrier, how do you do?* and *many happy returns* do not contrast in the usual way with other sentences in the language, e.g. *few happy returns, how will you do?* Such FOSSILISED structures, often used in limited social situations, may also be referred to as 'stereotyped' sentences. See Quirk *et al* 1972: Ch. 7.

form word A term sometimes used in WORD classification for a word whose role is largely or wholly grammatical, e.g. ARTICLES, PRONOUNS, CONJUNCTIONS. Several such terms exist for this notion (e.g. FUNCTION WORD, GRAMMATICAL WORD, FUNCTOR); all contrast with the LEXICAL words in a language, which carry the main SEMANTIC content. See Bolinger 1975: Ch. 5.

fortis A term used in the PHONETIC classification of CONSONANT sounds on the basis of their MANNER OF ARTICULATION: it refers to a sound made with a relatively strong degree of muscular effort and breath force, compared with some other sound (known as LENIS). The distinction between TENSE and LAX is used similarly. The labels 'strong' and 'weak' are sometimes used for the contrast involved, but these are more prone to AMBIGUITY. In English, it is the VOICELESS consonants ([p], [t], [f], [s], etc.) which tend to be produced with fortis articulation (their voiced counterparts being relatively weak), and often, when the voicing distinction is reduced, it is only the degree of articulatory strength which maintains a contrast between sounds.

fossilised

The term 'fortis' is sometimes used loosely to refer to strong VOWEL articulation also, but this is not a standard practice. See Gimson 1970: Ch. 4.

fossilised A term used in GRAMMAR and LEXICOLOGY to refer to a type of CONSTRUCTION which is no longer PRODUCTIVE in a LANGUAGE. In English, for example, fossilised SENTENCES include *so be it*, *long live the Queen*, and *least said*, *soonest mended*; fossilised LEXICAL items include such REDUPLICATIVE forms as *goody-goody*, *hocus-pocus*, and several types of IDIOM. See Lyons 1977b: Ch. 13; Quirk *et al* 1972: App.

frame A term used in some MODELS of GRAMMATICAL DESCRIPTION to refer to the STRUCTURAL CONTEXT within which a CLASS of ITEMS can be used. For example, the frame *He saw — box* provides an ENVIRONMENT for the use of DETERMINERS (*the*, *a*, *my*, etc.). The terms **syntactic frame** and **substitution frame** are also used. In CASE grammar, the array of cases which specifies the structural context for VERBS is known as a **case frame**. In LEXICAL entries for verbs, in this theory, abbreviated statements called **frame features** indicate the set of case frames into which the various verbs may be inserted. See Lyons 1968: Ch. 4; Bolinger 1975: Ch. 15.

free A term used in a range of LINGUISTIC contexts to refer to a PHONOLOGICAL or GRAMMATICAL feature lacking a specific type of FORMAL CONSTRAINT. For example, a 'free FORM' or 'free MORPHEME' is a minimal grammatical UNIT which can be used as a WORD without the need for further MORPHOLOGICAL modification (opposed to BOUND); 'free word order' occurs when the word ORDER in a LANGUAGE can be altered without a consequent change of MEANING (opposed to FIXED); 'free stress' occurs whenever there is no fixed place for the primary STRESS to fall in a POLYSYLLABIC word.

The main use of the term is in the phrase **free variation** in phonology, referring to the SUBSTITUTABILITY of one sound for another in a given ENVIRONMENT, with no consequent change in the word's MEANING, as when a speaker articulates a word like *sit* with an unreleased or a released PLOSIVE, or different pronunciations are given to *either* (/iːðə/ vs. /aɪðə/). These different phonetic realisations of a PHONEME are called 'free variants' (opposed to the 'contextual variants' found in cases of COMPLEMENTARY DISTRIBUTION). In traditional phonological study, free variation has been considered to be an area of little importance; but in recent SOCIOLINGUISTIC studies, it is suggested that free variants need to be described, in terms of the frequency with which they occur, because the choice of one variant rather than another may be made on sociological grounds, as when one 'chooses' a careful rather than a 'casual' speech style.

The term 'free variation' is occasionally applied analogously in grammar and SEMANTICS, as when SYNONYMOUS expressions might be said to be in 'free variation'. See Hyman 1975: Ch. 3; Lyons 1968: Chs. 2, 3.

frequentative A term sometimes used in the GRAMMATICAL classification of VERBS to refer to the expression of repeated action. In some LANGUAGES (e.g. Russian) the class may be marked MORPHOLOGICALLY, but in English the MEANING is normally expressed through ADVERBIALS of frequency, e.g. *again*, *regularly*, *often*. See Lyons 1968: Ch. 7.

fricative A term used in the PHONETIC classification of CONSONANT sounds on the basis of their MANNER OF ARTICULATION: also known as 'spirant', it refers to sounds made when two organs come so close together that the air moving between them produces audible FRICTION. There is no complete CLOSURE between the organs (in which case a PLOSIVE articulation would be produced): there is simply a STRICTURE, or narrowing. There are several such sounds in English, both VOICED and voiceless, as in *fin* [f], *van* [v], *thin* [θ], *this* [ð], *sin* [s], *zoo* [z], *ship* [ʃ], *measure* [ʒ], *hoop* [h]. Other fricative sounds may be heard in English, in restricted CONTEXTS or speech STYLES, such as the PALATAL fricative [ç], and several other fricatives may be heard in other languages, e.g. a voiceless VELAR fricative [x] in Welsh or German, a voiceless pharyngeal (cf. PHARYNX) fricative [ħ] in Arabic, a voiced BILABIAL fricative [β] in Spanish. The fricative manner of articulation produces a wider range of speech sounds than any other. They are sounds with a potential for considerable DURATION (e.g. *s-s-s*), and from this point of view, the opposite of fricative (i.e. a continuant sound lacking friction) is called a FRICTIONLESS CONTINUANT. See Gimson 1970: Chs. 4, 8; Catford 1977: Ch. 7.

friction A term used in PHONETICS to refer to the sound produced when air passes a CONSTRICTION made in the VOCAL TRACT. The occurrence of **audible friction** is part of the phonetic definition of CONSONANTS; the phonetic definition of VOWELS requires that they be FRICTIONLESS. Various types of friction can be identified, in terms of anatomical point of origin, e.g. BILABIAL friction, pharyngeal (cf. PHARYNX) friction; friction above the GLOTTIS may be referred to as SUPRAGLOTTAL friction. See Catford 1977: Ch. 7.

frictionless

frictionless (continuant) A general term used in the PHONETIC classification of speech sounds on the basis of their MANNER OF ARTICULATION: it refers to any sound functioning as a CONSONANT but which lacks the CLOSURE or FRICTION which identify most consonantal articulations. In RECEIVED PRONUNCIATION, /r/ is often articulated in this way, with no audible friction. From a PHONETIC point of view, all VOWELS and vowel-like sounds are also technically 'frictionless' and 'continuant', but it is usual to restrict the term to those sounds which are consonantal in function. All NASALS and LATERALS are thus classifiable under this heading, as well as many varieties of /r/. In received pronunciation, the POST-ALVEOLAR /r/ is often articulated in this way, without audible friction, and is often described specifically as a 'post-alveolar frictionless continuant'. Some phoneticians use the term APPROXIMANT to refer to these sounds. See Gimson 1970: Chs. 4, 8; Abercrombie 1967: Ch. 4.

front(-ing, -ed) (1) In PHONETICS, classifications of front speech sounds are of two types: (a) those ARTICULATED in the front part of the mouth (as opposed to the BACK); (b) those articulated by the front part (or BLADE) of the TONGUE. Front sounds which satisfy both criteria would be front VOWELS, as in *see, hit, pet, cap*, and such front CONSONANTS as the initial sound of *two, do, see, zoo, this, thin*. Consonants such as those in *pay* and *bay* are however front in sense (a) only. Front vowels, it should be noted, are in traditional phonetic classification contrasted with CENTRAL and BACK vowels. In DISTINCTIVE FEATURE analyses of sound SYSTEMS, front in sense (a) is referred to as ANTERIOR, in sense (b) is referred to as CORONAL.

In some analyses of sound patterns, it is useful to talk about **fronting**, a process common in historical sound change, and when children are learning to speak, whereby a sound (or group of sounds) may come to be articulated further forward in the mouth than the accepted adult norms. It is also often useful to analyse one sound as being 'fronted' when compared with a back variant of the same PHONEME: for example the /k/ phoneme in English has both front and back VARIANTS (as in *key* and *car* respectively) owing to the influence of the following vowel. The analogous terms 'backing'/ 'backed', are not commonly used. See Gimson 1970: Ch. 2; Catford 1977: Chs. 8, 9.

(2) **Fronting** is also used as a term in GENERATIVE SYNTAX referring to any TRANSFORMATION which transposes a CONSTITUENT from the middle or end of a STRING to initial position. For example, the rule of '*Wh*-fronting' places a *wh*-word (e.g. *where, why*) in initial position, transposing it from an earlier end position (cf. *John walked there → John*

154

walked where → *where did John walk*). See Akmajian & Heny 1975: Ch. 10.

FSP The usual abbreviation for FUNCTIONAL SENTENCE PERSPECTIVE.

full A term sometimes used in the GRAMMATICAL CLASSIFICATION of WORDS to refer to one of two postulated major word classes in LANGUAGE, the other being EMPTY. 'Full words' are said to be those which contain LEXICAL MEANING (e.g. *table, man, go, red*) as opposed to empty words, which have a purely grammatical role. The distinction has come under criticism, largely on the grounds that the boundary between 'full' and 'empty' words is not as clear-cut as is suggested. Words like *while, but, in*, etc., are considered to be grammatical words, but they plainly do have some independently stateable meaning.

'Full' may also be encountered as part of the specification of types of grammatical UNIT, e.g. 'full verb' (i.e. the lexical VERB in the verb PHRASE), 'full sentence' (i.e. a MAJOR SENTENCE type, consisting of SUBJECT and PREDICATE). See Palmer 1971: Ch. 2; Robins 1971: Ch. 7.

function(al) One of the most widely used terms in LINGUISTICS, with a correspondingly wide range of meanings. There are three main areas of application:

(1) The relationship between a linguistic FORM and other parts of the linguistic pattern or SYSTEM in which it is used. In GRAMMAR, for example, the NOUN PHRASE can 'function' in CLAUSE structure as SUBJECT, OBJECT, COMPLEMENT, etc., these roles being defined distributionally. **Syntactic functions** (or 'syntactic relations') of this kind are a major feature of several MODELS of linguistic analysis, including the approaches of the PRAGUE SCHOOL, GLOSSEMATICS and RELATIONAL GRAMMAR, and the terms **functional analysis** and **functional linguistics** have been used to characterise theories which treat the notion of function as central (cf. also FUNCTIONAL SENTENCE PERSPECTIVE). More specifically, the term functional is used of an ELEMENT which is DISTINCTIVE, or CONTRASTIVE, within a language system, as in one definition of PHONOLOGY as **functional phonetics**. See Lyons 1968: Ch. 9; Bolinger 1975: Ch. 6.

(2) The use made of a linguistic contrast in a SYSTEM is sometimes referred to as its **functional load** or **yield**. The term is usually used with reference to phonology, where in English, for example, the contrast between /p/ and /b/ would be said to have a higher functional load than between /ʃ/ and /ʒ/: the former contrast distinguishes many MINIMAL PAIRS, whereas the latter contrast distin-

guishes only a few. Several criteria are used in making such quantitative judgements, such as the position within a WORD at which the contrast is found, and the frequency of occurrence of the words in the language. See Lyons 1968: Ch. 2.

(3) The role language plays in the context of society or the individual is also referred to by the term 'function' (**social function**). For example, language is used ('functions') to communicate ideas, to express attitudes, and so on. It may also be used to identify specific SOCIOLINGUISTIC situations, such as informality or intimacy, or VARIETIES of language such as science and law: in such cases, one might talk, for instance, of the 'function' of scientific language being to express a certain mode of experience in a certain way, and so on. Several detailed classifications of the social functions of language have been made, especially in recent HALLIDAYAN linguistics, and in relation to the theory of SPEECH ACTS. The traditional classification of SENTENCE functions falls between grammatical and SPEECH-ACT theory: sentences are said to 'function' as STATEMENTS, QUESTIONS, COMMANDS, etc. See Gumperz & Hymes 1971: Ch. 7; Bolinger 1975: Ch. 11.

functional sentence perspective (FSP) A theory of LINGUISTIC analysis associated with the modern exponents of the PRAGUE SCHOOL of linguistics. It refers to an analysis of UTTERANCES (or texts) in terms of the INFORMATION they contain, the role of each utterance part being evaluated for its SEMANTIC contribution to the whole. The notion of 'COMMUNICATIVE dynamism' has been developed as an attempt to rate these different LEVELS of contribution within a structure, particularly with reference to the concepts of RHEME and THEME. See Bolinger 1975: Ch. 15; Lyons 1977b: Ch. 12.

function word A term sometimes used in WORD classification for a word whose role is largely or wholly grammatical, e.g. ARTICLES, PRONOUNS, CONJUNCTIONS. Several such terms exist for this notion (e.g. FORM WORD, GRAMMATICAL WORD, FUNCTOR); all contrast with the LEXICAL words in a language, which carry the main SEMANTIC content. See Bolinger 1975: Ch. 5.

functor A term sometimes used in WORD classification for words and BOUND MORPHEMES whose role in language is largely or wholly grammatical, such as PREPOSITIONS, ARTICLES, PRONOUNS, CONJUNCTIONS. Several such terms relate to this notion (e.g. FUNCTION WORD, GRAMMATICAL WORD, FORM WORD); all contrast with the LEXICAL words in a language, which carry the main SEMANTIC content. See Bolinger 1975: Ch. 5.

fundamental (frequency) A term derived from the study of the physics of sound, and used in ACOUSTIC PHONETICS, referring to the lowest frequency component in a complex sound wave (other components being known as the 'harmonics'). Frequency refers to the number of complete cycles (opening and closing movements) of VOCAL CORD vibration in a unit of time per second. The 'fundamental', or F_0 ('f nought'), is of particular importance in studies of INTONATION, where it displays a reasonably close correspondence with the PITCH movements involved. It is measured in Hertz (Hz), a term which has replaced the older 'cycles per second'. See Ladefoged 1975: Ch. 8; Catford 1977: Ch. 4.

fusional (fuse, fusion) A type of LANGUAGE sometimes distinguished in COMPARATIVE LINGUISTICS using STRUCTURAL (as opposed to historical) criteria, and focusing on the characteristics of the WORD: in **fusional languages**, words typically contain more than one MORPHEME, but there is no one-to-one correspondence between these morphemes and the linear SEQUENCE of MORPHS the words contain. Languages such as Latin and Sanskrit represent this type, also known as INFLECTING languages. For example, in Latin *amicus* 'friend', this form 'fuses' the features masculine, NOMINATIVE, and singular, in addition to the ROOT, in a manner which makes the word extremely difficult to segment morphologically (except by WORD AND PARADIGM techniques). As always in such classifications, the categories are not clear-cut: different languages will display the characteristic of 'fusion' to a greater or lesser degree.

The term is also used, independently of this classification, to refer to the merging of exponents within a linguistic unit, especially a word, e.g. *took* represents the 'fusion' of *take + past*; sounds may be 'fused' in some types of ASSIMILATION. See Robins 1971: Ch. 8; Matthews 1974: Ch. 6.

fuzzy A term derived from mathematics and used by some LINGUISTS to refer to the INDETERMINACY involved in the analysis of a linguistic UNIT or PATTERN. For example, several LEXICAL ITEMS, it is argued, are best regarded as representing a SEMANTIC CATEGORY which has an INVARIANT core with a variable (or 'fuzzy') boundary, this allowing for flexibility of APPLICATION to a wide range of entities, given the appropriate CONTEXT. The difficulty of defining the boundaries of *cup* and *glass* has been a well-studied example of this indeterminacy. Other items which lend 'fuzziness' to language include *sort of, rather, quite*, etc. The notion is seen as particularly important in NON-DISCRETE grammar. See Radford 1981: Ch. 3.

G

᭤᭤᭤᭤᭤᭤

gap A term used in LINGUISTICS to refer to the absence of a linguistic UNIT at a place in a pattern of relationships where one might have been expected. The term occurs especially in SEMANTICS, where a 'LEXICAL gap' can be illustrated by the absence of a male vs. female distinction within the term *cousin* (cf. *brother/sister, uncle/aunt*, etc.). An example of a PHONOLOGICAL 'gap' or 'hole in the pattern' would be a LANGUAGE where the PHONEMIC CONTRASTS /p/, /b/ and /t/, /d/ were not matched by a corresponding velar pair, only /k/ being found. See Lyons 1977b: Ch. 9.

gapping A term proposed in GENERATIVE GRAMMAR to refer to the DELETION of a repeated VERB in CLAUSES which have been CONJOINED – a 'gap' has been left in the reduced clause, e.g. *she went to London and he to New York*. See Akmajian & Heny 1975: Ch. 7.

geminate A term used in PHONETICS and PHONOLOGY for a SEQUENCE of identical adjacent SEGMENTS of a sound in a single MORPHEME, e.g. Italian *notte* /nɔtte/ 'night'. Because of the SYLLABLE division, a geminate sequence cannot be regarded as simply a 'long' CONSONANT, and TRANSCRIPTIONAL differences usually indicate this, e.g. [-ff-] is geminate, [-f:-] is long. See Catford 1977: Ch. 11: Robins 1971: Ch. 3.

gender A GRAMMATICAL CATEGORY used for the analysis of WORD classes displaying such CONTRASTS as masculine/feminine/neuter, ANIMATE/inanimate, etc. Discussion of this concept in LINGUISTICS has generally focused upon the need to distinguish **natural gender**, where items refer to the sex of real-world entities, and **grammatical gender**, which has nothing to do with sex, but which has an important role in signalling grammatical relationships between words in a SENTENCE (ADJECTIVES agreeing with NOUNS, etc.). The gender SYSTEMS of French, German, Latin, etc. are grammatical, and shown by the FORM of the ARTICLE (e.g. *le* vs. *la*) or of the noun (e.g. nouns ending in *-a* are feminine). Grammatical gender is not a feature of English, though some parts of the language can be analysed in such terms (e.g. the correlation between PRONOUNS, *he/she* co-occurring with *who/whose*, etc., whereas *it* co-occurs with *which*). English gender contrasts are on the whole natural, *viz he* refers to male people, animals, etc. The few cases of other kinds of usage (e.g. *a ship* being referred to as *she*) pose interesting problems which have attracted considerable discussion in linguistics. See Palmer 1971: App. A; Quirk *et al* 1972; Ch. 4; Lyons 1968: Ch. 7.

general (1) A commonly used characterisation of LINGUISTICS, when one wants to emphasise the UNIVERSAL applicability of linguistic theory and method in the study of LANGUAGES. **General linguistics** thus includes the theoretical, DESCRIPTIVE and COMPARATIVE biases of the subject. It is sometimes seen in contrast with those branches of linguistics where there is an interdisciplinary or applied orientation (as in SOCIOLINGUISTICS, APPLIED LINGUISTICS). A similar use of the term is in the phrase **general grammar** found in several early language studies (e.g. the PORT ROYAL GRAMMAR), and often used in GENERATIVE linguistic contexts in the sense of 'UNIVERSAL GRAMMAR'. **General semantics**, by contrast, has nothing to do with linguistics in its modern sense, referring to a philosophical movement developed in the 1930s by the American scholar Alfred Korzybski (1879–1950), which aimed to make people aware of the conventional relationship between words and things, as a means of improving systems of communication and clear thinking. See Robins 1971: Ch. 1; Bolinger 1975: Ch. 8.

(2) (**-ise, -ity, -isation**) A property of those linguistic analyses and descriptive statements which are applicable to a relatively wide range of DATA in a language, and which are expressed in relatively abstract terms. A statement which can be made only with reference to individual UNITS (e.g. LEXICAL ITEMS, sounds, CONSTRUCTIONS), or to small CLASSES of units, is said to 'lack generality'. The aim of the linguist is to make **generalisations** about his data which need as few qualifications as possible (e.g. about exceptions, or restricted CONTEXTS of use), and which are MEANINGFUL TO NATIVE SPEAKERS (i.e. they are LINGUISTICALLY SIGNIFICANT GENERALISATIONS). Likewise, linguistic theories should be as 'general' as possible, i.e. aiming to establish the universal characteristics of human language.

In language ACQUISITION, 'generalisation' refers to the process whereby a child extends his initial use of a linguistic feature to a class of items, as when, having learned to use an *-ing* ending on a VERB, the feature is, 'generally' applied to the class of verbs. **Overgeneralisation** takes place when the feature is extended beyond its limits in the adult grammar – as when the regular plural ending is applied to irregular FORMS, e.g. **mouses, *sheeps*. Bolinger 1975: Ch. 12.

(3) A type of TRANSFORMATIONAL RULE recognised in early MODELS

generative

of GENERATIVE grammar, where the rule operates with an input of two or more TERMINAL strings. Two types of **generalised transformation** are recognised: CONJOINING transformations handle CO-ORDINATION; EMBEDDING transformations handle SUBORDINATION. See Lyons 1968: Ch. 6.

generative (generate) (1) A term derived from mathematics, and introduced by Noam CHOMSKY, in his book *Syntactic Structures* (1957), to refer to the capacity of a GRAMMAR to define (i.e. specify the membership of) the set of grammatical SENTENCES in a LANGUAGE. Technically, a **generative grammar** is a set of FORMAL RULES which PROJECTS a finite set of sentences upon the potentially infinite set of sentences that constitute the language as a whole, and it does this in an EXPLICIT manner, ASSIGNING to each a set of STRUCTURAL DESCRIPTIONS. Several possible MODELS of generative grammar have been formally investigated, following Chomsky's initial discussion of three types – FINITE STATE, PHRASE STRUCTURE and TRANSFORMATIONAL grammars. There are two main branches of generative linguistics: **generative phonology** and **generative syntax**. The term 'generative semantics' is also used, but in a different sense (see (2) below).

(2) The **generative semantics** school of thought within GENERATIVE LINGUISTIC theory was propounded by several American linguists (primarily George Lakoff (b. 1941), James McCawley (b. 1938), Paul Postal (b. 1936) and John Ross (b. 1938)) in the early 1970s; it views the SEMANTIC COMPONENT of a grammar as being the generative base from which SYNTACTIC structure can be derived. One proceeds in an analysis by first providing a semantic REPRESENTATION of a SENTENCE, and this single LEVEL is all that is needed to specify the conditions which produce WELL-FORMED SURFACE STRUCTURES. The subsequent syntatic RULES are solely INTERPRETIVE, and there is no intermediate level. This puts the approach plainly in contrast with the claims of Noam Chomsky and others (in the STANDARD THEORY) who argued the need for a level of syntactic DEEP STRUCTURE as well as a semantic level of analysis. 'Generative' in this phrase has, accordingly, a narrower sense than in 'generative grammar' as a whole, as it specifically opposed to those MODELS which operate with a different, interpretive view of semantics. The proponents of this approach are known as 'generative semanticists'. See Lyons 1977a: Ch. 8; Huddleston 1976: Ch. 16.

generic A term used in GRAMMATICAL and SEMANTIC analysis for a LEXICAL stem or PROPOSITION which refers to a CLASS of entities, e.g. *the bat is an interesting creature*, **bats** *are horrid, the English/French...*, *the poor/rich/good...* See Quirk *et al* 1972: Ch. 4; Lyons 1977b: Ch. 7.

Geneva School (1) In LINGUISTICS, the name given to those who have developed the views of the Swiss linguist Ferdinand de SAUSSURE, who taught linguistics at the University of Geneva between 1906 and 1911. Scholars such as Charles Bally (1865–1947) have expounded Saussurean theories and applied them to several new areas, e.g. literary LANGUAGE. See Bolinger 1975: Ch. 15.

(2) In language ACQUISITION, the name given to those who have developed the views of the Swiss psychologist, Jean Piaget (b. 1896). Particular attention has been paid to experimental techniques designed to extend Piaget's observations on LANGUAGE development in children to a wider range of DATA and CONTEXTS in a wider range of languages. See Clark & Clark 1977: Ch. 8.

genitive One of the FORMS taken by a WORD, usually a NOUN or PRONOUN, in LANGUAGES which express GRAMMATICAL relationships by means of INFLECTIONS. The genitive CASE typically expresses a possessive relationship (e.g. *the boy's book*), or some other similarly 'close' connection (e.g. *a summer's day*); but there is a great deal of variation between languages in the way this case is used. The term may also apply to CONSTRUCTIONS formally related to the case form, as in the 'post-modifying' genitive with *of* in English, e.g. *the car of the general* (→ *the general's car*). In English LINGUISTICS, particular attention has been paid to the problems caused by the DISTRIBUTION of the genitive ending, as in *a book of my brother's* and *the King of England's hat*. See Lyons 1968: Ch. 7; Quirk *et al* 1972: Ch. 4.

geographical linguistics The study of LANGUAGES and DIALECTS in terms of their regional distribution is sometimes collectively referred to by this label, though the terms DIALECTOLOGY and AREAL LINGUISTICS are more commonly used. 'Geographical dialects' is an alternative term for 'regional dialects'. See Trudgill 1974: Ch. 7.

given A term used by some LINGUISTS in a two-part analysis of UTTERANCES in terms of INFORMATION structure; 'given' information is opposed to NEW. (The contrast between FOCUS and PRESUPPOSITION makes an analogous distinction.) 'Given' refers to information already supplied by the previous CONTEXT of speaking, whereas 'new' information, as its name suggests, has not been previously supplied. Given information will usually be relatively unstressed within the TONE UNIT, e.g. in the sequence A: *What are you looking at?* B: *I'm looking at a màn*, all but the final phrase is given; in A: *What are you doing?* B: *I'm looking at a man*, the context shows that only the first part of the sentence is given. Complications arise when the new information is PROSODICALLY 'spread' throughout a tone unit, however, as in *your*

glide

cóusin's had a bàby, and analyses in these terms are not without controversy. See Lyons 1977b: Ch. 12; Quirk *et al* 1972: Ch. 14.

glide A term used in PHONETICS to refer to a TRANSITIONAL sound as the VOCAL ORGANS move towards or away from an ARTICULATION (**on-glide** and **off-glide** respectively). An example is the [j] glide heard in some pronunciations of words like *tune*, *viz* [tʲuːn]. DIPHTHONGS are sometimes referred to as 'gliding vowels'. See Gimson 1970; Ch. 4.

global A term used in GENERATIVE LINGUISTIC theory in the early 1970s to refer to a type of RULE (**global rule**) which extends over entire DERIVATIONS, or parts of derivations, and cannot be satisfactorily stated in terms of TRANSFORMATIONAL operations that define the conditions of WELL-FORMEDNESS on individual PHRASE-MARKERS or pairs of adjacent phrase-markers in a derivation. Global rules (or 'global derivational CONSTRAINTS') thus contrast with PHRASE STRUCTURE and TRANSFORMATIONAL rules, as traditionally understood: they define the conditions of well-formedness on configurations of corresponding NODES in non-adjacent PHRASE-MARKERS. Several topics in PHONOLOGY, SYNTAX and SEMANTICS have been analysed in these terms (e.g. CASE AGREEMENT, CONTRACTED forms, placement of contrastive STRESS). See Hyman 1975: Ch. 4.

glossematics An approach to LANGUAGE developed primarily by Louis Hjelmslev (1899–1965) and associates at the Linguistic Circle of Copenhagen in the mid-1930s (the COPENHAGEN SCHOOL). The novel name was a reflection of the originality of the school's intention to develop a theory which would be applicable, not just for language, but for general study of the humanities ('semiology', the study of symbolic systems in general; cf. SEMIOTICS). Language, in this view, was seen as one kind of symbolic system, whose special features would be clarified only when it was compared with other, non-linguistic symbolic systems (e.g. logic, dancing). The philosophical and logical basis of glossematic theory, especially as FORMALISED by Hjelmslev in his *Prolegomena to a Theory of Language*, published in 1943, presenting language as a purely deductive system, is its most distinctive feature. The irreducible and invariant UNITS established by this procedure were called GLOSSEMES. See Bolinger 1975: Ch. 15; Dinneen 1967: Ch. 11.

glosseme A term used in GLOSSEMATICS to refer to the abstract minimal invariant FORMS set up by the theory as the bases of explanation in all areas of LINGUISTIC analysis. See Dinneen 1967: Ch. 11.

glossolalia A term used by some LINGUISTS to refer to the phenomenon of 'speaking in tongues', as practised by members of various religious groups. See Bolinger 1975: Ch. 11.

glottal(-ic, -ise, -isation, glottis) A term in the classification of CONSONANT sounds on the basis of PLACE OF ARTICULATION: it is a sound made in the LARYNX, due to the CLOSURE or narrowing of the **glottis**, the aperture between the VOCAL CORDS. The audible release of a complete closure at the glottis is known as a **glottal stop**, transcribed [ʔ]. This is often used in English, e.g. it may be heard before a forcefully articulated VOWEL, as in *are you*, or between adjacent vowels as in *co-operate*. In several ACCENTS of English, (e.g. those influenced by Cockney) the sound has PHONEMIC status, being used in some positions where RECEIVED PRONUNCIATION has a VOICE-LESS PLOSIVE ([t] and [k] especially), e.g. *bottle* /bɔʔl/ for /bɔtl/. Varying degrees of audible FRICTION may also originate at the glottis, as in whispered speech, or the [h] sound in English. Other glottal effects, due to the mode of vibration of the vocal cords, are an important feature of speech sounds, such as VOICING and PITCH variation, and BREATHY and CREAKY phonation.

Glottalisation is a general term for any articulation involving a simultaneous glottal CONSTRICTION, especially a glottal stop. In English, glottal stops are often used in this way to reinforce a voiceless plosive at the end of a word, as in *what?* [wɔtʔ]. However, if the opening of the glottis is delayed until after the release of the glottalised sound, a different sound effect is created. Such sounds, made while the glottis is closed, are produced without the direct involvement of air from the lungs. Air is compressed in the mouth or PHARYNX above the glottal closure, and released while the breath is still held: the resultant sounds produced in this **glottalic** AIR-STREAM MECHANISM are known as EJECTIVE sounds. They are also called 'glottalic' or 'glottalised' sounds (though the latter term is often restricted to sounds where the glottal feature is a SECONDARY ARTICULATION). They are transcribed with a following raised glottal stop sign or apostrophe, as in [p'], [t'], [s']. In English, such sounds have only STYLISTIC force (as when *I think* might be said in a clipped precise manner, producing an ejective [k'] in *think*), but in languages like Quechua and Hausa, ejective consonants are used as phonemes. A further category of sounds involving a glottalic air-stream mechanism is known as IMPLOSIVE.

In CHOMSKY & Halle's DISTINCTIVE FEATURE theory of PHONOLOGY, **glottal constrictions** constitute one of the types of sound set up to handle variations in place of articulation (CAVITY features). Glottal constrictions are formed by narrowing the glottis beyond its neutral position, as in the above sounds.

See Gimson 1970: Chs. 4, 8; Catford 1977: Ch. 5; Ladefoged 1975: Ch. 6.

glottochronology A term used in LINGUISTICS, referring to the quantification of the extent to which LANGUAGES have diverged from a common source. Using a technique known as LEXICOSTATISTICS, one studies the extent to which the hypothetically related languages share certain basic WORDS (COGNATES) and deduces from this the distance in time since the languages separated. The theory and methods involved are not widely used, and are highly controversial. See Robins 1971: Ch. 8.

goal A term used by some LINGUISTS as part of the SEMANTIC analysis of a SENTENCE: it refers to the entity which is affected by the action of the VERB, e.g. *the cat caught **a mouse***. Several other terms have been used for this idea, e.g. 'patient', 'recipient'. See Bolinger 1975: Ch. 6.

God's truth A phrase coined in the 1950s to characterise one of two extreme states of mind of a hypothetical LINGUIST when he sets up a DESCRIPTION of linguistic DATA; opposed to HOCUS-POCUS. A 'God's truth' linguist approaches his data with the expectation that the LANGUAGE has a 'real' STRUCTURE which is waiting to be uncovered. The assumption is that if one's procedure of analysis is logical and consistent, the same description would always emerge from the same data, any uncertainty being the result of defective observation or logic on the part of the analyst. In a hocus-pocus approach, by contrast, no such assumption is made. See Robins 1971: Ch. 2.

govern (1) (**-ment**) A term used in GRAMMATICAL analysis to refer to a kind of SYNTACTIC linkage whereby one WORD (or word CLASS) requires a specific MORPHOLOGICAL FORM of another word (or class). For example, PREPOSITIONS in Latin are said to 'govern' NOUNS, making a certain case form obligatory (e.g. *ad* plus ACCUSATIVE). The notion is, accordingly, not readily applicable to a LANGUAGE like English, where case endings are few – to say that in *the man kicked the ball, kicked* 'governs' *the ball*, is true only in a loose SEMANTIC sense (and even then, it is debatable whether this is a valid notion of government, when the relationship between other ELEMENTS is considered: almost any pairs of elements, e.g. *the man* and *kicked*, might be said to be displaying government, in this sense). The term is usually contrasted with AGREEMENT, where the form taken by one word requires a corresponding form in another. See Palmer 1971: Ch. 2.

(2) (**-ed, un-**) In GENERATIVE grammar (cf. ASPECTS), the terms **governed** and **ungoverned** are used to refer to whether or not a RULE has LEXICAL exceptions. For example, because not all ACTIVE TRANSITIVE SENTENCES take the PASSIVE (e.g. *they have a car, the hat suits you*), the passivisation rule would be said to be 'governed'. An example of an ungoverned rule is REFLEXIVISATION (e.g. *I shaved myself*, etc.). See Akmajian & Heny 1975: Ch. 6; Huddleston 1976: Ch. 10.

(3) (**-or**) In DEPENDENCY grammar, the **governor** refers to the superordinate NODE in a dependency tree, which 'governs' a set of 'dependent' nodes. Each combination of governor and dependent defines a specific structural relationship. For example, the VERB is seen as the governor of the NOUN PHRASES occurring in CLAUSE STRUCTURE, and each verb/noun phrase combination specifies a syntactic RELATION, e.g. SUBJECT, INDIRECT OBJECT. See Radford 1981: Ch. 4.

gradability ((un-)gradable) A term used in GRAMMAR and SEMANTICS to refer to an analysis of the SENSE relationship between LEXICAL items in terms of the possibility of comparison. In semantics, **gradable** terms are best illustrated by such opposites as *big/small, high/low* (cf. ANTONYMS). **Ungradable** terms can be illustrated by *single/married, north/south*, etc. In grammar, the term is used to refer to various types of grammatical MODIFICATION which can be used as criteria for comparative MEANINGS, e.g. *a piece/bit/chunk of…, a very/slightly/extremely…* See Lyons 1977b: Ch. 9; Quirk *et al* 1972: Chs. 4, 5.

gradience A term used by some LINGUISTS to refer to areas of LANGUAGE where there are no clear boundaries between sets of analytic categories. PHONETIC continua provide clear examples (such as the set of possible CONTRASTS between FALLING and RISING INTONATION patterns), but the term is also found in SEMANTICS (as in the study of continua, such as colour terms, or GRADABLE ANTONYMS), and in GRAMMAR (where the boundaries between WORD CLASSES are not clear-cut, e.g. noun-like words such as *rich, London, smoking, someone* make it difficult to circumscribe the class of NOUNS). See Bolinger 1975: Ch. 8.

gradual A type of OPPOSITION recognised by PRAGUE SCHOOL PHONOLOGY, distinguished from PRIVATIVE and EQUIPOLLENT. A gradual opposition is one where degrees of difference in a LANGUAGE are recognised along a scale of some kind, as in a language with four FRONT VOWELS /i/, /e/, /ɛ/ and /a/ where (according to N. Trubetskoy) it would not be desirable to analyse the four degrees of vowel height in terms of privative pairs, such as 'high' vs. 'low'. See Hyman 1975: Ch. 2.

grammar (gramma-tical, -rian) A central term in LINGUISTICS, but one which covers a wide range of phenomena. Several types of grammar can be distinguished.

(1) A **descriptive grammar** is, in the first instance, a systematic DESCRIPTION of a LANGUAGE as found in a sample of speech or writing (e.g. in a CORPUS of material, or as elicited from NATIVE-SPEAKERS). Depending on one's theoretical background, it may go beyond this and make statements about the language as a whole, and insofar as these statements are explicit and predictive of the speaker's COMPETENCE, the grammar can be said to be 'descriptively adequate' and GENERATIVE. In the older tradition, 'descriptive' is in contrast to the PRESCRIPTIVE approach of grammarians who attempted to establish RULES for the socially or STYLISTICALLY CORRECT use of language. Comprehensive descriptions of the SYNTAX and MORPHOLOGY of a language are known as 'reference grammars' or 'grammatical handbooks' (such as those produced this century by the North European grammarians, e.g. the Dane, Otto Jespersen (1860–1943), and more recently by Randolph Quirk *et al* (see p. 390)).

(2) A **theoretical grammar** goes beyond the study of individual languages, using language DATA as a means of developing theoretical insights into the nature of linguistic enquiry as such, and into the categories and processes needed for successful linguistic analysis. Such insights include the distinction between 'DEEP grammar' and 'SURFACE grammar', the notion of 'grammatical CATEGORIES' and 'grammatical MEANING'. Insofar as grammar concentrates on the study of linguistic FORMS (their STRUCTURE, DISTRIBUTION, etc.), it may be referred to as **formal grammar** (as opposed to 'NOTIONAL grammar'); but formal grammar also refers to the use of the FORMALISED techniques of logic and mathematics in the analysis of language.

(3) Other general notions include the distinction between DIACHRONIC and SYNCHRONIC grammars, based on whether or not grammars introduce a historical dimension into their analysis. **Comparative grammar**, which compares the forms of languages (or states of a language), relies on a combination of theoretical and descriptive methods. A 'pedagogical' or 'teaching grammar' is a grammar designed specifically for the purposes of teaching or learning a (foreign) language, or for developing one's awareness of the mother-tongue.

(4) The phrase **traditional grammar** is an attempt to summarise the range of attitudes and methods found in the pre-linguistic era of grammatical study. The term TRADITIONAL, accordingly, is found with reference to many periods, such as the Roman and Greek grammarians, renaissance grammars, and (especially) the 18th and 19th

century school grammars, in Europe and America. It is usually used with a critical ('non-scientific') implication, despite the fact that many antecedents of modern linguistics can be found in early grammars. Criticism is directed primarily at the PRESCRIPTIVE and PROSCRIPTIVE recommendations of authors, as opposed to the descriptive emphasis of linguistic studies.

In a restricted sense (the traditional sense in linguistics, and the usual popular interpretation of the term), grammar refers to a level of structural organisation which can be studied independently of PHONOLOGY and SEMANTICS, and generally divided into the branches of SYNTAX and MORPHOLOGY. In this sense, grammar is the study of the way WORDS, and their component parts, combine to form SENTENCES. It is to be contrasted with a general conception of the subject, where grammar is seen as the entire system of structural relationships in a language, as in such titles as STRATIFICATIONAL grammar, SYSTEMIC grammar, and (especially) GENERATIVE grammar. Here, 'grammar' subsumes phonology and semantics as well as syntax, traditionally regarded as separate linguistic LEVELS. 'A grammar', in this sense, is a device for generating a finite specification of the sentences of a language. Insofar as a grammar defines the total set of RULES possessed by a speaker, it is a grammar of his competence (**competence grammar**). Insofar as a grammar is capable of accounting for only the sentences a speaker has actually used (as found in a sample of his output, or CORPUS), it is a **performance grammar**. The study of PERFORMANCE grammars, in a PSYCHOLINGUISTIC context, goes beyond this, however, attempting to define the various psychological, neurological and physiological stages which enter into the production and perception of speech. Investigations which go beyond the study of an individual language, attempting to establish the defining (UNIVERSAL) characteristics of human language in general, have as their goal a **universal grammar**.

The student of grammar is a 'grammarian', and he carries out a 'grammatical' analysis (the term here having no implications of WELL-FORMEDNESS, as it has in the notion of GRAMMATICALITY). When it is necessary to differentiate entities in one's analysis as belonging to a grammatical level of description as opposed to some other (e.g. semantic, phonological), the term 'grammatical' is often used attributively, as in 'grammatical CATEGORY' (e.g. GENDER, CASE, VOICE), 'grammatical gender' (as opposed to 'natural gender'), 'grammatical FORMATIVE/ITEM/UNIT' (e.g. an INFLECTIONAL ending), 'grammatical SUBJECT/OBJECT...' (as opposed to 'logical' or 'semantic' subjects/objects...), 'grammatical word' (as opposed to LEXICAL word). See Palmer 1971; Lyons 1968: Ch. 4; Robins 1971: Chs. 5–7.

grammaticality (un-grammatical(ness)) In LINGUISTICS, the conformity of a SENTENCE (or part of a sentence) to the RULES defined by a specific GRAMMAR of a LANGUAGE. A preceding ASTERISK is commonly used to indicate that a sentence is **ungrammatical**, i.e. incapable of being accounted for by the rules of a grammar. In practice, deciding whether a sentence is grammatical or ungrammatical may cause difficulty, e.g. in cases such as *The bus he got off was a red one*, where NATIVE-SPEAKERS vary in their judgements. In GENERATIVE linguistics, the view is taken that a grammar is set up in the first instance to draw a dividing line between those sentences which are clearly grammatical and those which are clearly ungrammatical. Once this has been done, the cases of uncertainty can be investigated, and a decision made as to whether they can be incorporated into the grammar as they stand, and without further modification being introduced into the grammar. If they can, these sentences are thereby defined as grammatical, i.e. the grammar recognises them as such. If not, they will be said to be ungrammatical, with reference to that grammar.

An alternative term for 'grammatical' in this context, is WELL-FORMED (VS. ILL-FORMED): grammars adjudicate on the 'well-formedness' of sentences. Such decisions have nothing to do with the MEANING or ACCEPTABILITY of sentences. A sentence in this view may be well-formed, but nonsensical (as in CHOMSKY's famous *Colourless green ideas sleep furiously*); it may also be well-formed but unacceptable (for reasons of STYLISTIC inappropriateness, perhaps).

It should be emphasised that no social value judgement is implied by the use of 'grammatical', and this therefore contrasts with some popular uses of the term, as when sentences are said to be ungrammatical because they do not conform to the canons of the STANDARD language (as in the use of double NEGATIVES, such as *I haven't done nothing*). There is no PRESCRIPTIVE implication in the above use in linguistics. See Lyons 1977a: Chs. 4, 5.

graph A term used by some LINGUISTS to refer to the smallest DISCRETE SEGMENT in a stretch of writing or print – analogous to the notion of the PHONE in PHONETICS. The present line of type is composed of such graphs as *t*, *T*, *h*, *e*, and so on, as well as the punctuation marks. The linguistic analysis of these graphs into GRAPHEMES is the province of GRAPHOLOGY. See Lyons 1968: Ch. 2.

grapheme (graphemics) The minimal CONTRASTIVE UNIT in the writing SYSTEM of a LANGUAGE. The grapheme *a*, for example, is realised as several ALLOGRAPHS *A*, *a*, *a*, etc., which may be seen as units in COMPLEMENTARY DISTRIBUTION (e.g. upper case restricted to SENTENCE-initial position, proper names, etc.), or in FREE VARIATION (as in some styles of handwriting), just as in PHONEMIC analysis. 'Grapheme analysis' is the main business of 'graphemics' (or GRAPHOLOGY). See Bolinger 1975: Ch. 14.

graphetic(s) A term used by some LINGUISTS, on analogy with PHONETICS, for the analysis of the GRAPHIC SUBSTANCE of written LANGUAGE. For example, it is theoretically possible to define a UNIVERSAL set of graphic features which enter into the formation of DISTINCTIVE letter shapes. There are also several properties of the written MEDIUM which exercise a considerable influence on communication, e.g. colour, size of writing or print, spacing. There is plainly an overlap here with the field of graphics and typography (and 'graphics' is in fact sometimes used as a label for this field). So far little analysis of TEXTS in these terms has taken place, and the relationship between GRAPHETICS and GRAPHOLOGY remains unclear. See Robins 1971: Ch. 1.

graphic substance A term used by some LINGUISTS to refer to the written form of LANGUAGE as seen as a set of physically definable visual properties, i.e. marks on a surface. The analogous term for speech is PHONIC substance. The linguistic analysis of these graphic or 'graphetic' features is sometimes referred to as GRAPHOLOGY, on analogy with PHONOLOGY. See Lyons 1968: Ch. 2.

graphology (graphological) A term used by some LINGUISTS to refer to the writing SYSTEM of a LANGUAGE – on analogy with PHONOLOGY. A 'graphological' analysis would be concerned to establish the minimal CONTRASTIVE UNITS of visual language – defined as GRAPHEMES, graphemic FEATURES, or without using EMIC terms – using similar techniques to those used in phonological analysis. Graphology in this sense has nothing to do with the analysis of handwriting to determine the psychological characteristics of the writer – an activity for which the same term is often popularly used. See Bolinger 1975; Ch. 14.

grave One of the features of sound set up by JAKOBSON & Halle in their DISTINCTIVE FEATURE theory of PHONOLOGY, to handle variations in PLACE OF ARTICULATION; its opposite being ACUTE. Grave sounds are defined ARTICULATORILY and ACOUSTICALLY, as those involving a peripheral articulation in the VOCAL TRACT, and a concentration of acoustic energy in the lower frequencies. BACK VOWELS, and LABIAL and VELAR CONSONANTS are [+grave]; FRONT vowels, and DENTAL, ALVEOLAR, and PALATAL consonants are [−grave]. See Ladefoged 1975: Ch. 11; Hyman 1975: Ch. 2.

groove A term sometimes used in PHONETICS to refer to a type of FRICATIVE where the TONGUE is slightly hollowed (or 'grooved') along its central line, the passage of air producing a sound with a higher frequency than in other fricatives. In English, [s], [z], [ʃ], and [ʒ] are 'groove fricatives'. In SLIT fricatives (e.g. [f], [θ]), there is no such groove. See Dinneen 1967: Ch. 2.

group (1) A term used in HALLIDAYAN grammar to refer to a UNIT on the RANK scale intermediate between CLAUSE and WORD. For example, in the SENTENCE *the car was parked in the street*, *the car* is a 'NOMINAL group', *was parked* is a 'VERBAL group', and *in the street* is an 'ADVERBIAL group'. The term PHRASE is equivalent in most other approaches. See Bolinger 1975: Ch. 15.

(2) A **group genitive** is a general designation for the English CONSTRUCTION where the GENITIVE ending is added to the last ELEMENT in a noun PHRASE containing POSTmodification or CO-ORDINATION, e.g. *the University of London's grant, Morecambe and Wise's humour*. See Quirk *et al* 1972: Ch. 4.

H

꩜꩜꩜꩜꩜꩜

Hallidayan Characteristic of, or a follower of, the linguistic principles of the British LINGUIST, Michael Alexander Kirkwood Halliday (b. 1925). Much of Halliday's early thinking can be traced back to the teaching of J. R. Firth, and his approach is accordingly often called 'neo-FIRTHIAN'. His original conception of LANGUAGE, SCALE-AND-CATEGORY grammar, was published in article form in 1961: this contained a MODEL of language organisation in terms of LEVELS OF SUBSTANCE, FORM (GRAMMAR and LEXIS) and CONTEXT, and theoretical model of grammar in terms of three SCALES (of RANK, EXPONENCE and DELICACY) and four CATEGORIES (of UNIT, CLASS, STRUCTURE and SYSTEM). The central role of the last two has led to an alternative label for this approach – 'system-structure' theory. In the 1970s, the notion of 'system' became the central construct in an alternative model known as 'systemic' grammar: here, grammar is seen as a network of inter-related systems of classes; ENTRY conditions define the choices which can be made from within each system, and these choices become increasingly specific ('delicate') as the analysis proceeds. In recent years, attempts have been made to relate systemic grammar to the principles of TRANSFORMATIONAL grammar. The application of Hallidayan ideas has been widespread, e.g. in TEXT analysis (cf. COHESION), STYLISTICS (cf. REGISTER) and language ACQUISITION. See Robins 1971: Ch. 7; Bolinger 1975: Ch. 15.

haplology A term used in PHONOLOGY, in both SYNCHRONIC and HISTORICAL contexts, to refer to the omission of some of the sounds occurring in a sequence of similar ARTICULATIONS, as when *cyclists* is pronounced /saıklıs:/, *library* /laıbrı/, etc. Some PSYCHOLINGUISTS also use the term to refer to a TONGUE-SLIP where an omission of this kind has taken place, e.g. *running jump* becoming *rump*. See Clark & Clark 1977: Ch. 7; Bolinger 1975: Ch. 12.

hard consonant An impressionistic term sometimes used in the PHONETIC descriptions of particular LANGUAGES, referring to a CONSONANT which

head

lacks PALATALisation. Russian is a language which has several such hard (as opposed to SOFT) consonants. In Russian the ъ symbol ('hard sign') marks this lack of palatalisation on the preceding consonant. See Ladefoged 1975: Ch. 7.

head A term used in the GRAMMATICAL description of some types of PHRASE (ENDOCENTRIC phrases) to refer to the central element which is DISTRIBUTIONALLY equivalent to the phrase as a whole. The head also determines any relationships of CONCORD or GOVERNMENT in other parts of the phrase or SENTENCE. For example, the head of the NOUN phrase *a big man* is *man*, and it is the singular form of this ITEM which relates to the co-occurrence of singular verb-forms, such as *is, walks*, etc.; the head of the VERB phrase *has put* is *put*, and it is this verb which accounts for the use of OBJECT and ADVERBIAL later in the sentence (e.g. *put it there*). In phrases such as *men and women*, either item could be the head. See Quirk *et al* 1972: Ch. 13; Lyons 1968: Ch. 6.

heightened subglottal pressure One of the SOURCE FEATURES of sound set up by CHOMSKY & Halle in their DISTINCTIVE FEATURE theory of PHONOLOGY, to handle variations in sub-GLOTTAL pressure, as in the ASPIRATED STOPS of various LANGUAGES, such as Hindi. See Hyman 1975: Ch. 2; Ladefoged 1975: Ch. 11.

hesitation The general sense of this term is used in LINGUISTICS, and especially in PSYCHOLINGUISTICS, where the phenomenon is sub-classified into types, and the significance of 'hesitation phenomena' in terms of LANGUAGE processing is discussed. Types of hesitation include silence, FILLED PAUSES (e.g. *er*, elongated SYLLABLES (e.g. *we-e-ll*), repetitions (e.g. *the-the-thing*...), and so on. The DISTRIBUTION of these features is by no means random in speech, and it has been hypothesised that they occur at points where the speaker is planning new UTTERANCES. Based on the extent to which hesitations coincide with the boundaries between GRAMMATICAL, SEMANTIC, etc. CONSTITUENTS, the possibility has emerged that there may be more than one level of planning (e.g. syntactic, semantic, interactional) in SPEECH PRODUCTION. See Clark & Clark 1977: Ch. 7.

heteronym(y) A term sometimes used in SEMANTIC analysis to refer to words (LEXEMES) which display partial HOMONYMY, i.e. they differ in MEANING, but are identical in FORM in one MEDIUM only (*viz* speech or writing). Examples would be the HOMOGRAPHS *row* (sc. a boat) and *row* (sc. noise), or the HOMOPHONES *threw* and *through*. See Lyons 1977b: Ch. 1.

heuristic An application in LINGUISTICS and PHONETICS of the general use of this term in cybernetics, referring to a specific mode of investigation adopted as part of a process of discovery or problem-solving. In linguistics, the notion has been introduced mainly in the discussion of PROCEDURES of analysis, where BLOOMFIELDIAN DISCOVERY procedures are contrasted with the FORMAL analyses of GENERATIVE GRAMMAR. The term is also used in the looser sense of a 'working hypothesis', used to suggest or eliminate a possible explanation of events. A notion such as DISCOURSE, for example, cannot easily be given a formal or operational definition, but it can be seen as a 'heuristic device', and used as a pre-theoretical notion, thus enabling an investigation to proceed. See Lyons 1977a: Ch. 4.

hierarchy (hierarchical) A term derived from TAXONOMIC studies and applied in LINGUISTICS to refer to any CLASSIFICATION of linguistic UNITS which recognises a series of successively subordinate LEVELS. **Hierarchical structure** can be illustrated from any branch of linguistics, e.g. the analysis of a SENTENCE into IMMEDIATE CONSTITUENTS, or the analysis of the LEXICON into semantic fields of increasing specificity (as in *Roget's Thesaurus*). The relationship of inclusion which is involved can be seen in analyses of linguistic structure where DISCOURSES are seen to 'consist of' sentences, which in turn consist of CLAUSES or PHRASES; these consist of WORDS, which in turn consist of MORPHEMES. The term has a special status in RELATIONAL GRAMMAR, as part of the phrase 'ACCESSIBILITY hierarchy'. See Lyons 1968: Ch. 4; Bolinger 1975: Ch. 1.

high One of the features of sound set up by CHOMSKY & Halle in their DISTINCTIVE FEATURE theory of PHONOLOGY, to handle variations in PLACE OF ARTICULATION (CAVITY features). High sounds are a type of TONGUE-BODY feature, and defined ARTICULATORILY as those produced by raising the TONGUE above the level it holds in neutral position; CLOSE VOWELS and PALATAL/VELAR CONSONANTS are [+high]. Its opposite is **non-high** [−high], referring to sounds produced without any such raising, as in OPEN vowels and FRONT consonants. See Ladefoged 1975: Ch. 11; Hyman 1975: Ch. 2.

higher A term used in GENERATIVE GRAMMAR to refer to a CATEGORY which is introduced into a SENTENCE DERIVATION earlier than a further instance of the same category. In a TREE diagram representation of the derivation, the first instance of the category is seen to be higher up the tree than the other instance(s). For example, in the derivation of such sentences as *the idea that the man will resign surprises me*, the following (partial) tree might be used:

In this sentence, the 'higher verb' is *surprise*, and the 'higher clause' or 'higher sentence' is *the idea surprises me*. Alternative terms are MATRIX and 'superordinate'. The usual term for the 'lower' verb/clause is EMBEDDED. See Akmajian & Heny 1975: Ch. 8.

historical linguistics A branch of LINGUISTICS which studies the development of LANGUAGE and languages over time; also known as DIACHRONIC linguistics. The data of study are identical to that of COMPARATIVE PHILOLOGY, *viz* the extant records of older states of languages; but the methods and aims are not the same. Historical linguistics uses the methods of the various schools of SYNCHRONIC linguistics (including SOCIOLINGUISTICS and PSYCHOLINGUISTICS, especially in considering the reasons for language change). One thus encounters such sub-fields as 'historical PHONOLOGY/MORPHOLOGY/SYNTAX', etc. It also aims to relate its findings to GENERAL linguistic theory. See Robins 1971: Ch. 1; Bolinger 1975: Chs. 12–13.

hocus-pocus A phrase coined in the 1950s to characterise one of two extreme states of mind in a hypothetical LINGUIST when he sets up a DESCRIPTION of linguistic DATA; opposed to GOD'S TRUTH. A 'hocus-pocus' linguist approaches his data in the expectation that he will have to impose an organisation on it in order to show STRUCTURAL patterns. Different linguists, on this view, could approach the same data, and by virtue of their different backgrounds, INTUITIONS, PROCEDURES, etc. arrive at differing descriptions. In a God's truth approach, by contrast, the aim is to demonstrate an underlying structure really present in the data over which there could be no dispute. See Robins 1971: Ch. 2.

hold(ing) A term used in describing the ARTICULATION of some types of sound, where the VOCAL ORGANS maintain their position for a definable period, as in the CLOSURE stage in the production of a PLOSIVE or a long CONSONANT (cf. LENGTH). See Gimson 1970: Ch. 8.

holophrase (holophras -tic, -is) A term used in language ACQUISITION to refer to a GRAMMATICALLY unstructured UTTERANCE, usually consisting of a single WORD, which is characteristic of the earliest stage of LANGUAGE learning in children. Typical 'holophrastic' utterances include *dada, allgone, more, there.* Theoretical controversy centres on the extent to which these utterances may be analysed as SENTENCES ('one-word sentences'), or as a reduced version of a sentence, whose other ELEMENTS are 'understood' in the EXTRA-LINGUISTIC SITUATION (e.g. *daddy* means 'there is daddy', the *there is* being expressed by gesture, tone of voice, etc.). **Holophrasis** is also sometimes identified in adult utterances where there is no internal STRUCTURAL contrastivity, such as *thanks, please, sorry.* See Bolinger 1975: Ch. 1.

homograph(-y, -ic) (1) A term used in SEMANTIC analysis to refer to WORDS (i.e. LEXEMES) which have the same spelling, but differ in MEANING. 'Homographs' are a type of HOMONYMY. 'Homography' is illustrated from such pairs as *wind* (sc. blowing) and *wind* (sc. a clock). When there is AMBIGUITY on account of this identity, a **homographic clash** or 'conflict' is said to have occurred. See Lyons 1977b: Ch. 1.

(2) The term **homography** is also used to refer to a type of orthography where there is a one-to-one correspondence between symbols and sounds, as in a PHONETIC TRANSCRIPTION, or the systematically devised alphabets of some languages. In this sense, it is opposed to 'heterographic' systems, such as the spelling system of English, French, etc. See Abercrombie 1967: Ch. 7.

homonym(-y, ic) A term used in SEMANTIC analysis to refer to LEXICAL ITEMS which have the same FORM, but differ in MEANING. 'Homonymy' is illustrated from the various meanings of *bear* (= animal, carry) or *ear* (of body, of corn). In these examples, the identity covers both spoken and written forms, but it is possible to have partial homonymy (or 'heteronymy'), where the identity is within a single MEDIUM, as in HOMOPHONY and HOMOGRAPHY. When there is AMBIGUITY between homonyms (whether non-deliberate or contrived, as in riddles and puns), a **homonymic clash** or 'conflict' is said to have occurred. In semantic analysis, the theoretical distinction between homonymy and POLYSEMY (one form with different meanings) provides a problem which has attracted a great deal of attention. See Lyons 1977b: Chs. 1, 13.

homophone (homophon-y, -ic) A term used in SEMANTIC analysis to refer to WORDS (i.e. LEXEMES) which have the same pronunciation, but differ in MEANING. 'Homophones' are a type of HOMONYMY. **Homophony** is illustrated from such pairs as *threw/through* and *rode/rowed*. When there is AMBIGUITY on account of this identity, a **homophonic clash** or 'conflict' is said to have occurred. See Lyons 1977b: Ch. 1.

homorganic A general term in the PHONETIC classification of speech sounds, referring to sounds which are produced at the same PLACE OF ARTICULATION, such as [p], [b] and [m]. Sounds involving independent articulations may be referred to as 'heterorganic'. Sounds involving adjacent, and thus to some degree mutually dependent, articulations are also sometimes further distinguished as 'contiguous'. See Catford 1977: Ch. 10.

honorific A term used in the GRAMMATICAL analysis of some LANGUAGES (e.g. Japanese) to refer to SYNTACTIC or MORPHOLOGICAL distinctions used to express LEVELS of politeness or respect, especially in relation to the compared social status of the participants. The PRONOUN system of several European languages expresses a contrast of this kind, e.g. French *tu* vs. *vous*, Spanish *tú* vs. *usted*. See Lyons 1968: Ch. 7; 1977b: Ch. 15.

hypercorrection A term used in LINGUISTICS to refer to the movement of a linguistic FORM beyond the point set by the VARIETY of LANGUAGE that a speaker has as his target. The phenomenon usually takes place when speakers of a non-standard DIALECT attempt to use the STANDARD dialect and 'go too far', producing a version which does not appear in the standard, e.g. putting a long /ɑ/ in place of a short /æ/ in such words as *cap*, *mat*, etc. Analogous behaviour is encountered in second-language learning. See Gumperz & Hymes 1971: Ch. 19.

hypersememic One of the strata recognised in STRATIFICATIONAL GRAMMAR, dealing with the conceptual or REFERENTIAL properties of LANGUAGE. See Bolinger 1975: Ch. 15.

hyponym(y) A term used in SEMANTICS as part of the study of the SENSE relations which relate LEXICAL ITEMS. 'Hyponymy' is the relationship which obtains between specific and general lexical items, such that the former is 'included' in the latter (i.e. 'is a hyponym of' the latter). For example, a *cat* is a hyponym of *animal*, *flute* of *instrument*, *chair* of *furniture*, and so on. In each case, there is a superordinate term, with reference to which the subordinate term can be defined, as is the usual practice in dictionary definitions ('a cat is a type of animal...'). The set of terms which are hyponyms of the same superordinate term are **co-hyponyms**, e.g. *flute*, *clarinet*, *trumpet*, etc. Hyponymy is distinguished from such other sense relations as SYNONYMY and ANTONYMY. See Lyons 1977b: Ch. 9.

hypophonemic One of the strata recognised in STRATIFICATIONAL GRAMMAR, dealing with the PHONETIC properties of an UTTERANCE. See Bolinger 1975: Ch. 15.

hypotactic (hypotaxis) A term used in TRADITIONAL GRAMMATICAL analysis, and often found in DESCRIPTIVE LINGUISTIC studies, to refer to SUBORDINATE CONSTRUCTIONS where CONSTITUENTS have been linked through the use of CONJUNCTIONS. 'Hypotactic constructions' are opposed to PARATACTIC ones, where the linkage is conveyed solely by juxtaposition and punctuation/INTONATION. 'Hypotaxis' is illustrated by *The man laughed when the dog barked* (cf. *the man laughed; the dog barked*). See Quirk *et al* 1972: Ch. 9.

I

𝕊𝕊𝕊𝕊𝕊𝕊

IA The usual abbreviation for an ITEM AND ARRANGEMENT MODEL of description in MORPHOLOGY.

IC The usual abbreviation for IMMEDIATE CONSTITUENT.

iconic(ity) A suggested defining property of some SEMIOTIC SYSTEMS, but not LANGUAGE, to refer to signals whose physical FORM closely corresponds to characteristics of the entities to which they refer. This is the normal state of affairs in animal communication, for example, where a call expressing fear is only used in a fear-producing context. In language, only a small number of ITEMS could be argued to possess such directly symbolic ('iconic') properties, e.g. onomatapoeic expressions, such as *cuckoo*, *growl*, etc. See Lyon 1977b: Chs. 3, 4.

idealisation (ideal) A term used in LINGUISTICS to refer to the degree to which the linguist ignores certain aspects of the variability in his raw DATA, in order to arrive at an analysis that is as GENERALLY applicable as possible. 'Idealisation' is a major assumption of GENERATIVE linguistics, as it underlies the notion of COMPETENCE. A main aim of linguistics, in this view, is to account for the LANGUAGE of an 'ideal' speaker-hearer in an ideal (i.e. homogenous) SPEECH community, who knows his language perfectly, and is unaffected by memory limitations, distractions, errors, etc. in actually using his language. While some degree of idealisation is inevitable, if general statements are to be made, the decision as to what can be discounted in carrying out an analysis is often controversial. See Lyons 1968: Ch. 4.

ideational A term sometimes used in SEMANTICS as part of a classification of types of MEANING. It refers to that aspect of meaning which relates to the speaker's COGNITIVE awareness of the external world or (in a behavioural definition) to the objectively verifiable states of affairs in the external world, as reflected in LANGUAGE. This function of language, for the expression of CONTENT, is usually contrasted with INTERPERSONAL (or social), EXPRESSIVE and TEXTUAL meaning. Terms with similar meaning include 'conceptual' and COGNITIVE. See Lyons 1977b: Ch. 2.

idiolect A term used in LINGUISTICS to refer to the linguistic SYSTEM of an individual speaker – his personal DIALECT. A dialect can be seen as an abstraction deriving from the analysis of a large number of idiolects. Some linguists give the term a more restricted definition, referring to the speech habits of a person as displayed in a particular VARIETY at a given time. See Robins 1971: Ch. 2; Trudgill 1974: Ch. 1.

idiom(-atic) A term used in GRAMMAR and LEXICOLOGY to refer to a SEQUENCE of WORDS which is SEMANTICALLY and often SYNTACTICALLY restricted, so that they function as a single UNIT. From a semantic viewpoint, the MEANINGS of the individual words cannot be summed to produce the meaning of the 'idiomatic' expression as a whole. From a syntactic viewpoint, the words often do not permit the usual variability they display in other CONTEXTS, e.g. *it's raining cats and dogs* does not permit **it's raining a cat and a dog/dogs and cats*, etc. Because of their lack of internal CONTRASTIVITY, some linguists refer to idioms as 'ready-made UTTERANCES'. An alternative terminology refers to idioms as 'habitual COLLOCATIONS'. A point which has attracted considerable discussion is the extent to which degrees and kinds of idiomaticness can be established: some idioms do permit a degree of internal change, and are somewhat more literal in meaning than others (e.g. *it's worth his while/the job will be worth my while*, etc.). See Lyons 1968: Ch. 5; Bolinger 1975: Ch. 5.

idiophone A term used by some LINGUISTS to refer to a speech sound identifiable with reference to a single IDIOLECT. See Bolinger 1975: Ch. 11.

ill-formed(ness) A term used in LINGUISTICS, especially in GENERATIVE GRAMMAR, to refer to the ungrammaticality ('ill-formedness' or DEVIANCE) of a SENTENCE. A sentence is ill-formed if it cannot be generated by the RULES of a grammar; it is WELL-FORMED if it can be. The term applies equally to SYNTAX, SEMANTICS and PHONOLOGY. See Lyons 1977a: Ch. 5; Huddleston 1976: Ch. 1.

illocutionary A term used in the theory of SPEECH-ACTS to refer to an act which is performed by the speaker by virtue of his UTTERANCE having been made. Examples of **illocutionary acts** (or **illocutionary**

force) include promising, commanding, requesting, baptising, arresting, etc. The term is contrasted with LOCUTIONARY (the act of 'saying') and PERLOCUTIONARY (where the act is defined by reference to the effect it has on the hearer). See Lyons 1977b: Ch. 16; Clark & Clark 1977: Ch. 3.

imitation An application of the general sense of this term to LANGUAGE ACQUISITION, where it refers to the child's behaviour in copying the language he has around him. The importance of the notion is twofold. First, it has been shown that imitation cannot by itself account for the facts of language development (despite a popular view to the contrary, that children learn language by imitating their parents): FORMS such as *mouses and *wented, and SENTENCES such as *Me not like that, show that some internal process of construction is taking place. Secondly, the skills a child shows when he is actually imitating are often different, in important aspects, from those he displays in spontaneous SPEECH PRODUCTION, or in COMPREHENSION. The relationship between imitation, production and comprehension has been a major focus of experimental and descriptive interest in acquisition studies. See Clark & Clark 1977: Ch. 9.

immediate constituent (IC) A term used in GRAMMATICAL analysis to refer to the major divisions that can be made within a SYNTACTIC CONSTRUCTION, at any LEVEL. For example, in analysing the SENTENCE *The boy is walking*, the immediate constituents would be *the boy* and *is walking*. These in turn can be analysed into immediate constituents (*the + boy*, *is + walking*), and the process continues until irreducible constituents are reached. The whole procedure is known as **immediate constituent analysis** (or 'CONSTITUENT analysis'), and was a major feature of BLOOMFIELDIAN STRUCTURALIST linguistics. See Lyons 1968: Ch. 6; 1977a: Ch. 6.

imperative A term used in the GRAMMATICAL classification of SENTENCE types, and usually seen in contrast to INDICATIVE, INTERROGATIVE, etc. MOODS. It refers to VERB FORMS or sentence/CLAUSE types used in the expression of COMMANDS, e.g. *Go away!* See Quirk *et al* 1972: Ch. 7; Lyons 1977b: Ch. 1.

implicature A term derived from the work of the philosopher H. P. Grice and now frequently used in LINGUISTICS as part of the study of conversational structure. **Conversational implicatures** refer to the implications which can be deduced from the FORM of an UTTERANCE, on the basis of certain CO-OPERATIVE PRINCIPLES which govern the efficiency and normal ACCEPTABILITY of conversations, as when the sentence *There's some chalk on the floor* is taken to mean 'you ought to pick it up'. Several types of implicature have been discussed, in the context of the relationship between language and logical expression, and of the conditions which affect the APPROPRIATENESS of utterances; but relatively little detailed linguistic investigation has yet taken place. See Clark & Clark 1977: Ch. 3; Lyons 1977b: Ch. 14.

implosive A term used in the PHONETIC classification of CONSONANT sounds on the basis of their MANNER OF ARTICULATION: it refers to the series of PLOSIVE sounds it is possible to make using an AIR-STREAM involving an inwards movement of air in the mouth (an INGRESSIVE air-stream). A complete CLOSURE is made in the mouth, as with any plosive sound, but the air behind the closure is not compressed, ready for outwards release; instead, a downwards movement of the LARYNX takes place, and the air inside the mouth is accordingly rarefied. Upon release of the closure, air is then sucked into the mouth at the same time as the GLOTTIS is released, allowing lung air to produce some VOCAL CORD vibration. It is this combination of movements that results in the characteristically 'hollow' auditory effect of the implosive consonants. Such consonants are usually VOICED and occur PHONEMI-CALLY in such languages as Sindhi and Igbo. They are transcribed with a right-facing hook attached to the consonant symbol, as in [ɠ], [ɗ], [ɓ]. Alternative terms are 'ingressive stop' and 'suction stop' consonants. There is no opposite technical term 'explosive'. See Gimson 1970: Ch. 4; Catford 1977: Ch. 5.

inalienable A term used in GRAMMATICAL analysis to refer to a type of possessive relationship formally marked in some languages (e.g. Chinese). If a possessed item is seen as being in a permanent or necessary relationship to its possessor, the relationship is said to be 'inalienable' (e.g. *the man's head, the town centre*), otherwise it is ALIENABLE. See Lyons 1968: Ch. 7; 1977b: Ch. 9.

inceptive, inchoative Terms used in the GRAMMATICAL analysis of VERBS, to refer to a type of ASPECTUAL relationship in which the beginning of an action is specified. In LANGUAGES which mark 'inceptive' (or 'inchoative') aspects, the MEANINGS might be translated into English by 'be about to' or 'be on the point of' – for example, Latin *-escere*. See Lyons 1968: Ch. 7.

inclusion (inclu-ded, -sive) (1) A SEMANTIC relationship which identifies the SENSE relation of HYPONYMY, e.g. to say that a *car* is a kind of *vehicle*, is to say that the class of cars is 'included' within that of vehicles. See Lyons 1977b: Ch. 9.

(2) In GRAMMATICAL analysis, the term **included** is mainly used to refer to a LINGUISTIC FORM which occurs as a CONSTITUENT of a CONSTRUCTION: it is in the 'included position'. For example, the CLAUSE *parked in the street* is in the included position in the SENTENCE *The car parked in the street was a Hillman*. See Robins 1971: Ch. 6.

(3) With reference to PRONOUNS, the term **inclusive** is used (in contrast with 'exclusive') to refer to a first PERSON role where the speaker and addressee are both included, e.g. *we* = 'me and you'. See Lyons 1968: Ch. 7.

incompatibility (incompatible) A term used in SEMANTICS as part of the study of the SENSE relations between LEXICAL ITEMS. It refers to sets of items where the choice of one item excludes the use of all the other items from that set (unless there is to be a contradiction). Colour terms provide a well-studied example: to say *the car is red* excludes *the car is green/blue*, etc. – and the set of items which contrast in this way are said to be 'incompatible'. 'Incompatibility' has been less investigated than other sense relations (such as ANTONYMY and SYNONYMY), but some linguists have pointed to the existence of different types of many-member (as opposed to binary) sets, such as ranks (e.g. military), scales (e.g. value judgements) and cycles (e.g. seasons). See Lyons 1977b: Ch. 9.

incorporating A type of LANGUAGE sometimes distinguished in COMPARATIVE LINGUISTICS using STRUCTURAL (as opposed to HISTORICAL) criteria, and focusing on the characteristics of the WORD: 'polysynthetic' or **incorporating languages** demonstrate MORPHOLOGICALLY complex, long word forms, as in the CONSTRUCTIONS typical of many American Indian languages, and encountered occasionally in English, in coinages such as *anti/dis/establish/ment/arian/ism/s*. Some linguists, however, prefer to see such constructions handled as a complex of 'incorporated' AGGLUTINATIVE and FUSIONAL characteristics, and do not regard this category of language as typologically distinct. As always in such classifications, the categories are not clear-cut: different languages will display the characteristic of 'incorporation' to a greater or lesser degree. See Robins 1971: Ch. 8; Bolinger 1975: Ch. 2.

indeterminacy (indeterminate) A term used in LINGUISTICS to refer to a state of affairs in linguistic study in which there is uncertainty on the part of a NATIVE-SPEAKER, or disagreement between native-speakers, as to what is GRAMMATICAL or ACCEPTABLE; or in which there is uncertainty on the part of a linguist, or between several linguists, as to how and where a boundary-line between different types of STRUCTURE might best be drawn. Indeterminacy poses a major difficulty for linguistic theories which attempt to define the limits of grammaticality in an unequivocal way (as in GENERATIVE grammar). It is a major focus of attention in NON-DISCRETE grammar. See Lyons 1968: Ch. 4.

indexical (indices) A term used by some LINGUISTS to refer to features of speech or writing which reveal the personal (biological, psychological or social) characteristics of a LANGUAGE user, as in VOICE QUALITY or handwriting. More generally, the term may be used to refer to the membership-identifying characteristics of a group, such as regional, social or occupational 'indices'. See Lyons 1977b: Ch. 4; Abercrombie 1967: Ch. 1.

indicative A term used in the GRAMMATICAL classification of SENTENCE types, and usually seen in contrast to IMPERATIVE, SUBJUNCTIVE, etc. MOODS. It refers to VERB forms or sentence/CLAUSE types used in the expression of STATEMENTS and QUESTIONS, e.g. *the man is walking*. Alternatively, the term 'declarative' may be used. See Quirk *et al* 1972; Lyons 1977b: Ch. 1.

indirect (1) A term used in GRAMMATICAL description to refer to one of the two types of OBJECT ELEMENT which can function in CLAUSE STRUCTURE, the other being labelled DIRECT. **Indirect objects** in English usually appear before the direct object (e.g. *the man gave the boy a book*), but may also follow it (e.g. *the man gave a book to the boy*). See Quirk *et al* 1972: Chs. 2, 11.

(2) The opposition between direct and indirect is also used to identify the two main ways of reflecting a person's speech: **indirect speech** (or 'reported speech') refers to the use of a grammatical CONSTRUCTION where the WORDS of the speaker are SUBORDINATED to a VERB in a main CLAUSE, e.g. *he said that he had a cold*, where the 'direct speech' would have been *I have a cold*. See Quirk *et al* 1972: Ch. 11.

(3) In the classification of SPEECH-ACTS, the term refers to an UTTERANCE whose linguistic FORM does not directly reflect its communicative purpose, as when *I'm feeling cold* functions as a request for someone to close a door. If, on the other hand, someone produced the same sentence to express, literally the fact that he was feeling cold, then the speech-act would be direct – an assertion. See Clark & Clark 1977: Ch. 3; Lyons 1977b: Ch. 16.

infinitive A traditional term for the non-FINITE FORM of the VERB usually cited as its unMARKED or BASE form, e.g. *go, walk, kick*, though some LANGUAGES mark it SYNTACTICALLY or MORPHOLOGICALLY. In English, the infinitive form may be used alone or in conjunction with the PARTICLE *to* (the '*to*-infinitive'), e.g. *he saw her come* vs. *he wants to come*. See Quirk *et al* 1972: Ch. 12.

infix(-ing/ation) A term used in MORPHOLOGY referring to an AFFIX which is added within a ROOT or STEM. The process of **infixation** is not encountered in European LANGUAGES, but it is commonly found in Asian, American Indian and African languages (e.g. Arabic). See Robins 1971: Ch. 5; Matthews 1974: Ch. 7.

inflection(al) (inflexion(al), inflect) (1) A term used in MORPHOLOGY to refer to one of the two main CATEGORIES or processes of WORD-FORMATION, the other being DERIVATION(AL). These terms also apply to the two types of AFFIX involved in word-formation. Inflectional affixes signal GRAMMATICAL relationships, such as plural, past TENSE and possession, and do not change the grammatical CLASS of the STEMS to which they are attached; that is, the words constitute a single PARADIGM, e.g. *walk, walks, walked*. A word is said to 'inflect for' past tense, plural, etc. In traditional (pre-linguistic) grammatical studies, the term 'accidence' was used in this sense. See Matthews 1974: Ch. 7; Robins 1971: Ch. 5.

(2) In the phrase **inflecting language** ('inflectional' or 'inflected' languages), the term refers to a type of LANGUAGE established by COMPARATIVE LINGUISTICS using STRUCTURAL (as opposed to HISTORICAL) criteria, and focusing on the characteristics of the WORD. In this kind of language, words display grammatical relationships morphologically: they typically contain more than one MORPHEME, but unlike AGGLUTINATIVE languages, there is no one-to-one correspondence between these morphemes and the linear SEQUENCE of MORPHS. In languages such as Latin, Greek, Arabic, etc., the inflectional forms of words may represent several morphological OPPOSITIONS, e.g. in Latin *amo* 'I love', the form simultaneously represents present TENSE, ACTIVE, 1st PERSON singular, INDICATIVE. This 'fusing' of properties has led to such languages being called FUSIONAL, and has motivated the WORD AND PARADIGM MODEL of analysis. As always in such classifications, the categories are not clear-cut: different languages will display the characteristic of inflection to a greater or lesser degree. See Robins 1971: Ch. 8; Lyons 1968: Ch. 5.

informant Someone who acts as a source of DATA for LINGUISTIC analysis, usually a NATIVE-SPEAKER of a LANGUAGE. It may be the linguist himself, but more usually an attempt is made to construct or verify hypotheses by referring directly to a range of informants, who provide, it is hoped, a representative sample of the language one is investigating. In fieldwork on previously unstudied languages, the informant is of fundamental importance, and several sophisticated techniques for ELICITING relevant but natural data from informants have now been devised. See Robins 1971: Ch. 9.

information LINGUISTICS has made several uses of this fundamental concept, both in a general sense, and also as formalised in statistical terms, derived from the mathematical theory of COMMUNICATION. Ideas derived from information theory (as formulated originally by Claude Shannon and Warren Weaver in their book *The Mathematical Theory of Communication* (1949)) have been applied in PHONETICS (e.g. in analysing the amount of information carried by the various features of the sound wave), GRAMMAR (e.g. in studies of the predictability of various parts of a SENTENCE), and SEMANTICS (e.g. in applying the notion of 'choice' between alternatives in the analysis of semantic CONTRASTS). The concept of REDUNDANCY, for example, ultimately derives from this approach.

In its general sense, the term is used by several linguists as a basis for a theoretical account of the STRUCTURE of messages. It is postulated that speech can be seen as displaying an 'information structure', with formally identifiable 'units of information'. INTONATION provides the main signal for such UNITS. The TONE UNIT represents an information unit, and the NUCLEAR tone marks the information FOCUS. Many sentences will be single units of information, e.g. *the box on the table is ready for pòsting/*, but altering the intonation, in this view, alters the number of informational units, e.g. *the box on the táble/is ready for pòsting/*. Even if one tone unit is retained, altering the TONICITY will change the information structure, e.g. *the bòx on the table is ready for posting/* (i.e. not the envelope). The further analysis of information structure is complex and controversial: a common next step is to distinguish between GIVEN and NEW information. Analysts who use this approach (e.g. HALLIDAYAN linguists) usually distinguish between information-structure and THEMATIC and grammatical structure. See Lyons 1968: Ch. 2; 1977b: Ch. 12; Quirk *et al* 1972: Ch. 14.

-ing form A term used in English GRAMMATICAL description to refer to the FORM of the VERB ending in *-ing*, e.g. *going, smoking*. Many such forms can be used without change as NOUNS (e.g. *smoking is prohibited*), and the purpose of the term is to provide a neutral DESCRIPTIVE label for this feature of English, thus avoiding the use of such traditional notions as 'gerund', which were originally devised for Latin grammar.

ingressive

The term 'verb(al)-noun' is sometimes used. See Quirk *et al* 1972: Ch. 3; Akmajian & Heny 1975: Ch. 4.

ingressive A term used in the PHONETIC classification of speech sounds, referring to all sounds produced using an inwards-moving AIR-STREAM. The opposite category is EGRESSIVE, which is the normal mode for speech production. Ingressive sounds are often heard incidentally, as when one speaks while breathing in, when out of breath, or vocalises upon a sudden intake of breath when expressing pain or surprise. Two types of ingressive sound are used as part of the PHONEMIC systems of some LANGUAGES: IMPLOSIVE consonants, such as [ɓ], [ɗ], [ɠ], made by an inward flow of air in conjunction with GLOTTAL vibration; and 'velaric' consonants (cf. VELAR), which constitute such CLICK sounds as [ʇ] (as in 'tut tut'), made by an inward flow of air in conjunction with contact made at the velum. See Gimson 1970: Chs. 2, 4; Catford 1977: Chs. 2, 5.

inherent features A term used in some MODELS of GENERATIVE GRAMMAR (cf. ASPECTS) to refer to one of the types of (BINARY) FEATURES which are contained in a LEXICAL entry (the others being CONTEXTUAL and RULE features), and which provides information about the essential characteristics of an ITEM likely to affect its SYNTACTIC functioning, e.g. [+Human], [+Abstract], [+Male]. These features are involved at several points in an analysis, e.g. in specifying SELECTIONAL restrictions, and in some non-lexical TRANS-FORMATIONS. See Huddleston 1976: Ch. 10.

initial The usual way of referring to the first ELEMENT in a LINGUISTIC UNIT, especially in PHONOLOGY. For example, the PHONEME /k/ occurs 'in initial position' (or 'initially') in the word *cat*; the word *the* occurs in initial position in the PHRASE *the big house*. Other positions are referred to as MEDIAL and FINAL. Other linguistic features which occur in this position are sometimes labelled accordingly, e.g. 'initial STRESS' (i.e. stress on the first SYLLABLE in a WORD). See Gimson 1971: Ch. 5.

initial symbol The first, undefined term in a GENERATIVE GRAMMAR, which appears on the left-hand side of the first REWRITE RULE. Standing for SENTENCE, the highest-level CONSTRUCTION recognised by the grammar, it is usually written Σ, or S. The contrast implied is with TERMINAL symbols, the items which occur in a terminal STRING generated by the grammar. Other starting-points than sentence have occasionally been suggested. See Lyons 1968: Ch. 6.

initiator (initiation) A term in PHONETICS for those VOCAL ORGANS which are the source of air movement. The lungs are the normal initiators for speech, but other AIR-STREAM MECHANISMS can be used. Initiation, from an aerodynamic point of view, is comparable to a bellows or piston. See Catford 1977: Ch. 5.

innate(ness) An application of the philosophical use of this term in PSYCHOLINGUISTICS, referring to the view that the child is born with a biological predisposition to learn LANGUAGE. The **innateness hypothesis** argues that the rapid and complex development of children's GRAMMATICAL COMPETENCE can be explained only by the hypothesis that they are born with an innate knowledge of at least some of the UNIVERSAL STRUCTURAL principles of human language. This view has received considerable support in GENERATIVE linguistics (cf. language ACQUISITION DEVICE), but controversy abounds over the nature of the early linguistic knowledge which might be attributable to the child, and whether this knowledge can be specified independently of other (e.g. cognitive) factors. See Clark & Clark 1977: Ch. 14.

insertion A basic SYNTACTIC operation within the framework of TRANS-FORMATIONAL GRAMMAR which inserts a new STRUCTURAL ELEMENT into a STRING; specific types of example include 'DO-insertion', 'NEGATIVE (*neg-*) insertion' and '*there*-insertion' (which inserts an empty *there* in SUBJECT-position in STATEMENTS, e.g. *there was a cat in the garden*). See Akmajian & Heny 1975: Ch. 7.

instantaneous A term sometimes used in DISTINCTIVE FEATURE theory of PHONOLOGY, as part of the phrase 'instantaneous release', referring to a sound released suddenly, without the ACOUSTIC turbulence of a FRICATIVE, as in PLOSIVE CONSONANTS. Its opposite is DELAYED RELEASE, used to characterise AFFRICATES. See Hyman 1975: Ch. 2.

instrumental In languages which express GRAMMATICAL relationships by means of INFLECTIONS, this term refers to the FORM taken by a WORD, usually a NOUN or PRONOUN, when it expresses such a notion as 'by means of' (as in Russian). The term has a special status in CASE grammar, where it refers to the SEMANTIC case of the inANIMATE entity causally involved in a verb's action (e.g. *the key* in *the key opened the door* or *the door was opened with a key*), and is contrasted with AGENTIVE, DATIVE, etc. See Lyons 1968: Ch. 8; Bolinger 1975: Ch. 15.

intensifier A term used in some GRAMMATICAL classifications of WORDS to refer to a CLASS of ADVERBS which have a heightening or lowering effect on the MEANING of another ELEMENT in the SENTENCE, e.g. *very, terribly, definitely, hardly, kind of*. See Quirk *et al* 1972: Ch. 8.

intension A term used in philosophy and logic, and now often used as part of a theoretical framework for LINGUISTIC SEMANTICS, to refer to the set of defining properties which determines the APPLICABILITY of a term. For example, 'legs', 'flat surface', etc. define the intension of *table*, and an 'intensional definition' would be based on such notions, e.g. 'A table is something with legs, a flat surface, etc.' See Lyons 1977b: Ch. 6.

intensive A term used in some GRAMMATICAL analyses to refer to STRUCTURES where there is a close SEMANTIC identity between ELEMENTS of structure, such as between SUBJECT and COMPLEMENT (e.g. *he is a fool*), OBJECT and complement (e.g. *they called him Fred*) or APPOSITION (e.g. *John the butcher...*). The verbs involved in 'intensive constructions' are called 'intensive verbs'. The term is opposed to EXTENSIVE. See Quirk *et al* 1972: Chs. 2, 7.

interchangeability A suggested defining property of a SEMIOTIC SYSTEM, including human LANGUAGE, to refer to the system's ability to be mutually transmitted and received by members of the same species. Some animal signals, by contrast, lack this property – for example, female calls which are not shared by the male members of the species. See Lyons 1977b: Ch. 3.

interdental A term used in the PHONETIC classification of CONSONANT sounds, referring to a sound made by the TIP of the TONGUE between the teeth, as in English *th* /θ/ and /ð/. See Gimson 1970: Chs. 4, 8.

interference A term used in SOCIOLINGUISTICS and foreign language learning to refer to the ERRORS a speaker introduces into one LANGUAGE as a result of his contact with another language. The most common source of error is in the process of learning a foreign language, where the native tongue interferes; but interference may occur in other CONTACT situations (as in MULTILINGUALISM). See Corder 1973: Ch. 6.

interjection A term used in the TRADITIONAL CLASSIFICATION of PARTS OF SPEECH, referring to a CLASS of WORDS which are UNPRODUCTIVE, do not entire into SYNTACTIC relationships with other classes, and whose FUNCTION is purely EMOTIVE, e.g. *Yuk!*, *Strewth!*, *Blast!*, *Tut tut!*. There is an unclear boundary between these ITEMS and other types of

EXCLAMATION, where some REFERENTIAL MEANING may be involved, and where there may be more than one word, e.g. *Excellent!*, *Lucky devil!*, *Cheers!*, *Well well!* Several alternative ways of analysing these items have been suggested, using such notions as MINOR SENTENCE, FORMULAIC LANGUAGE, etc. See Quirk *et al* 1972: Ch. 7.

inter-level A term used in HALLIDAYAN LINGUISTICS referring to a LEVEL of analysis lying in between the main levels recognised by the theory. In this veiw, PHONOLOGY would be seen as an inter-level relating PHONIC/GRAPHIC SUBSTANCE and linguistic FORM. See Bolinger 1975: Ch. 15.

intermediate A term used in the PHONETIC classification of VOWEL QUALITIES, to refer to a vowel which falls between two adjacent CARDINAL vowels. The vowel which occurs in the centre of the cardinal vowel area (cf. SCHWA) is also sometimes referred to as an 'intermediate vowel'. See Gimson 1970: Ch. 7.

internalise A term used in GENERATIVE LINGUISTICS to refer to the process whereby speakers come to possess knowledge of the STRUC-TURE of their LANGUAGE. The term is primarily used in the context of language ACQUISITION, where children are said to 'internalise' RULES, as when the use of such FORMS as *mans* and *mices* shows that a plural formation RULE has been acquired. COMPETENCE, on this account, can be seen as a SYSTEM of internalised rules. See Clark & Clark 1977: Ch. 8.

International Phonetic Association (IPA) An organisation founded in 1886 by a group of European phoneticians (Paul Passy (1859–1940) and others) to promote the study of PHONETICS. In 1889 it published the **International Phonetic Alphabet** which, in modified and ex-panded form, is today the most widely used system for transcribing the sounds of a LANGUAGE (cf. TRANSCRIPTION). See Gimson 1970: App.

interpersonal A term sometimes used in SEMANTICS as part of a classification of types of MEANING. It refers to those aspects of meaning which relate to the establishing and maintaining of social relations, e.g. social roles, STYLISTIC LEVEL, the expression of personality, etc. Some scholars also subsume EXPRESSIVE meaning under this heading. An alternative view sees the LINGUISTIC expression of social relationships as being a matter of SOCIOLINGUISTIC FUNCTION, and not semantics. See Lyons 1977b: Ch. 2.

interpretive A term used in GENERATIVE LINGUISTICS to refer to a mode of relationship between LEVELS of REPRESENTATION. Its original use can be defined with reference to the STANDARD theory of generative GRAMMAR. Here, the SEMANTIC RULES which relate SYNTACTIC DEEP STRUCTURE to the semantic COMPONENT, and the PHONOLOGICAL rules which relate syntactic SURFACE STRUCTURES to the phonological component are both 'interpretive', i.e. they 'interpret' the output of the syntactic structures by ASSIGNING them a (semantic or PHONETIC) representation, which is the basis from which the MEANING and pronunciation of the sentence is derived. In the **interpretive semantics** view, it is thus the level of syntax which contains all the generative POWER of the grammar. In the early 1970s, the term came to characterise any MODEL of this general sort, as opposed to those which claimed that it was the syntax, and not the semantics, which was interpretive – the view of GENERATIVE SEMANTICS. See Lyons 1977a: Ch. 8; Huddleston 1976: Ch. 16.

interrogative A term used in the GRAMMATICAL classification of SENTENCE types, and usually seen in contrast to DECLARATIVE. It refers to VERB FORMS or SENTENCE/CLAUSE types used in the expression of QUESTIONS, e.g. the inverted order of *is he coming?*, or the use of an 'interrogative word' (often sub-classified as interrogative ADJECTIVES; e.g. *which*; ADVERBS, e.g. *why*; and PRONOUNS, e.g. *who*). See Quirk *et al* 1972: Ch. 7; Lyons 1977b: Ch. 1.

interruptability A term used in GRAMMAR, to refer to a defining property of the WORD, seen as a grammatical UNIT, where it appears in the form **uninterruptability**. A more positive name for this criterion is COHESIVENESS. See Matthews 1974: Ch. 9; Lyons 1968: Ch. 5.

interrupted A term sometimes used in the DISTINCTIVE FEATURE theory of PHONOLOGY to refer to sounds produced with a complete CLOSURE of the VOCAL TRACT, as in PLOSIVES. Its opposite is CONTINUANT, used to characterise FRICATIVES, VOWELS, etc. See Hyman 1975: Ch. 2.

intervocalic A term used in PHONETICS to refer to a CONSONANT sound used between two VOWELS, as in the /t/ of *attack*. The phonetic characteristics of consonants in this position are often different from those in other positions, e.g. the amount of VOICING in a voiced consonant is likely to be greater. See Gimson 1970: Ch. 8.

intonation A term used in the study of SUPRASEGMENTAL PHONOLOGY, referring to the distinctive use of patterns of PITCH, or melody. Several ways of analysing intonation have been suggested: in some approaches, the pitch patterns are described as CONTOURS and analysed in terms of LEVELS of pitch as pitch PHONEMES and MORPHEMES; in others, the patterns are described as TONE UNITS or tone groups, analysed further as contrasts of NUCLEAR TONE, TONICITY, etc. The three variables of pitch range, height and direction are generally distinguished.

Intonation performs several functions in language. Its most important function is as a signal of GRAMMATICAL structure, where it performs a role similar to punctuation in writing, but involving far more contrasts. The marking of SENTENCE, CLAUSE and other boundaries, and the contrast between some grammatical structures, such as QUESTIONS and statements, may be made using intonation. For example, the change in meaning illustrated by 'Are you asking me or telling me' is regularly signalled by a contrast between RISING and FALLING pitch, e.g. *He's coming, isn't he?* (= I'm asking you) vs. *He's coming, isn't he!* (= I'm telling you). A second role of intonation is in the communication of personal attitude: sarcasm, puzzlement, anger, etc. can all be signalled by contrasts in pitch, along with other PROSODIC and PARALINGUISTIC features. Other roles of intonation in language have been suggested, e.g. as one of the ways of signalling social background.

Intonation patterns can be seen as a sequence of pitch levels, or 'tones', but this use of 'tone' is different from that encountered in the phrase TONE LANGUAGE, where it refers to the use of pitch to make contrasts of meaning at WORD level. See Crystal 1969; Bolinger 1975: Ch. 3.

intrinsic A term used in GENERATIVE GRAMMAR, referring to a type of CONSTRAINT imposed on the ORDERING of RULES (as opposed to a CONDITION where such rules are allowed to apply in a random order). An **intrinsic ordering** is one where the FORMAL or logical properties of a SYSTEM of rules dictate the SEQUENCE in which the rules apply: one rule (B) cannot apply until after another rule (A) has operated, because A supplies B with the properties B needs for its operation. Intrinsic ordering is opposed to EXTRINSIC ordering, where the order of application is not motivated by such considerations of formal consistency; the rules could logically occur in any order, but some ordering has to be imposed (taking into account the DATA of the LANGUAGE) in order for a correct output to emerge. See Akmajian & Heny 1975: Ch. 6; Huddleston 1975: Ch. 12; Hyman 1975: Ch. 4.

intrusion A term used occasionally in PHONETICS to refer to the addition of sounds in CONNECTED SPEECH which have no basis in the pronunciation of the SYLLABLES or WORDS heard in isolation. The most well-known example in English (RECEIVED PRONUNCIATION) is of the /r/ which is introduced as a LINKING FORM after a VOWEL when the following word begins with a vowel, when there is no historical justification for it (i.e. there is no *r* in the spelling). Examples such as *law(r) and order*, *India(r) and Pakistan*, and (within word) *draw(r)ings* are common, and attract much criticism, though the frequency with which such forms are heard (the critics not excluded) indicates that the tendency of this DIALECT to link words in this way is deep-rooted. But one may hear other cases of intrusion, such as the introduction of an unstressed, SCHWA vowel between CONSONANTS in such words as *athletics* /aθəletɪks/.

As with the opposite effect, ELISION, traditional rhetoric had devised a classification of types of intrusion in terms of the position of the extra sound in a word: in word-INITIAL position, it was termed *prothesis*, in word-MEDIAL position *anaptyxis* or *epenthesis*, and in word-FINAL position *paragogue*. In phonetic analyses of modern languages, too, reference to a 'prothetic' vowel or an 'epenthetic' vowel is often encountered. See Gimson 1970: Ch. 8.

intuition (intuitive) A term in LINGUISTICS referring to the judgement of a NATIVE-SPEAKER about his LANGUAGE, especially in deciding whether a SENTENCE is ACCEPTABLE or not, and how sentences are inter-related. It is sometimes referred to as tacit knowledge, or *Sprachgefühl*. Native-speaker intuitions are always a crucial form of evidence in linguistic analysis, but they are given a special theoretical status in GENERATIVE GRAMMAR, where in his later work Noam CHOMSKY sees them as part of the DATA which the grammar has to account for. It is important, in discussions of this topic, to distinguish the intuitions of the native-speaker from those of the linguist – a distinction which can be easily confused when the linguist is investigating his own language. The linguist's intuitions concerning the accuracy or elegance of his analysis are quite different in kind from those of the non-linguist, whose intuitions concern the sameness, difference and relatedness of MEANINGS. See Robins 1971: Ch. 1; Akmajian & Heny 1975: Ch. 1.

invariable (invariant) A term sometimes used in the GRAMMATICAL classification of WORDS to refer to one of two postulated major word CLASSES in LANGUAGE, the other being VARIABLE. Invariable or 'invariant' words are said to be those which are used without any MORPHOLOGICAL change, e.g. *under*, *but*, *them*. Variable words, by contrast, INFLECT, e.g. *house/houses*, *sit/sat*... See Robins 1971: Ch. 5.

invariance A principle in some approaches to PHONOLOGY whereby each PHONEME is seen as having a set of defining PHONETIC FEATURES, such that whenever a phoneme occurs the corresponding features will also occur. Along with the conditions of LINEARITY and BIUNIQUENESS, the invariance principle establishes a view of phonemic analysis which has been criticised by GENERATIVE phonologists, as part of a general attack on TAXONOMIC phonemics. See Hyman 1975: Ch. 3.

inventory A term used in LINGUISTICS and PHONETICS to refer to an unordered listing of the ITEMS belonging to a particular LEVEL or area of DESCRIPTION in a LANGUAGE, e.g. the listing of the PHONEMES of English would constitute that language's 'phonemic inventory'. See Robins 1971: Ch. 2.

inversion A term used in GRAMMATICAL analysis to refer to the process or result of SYNTACTIC change in which a specific SEQUENCE of CONSTITUENTS is seen as the reverse of another. In English, for example, one of the main ways of forming QUESTIONS is by inverting the order of SUBJECT and AUXILIARY, e.g. *Is he going?* See Quirk *et al* 1972: Ch. 14.

IP The usual abbreviation for an ITEM AND PROCESS MODEL of DESCRIPTION in MORPHOLOGY.

IPA An abbreviation which is used for both the INTERNATIONAL PHONETIC ASSOCIATION and the International Phonetic Alphabet of that Association.

irregular(ity) A term used in LINGUISTICS to refer to a linguistic FORM which is an exception to the pattern stated in a RULE. For example, VERBS such as *took*, *went*, *saw*, etc. are irregular, because they do not follow the rule which forms the past TENSE by adding -*ed*. GRAMMAR is concerned with the discovery of REGULAR PATTERNS in linguistic DATA: lists of 'irregularities' are usually avoided, and handled by incorporating the exceptional information into a dictionary-entry. See Robins 1971: Ch. 6.

iso- A PREFIX used in DIALECTOLOGY as part of the labelling of the various types of LINGUISTIC information which can be displayed on maps ('linguistic atlases'). The most widely-used notion is that of the **isogloss** (or 'isograph', or 'isoglottic line'), a line drawn on a map to mark the boundary of an area in which a particular linguistic feature is used. A number (or 'bundle') of isoglosses falling together in one place suggests the existence of a dialect boundary. Further distinctions can be made in terms of the kind of linguistic feature being isolated: an **isophone** is a line drawn to mark the limits of a PHONOLOGICAL feature: an **isomorph** marks the limits of a MORPHOLOGICAL feature; an **isolex** marks the limits of a LEXICAL ITEM; an **isoseme** marks the limits of a SEMANTIC feature (as when lexical items of the same phonological form take on different MEANINGS in different areas). Other distinctions have been suggested, based on the same principle. An alternative terminology talks of isophonic/isomorphic/ . . . 'lines'. An **isopleth** is a more general notion, being used by some SOCIO-LINGUISTS to refer to a line which marks the limits of a linguistic feature seen in association with relevant sociocultural features. An **isolect** is a term used by some sociolinguists to refer to a linguistic VARIETY (or LECT) which differs minimally from another variety (i.e. a single isogloss, whether of a regional or a social kind, differentiates them). See Gumperz & Hymes 1971: Intro; Robins 1971: Ch. 2.

isochrony/isochronism A term used by some PHONETICIANS to refer to the rhythmic characteristic of some LANGUAGES. In isochronous RHYTHM, the STRESSED SYLLABLES fall at approximately regular intervals throughout an UTTERANCE. This is 'subjective' isochrony, based on the perception of the listener – a more realistic interpretation of this notion than that of 'objective' isochrony, where the intervals would be measurably identical. One implication of this is that the theory predicts that unstressed syllables between stresses will be uttered in similar periods of time. If there are several unstressed syllables, accordingly, they will be articulated rapidly, to get them into the time span available. In such sentences as *The 'consequences of his 'action are 'several*, the speed of ARTICULATION of the five syllables after '*con*- will be greater than the two following '*ac*-. Isochrony is said to be a strong tendency in English, for example, which is accordingly referred to as a 'STRESS-TIMED' (as opposed to a 'syllable-timed') language. The UNITS of rhythm in such languages, i.e. the distances between stressed syllables, are called FEET (cf. FOOT), by some phoneticians. The theory is not without its critics, who doubt the extent of the principle's applicability, given the many variations in TEMPO heard in speech. See Catford 1977: Ch. 5; Abercrombie 1967: Ch. 6.

isolated A type of OPPOSITION recognised in PRAGUE SCHOOL PHONOLOGY, distinguished from PROPORTIONAL. The opposition between English /v/ and /l/ is isolated, because there are no other segments that are contrasted in this particular way, i.e. VOICED LABIO-DENTAL FRICATIVE vs. voiced LATERAL. The opposition between /f/ and /v/, however, is proportional, because there are other oppositions in the language which work in parallel, e.g. /s/ vs. /z/, /θ/ vs. /ð/. See Hyman 1975: Ch. 2.

isolating (isolation) A type of LANGUAGE established by COMPARATIVE LINGUISTICS using STRUCTURAL (as opposed to HISTORICAL) criteria, and focusing on the characteristics of the WORD: in **isolating languages**, all the words are invariable (and SYNTACTIC relationships are primarily shown by word order). Vietnamese, Chinese and many South-East Asian languages are often cited as good instances of isolating languages. As always with such general classifications, the CATEGORIES are not clear-cut: different languages will display the characteristics of 'isolation' to a greater or lesser degree. An alternative term is ANALYTIC, seen as opposed to SYNTHETIC types of language (AGGLUTINATIVE and INFLECTING), where words contain more than one MORPHEME. See Robins 1971: Ch. 8; Lyons 1968: Ch. 5.

isomorphism (isomorphic) A property of two or more STRUCTURES whose CONSTITUENT parts are in a one-to-one correspondence with each other, at a given level of abstraction. For example, a SYNTACTIC and a SEMANTIC analysis would be 'isomorphic' if for each syntactic UNIT there were a corresponding semantic unit, e.g. SUBJECT + VERB + OBJECT : ACTOR + Action + Goal. Likewise, a structural 'isomorphism' may occur between LANGUAGES or DIALECTS, e.g. in VOCABULARY (the kinship terms in language X may be isomorphic with those in language Y). See Lyons 1968: Ch. 2.

item A term used in LINGUISTICS to refer to an individual linguistic FORM, from the viewpoint of its occurrence in an inventory and not in a CLASSIFICATION. For example, the vocabulary of a LANGUAGE, as listed in a dictionary, can be seen as a set of 'LEXICAL items' (e.g. the headwords in this dictionary). GRAMMATICAL and PHONOLOGICAL UNITS may also be listed as items, though this is less common, as they are more readily analysable into classes. See Robins 1971: Ch. 1.

item and arrangement (IA) A MODEL of description used in MORPHOLOGY for the analysis of WORDS (and sometimes in SYNTAX for larger GRAMMATICAL UNITS). In this approach, words are seen as linear SEQUENCES ('arrangements') of MORPHS ('items'), e.g. *The boys kicked the ball* will be analysed as *the + boy + s + kick + ed + the + ball*. Problem cases, where this notion of sequence would not easily

item and process

apply, constituted a main part of discussion in LINGUISTICS of the 1940s and 1950s, e.g. whether *mice* can be seen as *mouse* + plural. The main alternatives to this way of proceeding are the ITEM AND PROCESS and WORD AND PARADIGM models. See Matthews 1974: Ch. 12.

item and process (IP) A MODEL of description used in MORPHOLOGY for the analysis of WORDS. In this approach, the relationships between words are seen as processes of DERIVATION, e.g. the 'item' *took* is derived from the item *take* by a 'process' involving VOWEL change. For some LINGUISTS this label is applicable to any approach which makes use of derivational processes in its formulation, such as GENERATIVE grammar; but its original use was in the context of morphology. See Matthews 1974: Ch. 12.

J

⌘⌘⌘⌘⌘⌘

Jakobsonian Characteristic of, or a follower of, the linguistic principles of the American LINGUIST, **Roman Jakobson** (b. 1896), a principle founder of the PRAGUE SCHOOL, and a major influence in contemporary linguistics since. Two terms in particular are associated with his name. 'Jakobsonian DISTINCTIVE FEATURE theory' refers to the use he and other scholars made of the notion of distinctive feature in the mid-1950s, in which features are defined primarily in ACOUSTIC terms. In this dictionary, the main reference to this approach is cited as 'Jakobson & Halle' (i.e. R. Jakobson & M. Halle, *Fundamentals of Language* (1956)). In LANGUAGE ACQUISITION, the **Jakobsonian hypothesis** concerns the order in which he predicted OPPOSITIONS between sounds would appear (and also be lost, in cases of language breakdown). See Clark & Clark 1977: Ch. 10.

juncture A term used in PHONOLOGY to refer to the PHONETIC boundary features which may demarcate GRAMMATICAL UNITS such as MORPHEME, WORD or CLAUSE. The most obvious junctural feature is silence, but in CONNECTED SPEECH this feature is not as common as the use of various MODIFICATIONS to the beginnings and endings of grammatical units. Word-division, for example, can be signalled by a complex of PITCH, STRESS, LENGTH and other features, as in the potential contrast between *that stuff* and *that's tough*. In a SEGMENTAL phonological TRANSCRIPTION, these appear identical, /ðætstʌf/, but there are several phonetic modifications which can differentiate them in speech. In *that stuff*, the /s/ is strongly ARTICULATED, and the /t/ is unaspirated, whereas in *that's tough*, the /s/ is relatively weak, and the /t/ is ASPIRATED. In rapid speech such distinctions may disappear: they are only potentially CONTRASTIVE.

There have been several attempts to establish a typology of junctures. A commonly used distinction is between 'open' or 'plus' juncture (the features used at a word boundary, before silence), as illustrated in the above example (usually transcribed with a plus sign ⟨+⟩), and 'close' juncture (referring to the normal TRANSITIONS between sounds within a word). To handle the special cases of an open transition within a word, as in *co-opt*, the notion of 'internal open juncture' may be used. A more general distinction sometimes used to handle these possibilities is that between open and close transition.

In some American analyses of the INTONATION patterns of larger grammatical units than the word, several types of juncture are distinguished: 'single-bar' or 'sustained' juncture is recognised when the pitch pattern stays level within an UTTERANCE (transcribed with a single oblique $\langle / \rangle$ or level arrow $\langle \rightarrow \rangle$; 'double-bar' or 'rising' juncture is recognised when the pitch pattern rises before a silence (transcribed with a double slash $\langle // \rangle$ or a rising arrow $\langle \nearrow \rangle$); a 'terminal', 'double-cross', 'falling', or 'fading' juncture is recognised when the pitch pattern falls before a silence (transcribed with a double cross $\langle \# \rangle$ or a falling arrow $\langle \searrow \rangle$). See Gimson 1970: Ch. 11; Robins 1971: Ch. 4.

K

᭤᭤᭤᭤᭤᭤

Katz–Postal hypothesis A proposed property of TRANSFORMATIONS
claimed by the American LINGUISTS Jerrold Katz and Paul Postal in
1964 in their book *An Integrated Theory of Linguistic Descriptions*, which
has had considerable influence on subsequent discussions of the
relationship between SYNTACTIC and SEMANTIC analysis. Essentially,
the hypothesis argued that all transformations should not change
MEANING (they should be MEANING-PRESERVING). In relation to the
MODEL of GRAMMAR expounded by Noam CHOMSKY in *Aspects of the
Theory of Syntax* (1965), it came to be argued that whenever two
SENTENCES differ in meaning, they will differ in DEEP STRUCTURE; and
that accordingly from a consideration of deep structure, the
grammatical meaning of a sentence can be deduced, which can then
provide the input to the semantic COMPONENT. The removal of
meaning-changing transformations, on this view, would thus simplify
the functioning of the semantic RULES. There are, of course, several
areas of syntax which provide apparent COUNTER-EXAMPLES to this
hypothesis (such as TAG QUESTIONS, or the introduction of CONJUNC-
TIONS), and these have provided the grounds of much subsequent
discussion as to the validity of this and similarly-motivated hypotheses.
Considerable effort has been made to apply the hypothesis to such
cases, by re-formulating the analyses (usually by adding extra ELEMENTS
to the UNDERLYING structures involved). See Akmajian & Heny 1975:
Ch. 7; Huddleston 1976: Ch. 6.

kernel A term used in early GENERATIVE GRAMMAR to refer to a type of
STRUCTURE produced by the PHRASE-STRUCTURE RULES of a grammar.
The output of these rules is a 'kernel STRING'. The basic type of
SENTENCE generated from this string without any OPTIONAL TRANS-
FORMATIONS (as defined in the *Syntactic Structures* MODEL, e.g. NEGATIVE
or PASSIVE) is a **kernel sentence** – corresponding to the SIMPLE,
ACTIVE, AFFIRMATIVE DECLARATIVE (SAAD) sentences of LANGUAGE.
See Lyons 1968: Ch. 6.

key A term used by some SOCIOLINGUISTS as part of a classification of variations in spoken interaction: it refers to the tone, manner, or spirit in which a SPEECH-ACT is carried out, e.g. the contrast between mock and serious STYLES of activity. In a more restricted sense, the term is used by some LINGUISTS to subsume the various LEVELS of FORMALITY found in speech. One proposal analyses speech in terms of five such keys: 'frozen', 'formal', 'consultative', 'casual' and 'intimate'. See Bolinger 1975: Ch. 11; Gumperz & Hymes 1972: Ch. 1.

kinesics (kine, -me) A term in SEMIOTICS for the systematic use of facial expression and body gesture to communicate MEANING, especially as this relates to the use of LANGUAGE (e.g. when a smile vs. a frown alters the interpretation of a SENTENCE). Some analysts have applied the full EMIC terminology to this area, distinguishing 'kinemes', 'kines' and 'ALLOkines'; but the extent to which one can handle 'body language' in these terms is controversial, as analytic criteria are less clear than in PHONOLOGY, and kinesic TRANSCRIPTIONS raise several problems of interpretation. See Bolinger 1975: Ch. 1; Gumperz & Hymes 1971: Ch. 13.

L

⌘⌘⌘⌘⌘⌘

label(-led, -ling) A term in GRAMMATICAL analysis for the explicit marking of the parts or stages in a STRUCTURAL analysis of a SENTENCE. For example, the main structural divisions in the sentence *men ran* can be signalled using such methods as BRACKETING or a TREE diagram, e.g.[[men] [ran]]; but this analysis is made more meaningful if a structural description is added (ASSIGNED) to the brackets, e.g. [[men]$_N$[ran]$_V$]$_S$, where N = NOUN, V = VERB, and S = sentence. Such a **labelled bracketing** is used in PHRASE-STRUCTURE grammars. In a tree diagram, NODES can be labelled similarly. See Lyons 1968: Ch. 6.

labial(-ise, -isation) A general term in the PHONETIC classification of speech sounds on the basis of their PLACE OF ARTICULATION: it refers to active use of one lip (as in LABIO-DENTAL sounds, such as [f]) or both lips (as in BILABIAL CONSONANTS, such as [b], or ROUNDED VOWELS, such as [u]). In an empty sense, all ORAL sounds are labial, in that the air-flow has to pass through the lips: the important qualification in the above definition is that the lips are *actively* involved. From a position of rest, there must be a marked movement to qualify as a labial sound, and it is lip-rounding which is the most common and noticeable feature. Similarly, **labialisation** is a general term referring to a SECONDARY ARTICULATION involving any noticeable lip-rounding, as in the initial [k] of *coop*, or *sh-* [ʃ] of *shoe*, which are here 'labialised', because of the influence of the labialisation in the following vowel, [u]. Labialisation is applied both to cases where the lip-rounding is an essential feature of a sound's identity, as in [u], as well as to cases where the lip-rounding is found only in specific contexts, as in the [k] example above – in *kill*, there is no labialisation. The DIACRITIC for labialisation is [ʷ], underneath the main symbol, but a raised [ʷ] is often used. See Gimson 1970: Ch. 4; Catford 1977: Ch. 8.

labio-dental A term used in the PHONETIC classification of speech sounds on the basis of their PLACE OF ARTICULATION: it refers to a sound in

labio-velar

which one lip is actively in contact with the teeth. The usual way is for the lower lip to articulate with the upper teeth, as in [f] and [v]. The opposite effect, upper lip against lower teeth, is possible in theory, but not recognised in the usual phonetic classifications. The term is also applied to articulations where the lip approaches close to the teeth, but without actual contact, as in the sound [ʋ], which is a VOWEL-like sound mid-way between [w] and [v]. See Gimson 1970: Ch. 4; Catford 1977: Ch. 8.

labio-velar A term used in the PHONETIC classification of speech sounds on the basis of their PLACE OF ARTICULATION: it refers to a sound made at the velum (cf. VELAR) with the simultaneous accompaniment of lip ROUNDING. A 'labio-velar SEMI-VOWEL' occurs in English as /w/, e.g. *well*, *wasp*; some DIALECTS preserve a VOICELESS PHONEME for words written with *wh*, and thus CONTRAST such pairs as *Wales* and *whales*. See Gimson 1970: Ch. 8.

LAD The usual abbreviation for LANGUAGE ACQUISITION DEVICE.

lag A term used in ACOUSTIC PHONETICS as part of the study of VOICE onset time variations in INITIAL PLOSIVE CONSONANTS: **voicing lag** refers to the occurrence of voicing after the plosive release (BURST); it contrasts with 'voicing lead'. See Ladefoged 1975: Ch. 6.

laminal (lamin-a, -o) A term used in PHONETIC classification, referring to a sound made with the BLADE or 'lamina' of the TONGUE in contact with the upper lip, teeth and alveolar ridge, as in ALVEOLAR (sc. 'lamino-alveolar') or DENTAL (sc. 'lamino-dental') sounds. See Catford 1977: Ch. 8.

language The everyday use of this term involves several different senses, which LINGUISTICS is careful to distinguish. At its most specific level, it may refer to the concrete act of speaking, in a given situation – the notion of PAROLE, or PERFORMANCE. The linguistic SYSTEM underlying an individual's use of language in a given time and place is identified by the term IDIOLECT – and this is often extended to the SYNCHRONIC analysis of the whole of a person's language (as in 'Shakespeare's language'). A particular VARIETY, or LEVEL of speech/writing may also be referred to as 'language' (e.g. 'scientific language', 'bad language'), and this is related to the SOCIOLINGUISTIC or STYLISTIC restrictiveness involved in such terms as 'trade language' (cf. PIDGIN), the teaching of 'languages for special purposes' (in APPLIED LINGUISTICS), etc. In such phrases as 'first language', 'the English language', the sense is the abstract system underlying the collective totality of the speech/ writing behaviour of a community (the notion of LANGUE), or the knowledge of this system by an individual (the notion of COMPETENCE). This may be seen both in a synchronic sense (e.g. 'the English language today') and a DIACHRONIC sense (e.g. 'the English language since Chaucer'). Higher-order groupings can be made, as in such notions as 'the Romance languages', 'CREOLE languages'. All of these examples would fall under the heading of 'natural languages' – a term which contrasts with the artificially constructed systems used to expound a conceptual area (e.g. 'formal', 'logical', 'computer' languages) or to facilitate communication (e.g. Esperanto).

In contrast with these instances of individual languages, DIALECTS, VARIETIES, etc., there is also the abstract sense of 'language', referring to the biological faculty which enables individuals to learn and use their language – implicit in the notion of language ACQUISITION DEVICE in PSYCHOLINGUISTICS. At a comparably abstract level 'language' is seen as a defining feature of human behaviour – the UNIVERSAL properties of all speech/writing systems, especially as characterised in terms of 'design features' (e.g. PRODUCTIVITY, DUALITY, LEARNABILITY) or 'language universals' (FORMAL, SUBSTANTIVE, etc.). Linguistics does not however follow the popular application of the term to human modes of communication other than by speech and writing (cf. such phrases as 'body language', 'eye language'), on the grounds that the behaviours involved are different in kind (as the criteria of productivity and duality suggest). Nor is 'language' a term generally applied to natural animal communication (cf. ZOÖSEMIOTICS).

The term enters into several technical phrases, most of which are self-evident, e.g. 'language teaching', 'language learning'. Some, however, require a minimum of elucidation. For example, **first language** (sc. mother-tongue) is distinguishable from **second language** (a language other than one's mother tongue used for a special purpose, e.g. for education, government). **Language planning** is a term used in sociolinguistics to refer to a systematic attempt to solve the communication problem of a community by studying the various languages or dialects it uses and developing a realistic policy concerning the selection and use of different languages. **Language laboratory** is a term used in foreign language learning to refer to a specially-equipped classroom (a set of booths containing recording and play-back facilities, capable of being monitored at a central console) which provides students with a means of listening and responding instantly to UTTERANCES made in the foreign language. See Robins, 1971: Ch. 1; Bolinger 1975: Ch. 2.

langue A term introduced into LINGUISTICS by the Swiss linguist Ferdinand de SAUSSURE, to distinguish one of the senses of the word 'LANGUAGE'. It refers to the language SYSTEM shared by a community of speakers, and is contrasted with PAROLE, which is the concrete act of speaking in actual situations by an individual speaker (cf. also PERFORMANCE). See Lyons 1968: Ch. 1; Robins 1971: Ch. 2.

larynx The part of the windpipe, or trachea, containing the VOCAL CORDS. The larynx, or 'voice box', is a casing of muscle and cartilage, which at the front is most noticeable in the protruberance in the adult male neck known as the 'Adam's apple'. Its functions are both biological and LINGUISTIC. Under the former heading, the larynx acts as a valve to shut off the lungs, e.g. to aid in the process of exertion. Under the latter heading, the larynx is involved in the production of several types of sound effect (e.g. VOICING, PITCH, whisper, GLOTTAL stop, GLOTTALIC sounds): these functions are described more fully under VOCAL CORDS. Speech sounds made in the larynx are sometimes referred to as **laryngeals**. **Laryngealisation** refers to variation in the mode of vibration of the vocal cords, over and above their normal vibratory mode in the production of voice, as in CREAKY voice. Laryngealised sounds are sometimes used CONTRASTIVELY with non-laryngealised sounds in LANGUAGE, e.g. in Hausa. The traditional method of examining the inside of the larynx is by using the **laryngoscope**, a mirror placed at an angle inside the mouth: several high-speed films of vocal cord activity have been made using this technique. The fibre-optic laryngoscope allows a more direct and flexible inspection to be made: the fibres are inserted through the nose, and thus interfere less with normal speech. The **laryngograph** is a device for recording vocal cord vibrations visually, using electrodes placed against the appropriate part of the neck. See Gimson 1970: Ch. 2; Ladefoged 1975: Ch. 6.

lateral(-ly) A term used in the PHONETIC classification of CONSONANT sounds on the basis of their MANNER OF ARTICULATION: it refers to any sound where the air escapes around one or both sides of a CLOSURE made in the mouth, as in the various types of *l* sound. Air released around only one side of the TONGUE produces **unilateral** sounds; around both sides **bilateral** sounds. Lateral sounds may be VOICED, as in *lady, pool*, or VOICELESS, as in *play*, where the [l] has been devoiced due to the influence of the preceding voiceless consonant: [l̥]. An independent voiceless *l* sound occurs with Welsh *ll*, as in *Llandudno*, but here there is much accompanying friction, and the sound is best described as a 'lateral FRICATIVE' [ɬ]. /t/ and /d/ followed by /l/ in English are often released 'laterally', the phenomenon of 'lateral PLOSION': the air escapes round the sides of the tongue, the closure between tongue and ALVEOLAR ridge remaining, as in *bottle*, *cuddle*. It is possible to say the final SYLLABLE of such words without moving the front of the tongue from its contact at all.

In some DISTINCTIVE FEATURE approaches to PHONOLOGY, the term 'lateral' is specifically opposed to **non-lateral** (i.e. sounds which do not have a lateral release, as described above), these being postulated as two of the contrasts needed in order to specify fully the sound system of a language. In CHOMSKY & Halle's theory, for example, 'lateral' is classified as a CAVITY feature, along with NASAL, under the specific heading of SECONDARY APERTURES. See Gimson 1970: Chs. 4, 8; Catford 1977: Ch. 8; Hyman 1975: Ch. 2.

lax One of the features of sound set up by JAKOBSON & Halle in their DISTINCTIVE FEATURE theory of PHONOLOGY, to handle variations in MANNER OF ARTICULATION. Lax sounds are those produced with less muscular effort and movement, and which are relatively short and indistinct, compared to tense sounds (cf. TENSION). Examples are VOWELS articulated nearer the CENTRE of the vowel area (as in *bit*, *put*). See Ladefoged 1975: Ch. 11; Hyman 1975: Ch. 2.

layering A term used by some LINGUISTS to refer to the successive HIERARCHICAL LEVELS in an IMMEDIATE CONSTITUENT analysis. In TAGMEMIC GRAMMAR, it refers to the inclusion of a tagmemic CONSTRUCTION within another construction at the same level, as in *the car in the road*, where a PHRASE is within a phrase. Here it contrasts with LOOPBACK and LEVEL-SKIPPING. Bolinger 1975: Ch. 6.

lead A term used in ACOUSTIC PHONETICS as part of the study of VOICE onset time variations in INITIAL PLOSIVE CONSONANTS: **voicing lead** refers to the occurrence of voicing before the plosive release (BURST); it contrasts with 'voicing lag'. See Ladefoged 1975: Ch. 6.

learnability A suggested defining property of human LANGUAGE (contrasting with the properties of other SEMIOTIC SYSTEMS), referring to the way any language can in principle be acquired by any normal child given the opportunity to do so. See Lyons 1977b: Ch. 3.

lect A term used by some SOCIOLINGUISTS to refer to a collection of LINGUISTIC phenomena which has a functional identity within a SPEECH

COMMUNITY, but without specifying the basis on which the collection was made (e.g. whether the lect was regional (cf. DIALECT), social (cf. SOCIOLECT), etc.). See Bolinger 1975: Ch. 11.

left-branching A term used in GENERATIVE GRAMMAR to refer to a CONSTRUCTION whose DERIVATION involves a series of structural operations which would be represented as increasing complexity of the left-hand side of a TREE diagram. The type of RULE involved can be represented by X → (X) + Y. For example, the phrase *my friend's aunt's pen* is a 'left-branching' or 'left recursive' structure; it contrasts with the RIGHT-BRANCHING character of *the pen of the friend of my aunt*. See Lyons 1977a: Ch. 9.

length (1) A term used in PHONETICS to refer to the physical duration of a sound or UTTERANCE, and in PHONOLOGY to refer to the relative DURATIONS of sounds and SYLLABLES when these are linguistically contrastive; also referred to as QUANTITY. Sometimes the term is restricted to phonological contexts, the phonetic dimension being referred to as 'duration'. Phonologically 'long' and 'short' values are conventionally recognised, both for VOWELS and CONSONANTS. LANGUAGES often have one degree of phonological length, and may have more than one. Long vowels (transcribed with the DIACRITIC [:] occur in Arabic and Finnish; long (or 'double') consonants in Lithuanian and Luganda. In English, the so-called distinction between long and short vowels (as in *beat* vs. *bit*) is not strictly a contrast in length, as QUALITY variations are always involved. See Catford 1977: Ch. 10; Gimson 1970: Ch. 3.

(2) The notion of physical length has also been used in PSYCHO-LINGUISTIC, SOCIOLINGUISTIC and STYLISTIC studies of GRAMMAR and VOCABULARY, in an attempt to quantify variations in the apparent COMPLEXITY of SENTENCES, WORDS, etc. Notions such as **sentence length** and **mean length of utterance**, have been studied in terms of the number of CONSTITUENT words, MORPHEMES, SYLLABLES, etc. which they contain. These quantifications have been criticised by many LINGUISTS, on the grounds that there is no necessary correlation between the length of a linguistic UNIT and its STRUCTURAL or FUNCTIONAL COMPLEXITY. See Clark & Clark 1977: Chs. 8, 9.

lenis A general term used in the PHONETIC classification of CONSONANT sounds on the basis of their MANNER OF ARTICULATION: it refers to a sound made with a relatively weak degree of muscular effort and breath force, compared with some other sound (known as FORTIS). The distinction between LAX and TENSE is used similarly. The labels 'weak' and 'strong' are sometimes used for the contrast involved, but these are more prone to ambiguity. In English, it is the VOICED CONSONANTS ([b], [d], [v], [z], etc.) which tend to be produced with lenis articulation (their voiceless counterparts being relatively strong), and often, when the voicing distinction is reduced, it is only the degree of articulatory strength which maintains a contrast between sounds. The term 'lenis' is sometimes used loosely to refer to weak vowel articulation also, but this is not a standard practice. See Gimson 1970: Ch. 4.

level (1) A general term in LINGUISTICS to refer to a major dimension of STRUCTURAL organisation held to be susceptible of independent study. The most widely recognised 'levels of analysis' are PHONOLOGY, GRAMMAR and SEMANTICS, but often PHONETICS is distinguished from phonology, LEXIS from semantics, and MORPHOLOGY and SYNTAX are seen as separate levels within grammar. Some linguistic MODELS make even more specific divisions, identifying MORPHOPHONOLOGY, for example, as a separate level. An analogous notion is found in all theories, e.g. the COMPONENTS of a GENERATIVE grammar, or the STRATA of STRATIFICATIONAL grammar. There is considerable difference of opinion concerning not only the number, but also the way these levels should be inter-related in a linguistic theory. BLOOMFIELD-IAN linguistics, for example, saw analysis as a matter proceeding unidirectionally from the 'lower' levels of phonetics through the progressively 'higher' levels of phonology, morphology and syntax towards semantics. In this approach, the 'mixing of levels' was disallowed: phonology, for example, was to be analysed without reference to higher levels of description. In HALLIDAYAN linguistics, phonology is seen as an **inter-level**, linking the level of phonic/graphic SUBSTANCE with that of grammatical/lexical FORMS. 'Double ARTICU-LATION' theories recognise the main levels only. When criteria of analysis from different levels coincide in establishing a linguistic UNIT (as when phonological and grammatical criteria are found to agree in identifying the WORDS in a language), the term 'CONGRUENCE of levels' is sometimes used. See Robins 1971: Ch. 1.

(2) In GENERATIVE linguistics, the term is used to refer to the different types of REPRESENTATION encountered within the DERIVATION of a SENTENCE. For example, DEEP and SURFACE STRUCTURE 'levels of representation' are commonly recognised, as are SYSTEMATIC PHONEMIC and PHONETIC levels. Linguistic operations, such as TRANS-FORMATIONS, can be described as taking place at certain 'levels of depth'. See Hyman 1975: Ch. 1.

(3) The different STRUCTURAL layers within a linguistic HIERARCHY are often referred to as 'levels', e.g. within GRAMMAR one might talk

of the levels (or RANKS) of SENTENCE, CLAUSE, PHRASE, WORD and MORPHEME. This view is a central feature of TAGMEMIC analysis. See Bolinger 1975: Ch. 15; Lyons 1968: Ch. 5.

(4) The various degrees of progress which it is anticipated linguistics can achieve are referred to as 'levels' of ADEQUACY. See Hyman 1975: Ch. 3.

(5) Within PHONETICS and PHONOLOGY, 'level' may be used to characterise (i) the degree of PITCH height of an UTTERANCE, or SYLLABLE, e.g. 'average pitch level', 'four pitch levels', or (ii) the degree of loudness of a sound, e.g. 'three levels of STRESS'. 'Level tone' is used by some INTONATION analysts to refer to a NUCLEAR tone which has neither a FALLING nor a RISING component (as in the tone of boredom or sarcasm in English, e.g. *re͞ally*). 'Level stress' is sometimes used to refer to COMPOUNDS where the two items have a major stress feature, e.g. *washing-machine*. See Crystal 1969: Ch. 4.

(6) In STYLISTICS and SOCIOLINGUISTICS, 'level' is often used to refer to a mode of expression felt to be appropriate to a type of social SITUATION, e.g. 'FORMAL level', 'intimate level'. Sometimes, several such stylistic levels are distinguished within the range of formality (e.g. 'frozen', 'casual', 'deliberative'). See Bolinger 1975: Ch. 11.

level-skipping A term used in TAGMEMIC GRAMMAR to refer to a process of SYNTACTIC CONSTRUCTION where a LEVEL has been omitted. In such cases, a FILLER from a lower level construction is used in a higher level one, as when a GENITIVE ending (from the MORPHEME level) is attached to a PHRASE, rather than a WORD (e.g. *the King of Spain's daughter*). It is contrasted with LOOPBACK and LAYERING. See Bolinger 1975: Ch. 15.

lexeme A term used by some LINGUISTS to refer to the minimal DISTINCTIVE UNIT in the SEMANTIC SYSTEM of a LANGUAGE. Its original motivation was to reduce the AMBIGUITY of the term WORD, which applied to orthographic/PHONOLOGICAL, GRAMMATICAL and LEXICAL LEVELS, and to devise a more appropriate term for use in the context of discussing a language's vocabulary. The lexeme is thus postulated as the abstract unit underlying such sets of grammatical VARIANTS as *walk, walks, walking, walked*, or *big, bigger, biggest*. IDIOMATIC phrases, by this definition, are also considered lexemes (e.g. *kick the bucket* (= 'die')). Lexemes are the units which are conventionally listed in dictionaries as separate entries. See Lyons 1977b: Ch. 1; Matthews 1974: Ch. 2.

lexicon In its most general sense, the term is synonymous with VOCABULARY. It has a special status in GENERATIVE GRAMMAR, where it refers to the COMPONENT containing all the information about the STRUCTURAL properties of the LEXICAL ITEMS in a LANGUAGE, i.e. their specification SEMANTICALLY, SYNTACTICALLY and PHONOLOGICALLY. In later MODELS (cf. ASPECTS), these properties are formalised as FEATURES, and put in square brackets, e.g. WORD CLASS assignments include NOUN [+N], etc. Given this component, the TERMINAL symbols in PHRASE-MARKERS can then be related directly to the lexicon, through the use of lexical TRANSFORMATIONS, e.g. any item in the lexicon specified by [+D] can be attached to the NODE D, and so on. See Akmajian & Heny 1975: Ch. 2; Lyons 1977b: Ch. 13.

lexicostatistics A technique used in GLOTTOCHRONOLOGY with which one attempts to make quantitative comparisons between the rates of change within sets of LEXICAL ITEMS in hypothetically related LAN-GUAGES, and thus to deduce the distance in time since the languages separated. Other types of lexical comparison (e.g. to determine the mutual intelligibility of languages) may also be referred to by this label. See Robins 1971: Ch. 8.

lexis (lexic-al (-ise, -ist), -ology, -ography) A term used in LINGUISTICS to refer to the vocabulary of a LANGUAGE, and used adjectivally in a variety of technical phrases. A UNIT of vocabulary is generally referred to as a **lexical item**, or LEXEME. A complete inventory of the lexical items of a language constitutes that language's dictionary, or LEXICON – a term particularly used in generative grammar: items are listed 'in the lexicon' as a set of **lexical entries**. The way lexical items are organised in a language is the **lexical structure** or **lexical system**. A group of items used to identify the network of contrasts in a specific semantic or **lexical field** (e.g. cooking, colour) may also be called a 'lexical SYSTEM'. Specific groups of items, sharing certain FORMAL or semantic features, are known as **lexical sets**. The absence of a lexeme at a specific STRUCTURAL place in a language's lexical field is called a **lexical gap** (e.g. *brother* vs. *sister*, *son* vs. *daughter*, etc., but no separate lexemes for 'male' vs. 'female' *cousin*). The mutual restriction govern-ing the CO-OCCURRENCE of sets of lexical items is known as **lexical selection** (e.g. ANIMATE NOUNS being compatible with animate VERBS). The insertion of particular lexemes at particular places in grammatical structures is carried out by a process of **lexical substitution** or **lexical transformation**. In comparing languages, it may be said that one language may **lexicalise** a contrast, whereas another may not – that is, the contrast is identified using lexemes, as in the many terms for 'snow' available in Eskimo.

Lexis may also be seen in contrast with GRAMMAR, as in the distinction between 'grammatical WORDS' and **lexical words**: the former refers to words whose sole function is to signal grammatical relationships (a role which is claimed for such words as *of*, *to* and *the* in English); the latter refers to words which have **lexical meaning**, i.e. they have semantic CONTENT. HALLIDAYAN linguistics makes a theoretical distinction between grammar and lexis, seen as two sub-divisions within linguistic FORM: lexis here is studied with reference to such formal concepts as COLLOCATION, and not in semantic terms. In GENERATIVE linguistics, in the mid-1970s, there developed a **lexicalist** conception of grammar, in which the identity of a separate lexicon was preserved alongside the notion of deep structure; this came into conflict with the generative semantics conception, where a more direct relationship between meaning and form was postulated.

Lexicology is a term sometimes used to refer to the overall study of a language's vocabulary (including its history). It is distinguished here from **lexicography**, which is the art and science of dictionary-making. Lexicography could accordingly be seen as a branch of 'applied lexicology'. The term 'lexicologist' is however little used: someone interested in vocabulary would normally be considered a species of semanticist. See Lyons 1968: Ch. 9; 1977b: Chs. 8, 9; Robins 1971: Ch. 2.

liaison A term used in PHONOLOGY to refer to one type of TRANSITION between sounds, where a sound is introduced at the end of a WORD if a certain CONTEXT follows. It is a notable feature of French, e.g. the final *t* of *c'est* is pronounced when followed by a VOWEL. It may be heard in English where a 'linking /r/' is often found in words ending with an *r* in the spelling, when they occur before words beginning with a vowel, e.g. *hear* /hɪə/ usually becomes /hɪər/ in such phrases as *here are*. See Gimson 1970: Ch. 11.

linear(ity) A term used in LINGUISTICS to describe the characteristic REPRESENTATION of LANGUAGE as a unidimensional SEQUENCE of ELEMENTS or RULES. The assumption is made that it is possible to order rules in a sequence, and to adhere strictly to this ordering in constructing DERIVATIONS without any loss of GENERALITY (compared to an unordered set of rules or a set ordered on a different principle, e.g. one of simultaneous application). It is also claimed that linear ordering makes it possible to formulate grammatical processes that would otherwise not be expressible with complete generality. In PHONOLOGY, **linearity** is an organisational principle, whereby each occurrence of a PHONEME is associated with a specific sequence of PHONES (minimally, one phone) which realise that phoneme. If phoneme A precedes phoneme B, then phone(s) A' will precede phone(s) B′. Linearity is thus one of the preconditions of BIUNIQUENESS. The principle has been criticised by GENERATIVE phonologists, as part of a general attack on TAXONOMIC phonemics. See Dinneen 1967: Ch. 1; Hyman 1975: Ch. 3.

lingua franca A term used in SOCIOLINGUISTICS, and often in everyday speech, to refer to an auxiliary LANGUAGE used to enable routine communication to take place between groups of people who speak different native languages. English is the world's most common lingua franca, followed by French; but other languages are also widely used. In East Africa, for example, Swahili is the lingua franca; in many parts of West Africa, Hausa is used. See Trudgill 1974: Ch. 6.

lingual (linguo-) A general term sometimes used in the PHONETIC classification of speech sounds, referring to a sound made with the TONGUE. A 'lingual roll/trill', for example, is the trilled [r] made with the TIP of the tongue against the ALVEOLAR ridge. The term **linguo-** is sometimes used as a PREFIX in the definition of PLACE OF ARTICULA-TION (e.g. 'linguolabial', where the tongue would be in contact with the lips, as in 'blowing raspberries'), but usually more specific prefixes are used (e.g. APICO-, LAMINO-). See Catford 1977: Ch. 8.

linguist The normal term for a student or practitioner of the subject of LINGUISTICS. 'Linguistician' is often cited for this purpose, but it is never used by the professional linguist about himself. Ironically, confusion sometimes arises from the earlier, and still current, sense of someone proficient in several languages.

linguistic A term which has to be used with care because of its ambiguity: it can be (i) the adjective from LANGUAGE, as in such phrases as 'linguistic philosophy', 'linguistic skill' and 'linguistic minority', or (ii) the adjective from LINGUISTICS, where it refers to an approach characterised by the scientific attributes of that subject, as in 'linguistic analysis'. In such phrases as 'linguistic intuition', however, either sense could apply: (a) intuitions about language, or (b) 'intuitions about how to analyse language linguistically'. Similarly, a 'linguistic atlas' may or may not be based on the techniques, findings, etc. of linguistics. See Robins 1971: Ch. 1; Lyons 1968: Ch. 1.

linguistically significant generalisation A term used especially in GENERATIVE GRAMMAR to refer to the kind of analytic statement which it is hoped the grammatical analysis will provide. The aim of the grammar is not just to generate all and only the grammatical

SENTENCES of a language, but to do this in such a way that those relationships felt to be significant by NATIVE-SPEAKERS are expressed in an economical way. For example, a grammar which generated ACTIVE sentences separately from PASSIVE ones, or QUESTIONS from STATEMENTS, and which failed to show how these are inter-related, would be missing linguistically significant generalisations. This is one of the reasons for the introduction of TRANSFORMATIONS into linguistic analysis. The extent to which a grammar expresses the linguistically significant generalisations about a language would be one measure of the grammar's ADEQUACY. See Huddleston 1976: Ch. 1; Akmajian & Heny 1975: Ch. 3.

linguistics The scientific study of LANGUAGE. As an academic discipline, the development of this subject has been recent and rapid, having become particularly widely known and taught in the 1960s. This reflects partly an increased popular and specialist interest in the study of language and communication in relation to human beliefs and behaviour (e.g. in theology, philosophy, information theory, literary criticism), and the realisation of the need for a separate discipline to deal adequately with the range and complexity of linguistic phenomena; partly the impact of the subject's own internal development at this time, arising largely out of the work of the American linguist, Noam CHOMSKY, and his associates, whose more sophisticated analytic techniques and more powerful theoretical claims gave linguistics an unprecedented scope and applicability.

Different branches may be distinguished according to the linguist's focus and range of interest. A major distinction, introduced by Ferdinand de SAUSSURE, is between **diachronic** and **synchronic linguistics**, the former referring to the study of language change (also called **historical linguistics**), the latter to the study of the state of language at any given point in time. Insofar as the subject attempts to establish general principles for the study of all languages, and to determine the characteristics of human language as a phenomenon, it may be called **general linguistics**. When it concentrates on establishing the facts of a particular language system, it is called **descriptive linguistics**. When its purpose is to focus on the differences between languages, especially in a language-teaching context, it is called **contrastive linguistics**. When its purpose is primarily to identify the common characteristics of different language or language families, the subject goes under the heading of **comparative** (or **typological**) **linguistics**.

When the emphasis in linguistics is wholly or largely historical, the subject is traditionally referred to as COMPARATIVE PHILOLOGY (or simply PHILOLOGY), though in many parts of the world 'philologists' and 'historical linguists' are people with very different backgrounds and attitudes. The term **structural linguistics** is widely used, sometimes in an extremely specific sense, referring to the particular approaches to SYNTAX and PHONOLOGY current in the 1940s and 1950s, with their emphasis on providing DISCOVERY PROCEDURES for the analysis of a language's SURFACE STRUCTURE; sometimes in a more general sense, referring to any SYSTEM of linguistic analysis that attempts to establish explicit systems of RELATIONS between linguistic UNITS in surface structure. When the emphasis in language study is on the classification of structures and units, without reference to such notions as DEEP STRUCTURE; some linguists, particularly within GENERATIVE grammar, talk pejoratively of **taxonomic linguistics**.

In recent years the term **linguistic sciences** has come to be used by many as a single label for both linguistics and PHONETICS – the latter being seen here as a strictly pre-language study. Equally, there are many who do not see the divide between linguistics and phonetics being as great as this label suggests: they would be quite happy to characterise the subject as **linguistic science**. 'Linguistics' is still the preferred name.

The overlapping interests of linguistics and other disciplines has led to the setting up of new branches of the subject, such as **anthropological linguistics, biolinguistics, computational linguistics, ethnolinguistics, mathematical linguistics, neurolinguistics, psycholinguistics, sociolinguistics**. When the subject's findings, methods, or theoretical principles are applied to the study of problems from other areas of experience, one talks of **applied linguistics**; but this term is often restricted to the study of the theory and methodology of foreign-language teaching. See Robins 1971: Ch. 1; Lyons 1968: Ch. 1.

linking A term used in PHONOLOGY to refer to a sound which is introduced between LINGUISTIC UNITS, usually for ease of pronunciation. In English, the 'linking /r/' is the most familiar example of this process, as when the r in *car* is pronounced before a VOWEL, or when an /r/ is introduced without there being justification in the writing (e.g. *Shah of* . . . /ʃɑːr ɔv. . ./). In French, a linking /t/ is introduced in the third PERSON QUESTION form of VERBS, when this ends in a vowel, e.g. *il a* 'he has' → *a-t-il*. In SYNTAX, the COPULA *be*, and sometimes such verbs as *seem, become*, etc. may be referred to as 'linking verbs'. See Gimson 1970: Ch. 8.

liquid

liquid A term used by some PHONETICIANS in the classification of speech sounds, referring collectively to all the APICO-ALVEOLAR sounds of the types [l] and [r]. See Ladefoged 1975: Ch. 4.

loan A LINGUISTIC UNIT (usually a LEXICAL ITEM) which has come to be used in a LANGUAGE or DIALECT other than the one where it originated. Several types of loan process have been recognised, such as **loan words** (where both FORM and MEANING are borrowed, or 'assimilated', with some adaptation to the PHONOLOGICAL system of the new language, e.g. *sputnik*); **loan blends** (where the meaning is borrowed, but only part of the form, e.g. *restaurant* with a simulated French ending /ˈrestərɔ̃/); **loan shifts** (where the meaning is borrowed, and the form is native, e.g. *restaurant* as /ˈrestrənt/); and **loan translations** (where the MORPHEMES in the borrowed word are translated item by item, e.g. *Superman* from *Übermensch* – also known as a CALQUE). See Bolinger 1975: Ch. 12; Robins 1971: Ch. 8.

local A type of TRANSFORMATION, introduced by Noam CHOMSKY (in ASPECTS), which affects only a sub-STRING DOMINATED by a single CATEGORY symbol: the applicability of the RULE is thus determined by the PHRASE STRUCTURE of the string, not just by the SEQUENCE of elementary symbols of which the string is composed. For example, the way in which the rules of the transformational CYCLE in PHONOLOGY are applied to assign STRESS depends on the way the FORMATIVES are categorised, e.g. as NOUN, VERB, ADJECTIVE, etc. in the phrase structure TREE. See Huddleston 1976: Ch. 11.

localism (localist) An approach to LINGUISTIC analysis which proposes that expressions of location (in space and time) are more basic to a GRAMMATICAL or SEMANTIC analysis than are other types of expressions, which are viewed as derived. In this 'localist' view, distinctions such as TENSE, ASPECT, possession and existence are interpreted as having underlying locational features, as is most evident in such relations as *John has a dog/John's dog...*, and *there are four legs on that table/that table has four legs*. See Lyons 1977b: Ch. 15.

locative In LANGUAGES which express GRAMMATICAL relationships by means of INFLECTIONS, this term refers to the FORM taken by a WORD, usually a NOUN or PRONOUN, when it typically expresses the idea of location of an action. English does not have a locative CASE form, using such PREPOSITIONS as *at* instead. Structures which express locational MEANING may also be referred to as locative, e.g. in *The man was standing at a bus-stop*, *at a bus-stop* could be called a 'locative PHRASE'. Some

LINGUISTS see locative CONSTRUCTIONS as having particular importance in developing a LINGUISTIC theory, interpreting such notions as 'being', 'having', etc. as involving a fundamental locative feature. The term is also given special status in CASE grammar. See Lyons 1968: Chs. 7, 8; Bolinger 1975: Ch. 15.

locus A term used in ACOUSTIC PHONETICS to refer to the apparent point of origin of a FORMANT for a given PLACE OF ARTICULATION, as displayed on a SPECTROGRAM. The formants which identify VOWELS are bent in characteristic directions, depending on the CONSONANTS adjacent to them; but for any single consonant, these bends, or TRANSITIONS, all point in the same direction, at a hypothetical natural frequency range for the consonant. It is this hypothetical point of origin which is referred to as the 'locus' of the consonant. See Bolinger 1975: Ch. 3.

locutionary A term used in the theory of SPEECH-ACTS to refer to an act of making a MEANINGFUL UTTERANCE. The point of the term is in its contrast with ILLOCUTIONARY and PERLOCUTIONARY acts, where there is more involved than merely 'speaking'. See Lyons 1977b: Ch. 16; Clark & Clark 1977: Ch. 3.

loopback (backlooping) A term in TAGMEMIC GRAMMAR for the inclusion of higher LEVEL CONSTRUCTIONS within the SLOTS of a lower level construction, as in the use of RELATIVE CLAUSES within the NOUN PHRASE (e.g. *the man who was talking*...). It is distinguished from LEVEL-SKIPPING and LAYERING. See Bolinger 1975: Ch. 15.

loudness The attribute of auditory sensation in terms of which a sound may be ordered on a scale from soft to loud. It is an AUDITORY PHONETIC feature, corresponding to some degree with the ACOUSTIC feature of intensity (measured in decibels (dB)), which in the study of speech is based on the size of the vibrations of the VOCAL CORDS, as a result of variations in air pressure. There is however no direct or parallel correlation between loudness (or 'volume') and intensity: other factors than intensity may affect our sensation of loudness, e.g. increasing the FREQUENCY of vocal cord vibrations may make one sound seem louder than another.

The linguistic use of loudness is of particular interest to the PHONOLOGIST, and this is studied under the heading of STRESS. See Ladefoged 1975: Ch. 8; Bolinger 1975: Ch. 3.

low One of the features of sound set up by CHOMSKY & Halle in their DISTINCTIVE FEATURE theory of PHONOLOGY, to handle variations in PLACE OF ARTICULATION (CAVITY features). Low sounds are a type of TONGUE-BODY feature, and defined ARTICULATORILY, as those produced by lowering the TONGUE to below the level it holds in neutral position; OPEN VOWELS and the GLOTTAL FRICATIVES are [+low]. Its opposite is **non-low** ([−low]), referring to sounds produced without any such lowering and thus covers MID and CLOSE vowels, and most CONSONANTS. See Ladefoged 1975: Ch. 11; Hyman 1975: Ch. 2.

lower A term used in GENERATIVE GRAMMAR to refer to the introduction into a SENTENCE DERIVATION of a CATEGORY which has already been used once in the derivation. In a TREE diagram representation of the derivation, the category that has been introduced later will appear to be lower down the tree than the earlier (HIGHER) category. Lower, or EMBEDDED, sentences (CLAUSES, VPS, NPS, etc.) can be illustrated by *the car **which I left in the street** has been stolen*. See Akmajian & Heny 1975: Ch. 8.

M

𝕊𝕊𝕊𝕊𝕊𝕊

macrolinguistic(s) A term used by some LINGUISTS, especially in the 1950s, to identify an extremely broad conception of the subject of linguistic enquiry. LINGUISTICS is seen in its overall relation to PHONETIC and EXTRALINGUISTIC experience. It is divided into three main sub-FIELDS: PRELINGUISTICS (whose primary subject-matter is PHONETICS), MICROLINGUISTICS (whose primary subject-matter is PHONOLOGY, MORPHOLOGY and SYNTAX), and METALINGUISTICS (whose subject-matter is the relationship between LANGUAGE and all extra-linguistic features of communicative behaviour, e.g. including what would now be called SOCIOLINGUISTICS). Some sociolinguists (e.g. Joshua Fishman (b. 1926)) distinguish between the broad concerns of 'macrosociolinguistics' (e.g. MULTILINGUALISM, language plan-ning) and the detailed investigation of 'microsociolinguistics' (e.g. speech events, conversations). See Crystal 1969: Ch. 2; Gumperz & Hymes 1971: Ch. 15.

main A term used in GRAMMATICAL analysis as part of the CLASSIFICATION of CLAUSE types: opposed to SUBORDINATE or DEPENDENT. A **main clause** is an independent clause, i.e. it can stand on its own as a SENTENCE. The term is also used to identify the more important STRUCTURAL member of a SEQUENCE of ITEMS all belonging to the same CLASS, e.g. 'main VERB' (VS. AUXILIARY verb). See Quirk *et al* 1972: Ch. 11.

major A term used by some LINGUISTS in the CLASSIFICATION of SENTENCE types to refer to the most PRODUCTIVE sentence pattern in a LANGUAGE. In English, the SUBJECT + PREDICATE (NP + VP) pattern is the **major sentence** (or FAVOURITE) type, e.g. *The elephant is running, A book is on the table.* Other types may be referred to as MINOR. See Quirk *et al* 1972: Ch. 2.

major class feature One of the five main dimensions of classification in CHOMSKY & Halle's DISTINCTIVE FEATURE theory of PHONOLOGY (the

manifest

others being CAVITY FEATURES, MANNER OF ARTICULATION FEATURES, SOURCE FEATURES and PROSODIC FEATURES). The term refers to the main types of sound produced by the open vs. closed possibilities of VOCAL TRACT variation. There are three such features, all defined as OPPOSITIONS: SONORANT vs. non-sonorant (OBSTRUENT), VOCALIC vs. non-vocalic, and CONSONANTAL vs. non-consonantal. Using these features, sounds can be subdivided into the major classes of VOWELS, CONSONANTS, OBSTRUENTS, SONORANTS, GLIDES and LIQUIDS. See Ladefoged 1975: Ch. 11.

manifest(ation) A term used by some linguists to refer to the physical expression of an abstract LINGUISTIC UNIT, e.g. PHONEMES are 'manifested' in PHONIC SUBSTANCE as PHONES, MORPHEMES as MORPHS. Any UNDERLYING FORM may be seen as having a corresponding manifestation in substance. In TAGMEMICS, the term has a special status, referring to the ETIC (physical) expression of EMIC (abstract) units (the **manifestation mode**). Elsewhere, the term REALISATION is widely used. See Lyons 1968: Ch. 2; Bolinger 1975: Ch. 15.

manner (1) (**of articulation**) One of the main parameters in the PHONETIC or PHONOLOGICAL classification of speech sounds, referring to the kind of ARTICULATORY process used in a sound's production. The distinction between CONSONANT and VOWEL is usually made in terms of manner of articulation. Within consonants, several articulatory types are recognised, based on the type of CLOSURE made by the VOCAL ORGANS. If the closure is complete, the result is a PLOSIVE, AFFRICATE or NASAL. If the closure is partial, the result is a LATERAL. If the closure is intermittent, the result is a ROLL (TRILL), or FLAP. And if there is narrowing without complete closure, the result is a FRICATIVE. Within VOWELS, classification is based on the number of auditory qualities distinguishable in the sound (PURE VOWELS, DIPHTHONG, TRIPHTHONG), the position of the soft PALATE, and the type of lip position (see ROUNDING). Sounds which are vowel-like in manner of articulation, but consonantal in function, are classified as SEMIVOWELS or FRICTIONLESS CONTINUANTS.

The term has special status in recent DISTINCTIVE FEATURE theory in PHONOLOGY, where it constitutes one of the five main dimensions in terms of which features of speech sound are analysed (the others being MAJOR CLASS FEATURES, CAVITY features, SOURCE features and PROSODIC features). The features subsumed under this heading, all analysed as OPPOSITIONS, are: CONTINUANT, RELEASE features (INSTANTANEOUS and DELAYED), SUPPLEMENTARY MOVEMENTS

(SUCTION and PRESSURE) and TENSE. See Gimson 1970: Ch. 4; Ladefoged 1975: Chs. 7, 11; Hyman 1975: Ch. 2.

(2) Several linguists use this term in the classification of LANGUAGE VARIETIES (more fully, **manner of discourse**), referring to the relations among the participants in a language activity, especially the LEVEL of FORMALITY they adopt (colloquial, formal, etc.). Alternative labels which have been proposed for this area are STYLE or TENOR of discourse. See Bolinger 1975: Ch. 17.

(3) **Manner adverbials** are usually recognised in GRAMMATICAL description, e.g. *in an X manner/way, quickly, angrily* – all able to answer the question 'How?' Certain other SEMANTIC CLASSES of adverbial are closely related (e.g. instrument, means), and sometimes subsumed under the heading of manner. Some GENERATIVE linguists see adverbials of manner as particularly significant, proposing a relationship between them and the PASSIVE construction. See Quirk *et al* 1972: Ch. 8.

map(-ping, -ped) This term, used to characterise a feature of MODEL construction in scientific enquiry, has been applied in several areas of LINGUISTICS and PHONETICS. **Mapping** refers to the correspondence between the ELEMENTS defined in a model of a situation, and the elements recognised in the situation itself. If these elements are in a one-to-one correspondence, at a given level of abstraction, then the mapping is said to be ISOMORPHIC; if there is selectivity of representation (again, at a given level of abstraction), the mapping is 'homomorphic'. For example, one could evaluate the extent to which an isomorphic relationship existed between SYNTACTIC and SEMANTIC LEVELS of REPRESENTATION of SENTENCE STRUCTURE. In TRANSFORMATIONAL grammar, the term is used specifically to refer to the process whereby a particular stage in the DERIVATION of a sentence is formally related to a subsequent stage, e.g. an input phrase is 'mapped' by a set of transformations onto a derived PHRASE-MARKER. See Huddleston 1976: Ch. 1.

margin The collective term for the sound SEGMENTS which form the boundaries of a SYLLABLE. In the WORD *cup*, for example, the CONSONANTS [k] and [p] constitute the syllable margins, as opposed to the VOWEL, which constitutes the syllable CENTRE. See Ladefoged 1975: Ch. 10.

markedness (mark-ing, -ed) An analytic principle in LINGUISTICS whereby pairs of linguistic FEATURES, seen as OPPOSITIONS, are given different values of POSITIVE (**marked**) and NEUTRAL or NEGATIVE (**unmarked**). In its most general sense, this distinction refers to the presence versus the absence of a particular linguistic feature. There is a formal feature marking plural in most English nouns, for example; the plural is therefore 'marked', and the singular is 'unmarked'. The reason for postulating such a relationship becomes clear when one considers the alternative, which would be to say that the opposed features simply operate in parallel, lacking any directionality. Intuitively, however, one prefers an analysis whereby *dogs* is derived from *dog* rather than the other way round – in other words, to say that '*dogs* is the plural of *dog*', rather than '*dog* is the singular of *dogs*'. Most of the theoretical discussion of markedness, then, centres on the question of how far there is intuitive justification for applying this notion to other areas of language (cf. *prince/princess, happy/unhappy, walk/walked,* etc.).

One of the earliest uses of the notion was in PRAGUE SCHOOL PHONOLOGY, where a sound would be said to be marked, if it possessed a certain DISTINCTIVE FEATURE (e.g. VOICE), and unmarked if it lacked it (this unmarked member being the one which would be used in cases of NEUTRALISATION). In GENERATIVE phonology, the notion has developed into a central criterion for formalising the relative NATURAL-NESS of alternative solutions to phonological problems. Here, evidence from frequency of occurrence, HISTORICAL LINGUISTICS, and language ACQUISITION is used to support the view that marking is a basic principle for assigning UNIVERSAL (and possibly innate) values to PHONETIC features (by contrast with the language-specific, phonological approach of the Prague School). The distinctive features are each assigned marking values, e.g. [+voice] is seen as marked, [−voice] as unmarked. SEGMENTS, in this view, can then be seen as combinations of marked or unmarked features, and thus be compared with each other, e.g. /a/ is the maximally unmarked vowel because it is [−high], [−back] and [−round]; /ɔ/ is more complex because it is [+low] and [+round], and so on.

Several other interpretations of the notion of marking are found in the literature, where the concept of 'presence vs. absence' does not readily apply. One interpretation relates marking to frequency of occurrence, as when one might say a FALLING INTONATION pattern was unmarked, compared with a RISING one, because it is more common. Another is found in the SEMANTIC analysis of LEXICAL ITEMS, where pairs of items are seen as unmarked and marked respectively, on the grounds that one member is more specific than the other (e.g. *dog/bitch,* where the latter is marked for sex – one can say *male/female dog,* but these ADJECTIVES are inapplicable with *bitch*). A third, related sense occurs when the DISTRIBUTION of one member of an opposition is restricted, compared with the other: the restricted item is then said to be marked – several COMPARATIVE SENTENCES illustrate this, e.g. *How tall is John?* (where *How short is John?* is abnormal). See Lyons 1977b: Ch. 9; Hyman 1975: Ch. 5.

marker A term used by some GENERATIVE LINGUISTS as part of a (controversial) two-way classification of the SEMANTIC COMPONENTS of LEXICAL ITEMS. Markers are those components of the meaning of a lexical item which are systematic for the language, i.e. the relations into which the item enters are systematic, in that the analysis of other lexical items makes reference to them. For example, [animate] is a marker, as can be seen by SELECTIONAL restrictions on the CO-OCCURRENCE of [+animate] lexical items with [−animate] ones, e.g. **the stone slept.* Components of meaning which do not operate in this way were called DISTINGUISHERS. See Lyons 1977b: Ch. 9.

mass A term used in the GRAMMATICAL classification of NOUNS; opposed to COUNT. The term refers to those nouns which the speaker treats as continuous entities, having no natural bounds (contrasting with the separable 'countable' quality of count nouns): but the distinction is not made on SEMANTIC grounds alone; the contrasting pattern of co-occurrence with DETERMINERS, QUANTIFIERS, etc. is the main evidence, e.g. **an anger* vs. *some anger* shows this to be a mass noun. There is no logical reason why nouns should be count or mass: a concept may be countable in one language, but mass in another, as in the case of *information*, which is mass in English, but countable in French (*des informations*). See Quirk *et al* 1972: Ch. 4; Palmer 1971: App. B; Lyons 1968: Ch. 7.

mathematical linguistics A branch of LINGUISTICS which studies the mathematical properties of LANGUAGE, usually employing concepts of a statistical or algebraic kind. A contribution has also come from information theory (e.g. quantification of such notions as REDUNDANCY and FUNCTIONAL load) and from computational analysis (e.g. the use of ALGORITHMS). The main application of mathematical notions has been in the FORMALISATION of linguistic theory, as developed in relation to GENERATIVE linguistics; but several other areas of language study have been investigated using these methods. Statistical studies of the DISTRIBUTION and frequency of linguistic ITEMS have led to the development of several empirical laws and specific techniques, e.g. in authorship studies (cf. STYLOSTATISTICS) and COMPARATIVE language study (cf. LEXICOSTATISTICS). See Lyons 1968: Ch. 2; 1977a: App.

matrix (1) A term derived from mathematics to refer to a rectangular array of entities (usually symbols) made up of rows and columns, and used in all branches of LINGUISTICS as an aid in DESCRIPTION or analysis. In PHONOLOGY, for example, DISTINCTIVE FEATURES are usually described within a matrix, where the columns are SEGMENTS and the rows are features: the cells of the matrix are then filled with pluses or minuses (or in some cases, zero) corresponding to whether a feature is or is not used. See Hyman 1975: Ch. 2.

(2) A term used in linguistics, and especially in GENERATIVE GRAMMAR, to refer to the superordinate SENTENCE within which another sentence is EMBEDDED, e.g. *The man who shouted came*, where *the man came* is the **matrix sentence**, and *the man shouted* is the embedded sentence. See Lyons 1968: Ch. 6.

MDP An abbreviation often used in language ACQUISITION studies for MINIMAL-DISTANCE PRINCIPLE.

meaning(-ful) This basic notion is used in LINGUISTICS both as a datum and as a criterion of analysis: linguists study meaning, and also use meaning as a criterion for studying other aspects of LANGUAGE (especially through such notions as CONTRASTIVITY and DISTINCTIVENESS). The topic of 'meaning' in the context of language, however, necessitates reference to non-linguistic factors, such as thought, situation, knowledge, intention and use. It is the difficulty in drawing clear dividing-lines between such notions that indicates why so many other academic disciplines are involved in the study of meaning along with linguistics – philosophers, and logicians especially, but also psychologists, sociologists, literary critics, theologians and others. The linguist's primary interest is distinguished by the attention he pays to the analysis of meaning in the context of everyday speech (rather than, say, in the context of literature, or abstract reasoning), by his comparative interests (comparing the way meaning is structured in a range of languages, and how meaning changes over time), and by his attempt to integrate meaning with the other COMPONENTS of a general linguistic theory (especially with GRAMMAR). These emphases characterise the linguistic study of meaning, SEMANTICS.

Linguistics shares with other disciplines the concern to isolate the several factors which contribute to the total interpretation, or signification, of a message, as this provides the essential perspective within which the specifically intralinguistic properties of meaning can be identified. These factors – the 'meanings of meaning' as they are sometimes called – have been variously labelled; and while it is impossible to generalise about usage (in view of the many technical

senses these labels have in various theories), labels do cluster around
three major themes. When the emphasis is on the relationship between
language, on the one hand, and the entities, events, states-of-affairs,
etc. which are external to the speaker and his language, on the other,
terms such as 'REFERENTIAL/DESCRIPTIVE/DENOTATIVE/EXTENSIONAL/
factual/objective meaning' have been used. When the emphasis is on
the relationship between language and the mental state of the speaker,
two sets of terms are used: the personal, emotional aspects are handled
by such terms as 'ATTITUDINAL/AFFECTIVE/CONNOTATIVE/EMOTIVE/
EXPRESSIVE meaning'; the intellectual, factual aspects involve such
terms as 'COGNITIVE/IDEATIONAL meaning'. When the emphasis is on
the way variations in the EXTRALINGUISTIC situation affect the
understanding and interpretation of language, terms such as 'CON-
TEXTUAL/FUNCTIONAL/interpersonal/social/SITUATIONAL' have been
used. 'Contextual', along with 'TEXTUAL meaning', is also used to refer
to these factors which affect the interpretation of a sentence which
derive from the rest of the DISCOURSE or TEXT within which the
sentence occurs.

Within linguistics, the role each linguistic LEVEL plays in the total
interpretation of a sentence is often referred to as the 'meaning' of
that level. The main levels involved are 'LEXICAL meaning', the
meaning of lexical ITEMS; and 'GRAMMATICAL meaning' (or 'STRUC-
TURAL meaning'), the meaning of grammatical structures. This approach has been extended by some linguists (e.g. FIRTHIANS) to include
other linguistic levels, e.g. 'PHONETIC meaning' (cf. SOUND-SYMBOLISM),
'PHONOLOGICAL meaning' (as in the structural use of alliteration or
rhyme in poetry). The term 'semantic meaning' may be used whenever
one wants to emphasise the content, as opposed to the form or
reference, of linguistic units. Specific aspects of the content of
sentences may be singled out for special attention, e.g. the notion of
'PROPOSITIONAL meaning'. See Lyons 1977b: Ch. 1; Bolinger 1975:
Ch. 7.

meaning-changing (-preserving) A theoretical distinction introduced
in early GENERATIVE GRAMMAR between two types of TRANSFORMA-
TIONS. If the operation of a transformation involves a change in the
MEANING between input and DERIVED SENTENCES, the transformation
is said to be 'meaning-changing'; in 'meaning-preserving' transformations, there is no such change (cf. KATZ–POSTAL HYPOTHESIS). An
example of the former would be in deriving IMPERATIVE sentences
from an UNDERLYING (DECLARATIVE) STRUCTURE by using a *you-*
DELETION transformation (e.g. *see* from *you see*); here is a plain contrast
between declarative and imperative 'meanings', and the reason for the

appearance of this contrast in the grammar is the use of the transformation. On the other hand, if the imperative is derived from an underlying structure where its 'imperativeness' has been represented, then the application of the *you*-deletion transformation would no longer change the structure's meaning, but simply make tangible an element of meaning which was already present (*viz* Imp + *see* → *see*). See Huddleston 1976: Ch. 6.

mean length of utterance (MLU) A measure introduced by the American psychologist Roger Brown (b. 1925) into LANGUAGE ACQUISITION studies, which computes the LENGTH of an UTTERANCE in terms of MORPHEMES. The technique is then used to show the increasing length of a child's utterances over time, as a base-line for carrying out studies on the developmental complexity of SENTENCE STRUCTURE. See Clark & Clark 1977: Ch. 8.

medial The usual way of referring to an ELEMENT occurring within a LINGUISTIC UNIT, other than in INITIAL and FINAL positions. The term is especially used in PHONOLOGY, e.g. the PHONEME /i/ occurs 'in medial position' (or 'medially') in the word *seat*. See Gimson 1970: Ch. 4.

medium A term used in the study of COMMUNICATION to refer to the functionally distinct dimensions in which a message is transmitted. In LINGUISTICS, the basic media are speech and writing, but others are not excluded (e.g. signing). Of these, speech is generally held in linguistics to be the 'primary medium', writing the 'secondary' or 'derived' medium, and the analysis of the differences between these media in STRUCTURAL and FUNCTIONAL terms is an important topic in linguistics. The term is usually distinguished from 'channel' (as used in communication theory), which refers to the physical means whereby a (spoken or written) message is transmitted, such as a wire, air, light, etc. See Lyons 1977b: Ch. 3; Abercrombie 1967: Ch. 1.

mellow One of the features of sound set up by JAKOBSON & Halle in their DISTINCTIVE FEATURE theory of PHONOLOGY, to handle variations in PLACE OF ARTICULATION; its opposite being STRIDENT. Mellow sounds are defined ARTICULATORILY and ACOUSTICALLY, as those involving a less complex or 'smooth-edged' CONSTRICTION at the point of articulation, and marked by acoustic energy of relatively low FREQUENCY and intensity, compared with strident sounds. PLOSIVES and NASALS are examples. See Hyman 1975: Ch. 2.

mentalism In LINGUISTICS, the influence of this school of thought (that mental states and processes exist independently of their manifestations of behaviour, and can explain behaviour) is most marked in the work of Noam CHOMSKY, especially in his notions of COMPETENCE and INNATENESS, and in his general views of the relationship between LANGUAGE and mind. In this respect, **mentalistic linguistics** is opposed to the BEHAVIOURISM of earlier psychological work on language. See Lyons 1977b: Ch. 5.

merger (merge) A term used in LINGUISTICS, especially in HISTORICAL studies, to refer to the coming together (or CONVERGENCE) of linguistic UNITS which were originally distinguishable. In cases of two PHONEMES coming together, the phrase **phonemic merger** is often used (the opposite phenomenon being referred to as 'phonemic split'). For example, the /æ:/ and /e:/ vowels in Old English have now merged in modern English /i:/, as in *meet* and *clean*. Analogous terms include COALESCENCE, FUSION and NEUTRALISATION. See Bolinger 1975: Ch. 13.

metalanguage (metalinguistic(s)) (1) LINGUISTICS, as other sciences, uses this term in the sense of a higher level language for describing an object of study (or 'object language') – in this case the object of study is itself language, *viz* the various language samples, INTUITIONS, etc. which constitute our linguistic experience. The subject of this dictionary is **linguistic metalanguage**. 'Metalinguistics' is the study of metalanguage, in this general sense. See Matthews 1974: Ch. 4; Lyons 1977b: Ch. 1.

(2) The general term **metalinguistics** has a more specific sense within linguistics, where some linguists have used it, especially in the 1950s, to refer to the overall relation of the linguistic system to the other systems of behaviour in the associated culture (cf. the similar notion of CONTEXT OF SITUATION). In this view, only such a total account will constitute the full statement of the MEANINGS of the linguistic FORMS. See Crystal 1969: Ch. 2.

metathesis A term used in LINGUISTICS to refer to an alteration in the SEQUENCE of ELEMENTS in a SENTENCE – usually of sounds, but sometimes of SYLLABLES, WORDS, or other UNITS. 'Metatheses' are well-recognised in HISTORICAL LANGUAGE studies (e.g. Old English *brid* becoming *bird*), but they can also be seen in PERFORMANCE ERRORS – in such TONGUE SLIPS as *aks* for *ask*, or in the phenomenon of 'spoonerisms' (cf. *the dear old queen* becoming *the queer old dean*). See Bolinger 1975: Ch. 12.

metrics The traditional sense of this term – the study of versification – is interpreted in LINGUISTICS as the analysis of metrical structure using the whole range of linguistic techniques, especially those belonging to SEGMENTAL and SUPRASEGMENTAL PHONOLOGY. See Robins 1971: Ch. 9.

microlinguistic(s) A term used by some linguists, especially in the 1950s, to refer to the main areas of LINGUISTICS, especially PHONOLOGY, MORPHOLOGY and SYNTAX, these being seen as constituting a sharply defined field of study differentiable from PRELINGUISTICS and META-LINGUISTICS. In this frame of reference, it was seen as a branch of MACROLINGUISTICS. More broadly, the term can be used to distinguish complementary views of a subject, one being strictly linguistic, the other being broader, e.g. a study of MEANING which concentrates on DENOTATIVE meaning and does not take SOCIOLINGUISTIC, etc. factors into account might be called 'microlinguistic' (as opposed to 'macro-linguistic') semantics.

The term 'microlinguistic' is sometimes used outside this frame-work in a general sense, to refer to any analysis of linguistic data involving a maximum depth of detail. Likewise, the term 'micro-sociolinguistic' (opposed to 'macro-') is sometimes found. See Crystal 1969: Ch. 2; Lyons 1977b: Ch. 14.

mid A term used in the three-fold PHONETIC classification of vertical TONGUE movement in VOWEL sounds, the others being 'high' and 'low'. It refers to vowels made in the middle area of ARTICULATION, as in *get*, *say*, *go* or *got*. See Gimson 1970: Ch. 4; Catford 1977: Ch. 9.

minimal-distance principle (MDP) A term used in PSYCHOLINGUIST-ICS, referring to a principle assumed to be generally applicable in the analysis of COMPLEMENT structures of the type *John wants Jim to go*, where the SUBJECT of the complement CLAUSE is *Jim*, i.e. the nearest NOUN PHRASE to the left of the complement VERB. Most complement-taking verbs conform to this principle (e.g. *like*, *hope*, *make*), which is used especially in child language studies to explain apparent anomalies in the ACQUISITION of complements and other similar types of STRUCTURE. For example, in *John promised Jim to go*, the subject of *go* is *John*: this breaks the minimal-distance principle, and it is hypothesised that children will have greater difficulty learning structures involving such verbs, since they constitute exceptions to the general rule. See Clark & Clark 1977: Ch. 9.

minimal free form A term introduced into LINGUISTICS by the American linguist Leonard BLOOMFIELD as part of his definition of

WORD. The phrase can be glossed as 'the smallest linguistic FORM which can stand on its own as an UTTERANCE'. See Lyons 1968: Ch. 5.

minimal pair (test) One of the DISCOVERY PROCEDURES used in PHONOLOGY to determine which sounds belong to the same class, or PHONEME. Two words which differ in only one sound are referred to as a 'minimal pair', e.g. *pin* vs. *bin*, *cot* vs. *cut*. A group of words differentiated by each having only one sound different from all others, e.g. *big, pig, rig...* is sometimes called a 'minimal set'. See Hyman 1975: Ch. 3; Bolinger 1975: Ch. 3.

minor A term used by some LINGUISTS in the classification of SENTENCE types to refer to a sentence (a **minor sentence**) with limited PRODUCTIVITY (e.g. *Please, Sorry*) or one which lacks some of the CONSTITUENTS of the LANGUAGE'S MAJOR (or FAVOURITE) sentence type (e.g. VOCATIVES, ELLIPTICAL CONSTRUCTIONS). See Quirk *et al* 1972: Ch. 7.

misderivation A term used by some PSYCHOLINGUISTS to refer to a type of TONGUE-SLIP where the wrong AFFIX is attached to a WORD, as in *kingness* for *kingship*. See Clark & Clark 1977: Ch. 7; Bolinger 1975: Ch. 12.

MIT The abbreviation for Massachusetts Institute of Technology, used in LINGUISTICS as a label characterising GENERATIVE linguistic theory and method. The 'MIT school' is so called because of the influence of the work of Noam CHOMSKY and his associates at MIT since the late 1950s. See Bolinger 1975: Ch. 15.

MLU The usual abbreviation for MEAN LENGTH OF UTTERANCE.

modal(ity) A term used in GRAMMATICAL and SEMANTIC analysis to refer to contrasts in MOOD signalled by the VERB and associated categories. In English, modal contrasts are primarily expressed by a sub-class of AUXILIARY verbs, e.g. *may, will, can*. This sub-class is symbolised as M in the PHRASE-STRUCTURE RULES of a GENERATIVE grammar. In CASE grammar, **modality** refers to one of the two major CONSTITUENTS of a sentence's DEEP STRUCTURE, the other being PROPOSITION. See Lyons 1968: Ch. 7; Quirk *et al* 1972: Ch. 3.

mode (1) A term used in the HALLIDAYAN classification of LANGUAGE VARIETIES, referring to the MEDIUM of the language activity which determines the role played by the language in a situation. Mode (more fully, **mode of discourse**) primarily includes the choice of speech vs. writing (along with other possible sub-divisions, such as reading model

aloud, speech from notes, etc.), but also includes choice of format (as in newspapers, commentary, poetry, etc.). The main terms with which it contrasts are FIELD and STYLE. See Bolinger 1975: Chs. 11, 15.

(2) A term used in TAGMEMIC analysis to label the various dimensions recognised by the theory, e.g. the distinction between PHONOLOGICAL, LEXICAL and GRAMMATICAL 'modes' (which constitute the main components of the theory), and between FEATURE, MANIFESTATION and DISTRIBUTION 'modes' (which are used to handle the UNITS of linguistic description). See Bolinger 1975: Ch. 15.

model (1) This central notion of scientific enquiry has been applied in several areas of LINGUISTICS and PHONETICS. A model is a specially designed representation of concepts or entities, used to discover or explain their structure or function. All models involve the MAPPING in a new conceptual dimension of a set of ELEMENTS recognised in the situation being modelled. For example, the PHONOLOGIST builds models of the organisation of the speech continuum, using such contrasts as PHONEMES (sc. the 'phonemic model of analysis') or DISTINCTIVE FEATURES (sc. the 'distinctive feature model'); the GRAMMARIAN uses TREE diagrams, BRACKETS and other such devices to help model SYNTACTIC STRUCTURE. One of the earliest uses of the term in linguistics was by the American linguist, Charles Hockett (b. 1916), in a discussion of models of DESCRIPTION in MORPHOLOGY – a distinction being made between the 'ITEM AND ARRANGEMENT model' and the 'ITEM AND PROCESS model' (and later, the 'WORD AND PARADIGM model'). In discussion of GENERATIVE grammar, and related developments in linguistic theory, the term is often used in the sense of 'formal representation of a theory', as when one contrasts the '*Syntactic Structures* model' of generative grammar with the '*Aspects* model'. Sometimes, though, the term 'model' is used synonymously with 'theory' by some authors; usage is not entirely consistent. However, there is now increasing awareness of the role of models in linguistic enquiry, and of their strengths and limitations in generating testable hypotheses. See Lyons 1977a: App.

(2) In several areas of APPLIED LINGUISTICS, one encounters the traditional sense of a model as someone or something used as an exemplar of a level of language achievement. For example, foreign language teaching may use a NATIVE-SPEAKER, or a STANDARD DIALECT, as a model of the language to be learned; a speech therapist may use herself as a model for a language disordered patient; an English teacher may use a certain piece of writing as a model of attainment for his class. See Corder 1973: Ch. 9.

modification (modif-y, -ier) (1) A term used in SYNTAX to refer to the STRUCTURAL dependence of one GRAMMATICAL UNIT upon another – but with different restrictions in the scope of the term being introduced by different approaches. Some reserve the term for structural dependence within any ENDOCENTRIC PHRASE, e.g. in *the big man in the garden*, both *the big* and *in the garden* 'modify' *man* – PREMODIFICATION and POSTmodification respectively. Some LINGUISTS reserve the term for the premodifying structures only: in HALLIDAYAN grammar, for example, the above phrase would have the structure M–H–Q, standing for modification–HEAD–QUALIFICATION. TRADITIONAL grammar reserved the term for ADVERBIAL units which were dependent on the VERB, and this tradition is sometimes encountered. See Lyons 1968: Ch. 6.

(2) The term is also used in MORPHOLOGY to refer to a process of change within the ROOT or STEM of a FORM, as in the VOWEL changes between the singular and plural of some nouns in English (*man* ~ *men*), or in cases of SUPPLETION. In this, and related senses, the term is also found in HISTORICAL LANGUAGE studies. See Matthews 1974: Ch. 7.

(3) In PHONETICS, factors which influence the air flow in the VOCAL TRACT are often referred to as **modifications**, e.g. the movement of the soft PALATE, the degree of CLOSURE of the GLOTTIS. The term is also sometimes used to refer to any factors which alter the typical actions of the VOCAL ORGANS in producing the PHONEMES of a language, as in PROSODIC features, SECONDARY ARTICULATIONS, and TRANSITIONS between sounds. See Dinneen 1977: Ch. 9.

(4) Also in phonetics, the range of DIACRITIC marks which indicate variations in VOWEL and CONSONANT quality are referred to as **modifiers**, in the INTERNATIONAL PHONETIC alphabet. See Gimson 1970: App.

modulation A term sometimes used in LINGUISTICS to refer to the SUPRASEGMENTAL alterations introduced into an UTTERANCE for a particular attitudinal or social effect, e.g. whispering, shouting. See Lyons 1977b: Ch. 3.

mono- A PREFIX used in PHONETICS and LINGUISTICS when one wants to contrast the unitary manifestation of a linguistic concept with a multiple one. Examples of this contrast are: **monosyllabic** WORDS (or 'monosyllables') vs. POLYSYLLABLES; **monomorphemic** words (i.e. consisting of a single MORPHEME) vs. bimorphemic, etc.; **monosystemic** PHONOLOGY (consisting of a single SYSTEM of PHONEMES) vs. POLYSYSTEMIC; **monosemy** (consisting of a single MEANING) vs. POLYSEMY; and so on.

monophthong A term used in the PHONETIC classification of VOWEL sounds on the basis of their MANNER OF ARTICULATION: it refers to a vowel (a PURE VOWEL) where there is no detectable change in quality during a SYLLABLE, as in English *cart, cut, cot*. Vowels which change in quality are known as DIPHTHONGS (or TRIPHTHONGS). In some DIALECT and HISTORICAL studies, a process of **monophthongisation** can be found, i.e. a change in VOWEL QUALITY from a diphthong to a monophthong. See Ladefoged 1975: Ch. 4; Gimson 1977: Ch. 4.

Montague grammar A movement in LINGUISTIC theory in the mid-1970s which owes its impetus to the thinking of the American logician Richard Montague (1930–1970). The approach uses a conceptual apparatus derived from the study of the SEMANTICS of FORMAL (logical) LANGUAGES, and applies it to the analysis of natural languages. The GRAMMAR contains a SYNTACTIC and a SEMANTIC COMPONENT, which are strictly related, in that there is a one-for-one correspondence between CATEGORIES set up at the two levels. The syntax is introduced through CATEGORIAL RULES which define syntactic categories, and build up a PHRASE-STRUCTURE grammar. The corresponding semantic rules construct a PROPOSITIONAL interpretation of these sentences, using the notions of truth-conditional predicate logic. At the time of writing, this approach has attracted a great deal of interest among linguists, and several developments of it are forthcoming (e.g. introducing TRANSFORMATIONAL operations). See Lyons 1977b: Ch. 11.

mood/modal(ity) A term used in the theoretical and descriptive study of SENTENCE/CLAUSE types, and especially of the VERBS they contain. Mood ('modality', or 'mode') refers to a set of SYNTACTIC and SEMANTIC CONTRASTS signalled by alternative PARADIGMS of the verb, e.g. INDICATIVE (the unMARKED form). SUBJUNCTIVE, IMPERATIVE. Semantically, a wide range of meanings is involved, especially attitudes on the part of the speaker towards the factual content of his utterance, e.g. uncertainty, definiteness, vagueness, possibility. Syntactically, these contrasts may be signalled by alternative INFLEC-TIONAL forms of a verb, or by using AUXILIARIES. English mainly uses 'modal' auxiliaries, e.g. *may, can, shall, must*, but makes a little use of inflection (e.g. *if I were you* vs. *I was*. . .). The semantic analysis of modal verbs, and the study of their distribution in everyday speech, is a topic which has attracted a great deal of recent attention in LINGUISTICS, and several classifications involving such notions as necessity, possibility, certainty, etc. have been proposed. The results of such studies have implications for fields other than linguistics; for example, theoretical modal distinctions involving such notions have been a major concern of logicians. See Lyons 1968: Ch. 7; Quirk *et al* 1972: Ch. 3.

morpheme (morph, -emics) The minimal DISTINCTIVE UNIT of GRAMMAR, and the central concern of MORPHOLOGY. Its original motivation was as an alternative to the notion of the WORD, which had proved to be difficult to work with in comparing LANGUAGES. Words, moreover, could be quite complex in STRUCTURE, and there was a need for a single concept to inter-relate such notions as ROOT, PREFIX, COMPOUND, etc. The morpheme, accordingly, was seen primarily as the smallest functioning unit in the composition of words.

Morphemes are commonly classified into **free forms** (morphemes which can occur as separate words) and **bound forms** (morphemes which cannot so occur – mainly AFFIXES): thus *unselfish* consists of the three morphemes *un*, *self*, and *ish*, of which *self* is a free form, *un-* and *-ish* bound forms. A word consisting of a single (free) morpheme is a **monomorphemic** word: its opposite is **polymorphemic**. A further distinction may be made between 'lexical' and 'grammatical morphemes'; the former are morphemes used for the construction of new words in a language, such as in COMPOUND words (e.g. *blackbird*), and affixes such as *-ship*, *-ise*; the latter are morphemes used to express grammatical relationships between a word and its CONTEXT, such as plurality or past TENSE (i.e. the INFLECTIONS on words). Grammatical morphemes which are separate words are called (*inter alia*) FUNCTION WORDS.

As with all EMIC notions, morphemes are abstract units, which are realised in speech by DISCRETE units, known as MORPHS. The relationship is generally referred to as one of EXPONENCE, or REALISATION. Most morphemes are realised by single morphs, as in the example above. Some morphemes, however, are realised by more than one morph according to their position in a word or sentence, such alternative morphs being called ALLOMORPHS, or 'morphemic variants'. Thus the morpheme of plurality represented orthographically by the *-s* in e.g. *cots*, *digs*, and *forces* has the allomorphs represented phonetically by {-s}, {-z}, and {-iz} respectively (morphemes are usually symbolised using brace brackets). In this instance the allomorphs result from the phonetic influence of the sounds with which the singular forms of the words terminate, the process being referred to as one of 'phonological conditioning'. The study of the arrangement of morphemes in linear sequence, taking such factors into account, is **morphotactics**.

The application of morphemic ideas to the analysis of languages was particularly extensive in the 1940s and 1950s in post-BLOOMFIELDIAN linguistics, when the approach came to be called **morphemics**, and several analytical difficulties emerged. The English plural morpheme illustrates some of these. When the plurality is simply added to the root, as in the above examples, the correspondence between morpheme and morph is straightforward. But in cases like *mouse* ~ *mice* and *sheep* ~ *sheep* it is more problematic. Several solutions have been proposed to handle such cases: in the case of *sheep*, for example, a **zero morph** of plurality may be recognised, to preserve the notion of 'sheep + plural', this being symbolised as ϕ. Other concepts which have proved to be of importance in 'morphemic analysis' include (i) the **empty morph**, set up to handle cases where a FORMAL feature in a word cannot be allocated to any morpheme, and (ii) the **portmanteau morph**, set up to handle cases where a formal feature can be allocated to more than one morpheme. See Matthews 1974: Ch. 5; Robins 1971: Ch. 5; Bolinger 1975: Ch. 5.

morpheme structure rules/conditions Terms used in GENERATIVE PHONOLOGY, to refer to the processes which have attempted to cope with REDUNDANCY in carrying out an analysis. When SEGMENTS co-occur, the presence of a FEATURE characterising one segment may make it unnecessary to specify a certain feature in another segment: the CONSTRAINTS involved are handled by MORPHEME structure (or 'LEXICAL redundancy') rules. For example, given an English morpheme which has an AFFRICATE in INITIAL position, it is predictable that the following segment will be a VOWEL. It would then be possible to leave the features for vowels (e.g. [−consonantal], [+sonorant]) blank in the UNDERLYING FORM of the morpheme, the apppropriate values being filled in automatically by the application of the relevant morpheme structure rule at some subsequent point in the DERIVATION. Several problems with this view have led to the more recent proposal to handle these redundancies in terms of **morpheme structure conditions**, which state more explicitly the processes constraining the correspondences between segments, without recourse to the blank-filling procedure. See Hyman 1975: Ch. 4.

morphology (morphological) The branch of GRAMMAR which studies the STRUCTURE or FORMS of WORDS, primarily through the use of the MORPHEME construct. It is traditionally distinguished from SYNTAX, which deals with the RULES governing the combination of words in SENTENCES. It is generally divided into two fields: the study of INFLECTIONS ('inflectional morphology'), and of WORD-FORMATION ('lexical' or 'derivational morphology'). When emphasis is on the technique of analysing words into morphemes, particularly as practised by American STRUCTURALIST linguists in the 1940s and 1950s, the term **morphemics** is used. 'Morphemic analysis' in this sense is part of a SYNCHRONIC linguistic study; **morphological analysis** is the more general term, being applied to HISTORICAL studies as well. Morphological analysis may take various forms. One approach is to make a DISTRIBUTIONAL study of the morphemes and morphemic variants occurring in words (the analysis of 'morphotactic arrangements'), as in **item and arrangement models** of description. Another approach sets up 'morphological processes' or 'operations', which see the relationships between word-forms as one of replacement (e.g. replace the /ei/ of *take* with the /ʊ/ of *took*), as in ITEM AND PROCESS models.

In GENERATIVE linguistics, morphology and syntax are not seen as two separate LEVELS; the syntactic RULES of the grammar apply to the structure of words, as they do to PHRASES and sentences, and morphological notions emerge only at the point where the output of the syntactic component has to be given a PHONOLOGICAL REPRESENTATION via the MORPHOPHONOLOGICAL rules). See Matthews 1974; Robins 1971: Ch. 5.

morpho(-)phoneme The basic unit recognised in a MORPHOPHONEMIC LEVEL of analysis. It is usually symbolised by the use of a capital letter within brace BRACKETS, e.g. {F}, {T}. One of the original examples used in order to justify establishing this entity was the **alternation** between /f/ and /v/ in some English plurals, such as *knife ~ knives*. There is no predictable alternation between /f/ and /v/ for English WORDS in general, but only in this specific GRAMMATICAL CONTEXT. This fact, it is argued, can be captured by setting up a morphophoneme {F}, as in {naɪF}: in a singular context this is realised as /f/, in a plural context as /v/. Each morphophonemic symbol thus represents the class of PHONEMES which occurs within a particular set of grammatical ENVIRONMENTS. In recent linguistic theory, the term SYSTEMATIC PHONEME is more widespread. See Hyman 1975: Ch. 3; Bolinger 1975: Ch. 3.

morpho(-)phonemics (morpho(-)(pho)nology) A branch of LINGUISTICS referring to the analysis and classification of the PHONOLOGICAL factors which affect the appearance of MORPHEMES, or, correspondingly, the GRAMMATICAL factors which affect the appearance of PHONEMES. In the European tradition, **morphophonology** (or 'morphonology') is the preferred term; in the American tradition, it is **morphophonemics**. In some theories, morphophonemics is seen as a separate level of linguistic structure intermediate between grammar and phonology. In early versions of GENERATIVE grammar, **morphophonemic rules** were distinguished as a separate COMPONENT in the DERIVATION of SENTENCES, whereby a TERMINAL STRING of morphemes would be converted into their correct phonological form. In later generative theory, the term SYSTEMATIC PHONEMICS became standard. See Hyman 1975: Ch. 3; Bolinger 1975: Ch. 3; Matthews 1974: Ch. 9.

morphosyntactic A term used in LINGUISTICS to refer to GRAMMATICAL categories or properties for whose definition criteria of MORPHOLOGY and SYNTAX both apply, as in describing the characteristics of WORDS. The distinctions under the heading of NUMBER in NOUNS, for example, constitute a morphosyntactic category: on the one hand, number CONTRASTS affect syntax (e.g. singular subject requiring a singular verb); on the other hand, they require morphological definition (e.g. add -*s* for plural). Traditional properties such as singular, PERFECT, INDICATIVE, PASSIVE, ACCUSATIVE, 3rd PERSON are examples. See Matthews 1974: Ch. 4.

motor theory A term used in PHONETICS and PSYCHOLINGUISTICS to refer to a theory of SPEECH PERCEPTION which proposes that the brain of the listener constructs a MODEL of the ARTICULATORY ('motor') movements being produced by the speaker. It is not usually interpreted as someone having to 'talk in parallel' (i.e. sub-vocally) while he is listening – a view for which there is little support; but rather, as an abstract mechanism, or model, which can help explain the indirect correspondences between the feature of the ACOUSTIC signal and the SEGMENTS the listener actually perceives. See Clark & Clark 1977: Ch. 5.

movement A term often used within the framework of TRANSFORMA-TIONAL GRAMMAR to refer to a basic kind of transformational operation. 'Movement transformations' have the effect of moving CONSTITUENTS (usually one at a time) from one part of a PHRASE-MARKER to another, as in the formation of PASSIVE sentences, the placement of NEGATIVES and AFFIXES. An alternative term is RE-ORDERING or PERMUTATION. In some recent approaches this notion is broken down into the more basic operations of ADJUNCTION and DELETION. See Akmajian & Heny 1975: Ch. 7; Huddleston 1976: Ch. 12.

multidimensional scaling A statistical technique which has been applied in PSYCHOLINGUISTICS to quantify the MEANINGS of related

LEXICAL ITEMS and define the SEMANTIC space within which these items work. INFORMANTS rate numerically a set of items (e.g. kinship terms, colours) in terms of their mutual similarity; the more similar the average ratings are, the closer these items are placed in the hypothetical space. In this inductive manner, it is hoped to establish classificatory criteria for lexical sets which might otherwise not emerge, and to develop more illuminating models of semantic STRUCTURE than are available using conventional analytic techniques. See Clark & Clark 1977: Ch. 11.

multilateral A type of OPPOSITION recognised in PRAGUE SCHOOL PHONOLOGY, distinguished from BILATERAL. The opposition between English /t/ and /v/ is multilateral, because there are several possibilities of CONTRAST involving the same set of FEATURES, e.g. /d/ vs. /f/. The opposition between /t/ and /d/, however, is bilateral, because these are the only units in the system which are ALVEOLAR/ PLOSIVE, and they are differentiated by the single feature of VOICING. See Hyman 1975: Ch. 2.

multilingual(ism) A term used in SOCIOLINGUISTICS to refer, in the first instance, to a SPEECH community which makes use of two or more LANGUAGES, and then to the individual speakers who have multilingual ability. 'Multilingualism' (or 'plurilingualism') in this sense may subsume BILINGUALISM, but it is often contrasted with it (i.e. a community or individual in command of *more* than two languages). A further distinction is sometimes made between a multilingualism which is internal to a speech community (i.e. for routine domestic communicative purposes), and one which is external to it (i.e. an additional language being used to facilitate communication with other nations, as in the use of a LINGUA FRANCA). Sociolinguistic studies have emphasised both the frequency and complexity of the phenomenon: on the one hand, there are very few speech communities which are totally monolingual (because of the existence of linguistic minority groups within their boundaries); on the other hand, the multilingual abilities demonstrated are of several levels of proficiency, and raise different kinds of political, educational and social problems, depending on the numbers, social standing, and national feeling of the groups concerned. See Trudgill 1974: Ch. 5; Gumperz & Hymes 1971: Ch. 15.

mutation A term used in LINGUISTICS, especially in HISTORICAL LAN- GUAGE studies, to refer to the change in a sound's QUALITY due to the influence of sounds in adjacent MORPHEMES or WORDS. For example, in the period when Old English was developing, the influence of an /i/ VOWEL in certain circumstances caused other vowels to 'mutate' in the direction of the CLOSE vowel, e.g. *foti became *feet*. The term is also occasionally used in SYNCHRONIC CONTEXTS, as in the mutation of various INITIAL CONSONANTS in Welsh after certain words, e.g. *pen* 'head' → *fy mhen* 'my head'. See Robins 1971: Ch. 5.

N

🅖🅖🅖🅖🅖🅖

nasal(-ised, -isation, -ity) A term used in the PHONETIC classification
of speech sounds on the basis of MANNER OF ARTICULATION: it refers
to sounds produced while the soft PALATE is lowered to allow an
audible escape of air through the nose. Both CONSONANTS and VOWELS
may be articulated in this way. Nasal consonants occur when there
is a complete CLOSURE in the mouth, and all the air thus escapes
through the nose. Examples in English are the final consonants of *ram*,
ran, *rang* [ram, ran, raŋ], where the closures are in BILABIAL, ALVEOLAR
and VELAR positions respectively. Several other nasal sounds are
possible, e.g. in PALATAL positions [ɲ], as in Spanish *mañana*. VOICELESS
nasal sounds also occur, as when a nasal consonant follows [s] in
English, e.g. *small*, *snooze*. In nasal (or 'nasalised') vowels, air escapes
through nose and mouth simultaneously; the vowels are transcribed
with [˜] above the symbol, e.g. [ã]. Nasal vowels are opposed to ORAL
vowels in a language, as in French and Portuguese. English has no
distinct nasal vowels, but **nasalisation** is often heard on English
vowels, when they display the articulatory influence of an adjacent
nasal consonant, as in *mat* or *hand*. The vowel in a word like *man* may
be articulated with the soft palate lowered throughout, because of this
influence. Such cases, where the nasality comes from other sounds,
would be referred to as 'nasalised' vowels; the term 'nasal vowel',
on the other hand, suggests that the nasality is an essential identifying
feature of the sound. A 'nasalised consonant', likewise, would refer
to a consonant which, though normally oral in a language, was being
articulated in a nasal manner because of some adjacent nasal sound.
The opposite term is 'denasalised', which would be applied only to
sounds which normally were articulated with a nasal component (as
when one speaks through a blocked nose). In certain clinical
conditions, such as cleft palate, abnormal degrees of nasalisation may
be present: excessively nasal (or 'hypernasal') speech is here opposed
to reduced nasality (or 'hyponasal' speech).

Other nasal effects may be heard in a language. A PLOSIVE sound,
for example, when followed by a nasal articulated in the same position,

may be released through the nose instead of the mouth, and the resulting auditory effect is one of 'nasal plosion', as in *sudden* [sʌdn̩], which is rather more likely than [sʌdən]. 'Nasal twang' is not a term with a precise phonetic definition, as it refers to any degree of nasal effect in a speaker or DIALECT, seen in contrast with speech which is more oral in character.

The opposition between 'nasal' and 'oral' is given a special technical status in the DISTINCTIVE FEATURE theory of PHONOLOGY, where it works alongside other two-way CONTRASTS as part of the complete specification of a sound system. In CHOMSKY & Halle's theory, for example, it is classified as a CAVITY feature, and grouped along with LATERAL under the specific heading of SECONDARY APERTURES. See Gimson 1970: Chs. 4, 8; Catford 1977: Ch. 8; Hyman 1975: Ch. 2.

native-speaker Term used in LINGUISTICS to refer to someone for whom a particular LANGUAGE is a 'native language' (also called 'first language', 'mother tongue'). The implication is that this language, having been acquired naturally during childhood, is the one about which a speaker will have the most reliable INTUITIONS, and whose judgements about the way the language is used can therefore be trusted. In investigating a language, accordingly, one is wise to try to obtain information from 'native-speaking' informants, rather than from those who may have learned it as a SECOND or foreign language (even if they are highly proficient). Many people do however develop a 'native-like' command of a foreign language, and in BILINGUALISM one has the case of someone who has a native command of two languages. See Robins 1971: Ch. 9.

naturalness/natural class A notion introduced into (especially GEN-ERATIVE) LINGUISTIC theory to refer to the PHONETIC plausibility of an analysis, which is seen as an important criterion in evaluating analyses alongside such other criteria as SIMPLICITY. An analysis, it is argued, must make phonetic sense, if it is to have any explanatory role in relation to the speaker's behaviour, e.g. such factors as relative ease of ARTICULATION must be taken into account. One of the first steps in defining naturalness more formally is to recognise the notion of 'natural class'. A set of SEGMENTS is said to constitute a natural class if fewer phonetic FEATURES are needed to specify the set as a whole than to specify any one member of the set. The set of VOICED PLOSIVE segments in English are a natural class, on this basis: /b/, /d/ and /g/ all share the features of VOICING, INSTANTANEOUS RELEASE, and

INTERRUPTED; but to specify any one of these, further features would be required (e.g. /d/ would be CORONAL, in addition).

The term in this sense applies to any set of speech segments which can be shown to have a highest common factor in this way; but as it stands the criterion needs to be supplemented by others, as it is too general (e.g. it would allow for all sounds in a language to be considered a natural class, on the grounds that they are all PULMONIC EGRESSIVE). Several other relevant criteria have been suggested, e.g. that the set of sounds all turn up in the same PHONOLOGICAL RULES, undergoing similar processes together. Also, there are several difficulties in working with the notion in terms of features, e.g. the more natural solution is not always the simpler. The notion of naturalness has thus been developed to take into account the relative naturalness of (i) segments (mainly through the use of the MARKING convention), (ii) sound SYSTEMS (by computing the relative complexity of its units, this being defined in terms of marking values), and (iii) phonological rules (based on the tendency for some phonological processes to be more frequent and phonetically more expected than others, e.g. /i/ becoming /u/ rather than /ɯ/, or certain types of ASSIMILATION or SYLLABLE structures being preferred). These developments are continuing. See Hyman 1975: Ch. 5.

negation (negative) A process or construction in GRAMMATICAL and SEMANTIC analysis which typically expresses the contradiction of some or all of a sentence's meaning. In English grammar, it is expressed by the insertion of the 'negative PARTICLE' *not* or *n't* (the CONTRACTED negative); in LEXIS, there are several possible means, e.g. PREFIXES such as *un-*, *non-*, or words such as *deny*. Some LANGUAGES use more than one particle to express negation (as in French *ne...pas*), and similar 'double negative' features are characteristic of some English DIALECTS, e.g. *I'm not unhappy* (which is a STYLISTICally MARKED mode of assertion) and *I've not done nothing* (which is not acceptable in STANDARD English).

In recent LINGUISTICS, a topic of particular interest has been the range of sentence STRUCTURE affected by the insertion of a negative particle, e.g. *I think John isn't coming* vs. *I don't think John is coming*: such variations in the 'scope' of negation affect the logical structure as well as the semantic analysis of the sentence. The opposite 'pole' to negative is POSITIVE (or AFFIRMATIVE), and the system of contrasts made by a language in this area is often referred to as POLARITY. See Quirk *et al* 1972: Ch. 2; Lyons 1977b: Ch. 6.

neogrammarian(s) A follower of, or characteristic of the principles of, a 19th-century school of thought in COMPARATIVE PHILOLOGY, initiated by the German scholars K. Brugmann (1894–1919) and S. A. Leskien (1840–1916). Their main tenet was that sound laws admitted no exceptions (the **neogrammarian hypothesis**). Their nickname in German *Junggrammatiker* ('young grammarians') arose from the attitude of older scholars who, while not necessarily rejecting the principle, objected to the forceful way in which it was promulgated. See Robins 1971: Ch. 8.

nesting (nested) A term used in LINGUISTICS to refer to the INSERTION of one or more linguistic UNITS (usually PHRASES or CLAUSES) within the STRUCTURE of an ENDOCENTRIC phrase. A phrase such as *the table in the corner with the candlesticks near the window* ... shows several MODIFYING phrases RECURSIVELY 'nested' (cf. EMBEDDED). See Lyons 1968: Ch. 6.

neurolinguistics A branch of LINGUISTICS, sometimes called **neurological linguistics**, which studies the neurological basis of LANGUAGE development and use in man, and attempts to construct a MODEL of the brain's control over the processes of speech and hearing. The main approach has been to postulate the stages of a 'neural program', which would explain the observed phenomena of temporal ARTICULATORY co-ordination, SEQUENCING and other features of SPEECH PRODUCTION. Central to this approach has been the research findings from two main areas: the study of CLINICAL LINGUISTIC conditions (such as aphasia, dysarthria, stuttering), in an attempt to deduce the nature of the underlying system from the analysis of its various stages of breakdown; and the study of speech production in PARAMETRIC articulatory phonetic terms – especially of the 'normal' ERRORS which are introduced into speech (e.g. TONGUE SLIPS, HESITATIONS). See Clark & Clark 1977: Ch. 6; Catford 1977: Ch. 12.

neutral (1) A term used in the classification of lip position in PHONETICS, referring to the visual appearance of the lips when they are held in a relaxed position, with no lip-ROUNDING, and a medium lowering of the lower jaw, as in the vowels of *pet* or *bird*. It is contrasted with SPREAD, OPEN and ROUNDED lip positions. See Gimson 1970: Ch. 2.

(2) A term used in the classification of VOWEL sounds, to refer to a LAX vowel made in the centre of the vowel ARTICULATION area, with the TONGUE neutral with respect to FRONT, BACK, HIGH or LOW positions. The most widely encountered vowel of this quality is heard in the first vowel of *asleep*, *balloon*, or the last vowel in *mother*, *cover*.

It is usually referred to as SCHWA [ə]. Several terms for this quality have been proposed, including 'central', 'medium' and 'murmured' vowel. See Gimson 1970. Ch. 7.

neutralisation (neutralis-e, -able) A term used in PHONOLOGY to describe what happens when the distinction between two PHONEMES is lost in a particular ENVIRONMENT. For example, in English, the contrast between ASPIRATED (voiceless) and unaspirated (VOICED) PLOSIVES is normally crucial, e.g. *tip* vs. *dip*, but this contrast is lost, or 'neutralised', when the plosive is preceded by /s/, as in *stop*, *skin*, *speech*, and as a result, there are no pairs of words in the language of the type /skɪn/ vs. /*sgɪn/. From a PHONETIC point of view, the explanation lies in the phonetic change which happens to /k/ in this position: the /k/ lacks aspiration, and comes to be physically indistinguishable from /g/. In the original PRAGUE SCHOOL formulation of this notion, 'neutralisable' was seen as a type of OPPOSITION, and contrasted with CONSTANT. See Lyons 1968: Ch. 3; Hyman 1975: Ch. 3.

new A term used by some LINGUISTS in a two-part analysis of utterances in terms of INFORMATION structure: 'new' information is opposed to GIVEN. (The contrast between FOCUS and PRESUPPOSITION makes an analogous distinction.) 'New', as its name suggests, refers to information which is additional to that already supplied by the previous CONTEXT of speaking; 'given', by contrast, refers to the information already available. In the clearest cases, new information is identified by INTONATIONAL emphasis within the TONE UNIT, the NUCLEAR tone (or primary STRESS) signalling its focus, e.g. *I've got thrèe books in my bag* vs. *I've got three books in my bàg*, and so on. Several problems arise in determining the scope of the new information, with reference to the previous CONTEXT, however, which have been the subject of much discussion, e.g. A: *What can you see?* B: *I can see 'three mèn*, where the *three* is plainly part of the new information, but does not carry the nuclear tone. See Lyons 1977b: Ch. 12; Quirk *et al* 1972: Ch. 14.

node A term used in GENERATIVE GRAMMAR to refer to the LABELLED BRANCHING points in a TREE diagram. A 'family' metaphor is often used in the discussion of nodes. A node directly DOMINATED by another is called a 'daughter' node; if two nodes are directly dominated by the same node, they are 'sister' nodes. (The term 'mother' node, however regrettably, is not used!) The topmost node of the tree diagram is the 'root'. Nodes which do not dominate other CATEGORIES are 'TERMINAL nodes'. See Akmajian & Heny 1975: Ch. 2.

nominal

nominal(isation) A term used in some GRAMMATICAL descriptions as a substitute for NOUN (e.g. 'nominal group' = 'noun phrase'). In a more restricted sense, it refers to WORDS which have some of the attributes of nouns, but not all, e.g. *the poor are many*, where the HEAD word of this PHRASE does not pluralise (**the poors*). **Nominalisation** refers to the process of forming a noun from some other word class (e.g. *red + ness*) or (in GENERATIVE grammar especially) the DERIVATION of a noun PHRASE from an underlying CLAUSE (e.g. *His answering of the letter*... from *He answered the letter*). See Lyons 1968: Ch. 8; Quirk *et al* 1972: Ch. 13.

nominative In languages which express GRAMMATICAL relationships by means of INFLECTIONS, this term refers to the FORM taken by a WORD, usually a NOUN or PRONOUN, when it is the SUBJECT of a VERB. It is usually the first form to be listed in a grammatical PARADIGM, or in a dictionary, and is often the UNMARKED form (cf. OBLIQUE), e.g. in Latin, *homo* 'man' is nominative singular (cf. *hominem, hominis*, etc.). See Lyons 1968: Ch. 7.

nonce A LINGUISTIC FORM which a speaker consciously invents or accidentally uses on a single occasion is known as a 'nonce word' or a 'nonce formation' (which may involve UNITS larger than the WORD). Many factors account for their use, e.g. a speaker cannot remember a particular word, so coins an alternative approximation (as in *linguistified*, heard recently from a student who felt he was getting nowhere with linguistics), or he is constrained by circumstances to produce a new form (as in newspaper headlines). Nonce formations have occasionally come to be adopted by the community – in which case they cease by definition to be 'nonce' (forms used 'for the (n)once'). See Quirk *et al* 1972: App. 1.

nondiscrete grammar The name given to a LINGUISTIC MODEL suggested by the American linguist John Robert Ross (b. 1938) in the early 1970s (as an alternative to the EXTENDED STANDARD THEORY of TRANSFORMATIONAL GRAMMAR), which analyses LANGUAGE as a series of DISCRETE contrasts (e.g. grammatical vs. ungrammatical, applicability vs. non-applicability of RULES). In nondiscrete grammar, however, such notions as grammaticality, rule applicability, CLASS membership, etc. are seen as matters of degree. Accounting for the existence of marginally grammatical sentences, SEMI-SENTENCES, and so on, is conceived as a major aim of linguistic theory, and INDETERMINACY of this kind is seen as an essential feature of COMPETENCE. The idiosyncratic terminology which this model uses (e.g. SQUISH, 'nouniness', 'clausematiness', etc.) has endeared it to some, and been a source of irritation to others. Its emphasis on the analysis of problematic DATA has been welcomed, but so far there has been relatively little development of the approach in linguistics as a whole, and its theoretical significance is controversial. See Radford 1981: Ch. 3.

nonsense In several contexts in LINGUISTICS and PHONETICS, this term is used in a rather more restricted sense than in everyday use. In phonetics, it is applied to the invented phonetic SEQUENCES ('nonsense words') used as part of EAR-TRAINING exercises. In linguistics, it refers, first, to SENTENCES which may be GENERATED by a GRAMMAR (i.e. they are grammatical), but which are not SEMANTICALLY ACCEPTABLE, e.g. *the stone is sleeping*, *he drank the car in a table*. Such meaningless sentences are often called 'anomalous'. The term is also used in grammar, as part of a technique for identifying PRODUCTIVE grammatical UNITS. Often used here is an extract from Lewis Carroll's *Jabberwocky*, where phrases such as *all mimsy were the borogroves* display WORD-CLASS identities clearly, e.g. *mimsy* (adjective) and *borogroves* (nouns). The technique is also used in language ACQUISITION, e.g. in language production tasks, to see if the child has acquired a grammatical unit (as in the WUGS experiment). See Lyons 1968: Ch. 9; Clark & Clark 1977: Chs. 2, 13.

norm(ative) The general sense of this term is used in LINGUISTICS to refer to a standard practice in speech or writing. The 'norm' in question may apply to groups of varying size within a SPEECH community, or to the community as a whole. For example, several kinds of scientific English make use of impersonal CONSTRUCTIONS much more frequently than is the case in conversational English, which may be seen as the norm for purposes of STYLISTIC comparison. Often, the norms of different groups conflict, and 'normative rules' may be imposed by one group on another (e.g. stating the 'correct' use of *whom*, *shall* or *will*, insisting on PREPOSITIONS at the end of SENTENCES). A collection of such rules is known as a 'normative GRAMMAR'; such grammars were particularly current in the 18th and 19th centuries, and this tradition still exercises considerable influence. In contrast with this PRESCRIPTIVE concern to maintain an imagined set of linguistic standards, linguistics emphasises the description of actual USAGE in the community, and SOCIOLINGUISTICS emphasises the need to take into account the relative APPROPRIATENESS of different VARIETIES of language in different situations. See Lyons 1977b: Ch. 10; Bolinger 1975: Ch. 16.

notation(al) A term used in LINGUISTICS and PHONETICS to refer to any system of GRAPHIC representation of speech (as in a 'PHONEMIC notation', where the term TRANSCRIPTION is widely used). Specifically, it refers to the set of symbols which represent a mode of linguistic analysis, as in the 'PHRASE-STRUCTURE notation' in GENERATIVE GRAMMAR. An analytic convention, in this sense, which is introduced into an analysis to facilitate the formulation of a statement, such as a RULE, is often called a 'notational device', e.g. the use of ( ) to indicate OPTIONALITY in generative syntax. See Lyons 1968: Ch. 4.

notional A characteristic of much TRADITIONAL grammatical analysis, which assumed that there existed EXTRALINGUISTIC categories in terms of which the UNITS of GRAMMAR could be defined. Well-known notional definitions are of the NOUN as the name of a 'person, place, or thing', of the VERB as a 'doing word', of a SENTENCE as a 'complete thought', and so on. LINGUISTICS is critical of the notional approach insofar as the 'notions' involved are incapable of systematic and consistent exposition, and replaces it with an emphasis on FORMAL criteria. See Lyons 1968: Ch. 4.

noun A term used in the GRAMMATICAL classification of WORDS, traditionally defined as the 'name of a person, place, or thing', but the vagueness associated with the notions of 'name' and 'thing' (e.g. is *beauty* a thing?) has led LINGUISTIC descriptions to analyse this class in terms of the FORMAL and FUNCTIONAL criteria of SYNTAX and MORPHOLOGY. In linguistic terms, then, nouns are ITEMS which display certain types of INFLECTION (e.g. of CASE or NUMBER), have a specific DISTRIBUTION (e.g. they may follow PREPOSITIONS but not, say, MODALS), and perform a specific syntactic function (e.g. as SUBJECT or OBJECT of a sentence). Nouns are generally subclassified into COMMON and PROPER types, and analysed in terms of NUMBER, GENDER, CASE and COUNTABILITY.

The CONSTRUCTIONS into which nouns most commonly enter, and of which they are the HEAD word, are generally called **noun phrases** (NP) or 'nominal groups'. The structure of a noun phrase consists minimally of the noun (or noun substitute, such as a PRONOUN); the constructions preceding and following the noun are often described under the headings of PREMODIFICATION and POSTmodification respectively. See Quirk *et al* 1972: Chs. 4, 13; Lyons 1968: Ch. 7.

NP The usual abbreviation for NOUN PHRASE, and encountered especially in the opening RULES of a GENERATIVE GRAMMAR.

nucleus (nuclear) A term used by some INTONATION analysts, particularly those working within the British tradition, to refer to the
SYLLABLE in a TONE UNIT which carries maximal PROMINENCE, usually
due to a major PITCH change. The **nuclear syllable** is also referred
to as the TONIC syllable. In GENERATIVE PHONOLOGY, the analogous
notion is **nuclear stress**, with the relevant STRESS ASSIGNMENT RULE
referred to as the **nuclear stress rule**. In the normal, unemphatic
version of the sentence *the lady saw the **tramp***, the last word is nuclear,
and will carry one of the possible **nuclear tones** in English. The
nuclear tone is the most prominent pitch movement in a tone unit.
In English, analyses of nuclear tones vary, but most recognise such
contrasts as FALLING (transcribed with ` above or before the SYLLABLE
in question), RISING ´, rising-falling ^, falling-rising ˅ and level ˉ.
Others are possible, including distinctions within these types, such as
'high' vs. 'low' fall. See Crystal 1969: Ch. 4; Gimson 1970: Ch. 10.

number A GRAMMATICAL CATEGORY used for the analysis of WORD
CLASSES displaying such CONTRASTS as singular, plural, dual, etc., as
in English *boy* vs. *boys*, *he walks* vs. *they walk*. The contrasts generally
correspond to the number of real-world entities referred to, but
LINGUISTIC discussion has drawn attention to the problems involved
in proposing any such straightforward one-to-one correlation. A
NOUN, for example, may 'look' singular, but refer to a multiplicity of
entities (e.g. *the committee are agreed*, cf. COLLECTIVE), and nouns which
'look' plural may refer to a single entity (e.g *billiards*). There are in
addition several analytical difficulties in relating the notion of number
to that of COUNTABILITY (to explain the absence of such forms as **a
butter*). See Palmer 1971: App. B; Quirk *et al* 1972: Ch. 4; Lyons 1968:
Ch. 7.

O

᠅᠅᠅᠅᠅᠅

object(ive) A term used in the analysis of GRAMMATICAL FUNCTIONS, to refer to a major CONSTITUENT of SENTENCE or CLAUSE structure, traditionally associated with the 'receiver' or 'goal' of an action, as in *The cat bit **the dog***. Traditional analysis distinguishes a **direct** vs. an **indirect object**, to allow for sentences such as *The man gave a letter to the boy / The man gave the boy a letter*, which is marked in English by a contrast using PREPOSITIONS and WORD order, and in INFLECTING languages by different CASES (typically, the object case being ACCUSATIVE, the indirect object case being DATIVE). Much discussion in LINGUISTICS has focused on clarifying the notion of 'receiving' an action, in relation to the other ELEMENTS of clause structure (SUBJECT, COMPLEMENT, etc.) distinguishing various kinds of VERB-object relationship, both in terms of SURFACE and UNDERLYING structure. Examples of problem sentences are *John is easy to please* (where *John* is the underlying object of *please*) and *The plants are selling well* (where in reality it is the plants which are the 'logical receivers' of the action).

In the study of inflected languages, **objective** may be used as an alternative to ACCUSATIVE, e.g. in English, the contrast between subject and object forms of PRONOUNS (e.g. *he ~ him*) is sometimes referred to as a distinction between SUBJECTIVE and objective case.

The term 'objective' has a special status in CASE grammar, where it refers to the semantically most neutral case, i.e. a noun whose role in the action is identified by the SEMANTIC interpretation of the verb itself. See Lyons 1968: Ch. 8; Quirk *et al* 1972: Chs. 2, 7; Bolinger 1975: Ch. 15.

obligatory One of two types of TRANSFORMATIONAL RULE postulated by Noam CHOMSKY in his book *Syntactic Structures* (1957), the other being OPTIONAL. An **obligatory transformation** is one which *must* apply at a given stage in a DERIVATION, when its STRUCTURAL DESCRIPTION is met, if a WELL-FORMED SENTENCE is to result, e.g. the rule which attaches AFFIXES to their BASE forms. In later versions of transformational grammar, the range of this notion changes as SURFACE

STRUCTURES come to be derived from DEEP STRUCTURES by obligatory transformations, and the notion of optional selection comes to be replaced by choices made between the rules of the base COMPONENT. See Lyons 1968: Ch. 6.

oblique In languages which express GRAMMATICAL relationships by means of INFLECTIONS, this term refers to the FORM taken by a WORD, usually a NOUN or PRONOUN, when it refers collectively to all the CASE forms of a word except that of the unMARKED case, or NOMINATIVE. See Lyons 1968: Ch. 7.

obstruent A term used in the PHONETIC classification of speech sounds to refer to sounds involving a CONSTRICTION which impedes the flow of air through nose or mouth, as in PLOSIVES, FRICATIVES and AFFRICATES. In the DISTINCTIVE FEATURE approach of CHOMSKY & Halle, the term is used in the same sense, but its status is that of PHONOLOGICAL opposition to SONORANT. See Ladefoged 1975: Ch. 11; Hyman 1975: Ch. 2.

obviative A term used in LINGUISTICS to refer to a fourth person FORM used in some languages (e.g. some North American Indian languages). This form (of a PRONOUN, VERB, etc.) usually contrasts with the third person, in that it is used to refer to an entity distinct from that already referred to by the third person form – the general sense of 'someone/something else'. See Robins 1971: Ch. 7.

occlusion (occlusive) A term used in PHONETICS referring to the duration of the CLOSURE which is made while a PLOSIVE CONSONANT is being articulated. Plosives are sometimes referred to as 'occlusives'. See Catford 1977: Ch. 7.

oesophageal A term used in PHONETICS for sounds or VOICE initiated at or below the oesophagus; also spelled **esophageal**. An oesophageal technique of voice PRODUCTION is often taught to patients following laryngectomy. See Gimson 1970: Ch. 2.

off-/on-glide Terms used in PHONETICS to refer to the AUDITORY effect of ARTICULATORY movement at points of TRANSITION between sounds. An **off-glide** is a movement which occurs as the VOCAL ORGANS leave the position taken up by one speech sound and travel towards the position required for the next sound (or towards a position of rest). An **on-glide** is the correlative movement which occurs as the vocal organs approach their TARGET position for the articulation of a sound, either from a previous sound, or from the position of rest. See Gimson 1970: Ch. 8.

onomasiology A term sometimes used in SEMANTICS to refer to the study of sets of associated concepts in relation to the LINGUISTIC FORMS which designate them, e.g. the various ways of organising LEXICAL ITEMS conceptually in thesauri. See Lyons 1977b: Ch. 4.

onomastics A branch of SEMANTICS which studies the ETYMOLOGY of institutionalised ('proper') names, such as the names of people ('anthroponymy') and places ('toponymy'). See Lyons 1977b: Ch. 7.

onset A term used in PHONETICS and PHONOLOGY to refer to the opening SEGMENT of a LINGUISTIC UNIT (e.g. a SYLLABLE, a TONE UNIT) or to the ARTICULATORY movement which initiates a speech sound (e.g. the CLOSURE phase of an AFFRICATE). See Gimson 1970: Ch. 4.

ontogeny (ontogene-tic, -sis) The application of this general term in LINGUISTICS refers to the chronological ACQUISITION, development and decay of LANGUAGE in the individual, as opposed to in the SPEECH COMMUNITY as a whole (PHYLOGENY). It is particularly encountered in child language studies. See Bolinger 1975: Ch. 1.

open (1) A term used in the four-level PHONETIC classification of vertical TONGUE movement in VOWEL sounds based on the CARDINAL VOWEL SYSTEM, the others being CLOSE, 'half-close' and 'half-open'. It refers to a vowel made with the tongue in the lowest possible position, i.e. the mouth as wide open as possible, as in [a] and [ɑ]: the most open vowels in English are in words like *cat* and *cart*. The area of articulation immediately above 'open' is known as 'half-open' or 'mid-open', as in [ɛ] and [ɔ] (the nearest English vowels being in words like *get* and *got* respectively). In a three-level classification of vowel sounds, the lowest group are known as 'low' vowels (as opposed to 'high' and 'mid'). See Gimson 1970: Ch. 4; Catford 1977: Ch. 9.

(2) A term used in the classification of lip positions, referring to the visual appearance of the lips when they are held relatively wide apart, but without any noticeable ROUNDING, as in such sounds as the [ɑ] in *part*. It is contrasted with SPREAD, NEUTRAL and ROUNDED positions. See Gimson 1970: Ch. 2.

(3) A term used in the two-way classification of SYLLABLE structure, referring to a syllable which ends in a VOWEL, as opposed to the CLOSED syllable, which ends in a CONSONANT. This feature is sometimes

referred to as a 'free' syllable. The open syllable is the first syllable type to be productively used by children, in the early stages of PHONOLOGICAL development. It also constitutes a syllable type (consonant + vowel) which seems to be a UNIVERSAL feature of LANGUAGE. See Ladefoged 1975: Ch. 4.

(4) A term sometimes used in the GRAMMATICAL CLASSIFICATIONS of WORDS to refer to one of two postulated major word classes in language, the other being CLOSED. An **open class** is one whose membership is in principle indefinite or unlimited. New items are continually being added, as new ideas, inventions, etc. emerge. NOUNS, VERBS, ADJECTIVES and ADVERBS are open-class items, whereas CONJUNCTIONS, PRONOUNS, etc. are closed. The distinction is not quite as clear-cut as it seems, as the class of PREPOSITIONS in English, for example, is relatively open (e.g. *in accordance with, on account of*, and many more), and within the so-called open classes of words, there are several closed sub-systems, e.g. AUXILIARY verbs. But the contrast between 'open' and 'closed' is widely recognised. See Quirk *et al* 1972: Ch. 2; Robins 1971: Ch. 6.

(5) In language ACQUISITION studies of the two-word stage of grammatical development, the term refers to the variable ELEMENT in a CONSTRUCTION, the other being referred to as the PIVOT. For example, in the set *daddy there, cat there, drink there, there* is the pivot word (a member of a small, 'closed' class), and *daddy*, etc. are members of an **open class**. See Clark & Clark 1977: Ch. 8.

opposition A term used in LINGUISTICS to refer to linguistically important differences betwen UNITS. The term is used primarily in PHONOLOGY, where contrasts between DISTINCTIVE FEATURES of sound, or between the presence and absence of a feature, are referred to as oppositions. The difference between /p/ and /s/, for example, can be seen as a combination of two oppositions – PLACE and MANNER OF ARTICULATION. One of the first attempts to classify the oppositions in this sense was in the PRAGUE SCHOOL's theory of **distinctive oppositions**, as first formulated in Nikolai Trubetzkoy's *Principles of Phonology* (1939). The main types of opposition recognised are:

(1) **bilateral** vs. **multilateral**: the opposition between English /t/ and /d/, for example, is *bilateral*, because these are the only units in the system which are ALVEOLAR/PLOSIVE, and they are differentiated by the single feature of VOICING; the opposition between, say, /t/ and /v/, however, is *multilateral*, because there are other possibilities involving the same set of features, e.g. /d/ vs. /f/.

(2) **proportional** vs. **isolated**: the opposition between /f/ and /v/ in English is *proportional*, because there are other oppositions in the

optional

language which work in parallel, e.g. /s/ vs. /z/, /ʃ/ vs. /ʒ/; on the other hand, the opposition between, say, /v/ and /l/ is *isolated* – there are no other segments that are contrasted in this particular way, i.e. VOICED LABIO-DENTAL FRICATIVE vs. voiced LATERAL.

(3) **privative, gradual** and **equipollent**: a *privative* opposition is a BINARY one, where one member is seen as MARKED by the presence of a feature, which its opposite member lacks (i.e. it is 'unmarked'), as in the /p/ vs. /b/ distinction in English; in a *gradual* opposition, degrees of difference in a language are recognised along a scale of some kind, as in a language with four front vowels /i/, /e/, /ɛ/ and /æ/ where (according to Trubetskoy) it would not be desirable to analyse the four degrees of vowel height in terms of privative pairs, such as 'high' vs. 'low'; in an *equipollent* opposition, the members are seen as logically equivalent to each other, contrasted neither gradually nor by a binary feature: e.g. the distinction between /p/ and /k/ cannot be analysed, according to Trubetskoy, as a difference along a single phonetic continuum, nor can /p/ be seen as 'non-velar', or /k/ as 'non-bilabial'.

(4) **constant** and **neutralisable**: a *constant* opposition exists when its members can occur in all possible positions, e.g. wherever /p/ might be found in a language, a contrast with /b/ will also be found; in English, the /t/ vs. /d/ distinction is *neutralisable*, because in some positions, there is no such contrast, the opposition being realised by the same sound, as when /t/ follows initial /s/, e.g. *stick* does not contrast with **sdick*. See Hyman 1975: Ch. 2; Gimson 1970: Ch. 5.

optional One of two types of TRANSFORMATIONAL RULE postulated by Noam CHOMSKY in his book *Syntactic Structures* (1957), the other being OBLIGATORY. **Optional transformations** may apply at a certain stage in a DERIVATION; but it is not essential for the WELL-FORMEDNESS of the SENTENCE that they do so, e.g. the transformation from POSITIVE to NEGATIVE, ACTIVE to PASSIVE, or DECLARATIVE to INTERROGATIVE. In later versions of transformational GRAMMAR, the range of this notion changes, as more structural rules come to be incorporated into the BASE component of the grammar, and are thus handled by obligatory rules. A few rules handling STYLISTIC alternatives remain optional. See Lyons 1968: Ch. 6.

oral (1) In phonetics, 'oral' is opposed to NASAL, referring either to the ARTICULATORY area of the mouth, as in the phrases 'oral CAVITY', 'oral chamber', or to the specific sounds that are made there. The opposition is usually with the nasal cavity (and with nasal sounds), but the PHARYNX, oesophagus and lungs are also excluded from the notion of 'oral'. In DISTINCTIVE FEATURE theory of PHONOLOGY, 'oral' is specifically opposed to 'nasal', these being postulated as two of the contrasts needed in order to specify fully the sound SYSTEM of a language. See Gimson 1970: Ch. 2; Catford 1977: Ch. 8.

(2) The usual adjective for the manifestation of LANGUAGE in its spoken, as opposed to its written form. The term **oracy** has been coined, on analogy with 'literacy', to refer to ability in speech and listening comprehension, but this term is used more in discussion of language skills and curricula in mother-tongue education, and will not generally be found in technical studies in LINGUISTICS and PHONETICS.

order(-ing, -ed) (1) A term used in LINGUISTICS to refer to the pattern of relationships constituting or UNDERLYING a LINEAR SEQUENCE of linguistic UNITS. Sometimes, no distinction is made between the sequential arrangement of observable FORMAL ELEMENTS (defined, for example, in terms of SURFACE STRUCTURE) and the abstract pattern of relationships assumed to underlie the surface arrangement: notions such as 'WORD order', 'MORPHEME order', 'SUBJECT-VERB-OBJECT order', etc. are often seen in this way. Usually, however, a systematic distinction is made between these two LEVELS of analysis, the former being referred to as SEQUENCE, and the latter as order. That there is no necessary one-to-one correspondence between surface sequence and underlying order can be shown in such sentences as *he took off his hat/he took his hat off, his hat he took off*, etc., where the same basic subject–verb–object order is REALISED in different surface sequences. This notion, that there is an underlying abstract 'ordering' of elements from which several surface arrangements can be derived, is a fundamental insight of TRANSFORMATIONAL GRAMMAR. In this approach, also, the term **ordering** is used to refer to the application of the RULES of a grammar in a given succession, a crucial principle which prevents the generation of unACCEPTABLE STRINGS, and enables SIMPLER analyses to be made. Several specific ordering conventions have been suggested (cf. the notions of CYCLICAL, LINEAR, CONJUNCTIVE, DISJUNCTIVE, BLEEDING, FEEDING, EXTRINSIC and INTRINSIC ordering). See Lyons 1968: Ch. 6.

(2) In PSYCHOLINGUISTICS, the phrase **order of mention** refers to a use of language where the order in which events in the outside world occur is paralleled by the same order in the sequence of SEMANTIC UNITS within SENTENCES. For example: *After John shut the door, he spoke* follows the 'order of mention'; *Before John spoke, he shut the door* does not. See Clark & Clark 1977: Ch. 13.

ordinal A term used in some models of GRAMMATICAL description referring to the class of numerals *first, second*, etc., by contrast with the cardinal numbers *one, two*, etc. See Quirk *et al* 1972: Ch. 4.

overextension A term used in language ACQUISITION studies to refer to one type of relationship between adult and child MEANING, as expressed in LEXICAL ITEMS. In 'overextension', the child's lexical item has a wider range of APPLICATION than the equivalent term in adult language, e.g. when *dog* is used for other animals apart from dogs. The term is usually contrasted with UNDEREXTENSION. See Clark & Clark 1977: Ch. 13.

overgeneralisation A term used in language ACQUISITION studies, referring to the process whereby a child extends his use of a GRAMMATICAL feature to CONTEXTS beyond those found in the adult language, e.g. 'overgeneralising' the regular past TENSE FORM in such items as **goed, *wented, *goned*. See Bolinger 1975: Ch. 12.

overlapping (1) A term used in PHONOLOGY to refer to the possibility that a PHONE may be assigned to more than one PHONEME (**phonemic overlapping**). The notion was introduced by American STRUCTURAL LINGUISTS in the 1940s. The overlapping (or 'intersection') of phonemes was said to be 'partial' if a given sound is assigned to phoneme A in one PHONETIC CONTEXT and to phoneme B in another; it would be 'complete' if successive occurrences of the sound in the *same* context are assigned sometimes to A, and sometimes to B (cf. the notion of NEUTRALISATION). An example of partial overlap is found between /r/ and /t/ in some DIALECTS of English, where both are realised by the TAP [ɾ] in different contexts: /r/ → [ɾ] after DENTAL FRICATIVES, as in *through*; /t/ → [ɾ] between VOWELS, as in *bitter*. An example of complete overlap occurs in the case of [ə], which may stand for most occurrences of English STRESSED vowels, when they occur in unstressed positions (e.g. *telegraph – telegraphy*, where the first and third vowels reduce to [ə]). The notion of complete overlap was generally rejected, on the grounds that it would lead to an unacceptable INDETERMINACY in phonemics which would destroy the principle of phonemic analysis as an independent LEVEL. One would not be able to tell, on the basis of pronunciation alone, which phoneme a phone belonged to. The need to preserve some kind of phonemic integrity for successive instances of the same sound led to the maxim 'Once a phoneme, always a phoneme', and to the notion of BIUNIQUENESS (or one-to-one correspondence between phones and phonemes). However, even partial overlap provides considerable difficulties for the notion of INVARIANCE, which is fundamental to the biuniqueness hypothesis, as has been argued by CHOMSKY, amongst others. It is evident that it is not always possible to predict the phoneme a phone belongs to, simply by considering its phonetic properties. See Hyman 1975: Ch. 3.

(2) A term used in language ACQUISITION studies to refer to one type of relationship between adult and child MEANING, as expressed in LEXICAL ITEMS. 'Overlapping' meanings, or 'overlap', as the name suggests, occur when the meaning of a lexical item for the child is not identical with that for the adult (cf. OVEREXTENSION and UNDEREXTENSION). In cases of no overlap, a child's lexical item has no point of contact at all with the meaning of that item in the adult language, e.g. one child used *door* to mean 'walk'. See Clark & Clark 1977: Ch. 13.

overt A term used in LINGUISTIC analysis to refer to the relationships between linguistic FORMS which are observable in the SURFACE STRUCTURE of a SENTENCE; opposed to COVERT. Examples of overt relations include WORD ORDER, CONCORD and PHONOTACTIC SEQUENCE. See Robins 1971: Ch. 6.

P

࿇࿇࿇࿇࿇࿇

palate (palatogra-phy, -m) The arched bony structure which forms the roof of the mouth, and which is much used for the ARTICULATION of speech sounds. The delimitation and classification of the PALATAL area has not been without controversy, as is shown by the several different classificatory systems for describing the types of pathological condition known as cleft lip and palate. In one such system, the whole of the upper oral area (including lips and alveolum) is referred to as palatal, on the grounds that this constituted a single embryological process. In PHONETICS, a much more restricted sense is used: here, the term applies to the whole area from behind the ALVEOLAR ridge to the UVULA. It is divided into two parts, the **hard palate**, which is the immobile bony area immediately behind the alveolar ridge, and the **solf palate** or 'velum', which is the mobile fleshy continuation of this culminating in the uvula. Only sounds articulated in the area of the hard palate are called 'palatal' sounds; soft palate sounds are either VELAR or UVULAR. The soft palate is particularly important in the production of speech, as it is under muscular control which enables it to be raised (closing the upper part of the PHARYNX) for the production of ORAL sounds, or lowered (keeping the passage to the nose open) for the production of NASAL sounds. Poor control of the soft palate (which may result from several neurological or anatomical conditions, such as cleft palate) leads to abnormal nasal resonance or friction.

It is difficult to see or sense what is going on inside the mouth when the TONGUE is making contact with the palate. **Palatography** is the instrumental study of articulation in this area. Several techniques have been tried to produce accurate pictures of TONGUE contact with the palate – **palatograms**: a standard technique involves spraying the roof of the mouth with a dark powdery substance; an articulation is then made, which, if in the palatal or alveolar area, rubs off some of the substance; the roof of the mouth is then photographed to pinpoint the place of articulation. Apart from the inconvenience of this method, its biggest drawback is that it is static: it disallows any observation of the movement of the tongue in connected speech. More recently, ELECTRO-PALATOGRAPHIC techniques have been devised which enable a continuous record to be made of tongue contact in this area. The potential of the device used, known as an **electro-palatograph**, is very great, but the research is still in its infancy. See Catford 1977: Chs. 8, 12.

palatal(isation) A term used in the PHONETIC classification of speech sounds on the basis of their PLACE OF ARTICULATION: it refers to a sound made when the FRONT of the TONGUE is in contact with or approaches the hard PALATE. Slavic languages usually illustrate a range of palatal sounds; in German, *ich* ('I') exemplifies a VOICELESS palatal [ç]; in English, palatal sounds are heard only in restricted contexts, as variants of a PHONEME, e.g. /k/ is normally described as VELAR, but the *k* in such words as *keep* is often quite palatal in its articulation, because of the influence of the following FRONT VOWEL. One may also hear palatal GLIDES in such words as *cute* [kj-] or *huge* [ç]. 'Palatal' is sometimes used with reference to vowels or SEMI-VOWELS articulated in the hard palate area (front CLOSE vowels), as in the [iː] of *seat* or the initial sound of *yet* [j]; but the commoner use is in relation to CONSONANTS.

Palatalisation is a general term referring to any articulation involving a movement of the tongue towards the hard palate. It may be used to describe the altered articulation illustrated by *k* above, but its more common use is in relation to SECONDARY ARTICULATIONS. Here, the primary place of articulation is elsewhere in the mouth; for example, a [t] sound, normally made in ALVEOLAR position, is said to be 'palatalised' if during its articulation the front of the tongue is raised towards the hard palate: in the case of [t], the palatalisation would be most noticeable when the plosive was released, as a palatal GLIDE would then be heard before the onset of the next main sound. Several languages, such as Russian, have sets of palatalised consonants operating as phonemes. Because of the auditory effect involved, the labels SOFT and HARD are often used to describe the contrasting qualities of palatalised and non-palatalised CONSONANTS respectively. (These labels have no relation to their use in the terms 'hard palate' and 'soft palate', which are anatomically based: see PALATE.) In phonetic TRANSCRIPTION, there are several ways of representing palatalisation: for instance [ţ], [ṫ], [tʲ] and [t'] have all been used to represent a palatalised [t]. See Gimson 1970: Ch. 4; Catford 1977: Ch. 8.

palato-alveolar A term used in the PHONETIC classification of CONSONANT sounds on the basis of their PLACE OF ARTICULATION: it refers to a sound made by a double movement of the TONGUE towards the area between the ALVEOLAR ridge and hard PALATE: the BLADE of the tongue (or the TIP and blade together) makes contact with the alveolar ridge, while the FRONT of the tongue is raised in the direction of the hard palate. Examples in English are the *sh-* [ʃ] of *ship*, the *-s-* [ʒ] of *treasure*. Several other varieties of sound may be articulated in this part of the mouth by slightly varying the position and shape of the tongue, e.g. ALVEO(LO)-PALATAL sounds, which are important in some LANGUAGES, such as Polish. See Gimson 1970: Ch. 4; Catford 1977: Ch. 8.

pandialectal A term used primarily in DIALECTOLOGY and SOCIOLINGUISTICS to characterise any LINGUISTIC FEATURE, RULE, etc. which is applicable to all the dialects of a LANGUAGE. See Trudgill 1974: Ch. 7.

panlectal A term used by some SOCIOLINGUISTS, to refer to a general MODEL of GRAMMAR within which individual VARIETIES (or LECTS) can be inter-related. See Bolinger 1975: Ch. 11.

paradigmatic (paradigm) (1) A basic term in LINGUISTICS for the set of relationships a linguistic UNIT has with other units in a specific CONTEXT. **Paradigmatic relations** can be established at all LEVELS of analysis, e.g. the selection of /p-/ as opposed to /b-/, /n-/, etc. in the context /-it/, or of *the* as opposed to *a*, *this*, *much*, etc. in the context – *cake*. Paradigmatic RELATIONS, together with SYNTAGMATIC relations, constitute the statement of a linguistic unit's identity within the language SYSTEM. CLASSES of paradigmatically related elements are often referred to as SYSTEMS, e.g. the 'PRONOUN system', 'CASE system'. A set of GRAMMATICALLY conditioned FORMS all derived from a single ROOT or STEM is called a **paradigm**. See Lyons 1968: Ch. 2; Robins 1971: Ch. 2.

(2) In PSYCHOLINGUISTICS, the term is used to refer to a class of ASSOCIATIVE responses which people make when hearing a stimulus word, *viz* those which fall into the same WORD-CLASS as the stimulus. A **paradigmatic response** or **association** would be *girl* following *boy*, *white* following *black*, etc. The SYNTAGMATIC association, by contrast, involves a change of word-class in the response. See Clark & Clark 1977: Ch. 12.

paralanguage (paralinguistic) A term used in SUPRASEGMENTAL PHONOLOGY to refer to variations in TONE of voice which seem to be less systematic than PROSODIC features (especially INTONATION and STRESS).

Examples would include the controlled use of BREATHY or CREAKY voice, spasmodic features (such as giggling while speaking), and the use of secondary ARTICULATIONS (such as lip-ROUNDING or NASALisation) to produce a tone of voice signalling attitude, social role, or some other language-specific meaning. Some analysts broaden the definition of paralanguage to include KINESIC features; some exclude paralinguistic features from LINGUISTIC analysis. See Crystal 1969: Ch. 4; Lyons 1977b: Ch. 3.

parametric phonetics An approach to PHONETICS which sees speech as a single physiological SYSTEM, in which the range of ARTICULATORY variables (or 'parameters') in the VOCAL TRACT is seen as being continually in operation, interacting in various ways along the time dimension to produce a continuum of sound which listeners SEGMENT according to the RULES of their LANGUAGE. It thus contrasts with the traditional view of speech, where articulation is seen in advance as a sequence of speech 'postures', or segments, each of which is independently definable with reference to a set of isolatable FEATURES (PLACE OF ARTICULATION, MANNER OF ARTICULATION, etc.). This 'static' model contrasts with the DYNAMIC parametric model, which has led to fresh interest in the nature of NEUROLINGUISTIC control mechanisms. See Ladefoged 1975: Ch. 3.

paraphrase A term used in LINGUISTICS for the result or process of producing alternative versions of a SENTENCE or TEXT without changing the MEANING. One SENTENCE may have several paraphrases, e.g. *The dog is eating a bone*, *A bone is being eaten by the dog*, *It's the dog who is eating a bone*, and so on. Most SEMANTIC theories would treat all these sentences as having a single semantic REPRESENTATION (though variations in FOCUS and PRESUPPOSITION could differentiate them). Linguists use syntactic paraphrase as a major procedure for establishing certain types of TRANSFORMATIONAL relations. See Clark & Clark 1977: Ch. 1.

paratactic (parataxis) A term used in TRADITIONAL GRAMMATICAL analysis, and often found in DESCRIPTIVE LINGUISTIC studies, to refer to CONSTRUCTIONS which are linked solely through juxtaposition and punctuation/INTONATION, and not through the use of CONJUNCTIONS. 'Paratactic constructions' are opposed to HYPOTACTIC ones, where conjunctions are used. 'Parataxis' is illustrated by *He bought tea, coffee, eggs and milk* (cf. . . . *tea and coffee and eggs* . . .). See Quirk *et al* 1972: Ch. 9.

parole

parole A term introduced into LINGUISTICS by the Swiss linguist
Ferdinand de SAUSSURE (1857–1913), to distinguish one of the senses
of the word 'language'. It refers to the concrete UTTERANCES
produced by individual speakers in actual situations, and is distinguished from LANGUE, which is the collective LANGUAGE SYSTEM of a
SPEECH community. An analogous term is PERFORMANCE. See Lyons
1968: Ch. 1; Robins 1971: Ch. 2.

parsing In TRADITIONAL GRAMMAR, this term refers to the pedagogical
exercise of labelling the grammatical ELEMENTS of single SENTENCES,
e.g. SUBJECT, PREDICATE, past TENSE, NOUN, VERB. LINGUISTICS, by
contrast, is less concerned with labels, and more with the criteria of
analysis which lead to the identification of these elements, and with
the way in which speakers use these elements to relate sentences in
the LANGUAGE as a whole. See Lyons 1968: Ch. 6.

participle (participial) A traditional GRAMMATICAL term referring to
a word derived from a VERB and used as an ADJECTIVE, as in *a laughing
face*. It is thus distinct from the traditional notion of 'gerund', where
the word derived from a verb is used as a NOUN, as in *smoking is
forbidden*. In LINGUISTICS the term is generally restricted to the
non-FINITE forms of verbs other than the INFINITIVE, *viz* present and
past, as in *I am going* and *I have walked* respectively, but, even here,
there is a strong tendency to avoid the use of the traditional labels
'present' and 'past' participles, with their Latinate associations of time
(inapplicable, for example, in a passive sentence like *I shall be kicked*,
where the participle can hardly be 'past'), and to use instead a neutral
set of terms, such as -ING FORMS or -ED/-EN FORMS. See Quirk
et al 1972: Ch. 3.

particle (1) A term used in GRAMMATICAL description to refer to an
INVARIABLE ITEM with grammatical FUNCTION, especially one which
does not readily fit into a standard classification of PARTS OF SPEECH.
In English, for example, the marker of the INFINITIVE, *to*, is often
called a particle because, despite its surface similarity to a PREPOSITION,
it really has nothing in common with that or any other WORD CLASS.
Likewise, the unique characteristics of *not* have prompted some to label
it a 'NEGATIVE particle', and the subordinate units in PHRASAL VERBS
'verbal particles'. See Quirk *et al* 1972: Ch. 11; Lyons 1968: Ch. 1.

(2) A term used in TAGMEMIC analysis to refer to a linguistic UNIT
seen as a DISCRETE entity, definable in terms of FEATURES. It is
contrasted with WAVE (where the unit's CONTEXTUAL variability is

analysed) and FIELD (where its DISTRIBUTION is described). See Bolinger 1975: Ch. 15.

part of speech The TRADITIONAL term for a GRAMMATICAL CLASS of WORDS. The main 'parts of speech' recognised by most school grammars derive from the work of the ancient Greek and Roman grammarians, primarily the NOUN, PRONOUN, VERB, ADVERB, ADJECTIVE, PREPOSITION, CONJUNCTION and INTERJECTION, with ARTICLE, PARTICIPLE and others often added. Because of the inexplicitness with which these terms were traditionally defined (e.g. the use of unclear NOTIONAL criteria), and the restricted nature of their definitions (reflecting the characteristics of Latin or Greek), LINGUISTS tend to prefer such terms as WORD-class or FORM-class, where the grouping is based on FORMAL criteria of a more UNIVERSALLY applicable kind. See Lyons 1968: Ch. 7.

passive (passiv-ise, -ation) A term used in the GRAMMATICAL analysis of VOICE, referring to a SENTENCE, CLAUSE or VERB FORM where the grammatical SUBJECT is typically the recipient or 'goal' of the action denoted by the verb, e.g. *the letter was written by a boy*. It is contrasted with ACTIVE, and sometimes with other forms, e.g. 'middle' (as in Greek). A full linguistic statement of the CONSTRAINTS affecting these relationships is a complex matter. In English, for example, there are active sentences that do not have passive counterparts (e.g. *the boy fell, they have a car*), passive sentences which have an unclear active counterpart (e.g. *the house was sold*), and so on. In addition, there is the problem that the central type of passive construction (using the verb *to be*, e.g. *he was pushed*) is closely related to other types of construction (cf. *he got pushed, he was interested*), and a boundary line is sometimes difficult to establish. Passive constructions which take an agent are **agentive passives** (e.g. *he was kicked (by the dog)*), as opposed to 'non-AGENTIVE' or 'agentless' passives, where there is no need for (and sometimes no possibility of) an agentive phrase being added, since the speaker does not have a 'performer of the action' in mind (e.g. *the city is industrialised now*). In GENERATIVE grammar, the TRANSFORMATION of a sentence from its active to its passive form is known as **passivisation**. A verb or sentence which undergoes such a process is said to 'passivise'. See Quirk *et al* 1972: Ch. 12; Lyons 1968: Ch. 8.

path A term used in GENERATIVE GRAMMAR referring to an unbroken series of BRANCHES and NODES moving in a single direction with respect to the top of a TREE diagram. See Akmajian & Heny 1975: Ch. 2.

patient A term used by some LINGUISTS as part of the GRAMMATICAL analysis of a SENTENCE: it refers to the entity which is affected by the action of the VERB, e.g. *the dog bit **the man***. 'Goal' is an alternative term. See Bolinger 1975: Ch. 6.

pattern In the general sense of 'a systematic arrangement of UNITS', this term is found in LINGUISTICS and PHONETICS, without any special implication. Certain theoretical implications may be added in some contexts, however. For example, in language teaching, **pattern drills** (or 'structure drills') refer to the use of a SUBSTITUTION-frame technique for the practise of a particular STRUCTURE. Also, in PHONO-LOGY, the term has been used to refer specifically to any demonstrable neatness of arrangement that can be demonstrated in a sound SYSTEM – a UNIT such as a PHONEME being seen as a point in a pattern of sound-relationships. It is felt that a phonemic pattern ought to be regular and symmetrical, and that the demonstration of **pattern congruity** in an analysis is a desirable feature. Whether a sound-cluster should be analysed as one phoneme or two, for example, may depend on the parallel patterns that can be demonstrated between this CLUSTER and other phonemes, e.g. English /tʃ/ and /dʒ/ on this criterion would be analysed as single phonemes, as a STOP + FRICATIVE analysis would receive little support elsewhere in the system. The phrase 'gap/hole in the pattern' is often used to refer to a lacuna which spoils the symmetry of an analysis, as when a series of unrounded VOWELS might have a corresponding series of ROUNDED vowels except for one case. See Hyman 1975: Ch. 3.

pause The general sense of this term applies in LINGUISTICS, PHONETICS and PSYCHOLINGUISTICS, where an attempt is made to give a precise account of the types and DISTRIBUTION of 'pausal phenomena' and to draw conclusions concerning their FUNCTION in speech. A distinction has been drawn between **silent pauses** and **filled pauses** (e.g. *ah, er*), and several functions of pause have been established, e.g. for breathing, to mark GRAMMATICAL boundaries, and to provide time for the planning of new material. Investigations of pausal phenomena have been particularly relevant in relation to developing a theory of SPEECH PRODUCTION. In GRAMMAR, the notion of **potential pause** is sometimes used as a technique for establishing the WORD UNITS in a LANGUAGE – pauses being more likely at word-boundaries than within words. See Clark & Clark 1977: Ch. 7; Lyons 1968: Ch. 5.

perception (perceptual) The general sense of this term is found in PHONETICS and PSYCHOLINGUISTICS, where it refers to the process of receiving and decoding SPEECH input. The process requires that the listener takes into account not only the ACOUSTIC CUES present in the speech signal, but also his own knowledge of the sound patterns of his LANGUAGE, in order to interpret what he hears. The term is usually contrasted with PRODUCTION. See Clark & Clark 1977: Ch. 5.

perfect(ive) A term used in the GRAMMATICAL description of VERB FORMS, referring to a contrast of a temporal or durative kind, and thus sometimes handled under the heading of TENSE (e.g. PERFECT, 'future perfect' 'pluperfect') and sometimes under ASPECT (e.g. PERFECTIVE, 'non-perfective'). It is illustrated in English by the contrast between *I go* vs. *I have gone*, or *I have gone* vs. *I had gone*. LINGUISTS prefer an aspectual analysis here, because of the complex interaction of durational, completive and temporal features of meaning involved; TRADITIONAL grammars, however, refer simply to 'perfect tense', etc., and thus imply a meaning which is to some degree an oversimplification.

The analysis of the above forms in terms of aspect is more problematic than in the case of such LANGUAGES as Russian and Polish, where a contrast between **perfective** and **imperfective** is fundamental to verb classification, and is formally marked MORPHOLOGICALLY. For example, the PREFIX про- before the verb 'read' produces a 'perfective verb' where the meaning is that the action (of reading) is completed; in the 'imperfective verb' which lacks the prefix, there is no such implication. See Lyons 1968: Ch. 7; Quirk *et al* 1972: Ch. 3.

performance (1) A term used in LINGUISTIC theory, and especially in GENERATIVE GRAMMAR, to refer to LANGUAGE seen as a set of specific UTTERANCES produced by NATIVE-SPEAKERS, as encountered in a CORPUS. It is opposed, in this sense, to the idealised conception of language known as COMPETENCE. The utterances of performance will contain features irrelevant to the abstract RULE system, such as hesitations and unfinished structures, arising from the various psychological and social difficulties acting upon the speaker (e.g. lapses of memory, or biological limitations, such as PAUSES being introduced through the need to breathe). These features must be discounted in a grammar of the language, which deals with the systematic processes of SENTENCE CONSTRUCTION. The possible implication of this view, that performance features are unimportant, has been strongly criticised in recent years, and the factors which contribute to **performance grammars** are now of considerable interest, especially in PSYCHOLINGUISTICS. See Palmer 1971: Ch. 4; Huddleston 1976: Ch. 1.

(2) A technique used in PHONETICS whereby aspiring practitioners

of the subject are trained to control the use of their VOCAL ORGANS so as to be able to produce the whole range of human speech sounds. The correlative technique of discriminating and identifying the sounds is known as EAR-TRAINING. See Ladefoged 1975: Ch. 1.

performative A term used by the philosopher J. E. Austin (1911–60), and now found in GRAMMATICAL and SEMANTIC analysis, to refer to a type of SENTENCE where an action is 'performed' by virtue of the sentence having been uttered, e.g. *I apologise, I baptise you...*, *I promise...* The original distinction was drawn between **performance utterances** and CONSTATIVE UTTERANCES: the latter are descriptive statements which can be analysed in terms of truth values; performatives, on the other hand, are expressions of activity which are not analysable in truth-value terms. **Performative verbs** (*apologise*, etc.) have a particular significance in SPEECH-ACT theory, as they mark the ILLOCUTIONARY force of an utterance in an explicit way. Some TRANSFORMATIONAL analysts have even proposed a 'performative analysis' of sentences, such that a performative VERB is present in UNDERLYING structure, e.g. an underlying (deletable) verb such as 'I assert that...'; but the advantages of adopting such a procedure have still to be fully explored. See Huddleston 1976: Ch. 9; Lyons 1977b: Ch. 16.

periphrasis (periphrastic) A term used in GRAMMATICAL DESCRIPTION to refer to the use of separate WORDS instead of INFLECTIONS to express the same grammatical relationship. In English, for example, the COMPARISON OF ADJECTIVES involves both inflection (e.g. *happier*, *happiest*) and periphrasis (e.g. *more happy*, *most happy* – the 'periphrastic forms'). See Quirk *et al* 1972: Ch. 5.

perlocutionary A term used in the theory of SPEECH-ACTS to refer to an act which is performed when an UTTERANCE achieves a particular effect on the behaviour, beliefs, feelings, etc. of a listener. Examples of **perlocutionary acts** (or **perlocutionary effects**) include utterances which frighten, insult, ridicule, sympathise, persuade, etc. A distinction may then be made between the intended and the actual perlocutionary effect of an utterance (e.g. a speaker may intend to persuade X to do Y, but may succeed in getting X to do Z). The term is contrasted with LOCUTIONARY (the act of 'saying') and ILLOCUTIONARY (where the act is defined with reference to the speaker's purpose). See Lyons 1977b: Ch. 16; Clark & Clark 1977: Ch. 3.

permutation A term often used within the framework of TRANSFORMA-
TIONAL GRAMMAR to refer to a basic kind of transformational operation.
'Permutation transformations' have the effect of moving CONSTI-
TUENTS (usually one at a time) from one part of a PHRASE-MARKER to
another, as in the formation of PASSIVE sentences, or the placement
of NEGATIVES and AFFIXES. An alternative term is MOVEMENT or RE-
ORDERING. In some recent approaches this notion is broken down into
the more basic operations of ADJUNCTION and DELETION. See Akmajian
& Heny 1975: Ch. 7; Huddleston 1976: Ch. 12.

perseveration A term used by some PSYCHOLINGUISTS to refer to a type
of TONGUE-SLIP where an earlier LINGUISTIC UNIT is carried over, as
when *stop the car* might become *stop the star*. See Clark & Clark 1977:
Ch. 7; Bolinger 1975: Ch. 12.

person(-al) A category used in GRAMMATICAL description to indicate the
nature of the participants in a SITUATION. The contrasts are DEICTIC,
i.e. refer directly to features of the situation of UTTERANCE. Distinctions of person are usually marked in the VERB and/or in the associated
PRONOUNS ('personal' pronouns). Usually a three-way contrast is
found: **first person**, in which the speaker refers to himself, or to a
group usually including himself (e.g. *I*, *we*); **second person**, in which
the speaker typically refers to the person he is addressing (e.g. *you*);
and **third person**, in which other people or things are referred to (e.g.
he, *she*, *it*, *they*). Other formal distinctions may be made in languages,
such as 'inclusive' vs. 'exclusive' *we* (e.g. speaker, hearer and others
vs. speaker and others, but not hearer); FORMAL (or 'honorific') vs.
informal (or 'intimate') e.g. French *vous* vs. *tu*; male vs. female;
definite vs. indefinite (cf. *one* in English); and so on. There are also
several stylistically restricted uses, as in the 'royal' and authorial uses
of *we*. Other word classes than personal pronouns may show person
distinction, as with the REFLEXIVE and possessive pronouns in English
(*myself*, etc., *my*, etc.). Verb constructions which lack person contrast,
usually appearing in the third person, are called **impersonal**. See
Lyons 1968: Ch. 7; Palmer 1971: Ch. 2.

pharyngeal(-ise, -ation, pharynx) A term used in the PHONETIC
classification of CONSONANT sounds on the basis of their PLACE OF
ARTICULATION: it refers to a sound made in the **pharynx**, the tubular
cavity which constitutes the throat above the LARYNX. Pharyngeal
consonants occur in Arabic, for example. They do not occur as speech
sounds in English, but similar effects can be heard in stage whispers,
as when *hey*, said forcefully in a whisper, is produced with a pharyngeal

'rasp'. The general term **pharyngealisation** refers to any articulation involving a constriction of the pharynx. A 'pharyngealised' [s], for example, is a SECONDARY ARTICULATION produced by simultaneously constricting the pharynx while making the [s] articulation; the auditory result would be a sound with a somewhat central and husky resonance (transcribed [s]). Pharyngealised sounds are transcribed with [∼] placed through the letter. See Catford 1977: Ch. 8.

phatic communion A term introduced by the anthropologist Bronislaw Malinowski (1884–1942) and used subsequently by many LINGUISTS to refer to LANGUAGE used for establishing an atmosphere or maintaining social contact rather than for exchanging information or ideas (e.g. comments on the weather, or enquiries about health). 'Phatic language' (or the 'phatic function' of language) is of particular relevance to the SOCIOLINGUISTIC analysis of linguistic FUNCTIONS. See Bolinger 1975: Ch. 15; Lyons 1977b: Ch. 2.

philology (philologist) The traditional term for the study of LANGUAGE history, as carried on by 'COMPARATIVE philologists' since the late 18th century. The study of literary texts is also sometimes included within the term (though not in Britain), as in the study of texts as part of cultural, political, etc. research. See Robins 1971: Ch. 1.

philosophical linguistics A little-developed branch of LINGUISTICS which studies, on the one hand, the role of LANGUAGE in relation to the understanding and elucidation of philosophical concepts, and on the other hand, the philosophical status of linguistic theories, methods and observations. When these topics are studied by philosophers, rather than linguists, the terms **linguistic philosophy** and the **philosophy of language** are used. When the term 'philosophical' is used in association with the various fields of linguistic enquiry, a contrast is usually intended with 'linguistic' e.g. 'philosophical GRAMMAR' (i.e. NOTIONAL, as opposed to DESCRIPTIVE grammar), 'philosophical SEMANTICS' (which includes such matters as the truth and validity of PROPOSITIONS, normally taken for granted by linguistic semantics). See Lyons 1977b: Ch. 6.

phonaesthetics (phonaesth-eme, -esia) A term sometimes used in LINGUISTICS to refer to the study of the aesthetic properties of sound, especially the SOUND SYMBOLISM attributable to individual sounds. Cases such as the [iː] vowels in a LANGUAGE signalling smallness (cf. *teeny*, *weeny*, etc.) have been suggested as evidence for a limited sound/MEANING correspondence in language ('phonaesthesia' or

SYNAESTHESIA), the sound units concerned being referred to as 'phonaesthemes'. The branch of STYLISTICS which studies such EXPRESSIVE effects (e.g. the onomatopoeia of poetry) is known as phonoSTYLISTICS. See Bolinger 1975: Ch. 7.

phonation A general term used in PHONETICS to refer to any vocal activity in the LARYNX whose role is one neither of INITIATION nor of ARTICULATION. The various kinds of VOCAL CORD vibration (VOICING) are the main phonatory activities, and the study of **phonation types** is aimed at accounting for the various laryngeal possibilities, such as BREATHY and CREAKY voice. Some phoneticians would also include under this heading the MODIFICATIONS in phonation which stem from variations in the length, thickness and tension of the vocal cords, as displayed in the various REGISTERS of speech (e.g. falsetto, soprano). See Catford 1976: Ch. 6; Ladefoged 1975: Ch. 6.

phone A term used in PHONETICS to refer to the smallest perceptible DISCRETE SEGMENT of sound in a stream of speech ('phonic continuum' or PHONIC SUBSTANCE). From the viewpoint of segmental PHONOLOGY, phones are the physical REALISATIONS of PHONEMES; phonic variants of a phoneme are referred to as ALLOphones. See Robins 1971: Ch. 4.

phonematic unit One of the two analytic categories used in the FIRTHIAN theory of PROSODIC PHONOLOGY, the other being the PROSODY. Phonematic UNITS comprise CONSONANTS and VOWELS, occurring in LINEAR SEQUENCE, which cannot be handled in terms of prosodies. Despite the resemblance of the term to PHONEME, the two terms are conceptually quite different, as no attempt is made with this unit to analyse speech totally into a single system of phonological OPPOSITIONS, valid for all places in structure (as is the case with the phoneme), and some features which would be included in a phonemic analysis would not be included in an analysis into phonematic features (e.g. lip-ROUNDING). See Robins 1971: Ch. 4.

phoneme (phonemic(s)) The minimal unit in the sound SYSTEM of a LANGUAGE, according to traditional PHONOLOGICAL theories. The original motivation for the concept stemmed from the concern to establish patterns of organisation within the indefinitely large range of sounds heard in languages. The PHONETIC specifications of the sounds (or PHONES) heard in speech, it was realised, contain far more detail than is needed to identify the way languages make CONTRASTS in MEANING. The notion of the phoneme allowed linguists to group together sets of phonetically similar phones as VARIANTS, or 'members' of the same underlying unit. The phones were said to be REALISATIONS of the phonemes, and the variants were referred to as **allophones** of the phonemes (cf. ALLO-). Each language can be shown to operate with a relatively small number of phonemes; some languages have as few as 15 phonemes; others as many as 50. An analysis in these terms will display a language's **phonemic structure** or **phonemic system**. No two languages have the same phonemic system.

Sounds are considered to be members of the same phoneme if they are phonetically similar, and do not occur in the same ENVIRONMENT (i.e. they are in COMPLEMENTARY DISTRIBUTION) – or if they do, the substitution of one sound for the other does not cause a change in meaning (i.e. they are in FREE VARIATION). A sound is considered 'phonemic', on the other hand, if its substitution in a word does cause a change in meaning. In a **phonemic transcription**, only the phonemes are given symbols (compared with phonetic TRANSCRIPTIONS, where different degrees of allophonic detail are introduced, depending on one's purpose). Phonemic symbols are written between oblique brackets, compared with the square brackets used for phonetic transcriptions, e.g. the phoneme /d/ has the allophones [d] (i.e. an ALVEOLAR VOICED variant), [d̥] (i.e. an alveolar devoiced variant), [d̪] (i.e. a DENTAL variant) in various complementary positions in English words. Putting this another way, it is not possible to find a pair of words in English which contrast in meaning solely on account of the difference between these features (though such contrasts may exist in other languages). The emphasis on transcription found in early phonemic studies is summarised in the sub-title of one book on the subject: 'a technique for reducing languages to writing'. The extent to which the relationship between the phonemes and the GRAPHEMES of a language is regular is called the 'phoneme–grapheme correspondence'.

On this general basis, several approaches to **phonemic analysis**, or **phonemics**, have developed. The PRAGUE SCHOOL defined the phoneme as a BUNDLE of abstract DISTINCTIVE FEATURES, or OPPOSITIONS between sounds (such as VOICING, NASALITY), an approach which was developed later by JAKOBSON & Halle, and GENERATIVE phonology. The approach of the British phonetician, Daniel Jones (1881–1967), viewed the phoneme as a 'family' of related sounds, and not as oppositions. American linguists in the 1940s also emphasised the phonetic reality of phonemes, in their concern to devise PROCEDURES of analysis, paying particular attention to the DISTRIBUTION of sounds in an UTTERANCE. Apart from the question of definition, if the view is taken that all aspects of the sound system of a language can be analysed in terms of phonemes – that is, the SUPRASEGMENTAL as well as the segmental features – then 'phonemics' becomes equivalent to phonology (= **phonemic phonology**). This view was particularly common in later developments of the American STRUCTURALIST tradition of linguistic analysis, where linguists adopting this 'phonemic principle' were called **phonemicists**. Many phonologists, however (particularly in the British tradition), prefer not to analyse suprasegmental features in terms of phonemes, and in recent years, approaches have developed which do without the phoneme altogether ('nonphonemic phonology', as in PROSODIC and DISTINCTIVE FEATURE theories).

The term **phonemic clause** is a unit which has been used primarily in PSYCHOLINGUISTIC research into the distribution and function of PAUSES: it refers to a GRAMMATICAL structure produced within a single INTONATION CONTOUR, and bounded by JUNCTURES. See Robins 1971: Ch. 4; Hyman 1975: Ch. 3; Gimson 1970: Ch. 5.

phonetics (phonetic, -ian) The science which studies the characteristics of human sound-making, especially those sounds used in speech, and provides methods for their DESCRIPTION, CLASSIFICATION and TRANSCRIPTION. Three branches of the subject are generally recognised: (1) **articulatory phonetics** is the study of the way speech sounds are made ('articulated') by the vocal organs; (2) **acoustic phonetics** studies the physical properties of speech sound, as transmitted between mouth and ear; (3) **auditory phonetics** studies the perceptual response to speech sounds, as mediated by ear, auditory nerve and brain. The term **instrumental phonetics** is used for the study of any of these aspects of the subject using physical apparatus, such as devices for measuring air-flow, or for analysing sound waves. People engaged in the study of phonetics are known as **phoneticians**.

Phonetic categories are generally defined using terms which have their origins in other subjects, such as anatomy, physiology and acoustics. CONSONANT sounds, for example, are described with reference to anatomical place of articulation (as in PLOSIVE, FRICATIVE, etc.), or to their physical structure (the frequency and amplitude characteristics of the sound waves). Because these methods of analysis are equally valid for all human speech sounds, regardless of the LANGUAGE or speaker, the subject is often referred to as **general phonetics**. This term also reflects the aim of the phonetician to discover universal principles governing the nature and use of speech sounds. **Experimental phonetics** is another term which reflects the general nature of this 'pure' scientific endeavour.

Work in phonetics can, accordingly, be classified into two broad types: (1) general studies of the articulation, acoustics or perception of speech, and (2) studies of the phonetic properties of specific languages. In this latter sense, it is evident that a further dimension will be required, in order to study how the sounds are used within the pronunciation SYSTEM of a language. This 'functional' approach to phonetics is usually carried on under the heading of PHONOLOGY. However, insofar as phoneticians have a specific interest in the study of individual (groups of) LANGUAGES or DIALECTS, it might then be argued that phonetics is a branch of LINGUISTICS.

It is this two-fold character of phonetic enquiry which gives rise to a difficulty: is phonetics an autonomous subject, or is it to be seen as a branch of linguistics? In terms of methods, it is certainly very different, and phonetic research of type (1) above often has little to do with the aims of linguistic analysis. But phonetic research of type (2) is plainly a part of linguistic enquiry – some would say, an indispensable foundation. Depending on their traditions, emphases and aims, then, some university departments have been called 'Departments of Linguistics', some have been called 'Departments of Linguistics and Phonetics' – a distinction which should not be taken to mean that phonetics is not taught in the former! One compromise has been to talk of the 'linguistic sciences' – that is, linguistics and phonetics. See Ladefoged 1975; Catford 1977.

phonic substance A term used by some PHONETICIANS and LINGUISTS to refer to speech seen as a set of physically definable ACOUSTIC, ARTICULATORY or AUDITORY properties. The importance of this notion is that it constitutes an empirical datum to which theories of LANGUAGE must ultimately relate. To be plausible, an account of the English sound SYSTEM, for example, needs to correlate well with the PHONETIC facts (as defined in acoustic, articulatory or auditory terms); and 'phonic' (or 'phonetic') substance is a convenient label to summarise this physical level of investigation. The analogous term for the written language is GRAPHIC SUBSTANCE. See Catford 1977: Ch. 1; Lyons 1968: Ch. 2.

phonology (phonolog-ical, -ist) A branch of LINGUISTICS which studies the sound SYSTEMS of LANGUAGES. Out of the very wide range of sounds the human vocal apparatus can produce, and which are studied by PHONETICS, only a relatively small number are used DISTINCTIVELY in any one language. The sounds are organised into a system of CONTRASTS, which are analysed in terms of PHONEMES, DISTINCTIVE FEATURES, or other such 'phonological UNITS', according to the theory used. The aim of phonology is to demonstrate the patterns of distinctive sound found in a language, and to make as general statements as possible about the nature of sound systems in the languages of the world. Putting this another way, phonology is concerned with the range and function of sounds in specific languages (and often therefore referred to as 'functional phonetics'), and with the rules which can be written to show the types of phonetic relationships that relate and contrast words and other linguistic units. The student of phonology is known as a **phonologist**.

In linguistic theories, phonology is seen in one of two main ways: (i) as a LEVEL of linguistic organisation, contrasted with the levels of PHONETICS, GRAMMAR and SEMANTICS in the first instance, (ii) as a COMPONENT of a GENERATIVE grammar (the **phonological component**), contrasted with the SYNTACTIC and semantic components. Within phonology, two branches of study are usually recognised: SEGMENTAL and SUPRASEGMENTAL. **Segmental phonology** analyses speech into DISCRETE segments, such as phonemes; **suprasegmental phonology** analyses those features which extend over more than one segment, such as INTONATION CONTOURS. Another distinction is made between SYNCHRONIC and DIACHRONIC phonology, the former studying patterns of sound change in the history of language, the latter studying sound patterns regardless of the processes of historical change.

The history of phonology is largely taken up with the development of ideas concerning the phoneme, as originally propounded in PRAGUE SCHOOL and BLOOMFIELDIAN phonological theory, and the subsequent alternative views proposed, especially in generative and PROSODIC phonology, both of which reject the concept of the phoneme. In prosodic phonology, the notions of PHONEMATIC UNIT and PROSODY are proposed. In GENERATIVE phonology, different LEVELS of REPRESENTATION (such as the SYSTEMATIC PHONEMIC and the SYSTEMATIC PHONETIC) have been recognised, and an AUTONOMOUS phonemic level rejected. The purpose of the phonological component of a generative GRAMMAR is to take the output of the syntactic component and interpret it phonetically, making reference only to the SURFACE structure properties of the FORMATIVES involved. These surface structure properties include a specification of the segmental (VOWEL/CONSONANT) structure of the formatives (which comes from the LEXICON), and a specification of the SYNTACTIC FEATURES involved (which comes from the syntactic RULES). The phonological rules of the component apply to the segmental representation, using the principle of the TRANSFORMATIONAL CYCLE. At the end of this cycle, all the BRACKETS marking structure have been removed, STRESSES have been assigned, and the resulting STRING of elements is represented as a set of phonetic segments (defined in terms of DISTINCTIVE features). See Robins 1971: Ch. 4; Hyman 1975.

phonotactics A term used in PHONOLOGY to refer to the specific ARRANGEMENTS (or 'tactic behaviour') of sounds or PHONEMES which occur in a language. In English, for example, CONSONANT sequences such as /fs/ and /spm/ do not occur INITIALLY in a word, and there are many restrictions on the possible consonant + VOWEL combinations which may occur, e.g. /ŋ/ occurs only after some short vowels /ɪ, æ, ʌ, ɒ/. These 'sequential constraints' can be stated in terms of 'phonotactic RULES'. See Gimson 1970: Ch. 9.

phrasal verb A type of VERB consisting of a SEQUENCE of a LEXICAL element plus one or more PARTICLES, e.g. *come in, get up, look out for*. Sub-types may be distinguished on SYNTACTIC grounds (for instance, the particles may be classified into PREPOSITIONAL or ADVERBIAL types), and the definition of 'phrasal' varies somewhat within different descriptions. But the overall syntactic and SEMANTIC unity of these sequences is readily demonstrable, using TRANSFORMATIONAL and SUBSTITUTION criteria (cf. *He **got up** at six*/*He **rose** at six*/*What time did he **get up**?* etc.). See Quirk *et al* 1972: Ch. 12.

phrase (phrasal) A term used in GRAMMATICAL analysis to refer to a single ELEMENT of STRUCTURE containing more than one WORD, and lacking the SUBJECT-PREDICATE structure typical of CLAUSES. Traditionally, it is seen as part of a structural HIERARCHY, falling between clause and word, several types being distinguished, e.g. 'ADVERBIAL phrase' (e.g. *yesterday morning*,...), 'ADJECTIVAL phrase' (e.g. *the house, old and derelict*,...), 'PREPOSITIONAL phrase' (e.g. *in the morning*,...). In GENERATIVE grammar, the term has a broader function, being used as part of a general characterisation of the initial stage of analysis (PHRASE-STRUCTURE GRAMMAR, PHRASE-MARKER) and of the analytic units involved (NOUN phrase, VERB phrase). See Lyons 1968: Ch. 5; Quirk *et al* 1972: Ch. 2.

phrase-marker (PM) A term used in GENERATIVE LINGUISTICS to refer to the STRUCTURAL REPRESENTATION of SENTENCES in terms of a LABELLED BRACKETING, as ASSIGNED by the RULES of the GRAMMAR. Phrase-markers EXPLICITLY specify the HIERARCHICAL structure of sentences, at the various stages of their DERIVATION, and analyse them into a LINEAR SEQUENCE of MORPHEMES, or FORMATIVES. They are usually presented in the form of a TREE diagram. See Lyons 1968: Ch. 6; Huddleston 1976: Ch. 3.

phrase-structure (PS) grammar A type of GRAMMAR discussed by Noam CHOMSKY in his book *Syntactic Structures* (1957) as an illustration of a GENERATIVE DEVICE. Phrase-structure grammars contain RULES which are capable not only of generating STRINGS of LINGUISTIC ELEMENTS, but also of providing a CONSTITUENT analysis of the strings, and hence more information than FINITE-STATE grammars. They are not, however, as POWERFUL as TRANSFORMATIONAL grammars, as the latter are more capable of displaying certain types of INTUITIVE relationship between SENTENCES, and may ultimately be demonstrable as SIMPLER. In a related sense, the 'phrase-structure COMPONENT' of a transformational grammar specifies the HIERARCHICAL structure of a SENTENCE, the linear sequence of its constituents, and indirectly (through the notion of DOMINANCE) some types of SYNTACTIC RELATIONS.

The main difference between the phrase-structure grammars (PSGs) of Chomsky as opposed to the IMMEDIATE CONSTITUENT analysis of earlier linguists is that Chomsky's MODEL is FORMALISED as a system of generative RULES, and aims to avoid the emphasis on DISCOVERY PROCEDURES characteristic of the earlier approach. In their original formulation, PSGs took the form of a set of REWRITE rules (with the abbreviations expanded here), such as:

Sentence → Noun Phrase + Verb Phrase
Verb Phrase → Verb + Noun Phrase
Noun Phrase → Determiner + Noun

Various distinctions have been made in the classification of phrase-structure grammars, of which the main division is into **context-free** and **context-sensitive** types: a grammar consisting wholly of context-free rules (rules which are of the form 'Rewrite X as Y', i.e. regardless of CONTEXT) is much less constrained (and thus less strongly ADE-QUATE) than a grammar containing context-sensitive rules (rules which are of the form 'Rewrite X as Y in the context of Z'). See Lyons 1968: Ch. 6; Huddleston 1976: Ch. 3.

phylogeny (phylogene-tic, -sis) The application of this general term in LINGUISTICS refers to the HISTORICAL development and decay of LANGUAGE in SPEECH communities, or as represented in historical TEXTS. The term contrasts with ONTOGENY, for the study of develop-ment in the individual, as carried on in language ACQUISITION. See Bolinger 1975: Ch. 13.

pidgin(ise) A term used in SOCIOLINGUISTICS to refer to a LANGUAGE with a markedly reduced GRAMMATICAL STRUCTURE, LEXICON and STYLISTIC range, compared with other languages, and which is the native language of no-one. Structures which have been reduced in this way are said to be 'pidginised'. Pidgins are formed by two SPEECH communities attempting to communicate, each successively approximating to the more obvious features of the other's language. Such developments need considerable motivation on the part of the speakers, and it is therefore not surprising that **pidgin languages** flourish in areas of economic development, as in the pidgins based on English, French, Spanish and Portuguese, in the East and West Indies, Africa and the Americas. Pidgins become CREOLISED when they become the mother-tongue of a community. See Trudgill 1974: Chs. 3, 7.

pitch The attribute of auditory sensation in terms of which a sound may be ordered on a scale from 'low' to 'high'. It is an AUDITORY PHONETIC feature, corresponding to some degree with the acoustic feature of FREQUENCY, which in the study of speech is based upon the number of complete cycles of vibration of the VOCAL CORDS. Frequency is measured in Hertz (Hz), e.g. 440 Hz = 440 cps (cycles per second). The frequency of a sound can be determined automatically using a 'FUNDAMENTAL FREQUENCY analyser', or 'pitch meter'. There is however no direct or parallel correlation between pitch and frequency: other factors than frequency may affect our sensation of pitch (measured in units known as *mels*). Variations of pitch are more easily produced using VOICED sounds, because of their regular waveform. It is however possible to hear pitch contrasts in voiceless sounds; and even in whispered speech, impressions of FALLING, RISING, etc. pitches can be heard, reflecting the changing configurations of the VOCAL TRACT.

The linguistic use of pitch is of particular interest to the PHONOLOGIST, and this is studied under the headings of INTONATION and TONE. See Ladefoged 1975: Ch. 8; Bolinger 1975: Ch. 3.

pivot A term introduced into language ACQUISITION studies of the 1960s, to refer to a primitive WORD-CLASS thought to characterise the early two-word combinations produced by children. Analysis of these combinations suggested that children used a few words very frequently, and in a fixed position, e.g. *my daddy, my car, my drink; shoe gone, car gone*, etc. These common elements were seen as 'pivots' on which the rest of a SENTENCE (the 'OPEN class' word) depended, the STRUCTURE of the whole SENTENCE being seen as either Pivot + Open or Open + Pivot. This analysis is no longer popular, for several reasons (e.g. it fails to relate to the analysis of adult grammatical structures, ignores the SEMANTIC structure of such sentences, and seems to apply to only certain types of sentence in certain children). See Clark & Clark 1977: Ch. 8.

place of articulation One of the main parameters used in the PHONETIC classification of speech sounds, referring to where in the vocal apparatus a sound is produced. It is usual to represent this parameter horizontally, though as a result this dimension does omit some of the variations which can only be identified transversely, e.g. whether one or both sides of the tongue is involved in an ARTICULATION (see LATERAL). The conventionally recognised places, or 'points' of articulation for CONSONANTS correspond to main anatomical divisions, *viz* LABIAL, LABIO-DENTAL, DENTAL, ALVEOLAR, PALATAL, VELAR, UVULAR, PHARYNGEAL, GLOTTAL, but other places relative to these are also recognised, such as POSTalveolar and RETROFLEX. The analogous classification of VOWELS is done in terms of AUDITORY criteria, using the horizontal scale of FRONT and BACK, and the vertical scale of CLOSE and OPEN; but because of the lack of a clear anatomical correlate, it is less usual to talk about vowels in terms of articulatory 'places' or 'points', except in a loose way. See Gimson 1970: Chs. 2, 4; Catford 1977: Ch. 8.

plain One of the features of sound set up by JAKOBSON & Halle in their DISTINCTIVE FEATURE theory of PHONOLOGY, to handle variations in MANNER OF ARTICULATION, its opposite being FLAT or SHARP, depending on the contrast involved. 'Plain' is defined articulatorily and ACOUSTICALLY; in contrast to flat, it refers to sounds involving a relatively wide mouth opening, and a relatively strong high-frequency component of the sound spectrum, as in sounds lacking lip-ROUNDING: in contrast to sharp, it refers to sounds lacking any PALATALISATION feature. See Hyman 1975: Ch. 2.

plereme A term used by some LINGUISTS to refer to the minimal UNITS of MEANING in COMPONENTIAL SEMANTIC analysis – what are often called 'semantic FEATURES' or 'semantic COMPONENTS'. In GLOSSEMATICS, the term refers to the minimal unit of meaningful EXPRESSION (cf. MORPHEME). See Lyons 1968: Ch. 10.

plosive (plosion) A term used in the PHONETIC classification of CONSONANT sounds on the basis of their MANNER OF ARTICULATION: it refers to a sound made when a complete CLOSURE in the VOCAL TRACT is suddenly released; the air pressure which has built up behind the closure rushes out with an explosive sound, hence the term. Examples

plurisegmental

in English are [p, b, t, d, k, g, ʔ]. 'Plosion' is the term used to refer to the outwards movement of air upon release. Plosive consonants are also called STOP consonants. It is also possible, using a different AIR-STREAM MECHANISM than the one which produces an outwards flow of lung air, to produce plosives (IMPLOSIVES) where the air upon release moves inwards. See Gimson 1970: Ch. 4; Catford 1977: Ch. 7.

plurisegmental A term used by some PHONETICIANS to refer to a vocal effect which extends over more than one sound SEGMENT in an UTTERANCE, such as an INTONATION CONTOUR. The term SUPRASEGMENTAL is more widely used. See Bolinger 1975: Ch. 3.

PM An abbreviation sometimes used in GENERATIVE LINGUISTICS, standing for PHRASE-MARKER.

poetics A term used in LINGUISTICS to refer to the application of linguistic theory and method to the analysis of poetry. However, some linguists (such as Roman JAKOBSON) have given the term a broader interpretation, including within the 'poetic function' of LANGUAGE any aesthetic or creative linguistic use of the spoken or written MEDIUM. See Lyons 1977b: Ch. 2; Gumperz & Hymes 1971: Ch. 2.

polarity A term used by some LINGUISTS for the SYSTEM of POSITIVE/ NEGATIVE CONTRASTIVITY found in a LANGUAGE. The distinction between 'positive' and 'negative polarity' may be expressed GRAMMATICALLY (e.g. *not* in English), LEXICALLY (e.g. *happy* vs. *unhappy*) or SEMANTICALLY (e.g. *high* vs. *low*). See Lyons 1977b: Ch. 9; Quirk *et al* 1972: Ch. 2.

polylectal A term used by some SOCIOLINGUISTS to refer to a proposed MODEL of GRAMMAR which would account for the VARIETIES of LANGUAGE used by the individual (and, by extension, in the community as a whole). The contrast intended is with grammars which ignore regional and social variations, and which analyse language as if it were in a hypothetical homogenous state. See Bolinger 1975: Ch. 11.

polysemy (polysem-ia, -ic, -ous) A term used in SEMANTIC analysis to refer to a LEXICAL ITEM which has a range of different MEANINGS, e.g. *plain* = 'clear', 'unadorned', 'obvious'... A large proportion of a language's vocabulary is 'polysemic' (or 'polysemous'). The theoretical problem for the LINGUIST is how to distinguish 'polysemy' or 'polysemia' (one FORM – several meanings) from HOMONYMY (two lexical items which happen to have the same PHONOLOGICAL form). Several criteria have been suggested, such as ETYMOLOGY (the antecedents of homonymous items would be formally distinct), and the closeness of the relationship between the meanings in question (the meanings of homonymous items would be further apart, or unrelated – cf. the related senses of *plain* above with the homonyms *plane* = 'carpenter's tool' and *plane* = 'aeroplane'). But all such criteria involve analytic problems, and the distinction between polysemy and homonymy thus remains a source of theoretical discussion in LINGUISTICS. See Lyons 1977b: Ch. 13.

polysyllable (polysyllabic) A term used in PHONETICS and PHONOLOGY to refer to a WORD consisting of more than one SYLLABLE. 'Polysyllabic' or 'multisyllabic' words are contrasted with MONOSYLLABLES. See Gimson 1970: Ch. 9.

polysynthetic A type of LANGUAGE sometimes distinguished in COMPARATIVE LINGUISTICS using STRUCTURAL (as opposed to HISTORICAL) criteria, and focusing on the characteristics of the WORD: 'polysynthetic' or 'incorporating' languages demonstrate MORPHOLOGICALLY complex, long word-forms, as in the constructions typical of many American Indian languages, and encountered occasionally in English, in coinages such as *anti/dis/establish/ment/arian/ism/s*. The term is opposed to SYNTHETIC and ANALYTIC type languages. Some linguists, however, prefer to see such constructions handled as a complex of AGGLUTINATIVE and FUSIONAL characteristics, and do not regard this category of language as typologically distinct. As always in such classifications, the categories are not clear-cut: different languages will display the characteristic of 'polysynthesis' to a greater or lesser degree. See Robins 1971: Ch. 8; Bolinger 1975: Ch. 2.

polysystemic(ism) A term used to identify an approach to LINGUISTIC analysis proposed by J. R. FIRTH, in which different linguistic SYSTEMS are set up at different places in STRUCTURE, no attempt being made to identify the systems with each other. The approach has been developed primarily in relation to PHONOLOGY, where it is known as PROSODIC analysis. 'Polysystemic' is opposed to 'monosystemic', as in phonemic theories of phonology, where a single basic phonological unit is used (the PHONEME), and the set of phonemes is seen as a single system of CONTRASTS, applicable to the analysis and TRANSCRIPTION of LINEAR SEQUENCES of speech sounds, regardless of the GRAMMATICAL or LEXICAL structures involved. In 'polysystemicism', on the other hand, different phonological systems are set up as required at different places

portmanteau

in the structure of SYLLABLES, WORDS and other UNITS, and within different areas of the vocabulary or grammar. There is little emphasis on transcription, and a correspondingly greater emphasis on relating phonology to other levels of linguistic structure. In this approach, the set of sounds needed to define the contrastive possibilities at the beginning of words in a language may be quite different from those required in the middle or at the end of words. There is little evidence of the need for this analysis in English (apart from occasional contrasts such as /ŋ/ and /h/, which do not occur in the same ENVIRONMENTS), but several languages, such as many in South-East Asia, have been fruitfully analysed in these terms. See Robins 1971: Ch. 4.

portmanteau A term used in MORPHOLOGICAL analysis referring to cases where a single MORPH can be analysed into more than one MORPHEME, as in French *au, aux*, etc. (= *à le *à les 'to the'). See Palmer 1971: Ch. 3.

Port Royal The name given to a group of 17th-century scholars, based at the convent of Port Royal, south of Versailles, who, following the ideas of Descartes, developed a view of LANGUAGE in which grammatical CATEGORIES and STRUCTURES were seen as relatable to UNIVERSAL logical patterns of thought (an influential work was the *Grammaire générale et raisonné* of C. Lancelot, A. Arnauld and others, published in 1660). The ideas of this school of thought became widely known in the 1960s, when CHOMSKY drew certain parallels between them and his own conception of the relationship between LANGUAGE and mind. See Lyons 1968: Ch. 1.

position(al) (1) A term used in LINGUISTICS to refer to the FUNCTIONALLY CONTRASTIVE places within a linguistic UNIT, e.g. PHONEMES within the SYLLABLE or WORD, MORPHEMES within the word, words within the SENTENCE. It is common to talk of ELEMENTS occurring in INITIAL, MEDIAL or FINAL 'positions' within the higher-order unit. A 'positional variant' refers to the FORMAL variations introduced into a linguistic unit (usually a phoneme or morpheme) because of the CONDITIONING influence of its linguistic CONTEXT. See Lyons 1968: Ch. 2.

(2) In phonetics, the term is used to refer to the arrangement of the VOCAL ORGANS during the ARTICULATION of a sound: the various articulators (lips, TONGUE, etc.) are said to be in certain positions, based on their PLACE and MANNER of articulation. See Ladefoged 1975: Ch. 1.

positional mobility A term often used in GRAMMAR to refer to a defining property of the WORD, seen as a grammatical UNIT. The criterion states that the CONSTITUENT elements of complex words are not capable of rearrangement (e.g. *unsuccessful* cannot vary to produce *full-un-success*, etc.), thus contrasting with the way words themselves are mobile in SENTENCES, i.e. they can occur in many contrasting positions. See Matthews 1974: Ch. 9; Lyons 1968: Ch. 5.

positive (1) A term used in GRAMMATICAL description to refer to a type of SENTENCE or VERB which has no marker of negation, i.e. it is expressing an assertion. The positive, or AFFIRMATIVE 'pole' of this contrast is opposed to NEGATIVE, and the grammatical system involved is often referred to under the heading of POLARITY. See Quirk *et al* 1972: Ch. 2.

(2) The unMARKED term in the three-way grammatical description of ADJECTIVES and ADVERBS into DEGREES, specifying the extent of their application. The positive or 'absolute' degree implies no comparative quality, and contrasts with such terms as COMPARATIVE and SUPERLATIVE. In English, the adjective with no formal MODIFICATION is used as the positive form, and this is generally the case in languages. See Quirk *et al* 1972: Ch. 2.

post- A PREFIX used commonly in PHONETICS and LINGUISTICS, referring to relative POSITION in a SEQUENCE; opposed to PRE-. In phonetics, it refers to an ARTICULATION a little behind a recognised PLACE OF ARTICULATION, e.g. 'post-ALVEOLAR', 'post-PALATAL'. The terms 'post-VOCALIC', 'post-CONSONANTAL', however, do not refer to points of articulation, but to sounds occurring in a specific SYLLABIC position, *viz* after a VOWEL/CONSONANT respectively.

In LINGUISTICS, the term is found in relation to several GRAMMATICAL contexts. **Postmodification** is used in some grammatical DESCRIPTIONS to refer to all the ITEMS which occur after the HEAD of a PHRASE (an ENDOCENTRIC phrase), e.g. *The cars **in the garage** are expensive*. In English, three main types of 'postmodifying' structure are recognised, PREPOSITIONAL phrases (e.g. *the cars **in the garage**...*), FINITE (RELATIVE) CLAUSES (e.g. *the car **which was in the garage**...*) and non-finite (INFINITIVE or PARTICIPIAL) clauses, e.g. *the car **parked in the street**..., the car **to buy**...*

The term **postposition** is used in the grammatical classification of WORDS, referring to the CLOSED set of items which follow NOUN phrases (or single nouns or PRONOUNS) to form a single CONSTITUENT of structure. The analogous construction in English involves PREPOSITIONS. Many languages make regular use of postpositions, e.g. Japanese, Hindi. Other terms involving this prefix include 'post-determiner', 'post-article', 'post-verbal', etc. See Quirk *et al* 1972: Chs. 6, 13; Lyons 1968: Ch. 7.

postulates An application in LINGUISTICS of the general use of this term in the branch of logic known as axiomatics. It refers to a set of initial PROPOSITIONS which a theory assumes to be true; these initial statements, and the subsequent deductions made from them, are collectively known as the 'postulational method' (cf. AXIOMATIC). In linguistics, several 'sets of postulates' have been proposed, in attempts to systematise ideas about LANGUAGE, the most well-known being those propounded by the American linguists Leonard BLOOMFIELD (in 1926) and Bernard Bloch (in 1948). See Dinneen 1967: Ch. 1.

potential pause A term often used in GRAMMAR, to refer to a defining property of the WORD, seen as a grammatical UNIT. The criterion states that, in normal speech, PAUSES are not introduced within the STRUCTURE of the word, but are always possible (and often present) at word boundaries. See Matthews 1974: Ch. 9; Lyons 1968: Ch. 5.

power(ful) A term used in the formal evaluation of GRAMMARS, and particularly found in discussion of GENERATIVE theories. Basically, grammar A would be said to be more powerful than grammar B if it can generate more LANGUAGES (SENTENCES, etc.) than B. A further distinction is often introduced, between 'weak' and 'strong' generative power. In the notion of 'weak' generative power, a grammar (or RULE, or set of rules, etc.) is said to be more powerful than another if it GENERATES more grammatical sentences. In the notion of 'strong' generative power, a grammar is said to be more powerful if it assigns to these sentences a set of STRUCTURAL DESCRIPTIONS which more satisfactorily shows their relationships. It is important, however, that a grammar should not become too powerful, in the sense that it generates sentences which are ungrammatical, structural descriptions which are intuitively implausible, or a characterisation of natural language that is too broad (e.g. including features of non-language systems). FORMAL constraints therefore have to be built into grammatical MODELS to restrict the power of grammars in specific ways, and much current discussion is focused on this subject. See Lyons 1968: Ch. 6; 1977a: Ch. 8.

pragmatics One of the three major divisions of SEMIOTICS (along with SEMANTICS and SYNTACTICS). In LINGUISTICS the term has come to be applied to the study of LANGUAGE from the point of view of the user, especially of the choices he makes, the CONSTRAINTS he encounters in using language in social interaction, and the effects his use of language has on the other participants in an act of communication. Several SOCIOLINGUISTIC and PSYCHOLINGUISTIC studies since the mid-1970s have attached particular importance to these factors, but the difficulties involved in formulating the behavioural variables in a precise way have limited the growth of the subject. Some semanticists now see pragmatics as contrasting with TRUTH-CONDITIONAL SEMANTICS, it being suggested that the difficulties which arise in relation to the latter (e.g. how it handles the notion of PRESUPPOSITION) are more readily explicable with reference to the former. See Lyons 1977b: Ch. 4; Gumperz & Hymes 1971: Ch. 14.

Prague School The name given to the views and methods of the Linguistic Circle of Prague and the scholars it influenced. The circle was founded in 1926 by Vilém Mathesius (1882–1946), a professor of English at Caroline University, and included such LINGUISTS as Roman JAKOBSON (b. 1896) and Nikolai Trubetskoy (1890–1938). The 'Praguean' influence has been widespread and long-lasting, as the frequent reference to it throughout this dictionary testifies. Its main emphasis lay on the analysis of LANGUAGE as a SYSTEM of FUNCTIONALLY related UNITS, an emphasis which showed SAUSSUREAN influence. In particular, it led to the distinction between the PHONETIC and the PHONOLOGICAL analysis of sounds, the analysis of the PHONEME into DISTINCTIVE FEATURES, and such associated notions as BINARITY, MARKING and MORPHOPHONEMICS. Since the 1950s, Prague School ideas have been received and developed, particularly with reference to the SYNTAX, SEMANTICS and STYLISTICS of English and Slavonic languages, and illustrated in the work of Josef Vachek (b. 1909), Jan Firbas (b. 1921) and others. Of particular note here is the formulation of a theory of FUNCTIONAL SENTENCE PERSPECTIVE, wherein sentence analysis is seen as a complex of functionally contrastive CONSTITUENTS. A representative reader is J. Vachek (ed.), *A Prague School Reader in Linguistics* (1964), but the early book by Trubetskoy, *Grundzüge der Phonologie* (1939), translated in 1969 as *Principles of Phonology*, is seminal.

pre- A PREFIX used commonly in PHONETICS and LINGUISTICS, referring to relative POSITION in a SEQUENCE; opposed to POST-. In phonetics, it refers to an ARTICULATION a little in front of a recognised PLACE of articulation, e.g. 'pre-PALATAL', 'pre-VELAR'. The terms 'pre-VOCALIC', 'pre-CONSONANTAL', however, do not refer to points of articulation, but to sounds occurring in a specific SYLLABIC position, *viz* before a VOWEL/CONSONANT respectively. In LINGUISTICS, the term is found in relation to several GRAMMATICAL contexts. **Pre-determiner**, for example, is used in some MODELS of grammatical DESCRIPTION, referring to a CLASS of ITEMS which occur before a DETERMINER in the NOUN PHRASE, e.g. *all/both/half* in *all the man*, etc.

predicate

Other terms include 'pre-article', 'pre-verbal', PRE-LEXICAL, PRE-LINGUISTIC, PREMODIFICATION – and, of course, PREPOSITION. See Quirk *et al* 1972: Ch. 4.

predicate (predicat-ion, -ive, -or) (1) A term used in the analysis of GRAMMATICAL FUNCTIONS, to refer to a major CONSTITUENT of SENTENCE structure, traditionally associated with a two-part analysis in which all obligatory CONSTITUENTS other than the SUBJECT were considered together. For example, *John walked/John kicked the ball/John went on holiday*... would all be seen as Subject (*John*) + Predicate constructions. These sentences would also be labelled 'predicative' in a classification of EXOCENTRIC constructions. There are several points of contact here with the philosophical analysis of propositions in terms of **predication** (i.e. properties being 'predicated' of entities), and recent linguistic discussion has focused on the extent to which there are parallels between the SYNTACTIC and the SEMANTIC dimensions of analysis (using such distinctions as GIVEN/NEW and TOPIC/COMMENT). At a more detailed level, in syntax, distinctions are sometimes made between **predicative** and 'non-predicative' functions of words, e.g. the ADJECTIVE in *the man is **big*** is predicative, whereas in *the **big** man* it is ATTRIBUTIVE. However, terminology varies a great deal here, depending on the model of description used. The term **predicator** has also been suggested by some theorists to refer to the verbal element in Subject–Verb–Object constructions, *viz* Subject–Predicator–Object, on the grounds that this avoids using 'Verb' in both a functional and a FORMAL sense (cf. 'a Subject may have a noun as its exponent' with the undesirability of 'a Verb may have a verb as its exponent'). See Lyons 1968: Ch. 8; Quirk *et al* 1972: Chs. 2, 7.

(2) The term is also used in linguistics where notions from the logical system of **predicate calculus** are sometimes used as a framework for aspects of GRAMMATICAL and SEMANTIC analysis. A logical calculus presents a set of logical laws or truths in systematic deductive form: in predicate calculus, rules for representing the internal structure of simple PROPOSITIONS (especially for handling QUANTIFICATION) are presented (usually axiomatically) in a FORMAL notation. A 'predicate' is that term in a proposition which provides information about the individual or entity, e.g. *the car is **stolen/big/beautiful**...*: it is seen as a device whereby simple propositions can be formed out of names. A simple proposition is then said to be a FUNCTION of its component name(s), the name(s) being its argument(s). The terms 'one-place/two-place, etc. predicates' are then used, depending on the number of arguments contained within the proposition, e.g. *Jules saw Jim* is a two-place predicate, *Jules* and *Jim*

being arguments of the predicate *saw*. MODELS based on this principle are used in several linguistic theories, e.g. CASE GRAMMAR, DEPENDENCY GRAMMAR. See Lyons 1977b: Ch. 6.

prefix(-ing, -ation) A term used in MORPHOLOGY referring to an AFFIX which is added initially to a ROOT or STEM. The process of 'prefixation' is common in English, for forming new LEXICAL items (e.g. *para-*, *mini-*, *un-*), but English does not INFLECT words using prefixes. Languages which do inflect in this way include German (e.g. the *ge-* of PERFECTIVE forms), Greek, and many American Indian langages (e.g. the Athapaskan family). See Robins 1971: Ch. 5; Matthews 1974: Ch. 7.

pre-lexical structures A term used in some MODELS of GENERATIVE GRAMMAR (cf. ASPECTS) to refer to the first stage in a two-stage generation of DEEP STRUCTURES. In this stage, PHRASE-MARKERS are generated in which the TERMINAL NODES are expressed as a Δ (DELTA) ELEMENT. In the second stage, LEXICAL ITEMS are inserted into these positions, in the form of COMPLEX SYMBOLS (i.e. 'lexical TRANSFORMATIONS'). See Huddleston 1976: Ch. 10.

prelinguistic(s) (1) A term used by some linguists, especially in the 1950s, to refer to the ARTICULATORY and ACOUSTIC study of sound, as opposed to the strictly LINGUISTIC studies of PHONOLOGY, etc. (MICROLINGUISTICS). In this frame of reference, it was seen as a branch of MACROLINGUISTICS. The term 'prelinguistic' is sometimes used outside this framework to refer to any construct which needs to be taken into account as a preliminary consideration before linguistic analysis proceeds, e.g. the obtaining of adequate DATA samples. See Crystal 1969: Ch. 2.

(2) In the study of PERFORMANCE MODELS of language, the term has also been used with reference to hypothetical stages in SPEECH PRODUCTION which precede those involved with language organisation. Psychological factors, such as cognitive awareness and attention, could be seen as prelinguistic in this sense. See Clark & Clark 1977: Ch. 6.

(3) In language ACQUISITION, the period immediately preceding the emergence of linguistic patterning in children's VOCALISATION is considered a 'prelinguistic' stage of development, *viz* much of the second half of the first year of life. See Clark & Clark 1977: Ch. 8.

premodification (premodify) A term used in some MODELS of GRAMMATICAL description to refer to all the ITEMS which occur before the HEAD of a PHRASE (an ENDOCENTRIC phrase), e.g. ***All those big red***

foreign cars have been sold. DETERMINERS and ADJECTIVES are the main CLASSES occurring in premodifying position in English, but there are several other categories involved in the full description of this complex area, e.g. QUANTIFIERS, INTENSIFIERS. See Quirk *et al* 1972: Chs. 4, 5, 13.

preposition(al) A term used in the GRAMMATICAL classification of WORDS, referring to the CLOSED set of ITEMS which precede NOUN PHRASES (or single nouns or PRONOUNS) to form a single CONSTITUENT of STRUCTURE. The resulting 'prepositional phrase' (or 'prepositional group') can then be described in terms of DISTRIBUTION (e.g. their use following a noun, as in *the man in the corner*) or SEMANTICALLY (e.g. the expression of possession, direction, place). Prepositional sequences of the type illustrated by *in accordance with* are often called **complex prepositions**. POSTpositions refer to structures where a PARTICLE, similar in function to a preposition, is placed after a noun, as in Japanese. See Quirk *et al* 1972: Ch. 6; Lyons 1968: Ch. 7.

prerequisites A term used in LINGUISTICS to refer to the concepts on which an analysis at a specific linguistic LEVEL depends. Its main application is in the context of PHONOLOGICAL PROCEDURES, where the American STRUCTURALIST view of the 1940s, that phonological analysis should proceed solely on the basis of PHONETIC criteria, came to be opposed by a view which stressed the importance of 'GRAMMATICAL prerequisites' – the PRESUPPOSITIONS about the identity of such notions as WORD and SENTENCE which had to be made before techniques such as the MINIMAL PAIR test could be used. See Hyman 1975: Ch. 3; Robins 1971: Ch. 4.

prescriptive (prescriptiv-ism, -ist) A term used by LINGUISTS to characterise any approach which attempts to lay down RULES of CORRECTNESS as to how LANGUAGE should be used. Using such criteria as purity, logic, history, or literary excellence, 'prescriptivism' aims to preserve imagined standards by insisting on NORMS of USAGE and criticising departures from these norms. **Prescriptive grammars** include such recommendations as: *I* should be used after the VERB *be*, e.g. *It is I;* *whom* should be used as the RELATIVE PRONOUN in OBJECT FUNCTION, e.g. *the man whom I saw*; and so on. A distinction is sometimes made between 'prescriptive' and PROSCRIPTIVE rules, the latter being rules which forbid, rather than command. Linguistics has been wholly critical of the 'prescriptivist' approach, emphasising instead the importance of DESCRIPTIVELY accurate studies of usage, and of the need to take into account SOCIOLINGUISTIC variation in explaining attitudes to language. The term 'prescriptive' is sometimes used in sociolinguistics (e.g. the 'prescriptions' of a sociolinguistically realistic language planning programme), but on the whole the term is pejorative in linguistic contexts. See Lyons 1968: Ch. 1; Bolinger 1975: Ch. 15.

pressure One of the features of sound set up by CHOMSKY & Halle in their DISTINCTIVE FEATURE theory of PHONOLOGY, under the heading of SUPPLEMENTARY MOVEMENTS, to handle variations in MANNER OF ARTICULATION. It refers to articulatory movements of the GLOTTIS or VELUM (cf. VELAR) where the air flow is directed outwards, as in EJECTIVES. See Ladefoged 1975: Ch. 11; Hyman 1975: Ch. 2.

presupposition The philosophical uses of this term will be found in SEMANTIC discussion, *viz* a condition which must be satisfied if a particular state of affairs is to obtain, or (in relation to language) what a speaker assumes in saying a particular sentence, as opposed to what he actually asserts. It is also analysed as a certain type of logical relationship between statements, contrasting with ENTAILMENT. Some linguists have come to use the term in a narrower sense, in a two-part analysis of sentences which contrasts the INFORMATION assumed (or 'presupposed') by the speaker, and that which is at the centre of his communicative interest; in this sense, 'presupposition' is opposed to FOCUS. (The contrast between GIVEN and NEW information makes an analogous distinction.) For example, in one interpretation of this notion, the sentence *Where's the salt?* is said to presuppose that the salt is not present to the speaker, that there is someone whom he thinks might know where the salt is, and so on. This total study of the factors in the communicative context which affect the meaning of an utterance has attracted increasing interest from linguists in recent years, partly in SEMANTICS and partly under the heading of PRAGMATICS. Controversial aspects of analysing language in these terms abound, in particular over the extent to which the notion of presupposition can or ought to be restricted to certain kinds of logical or behaviourally demonstrable factors. See Lyons 1977b: Ch. 14.

prevarication A suggested defining property of human LANGUAGE (contrasting with the properties of other SEMIOTIC SYSTEMS), referring to the way languages can be used to misinform, as in lying, irony, etc. See Lyons 1977b: Ch. 3.

primitive (prime) An application in LINGUISTICS and PHONETICS of the general use of this term in scientific investigation, where certain constructs are taken as 'given', by a theory, the purpose of the theoretical exposition being to explicate them. The PROPOSITIONS which contain such undefined terms are referred to as POSTULATES, or AXIOMS. Examples of terms often taken as primitive include 'UT-TERANCE', 'acceptable', 'sound', 'meaningful', 'mouth', 'vocalisa-tion', 'distinctiveness', etc. – though any of these might become the focus of controversy in an investigation, and could not thereby be assumed to have primitive status. The distinction between primitive and **non-primitive** terms is of particular importance in attempts to FORMALISE linguistic theory, and has been much discussed in GENERA-TIVE GRAMMAR. Here, the terms which appear in the STRUCTURAL DESCRIPTIONS of a SENTENCE are primitive, e.g. 'sentence', 'NOUN PHRASE', 'VERB phrase', ' + ', ' → ', ('REWRITE'). Terms such as SUBJECT, OBJECT, SUBORDINATE, CO-ORDINATE, etc. are DERIVED or non-primitive, in this MODEL. See Huddleston 1976: Ch. 3; Lyons 1968: Ch. 4.

privative A type of OPPOSITION recognised in PRAGUE SCHOOL PHONO-LOGY, distinguished from GRADUAL and EQUIPOLLENT. A privative opposition is a BINARY one, where one member is seen as MARKED by the presence of a FEATURE, which its opposite member lacks (i.e. it is 'unmarked'), as in the /p/ vs. /b/ DISTINCTION in English, where the former is seen as marked for VOICING. See Hyman 1975: Ch. 2.

privilege of occurrence A term used in LINGUISTICS to refer to the FORMAL ENVIRONMENT in which a linguistic ITEM may be used. Items which share the same 'privileges of occurrence' belong to the same CLASS, e.g. *black, nice, big, angry*, etc. in the CONTEXT *the – dog*. See Robins 1971: Ch. 6.

procedure A term used in LINGUISTICS referring to a particular way of arriving at a linguistic analysis or decision. Different views about the goals of a linguistic theory can be clarified by phrasing the question in terms of procedures, of which three types have attracted particular interest, since their first formulation by Noam CHOMSKY:

(1) **discovery procedure**: a technique which can be automatically or 'mechanically' applied to a sample of LANGUAGE and which would produce a CORRECT analysis. Attempts to develop such a procedure characterised the work of many BLOOMFIELDIAN linguists, and were strongly criticised in early formulations of GENERATIVE GRAMMAR. It is argued that it is never possible to identify with certainty all the factors which lead a linguist in the direction of a particular analysis.

Nor is it desirable to seek such a procedure, as the analysis itself can be evaluated regardless of the means by which it was obtained.

(2) **decision procedure**: a technique which could be automatically applied to a series of grammars of a language, to decide which was the best grammar. It is suggested that such a goal is impossible, in the present state of linguistic knowledge, and that linguists must content themselves with relative and not absolute decisions, as in (3) below.

(3) **evaluation procedure**: a technique which provides criteria for choosing the better of two analyses of a set of DATA, as when it is argued that one analysis is simpler, more plausible, or more elegant than another. In generative linguistics, a few (controversial) procedures have been suggested (cf. SIMPLICITY) which attempt to FORMALISE the properties of alternative DESCRIPTIONS so that precise evaluations can be made. See Lyons 1977a: Ch. 4; Huddleston 1976: Ch. 1.

process Any approach to LINGUISTIC DESCRIPTION which sees some ELEMENTS (STRUCTURES, etc.) as being the result of a change operating on some other element in the LANGUAGE. The process of change may be real (as in ATTESTED processes of HISTORICAL change) or part of the abstract system of relationships found in a particular MODEL of description (as when plural NOUNS are derived from singulars by a process of pluralisation). This notion is fundamental to the ITEM AND PROCESS model of linguistic description, and several important terms in contemporary linguistics reflect a process approach, e.g. DERIVATION, REWRITE RULE, BLEND, and the many terms ending in -*ation*, such as LABIALISATION, PASSIVISATION. In PSYCHOLINGUISTICS, considerable discussion has taken place concerning the extent to which the linguistic processes encountered in a linguistic model can be related to processes of a psychological kind (cf. PERFORMANCE GRAMMAR, CORRESPONDENCE hypothesis). See Lyons 1968: Ch. 2; Clark & Clark 1977: Chs. 2, 9.

production (productive) The general sense of this term is found in PHONETICS and PSYCHOLINGUISTICS, where it refers to the process of planning and executing the act of SPEECH. The study of **speech production** includes not only the neuroanatomical and neurophysiological activities involved in speaking, but also the construction and testing of MODELS of the neural control system in the brain's organisation of speech. A particular strategy is to analyse certain characteristics of speech output (e.g. PAUSE, TONGUE-SLIPS, DYNAMIC features), as a means of inferring the properties of this system.

productivity

Production is usually contrasted with speech PERCEPTION and COM-PREHENSION. See Clark & Clark 1977: Chs. 6, 7.

productivity (productive, non-/un-) A general term used in LINGUIS-TICS to refer to the CREATIVE capacity of LANGUAGE users to produce and understand an indefinitely large number of SENTENCES. It contrasts particularly with the 'unproductive' communication systems of animals, and in this context is seen by some linguists as one of the design features of human language. The term is also used in a more restricted sense with reference to the use made by a language of a specific feature or pattern. A pattern is 'productive' if it is repeatedly used in language to produce further instances of the same type (e.g. the past TENSE AFFIX -ed in English is productive, in that any new VERB will be automatically assigned this past tense form). **Non-productive** (or 'unproductive') patterns lack any such potential, e.g. the change from *mouse* to *mice* is not a productive plural formation – new NOUNS would not adopt it, but would use instead the productive *s*-ending pattern. **Semi-productive** forms are those where there is a limited or occasional creativity, as when a PREFIX such as *un-* is sometimes, but not universally, applied to words to form their opposites, e.g. *happy* → *unhappy*, but not *sad* → **unsad*. See Lyons 1977a: Ch. 2; 1977b: Ch. 3; Matthews 1974: Ch. 3.

pro-form A term used in some models of GRAMMATICAL description to refer collectively to the ITEMS in a SENTENCE which substitute for other items or CONSTRUCTIONS. The central class of examples (from which the term is derived by analogy) is PRONOUNS, which substitute for NOUN PHRASES. Other pro-forms replace ADVERBIALS (e.g. *them, there*), PREDICATES (e.g. *do*, as in *I like films. So do I* (sc. 'so do I like films')), and even whole CLAUSES or sentences (e.g. *so*, as in *I said so*). Terminology such as 'pro-verb', 'pro-nominal', 'pro-locative', etc. is therefore likely to be encountered. See Quirk *et al* 1972: Chs. 2, 10; Palmer 1971: Ch. 2.

progressive (1) A term used in the GRAMMATICAL description of VERB FORMS, referring to a contrast of a temporal or durative kind, and thus sometimes handled under the heading of TENSE and sometimes under ASPECT. The usual contrast recognised is between 'progressive' or 'continuous' (e.g. *I am going*) and **non-progressive** or 'simple' (e.g. *I go*). LINGUISTS prefer an aspectual analysis here, because of the complex interaction of durational, completive and temporal features of meaning involved; TRADITIONAL grammars, however, merely refer to 'simple tense forms', etc., and thus imply a meaning which is to some degree an oversimplification. See Quirk *et al* 1972: Ch. 3; Lyons 1968: Ch. 7.

(2) A term used in PHONETICS and PHONOLOGY as part of the classification of types of ASSIMILATION. In **progressive assimilation**, a sound changes because of the influence of the preceding sound, as when [s] becomes [ʃ] following [ʤ], in such phrases as *Goodge Street*. It is opposed to REGRESSIVE and COALESCENT assimilations. See Gimson 1970: Ch. 11.

project(ion) A term used in GENERATIVE LINGUISTICS to characterise the capability of a GRAMMAR to extend the analysis of any given set of SENTENCES so that it applies also to the potentially infinite number of sentences in the LANGUAGE as a whole. The main means of doing this is the generative RULE. In some MODELS of generative grammar, a more restricted sense is found: **projection-rules** are established as part of the SEMANTIC COMPONENT, their function being to assign a semantic INTERPRETATION to each STRING of FORMATIVES generated by the SYNTACTIC component. See Lyons 1977a: Ch. 4; 1977b: Ch. 10.

prominence (prominent) A term used in AUDITORY PHONETICS to refer to the degree to which a sound or SYLLABLE stands out from others in its ENVIRONMENT. Variations in LENGTH, PITCH, STRESS and inherent SONORITY are all factors which contribute to the relative prominence of a UNIT. See Gimson 1970: Ch. 3.

pronoun A term used in the GRAMMATICAL classification of WORDS, referring to the CLOSED sets of ITEMS which can be used to substitute for a NOUN PHRASE (or single noun). There are many types of pronoun, with terminology varying somewhat between grammars. **Personal pronouns** include *I*, *you*, etc. in their variant FORMS (e.g. *I/me*); in their form *my/mine*, the term **possessive pronoun** is often used. Other classes of pronoun regularly recognised include: **demonstrative pronouns**, e.g. *this/that* (in certain of their uses); **interrogative pronouns**, e.g. certain uses of *who/which/what*; **reflexive pronouns**, e.g. *myself/yourself*; **indefinite pronouns**, e.g. *anyone/nobody*; and **relative pronouns**, e.g. *who/whom/that*. The grammatical statement of pronominal distribution in a language is usually quite complex. It is often discussed with reference to the more general notions of PRO-FORM and DEIXIS. See Quirk *et al* 1972: Ch. 4.

prop A term used in some GRAMMATICAL descriptions to refer to a meaningless ELEMENT introduced into a structure to ensure its GRAMMATICALITY, e.g. the *it* in *it's a lovely day*. Such words are also proper

referred to as EMPTY, because they lack any SEMANTICALLY independent MEANING. SUBSTITUTE WORDS, which refer back to a previously occurring element of structure, are also often called prop words, e.g. *one* or *do* in *he does, he's got one*, etc. See Quirk *et al* 1972: Chs. 10, 14.

proper A term used in the GRAMMATICAL classification of NOUNS, opposed traditionally to a set of terms including COMMON, abstract, etc., but in LINGUISTIC analyses usually contrasting with 'common' alone. The alternative term, **proper name**, reflects its traditional SEMANTIC definition: the name of an individual person, place, etc. Modern grammars aim to provide a FORMAL treatment of these distinctions: proper nouns, for example, cannot be used with DETER-MINERS in the way common nouns can, cf. *the/a boy* with **the/a London*, etc. See Quirk *et al* 1972: Ch. 4.

proportional A type of OPPOSITION recognised in PRAGUE SCHOOL PHONOLOGY, distinguished from ISOLATED. The opposition between /f/ and /v/ in English is proportional, because there are other oppositions in the language which work in parallel, e.g. /s/ vs. /z/, /ʃ/ vs. /ʒ/; on the other hand, the opposition between, say /v/ and /l/ is isolated – there are no other segments that are contrasted in this particular way, i.e. VOICED LABIO-DENTAL FRICATIVE vs. voiced LATERAL. See Hyman 1975: Ch. 2.

proposition(al) A term derived from philosophy, where its status is controversial, and often used in LINGUISTICS as part of a GRAMMATICAL or SEMANTIC analysis. It refers to the UNIT of MEANING which constitutes the subject-matter of a STATEMENT in the form of a SIMPLE DECLARATIVE sentence. Two 'terms' are involved in the analysis of propositions: the expression of a single action or state (a PREDICATE), and one or more entities ('names') which delimit the effects of this action or state. The logical system of **propositional calculus** may then be used as a framework for aspects of grammatical and semantic analysis. A logical calculus presents a set of logical laws or truths in systematic deductive form; in propositional calculus, rules for determining the relations between combinations of propositions are presented (usually AXIOMatically) in a formal notation. Particular emphasis is placed on the analysis of the logical CONNECTIVES used in forming these combinations (negation, conjunction, disjunction and implication), and on the possible truth-values which 'single' or 'complex' propositions may have.

In linguistics, the interest is primarily in the way in which different linguistic FORMS can be shown to express the same proposition (e.g. *the cat ate the meat, the meat was eaten by the cat*, and so on), and how a single linguistic form can be analysed in terms of several propositions (e.g. *Those nice red apples cost a lot* expresses the propositions that 'the apples cost a lot', 'the apples are nice' and 'the apples are red'). The notion of 'proposition' is fundamental to CASE GRAMMAR, where it is used as one of the two main UNDERLYING CONSTITUENTS of sentences (Sentence → Modality + Proposition): each proposition is analysed in terms of a predicate word and its associated ARGUMENTS (i.e. case roles). Also of interest is the distinction to be made between the 'propositional meaning' of a sentence on the one hand, and the use made of the sentence (e.g. in various SPEECH-ACT situations) on the other. Linguists are not primarily concerned with the evaluation of a proposition in terms of truth-values, nor with the question of the referential or cognitive status of the notion. See Lyons 1977b: Ch. 6; Clark & Clark 1977: Ch. 1.

proscriptive A term used by LINGUISTS to characterise any approach which attempts to lay down RULES of CORRECTNESS, emphasising how LANGUAGE should *not* be used. For example, the view that 'SENTENCES should not end with PREPOSITIONS' is a 'proscriptive RULE'. These NORMATIVE statements are usually made within the overall context of a PRESCRIPTIVE GRAMMAR. See Bolinger 1975: Ch. 16.

prosody/prosodic (feature) A term used in SUPRASEGMENTAL PHONETICS and PHONOLOGY to refer collectively to variations in PITCH, LOUDNESS, TEMPO and RHYTHM. Sometimes, it is used loosely as a synonym for 'suprasegmental', but in a narrower sense it refers only to the above variables, the remaining suprasegmental features being labelled PARA-LINGUISTIC. The narrow sense is close to the traditional use of the term 'prosody', where it referred to the characteristics and analyses of verse structure.

In the theory of phonology proposed by J. R. FIRTH (**prosodic phonology**), the notion of prosody is given special status. It is distinguished in this approach from PHONEMATIC UNIT: this is a SEGMENTAL unit, such as consonant or vowel, whereas **prosodies** are features extending over stretches of utterance (one talks of 'sentence prosodies', 'syllable prosodies', etc.). Not only pitch, STRESS and JUNCTURE patterns would be subsumed under the heading of prosody, but such features as SECONDARY ARTICULATIONS would also be included, e.g. lip-ROUNDING or nasalisation (cf. NASAL), when these are used to account for phonotactic restrictions, or to characterise GRAMMATICAL structure (as in the notion of 'VOWEL harmony').

prothetic

Another feature of Firth's prosodic analysis is its POLYSYSTEMIC principle: it permits different phonological systems to be set up at different places in grammatical, lexical or phonological structure, e.g. the contrasts which occur at the beginning of a WORD may not be the same as those which occur at the end, and this fact is given special attention in this approach.

In PHONEMIC phonology, linguistically contrastive prosodic features are often referred to as **prosodemes**. In GENERATIVE phonology, prosodic features are considered to be one of the five main dimensions of classification of speech sounds (the others being MAJOR CLASS FEATURES, CAVITY FEATURES, MANNER OF ARTICULATION FEATURES and SOURCE FEATURES). See Robins 1971: Ch. 4; Crystal 1969.

prothetic A term used in PHONETICS and PHONOLOGY to refer to a type of INTRUSION, where an extra sound has been inserted initially in a WORD. The phenomenon is common both in historical change and in CONNECTED SPEECH (e.g. *left turn* pronounced as /ˀleft tɜːn/). See Bolinger 1975: Ch. 12.

proto- A prefix used in HISTORICAL LANGUAGE studies to refer to a LINGUISTIC FORM or STATE of a language said to be the ancestor of ATTESTED forms/languages, e.g. Proto-Indo-European, Proto-Romance. More recently, some linguists have begun to use the term analogously in the context of language ACQUISITION, to refer to the emerging linguistic system of the young child, in such uses as 'proto-conversion', 'proto-sentence'. See Bolinger 1975: Ch. 13.

proxemics A term used in SEMIOTICS to refer to the study of variations in posture, distance and tactile contact in human COMMUNICATION. These variations in interpersonal space are often culture-specific, and can be analysed in terms of sex, age, intimacy, social role and other such factors. See Lyons 1977b: Ch. 3; Gumperz & Hymes 1971: Ch. 13.

PS(G) The usual abbreviations for PHRASE-STRUCTURE or 'phrase-structure GRAMMAR'.

pseudo-cleft sentence A term used in GRAMMATICAL description to refer to a CONSTRUCTION which resembles a CLEFT SENTENCE, in that a single CLAUSE has been divided into two separate sections, each with its own VERB, but with the essential difference that the two sections can be analysed as having a MAIN clause–SUBORDINATE clause relationship. For example, the sentence *You are a fool* is related to *What you are is a* *fool* or *A fool is what you are.* See Quirk *et al* 1972: Ch. 14; Akmajian & Heny 1975: Ch. 9.

pseudo-procedure A term sometimes used in LINGUISTICS and PHONETICS to refer to an analytic procedure which claims to work in a certain way, but which is in fact incapable of doing so, e.g. to assume that PHONOLOGICAL distinctions can be established by scrutinising the ACOUSTIC patterns displayed on a SPECTROGRAM, or that it is possible to do GRAMMATICAL analysis without reference to MEANING. See Palmer 1971: Ch. 4.

psycholinguistics A branch of LINGUISTICS which studies the correlation between linguistic behaviour and the psychological processes thought to underlie that behaviour. There are two possible directions of study. One may use LANGUAGE as a means of elucidating psychological theories and processes (e.g. the role of language as it affects memory, perception, attention, learning, etc.), and for this the term **psychological linguistics** is sometimes used. Alternatively, one may investigate the effects of psychological constraints on the use of language (e.g. how memory limitations affect SPEECH PRODUCTION and COMPREHENSION). It is the latter which has provided the main focus of interest in linguistics, where the subject is basically seen as the study of the mental processes underlying the planning, production, perception and comprehension of speech. The most well-developed branch of the subject is the study of language ACQUISITION in children, but several other topics have attracted considerable interest (e.g. the notion of linguistic COMPLEXITY, the relationship between linguistic and cognitive UNIVERSALS, the study of reading). See Clark & Clark 1977; Robins 1971: Ch. 9.

pulmonic In PHONETICS this is the usual adjective to describe activity associated with the lungs. The pulmonic AIR-STREAM MECHANISM, for example, refers to the use of the lungs to initiate an air-flow for SPEECH PRODUCTION. Most human speech involves pulmonic sounds. See Gimson 1970: Ch. 2; Catford 1977: Ch. 5.

pure vowel A term used in PHONETICS referring to a VOWEL sound with no perceived change in quality during a SYLLABLE, as in *pot* or *pit*. Alternatively known as a MONOPHTHONG, its opposite is 'gliding vowel' (cf. GLIDE) or DIPHTHONG. See Ladefoged 1975: Ch. 4; Gimson 1970: Ch. 4.

purism (purist) A term used pejoratively in LINGUISTICS to characterise a school of thought which sees a LANGUAGE as needing preservation from the external processes which might infiltrate it and thus make it change, e.g. the pressures exercised by other DIALECTS and languages (as in LOAN words) and the variations introduced by colloquial speech. This 'purist' concern is considered misplaced by linguists, who point to the inevitability of language change, as a reflex of social, cultural and psychological development. See Bolinger 1975: Ch. 11.

Q

𝔊𝔊𝔊𝔊𝔊𝔊

qualification (qualifier) A term used in SYNTAX to refer to certain types of STRUCTURAL DEPENDENCE of one grammatical UNIT upon another. In some TRADITIONAL GRAMMARS, for example, dependent ITEMS in a NOUN PHRASE (such as ADJECTIVES, PREPOSITIONAL phrases) were said to 'qualify' the noun. In HALLIDAYAN grammar, on the other hand, the term is reserved for structures following the HEAD of the noun phrase: *the man in the street* would be analysed in terms of M–H–Q, standing for MODIFICATION–head–qualification. See Quirk *et al* 1972: Ch. 4.

quality A term used in AUDITORY PHONETICS and PHONOLOGY to refer to the characteristic resonance, or TIMBRE, of a sound, which is the result of the range of FREQUENCIES constituting the sound's identity. Variations in both VOWELS and CONSONANTS are describable in terms of quality, e.g. the distinction between [i], [e], etc. would be called a 'qualitative' difference. In this sense, the term 'quality' is generally opposed to QUANTITY or LENGTH.

Voices are also described as having a characteristic 'quality', though this notion has no linguistic status (cf. VOICE QUALITY). See Ladefoged 1975: Ch. 4.

quantifier (quantification) A term used in SEMANTIC or logical analysis, referring to a set of ITEMS which express contrasts in quantity, such as *all, some, each*. The status of some of these items has particular significance in the construction of logical systems, and the distinctions made in logic between **universal quantification** (i.e. 'for all x, it is the case that...') and **existential quantification** (i.e. 'for some x, it is the case that ...') may be found in semantic studies. In some MODELS of GRAMMATICAL description, 'quantifiers' refer to a class of items expressing contrasts in quantity occurring with restricted DISTRIBUTION in the NOUN PHRASE, e.g. *much/many, several, a lot of*. The rule of **quantifier-floating** has been proposed by some TRANSFORMATIONAL LINGUISTS, to handle the mobile properties of quantifiers in SENTENCES, as in *All the people arrived* vs. *The people all arrived*. See Lyons 1977b: Ch. 6; Quirk *et al* 1972: Ch. 4.

quantitative linguistics A branch of LINGUISTICS which studies the frequency and DISTRIBUTION of linguistic UNITS using statistical techniques. The subject has both a pure and an applied side: the former aims to establish general principles concerning the statistical regularities governing the way WORDS, sounds, etc. are used; the latter investigates the way statistical techniques can be used to elucidate linguistic problems (such as FUNCTIONAL LOAD, STYLISTIC DISTINCTIVENESS, authorship identity). See Lyons 1968: Ch. 2.

quantity A term used in PHONOLOGY to refer to the relative DURATIONS of sounds and SYLLABLES when these are linguistically contrastive; also referred to as LENGTH. The term is particularly used in historical studies of VOWEL and syllable length, and is contrasted with the notion of QUALITY. See Catford 1977: Ch. 10; Gimson 1970: Ch. 3.

question A term used in the classification of SENTENCE FUNCTIONS, and defined sometimes on GRAMMATICAL and sometimes on SEMANTIC or SOCIOLINGUISTIC grounds. SYNTACTICALLY, in English, a question is a SENTENCE with INVERSION of the SUBJECT and first VERB in the verb PHRASE (*'yes–no* questions', such as *is he coming?*), commencing with a **question word** (WH-QUESTIONS, such as *where is he?*), or ending with a question TAG (e.g. *he's coming, isn't he?*). Some would include the use of sentences with a rising INTONATION to be a class of question. Semantically, questions express a desire for more information, usually requesting a reply from the listener (exceptions include 'rhetorical questions' (e.g. *isn't that awful?*)). The term is usually contrasted with three other major sentence functions: STATEMENT, COMMAND, EXCLAMATION. In grammatical discussion, questions are usually referred to as INTERROGATIVE in form. See Quirk *et al* 1972: Ch. 7; Lyons 1977b: Ch. 1.

R

᭠᭠᭠᭠᭠᭠

raising A type of RULE recognised in some MODELS of TRANSFORM-
ATIONAL GRAMMAR. In a 'raising to object' (or **object-raising**) rule,
the LINEAR CONSTITUENTS in a STRING consisting of a main
CLAUSE + COMPLEMENT clause (e.g. *he believes John to be honest*) are
BRACKETED so that the SUBJECT of the complement clause appears to
have been 'raised' to become the OBJECT of the HIGHER clause (*he
believes it + John is honest* becoming *he believes John + to be honest*). In a
subject-raising rule, an underlying subject complement clause has the
subject taken from it and 'raised' to be the subject of the main clause.
For example, in relating such sentences as *it seems that the man is angry*
to *the man seems angry*, one may begin with

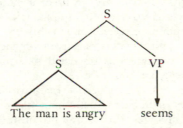

Subject-raising (in association with other transformational operations,
omitted here) places *the man* as subject of *seems*, producing (*the
man*) (*seems*) (*to be angry*). The FORMALISATION of such rules is controversial, as is the extent of their application (they are both GOVERNED
rules, applying to small classes of verb only). See Huddleston 1976:
Ch. 8; Akmajian & Heny 1975: Ch. 9.

rank In HALLIDAYAN LINGUISTICS, this term is used to refer to one of
the SCALES of analysis which inter-relates the CATEGORIES of the theory,
viz the HIERARCHICAL arrangement of linguistic UNITS within a
linguistic LEVEL. The GRAMMATICAL **rank scale**, for instance, recog-

nises SENTENCE—CLAUSE—GROUP—WORD—MORPHEME in a relationship of inclusion (i.e. a sentence consists of one or more clauses, etc.). Other scales in this approach are labelled EXPONENCE and DELICACY. The term **rankshift** is used to refer to a linguistic process when a given unit is 'shifted' down the rank scale, so that it operates within the structure of a lower unit (or one of equal rank), e.g. a clause working within a group (as in RELATIVE clauses, e.g. *the man **who came in** asked...*) is said to be a 'rankshifted' clause. See Lyons 1968: Ch. 5; Robins 1971: Ch. 7.

rate An application of the general sense of this term in PHONETICS and PHONOLOGY to refer to speed of speaking; alternatively known as TEMPO. LANGUAGES and people vary in their overall rate of ARTICULATION (measured in such terms as SYLLABLES per second, WORDS per minute, incidence of PAUSES). Within a given NORM, however, it is possible to vary one's rate for particular SEMANTIC or social effects, e.g. the 'meditative' sense of *we-e-ll*, produced very slowly. Rate thus forms part of the CONTRASTIVITY studied by SUPRASEGMENTAL phonology. See Bolinger 1975: Ch. 3.

realisation (realise) (1) The physical expression of an abstract LINGUISTIC UNIT, e.g. PHONEMES are 'realised' in PHONIC SUBSTANCE as PHONES, MORPHEMES as MORPHS. Any UNDERLYING FORM may be seen as having a corresponding realisation in substance. Alternative terms are ACTUALISATION, MANIFESTATION, EXPONENCE and REPRESENTATION, though the latter two are not restricted to expression solely at a physical level. See Lyons 1968: Ch. 2.

(2) In STRATIFICATIONAL GRAMMAR, **realisational analysis** is one of two main types of linguistic patterning (the other being TACTIC analysis), which involves the setting-up of four basic types of operation: 'horizontal grouping' (e.g. $d+o+g \rightarrow dog$), 'horizontal splitting' (e.g. French *des* realises *de+les*), 'vertical grouping' (two or more lower LEVEL UNITS realise one higher level unit, e.g. the various forms of the plural MORPHEME), and 'vertical splitting' (two or more higher level units are realised by one lower level unit, e.g. *-s* realising both plural and possessive). See Bolinger 1975: Ch. 15.

received pronunciation (RP) The name given to the regionally neutral ACCENT in British English, historically deriving from the prestige speech of the Court and the public schools. The term indicates that its prestige is the result of social factors, not linguistic ones. RP is in no sense linguistically superior or inferior to other accents; but it is the accent which tends to be associated with the more well-educated parts of society, and is the one most often cited as a norm for the description of British English, or in teaching that DIALECT to foreigners. The BBC originally adopted RP for its announcers because it was the form of pronunciation most likely to be nationally understood, and to attract least regional criticism – hence the association of RP with the phrase 'BBC English'. These days, the BBC, as indeed educated speech at large, displays considerable regional variation, and many **modified** forms of RP exist. RP no longer has the prestigious social position it once held. In the eyes of many (especially of the younger generations), regionally marked forms of accent are more desirable. The present-day situation is plainly one of rapid change. See Gimson 1970: Ch. 6.

reciprocal (1) A term used in PHONETICS and PHONOLOGY as part of the classification of types of ASSIMILATION. In reciprocal (or 'coalescent') assimilation, each of two adjacent ARTICULATIONS influences the other. An example is the fusion of *d* and *j* to produce [ʤ] in such phrases as *could you*. See Gimson 1970: Ch. 11.

(2) In some models of GRAMMATICAL description, the term is used to refer to classes which express the meaning of mutual relationship, e.g. 'reciprocal PRONOUNS', such as *each other*, or 'reciprocal VERBS', such as *meet*. See Quirk *et al* 1972: Ch. 4.

reconstruct(-ion) A method used in HISTORICAL LINGUISTICS and COMPARATIVE PHILOLOGY in which a hypothetical SYSTEM of sounds or FORMS representing an earlier, non-extant state of a LANGUAGE ('PROTO-forms' in a 'proto-language') is established deductively from an analysis of the attested sounds and forms of extant TEXTS. This process of **comparative reconstruction** is dependent on the existence of good written records or several known related languages. When these do not exist, as in many African and American Indian languages, it is still possible to hypothesise about the historical development of the languages by analysing the STRUCTURAL regularities and irregularities of their contemporary states, and deducing UNDERLYING forms which might reflect earlier states – a process of 'internal reconstruction'. See Robins 1971: Ch. 8; Bolinger 1975: Ch. 13.

recursive(ness) A term used in GENERATIVE LINGUISTICS to refer to RULES which are capable of repeated application in generating a SENTENCE, and also to the STRUCTURES thus generated. There is no limit, for example, to the number of ADJECTIVES which may be used before a NOUN in English, or the number of ADVERBS which may MODIFY a VERB. Such sequences would be introduced by the repeated ('recursive') application of the appropriate adjective – or adverb – insertion rules in the relevant section of the GRAMMAR. The importance of the notion is that recursive rules are the main FORMAL means of accounting for the CREATIVITY OF LANGUAGE: by using this device, an infinite set of sentences can be generated from a finite set of rules. A simple illustration of how this can be formalised is in the following rules:

$$NP \rightarrow Det + N \; (+Prep \; Phrase)$$
$$Prep \; Phrase \rightarrow Prep + NP$$

These rules say, in effect, that there is in principle no limit to the number of PREPOSITIONAL PHRASES which may occur following a noun in a noun phrase, e.g. *the man in a coat on a bus with his wife*... See Akmajian & Heny 1975: Ch. 2; Huddleston 1976: Ch. 7.

reduced A term used in the PHONOLOGICAL classification of VOWEL sounds, referring to a vowel which can be analysed as a centralised VARIANT of a vowel in a related form (cf. CENTRE). For example, the pronunciation of /ɔv/ becomes /əv/ when unstressed; the STRESSED vowels in *'telegraph* become reduced in the related word *te'legraphy* /'telɔgrɑːf/ → /tə'legrəfɪ/. See Gimson 1970: Ch. 7; Bolinger 1975: Ch. 3.

redundancy A term derived from information theory and applied to the analysis of the range of features used in making LINGUISTIC contrasts. A feature (of sound, GRAMMAR, etc.) is redundant if its presence is unnecessary in order to identify a linguistic unit. For example, the contrast between the /p/ and /b/ PHONEMES of English, as in *pin* vs. *bin*, may be defined in terms of VOICING, muscular TENSION and ASPIRATION: but only one of these features is necessary to specify the contrast involved, and once this decision has been made (e.g. voicing), the other features would be seen as redundant, in respect of this contrast. Features of sound (grammar, MEANING) which are not considered redundant are DISTINCTIVE. It should be noted that circumstances may arise which will affect the GENERALITY of an analysis: for instance, in other positions in the word, other features may become less redundant (e.g. muscular tension in final position, as in such contrasts as *rip* vs. *rib*), and in some VARIETIES of speech (such as public speaking, or in very noisy situations) the speaker may need to use all the available features in order to be ACCEPTABLE or intelligible.

Similar principles apply to the analysis of grammar and SEMANTICS in terms of redundancy. In grammar, for example, SENTENCES such as *the boy sits* display redundancy, in that both the SUBJECT and the VERB are MARKED for singularity: in theory, it would be possible for English to use, e.g. *the boy sit* vs. *the boys sit* to keep a singular/plural distinction clear. In semantics, the issue is more complex: what to one person might appear a totally unnecessary (and hence redundant) use of a word or phrase, may to someone else provide an additional nuance, and thus be distinctive. In GENERATIVE linguistics, the notion of redundancy has been formalised in terms of RULES (**redundancy rules**) which simplify the form of descriptions. For example, in generative PHONOLOGY, when certain features of a SEGMENT are predictable (because of the occurrence of other features in some CO-OCCURRING segment), the specification of these features is unnecessary: such redundant feature specifications would be left blank in the UNDERLYING representation of MORPHEMES (the RULES subsequently involved in inserting the redundant features being referred to as 'LEXICAL redundancy rules' or MORPHEME STRUCTURE RULES).

Various mathematical methods are available to demonstrate the nature and extent of redundancy in linguistic analysis. See Lyons 1968: Ch. 2; Hyman 1975: Ch. 1.

reduplication (reduplicat-e, -ive) A term in MORPHOLOGY for a process of repetition whereby the form of a PREFIX/SUFFIX reflects certain PHONOLOGICAL characteristics of the ROOT. This process may be found in Greek, where the initial CONSONANT of the root is reduplicated in certain GRAMMATICAL CONTEXTS (PERFECTIVE forms), e.g. /'lu:o:/ (λύω) 'I loose' becomes /'leluka/ (λέλυκα) 'I have loosed'. In English, the nearest one gets to this is in 'reduplicative compound' words, such as *helter-skelter*, *shilly-shally*. See Matthews 1974: Ch. 7; Robins 1971: Ch. 5.

referent (referen-ce, -tial) (1) A term used in philosophical LINGUISTICS and SEMANTICS for the entity (object, state of affairs, etc.) in the external world to which a linguistic EXPRESSION refers; for example, the referent of the WORD *table* is the object 'table'. The term is found both as part of a two-term analysis of MEANING (e.g. words ~ things) and in three-term analyses (e.g. words ~ concepts ~ things). Several limitations in the notion of **referential meaning** have been pointed out, such as that several words have no obvious referents (e.g. *the*, *should*, *since*), and that the same referent may be referred to by several different linguistic expressions, none of which may be SYNONYMOUS (e.g. (pointing to a book) *that is a book/the answer/my authority/a disgrace...*). Other terms have been suggested in an attempt to avoid these limitations, e.g. DENOTATION, EXTENSION. In linguistics, care is usually taken to distinguish knowledge of the world from knowledge of language: the extralinguistic notion of 'reference' is contrasted with the intralinguistic notion of SENSE, a property arising from the meaning relations between LEXICAL ITEMS and SENTENCES. See Robins 1971: Ch. 1; Lyons 1977b: Ch. 7.

(2) In GRAMMATICAL analysis, the term **reference** is often used to state a relationship of identity which exists between grammatical UNITS, e.g. a PRONOUN 'refers' to a NOUN or noun PHRASE. When the reference is to an earlier part of the DISCOURSE, it may be called 'back-reference' (or ANAPHORA); correspondingly, reference to a later part of the discourse may be called 'forward-reference' (or CATAPHORA). See Quirk *et al* 1972: Ch. 10.

referential indices A term used in GENERATIVE GRAMMAR (since ASPECTS) to refer to markers attached to a set of items in a SENTENCE to show identity or difference of REFERENCE. For example, both the sentences (i) *The man kicked the man* and (ii) *The man kicked himself* could, on one analysis be derived from the same UNDERLYING structure *The man kicked the man*. To mark the difference, sentence (i) would be marked as *The man$_i$ kicked the man$_j$*, whereas (ii) would be *The man$_i$ kicked the man$_i$*. Items marked with the same referential index variable are CO-REFERENTIAL; with different indices they are 'non-co-referential'. See Huddleston 1976; Ch. 7.

reflexive(-ness, reflexiv-ity, -isation) (1) A term used in GRAMMATICAL description to refer to a VERB or CONSTRUCTION where the SUBJECT and the OBJECT relate to the same entity. English uses reflexive PRONOUNS to express this relationship (e.g. *he kicked **himself***), but the same verbal MEANING is often present without the pronoun (e.g. *I shaved (myself)*). Other LANGUAGES use a variety of FORMS for the expression of reflexive meaning, such as SUFFIXES, CASE endings and WORD order. In TRANSFORMATIONAL grammar, **reflexivisation** refers to a RULE which introduces the reflexive pronouns into a sentence – in one formulation by changing the syntactic feature on the object personal PRONOUN, from [−reflexive] to [+reflexive], when it is CO-REFERENTIAL with the subject, e.g. *he saw him → he saw himself*. See Lyons 1968: Ch. 8.

(2) **reflexiveness** ('reflectiveness' or 'reflexivity') is also a suggested defining property of human LANGUAGE (contrasting with the properties of other SEMIOTIC SYSTEMS) whereby language can be used to 'talk about' language. The development of this METALANGUAGE leads to the terminology and notation which this dictionary is attempting to elucidate. If a linguistic form is used as a CITATION FORM, it is said to be used 'reflexively', as in *The cat is a noun phrase*. See Lyons 1977b: Ch. 1.

register (1) A term used in PHONETICS to refer to the VOICE QUALITY produced by a specific physiological constitution of the LARYNX. Variations in the length, thickness and tension of the VOCAL CORDS combine to produce (in singing) the differences between soprano, contralto, tenor, bass, etc. voices, and also (within one person) such differences as between 'head' ('falsetto') and 'chest' voice. Some phoneticians use the term in a functional way in relation to speech, to refer to types of PHONATION which the speaker varies in a controlled manner (as in CREAKY and BREATHY voice). See Catford 1977: Ch. 6; Abercrombie 1967: Ch. 6.

(2) In STYLISTICS and SOCIOLINGUISTICS, the term refers to a VARIETY of LANGUAGE defined according to its use in social SITUATIONS, e.g. a register of scientific, religious, FORMAL English. In HALLIDAYAN linguistics, the term is seen as specifically opposed to varieties of language defined according to the characteristics of the user (*viz* his regional or class DIALECT), and is given a sub-classification into FIELD, MODE and MANNER of DISCOURSE. See Gumperz & Hymes 1971: Ch. 1; Lyons 1977b: Ch. 14.

regressive A term used in PHONETICS and PHONOLOGY as part of the classification of types of ASSIMILATION. In **regressive** (or 'anticipatory') **assimilation**, a sound changes because of the following sound, as when [t] becomes [p] in *hot pies*. It is opposed to PROGRESSIVE and COALESCENT assimilations. See Gimson 1970: Ch. 11.

regular(ity) A term referring to LINGUISTIC FORMS when they are in conformity with the general RULES of a LANGUAGE, i.e. they are predictable. In English, for example, NOUNS such as *boy*, *girl*, *dog* are regular, in that they follow the rules governing the majority of nouns (e.g. take plurals in *-s*); nouns such as *mouse* and *sheep* are 'irregular', or 'exceptions'. In TRADITIONAL GRAMMARS, the notion was interpreted MORPHOLOGICALLY, e.g. 'regular verbs' were those whose VARIANT forms were in the majority, for a given CLASS. In linguistics, the notion includes both SYNTACTIC and morphological predictability. In HISTORICAL language studies, regularity is a major explanatory principle, in that one attempts to show systematic CORRESPONDENCES between languages and STATES of a language, which can be formulated in general terms. COMPARATIVE PHILOLOGISTS called such general correspondences SOUND LAWS, and much controversy took place in the late 19th century, when it was argued (by the NEOGRAMMARIANS) that sound laws admitted no exceptions which could not be explained by reference to other laws. The attempt to deal with exceptions by seeing them as variants of a general rule (conditioned by regional, social, or

reiteration

other factors) is a major preoccupation of contemporary linguistics. See Lyons 1968: Ch. 1.

reiteration A term used in HALLIDAYAN analysis of the COHESIVE characteristics of LANGUAGE to refer to the repeated use of a LEXICAL ITEM, or the use of a SYNONYMOUS lexical item, as a means of linking the various parts of a TEXT. An example is the use of *car* and *monstrosity* in the sequence *John saw a car. The car was very old. 'What a monstrosity!' he said.* There are other means of lexical linkage, e.g. COLLOCATION. See Quirk *et al* 1972: Ch. 10.

relation(-s, -al) A general term used in PHONETICS and LINGUISTICS to refer to the linguistically significant connections between two or more ELEMENTS in a LANGUAGE, such as EQUIVALENCE, CONTRAST, inclusion, GOVERNMENT. In GRAMMATICAL analysis, for example, the FUNCTIONAL role which a NOUN has in relation to a VERB can be identified by using such terms as SUBJECT, OBJECT, AGENT, COMPLEMENT, etc. These 'relational' notions are central to some theories (e.g. CASE grammar, RELATIONAL grammar), and of marginal importance in others (e.g. ASPECTS-type grammars). In SEMANTICS, the correspondences between LEXICAL items of similar, opposed, etc. MEANINGS are referred to as **sense relations**, and classified under such headings as SYNONYMY and ANTONYMY. At the most general level, linguistic relations can be classified into SYNTAGMATIC and PARADIGMATIC types. See Lyons 1968: Ch. 1.

relational grammar A development of GENERATIVE LINGUISTIC thinking of the mid-1970s which takes as central the notion of GRAMMATICAL RELATIONS (such as SUBJECT and OBJECT), rather than the categorial terms of standard PHRASE-MARKERS (e.g. NP, VP). TRANSFORMATIONS in this view are operations performed on unordered DEPENDENCY networks of grammatical relations, modelled as dependency trees. At the time of writing, the approach has received little publication, and it is unclear how widespread its influence will be; what is evident is that it is in marked contrast with most other versions of generative grammar, where the emphasis is on SYNTACTIC CATEGORIES such as NP and VP, and on LINEAR ORDERING, syntactic relations being specifiable only derivatively. See Lyons 1977a: Ch. 8; Radford 1981: Ch. 4.

relative (relativisation) A term used in GRAMMATICAL DESCRIPTION to characterise PRONOUNS which may be used to introduce a POSTMODIFY-ING CLAUSE within a NOUN PHRASE, and by extension to the clause as a whole. **Relative pronouns** in English include *who, which, whom, whose*

and *that*, as used in such **relative clauses** as *the man who went was...*
In TRANSFORMATIONAL LINGUISTICS, the process of forming a relative
clause CONSTRUCTION is known as 'relativisation'. See Quirk *et al* 1972:
Ch. 13.

relativity A term used to identify an influential view of the relationship
between LANGUAGE and thought, generally known as **linguistic
relativity**, which asserts, in its strongest form, that language determines the way people perceive and organise their worlds. This view (of
'linguistic determinism') was first expounded by the German
ethnologist, Wilhelm von Humboldt (1767–1835); in this century it
came to be known as the SAPIR–WHORF HYPOTHESIS. See Clark & Clark
1977: Ch. 14: Bolinger 1975: Ch. 8.

release A term used in PHONETICS to refer to the type of movement made
by the VOCAL ORGANS away from a point of ARTICULATION, particularly
with reference to PLOSIVES. English plosives, for example, may be
released with or without ASPIRATION, or as a LATERAL or NASAL (as
in *button* and *bottle*).

In the DISTINCTIVE FEATURE approach to PHONOLOGY of CHOMSKY
& Halle DELAYED and INSTANTANEOUS types of release are recognised.
See Gimson 1970: Ch. 8; Hyman 1975: Ch. 2.

relexification A term used in SOCIOLINGUISTICS to refer to a theory
concerning the origins of, and relationships between, PIDGIN (and
CREOLE) LANGUAGES. The 'relexification hypothesis' proposes that the
range of English, French, Spanish, etc. pidgins is derived from the
first widely-used pidgin language, Portuguese Pidgin, in the 15th
century in West Africa, by a process whereby the GRAMMAR of this
language was retained, but new LEXICAL ITEMS were introduced from
the other European languages. This view, it is maintained, provides
a satisfactory explanation for the grammatical similarities noted
between pidgin languages, and for the many lexical similarities which
seem to derive from an original West African source or from
Portuguese (e.g. *savvy?* – possibly from *sabe* 'know'). See Trudgill
1974: Ch. 7.

re-ordering (1) A term often used within the framework of TRANS-
FORMATIONAL GRAMMAR to refer to a basic kind of transformational
operation. 'Re-ordering transformations' have the effect of moving
CONSTITUENTS (usually one at a time) from one part of a PHRASE-
MARKER to another, as in the formation of PASSIVE sentences, the
placement of NEGATIVES and AFFIXES. An alternative term is

repertoire

MOVEMENT or PERMUTATION. In some recent approaches this notion is broken down into the more basic operations of ADJUNCTION and DELETION. See Akmajian & Heny 1975: Ch. 7; Huddleston 1976: Ch. 12.

(2) The term is also used in transformational analysis of LINGUISTIC change, referring to differences in the HISTORICAL SEQUENCE of RULES which must be postulated in order to explain the divergences between DIALECTS, FORMS, etc. The matter has been discussed mainly with reference to PHONOLOGY, and various types of rule-ordering relationships have been suggested, e.g. the distinction between FEEDING and BLEEDING rule ordering. See Hyman 1975: Ch. 4.

repertoire (repertory) A term used in SOCIOLINGUISTICS to refer to the range of LANGUAGES or VARIETIES of a language available for use by a speaker, each of which enables him to perform a particular social role. The term may also be applied collectively to the range of LINGUISTIC varieties within a SPEECH community. See Bolinger 1975: Ch. 11; Gumperz & Hymes 1971: Ch. 14.

replacive A term sometimes used in MORPHOLOGY to refer to a MORPH postulated to account for such problematic internal ALTERNATIONS as *man* ∼ *men*, *take* ∼ *took*, etc. The 'replacive morph' would be stated as *a → e*, etc. – a 'solution' which recent morphological theory has generally discounted. See Matthews 1974: Ch. 7.

representation A term used, especially in GENERATIVE LINGUISTICS, to refer to the relationship of correspondence existing between the successive levels of analysis which are recognised in generating a SENTENCE. The DATA of LANGUAGE are 'represented' as a configuration of ELEMENTS at a given level, (e.g. 'SEMANTIC/PHONOLOGICAL/DEEP STRUCTURAL/SYSTEMATIC PHONETIC... representation' of a sentence), and the RULES of the grammar assign STRUCTURAL DESCRIPTIONS to these representations. For example, in a phonetic representation, an UTTERANCE is analysed in terms of a MATRIX where the various rows are labelled by phonetic FEATURES and the columns are successive SEGMENTS. See Huddleston 1976: Ch. 1.

representative A term used in the theory of SPEECH-ACTS to refer to a type of UTTERANCE where the speaker conveys his belief about the truth of a PROPOSITION, as in *I state/hypothesise*... See Clark & Clark 1977: Ch. 3.

resonance A term derived from the physics of sound, and used in ACOUSTIC PHONETICS to refer to those vibrations of air movement in the VOCAL TRACT which are set in motion by a source of PHONATION. The main 'resonance chambers' of the vocal tract are the mouth, nose and PHARYNX, and these CAVITIES, in their various shapes, act to strengthen some of the frequencies present in the source of sound, producing the range of human sounds. See Catford 1977: Ch. 4.

resonant A term used by some PHONETICIANS to refer to speech sounds produced at the GLOTTIS with a relatively wide articulatory channel, so that no subsequent audible friction is produced, e.g. VOWELS, LATERALS, NASALS, FRICTIONLESS CONTINUANTS. The analogous term in DISTINCTIVE FEATURE theory is SONORANT. In this respect, the category can be opposed to OBSTRUENT, where CLOSURE or narrowing is the essential characteristic. See Catford 1977: Ch. 8.

restricted (1) A term used by the sociologist, Basil Bernstein (b. 1924), to refer to one of two VARIETIES (or CODES) of LANGUAGE use, introduced as part of a general theory of the nature of social systems and social roles, the other being ELABORATED. **Restricted code** is used in relatively informal situations, stresses the speaker's membership of a group, is very reliant on CONTEXT for its meaningfulness (e.g. there will be several shared expectations and assumptions between the speakers), and lacks STYLISTIC range. Linguistically, it is highly predictable, with a relatively high proportion of such features as PRONOUNS, TAG QUESTIONS, and use of gestures and INTONATION to convey MEANING. Elaborated code, by contrast, lacks these features. The correlation of restricted code with certain types of social class background, and its role in educational settings (e.g. whether children used to this code will succeed in schools where elaborated code is the norm – and what should be done in such cases) has brought this theory considerable publicity and controversy. See Gumperz & Hymes 1971: Ch. 17; Trudgill 1974: Ch. 2.

(2) The phrase **restricted language** is used by some LINGUISTS (especially FIRTHIANS) to refer to a reduced linguistic SYSTEM used for a special communicative purpose, as in the language of heraldry, or air-traffic control. Alternatively, the notion may be characterised with reference to 'restricted CONTEXTS'. See Lyons 1968: Ch. 9.

restrictive A contrast recognised in the GRAMMATICAL analysis of PHRASES, referring to the relationship of a MODIFYING structure to its accompanying HEAD word. In 'restrictive' modification, the LIN-GUISTIC identity of the head is dependent upon the accompanying modification; if it is not, the modification being inessential, the term **non-restrictive** is used. The contrast is illustrated by the two meanings of the sentence *Look at John's black dog*; with the emphasis on *dog*, the implication is that John has one dog with him, which happens to be black (i.e. the modification is non-restrictive); but with the emphasis on *black*, the implication is that John has more than one dog with him, and our attention is being drawn to the black one (i.e. the blackness is crucial to the identity of the dog, and the modification is thus restrictive). Several areas of grammar illustrate this contrast, such as RELATIVE clauses, and APPOSITIONAL constructions. See Quirk *et al* 1972: Chs. 9, 13.

retract(ed) A term used in PHONETICS to refer to the backwards movement of an ARTICULATOR, especially the BACK of the TONGUE towards the velum. 'Retracted' sounds are heard in VELARISATION, or the CENTRALISATION of FRONT VOWELS. See Catford 1977: Ch. 9.

retroflex(-ion, -ed) A term used in the PHONETIC classification of CONSONANT sounds on the basis of their PLACE OF ARTICULATION: it refers to a sound made when the TIP of the TONGUE is curled back in the direction of the front part of the hard PALATE – in other words, just behind the ALVEOLAR ridge. The degree of **retroflexion** varies considerably between sounds and DIALECTS. The quality of *r* sounds traditionally associated with American English, and with many rural British English dialects (especially in the South-west) illustrate one main group of retroflex sounds, and this quality may also be heard on any VOWELS preceding a **retroflexed** *r* (the vowel is said to be '*r*-coloured' or 'rhotacised'), as the tongue may begin to move to a retroflex position while the vowel is still being articulated. Other common retroflex consonants are the retroflexed correlates of [t] and [d] – [ṭ] and [ḍ] – heard in many Indian LANGUAGES, such as Hindi, and also in the English spoken by NATIVE-SPEAKERS of such languages. [n], [l], [s] and [z] may also be retroflexed. See Gimson 1970: Ch. 4; Catford 1972: Ch. 8.

reversal A term used by some PSYCHOLINGUISTS to refer to a type of TONGUE-SLIP where two LINGUISTIC UNITS are interchanged, as when *rabbits and chickens* might become *chabbits and rickens*. Traditionally, such errors are referred to as METATHESES or spoonerisms. See Clark & Clark 1977: Ch. 7; Bolinger 1975: Ch. 12.

Revised Extended Standard Theory The name given to the revised version of the EXTENDED STANDARD THEORY, proposed by Noam CHOMSKY in the mid-1970s, following the adoption of the TRACE convention on the application of MOVEMENT RULES. See Radford 1981: Ch. 5.

rewrite-rule (rewriting rule) A type of RULE in GENERATIVE GRAMMAR, which takes the form X → Y. The symbol to the left of the arrow represents a single STRUCTURAL ELEMENT; the symbol to the right of the arrow represents a STRING of one or more elements; and the arrow is an instruction to replace (or 'expand') X by Y. Such rules are conventionally read as 'Rewrite X as Y'. See Lyons 1968: Ch. 6.

rheme (rhematic) In the PRAGUE SCHOOL approach to LINGUISTICS of recent years, the term rheme is distinguished from THEME, as part of an analysis of the INFORMATION structure of messages, within an overall theoretical framework known as FUNCTIONAL SENTENCE PERSPECTIVE. The rheme is defined as the part of a sentence which adds most to the advancing process of communication (it has the highest degree of COMMUNICATIVE DYNAMISM); in other words, it expresses the largest amount of extra MEANING, in addition to what has already been communicated. The theme, by contrast, carries the lowest degree of communicative dynamism. Various transitional expressions, neither 'thematic' or 'rhematic', are also recognised. See Lyons 1977b: Ch. 12; Bolinger 1975: Ch. 15.

rhythm An application of the general sense of this term in PHONOLOGY, to refer to the perceived regularity of PROMINENT UNITS in speech. These regularities may be stated in terms of patterns of STRESSED vs. unstressed SYLLABLES, syllable LENGTH (long vs. short) or PITCH (high vs. low) – or some combination of these variables. Maximally regular patterns, such as are encountered in many kinds of poetry, are referred to as 'metrical'. See Bolinger 1975: Ch. 3.

right-branching A term used in GENERATIVE GRAMMAR to refer to a CONSTRUCTION whose DERIVATION involves a series of structural operations which would be represented in increasing complexity of the right-hand side of a TREE diagram. The type of rule involved can be represented by X → Y + (X). For example, the phrase *the book of the wife of the major . . .* is a 'right-branching', or 'right recursive' structure; it contrasts with *the major's wife's book*, which is LEFT-BRANCHING, and also with the notion of SELF-EMBEDDING. See Lyons 1977a: Ch. 9.

rim The edges of the TONGUE, the extent of whose contact with the roof of the mouth can affect the quality of several sounds, such as [s] and [l]. See Gimson 1970: Ch. 2; Catford 1977: Ch. 9.

rising

rising/rise (1) A term used in classifying the LINGUISTIC uses of PITCH, referring to a movement from relatively low to relatively high. Rising tones of various kinds (e.g. 'high/low rising', 'rising–falling') may be encountered in the study of INTONATION systems and of TONE LANGUAGES. See Bolinger 1975: Ch. 3.

(2) A term used in a two-way classification of DIPHTHONGS, referring to cases where the second element of the diphthong receives the maximum PROMINENCE. See Gimson 1970: Ch. 7.

roll(ed) A term used in the PHONETIC classification of CONSONANT sounds on the basis of their MANNER OF ARTICULATION: also known as a 'rolled' consonant, or a TRILL, it refers to any sound made by the rapid tapping of one organ of articulation against another. (VOCAL CORD vibration is not included in such a definition.) Several DIALECTS of English use an ALVEOLAR rolled [r], as in Welsh and Scots. French and German are examples of languages where a UVULAR rolled [R] can be heard. See Gimson 1970: Chs. 4, 8; Catford 1977: Ch. 8.

root (1) A term often used in LINGUISTICS (and traditionally used in HISTORICAL LANGUAGE study) as part of a classification of the kinds of ELEMENT operating within the STRUCTURE of a WORD. A root is the BASE FORM of a WORD which cannot be further analysed without total loss of identity. Putting this another way, it is that part of the word left when all the AFFIXES are removed. In the word *meaningfulness*, for example, removing *-ing*, *-ful* and *-ness* leaves the root *mean*. Roots (sometimes referred to as 'radicals') may be classified in several different ways. They may be 'free' MORPHEMES, such as *mean* (i.e. they can stand alone as a word), or they may be 'bound' morphemes, such as *-ceive* (e.g. *receive, conceive, deceive*, etc.). From another point of view, roots are sometimes classified as 'simple' (i.e. compositionally unanalysable in terms of morphemes) or 'complex'/'compound' (i.e. certain combinations of simple root forms, as in *blackbird, careful*, etc.), though for the latter the term STEM is commonly used. From a SEMANTIC point of view, the root generally carries the main component of MEANING in a word. From a historical viewpoint, the root is the earliest form of a word, though this information is not relevant to a SYNCHRONIC analysis (and may not always coincide with the results of it). The term **root-inflected** is sometimes applied to a type of language where the INFLECTIONS affect the internal PHONOLOGICAL structure of the root, as in Arabic, where roots are defined as a sequence of CONSONANTS (CvCvC), and variation in the intervening VOWELS signals such GRAMMATICAL differences as present vs. past TENSE. By contrast, a language such as Chinese may be said to be

root-isolating, i.e. the root morphemes are invariable, and grammatical relationships are signalled by other means, such as WORD ORDER. See Matthews 1974: Ch. 3; Robins 1971: Ch. 5.

(2) The furthest back part of the TONGUE, opposite the PHARYNGEAL wall, not normally involved in the production of speech sounds. See Abercrombie 1967: Ch. 4.

(3) In GENERATIVE GRAMMAR, the term is sometimes used to refer to the topmost NODE in a TREE diagram. In recent TRANSFORMATIONAL linguistics, it also refers to a type of transformation which applies only to full SENTENCE STRUCTURE and not to EMBEDDED sentences. A **root transformation** applies in the formation of *yes/no* QUESTIONS, for instance, where only the main CLAUSE is affected (e.g. *He said that there was trouble* → *Did he say that there was trouble?*). See Huddleston 1976: Ch. 3.

rounding (round-ed) A term used in the classification of lip position in PHONETICS, referring to the visual appearance of the lips when they assume a **rounded** shape, as in the 'close rounding' of [u] and the more 'open rounding' of [ɔ]. Each of the VOWEL positions on the CARDINAL VOWEL diagram has both a rounded and an **unrounded** form, e.g. [i] vs. [y], [e] vs. [ø]. Lip position is in fact of particular PHONOLOGICAL significance in the analysis of vowel and SEMI-VOWEL qualities.

The opposition rounded/non-rounded has special status in CHOMSKY & Halle's DISTINCTIVE FEATURE theory of PHONOLOGY, where it handles variations in PLACE OF ARTICULATION (CAVITY features), specifying lip position. 'Rounded' sounds are defined articulatorily, as those produced with a narrowing of the lips, as in [w], [u], etc. Its opposite is **non-rounded,** referring to sounds produced without any such narrowing, as in English FRONT VOWELS. See Ladefoged 1975: Ch. 11; Gimson 1970: Ch. 2.

RP The usual abbreviation for RECEIVED PRONUNCIATION.

rule A term used in LINGUISTICS, and especially in GENERATIVE GRAMMAR, to refer to a formal statement of correspondence between linguistic ELEMENTS or STRUCTURES. In the case of **generative rules**, there is more involved than a set of descriptive statements summarising one's observations; generative rules are predictive, expressing a hypothesis about the relationships between SENTENCES which will hold for the LANGUAGE as a whole, and which reflect the NATIVE-SPEAKER'S COMPETENCE. A grammar, accordingly, is seen as a set of rules (REWRITE-RULES) which will generate all and only the grammatical sentences of a language. The rules may be sub-classified in terms of the COMPONENTS of the grammar in which they appear (e.g. 'phonological rules', 'syntactic rules', 'lexical rules'.

Several types of rules have been recognised. The most basic types are PHRASE-STRUCTURE rules, of the form $X \rightarrow Y$, and TRANSFORMATIONAL rules, of the form $A \Rightarrow B$, where A and B are STRINGS of structural elements. In *Syntactic Structures* (1957), a distinction was made between OPTIONAL and OBLIGATORY rules. Other types of rule commonly cited include RECURSIVE, GLOBAL, and VARIABLE rules. In later MODELS of generative grammar, the notion of a **rule schema** is introduced. This is a means of specifying a set of rules without having to list them individually, e.g. $S \rightarrow S^n$, where ^{n} refers to any number of sentences (greater than 1) that can be the result of this rule (as in CO-ORDINATE sentences, which may be of any length).

The linguistic sense thus contrasts with the traditional use of the term, where rules are recommendations for correct usage, as in 'a preposition is not to be used at the end of a sentence'. No PRESCRIPTIVE or PROSCRIPTIVE implication is present in the linguistic sense of 'rule'. See Akmajian & Heny 1975: Ch. 1; Huddleston 1976: Ch. 7.

rule features A term used in some MODELS of GENERATIVE grammar (cf. ASPECTS) to refer to one of the types of (BINARY) FEATURES which are contained in a LEXICAL entry (the others being INHERENT features and CONTEXTUAL features), and which provides information as to whether a lexical ITEM is exceptional with reference to the applicability of a non-lexical TRANSFORMATION (e.g. PASSIVISATION). This type of feature is symbolised as [−Passive], [−Equi], etc. If a rule does have lexical exceptions, it is said to be GOVERNED (otherwise ungoverned). See Huddleston 1976: Ch. 10; Akmajian & Heny 1975: Ch. 6.

S

🔳🔳🔳🔳🔳🔳

S The usual abbreviation for SENTENCE.

SAAD An abbreviation sometimes used to refer to the KERNEL SENTENCES GENERATED by a GRAMMAR – standing for SIMPLE–ACTIVE–AFFIRMATIVE–DECLARATIVE.

sandhi A term used in SYNTAX and MORPHOLOGY, to refer to the PHONOLOGICAL MODIFICATION of GRAMMATICAL FORMS which have been juxtaposed. The term comes from a Sanskrit word meaning 'joining'. **Sandhi forms** are forms which have undergone specific modifications in specific circumstances (i.e. various **sandhi rules** have applied). ASSIMILATION and DISSIMILATION are two widespread tendencies which could be classified under this heading. The merit of the sandhi notion is that it can be used as a very general term within which can be placed a wide range of structural tendencies that otherwise it would be difficult to inter-relate. In languages where sandhi forms are complex, a distinction is sometimes made between 'external sandhi' (sandhi RULES which operate across word boundaries) and 'internal sandhi' (rules which operate within words). See Matthews 1974: Ch. 6; Robins 1971: Ch. 5; Gumperz & Hymes 1971: Ch. 18.

Sapir–Whorf hypothesis A theory of the relationship between LANGUAGE and thought expounded in its most explicit form by the American anthropological linguists Edward Sapir (1884–1939) and Benjamin Lee Whorf (1897–1941). Also known as the theory of linguistic RELATIVITY, the hypothesis states (in the words of Whorf) that 'we dissect nature along lines laid down by our native languages...by the linguistic systems in our minds'. The differences in world-view imposed by different languages have however proved extremely difficult to elucidate or test experimentally, and the fact of successful BILINGUAL translation weakens the force of the theory's claims; as a result, the Sapir–Whorf hypothesis has made little impact on contemporary PSYCHOLINGUISTICS. See Clark & Clark 1977: Ch. 14; Bolinger 1975: Ch. 8.

Saussurean Characteristic of, or a follower of, the principles of Ferdinand de Saussure (1857–1913), especially as outlined in his posthumous *Cours de linguistique générale* (Paris 1913), translated by W. Baskin as *Course in General Linguistics* (New York 1959). His conception of LANGUAGE as a SYSTEM of mutually defining entities was a major influence on several schools of LINGUISTICS (e.g. the PRAGUE SCHOOL, GENEVA SCHOOL, GLOSSEMATICS), and most of the theoretical distinctions he introduced have become foundations of linguistic study. Chief among these are the notions of LANGUE and PAROLE, SYNTAGMATIC and PARADIGMATIC, SYNCHRONIC and DIACHRONIC, and SIGNIFIANT and SIGNIFIÉ. See Bolinger 1975: Ch. 15; Lyons 1977b: Ch. 8.

SC An abbreviation used in GENERATIVE GRAMMAR to refer to STRUCTURAL CHANGE.

scale-and-category grammar A LINGUISTIC theory devised by the British linguist, M. A. K. HALLIDAY in the early 1960s in which the STRUCTURE of LANGUAGE is seen as an intersecting set of SCALES and CATEGORIES operating at different LEVELS. Several levels of organisation are recognised. At the level of SUBSTANCE, the physical DATA of speech or writing are defined in PHONIC or GRAPHIC terms. The organisation of substance into linguistic CONTRASTS is carried out at the level of FORM: GRAMMAR and LEXIS being the two main sub-divisions. PHONOLOGY is seen as an 'inter-level' connecting the level of substance and form. CONTEXT is a further 'inter-level', connecting the level of form with the extralinguistic SITUATION. Linguistic analysis in this view proceeds by establishing four theoretical 'categories': UNITS, STRUCTURES, CLASSES and SYSTEMS, inter-relating these by the 'scales' of RANK, EXPONENCE and DELICACY. In the late 1960s, parts of this approach were superseded by a SYSTEMIC MODEL of analysis. See Robins 1971: Ch. 7.

schwa, shwa (pron. [ʃwɑ:]) The usual name for the NEUTRAL VOWEL [ə], heard in English at the beginning of such WORDS as *ago*, *amaze*, or in the middle of *afterwards*. It is a particularly frequent vowel in English, as it is the one most commonly heard when a STRESSED vowel becomes unstressed, e.g. *telegraph* becoming *telegraphy* /ˈtelǝgrɑːf/ vs. /tǝˈlegrǝfi/. It is also the usual pronunciation of the vowel in such words as *the, a, an, and*. The term 'schwa' comes from the German name of a vowel of this CENTRAL quality found in Hebrew. See Gimson 1970: Ch. 7.

SD An abbreviation used in GENERATIVE GRAMMAR to refer to STRUCTURAL DESCRIPTION.

secondary apertures One of the types of sound feature set up by CHOMSKY & Halle in their DISTINCTIVE FEATURE theory of PHONOLOGY, to handle variations in PLACE OF ARTICULATION (CAVITY features). It subsumes NASAL and LATERAL features, both defined as OPPOSITIONS. See Ladefoged: Ch. 11; Hyman 1975: Ch. 2.

secondary articulation In a sound produced with two points of ARTICULATION, this term refers to the point of articulation involving the lesser degree of STRICTURE, e.g. LABIALisation, PALATALisation. It is opposed to 'primary articulation'. See Catford 1977: Chs. 8, 10.

secondary response A term introduced into LINGUISTICS by Leonard BLOOMFIELD to refer to UTTERANCES a person makes about his LANGUAGE. The term includes not only the METALINGUISTIC utterances of linguistics, but also the loosely organised, yet fairly uniform system of popular pronouncements about language, e.g. 'bad grammar', 'correct pronunciation'. It is distinguished from 'primary' responses (the use of language as such) and TERTIARY RESPONSES (the evaluation of secondary responses). See Bolinger 1975: Ch. 16.

segment(-al, -ation, -ator) A term used in PHONETICS and LINGUISTICS to refer to any DISCRETE UNIT that can be identified, either physically or auditorily, in the stream of speech. 'Segmentation' can take place using either physical or auditory criteria: in the former case, ACOUSTIC or ARTICULATORY change-points can be identified as boundaries of segments; in the latter case, perceptible changes in QUALITY or QUANTITY, often showing the influence of the language's PHONEMIC UNITS, are the basis of division. The term is especially used in phonetics, where the smallest perceptible discrete unit is referred to as a PHONE.

A **segmentator** is a device used in instrumental phonetics which plays back a recording of speech at varying small time intervals, thus allowing a more detailed study of the segments produced.

In PHONOLOGY, a major division is often made into segmental and SUPRASEGMENTAL (or 'non-segmental') categories. **Segmental phonology** analyses the speech into distinctive units, or PHONEMES

(= 'segmental phonemes') which have a fairly direct correspondence with phonetic segments (alternative approaches involve analysis in terms of DISTINCTIVE FEATURES and PROSODIES). **Suprasegmental phonology** analyses those features of speech which extend over more than one segment, such as INTONATION or (in some theories) VOWEL harmony. In GENERATIVE phonology, segments are defined similarly, as the vowel–CONSONANT structure of the FORMATIVES found in SURFACE STRUCTURE.

The above terminology has been applied analogously to the study of written texts, where GRAPHS and GRAPHEMES are some of the segments identified. The term is also found in the analysis of higher linguistic units, such as MORPHEMES or WORDS, as in STRUCTURALIST analyses of GRAMMAR (cf. IMMEDIATE CONSTITUENT analysis). See Catford 1977: Ch. 11; Hyman 1975: Ch. 1; Bolinger 1975: Chs. 3, 15.

selectional features/restrictions/rules A term in GENERATIVE GRAM-MAR for a type of CONTEXTUAL FEATURE, i.e. a SYNTACTIC feature which specifies the conditions relating to where in a DEEP STRUCTURE a LEXICAL ITEM can occur. Selectional features specify the restrictions on the permitted combinations of lexical items within a given GRAMMATICAL context. These restrictions are stated with reference to the relevant INHERENT features in an adjacent or nearby COMPLEX SYMBOL (within the same structural unit, i.e. they must be CLAUSE-MATES). For example, a SUBJECT NOUN which requires an ANIMATE VERB (cf. *the stone slept*) would have the restriction stated as part of its feature specification, e.g. as [—[− Animate]]. See Huddleston 1976: Chs. 1, 10.

selective listening A term derived from the notion of selective attention in psychology, and used in PSYCHOLINGUISTICS to refer to the process whereby people are able to pick out certain aspects of a speech signal and to ignore others. The COCKTAIL PARTY PHENOMENON characterises the problem – how a person is able to attend selectively to one out of several simultaneously occurring conversations. Analysis of the factors which affect this ability (e.g. the SEMANTIC content of the conversations, the speed of the speech) suggests several conclusions which are of major importance in developing a theory of speech perception – for instance, that CONNECTED SPEECH cannot be perceived as a series of isolated SEGMENTS. See Clark & Clark 1977: Ch. 5.

self-embedding A term used in GENERATIVE GRAMMAR to refer to a CONSTRUCTION whose DERIVATION involves a series of structural operations which are of the form $X \rightarrow Y + (X) + Z$. Self-embedding constructions can be illustrated from RELATIVE CLAUSES, such as *The dog that the cat scratched ran away*. Here, the SENTENCE which UNDERLIES the relative clause (*the cat scratched the dog*) is embedded within the sentence *the dog ran away*. The process can continue indefinitely, but as Noam CHOMSKY has pointed out, the ACCEPTABILITY of this construction deteriorates with the number of self-embeddings, cf. *?The dog that the cat that the man bought scratched ran away*. These problems have stimulated considerable discussion concerning the psychological mechanisms that need to be assumed to explain linguistic behaviour, reference being made to alternative processes of sentence formation, such as RIGHT-BRANCHING and LEFT-BRANCHING constructions. See Lyons 1977a: Ch. 9.

semantics (semantic, -ity) A major branch of LINGUISTICS devoted to the study of MEANING in LANGUAGE. The term is also used in philosophy and logic, but not with the same range of meaning or emphasis as in linguistics. **Philosophical semantics** examines the relations between linguistic expressions and the phenomena in the world to which they refer, and considers the conditions under which such expressions can be said to be true or false, and the factors which affect the interpretation of language as used. Its history of study, which reaches back to the writings of Plato and Aristotle, in recent years includes the work of such philosophers and logicians as Charles Peirce (1839–1914), Rudolf Carnap (1891–1970) and Alfred Tarski (b. 1902), particularly under the heading of SEMIOTICS and the 'philosophy of language'. 'Logical' or 'pure' semantics is the study of the meaning of expressions in terms of logical systems of analysis, or calculi, and is thus more akin to formal logic or mathematics than to linguistics.

In linguistics, the emphasis is on the study of the semantic properties of natural languages (as opposed to logical 'languages'), the term 'linguistic semantics' often being employed to make the distinction clear (though this is not a convention needed in this dictionary, where the term 'semantics' will be used without qualification to refer to its linguistic sense). Different linguists' approaches to meaning none-theless illustrate the influence of general philosophical or psychological positions. The 'behaviourist' semantics of Leonard BLOOM-FIELD, for example, refers to the application of the techniques of the BEHAVIOURIST movement in psychology, restricting the study of meaning to only observable and measurable behaviour. Partly because of the pessimism of this approach, which concluded that semantics was not yet capable of elucidation in behavioural terms, semantics came to be much neglected in post-Bloomfieldian linguistics, and has received proper attention only since the 1960s.

Of particular importance here is the approach of **structural semantics**, which displays the application of the principles of STRUCTURAL linguistics to the study of meaning through the notion of **semantic relations** (SENSE or 'meaning' relations such as SYNONYMY and ANTONYMY). 'Semantic meaning' may here be used, in contradistinction to 'GRAMMATICAL meaning'. The linguistic structuring of 'semantic space' is also a major concern of GENERATIVE linguistics, where the term 'semantic' is widely used in relation to the grammar's organisation (one section being referred to as the **semantic component**) and to the analysis of SENTENCES (in terms of a **semantic representation**) and of LEXICAL ITEMS (in terms of **semantic features**). Other terms used to distinguish features of meaning in this and other theories include 'semantic MARKERS/DISTINGUISHERS/properties' and (in an unrelated sense to the above) 'semantic components' (cf. COMPONENTIAL). The **semantic feature hypothesis** (SFH) is an application of this notion in the study of language ACQUISITION, where the order of appearance of a child's lexical items is held to be governed by the type and complexity of the semantic FEATURES they contain.

Semantic field theory is an approach which developed in the 1930s; it took the view that the VOCABULARY of a language is not simply a listing of independent items (as the headwords in a dictionary would suggest), but is organised into areas, or FIELDS, within which words inter-relate and define each other in various ways. The words denoting colour are often cited as an example of a semantic field: the precise meaning of a colour word can only be understood by placing it in relation to the other terms which occur with it in demarcating the colour spectrum.

Other areas of semantics include the HISTORICAL study of word meanings (ETYMOLOGY), the SYNCHRONIC analysis of word USAGE (LEXICOLOGY), and the compilation of dictionaries (LEXICOGRAPHY). The term 'semantic' has many other uses, however. In the phrase **semantic differential**, it has in fact very little to do with linguistic semantics, being a technique devised by psychologists to find out the emotional reactions of speakers to lexical items, and thus suggest the main AFFECTIVE dimension in terms of which a language's concepts are organised. In the phrase **semantic triangle**, it refers to a particular MODEL of meaning proposed by C. K. Ogden (1889–1957) and I. A. Richards (1893–1979) in the 1920s, which claimed that meaning is essentially a three-fold relationship between linguistic FORMS, concepts and REFERENTS. In the phrase **procedural semantics**, it refers to an approach in PSYCHOLINGUISTICS which models the notion of 'sense' in terms of a set of mental operations that decide on the applicability of a lexical item to an entity, state of affairs, etc. And the term

semanticity has a much broader sense, being suggested as a very general defining property of language (and other SEMIOTIC SYSTEMS), *viz* the ability of the system to convey meaning, by virtue of the associative ties which relate the system's signals to features of the external world. See Lyons 1977b; Bolinger 1975: Chs. 7, 8; Clark & Clark 1977: Ch. 11.

seme A term used by some European LINGUISTS (e.g. Eugene Coseriu (b. 1921)), to refer to minimal DISTINCTIVE SEMANTIC FEATURES operating within a specific semantic FIELD, e.g. the various defining properties of *cups* vs. *glasses*, such as 'having a handle', 'made of glass'. In this approach, semes contrast with CLASSEMES, which are features of a much more general kind, e.g. *male/female*. See Lyons 1977b: Ch. 9.

sememe (sememic(s)) A term used in some SEMANTIC theories to refer to a minimal UNIT of MEANING. For some, a sememe is equivalent to the meaning of a MORPHEME; for others it is a FEATURE of meaning, equivalent to the notion of 'semantic COMPONENT' or 'semantic feature' in some theories. The term **sememics** is used as part of the description of strata in STRATIFICATIONAL GRAMMAR; the 'sememic stratum', which handles the SYSTEMS of semantic relationship between LEXICAL ITEMS, is here distinguished from the HYPERSEMEMIC stratum, at which is analysed the relationship between LANGUAGE and the external world. 'Semotactics', in this approach, involves the study of the SEQUENTIAL arrangement of sememes. See Bolinger 1975: Ch. 15.

semiotics (semiotic) The scientific study of the properties of signalling-systems, whether natural or artificial. In its oldest sense, it refers to the study within philosophy of sign and symbol systems in general (also known as 'semiotic', 'semology', 'semasiology', 'semeiology', 'significs'). In this approach, LINGUISTIC, psychological, philosophical and sociological characteristics of communicative systems are studied together. The philosophers Charles Peirce (1834–1914), Charles Morris (b. 1901) and later Rudolf Carnap (1891–1970) saw the field as divisible into three areas: SEMANTICS, the study of the relations between linguistic expression and the objects in the world which they refer to or describe; SYNTACTICS, the study of the relation of these expressions to each other; and PRAGMATICS, the study of the dependence of the meaning of these expressions on their users (including the social situation in which they are used).

In recent years, the study of semiotics has come to be applied to the analysis of patterned human COMMUNICATION in all its sensory modes, i.e. hearing, sight, taste, touch and smell. 'Semiotic' studies in this sense vary in the degree to which they have progressed: this emphasis has been taken up mainly by anthropologists, linguists, psychologists and sociologists. The branch of the subject which has received most study is the VOCAL-AUDITORY mode, primarily through the subjects of PHONETICS and LINGUISTICS. The study of visual communication is known as KINESICS. The study of touch behaviour (and associated phenomena, such as body orientation and distance between people) is often called PROXEMICS. Gustatory (taste) and olfactory (smell) systems of communication have received more study in relation to animal communication.

Particularly in Europe, semiotic (or 'semiological') analysis has developed as part of an attempt to analyse all aspects of communication as SYSTEMS of signals ('semiotic systems'), such as music, eating, clothes, dance, as well as language. In this area, the French writer, Roland Barthes (b. 1915), has exercised particular influence.

The extension of the subject to the analysis of animal systems of communication is known as ZOÖSEMIOTICS. See Lyons 1977b: Chs. 3, 4; Crystal 1969: Ch. 3.

semi-sentence A term used by some LINGUISTS to refer to SENTENCES whose GRAMMATICALITY or ACCEPTABILITY is doubtful, but where there is sufficient plausibility of interpretation to make one unhappy about a definite judgement of ungrammaticality. For example, in certain CONTEXTS (e.g. poetry) a sentence might seem acceptable, which elsewhere would be rejected as ungrammatical (e.g. the breaking of SELECTIONAL RULES in *all the moon long*...). See Quirk *et al* 1972: Ch. 1.

semi-vowel A term used in the classification of CONSONANT sounds on the basis of their MANNER OF ARTICULATION: it refers to a sound functioning as a consonant but lacking the PHONETIC characteristics normally associated with consonants (such as FRICTION or CLOSURE); instead, its QUALITY is phonetically that of a VOWEL, though occurring as it does at the MARGINS of a SYLLABLE, its DURATION is much less than that typical of vowels. The common examples in English are [w] and [j], as in *wet* and *yet* respectively. Some phoneticians refer to these sounds as a type of APPROXIMANT. See Gimson 1970: Chs. 4, 8; Ladefoged 1975: Ch. 9.

semology A major COMPONENT recognised in STRATIFICATIONAL GRAMMAR, comprising the stratal SYSTEMS of SEMEMICS and HYPERSEMEMICS (or SEMANTICS). The component deals with the statement of MEANINGS, both in terms of semantic FEATURES, and in terms of REFERENTIAL/COGNITIVE meaning. See Bolinger 1975: Ch. 15.

sense In SEMANTICS, this term is usually contrasted with REFERENCE, as part of an explication of the notion of MEANING. Reference, or DENOTATION, is seen as EXTRALINGUISTIC – the entities, states of affairs, etc. in the external world which a linguistic EXPRESSION stands for. Sense, on the other hand, refers to the SYSTEM of linguistic relationships (**sense relations**) which a LEXICAL ITEM contracts with other lexical items – the PARADIGMATIC relationships of SYNONYMY, ANTONYMY, etc., and the SYNTAGMATIC relationships of COLLOCATION. See Lyons 1977b: Ch. 7.

sentence The largest STRUCTURAL UNIT in terms of which the GRAMMAR of a LANGUAGE is organised. Innumerable definitions of sentence exist, ranging from the vague characterisations of TRADITIONAL grammar (such as 'the expression of a complete thought') to the detailed structural descriptions of contemporary LINGUISTIC analysis. Most linguistic definitions of the sentence show the influence of the American linguist Leonard BLOOMFIELD, who pointed to the structural autonomy, or independence, of the notion of sentence: it is 'not included by virtue of any grammatical construction in any larger linguistic form'. Recent research has attempted to discover larger grammatical units (of DISCOURSE, or TEXT), but so far little has been uncovered comparable to the sentence, whose constituent structure is stateable in FORMAL, DISTRIBUTIONAL terms.

Linguistic discussion of the sentence has focused on problems of identification, classification and generation. Identifying sentences is relatively straightforward in the written language, but is often problematic in speech, where INTONATION and PAUSE may give uncertain clues as to whether a sentence boundary exists. Classification of sentence structure proceeds along many different lines, e.g. the binary constituent procedures of IMMEDIATE CONSTITUENT analysis, or the HIERARCHICAL analyses of HALLIDAYAN and other grammars (sentences being seen as composites of CLAUSES, which in turn are analysed into PHRASES, etc.). In GENERATIVE grammar, likewise, there are several models of analysis for sentence structure, with competing views as to the direction in which a sentence DERIVATION should proceed. Certain analytic problems are shared by all approaches, e.g. how to handle ELLIPTICAL sentences (or 'sentence fragments'), such as *To town* (in answer to *Where are you going?*); how to handle cross-reference between sentences, such as *He's coming* ('sentence CONNECTIVITY'); and how to handle the 'minor', non-PRODUCTIVE sentence types in a language (e.g. *Yes, Please, How do you do?*).

Most analysts agree on the need to recognise a FUNCTIONAL classification of sentences into STATEMENT, QUESTION, COMMAND and EXCLAMATORY types. Most analyses also recognise some such classification of 'sentence patterns' into simple vs. complex or compound types, i.e. consisting of one SUBJECT-PREDICATE unit, as opposed to more than one. Whether one calls this subject-predicate unit a CLAUSE, a 'simple' sentence, or uses some other term depends on one's model of analysis – but something analogous to this unit emerges in all theories, e.g. NP + VP, ACTOR–ACTION–GOAL, Subject–Verb–Object. Likewise, the number of formal sentence types recognised, and how they are best defined, has been and remains controversial. Several linguists insist on making a systematic distinction between sentence (a theoretical unit, defined by a grammar) and UTTERANCE (a physical unit, a matter of speech production, or PERFORMANCE): in this view, utterances can be analysed in terms of sentences, but utterances do not 'consist of' sentences. See Palmer 1971: Ch. 2; Lyons 1968: Ch. 5; Quirk *et al* 1972: Ch. 2.

sequence (sequencing) An application of the general sense of this term in LINGUISTICS and PHONETICS, referring to the observable succession of UNITS in an UTTERANCE or TEXT. This sequence may be LINEAR, where the dependencies are made between successive, adjacent units (*the-big-cat-is...*), but it may involve non-linear relationships, as in AGREEMENT between WORDS which are separated by other STRUCTURES. Sometimes, a specific sequential correspondence is given a separate label, as in the traditional term 'sequence of TENSES', referring to the dependencies between tense forms in successive CLAUSES (e.g. *if he enters, he will win*, but not *...he had won*), or the 'sequencing' patterns analysed in dialogue (as in the greeting ritual in conversational openings). **Sequencing** is also occasionally used, especially in psychologically influenced studies, to refer to the influence successive structures exercise upon each other (as seen, for example, in the difficulty some language-disordered patients have in sequencing appropriately a set of linguistic units). This use is quite different from the term 'sequencing' in language teaching, where it refers to the order in which a graded series of items is presented to the learner. The structure of linguistic sequences constitutes the province of SYNTAGMATIC analysis. The term is often distinguished from the more abstract notion of ORDER. See Lyons 1968: Ch. 2; Gumperz & Hymes 1971: Ch. 12.

series A term used in PHONETICS and PHONOLOGY to refer to any set of CONSONANT sounds which has at least one phonetic FEATURE in common, and distinguished in terms of PLACE OF ARTICULATION. For example, the VOICED PLOSIVE 'series' includes [b] – [d] – [g], the nasal series [m] – [n] – [ŋ], etc. See Gimson 1970: Ch. 4.

SFH The usual abbreviation in language ACQUISITION studies for 'SEMANTIC FEATURE hypothesis'.

sharp One of the features of sound set up by JAKOBSON & Halle in their DISTINCTIVE FEATURE theory of PHONOLOGY, to help handle SECONDARY ARTICULATIONS – in this case, PALATALISATION. Sharp CONSONANTS are defined both ARTICULATORILY and ACOUSTICALLY, as sounds produced with the TONGUE being raised towards the hard PALATE during their articulation, and with a relatively wide area behind the stricture; there is a consequent greater intensity of some of the higher frequencies of the sound spectrum. All palatalised consonants are [+sharp]. Its opposite term is PLAIN, which lacks these features, and thus corresponds to the whole range of non-palatalised sounds. The feature is not used in the CHOMSKY & Halle system. See Hyman 1975: Ch. 2.

sibilant (sibilance) A term in the PHONETIC classification of sounds on the basis of MANNER OF ARTICULATION. It refers to a FRICATIVE sound made by producing a narrow, GROOVE-like STRICTURE between the BLADE of the TONGUE and the back part of the ALVEOLAR ridge. These sounds, such as [s] and [ʃ], have a high-frequency hiss characteristic. Sounds which lack this feature could be called 'non-sibilant'. See Ladefoged 1975: Chs. 7, 12.

sign (1) **(if-y, -iant, -ié, -ics, -ication)** Several restricted applications of this general term are found in philosophical and LINGUISTIC studies of MEANING, the former especially discussing the types of possible contrast involved in such notions as 'signs', 'symbols', 'symptoms' and 'signals'. Sometimes 'sign' is used in an all-inclusive sense, as when SEMIOTICS is defined as 'the science of signs' (or 'significs'). In linguistic discussion, the most widespread sense is when linguistic EXPRESSIONS (WORDS, SENTENCES, etc.) are said to be 'signs' of the entities, states of affairs, etc. which they stand for (or, often, of the concepts involved). This relationship between sign and thing, or sign and concept, is traditionally known as 'signification'. The term **linguistic sign** is often used when a distinction is needed with other categories of sign (e.g. visual, tactile). The Swiss linguist, Ferdinand de SAUSSURE, introduced a terminological distinction which has exercised a major influence on subsequent linguistic discussion: **signifiant** (or 'signifier', or 'significans') was contrasted with **signifié** (or 'concept signified', 'significatum'), and the ARBITRARINESS of the relationship between the FORM and MEANING of signs was emphasised. See Lyons 1977b: Ch. 4.

(2) In such phrases as **sign language** and **sign system**, the term has a very restricted sense, referring to the system of manual communication devised by certain groups as an alternative to ORAL communication. Such groups include policemen (in traffic control), divers, monks vowed to silence, television studio directors, and so on; but the main application of the term is in relation to the deaf, where the claimed linguistic properties of the various natural and contrived deaf sign languages (e.g. American Sign Language, British Sign Language, Paget–Gorman Sign System) began to receive systematic investigation by linguists in the 1970s. See Clark & Clark 1977: Ch. 14.

(3) A more restricted sense of **significant** is found in linguistics, referring to the linguistic status of a spoken or written FEATURE: a feature is significant if it is CONTRASTIVE, i.e. where by substituting it for another feature, a difference in meaning is obtained. For example, the distinction between VOICED and voiceless is significant for many English CONSONANTS; WORD ORDER is significant in many types of SENTENCE. See Lyons 1968: Ch. 2.

simple A term sometimes used in GRAMMATICAL classification, especially of VERB FORMS, referring to the unMARKED member of an OPPOSITION, e.g. 'simple present' = the non-PROGRESSIVE ASPECT of the present TENSE form (as in *I go*); 'simple tense' = a VERB without any AUXILIARIES (as in *I take/took*); 'simple past' = the past tense form of the verb without auxiliary modification (as in *I took*). The term tends to be avoided in contemporary LINGUISTICS, because of its undesirable psychological associations, but the oppositions between simple and complex/compound SENTENCES (*viz* whether containing one CLAUSE or more than one), and simple and compound/complex PREDICATES (*viz* a predicate consisting wholly of a verb) are sometimes used. See Quirk *et al* 1972: Chs. 3, 7.

simplicity (metric) A measure proposed by GENERATIVE LINGUISTIC theory which would automatically assign factors to competing linguistic analyses that would determine which of them was the most satisfactory. Simplicity is here defined quantitatively, in terms of the number of constructs (symbols, RULES, etc.) used in formulating an analysis; this is also often referred to as an ECONOMY measure. Perhaps the most widespread criterion is the number of FEATURES required in order to state a PHONOLOGICAL GENERALISATION, and much thought has been given by generative phonologists to ways in which such generalisations can be more economically stated, using various kinds of notational abbreviation, e.g. ALPHA notation. But the measure relies on a notion of simplicity which still requires much theoretical and methodological elucidation. It is proving extremely difficult to evaluate simultaneously the many variables entering into an analysis, especially the closer that analysis gets to the language as a whole. A simplification made in one part of the analysis may lead to unexpected consequences, in terms of greater complexity (or COST) elsewhere. There is also the regular possibility that adult NATIVE-SPEAKERS, and children learning a language, will not always prefer the simpler of the two solutions; and little progress has been made in relating simplicity to other aspects of intuitive evaluation, such as NATURALNESS. Simplicity, then, and its FORMALISATION, remains a controversial topic. See Hyman 1975: Ch. 4.

single-base A type of TRANSFORMATIONAL RULE recognised in early MODELS of GENERATIVE GRAMMAR, where the rule operates with an input of one TERMINAL STRING. Single-base transformations are also known as SINGULARY transformations, and are opposed to DOUBLE-BASE types, where more than one string is involved. See Lyons 1968: Ch. 6.

singulary A type of TRANSFORMATIONAL RULE recognised in early MODELS of GENERATIVE GRAMMAR, where the rule operates with an input of one TERMINAL STRING. Singulary, or SINGLE-BASE transformations are contrasted with GENERALISED types, where more than one string is involved. See Lyons 1968: Ch. 6.

situation(al) In LINGUISTICS, this term is generally used to refer to the EXTRALINGUISTIC setting in which an UTTERANCE takes place – referring to such notions as number of participants, level of FORMALITY, nature of the ongoing activities, and so on. Linguistics emphasises the need to study LANGUAGE in its situation (or CONTEXT, or **context of situation**), for a full statement of MEANING to be obtained. SOCIO-LINGUISTICS is primarily concerned to correlate systematic variations in language with variations in social situation; and the term 'situation' may be used in a restricted sense to refer to the socially distinctive characteristics of the setting in which language is used. The **situational**

meaning of an utterance, in this sense, would be equivalent to its sociolinguistic interpretation, e.g. religious, political, informal 'situations'. See Lyons 1968: Ch. 7; 1977b: Ch. 12.

slit A term used by some PHONETICIANS to refer to a type of FRICATIVE where air is released over the surface of the ARTICULATORS through a narrow, horizontal opening. Such fricatives (e.g. [f], [θ], [ç]) are contrasted with GROOVE fricatives, where a hollowing of the active articulator is involved (e.g. [s], [ʃ]). See Dinneen 1967: Ch. 2.

slot A term used in GRAMMATICAL analysis to refer to a place in a CONSTRUCTION into which a CLASS of ITEMS can be INSERTED. For example, in the SENTENCE *The children – home*, the 'slot' marked by the dash can be 'filled' by *came, are, went*, etc. – a sub-class of VERBS. Approaches characterised by this emphasis are sometimes referred to as **slot-and-filler** MODELS. The analysis of SENTENCE STRUCTURE in terms of slots is a major feature of TAGMEMIC grammar, where the notion is used to identify the filler items (e.g. 'SUBJECT slot', 'OBJECT slot'). See Bolinger 1975: Chs. 6, 15.

sociolect A term used by some SOCIOLINGUISTS to refer to a linguistic VARIETY (or 'lect') defined on social (as opposed to regional) grounds, e.g. correlating with a particular social class, or occupational group. See Bolinger 1975: Ch. 11.

sociolinguistics A branch of LINGUISTICS which studies all aspects of the relationship between LANGUAGE and society. 'Sociolinguists' study such matters as the linguistic identity of social groups, social attitudes to language, STANDARD and non-standard forms of language, the patterns and needs of national language use, social VARIETIES and LEVELS of language, the social basis of MULTILINGUALISM, and so on. An alternative name for the subject (which suggests a greater concern with sociological rather than linguistic explanations of the above) is the **sociology of language**.

The term overlaps to some degree with ETHNOLINGUISTICS and ANTHROPOLOGICAL LINGUISTICS, reflecting the overlapping interests of the correlative disciplines involved – sociology, ethnology and anthropology. The study of DIALECTS is sometimes seen as a branch of sociolinguistics, and sometimes differentiated from it, under the heading of DIALECTOLOGY, especially when regional dialects are the focus of study. **Sociological linguistics** is sometimes differentiated from sociolinguistics, particularly in Europe, where the term reflects a concern to see language as an integral part of sociological theory. See Gumperz & Hymes 1972: Intro.; Bolinger 1975: Ch. 11.

soft consonant An impressionistic term sometimes used in the PHO-NETIC descriptions of particular LANGUAGES, referring to a CONSONANT which is PALATALISED. Russian is a language which has several such soft (as opposed to HARD) consonants. In Russian the ь symbol ('soft sign') marks the palatalisation (or 'softening') of the preceding consonant. See Ladefoged 1975: Ch. 7.

sonagraph (sonagram) The commercial name of the most widely used model of sound SPECTROGRAPH, its visual displays being referred to as 'sonagrams' (cf. 'spectrograms'). See Catford 1977: Ch. 12.

sonorant One of the major class features of sound set up by CHOMSKY & Halle in their DISTINCTIVE FEATURE theory of PHONOLOGY, to handle variations in MANNER OF ARTICULATION. Sonorant sounds are defined articulatorily, as those produced with a relatively free air flow, and a VOCAL CORD position such that spontaneous VOICING is possible, as in VOWELS, LIQUIDS, NASALS and LATERALS. Its opposite is **non-sonorant** (or OBSTRUENT), referring to sounds where there is a stricture impeding the air flow, as in PLOSIVES, FRICATIVES and AFFRICATES. An analogous term is RESONANT. See Ladefoged 1975: Ch. 11; Hyman 1975: Ch. 2.

sonority (sonorous) A term in AUDITORY PHONETICS for the overall LOUDNESS of a sound relative to others of the same PITCH, STRESS and DURATION. Sounds are said to have an 'inherent sonority', which accounts for the impression of a sound's 'carrying further', e.g. [s] carries further than [ʃ], [a] further than [i]. The notion has also been used in attempts to define the SYLLABIC STRUCTURE of UTTERANCES. It is, however, very difficult to define sonority objectively, and analyses involving this notion are usually somewhat controversial. See Ladefoged 1975: Ch. 10.

spectrograph (spectrogram) An instrument used in ACOUSTIC PHONE-TICS which provides a visual representation of the acoustic features that constitute the sounds in an UTTERANCE. The 'sound spectrograph' produces a three-dimensional visual record, or 'spectrogram', of an utterance, in which time is displayed horizontally, frequency vertically, and intensity by the relative blackness of the marks, on a sheet of sensitised paper. See Ladefoged 1975: Ch. 8.

sound change/law/shift Terms used in HISTORICAL LANGUAGE studies to describe the changes in a language's SOUND SYSTEM over a period of time. Many types of **sound change** have been recognised, e.g. whether the change affects the total number of PHONEMES (as when two phonemes MERGE into one, or one phoneme splits into two) or affects only the ALLOphones of a phoneme. Particular attention is paid to the nature of the ENVIRONMENTS which can be shown to restrict (or 'condition') the sound change. When a series of related sound changes take place at a particular stage of a language's history, the change is known as a **sound shift,** e.g. a VOWEL shift (as took place between Middle and Early Modern English – the Great Vowel Shift) or a CONSONANT shift (as in several of the changes between Latin and English). A regular series of changes is traditionally referred to in COMPARATIVE PHILOLOGY as a **sound law** – one hypothesis about such 'laws' (the NEOGRAMMARIAN hypothesis) being that they had no exceptions, i.e. at a given time, all WORDS containing a sound in a given PHONETIC environment would change in the same way, and any which did not could be explained by reference to a further law. Several apparent exceptions to the initial statement of such laws came to be explained by investigations which were carried out working on this premise. See Robins 1971: Ch. 8; Lyons 1968: Ch. 1.

sound-symbolism A term used in SEMIOTICS to refer to a direct association between the FORM and the MEANING of LANGUAGE: the sounds used reflect properties of the external world, as in cases of onomatopoeia (e.g. *cuckoo, murmur, crash*) and other forms of SYNAESTHESIA (e.g. *sl-* in such words as *slimy, slither*). See Robins 1977: Ch. 1.

sound system A term for the network, or SYSTEM, of PHONETICALLY REALISED CONTRASTS which constitute the PHONOLOGY of a LANGUAGE, DIALECT, etc. See Gimson 1970: Ch. 5.

source feature One of the five main dimensions of classification in CHOMSKY & Halle's DISTINCTIVE FEATURE theory of PHONOLOGY (the others being MAJOR CLASS FEATURES, CAVITY features, MANNER OF ARTICULATION features, and PROSODIC features). The term subsumes the feature OPPOSITIONS of HEIGHTENED SUBGLOTTAL PRESSURE, VOICE and STRIDENT. See Hyman 1975: Ch. 2; Ladefoged 1975: Ch. 11.

specialisation A suggested defining property of SEMIOTIC SYSTEMS, such as human LANGUAGE, referring to the extent to which the use of a signal and the behaviour it evokes are directly linked. Animal communication is said to lack specialisation, in that a signal triggers a behaviour; language, by contrast, is highly specialised, as the behavioural consequences of using a LINGUISTIC signal are less predictable (and often unpredictable). See Lyons 1977b: Ch. 3.

speech For the most part, the term is used in LINGUISTICS in its everyday sense, providing the subject with its primary DATA. There are two main interpretations of this data, which are complementary, rather than opposed. One interpretation is from the viewpoint of PHONETICS: here, speech is seen as a MEDIUM of transmission for LANGUAGE – the **spoken medium** or PHONIC SUBSTANCE of language (as opposed to writing). It is in this context that the term is used as part of the label for the many devices available in instrumental phonetics, e.g. the **speech stretcher** (which presents a slowed but otherwise undistorted recording of speech), or the **speech synthesiser** – a device which simulates the speech production process, either ARTICULATORILY (by modelling the VOCAL TRACT) or ACOUSTICALLY (using electronics), and, to the degree that it is successful, demonstrates the accuracy of the phonetician's analyses of speech production processes.

The other interpretation is from the viewpoint of linguistics, where **spoken language** (PERFORMANCE, or PAROLE) can be analysed in PHONOLOGICAL, GRAMMATICAL and SEMANTIC, as well as phonetic, terms. It is in this sense that terms such as **speech community** are used, referring to any regionally or socially definable human group identified by a shared linguistic SYSTEM. The term **speech-act**, also, has a more abstract sense than its name suggests: it is not in fact an 'act of speaking', but the activity which the use of language performs or promotes in the listener (respectively, the ILLOCUTIONARY force and PERLOCUTIONARY effect of the language). Similarly, the **speech event** is seen as the basic unit for the analysis of spoken interaction, i.e. the emphasis is on the role of the participants in constructing a DISCOURSE of verbal exchanges.

In recent years, phonetics and PSYCHOLINGUISTICS have come to pay increasing attention to constructing MODELS of the neurophysiological mechanisms hypothesised to underlie speech behaviour. In this respect, two main branches of speech analysis have developed: **speech production**, involving the planning and execution of acts of speaking; and **speech perception**, involving the perception and interpretation of the sound sequences of speech. The term **speech recognition** (or **speech reception**) is used to identify the initial stage of the decoding process involved in speech perception – and also to the automatic decoding of speech by machine. The whole activity of the perception and production of speech is known as **speech processing**. See Clark

speech

& Clark 1977: Chs. 5–7; Bolinger 1975: Chs. 2, 11; Gumperz & Hymes 1971: Intro.

speech(-)act A term derived from the work of the philosopher J. L. Austin (1911–60), and now used widely in LINGUISTICS, to refer to a theory which analyses the role of UTTERANCES in relation to the behaviour of speaker and hearer in interpersonal communication. It is not an 'act of speech' (in the sense of PAROLE), but a communicative activity, defined with reference to the intentions of the speaker while speaking (the ILLOCUTIONARY force of his utterances) and the effects he achieves on his listener (the PERLOCUTIONARY effect of his utterances). Several categories of speech-act have been proposed, *viz* DIRECTIVES (the speaker tries to get the listener to do something, e.g. begging, commanding, requesting), COMMISSIVES (the speaker commits himself to a future course of action, e.g. promising, guaranteeing), EXPRESSIVES (the speaker expresses his feelings, e.g. apologises, welcomes, sympathises), DECLARATIONS (the speaker's utterance brings about a new external situation, e.g. christening, marrying, resigning), and REPRESENTATIVES (the speaker conveys his belief about the truth of a PROPOSITION, e.g. asserts, hypothesises). The verbs which are used to indicate the speech-act intended by the speaker are sometimes known as PERFORMATIVE verbs. The criteria which have to be satisfied in order for a speech-act to be successful are known as FELICITY CONDITIONS. See Lyons 1977b: Ch. 16; Clark & Clark 1977: Chs. 1, 3.

spread(ing) A term in the classification of lip position in PHONETICS, referring to the visual appearance of the lips when they are held fairly close together and stretched sideways, as in a slightly open smile. Lip-spreading is noticeable in CLOSE VOWELS, as in the [i] of *see*, and is contrasted with NEUTRAL, OPEN and ROUNDED lip positions. See Gimson 1970: Ch. 2.

squish A term introduced into LINGUISTIC analysis by the American linguist John Robert Ross (b. 1938) in the early 1970s, as part of his notion of NONDISCRETE GRAMMAR: it refers to a continuum along which LEXICAL ITEMS can be placed, the poles being VERB and NOUN. Lexical items are seen as displaying degrees of verb-ness or noun-ness and SYNTACTIC RULES are seen as applying with varying PRODUCTIVITY to different parts of the continuum. For example, nouns used as PREMODIFIERS in noun PHRASES fall between the CLASSES of noun and ADJECTIVE (e.g. *the railway station, the town clock*), in that some but not all rules which apply to nouns can be used (cf. *the town's clock, *the towns* *clock*, etc.). What remains unclear, in this approach, is the extent to which these cases are sufficiently different from other problems of classification to warrant a radical reformulation of linguistic theory. See Radford 1981: Ch. 3.

standard(isation) A term used in SOCIOLINGUISTICS to refer to a prestige VARIETY of LANGUAGE used within a SPEECH COMMUNITY. 'Standard languages/dialects/varieties' cut across regional differences, providing a unified means of communication, and thus an institutionalised NORM which can be used in the mass-media, in teaching the language to foreigners, and so on. Linguistic FORMS or DIALECTS which do not conform to this norm are then referred to as **sub-standard** or (with a less pejorative prefix) **non-standard** – though neither term is intended to suggest that other dialect forms 'lack standards' in any linguistic sense. The natural development of a standard language in a speech community (or an attempt by a community to impose one dialect as a standard) is known as 'standardisation'. See Bolinger 1975: Chs. 11, 16; Trudgill 1974: Ch. 1.

standard theory/model A term used in GENERATIVE LINGUISTICS to refer to the MODEL of generative GRAMMAR proposed by Noam CHOMSKY in his 1965 book, *Aspects of the Theory of Syntax*. The importance of this formulation is such that, despite extensive subsequent modifications and alternatives provided by Chomsky and others, it is still viewed by many as the main statement concerning the aims and form of a TRANSFORMATIONAL GRAMMAR. It is usually contrasted with the EXTENDED STANDARD THEORY developed by Chomsky in later modifications of his own work, the REVISED EXTENDED STANDARD THEORY, and the various 'non-standard' versions of generative grammar (e.g. GENERATIVE SEMANTICS), which differ radically from the Aspects model. See Lyons 1977a: Ch. 8.

starred form A term used in LINGUISTICS to refer to a linguistic CONSTRUCTION that is unACCEPTABLE or unGRAMMATICAL, and marked thus by the use of an initial asterisk, e.g. **a boys have gone*. The term ASTERISKED FORM is an alternative. In HISTORICAL linguistics, starred forms indicate historical RECONSTRUCTIONS, the forms cited not being attested in any written records. See Robins 1971: Ch. 8; Bolinger 1975: Ch. 13.

state A term used in LINGUISTICS to refer to the condition of a LANGUAGE at a hypothetical point or period of time, e.g. Middle English, 16th statement

century, 1920s. States of languages (cf. ÉTAT DE LANGUE) thus constitute the subject-matter of SYNCHRONIC linguistics. See Lyons 1968: Ch. 1.

statement A term used in the classification of SENTENCE FUNCTIONS, and defined sometimes on GRAMMATICAL and sometimes on SEMANTIC or SOCIOLINGUISTIC grounds. SYNTACTICALLY, a statement is a sentence which contains a SUBJECT occurring before a VERB, e.g. *The man is coming.* Semantically, it is used primarily to convey information. The term is usually contrasted with three other major sentence functions: QUESTION, COMMAND, EXCLAMATION. In grammatical discussion, statements are usually referred to as DECLARATIVE or INDICATIVE in form. See Quirk *et al* 1972: Ch. 7; Lyons 1977b: Ch. 1.

statistical linguistics A branch of LINGUISTICS which studies the application of statistical techniques in linguistic theory and description. The study includes the analysis of frequency and DISTRIBUTION of linguistic UNITS in TEXTS with the aim of identifying the DISTINCTIVE characteristics of the speaker or writer (as in STYLOstatistics); but attempts have also been made to establish general laws concerning the statistical characteristics of languages, e.g. the relationship between WORD types (e.g. the word *up*) and word tokens (e.g. the number of instances of the word *up* in a sample), the relative frequency of ITEMS in different samples, the quantification of such notions as REDUNDANCY in statistical terms, and so on. See Lyons 1968: Ch. 2.

stative (stat-ivity, -ic) A term used in GRAMMATICAL classification, referring to one of two main ASPECTUAL categories of VERB use, the other being DYNAMIC. The distinguishing criteria for 'stativity' are mainly SYNTACTIC: for example, 'stative' or 'static' verbs do not usually occur in a PROGRESSIVE form (e.g. **I am knowing, *He is concerning*), nor in the IMPERATIVE (e.g. **know!*). On SEMANTIC grounds, they can be said to express states of affairs, rather than actions, i.e. the expression of relational processes (e.g. *be, belong to, involve, seem*) or of inactive perceptual or cognitive processes (e.g. *know, mean, realise, suppose*). The classification is complicated by the existence of verbs which have both a static and a dynamic use, e.g. *smell.* See Quirk *et al* 1972: Ch. 3; Lyons 1968: Chs. 7, 8.

stem A term often used in LINGUISTICS as part of a classification of the kinds of ELEMENTS operating within the structure of a WORD. The stem may consist solely of a single ROOT MORPHEME (i.e. a 'simple' stem, as in *man*), or of two root morphemes (i.e. a 'compound' stem, as in *blackbird*), or of a root morpheme plus a DERIVATIONAL AFFIX (i.e. a 'complex' stem, as in *manly, unmanly, manliness*). All have in common the notion that it is to the stem that inflectional affixes are attached. See Matthews 1974: Ch. 3; Robins 1971: Ch. 5.

stop A term used in the PHONETIC classification of speech sounds on the basis of their MANNER OF ARTICULATION. It refers to any sound which is produced by a complete CLOSURE in the VOCAL TRACT, and thus traditionally includes the class of PLOSIVES. Both NASAL and ORAL sounds can be classified as stops, though the term is usually reserved for the latter. A distinction is sometimes made between 'simple' and 'complex' stops, depending on whether the closure is made at one place or at two places simultaneously (e.g. the [gb] COARTICULATION heard in some African languages, or CONSONANTS produced with a simultaneous GLOTTAL stop). Other classifications of stop consonants involve taking into account the direction of air flow, whether INGRESSIVE or EGRESSIVE: 'ingressive stops' are often referred to as **suction stops**, 'egressive stops' as **pressure stops**.

In the DISTINCTIVE FEATURE theory of PHONOLOGY, the term 'stop' is sometimes used in opposition to CONTINUANT. See Ladefoged 1975: Chs. 3, 7, 11, 12.

stratificational (strat-um, -al) A LINGUISTIC theory devised by the American linguist Sydney M. Lamb (b. 1929), as expounded initially in *Outline of Stratificational Grammar* (1962), which models LANGUAGE as a SYSTEM of several related layers (or 'strata') of STRUCTURE. Six strata are recognised for English and many other languages: the component of PHONOLOGY comprises the HYPOPHONEMIC (or PHONETIC) and PHONEMIC strata; GRAMMAR comprises the MORPHEMIC and LEXEMIC strata; and SEMOLOGY comprises the SEMEMIC and HYPERSEMEMIC (or SEMANTIC) strata. Each stratum is organised in terms of a set of 'stratal systems', and each system deals with an aspect of linguistic structure which has to be stated independently of the structures operating at other strata. Two types of PATTERNING are recognised: TACTIC analysis (the patterns of sequential arrangement within each stratum) and REALISATIONAL analysis (the relationship between UNITS operating at higher and lower LEVELS between strata). A parallel terminology is used for each stratum: there is a 'hypophonemic / phonemic / morphomemic / lexemic / sememic / hypersememic' system consisting of various structural patterns (e.g. 'hypophonotactic/phonotactic', etc.), defined in terms of 'hypophonemes/phonemes', etc., and realised as 'hypophons/phons/morphons/lexons', etc. See Bolinger 1975: Ch. 15.

stress(ed) A term used in PHONETICS to refer to the degree of force used in producing a SYLLABLE. The usual distinction is between **stressed** and **unstressed** syllables, the former being more PROMINENT than the latter (and marked in TRANSCRIPTION with a raised vertical line, [']). The prominence is usually due to an increase in LOUDNESS of the stressed syllable, but increases in LENGTH and often PITCH may contribute to the overall impression of prominence. In popular usage, 'stress' is usually equated with an undifferentiated notion of 'emphasis' or 'strength'.

From the viewpoint of PHONOLOGY, the main function of stress is to provide a means of distinguishing degrees of emphasis or contrast in SENTENCES (**sentence stress**), as in *the **big** man looks angry*; the term **contrastive stress** is often used for this function. Many pairs of WORDS and word sequences can also be distinguished using stress variation (**lexical stress** or **word stress**), as in the contrast between *an increase in pay is needed* and *I'm going to increase his pay* – /'ɪŋkriːs/ vs. /ɪŋ'kriːs/ – or the distinction between *'black 'bird* and *'blackbird*. The analytical question here, which has attracted a great deal of attention in recent years, is how many degrees of stress need to be recognised in order to account for all such contrasts, and to show the inter-relationships between words derived from a common root, such as *'telegraph, tele'graphic* and *te'legraphy*. In the American STRUCTURALIST tradition, four such degrees are usually distinguished, and analysed as stress PHONEMES, namely (from strongest to weakest) (1) 'primary', (2) 'secondary', (3) 'tertiary' and (4) 'weak'. These contrasts are, however, demonstrable only on words in isolation, as in the compound *elevator*[1,4,3,4] *operator*[2,4,3,4] – one of several such phrases originally cited to justify analyses of this kind.

Alternative views recognised different kinds and degrees of stress, the simplest postulating a straight stressed vs. unstressed contrast, referring to other factors (such as INTONATION and VOWEL QUALITY) to explain such sequences as *elevator operator*. In DISTINCTIVE FEATURE theories of phonology, the various degrees of stress are assigned to the syllables of words by means of the repeated application of RULES (such as 'lexical', 'compound' and 'nuclear' stress rules). Some analysts maintain there is a distinction to be made between linguistic contrasts involving loudness (which they refer to as 'stress') and those additionally involving pitch (which they refer to as ACCENT). All the examples given above, they would argue, are matters of accent, not stress, because contrasts in pitch variation are normally involved. Similar problems arise in the analysis of TONE languages.

In cross-language comparison, it is useful to note variations in the typical place within the word where the stressed syllable falls. Some languages have a 'fixed' stress (or accent), e.g. Welsh, where the stressed syllable is almost always the penultimate, in polysyllabic words. Others, such as English, have a 'free' or 'moveable' stress (accent).

In the context of RHYTHM studies, the notion of a STRESS-TIMED language is often cited, i.e. one where the stresses fall at roughly regular intervals within an UTTERANCE. In analysing such a language in this way, the notion of **silent stress** is sometimes invoked, to handle cases where the omission of a stressed syllable in colloquial speech can nonetheless be 'felt'; a regularly cited case is the abbreviated version of *thank-you* /kjʊ/, which is said to be the unstressed residue of an unspoken stressed + unstressed combination. A sequence of syllables constituting a rhythmical unit, containing one primary stress, is known as a **stress group**. See Abercrombie 1967: Ch. 3; Gimson 1970: Ch. 9; Ladefoged 1975: Ch. 5; Hyman 1975: Ch 6.

stress-timed A very general term used in PHONETICS to characterise the pronunciation of LANGUAGES displaying a particular type of RHYTHM; it is opposed to SYLLABLE-TIMED languages. In stress-timed languages, it is claimed that the STRESSED SYLLABLES recur at regular intervals of time, regardless of the number of intervening unstressed syllables, as in English. This characteristic is referred to as ISOCHRONISM, or 'isochrony'. However, it is plain that this regularity is the case only under certain conditions, and the extent to which the tendency towards regularity in English is similar to that in, say, other Germanic languages remains unclear. See Catford 1977: Ch. 5; Abercrombie 1967: Ch. 6.

strict subcategorisation A type of SYNTACTIC FEATURE recognised in some MODELS of GENERATIVE GRAMMAR (cf. ASPECTS), its function being to specify a class of restrictions operating on the choice of LEXICAL items in DEEP STRUCTURE. Related notions include CATEGORY and SELECTIONAL features. See Huddleston 1976: Ch. 10.

stricture A general term used in PHONETICS to refer to an ARTICULATION which restricts the air stream to some degree, ranging from a complete CLOSURE to a slight narrowing. See Catford 1977: Ch. 6; Abercrombie 1967: Ch: 4.

strident One of the SOURCE FEATURES of sound set up by CHOMSKY & Halle in their DISTINCTIVE FEATURE theory of PHONOLOGY, to handle variations in the SIBILANCE of a sound. Strident sounds are defined ARTICULATORILY and ACOUSTICALLY, as those sounds produced by a

string

relatively complex STRICTURE, and marked by relatively high frequency and intensity, as in [f], [s] and [ʃ]. The opposite term in JAKOBSON & Halle's approach is MELLOW; in Chomsky & Halle's later system it is **non-strident**: these are sounds produced by a less complex stricture, and marked by noise of relatively low frequency and intensity, such as in PLOSIVES and NASALS. All vowels are also [−strident]. See Ladefoged 1975: Ch. 11; Hyman 1975: Ch. 2.

string A term used in LINGUISTICS, and especially in GENERATIVE GRAMMAR, to refer to a linear SEQUENCE of ELEMENTS of determinate length and constitution. Formal analysis also permits the notion of a string consisting of just one element, and also one consisting of no elements (cf. ZERO in linguistic description) – the 'empty' or 'null' string. A **substring** is any part of a string which is itself a string. For example, the following SENTENCE can be seen as a string of elements: *the + cat + sit + Past + on + the + mat*. Within this, several substrings could be recognised, e.g. *the + cat*, *the + cat + sit + Past*, etc. See Lyons 1968: Ch. 6; 1977a: App. 1.

strong form One of two possible pronunciations for a WORD, in the context of CONNECTED SPEECH, the other being WEAK. The strong form is that which is the result of a word being STRESSED. For example, most of the GRAMMATICAL WORDS of English occur in both forms, e.g. *I want bacon and eggs* vs. *I want bacon − AND eggs*. See Gimson 1970: Ch. 10.

structural(-ism, -ist) A term used in LINGUISTICS referring to any approach to the analysis of LANGUAGE that pays explicit attention to the way in which linguistic features can be described in terms of STRUCTURES and SYSTEMS ('structural' or 'structuralist linguistics'). In the general SAUSSUREAN sense, structuralist ideas enter into every school of linguistics. Structuralism does, however, have a more restricted definition, referring to the BLOOMFIELDIAN emphasis on the processes of SEGMENTING and CLASSIFYING the physical features of UTTERANCE (i.e. on what Noam CHOMSKY later called SURFACE structures), with little reference to the abstract UNDERLYING structures (Chomsky's DEEP structures) of language or their MEANING. It is this emphasis which the Chomskyan approach to language strongly attacked; for GENERATIVE linguists, accordingly, the term is often pejorative.

The contribution of this notion in linguistics is apparent in the more general concept of **structuralism,** especially as formulated in the work of the French anthropologist, Claude Lévi-Strauss (b. 1908), and others. Here, any human institution or behaviour (e.g. dancing, courtship, religion) is considered analysable in terms of an underlying network of relationships, and the structures demonstrated referrable to basic modes of thought. The crucial point is that the elements which constitute a network have no validity apart from the relations (of equivalence, contrast, etc.) which hold between them, and it is this network of relations which constitutes the structures of the system.

Within linguistics, 'structural' will be found in several contexts in PHONOLOGY, GRAMMAR and SEMANTICS. **Structural(ist) grammar**, as a general term, is now a largely dated conception of grammatical analysis, though the emphases which characterised it may still be seen in several areas of APPLIED LINGUISTIC studies (e.g. in the structural drills of foreign language teaching), and the term 'structural' is often given a special status as part of the exposition of a grammatical MODEL, e.g. the notion of STRUCTURAL DESCRIPTION in TRANSFORMATIONAL GRAMMAR. **Structural semantics** is an influential contemporary position, which is still in its early stages of analysing the SENSE relations that interconnect LEXEMES and SENTENCES. See Palmer 1971: Ch. 3; Lyons 1977b: Ch. 8.

structural ambiguity A term used in LINGUISTICS to refer to a CONSTRUCTION with more than one GRAMMATICAL interpretation in terms of CONSTITUENT analysis. A much-used example is *old men and women*, which is 'structurally ambiguous': it may be analysed as [*old men*] *and women* (i.e. only the men are old) or *old* [*men and women*] (i.e. both the men and women are old). In GENERATIVE grammar, this phenomenon is usually referred to as 'CONSTRUCTIONal homonymity'. See Lyons 1968: Ch. 6.

structural change (SC) A term used in GENERATIVE grammar to refer to the result of applying a TRANSFORMATIONAL RULE, i.e. the changes between the input and the output PHRASE-MARKERS. In the transformation of ACTIVE into PASSIVE SENTENCES, for example, the structural change is complex, involving the RE-ORDERING of the two NOUN PHRASES, and the INSERTION of new forms of the VERB, and the AGENT marker *by* (e.g. *the dog bit the cat* vs. *the cat was bitten by the dog*). See Akmajian & Heny 1975: Ch. 5; Huddleston 1976: Ch. 5.

structural description (SD) A term used in GENERATIVE GRAMMAR to refer to an analysis of a TERMINAL STRING in terms of a labelled BRACKETING. In TRANSFORMATIONAL analysis, the SD provides input to a transformational RULE: it specifies which PHRASE-MARKERS are to be affected by a rule, i.e. which will 'satisfy' or 'meet' the CONDITIONS of the rule. The terms 'structural analysis' and 'structure index' are also used. See Akmajian & Heny 1975: Ch. 5; Huddleston 1976: Ch. 1.

structure In its most general sense, and especially as defined by STRUCTURALIST studies of human institutions and behaviour, the term appies to the main abstract characteristic of a SEMIOTIC SYSTEM. A LANGUAGE, for example, is a structure, in the sense that it is a network of inter-related UNITS, the MEANING of the parts being specifiable only with reference to the whole. In this sense, the terms 'structure' and 'system' are often synonymous (and the phrase 'structured system' which is sometimes encountered – as in 'language is a structured system' – is a tautology). More specifically, the term is used to refer to an isolatable section of this total network, as in discussion of the structure of a particular GRAMMATICAL area (e.g. TENSES, PRONOUNS), and here 'structure' and 'system' are distinguished: one might talk of the 'structure' of a particular 'system'.

However, this application of the term to PARADIGMATIC relationships is not as widespread as the SYNTAGMATIC conception of 'structure'. Here a particular sequential pattern of linguistic ELEMENTS is referred to as 'a structure', definable with reference to one of the various 'structural LEVELS' recognised in a theory, e.g. 'PHONOLOGICAL structure', 'SYNTACTIC structure', 'MORPHOLOGICAL structure', 'SEMANTIC structure', etc. For example, CLAUSE structure can be defined in terms of STRINGS of such elements as SUBJECT, VERB, OBJECT, or NP, VP; SYLLABLE structure can be defined in terms of strings of CONSONANTS and VOWELS. The set of items which CONTRAST at a particular 'place' in a structure is then referred to as a system. This is the way in which the term is used in HALLIDAYAN linguistics, for example, where it has a special status, as the name of one of the four major CATEGORIES recognised by the theory (the others being UNIT, SYSTEM and CLASS): the category of structure accounts for the ways in which an occurrence of one syntactic unit can be made up out of occurrences of the unit below it (e.g. which kinds of GROUP structure can constitute which kinds of CLAUSE structure). In this sense, the MORPHEME has no structure, being the minimal unit in grammar. A narrower use of the term is found in the phrase **structure index**, sometimes used in TRANSFORMATIONAL GRAMMAR to refer to the FORMAL description of the input STRING to a transformational RULE – also known as a STRUCTURAL DESCRIPTION. See Robins 1971: Ch. 2; Lyons 1968: Ch. 2; Huddleston 1976: Ch. 5.

stylistics (styl-e, -istic, -o-) A branch of LINGUISTICS which studies the features of SITUATIONALLY-distinctive uses (VARIETIES) of LANGUAGE, and tries to establish principles capable of accounting for the particular choices made by individual and social groups in their use of language. **General stylistics** deals with the whole range (or REPERTOIRE) of non-DIALECTal varieties encountered within a language; **literary stylistics** deals with the variations characteristic of literature as a genre and of the 'style' of individual authors. The quantification of stylistic patterns is the province of **stylostatistics** (or 'stylometry') – a field which usually studies the statistical structure of literary texts, often using computers. The study of the expressive or aesthetic function of sound is sometimes called **phonostylistics**.

The term 'stylistics' is occasionally used in a very broad sense, to include all situationally-distinctive language – that is, including the variations of regional, social and historical dialects. It is more common, however, to see **style** used in a highly restricted sense – though the extremely broad and ambiguous reference of the term in everyday use has not made its status as a technical linguistic term very appealing. For example, in the HALLIDAYAN classification of language varieties, 'style' (more fully, 'style of DISCOURSE'), refers to the relations among the participants in a language activity, especially the level of FORMALITY they adopt (colloquial, formal, etc.). Alternative terms used by some linguists, presumably to avoid the ambiguity of an additional sense for the term 'style', include MANNER and TENOR. The main terms with which it contrasts in the Hallidayan model are MODE and FIELD. A similar conception of 'style' in terms of 'vertical' formality level is found in many SOCIOLINGUISTIC studies. See Bolinger 1975: Ch. 17; Lyons 1977b: Ch. 14.

subject A term used in the analysis of GRAMMATICAL FUNCTIONS to refer to a major CONSTITUENT of SENTENCE or CLAUSE structure, traditionally associated with the 'doer' of an action, as in *The cat bit the dog*. The oldest approaches make a two-fold distinction in sentence analysis between subject and PREDICATE, and this is still common, though not always in this terminology; other approaches distinguish subject from a series of other elements of STRUCTURE (OBJECT, COMPLEMENT, VERB, ADVERBIAL in particular). Linguistic analyses have emphasised the complexity involved in this notion, distinguishing, for example, the 'grammatical' from the UNDERLYING or 'logical' subject of a sentence, as in *The cat was kicked by the dog*, where *The cat* is the grammatical and *the dog* the logical subject. Not all subjects, moreover, can be analysed as doers of an action, as in such sentences as *Dirt attracts flies*, and *The books sold well*. The definition of subjects in terms of SURFACE

subjunctive

grammatical features (using WORD order or INFLECTIONAL criteria) is usually relatively straightforward, but the specification of their function is more complex, and has attracted much recent discussion (e.g. in RELATIONAL GRAMMAR).

In the study of inflected languages, 'subjective' may be used as an alternative to NOMINATIVE, e.g. in English, the contrast between subject and object forms of PRONOUNS (e.g. *he ~ him*) is sometimes referred to as a distinction between subjective and objective case. See Lyons 1968: Ch. 8; Quirk *et al* 1972: Chs. 2, 7.

subjunctive A term used in the GRAMMATICAL classification of SENTENCE types, and usually seen in contrast to INDICATIVE, IMPERATIVE, etc. MOODS. It refers to VERB forms or sentence/CLAUSE types used in the expression of many kinds of SUBORDINATE clause, for a range of attitudes including tentativeness, vagueness, uncertainty. In modern English, the examples which come nearest to the subjunctive occur in 'hypothetical' constructions of the type *if he **were** coming* (cf. *if he was coming*), in certain formulae (e.g. *So be it!*), and in some clauses introduced by that (especially in American English, e.g. *I insist that he **go** to town*). In many LANGUAGES, it is more PRODUCTIVE, e.g. in French. See Lyons 1968: Ch. 7; Quirk *et al* 1972: Ch. 3.

subordination (subordinat-e, -ing, -or) A term used in GRAMMATICAL analysis to refer to the process or result of linking LINGUISTIC UNITS so that they have different SYNTACTIC status, one being dependent upon the other, and usually a constituent of the other. (In this respect, it is usually distinguished from CO-ORDINATE linkage, where the units are equivalent.) **Subordinate clauses** are illustrated in the SENTENCE *John came when Mary left*; the marker of linkage is *when*, a **subordinating conjunction** (or **subordinator**). A wide range of subordinators exists in English, e.g. *although, since, because, while, after*. In ENDOCENTRIC PHRASES, the term 'subordinate' is also used to refer to the words which modify the HEAD, e.g. in *all the very big cars, all the very big* is subordinate to *cars*, and *very* is subordinate to *big*. See Quirk *et al* 1972: Ch. 11; Robins 1971: Ch. 6.

substance A term used in LINGUISTICS to refer to the undifferentiated raw material out of which LANGUAGE is constructed – the sound waves of speech ('PHONIC substance'), the marks of writing ('GRAPHIC substance'). 'Substance' is here opposed to FORM – the abstract pattern of relationships imposed on this substance by a language. In SAUSSURIAN theory, MEANING too is conceived as having substance, namely, the conceptual store of thoughts, feelings, etc. which exist independently of language. In modern linguistics, however, the term tends to be restricted to the PHONETIC and GRAPHIC MEDIA (as in HALLIDAYAN theory, where 'substance' is recognised as a separate LEVEL). See Lyons 1968: Ch. 2.

substantive (substantival) (1) A term used in LINGUISTIC theory to refer to a category of linguistic UNIVERSAL; opposed to FORMAL. **Substantive** (or **substantival**) **universals** are the PRIMITIVE ELEMENTS which a GRAMMAR establishes in order to analyse linguistic DATA, e.g. S, NP, VP, [+human], [+high] in GENERATIVE grammar, or SUBJECT, VERB, OBJECT, etc. in RELATIONAL MODELS. See Huddleston 1976: Ch. 13.

(2) In some DESCRIPTIVE grammars, 'substantive' is a term used in the CLASSIFICATION of WORDS, referring to the class of NOUNS (traditionally defined as 'substances', i.e. names of persons, places, things, etc.), and also to those ITEMS which function as nouns, though lacking some of the formal characteristics of that class (cf. the 'substantival function' of ADJECTIVES, in *the poor*, *the rich*, etc.). The set of PRONOUNS may also be included in this class. See Lyons 1968: Ch. 8.

substitution (substitut-e, -able, -ability) A term used in LINGUISTICS to refer to the process or result of replacing one ITEM with another at a particular place in a STRUCTURE. In GRAMMAR, the structural CONTEXT within which this replacement takes place is known as a **substitution frame**, e.g. *The — is angry*, and the set of items which can be used PARADIGMATICALLY at a given place is known as a **substitution class**. A WORD which refers back to a previously occurring element of structure (such as the PRONOUN *he* in *The man came in. He was cross.*) may be called a **substitute word**. In language teaching, exercises to improve the ability of learners to carry out this process of replacement are known as **substitution drills** (or 'pattern drills'). See Lyons 1968: Ch. 2.

substrate (substratum) A term used in SOCIOLINGUISTICS and HISTORICAL LANGUAGE studies to refer to a LINGUISTIC VARIETY or set of FORMS which has influenced the STRUCTURE or use of a more dominant variety or language within a community. A **substrate language** (**linguistic substrate** or **substratum**) is particularly evidenced when a language is imposed on a community, as a result of political or economic superiority, as can be seen in the many varieties of English spoken throughout the world which incorporate characteristics of a mother-tongue, e.g. in India, West Africa. The opposite effect is known as a SUPERSTRATUM. See Robins 1971: Ch. 8; Trudgill 1974: Ch. 3.

suction One of the features of sound set up by CHOMSKY & Halle in their DISTINCTIVE FEATURE theory of PHONOLOGY, under the heading of SUPPLEMENTARY MOVEMENTS, to handle variations in MANNER OF ARTICULATION. It refers to articulatory movements of the GLOTTIS or velum (cf. VELAR) where the air flow is directed inwards, as in IMPLOSIVES and CLICKS. See Ladefoged 1975: Ch. 11; Hyman 1975: Ch. 2.

suffix(-ing/-ation) A term used in MORPHOLOGY referring to an AFFIX which is added following a ROOT or STEM. The process of **suffixation** or **suffixing** is common in English, both for the DERIVATIONAL formation of new LEXICAL items (e.g. *-ise*, *-tion*) and for expressing GRAMMATICAL relationships (INFLECTIONAL endings such as *-s*, *-ed*, *-ing*). See Robins 1971: Ch. 5; Matthews 1974: Ch. 7.

superfix/suprafix A term used in PHONETICS and PHONOLOGY to refer to a vocal effect which extends over more than one sound SEGMENT in an UTTERANCE, such as a PITCH, STRESS, or JUNCTURE pattern, particularly when this is seen in the context of a specific GRAMMATICAL STRUCTURE. The term SUPRASEGMENTAL is however now widely used instead. See Bolinger 1975: Ch. 3.

superlative A term used in the three-way GRAMMATICAL description of ADJECTIVES and ADVERBS into DEGREES, specifying the extent of their application. The superlative form is used to express a comparison between more than two entities, and contrasts with COMPARATIVE, where only two entities are involved, and POSITIVE, where no comparison is implied. In English there is both an INFLECTION (*-est*) and a PERIPHRASTIC construction (*most*) to express this notion (e.g. *biggest*, *most interesting*). See Quirk *et al* 1972: Ch. 5.

superstratum A term used in SOCIOLINGUISTIC and HISTORICAL LANGUAGE studies to refer to a LINGUISTIC VARIETY or set of FORMS which has influenced the STRUCTURE or use of a less dominant variety or language within a community. A **linguistic superstratum** is usually the result of political, economic or cultural dominance, as illustrated by the influence of English, French, Arabic, etc. on the languages of the world at various periods in history. One of the most noticeable features of superstratal influence is the increased use of LOAN words. See Trudgill 1974: Ch. 8.

supplementary movements One of the types of sound feature set up by CHOMSKY & Halle in their DISTINCTIVE FEATURE theory of PHONOLOGY, to handle variations in MANNER OF ARTICULATION. They are sub-divided into SUCTION and PRESSURE types, a distinction made on the basis of the GLOTTAL or VELAR movement involved in sounds with two simultaneous CLOSURES, as in EJECTIVES and CLICKS. See Ladefoged 1975: Ch. 11; Hyman 1975: Ch. 2.

suppletion (suppletive) A term used in MORPHOLOGY to refer to cases where it is not possible to show a relationship between MORPHEMES through a general RULE, because the forms involved have different ROOTS. A **suppletive** is the grammar's use of an unrelated FORM (i.e. with a different root) to complete a PARADIGM, as in the present–past TENSE relationship of *go ~ went*, or the COMPARATIVE form *better* in relation to *good*. See Robins 1971: Ch. 5.

supraglottal A general term used in PHONETICS to refer to the whole area of the VOCAL TRACT above the GLOTTIS. See Ladefoged 1975: Ch. 1.

suprasegmental A term used in PHONETICS and PHONOLOGY to refer to a vocal effect which extends over more than one sound SEGMENT in an UTTERANCE, such as a PITCH, STRESS, or JUNCTURE pattern. In its contrast with 'segmental', it is seen as one of two main classes into which phonological UNITS can be divided. In American STRUCTURALIST theories, suprasegmentals were analysed as PHONEMES, and sequences of such features as MORPHEMES, but not all phonologists analyse these features in EMIC terms. Alternative terms are PLURISEGMENTAL, non-segmental and SUPERFIX. See Ladefoged 1975: Ch. 10; Bolinger 1975: Ch. 3; Hyman 1975: Ch. 6.

surface structure/grammar A central theoretical term in GENERATIVE GRAMMAR, opposed to DEEP STRUCTURE. The 'surface structure' (or 'surface grammar') of a sentence is the final stage in the SYNTACTIC REPRESENTATION of a sentence, which provides the input to the PHONOLOGICAL COMPONENT of the grammar, and which thus most closely corresponds to the structure of the sentence we articulate and hear. Analysing a surface STRING of MORPHEMES through CONSTITUENT analysis is a universal procedure which indicates many important facts about LINGUISTIC structure; but it by no means indicates everything, e.g. it cannot explain how we recognise AMBIGUOUS sentences, or how we INTUITIVELY relate sentences which have different surface FORMS but the same basic MEANING (e.g. *cats chase mice* and *mice are chased by cats*). For such reasons, linguists in the late 1950s postulated a deep

syllable

or 'underlying' structure for sentences – a LEVEL of structural organisation in which all the factors determining structural interpretation are defined and inter-related. The standard view is that a grammar operates by generating a set of abstract deep structures, subsequently converting these UNDERLYING REPRESENTATIONS into surface structures by applying a set of TRANSFORMATIONAL RULES. This two-level conception of grammatical structure is still widely held, though it has been much criticised in recent generative studies. An alternative conception is to relate surface structure directly to a SEMANTIC level of representation, by-passing deep structure altogether. See Lyons 1968: Ch. 6; 1977a: Ch. 8; Huddleston 1976: Chs. 4, 6.

syllable (syllab-ic, -(if)ication) A UNIT of pronunciation typically larger than a single sound and smaller than a WORD. A word may be pronounced 'syllable at a time', as in *ne-ver-the-less*, and a good dictionary will indicate where these **syllabic divisions** occur in writing, thus providing information about how a word may be hyphenated. The notion of syllable, in short, is very real to NATIVE SPEAKERS, and is often used in a quasi-technical sense in everyday conversation (e.g. *shall I put it in words of one syllable?*). **Syllabification** is the term which refers to the division of a word into syllables. A word containing a single syllable is called a **monosyllable**; if it contains more than one, the term **polysyllable** is used (or 'monosyllabic word'/'polysyllabic word' respectively.)

Providing a precise definition of the syllable is not an easy matter, and there are several theories in both PHONETICS and PHONOLOGY which have tried to clarify matters. From a phonetic viewpoint, attempts have been made to define the syllables of a LANGUAGE on the basis of the articulatory effort needed in order to produce them. The 'pulse' or 'motor' theory of syllable production proposed by the psychologist R. H. Stetson (1892–1950) argued that each syllable corresponds to an increase in air pressure, air from the lungs being released as a series of chest pulses. This can often be readily felt and measured, particularly in emphatic speech; but it is also often difficult to detect such a pulse in adjacent syllables, as when two VOWELS co-occur, e.g. *going* (which is two syllables, but usually said in a single muscular effort). An alternative phonetic approach attempts to define the syllable in auditory terms: the PROMINENCE theory argues that in a string of sounds, some are intrinsically more 'sonorous' than others, and that each 'peak' of SONORITY corresponds to the centre of a syllable. These peaks are best illustrated by vowels, which have the greater carrying-power. The less sonorous sounds provide 'valleys' of prominence, and are best illustrated by the closures and narrowings which produce consonants. This approach gives a useful general guideline, but it does not always indicate clearly where the boundary between adjacent syllables falls, e.g. in *busker*, the problem of whether to split the word as *bus-ker*, *bu-sker* or *busk-er* is not answerable using arguments based on perceived sonority. The problem remains, even if other acoustic features than sonority (such as pitch or length) are incorporated within the notion of prominence.

Phonetic approaches of this kind attempt to provide a definition of the syllable valid for all languages, and it is possible that more valid definitions in terms of speech production or perception will emerge. Phonological views of the syllable, on the other hand, focus on the ways sounds combine in individual languages to produce typical SEQUENCES. Here, two classes of sounds are usually established: sounds which can occur on their own, or at the centre of a sequence of sounds, and sounds which cannot occur on their own, or which occur at the edges of a sequence of sounds. The former include such sounds as [p], [g], [f], [ʧ], etc., and are generally referred to as CONSONANTS. A consonant–vowel (CV) sequence is a pattern which seems to be found in all languages: because the syllable is not 'closed' by another consonant, this type of syllable is often called an **open syllable** type. A CVC pattern is also very common in English. In such a case, the following terminology could be used:

the opening segment of a syllable = the **onset**,
the closing segment of the syllable = the **coda**,
the central segment of the syllable = the **centre** or **nucleus**.

A useful collective term for the opening and closing segments is the MARGINS of the syllable.

Using such methods, syllables can be defined in terms of the way the sound SEGMENTS of a language function. In this way, for instance, one can identify the various CLUSTERS of segments which may occur at syllabic margins, such as CV (*say*), CCV (*play*), CCCV (*stray*), etc. Exceptional syllables can also be identified, such as those where certain consonants occur alone to form the syllable – the NASALS and LATERALS in words such as *button* [bʌtn̩] and *bottle* [bɒtl̩], where [ˌ] indicates that the final consonant is a **syllabic consonant**.

The notion of syllable is widely used elsewhere in phonology, e.g. in relation to PROSODY and cross-linguistic studies of RHYTHM (cf. SYLLABLE-TIMED language).

In the DISTINCTIVE FEATURE theory of phonology proposed by CHOMSKY & Halle, **syllabic** is used to replace the earlier term 'vocalic', referring to all segments constituting a syllabic nucleus. Vowels, liquids and nasals would be [+syllabic] ([+syll]); all other segments would be [−syll].

See Gimson 1970: Ch. 5; Ladefoged 1975: Ch. 10.

syllable-timed A very general term used in PHONETICS to characterise the pronunciation of LANGUAGES displaying a particular type of RHYTHM; it is opposed to STRESS-TIMED languages. In syllable-timed languages, the SYLLABLES are said to occur at regular intervals of time, as in French; this characteristic is sometimes referred to as 'isosyllabism'. However, very little work has been done on the accuracy or general applicability of such properties, and the usefulness of the typology is questionable. See Catford 1977: Ch. 5; Abercrombie 1976: Ch. 6.

synaesthesia A term used in SEMANTICS to refer to a direct association between the FORM and the MEANING of LANGUAGE. For example, the *sl-* sound combination is often felt to express unpleasantness (cf. *slimy*, *slither*, etc. – and Lewis Carroll's *slithy*). Such SOUND-SYMBOLIC units are sometimes called PHONAESTHEMES. See Lyons 1977b: Ch. 4.

synchronic One of the two main temporal dimensions of LINGUISTIC investigation introduced by the Swiss linguist, Ferdinand de SAUSSURE, the other being DIACHRONIC. In **synchronic linguistics**, languages are studied at a theoretical point in time: one describes a 'state' of the language, disregarding whatever changes might be taking place. For example, one could carry out a synchronic description of the language of Chaucer, or of the 16th century, or of modern-day English. Most synchronic descriptions are of contemporary language states, but their importance as a preliminary to diachronic study has been stressed since Saussure. Linguistic investigations, unless specified to the contrary, are assumed to be synchronic. See Lyons 1968: Ch. 1; Robins 1971: Ch. 1.

syncretism (syncretise) A term originally used in HISTORICAL LINGUISTICS (referring to the merging of forms following the loss of INFLECTIONS), and now often used SYNCHRONICALLY to refer to identity between two forms of the same LEXEME, e.g. *walked* in *I walked* (where it is past TENSE) and *I've walked* (where it is past PARTICIPLE). The distinction is here 'syncretised', or 'neutralised'. See Matthews 1974: Ch. 2.

synonym(-y, -ous) A term used in SEMANTICS to refer to a major type of SENSE-relation between LEXICAL ITEMS: lexical items which have the same MEANINGS are synonyms, and the relationship between them is one of **synonymy**. For two items to be synonyms, it does not mean that they should be identical in meaning, i.e. interchangeable in all CONTEXTS, and with identical CONNOTATIONS – this unlikely possibility is sometimes referred to as 'total synonymy'. Synonymy can be said to occur if items are close enough in their meaning to allow a choice to be made between them in *some* contexts, without there being any difference for the meaning of the sentence as a whole. Linguistic studies of synonymy have emphasised the importance of context in deciding whether a set of lexical items is synonymous. For example, in the context *What a nice — of flowers*, the items *range, selection, choice,* etc. are synonymous; but in the context *His — of knowledge is enormous,* only *range* can be used, along with a different set of synonyms, e.g. *breadth*. Synonymy is distinguished from such other sense-relations as ANTONYMY, HYPONYMY and INCOMPATIBILITY. See Lyons 1968: Ch. 10; Bolinger 1975: Ch., 7.

syntagmatic (1) (**syntagm-a, -eme**) A fundamental term in LINGUISTICS, originally introduced by the Swiss linguist, Ferdinand de SAUSSURE, to refer to the SEQUENTIAL characteristics of speech, seen as a STRING of CONSTITUENTS (sometimes, but not always) in linear order. The relationships between constituents ('syntagms' or 'syntagmas') in a CONSTRUCTION are generally called **syntagmatic relations.** Sets of syntagmatically related constituents are often referred to as STRUC-TURES. Syntagmatic relations, together with PARADIGMATIC relations, constitute the statement of a linguistic UNIT's identity within the LANGUAGE SYSTEM. For example, the function of /p/ in English PHONOLOGY can be summarised by identifying its syntagmatic rela-tionships (e.g. *p-it, ni-p, a-p-t...*) and the paradigmatic relationships it contracts with other elements (e.g. *p-it, b-it, n-it...*). Syntagmatic relationships can be established at all LEVELS of analysis. In TAGMEMIC GRAMMAR, however, the term **syntagmeme** is used in a restricted sense, referring to a unit in a grammatical HIERARCHY seen from the viewpoint of the ELEMENTS (or tagmemes) it includes, e.g. the sentence is a syntagmeme for the CLAUSES that constitute it. See Lyons 1968: Ch. 2; Matthews 1974: Ch. 9; Bolinger 1975: Ch. 15.

(2) In PSYCHOLINGUISTICS, the term is used to refer to a class of ASSOCIATIVE responses which people make when hearing a stimulus word, *viz* those which fall into a different WORD-class from the stimulus, in that the response word could precede or follow the stimulus word in a SENTENCE. A **syntagmatic response** or **association** would be *drive* following *car, sheep* following *black,* etc. The **syntag-matic/paradigmatic shift** refers to a change in the patterns of response noted in children at around age seven, when the earlier pattern (of primarily syntagmatic associations) develops into the more adult-like pattern primarily involving PARADIGMATIC associations. See Clark & Clark 1977: Ch. 12.

syntax (syntactic(s)) A traditional term for the study of the RULES governing the way WORDS are combined to form sentences in a language. In this use, syntax is opposed to MORPHOLOGY, the study of word structure. An alternative definition (avoiding the concept of 'word') is the study of the inter-relationships between ELEMENTS of SENTENCE STRUCTURE, and of the rules governing the arrangement of sentences in SEQUENCES. In this use, one might then talk of the 'syntax of the word'. In GENERATIVE linguistics, the **syntactic component** is one of three major organisational units within a grammar (the others being PHONOLOGICAL and SEMANTIC), containing the PHRASE STRUCTURE and TRANSFORMATIONAL rules for the generation of **syntactic structures**. Syntactic structures (PATTERNS, or CONSTRUCTIONS) are analysable into sequences of **syntactic categories** or **syntactic classes**, these being established on the basis of the **syntactic relationships** linguistic ITEMS have with other items in a construction. Studying the sequential arrangements of syntax is sometimes referred to as 'syntactics', but there is a possibility of confusion here with the earlier use of this term as one of the three major divisions of SEMIOTICS (along with PRAGMATICS and SEMANTICS). The adjective form of 'syntax' in modern linguistics is 'syntactic', as in the above examples: 'syntactical' these days sounds quaint. See Lyons 1968: Ch. 5; Robins 1971: Ch. 6.

synthetic (1) A type of LANGUAGE sometimes distinguished in COMPARATIVE LINGUISTICS using STRUCTURAL (as opposed to HISTORICAL) criteria, and focusing on the characteristics of the WORD: in **synthetic languages**, words typically contain more than one MORPHEME (as opposed to ANALYTIC languages, where words are typically monomorphemic). Two types of synthetic language are usually recognised: AGGLUTINATIVE and INFLECTING – with POLYSYNTHETIC sometimes additionally distinguished. Examples include Latin, Greek, Arabic, Turkish. As always in such classifications, the categories are not clear-cut: different languages will display the characteristic of 'synthesis' to a greater or lesser degree. See Robins 1971: Ch. 8; Bolinger 1975: Ch. 2.

(2) Some use is made in SEMANTICS of the sense of 'synthetic' found in logic and philosophy, where **synthetic proposition/sentence** is one whose truth can be verified only by using empirical criteria, e.g. *It's raining, Those dogs are fierce*. The term contrasts with ANALYTIC, where the internal form of the PROPOSITION makes it necessarily true, without reference to external criteria. See Lyons 1977b: Ch. 6.

system(-atic, -ic) In its most general sense, the term refers to a network of patterned relationships constituting the organisation of LANGUAGE.

Language as a whole is then characterised as a system (cf. the 'linguistic system of English', etc.) – and often as a HIERARCHICALLY ordered arrangement of systems. In one view, the 'language system' is constituted by the phonological, grammatical and semantic systems; the PHONOLOGICAL system comprises the SEGMENTAL and SUPRASEG-MENTAL systems; the segmental system comprises the VOWEL and CONSONANT system; and so on. Within this totality, the term 'system' may be applied to any finite set of FORMALLY or SEMANTICALLY connected UNITS (referred to variously as the 'terms' or 'members' of the system), where the inter-relationships are mutually exclusive (i.e. two members of the same system cannot co-occur) and mutually defining (i.e. the meaning of one member is specifiable only with reference to others). For example, the set of personal PRONOUNS in a language constitute a system, according to these criteria. First, it is finite (in English, *I, you, he, she, it, we, they*); the system is 'closed', in the sense that new members are not normally created. Secondly, it is not possible to use more than one at a given place in STRUCTURE (cf. **I you came*, etc.). Thirdly, it is easier to define a member by referring to the other members of the system, rather than independently, e.g. *I* is 'the pronoun which is not *you/he/she/it/we/they*'. Other 'grammatical systems' would include DETERMINER/TENSE/MOOD/PREPOSI-TIONAL/NEGATION, etc. The term would not normally be applied to OPEN-class items, such as NOUNS, ADJECTIVES, SENTENCES, etc. unless it meant the set of formal grammatical relationships subsumed under that heading, e.g. the 'noun system' would mean the set of SYNTAG-MATIC and PARADIGMATIC relationships which define the CLASS of nouns. The analysis is also applicable in principle to the study of MEANINGS, and the term 'SEMANTIC system' is often used; but in the present state of knowledge it is often difficult to model the inter-relationship between semantic units according to criteria such as the above. A similar problem sometimes applies in grammatical analysis, where a full 'systemic' statement of certain areas is difficult to establish in certain areas (e.g. ADVERBIALS, APPOSITION), partly because of the INDETERMINACY of the notions involved.

In HALLIDAYAN linguistics, the notion of system receives a special status. In SCALE-AND-CATEGORY grammar, it is one of the four central categories recognised by the theory (the others being UNIT, STRUCTURE, and CLASS): 'systems' are finite sets of paradigmatically related items functioning in classes. In the later development of this approach, **systemic grammar**, the notion of system is made a central explanatory principle, the whole of language being conceived as a 'system of systems'. Systemic here should not be confused with 'systematic' (in either its general or technical uses; see below): systemic grammar is concerned to establish a network of systems of relationships, in the above sense, which will account for all the semantically relevant choices in the language as a whole.

The adjective 'systematic' is often used in linguistics in its everyday sense, but in certain contexts (usually in relation to PHONETICS and PHONOLOGY) it receives a restricted definition. In GENERATIVE grammar, it has been used to refer to TWO LEVELS of REPRESENTATION in the phonological COMPONENT of the grammar: SYSTEMATIC PHONEMIC and SYSTEMATIC PHONETIC levels are distinguished, the implication being that the terms of these analyses are being seen as in systemic correspondence with other aspects of the grammar (e.g. the MORPHO-LOGICAL relationships between items). See Lyons 1968: Ch. 1; Robins 1971: Ch. 2; Quirk *et al* 1972: Ch. 2.

systematic phonemics A level of REPRESENTATION in GENERATIVE PHONOLOGY which sets up a single UNDERLYING form capable of accounting for the phonological variations which relate GRAMMATICAL STRUCTURES (e.g. words). In such pairs of words as *divine* ~ *divinity*, *obscene* ~ *obscenity*, there is plainly a regular relationship of some kind, but it is not an easy relationship to state explicitly. CHOMSKY & Halle, in their approach to this problem, argue that the ROOT MORPHEME in each pair of words can be given a single underlying representation (/divīn/ and /obsēn/ in the above cases), and that this, along with the rules which relate such representations to the SURFACE ALTERNANTS, accounts for the native-speaker's awareness of the 'systematic' relationships which exist between grammar and phonology. (Such rules also often reflect sound changes which have taken place in the history of the language.) The units in these representations are referred to as **systematic phonemes**, as opposed to the 'autonomous' PHONEMES of traditional phonemic phonology, which are established without reference to grammatical structure. Some generative phono-logists (such as Chomsky & Halle) prefer the term 'phonological' to refer to this level of representation, because of the undesirable associations of the term 'phonemic' with traditional phonemic theory. See Hyman 1975: Ch. 3; Bolinger 1975: Ch. 4.

systematic phonetics A level of REPRESENTATION in GENERATIVE PHONOLOGY which provides a NARROW PHONETIC TRANSCRIPTION of the systematic features of pronunciation, i.e. excluding those which would be attributable to PERFORMANCE factors. It is related by the RULES of the GRAMMAR's phonological COMPONENT to the SYSTEMATIC PHONEMIC level of representation. See Ladefoged 1975: Ch. 2; Huddleston 1976: Ch. 11.

T

🕉🕉🕉🕉🕉🕉

T The usual abbreviation for TRANSFORMATION, as in such phrases as 'T RULES'.

T forms An abbreviation used in SOCIOLINGUISTICS as part of the study of terms of address in various LANGUAGES. Based on the distinction between *tu* and *vous*, the alternative forms of 'you' in French, and on similar CONTRASTS in many other languages (e.g. German *du/Sie*, Russian *ty/vy*), an OPPOSITION is set up between familiar (T) and formal (V) second PERSON VERB and PRONOUN FORMS. Hypotheses are then developed concerning the system of FORMALITY in use in the languages. See Gumperz & Hymes 1971: Ch. 7.

tacit A term used in GENERATIVE LINGUISTICS to characterise the NATIVE SPEAKER's knowledge of his LANGUAGE (his COMPETENCE). It refers to the fact that his INTUITIONS about the way his language is structured and functions are largely unconscious; it is usually used in the phrase **tacit knowledge**. See Huddleston 1976: Ch. 1.

tactic(s) (taxis) A general term used in PHONETICS and LINGUISTICS to refer to the systematic arrangements of UNITS in linear SEQUENCE at any linguistic LEVEL. The commonest terms based on this notion are: **phonotactics**, dealing with the sequential arrangements of sounds; **morphotactics** with MORPHEMES; and **syntactics** with higher grammatical units than the morpheme. Some linguistic theories give this dimension of analysis particular importance (e.g. STRATIFICATIONAL grammar, where several levels of tactic organisation are recognised, corresponding to the strata set up by the theory, *viz* 'hypophono-tactics', 'phonotactics', 'morphotactics', 'lexotactics', 'semotactics' and 'hypersemotactics'). See Bolinger 1975: Ch. 15; Robins 1971: Ch. 7.

tag A term used in GRAMMATICAL DESCRIPTION to refer to a QUESTION-structure (a **tag question**) usually consisting of an AUXILIARY VERB tagmemics

plus PRONOUN, attached to the end of a STATEMENT in order to convey a NEGATIVE or POSITIVE orientation. It may be invariable, as in French *n'est-ce pas*, German *nicht war*, or VARIABLE, as in English. In all cases, the INTONATION in which the tag is uttered determines its FUNCTION – the contrast between 'asking' and 'telling', illustrated by English *he's late, isn't he?* ('I am asking you if he is late') vs. *he's late, isn't he!* ('I am asking you to agree with me that he is late'). In English, in addition to this, the POLARITY of the tag is usually the reverse of that found in the MAIN CLAUSE: a positive clause takes a negative tag, and vice versa, e.g. *he's coming, isn't he/he isn't coming, is he*. Sometimes, two positive clauses are found (*he's coming, is he*), and, very rarely, two negatives (*he doesn't know, doesn't he*). Some grammars also recognise **tag statements** (e.g. *That was a lovely drink, that was; He's a nice man, is John*) and there are some close connections between this CONSTRUC-TION and such 'reinforcing' patterns as *They're all the same, these phoneticians!* See Quirk *et al* 1972: Chs. 7, 14.

tagmemics ((syn)tagmeme, tagma, -tics) A system of LINGUISTIC analysis developed by the American linguist Kenneth Lee Pike (b. 1912), and used by the Summer Institute of Linguistics for the training of linguists. LANGUAGE is seen as comprising three MODES – PHONOLOGY, LEXICON and GRAMMAR. The relationship phonology: PHONEME and lexicon: MORPHEME is paralleled by grammar: **tagmeme**. This basic grammatical UNIT consists of a 'functional slot' within a CONSTRUCTION frame, and a CLASS of substitutable items that can fill this SLOT ('fillers'). The identity of the tagmeme is in its correlation of FUNCTION and FORM, with both being explicitly labelled in the analysis (such functions as SUBJECT, PREDICATE, HEAD, MODIFIER, and such forms as PRONOUNS, NOUN PHRASES, INFINITIVES). **Tagmemic analysis** involves a distinction between essential units (the tagmemes) and the non-essential units (the minimal ETIC units, called **tagmas**, which are analysed as **allotagmas** of the tagmeme). The identification and CLASSIFICATION of tagmas is the province of **tagmatics**. The constructions which result from the stringing together of tagmemes are known as **syntagmemes**. Grammatical units are organised hier-archically into LEVELS (MORPHEMES, WORDS, PHRASES, CLAUSES, SEN-TENCES, etc.).

Units of language description, at any level in this approach, can be analysed simultaneously as PARTICLE (in terms of FEATURES), WAVE (in terms of their status as VARIANTS MANIFESTED in different CONTEXTS) and FIELD (in terms of their DISTRIBUTION). See Bolinger 1975: Ch. 15.

tap A term used in the PHONETIC classification of CONSONANT sounds on the basis of their MANNER OF ARTICULATION: it refers to any sound produced by a single rapid contact with the roof of the mouth by the TONGUE, resembling a very brief articulation of a STOP. It is commonly heard in many American English pronunciations of the medial /t/ or /d/ in *writer* and *rider*. Some phoneticians distinguish between taps and FLAPS in terms of the articulatory movements involved. See Ladefoged 1975: Ch. 7.

target (1) A term used in PHONETICS and PSYCHOLINGUISTICS to refer to a hypothetical ARTICULATORY state used as a reference point when describing SPEECH PRODUCTION in DYNAMIC terms. In CONNECTED SPEECH, the target articulatory features for a sound (e.g. ALVEOLARity, VOICING) may not be fully attained, because of the anticipatory influence of successive **target articulations**. The target MODEL postulates an idealised set of articulatory positions and a set of RULES which attempt to predict actual patterns of articulatory movement, taking into account such factors as speed of articulation, and the direction and distance between articulators. Similarly, models of SPEECH PERCEPTION have been proposed which use the construct of an **auditory target**, which enables the listener to identify the common factors in different ACCENTS, VOICE QUALITIES, etc. See Ladefoged 1975: Ch. 3; Clark & Clark 1977: Ch. 5.

(2) The LANGUAGE (or VARIETY, etc.) which is the focus of a linguistic process of change is known as the **target language**, e.g. the language into which one is translating or interpreting, the language (or variety, etc.) being taught to foreign learners, and so on. See Bolinger 1975: Chs. 11–13.

taxeme A term introduced by the American linguist, Leonard BLOOM-FIELD, on analogy with the PHONEME, to refer to a single minimal feature of GRAMMATICAL ARRANGEMENT. Examples of taxemes include WORD ORDER, CONCORD, the grammatical use of PITCH, and the constituents of the ACTOR–ACTION–GOAL relationship. Combinations of taxemes, occurring as a conventional grammatical unit, are **tactic forms**. Taxemes are distinguished in this approach from TAGMEMES, which are the smallest *meaningful* units of grammatical FORM. See Dinneen 1967: Ch. 9.

taxonomic (taxonomy) An application of the general sense of this term in biosystematics, to refer to an approach to LINGUISTIC analysis and DESCRIPTION which is predominantly or exclusively concerned with CLASSIFICATION. The basis of classification may be HISTORICAL,

AREAL, TYPOLOGICAL, FUNCTIONAL, etc., and the entities being classified may be linguistic FEATURES, ITEMS, UNITS, STRUCTURES – of whole VARIETIES, DIALECTS or LANGUAGES. The notion of 'taxonomy' has been fruitfully applied in many areas of linguistics (SOCIOLINGUISTICS, HISTORICAL linguistics, and SEMANTICS, in particular). The limitations of a taxonomic approach in linguistic analysis have however been emphasised by GENERATIVE linguists, who have criticised the over-reliance of STRUCTURALIST (or 'taxonomic') linguistics on PROCEDURES of SEGMENTATION and classification. In particular, the use of this label is intended to indicate the inability of structural linguistics to provide a level of explanation in terms of DEEP STRUCTURE. Such phrases as 'taxonomic PHONOLOGY', 'taxonomic SYNTAX', etc., when used in generative linguistics, invariably have a pejorative implication. See Gumperz & Hymes 1971: Ch. 1.

tempo An application of the general sense of this term in PHONETICS and PHONOLOGY to refer to speed of speaking; alternatively known as RATE. Contrasts in the tempo of UTTERANCE are analysed in SUPRASEGMENTAL phonetics and phonology, along with PITCH and LOUDNESS variation, as part of the overall study of RHYTHM. See Bolinger 1975: Ch. 3.

tenor A term used in the HALLIDAYAN classification of LANGUAGE VARIETIES (more fully **tenor of discourse**), referring to the relations among the participants in a language activity, especially the LEVEL of FORMALITY they adopt (colloquial, formal, etc.). Alternative labels which have been proposed for this area are STYLE or MANNER of discourse. See Bolinger 1975: Chs. 11, 15.

tense A CATEGORY used in the GRAMMATICAL description of VERBS (along with ASPECT and MOOD), referring primarily to the way the grammar marks the time at which the action denoted by the verb took place. Traditionally, a distinction is made between past, present and future tense forms, often with further divisions (perfect, pluperfect, etc.). In LINGUISTICS, the relationship between tense and time has been the subject of much study, and it is now plain that there is no easily stateable relationship between the two. Tense FORMS (i.e. variations in the MORPHOLOGICAL form of the verb) can be used to signal MEANINGS other than temporal ones. In English, for example, the past tense form (e.g. *I knew*) may signal a tentative meaning, and not past time, in some contexts (e.g. *I wish I knew* – that is, 'know now'). Nor is there a simple one-to-one relationship between tense forms and time: the present tense in English may help to refer to future or past time, depending on CONTEXT (e.g. *I'm going home tomorrow, Last week I'm* *walking down this street*...). Furthermore, if tenses are defined as forms of the verb, it becomes a matter of debate whether a language like English has a future tense at all: constructions such as *I will/shall go*, according to many, are best analysed as involving MODAL AUXILIARY verbs, displaying a different grammatical FUNCTION (e.g. the expression of intention or obligation, which may often involve futurity). English illustrates many such problems, as do other languages, where tense forms, if they exist, regularly display analytic difficulties, because of overlaps between tense and other verbal functions, such as aspect or mood. Alternative terminology (e.g. 'past' vs. 'non-past', 'future' vs. 'non-future', 'now' vs. 'remote') will often be needed. See Palmer 1971: App. C; Lyons 1968: Ch. 7.

tension (tense) A term used in the PHONETIC classification of speech sounds, referring to the overall muscular tension used in producing a sound. The contrasts are labelled variously, e.g. FORTIS VS. LENIS, tense vs. lax. This contrast is viewed as particularly important in DISTINCTIVE FEATURE theories of PHONOLOGY, where **tense** is one of the main features set up to handle variations in MANNER OF ARTICU-LATION. Tense sounds have been defined both ARTICULATORILY and ACOUSTICALLY: they are sounds produced with a relatively strong muscular effort, involving a greater movement of the (SUPRAGLOTTAL) VOCAL TRACT away from the position of rest (cf. FORTIS), and a relatively strong spread of acoustic energy. The VOWELS [i] and [u], for example, would be [+tense]; [ɪ] and [ʊ] would be [−tense]. ASPIRATED and long CONSONANTS (cf. LENGTH) would be [+tense]. The opposite term in JAKOBSON & Halle's system, is LAX; in CHOMSKY & Halle's later system, the term **non-tense** is also used: these are sounds produced with less muscular effort and movement, and which are relatively short and indistinct, involving a relatively weak spread of acoustic energy as in centralised vowels (cf. CENTRE). Sub-glottal tension in Chomsky & Halle's system is handled by the feature HEIGHTENED SUBGLOTTAL PRESSURE. See Ladefoged 1975: Ch. 11; Hyman 1975: Ch. 2.

terminal A term used in GENERATIVE LINGUISTICS to identify certain characteristics of the output of the SYNTACTIC COMPONENT of the GRAMMAR. A **terminal element** or **terminal symbol** refers to the units employed in the syntactic REPRESENTATION of a SENTENCE, after all the RULES have been applied, *viz* the MORPHEMES, FORMATIVES, FEATURES, such as *the*, *-en*, +, #, *man*. Terminal symbols are distin-guished from **non-terminal** (or 'auxiliary') elements, which are used in formulating rules. The former are usually written in lower case letters, the latter in upper case (e.g. NP, VP). A string consisting of terminal elements is known as a **terminal string**, i.e. the final STRING generated by a PHRASE-STRUCTURE grammar. See Lyons 1968: Ch. 6; Huddleston 1976: Ch. 3.

tertiary response A term introduced into LINGUISTICS by Leonard BLOOMFIELD to refer to the views a person displays when his utterances about language (his 'SECONDARY responses') are themselves subjected to evaluation. For example, someone who says 'That dialect is ugly/primitive', etc. is making a secondary response; if this is disputed, then his attempt to explain the basis of his statement (or, indeed, his general emotional reaction) would constitute a tertiary response. See Bolinger 1975: Ch. 16.

tessitura A term taken over by some PHONETICIANS from musical terminology and used to refer to the characteristic compass, or PITCH range, of a person's voice, when he is speaking normally. People are often impressionistically classified in this way (e.g. a 'very high-pitched' voice), as are languages. See Abercrombie 1967: Ch. 6.

text(ual) A pre-theoretical term used in LINGUISTICS and PHONETICS to refer to a stretch of language recorded for the purpose of analysis and description. What is important to note is that texts may refer to collections of written *or* spoken material (the latter having been transcribed in some way), e.g. conversation, monologues, rituals, and so on. The term **textual meaning** is sometimes used in SEMANTICS as part of a classification of types of MEANING, referring to those factors affecting the interpretation of a SENTENCE which derive from the rest of the text in which the sentence occurs – as when, at a particular point in a play or novel, a sentence or word appears whose significance can only be appreciated in the light of what has gone before. See Robins 1971: Ch. 9.

TG The usual abbreviation for TRANSFORMATIONAL GRAMMAR.

that*-clause** A term used in some MODELS of GRAMMATICAL DESCRIPTION to refer to a DEPENDENT DECLARATIVE CLAUSE, introduced by *that*. The main types are: SUBJECT clauses, e.g. ***that she came *surprises me*; OBJECT clauses, e.g. *she said **that she came***; APPOSITIONAL clauses, e.g. *your view, **that he'll come**, is rubbish*; subject COMPLEMENT *clauses*, e.g. *the trouble is **that it won't happen***; and ADJECTIVAL complement clauses, e.g. *I'm certain **that he'll go***. The *that* may be omitted in some circumstances, e.g. *he said **he would come***. See Quirk *et al* 1972: Ch. 11.

theme (thematic, thematisation) A term used in LINGUISTICS as part of an analysis of the structure of SENTENCES (their **thematic structure**): it refers, not to the subject-matter of a sentence (its everyday MEANING), but to the way a speaker identifies the relative importance of his subject-matter, and is defined as the first major CONSTITUENT of a sentence (seen here as a STRING of constituents). There is no necesssary correspondence with a FUNCTIONAL grammatical ELEMENT (though in English, theme and SUBJECT often coincide) e.g. ***The man is coming***, ***His hair*** I can't stand, ***Smith*** her name was, ***Under no condition*** will he... The process of moving an element to the front of the sentence in this way ('fronting'), to act as theme, is known as **thematisation** (sometimes TOPICALISATION). Some linguists systematically distinguish this notion from other ways of analysing the organisation of the sentence-structure of messages, such as the TOPIC/COMMENT distinction, or an analysis in terms of INFORMATION-structure.

In the PRAGUE SCHOOL approach to linguistics of recent years, theme is opposed to RHEME, producing a distinction similar to that of topic/comment, but interpreted with reference to the theoretical framework of FUNCTIONAL SENTENCE PERSPECTIVE. In this theory, the theme is defined as the part of a sentence which adds least to the advancing process of communication (it has the lowest degree of COMMUNICATIVE DYNAMISM); in other words, it expresses relatively little (or no) extra meaning, in addition to what has already been communicated. The rheme, by contrast, carries the highest degree of communicative dynamism. Various transitional expressions, neither 'thematic' nor 'rhematic', are also recognised. See Lyons 1977b: Ch. 12; Bolinger 1975: Ch. 15.

timbre The attribute of auditory sensation in terms of which a listener can judge the dissimilarity between sounds of otherwise identical PITCH, LOUDNESS and LENGTH. The best examples can be found in the characteristic timbres, or 'tonal qualities' of different instruments of the orchestra; but a similar set of timbres can be established to distinguish between the frequency characteristics of individual sounds (such as VOWELS, FRICATIVES) or individual speakers (as one of the features of VOICE QUALITY). The term is sometimes spelled **tambre** or **tamber**. An alternative term, more widely used in the context of SEGMENTAL studies, is QUALITY, as in 'vowel quality'. See Abercrombie 1967: Ch. 1; Crystal 1969: Ch. 3.

timing This general term is applied in PHONETICS and PSYCHOLINGUISTICS to the temporal constraints on the ARTICULATION and SEQUENCING of sounds in SPEECH PRODUCTION. Timing phenomena are therefore of relevance for an understanding of both SEGMENTAL and SUPRASEG-MENTAL phonetics and PHONOLOGY: timing is involved in the co-ordination of musculature required to produce an individual sound, in the programming of PHONOTACTIC SEQUENCES, and in such notions as RHYTHM and INTONATION. See Clark & Clark 1977: Ch. 7.

tip The end point of the TONGUE, also known as the APEX; used in the articulation of a few speech sounds, such as the TRILLED [r]. See Gimson 1970: Ch. 2; Catford 1977: Ch. 8.

tip-of-the-tongue phenomenon The everyday sense of this phrase is found in PSYCHOLINGUISTICS, where the phenomenon is subjected to experimental investigation as part of a theory of SPEECH PRODUCTION. It is shown that people having a tip-of-the-tongue experience are able to recall certain general characteristics of the WORD, e.g. the number of SYLLABLES it has, its STRESS pattern; also some PHONETIC SEGMENTS are recalled more readily than others. These results suggest that words vary in the ACCESSIBILITY of their PHONOLOGICAL REPRESENTATION in the brain, and that certain features of word structure are stored independently of others. See Clark & Clark 1977: Ch. 7.

tone(-eme, -emics, -etics) A term used in PHONOLOGY to refer to the DISTINCTIVE PITCH level of a SYLLABLE. In the study of INTONATION, a sequence of tones constitutes a CONTOUR or TONE UNIT. The most PROMINENT tone in a tone unit may be referred to as a NUCLEAR tone. In many LANGUAGES, the tone carried by a WORD is an essential feature of the MEANING of that word (**lexical tone**), e.g. in Peking Mandarin Chinese the word *ma* when pronounced in a level tone means 'mother', and in a FALLING–rising tone means 'horse' – two out of four possible tone contrasts in that language. Such languages, where word meanings or grammatical CATEGORIES (such as TENSE) are dependent on pitch level, are known as **tone languages**. Many languages of South-East Asia and Africa are tone languages, illustrating several types of tonal organisation. In such languages, sequences of adjacent tones may influence each other phonetically, e.g. a word which in isolation would have a low tone may be given a higher tone if a high-tone word follows: such a phenomenon is sometimes called **tone sandhi**.

The study of the phonetic properties of tone, in its most general sense, is sometimes referred to as **tonetics**. In the EMIC tradition of study, contrastive tones are classified as **tonemes**, and the study of such tones is known as **tonemics**. Features of tone, such as 'high', 'low' and 'mid' are proposed by DISTINCTIVE FEATURE theories of phonology. See Crystal 1969: Ch. 4; Ladefoged 1975: Ch. 10; Hyman 1975: Ch. 6.

tone group/unit A term used by some INTONATION analysts, particularly those working within the British tradition, to refer to a distinctive sequence of PITCHES, or TONES, in an utterance. The essential feature of a tone unit is the NUCLEAR tone, the most PROMINENT tone in the sequence; and this may be accompanied, depending on the length of the utterance, by other components, such as the **head** (i.e. the sequence of SYLLABLES between the first STRESSED syllable and the nuclear tone), **pre-head** (i.e. unstressed syllables at the very beginning of the tone unit) and **tail** (i.e. the syllables following the nuclear tone). This terminology can be illustrated by the sentence *the|man 'bought a|nèw |'clock|*, where the sequence of pre-head/head/nucleus/tail is marked by vertical lines. A tone unit usually corresponds to a CLAUSE or SENTENCE, but may be used on any grammatical unit, e.g. in an extremely irritated version of the above sentence, there might be several tone units, as in *the mán|bóught|a néw|clòck|*. See Crystal 1969: Ch. 4; Gimson 1970: Ch. 10.

tongue (1) From the PHONETIC point of view, the importance of the tongue is that it is the organ of articulation most involved in the production of speech sounds – all the VOWELS and the majority of the CONSONANTS (that is, excluding those made at the lips and in the throat). Different parts of the tongue are involved in articulating these sounds, and it has proved convenient to classify sounds with reference to these areas. From front to back, it is usual to distinguish the TIP (or APEX), BLADE (or FRONT), CENTRE (or 'top'), BACK (or DORSUM) and ROOT. The GROOVE running down the centre of the tongue is also significant, in that several sound contrasts can be made by altering its shape. Plotting tongue movements is difficult visually or kinaesthetically, but recent advances in phonetic instrumentation, such as the ELECTROPALATOGRAPH, can display many of these movements with accuracy. See Gimson 1970: Ch. 2; Catford 1977: Ch. 8.

(2) In CHOMSKY & Halle's DISTINCTIVE FEATURE theory of PHONO-LOGY, **tongue-body features** constitute one of the categories set up to handle variations in PLACE OF ARTICULATION (CAVITY features). The placement of the body of the tongue is characterised with reference to three features, all seen as OPPOSITIONS: HIGH, LOW and BACK. See Ladefoged 1975: Ch. 11.

tongue-slip (slip of the tongue) The everyday sense of this phrase is found in PHONETICS and PSYCHOLINGUISTICS, where the phenomenon is studied as part of a theory of SPEECH PRODUCTION. Such slips seem not to be random, e.g. SEGMENTS occurring initially in SYLLABLES seem to interfere only with other syllable-initial segments The suggestion is that tongue-slips are not just ERRORS OF ARTICULATION, but are rather the results of incorrect neural programming ('slips of the brain', as some would say). The analysis of these errors motivates hypotheses about the properties of the NEUROLINGUISTIC control governing speech (cf. ACCESSIBILITY). See Clark & Clark 1977: Ch. 7.

tonic(-ity) A term used by some INTONATION analysts, particularly those working within the British tradition, to refer to the SYLLABLE in a TONE UNIT which carries maximal PROMINENCE, usually owing to a major PITCH change. The tonic syllable is also referred to as the 'NUCLEAR syllable', or 'nucleus', in this tradition. Most words in a tone unit can carry the **tonic syllable**, depending on the meaning intended, although the usual position for this is at or towards the end of a sequence. Compare the different emphases in: *the **man** was walking to town* with *the man was walking to **town*** and *the man was **walking** to town*. The change in tonicity gives the sentence different implications (e.g. 'the *man*, not the woman, was walking...'), an important aspect of communication in conversation, where it draws attention especially to the NEW INFORMATION in a sentence. See Crystal 1969: Ch. 4; Gimson 1970: Ch. 10.

topic(alisation) (1) A term used in SEMANTICS and GRAMMAR as part of an alternative binary characterisation of SENTENCE STRUCTURE to that traditionally found in the SUBJECT/PREDICATE distinction; the opposite term is COMMENT. The topic of a sentence is the person or thing about which something is said, whereas the further statement made about this person/thing is the comment. The usefulness of the distinction is that it enables general statements to be made about the relationships between sentences which the subject/predicate distinction (along with other contrasts of this type) obscures. The topic often coincides with the subject of a sentence (e.g. ***A man*** / *is coming to the door*), but it need not (e.g. *there's **the man** / who gave you a lift*), and even when it is a subject, it need not come first in a sentence (e.g. *John Smith **my name** is*). It is sometimes referred to as the 'psychological subject'. Some languages mark the topic of a sentence using PARTICLES (e.g. Japanese, Samoan). The topic/comment contrast is, however, sometimes difficult to establish, owing to the effects of INTONATION (which has a 'competing' INFORMATION-signalling function), and in many types of sentence, the analysis is more problematic, such as in COMMANDS and QUESTIONS. See Lyons 1968: Ch. 8; Quirk *et al* 1972: Ch. 14.

(2) The phrase **topic sentence** is used in traditional studies of the structure of paragraphs, to refer to the sentence which introduces the paragraph's theme. Linguistic investigation of this and related notions

is relatively recent, but TEXT analysis of paragraphs indicates that the SEMANTIC and SYNTACTIC complexities of paragraph structure are much greater than this simple judgement suggests. See Quirk *et al* 1972: Ch. 10.

total accountability A principle of LINGUISTIC analysis, introduced into STRUCTURALIST discussion in the 1940s, whereby everything that is stated at one LEVEL of DESCRIPTION is predictable from another. The principle is presented with reference to the relationship between PHONOLOGY and MORPHOLOGY: every MORPH (and thus every PHONEME) must be capable of being determined by the morphemes and TAGMEMES of which an UTTERANCE is composed. Notions such as EMPTY and PORTMANTEAU morphs require special discussion in relation to this principle. See Robins 1971: Ch. 5.

***tough* movement** A term used in GENERATIVE GRAMMAR, referring to a RULE which involves moving a NOUN PHRASE out of the PREDICATE of a COMPLEMENT SENTENCE. *Tough* is one of a CLASS of ADJECTIVES (others being *hard, easy, simple, difficult, eager*, etc.) which have been the focus of discussion ever since Noam CHOMSKY's discussion of pairs such as *John is eager/easy to please*. Sentences such as *The ball was easy for John to catch* were said to be derived by *tough*-movement from the structure $_{NP}[it_S[$ *for John to catch the ball* $]_S]_{NP}$ *was easy*, via a rule which EXTRAPOSES the complement (*it was easy for John to catch the ball*). The rule of *tough*-movement took the non-SUBJECT noun phrase from the extraposed complement (i.e. *the ball*) and substituted it for the initial subject PRONOUN of the sentence as a whole (i.e. *it*). Other formulations of this rule have been suggested, and the extent of the rule's application is still a matter for debate. See Huddleston 1976: Ch. 15.

trace A term introduced into GENERATIVE LINGUISTIC theory of the mid-1970s to refer to a FORMAL means of marking the place a CONSTITUENT once held in a DERIVATION, before it was moved to another position by a TRANSFORMATIONAL operation. The position from which the constituent was moved is known as a 'trace' (*t* marks its place in the REPRESENTATION), which is said to be 'bound' by that constituent. For example, in a RULE which 'raises' the SUBJECT of an EMBEDDED CLAUSE to be the subject of the MAIN clause, the trace *t* marks the position of the embedded subject, e.g. *it is certain* [*the man to come*] → *the man is certain t to come*. Several arguments have been proposed to support a **trace theory** of movement rules, e.g. that it facilitates the statement of the conditions which affect the SEMANTIC INTERPRETATION of SURFACE structures, and that it permits a more

traditional

principled account of the operation of syntactic rules. At the time of writing, however, the extent of the convention's applicability (whether *all* removed constituents leave traces), and the kinds of insight and problem which the theory raises, remain sources of controversy. See Radford 1981: Ch. 5.

traditional A term used in LINGUISTICS, usually pejoratively, in relation to GRAMMAR (**traditional grammar**), to refer to the set of attitudes, procedures and PRESCRIPTIONS characteristic of the pre-linguistic era of language study, and especially of the European school grammars of the 18th and 19th centuries. The emphasis on such matters as CORRECTNESS, linguistic PURISM, literary excellence, the use of Latin models, and the priority of the written language, characterises this approach, and is in contrast with the concern of linguistics for DESCRIPTIVE accuracy, APPROPRIATENESS, CRITERIA of analysis, comprehensiveness, EXPLICITNESS, etc. On the other hand, several basic concepts of contemporary grammatical analysis have their origins in pre-20th century linguistic traditions, such as the notions of HIERARCHY, UNIVERSALS and WORD-CLASSIFICATION. The term 'traditional', too, has been applied to the major descriptive accounts of grammar in handbook form produced by several North European grammarians in the early 20th century (e.g. Otto Jespersen's *Modern English Grammar on Historical Principles* (1909–40). The pejorative use of the term, therefore, needs to be invoked with caution. See Bolinger 1975: Ch. 15.

transcription (-al, transcribe) A method of writing down speech sounds in a systematic and consistent way – also known as a 'notation' or 'script'. Two main kinds of transcription are recognised: PHONETIC and PHONEMIC. Square brackets enclose **phonetic transcription** (notation/script); oblique lines enclose **phonemic transcription** (notation/script). In the former, sounds are symbolised on the basis of their ARTICULATORY/AUDITORY identity, regardless of their FUNCTION in a LANGUAGE. In the latter, the only UNITS to be symbolised are those which have a linguistic function, i.e. the phonemes. A phonemic transcription looks simplest of all, as in this only the units which account for differences of MEANING will be represented, e.g. /pin/, /pen/, /pæn/. In a phonetic transcription on the other hand, the aim is not to judge the functional significance of sounds, in the context of some language, but to identify the sounds as such. A phonetic transcription of the English word *pen*, for example, might be [pʰɛ̃n]: this indicates some quite subtle features of pronunciation, such as the ASPIRATION following the PLOSIVE, and the slight NASALI-

SATION of the VOWEL – features which are not phonemes in their own right. If necessary, such a transcription could be made more detailed still, to incorporate any other articulatory or auditory features found in the pronunciation. Phonetic transcriptions which are relatively detailed are called **narrow transcriptions**; those which are less detailed are called **broad transcriptions**. In the broadest possible transcription, only those phonetic SEGMENTS would be notated which correspond to the functionally important units in the language – in other words, it would be equivalent to a phonemic transcription, and some phoneticians do use 'broad' in the sense of 'phonemic'. But in principle it is important to appreciate that the two transcriptions of [pen] and /pen/ refer to very different entities: the first is a broad phonetic transcription, representing a sequence of concrete, physical articulations; the second is a phonemic transcription, representing a sequence of abstract, functional units, and reflecting a particular theoretical point of view.

It is also important to remember that there are several possible ways of transcribing sounds phonemically, depending on the analyst's views as to what the salient contrasting features are. The contrast between *seat* and *sit*, for example, might be shown as /siːt/ vs. /sit/ or as /sit/ vs. /sɪt/: in the former case, the transcription indicates that the CONTRAST between these words is due to the different LENGTH of the vowels; in the latter case, the transcription suggests that it is not length but the QUALITY of the vowels which differentiates the words, /sɪt/ using a more OPEN vowel than /sit/. It would also be possible to have a third view, /siːt/ vs. /sɪt/, where both length and quality would be considered relevant. All these transcriptions will be found.

In any transcription (whether phonetic or phonemic), each distinguishable sound is given its own 'symbol'. The whole range of available phonetic symbols is known as a 'phonetic alphabet'. The most widely used such alphabet is the INTERNATIONAL PHONETIC alphabet.

Phonetic symbols are often the same as a letter of the alphabet, e.g. [b] as in *bit*, [k] as in *kettle*, but many new symbols have had to be invented to cope with the range of sounds heard in speech, e.g. [ʃ] for the *sh* sound in *ship*, [θ] for the *th* sound in *thin*. Most of the vowel sounds have had to be given a new symbol, to avoid overloading the five traditional vowel letters of the alphabet, and the generally 'alien' appearance of a phonetic transcription is largely due to this (see the range used in the CARDINAL VOWEL system, for example). See Gimson 1970: Ch. 5; Ladefoged 1975: Ch. 2.

transfer A term used in APPLIED LINGUISTICS to refer to a process in foreign LANGUAGE learning whereby learners carry over what they already know about their first language to their performance in their new language. This tendency may be an advantage, if the two languages have features in correspondence, as there will be 'positive transfer' (or 'facilitation'). Rather more noticeable, however, are the cases of 'negative transfer' (or INTERFERENCE), where the patterns of the two languages do not coincide. See Corder 1973: Ch. 6.

transformation(al) (transform) A FORMAL LINGUISTIC operation which enables two levels of structural REPRESENTATION to be placed in correspondence. A **transformational rule** (**T rule, transformation,** or **transform**) consists of a SEQUENCE of symbols which is rewritten as another sequence, according to certain conventions. The 'input' to the RULE is the STRUCTURAL DESCRIPTION ('structural analysis' or 'structure index'), which defines the class of PHRASE-MARKERS to which the rule can apply. The rule then operates a STRUCTURAL CHANGE on this input, by performing one or more of several basic operations. MOVEMENT (RE-ORDERING or PERMUTATION) transformations modify an input structure by re-ordering the elements it contains. When this operation is seen as one of moving elements to adjoining positions in a phrase marker, it is known as ADJUNCTION. INSERTION transformations add new structural elements to the input structure (as in element COPYING, or the insertion of *by* in the PASSIVE transformation below). DELETION transformations eliminate elements from the input structure. There is a certain amount of variation in the names given to these operations, and opinions differ concerning their status as fundamental operations within the theory.

One of the earliest illustrations of the operation of a transformational rule was the one which converted ACTIVE sentences into passive ones, which can be formulated as follows:

$$NP_1—Aux—V—NP_2 \rightarrow NP_2—Aux + be + en—V—by + NP_1$$

(where *be* is a form of the verb *to be*, and *en* represents the past participle ending of the LEXICAL verb). The rule is said to 'operate' on the first, UNDERLYING phrase-marker, converting it into a second, 'derived', phrase-marker. The string produced by the derived phrase-marker may then serve as the underlying string for further transformations, as the analysis of the SENTENCE proceeds. The sequence of phrase-markers assigned to a sentence constitutes its **transformational derivation** or **transformational history**.

A grammar which operates using this notion is a **transformational grammar**. This type of grammar was first discussed by Noam

CHOMSKY in *Syntactic Structures* (1957) as an illustration of a GENERATIVE device more POWERFUL than FINITE-STATE grammars or PHRASE-STRUCTURE grammars. In this view, very many sentence types can be ECONOMICALLY derived by supplementing the CONSTITUENT analysis rules of phrase-structure grammars with rules for transforming one sentence into another. The rule of passivisation above, for instance, is claimed to be a procedure both SIMPLER and INTUITIVELY more satisfactory than generating active and passive sentences separately in the same grammar. The arguments were persuasive, and as a result transformational grammars became the most influential type in the development of generative grammatical theory: indeed, the field as a whole has since been variously known as 'generative grammar', 'transformational grammar', 'transformational generative grammar' (or simply 'TG').

Several MODELS of transformational grammar have been presented since its first outline. The standard model, as presented by Chomsky in *Aspects of the Theory of Syntax* (1965), consists of three COMPONENTS: (a) a syntactic component, comprising a basic set of phrase-structure rules (sometimes called the BASE component) which together with lexical information provides the DEEP structural information about sentences, and a set of transformational rules for generating SURFACE structures; (b) a PHONOLOGICAL component, which converts strings of syntactic elements into pronounceable utterance; and (c) a SEMANTIC component, which provides a REPRESENTATION of the meaning of the LEXICAL ITEMS to be used in the sentence. The ways in which these components should be inter-related (especially the relationships between semantics and syntax) have proved to be a source of continuing controversy, since the appearance of *Aspects*, and alternative models of analysis have developed (cf. especially the distinction between GENERATIVE and INTERPRETIVE semantics).

As a result of these developments, the status and classification of transformations varied a great deal in the 1960s and 1970s. A distinction introduced early on is that between OPTIONAL and OBLIGATORY transformations, the former referring to a rule which *may* apply at a given stage in a derivation, the latter to a rule which *must* apply, if a WELL-FORMED sentence is to result. On the other hand, the classification and terminology of transformations in *Syntactic Structures* is different in many respects from that encountered in *Aspects*. In the former, two types of transformation are recognised: SINGULARY (or SINGLE-BASE), where the rule operates on only one TERMINAL string; and GENERALIZED (or DOUBLE-BASE), where the rule combines two or more terminal strings, as in CONJOINING and EMBEDDING transformations (which handle CO-ORDINATION and SUBORDINATION respectively).

In *Aspects*, however, other distinctions are introduced, some of which replace those found in the former book. Of particular importance is a distinction drawn in one of the models outlined in *Aspects* between LEXICAL and 'non-lexical' transformations: the former transform pre-lexical structures into DEEP structures containing COMPLEX SYMBOLS; the latter transform deep structures into SURFACE structures.

The theoretical status of transformations in generative linguistics is still a matter of debate, e.g. how to restrict the power of transformations, or whether all transformations need to be meaning-preserving (cf. the KATZ–POSTAL hypothesis). The potential fruitfulness of the notion, however, continues to be explored. See Lyons 1968: Ch. 6; 1977a: Ch. 7; Huddleston 1976: Ch. 4.

transition (1) A term used in PHONOLOGY to refer to the way adjacent sounds are linked. There are many ways in which the relationships between successive ARTICULATIONS may be described (cf. GLIDE, LIAISON): one general classification which has been suggested distinguishes between **close transitions** and **open transitions**, similar to the distinction between close and open JUNCTURE. Close transitions refer to those articulations where there is an articulatory continuity between successive sounds; in open transition, by contrast, there is a break in the continuity of the articulation. The distinction can be seen in the *s–s* sequences heard in *this sort* and *this assortment*, where the former illustrates a close, and the latter an open transition. See Catford 1977: Ch. 11.

(2) **(-al)** The term is also used in ACOUSTIC PHONETICS for the acoustic change which takes place to and from the articulatory positions of CONSONANTS, especially PLOSIVES. The transitional features, or **transients**, can be clearly seen on a SPECTROGRAM, by the way the FORMANTS of the adjacent VOWELS are bent upwards or downwards, depending on which consonant is articulated. See Ladefoged 1975: Ch. 8.

transitivity (transitive, intransitive) A category used in the GRAMMATICAL analysis of CLAUSE/SENTENCE CONSTRUCTIONS, with particular reference to the VERB's relationship to DEPENDENT elements of structure. The main members of this category are 'transitive', referring to a verb which can take a direct OBJECT (as in *he saw the dog*), and 'intransitive', where it cannot (as in **he went a ball*). Many verbs can have both a transitive and an intransitive use (cf. *we went a mile* vs. *we went*), and in some languages this distinction is marked MORPHOLOGICALLY. More complex relationships between a verb and the elements dependent upon it are usually classified separately. For example, verbs which take two objects are sometimes called 'ditransitive', as in *he gave me a pencil*. There are also several uses of verbs which are marginal to one or other of these categories, as in 'pseudo-intransitive' constructions (e.g. *the eggs are selling well*, where an AGENT is assumed – 'someone is selling the eggs' – unlike normal intransitive constructions, which do not have an agent transform – *we went*, but not **someone went us*). See Lyons 1968: Ch. 8; 1977b: Ch. 12; Quirk *et al* 1972: Chs. 2, 12.

tree (sub-) A two-dimensional diagram used in GENERATIVE GRAMMAR as a convenient means of displaying the internal HIERARCHICAL STRUCTURE of SENTENCES as generated by a set of RULES. The 'root' of the **tree diagram** is at the top of the diagram, consisting of the INITIAL SYMBOL S. From this topmost point, or NODE, branches descend corresponding to the CATEGORIES specified by the rules (e.g. NP, VP, etc.). The internal relationships of parts of the tree are described using 'family tree' terminology: if two CATEGORIES both derive from a single node, they are said to be 'sisters', and 'daughters' of the node from which they derive. A sub-section of a tree diagram, isolated for purposes of discussion, is referred to as a **subtree**, as in the enclosed area within the following example:

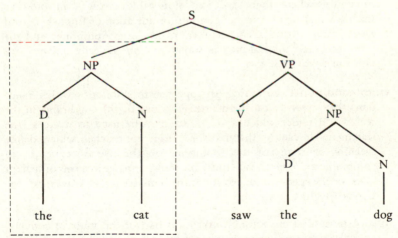

See Huddleston 1976: Ch. 3; Akmajian & Heny 1975: Ch. 2.

triadic A term used to characterise a theory of MEANING which postulates that there is an indirect relationship between LINGUISTIC FORMS and the entities, states of affairs, etc. to which they refer (i.e. REFERENTS).

Instead of a direct two-way relationship (a DUALIST theory), a third step is proposed, corresponding to the mental concept or SENSE of the linguistic form. The most well-known triadic MODEL is the 'semantic triangle' of C. K. Ogden (1889–1957) and I. A. Richards (1893–1979), presented in their book *The Meaning of Meaning* in 1923. See Lyons 1977b: Ch. 4.

trill(-ed) A term in the PHONETIC classification of CONSONANT sounds on the basis of their MANNER OF ARTICULATION: also known as a 'trilled' consonant, or a ROLL, it refers to any sound made by the rapid tapping of one organ of articulation against another. (VOCAL CORD vibration is not included in such a definition.) Several DIALECTS of English used the trilled *r*, as in Welsh and Scots. French and German are examples of LANGUAGES which have a UVULAR trill. The trill may also be accompanied by audible friction, and would then be called a 'FRICATIVE trill'. BILABIAL trills are also possible, as when one makes a 'freezing' noise, *brrr*, or imitates a car engine. See Gimson 1970: Chs. 4, 8; Catford 1977: Ch. 7.

triphthong A term used in the PHONETIC classification of VOWEL sounds on the basis of their MANNER OF ARTICULATION: it refers to a type of vowel where there are two noticeable changes in QUALITY during a SYLLABLE, as in a common pronunciation of English *fire* and *tower* /faɪə/, /taʊə/. The distinction between triphthongs and the more common DIPHTHONGS is sometimes phonetically unclear. See Gimson 1970: Chs. 4, 7.

truth-conditional semantics An approach to SEMANTICS which maintains that MEANING can be defined in terms of the conditions in the real world under which a SENTENCE may be used to make a true statement. It can be distinguished from approaches which define meaning in terms of the conditions on the use of sentences in communication, such as the function of the sentence in terms of SPEECH ACTS, or the speaker's beliefs about the sentence (cf. PRAGMATICS). See Lyons 1977b: Ch. 4.

turn A term used in SOCIOLINGUISTICS as part of the study of conversational structure: conversation is seen as a sequence of **conversational turns**, in which the contribution of each participant is seen as part of a co-ordinated and RULE-governed behavioural interaction. Some of the rules governing **turn-taking** are obvious (e.g. that only one person should talk at a time); others are less easy to discover, e.g. the rules which decide who should speak next in a group discussion. How children learn the conventions governing turn-taking is an issue which has recently attracted considerable interest in language ACQUISITION. See Clark & Clark 1977: Ch. 6; Gumperz & Hymes 1971: Ch. 12.

typological linguistics (typology) A branch of LINGUISTICS which studies the STRUCTURAL similarities between LANGUAGES, regardless of their history, as part of an attempt to establish a satisfactory CLASSIFICATION, or typology of languages. **Typological comparison** is thus distinguished from the historical comparison of languages – the province of COMPARATIVE PHILOLOGY and HISTORICAL linguistics – and its groupings may not coincide with those set up by the historical method. For example, in respect of the paucity of INFLECTIONAL endings, English is closer to Chinese than it is to Latin. One typological classification, proposed by the German linguist Wilhelm von Humboldt (1768–1835) in the early 19th century, established three main groups of languages on structural grounds: ISOLATING, AGGLUTINATIVE, and FUSIONAL; a fourth category, of POLYSYNTHETIC, has sometimes been suggested. The MORPHOLOGICAL orientation of this approach is however only one aspect of typological analysis, which can operate at all linguistic levels (e.g. a PHONOLOGICAL typology in terms of CONSONANT/VOWEL inventories or SYSTEMS, SYLLABLE structure, or SUPRASEGMENTAL patterns – as illustrated in such notions as 'TONE language' or 'CLICK language'). When one considers the many possible criteria of typological comparison, it is plain that no simple classification is likely to emerge, and that differences between languages are not clear-cut, but matters of degree. See Robins 1971: Ch. 8; Bolinger 1975: Ch. 1.

U

🔵🔵🔵🔵🔵🔵

UC The usual abbreviation for ultimate CONSTITUENT.

ultimate constituent (UC) A term used in STRUCTURALIST GRAMMATICAL analysis to refer to the irreducible ELEMENTS which are the result of an IMMEDIATE CONSTITUENT analysis. For example, in the SENTENCE *The girls stopped the bus*, the ultimate constituents would be *the + girl + s + stop + ed + the + bus*. See Lyons 1968: Ch. 6; 1977a: Ch. 6.

under-extension A term used in LANGUAGE ACQUISITION studies to refer to one type of relationship between adult and child MEANING, as expressed in LEXICAL ITEMS. In 'under-extension', the child's lexical item has a narrower range of APPLICATION than the equivalent term in adult language, e.g. when *cat* is used to refer to only one specific cat. See Clark & Clark 1977: Ch. 13.

underlying A term used in LINGUISTICS to refer to an abstract level of REPRESENTATION of a SENTENCE postulated in order to explain the patterns encountered in the empirical DATA of a LANGUAGE. The notion of **underlying forms** is central to GENERATIVE GRAMMAR, where several stages of **underlying structure** are recognised in the DERIVATION of sentences. In early TRANSFORMATIONAL grammar, the **underlying phrase-marker** refers to the STRUCTURAL DESCRIPTION of a sentence which is the result of the PHRASE-STRUCTURE rules; this **underlying string** then acts as the input to the transformational rules, which thereby produces 'derived' phrase-markers. Later, the term DEEP structure came to be used as a specific conception of underlying structure, in the context of *Aspects of the Theory of Syntax*, from which SURFACE structures are transformationally derived. The extent to which the various underlying representations of sentences have psychological reality has been and remains controversial. See Lyons 1968: Ch. 6; Hyman 1975: Ch. 3; Bolinger 1975: Ch. 4.

unit In a general, pre-theoretical sense, this term is often used in LINGUISTICS and PHONETICS, to refer to any entity which constitutes the focus of an enquiry. In HALLIDAYAN linguistics, however, the term has a special status, referring to one of the four main CATEGORIES recognised by that theory (the others being STRUCTURE, CLASS and SYSTEM). The unit is the stretch of language that carries grammatical patterns, and within which grammatical choices are made. For example, the unit SENTENCE consists of one or more instances of the unit CLAUSE, and so on (cf. RANK). In some grammatical descriptions, the term 'unit noun' is preferrred to COUNTABLE noun. See Lyons 1968: Ch. 5; Robins 1971: Ch. 7.

universal A term used in LINGUISTICS, and especially in GENERATIVE GRAMMAR, referring to a property claimed to be common for all LANGUAGES, to demonstrate the validity of which is a main goal of linguistic theory. **Universal grammar** is the term used to identify the main aim of those who hold that the ultimate purpose of linguistics is to specify precisely the possible form of a human grammar – and especially the restrictions on the form such grammars can take. In their broadest sense, then, **language universals** are equivalent to the general design-features of human language identified by some linguists under such headings as DUALITY, CREATIVITY, REFLEXIVENESS and DISPLACEMENT. In the generative literature, two main types of universal are recognised. **Formal universals** are the necessary conditions which have to be imposed on the construction of grammars in order for them to be able to operate. They include such notions as the number of COMPONENTS, types of RULES, ORDERING conventions (e.g. CYCLES), types of TRANSFORMATIONS, and so on. **Substantive universals**, on the other hand, are the PRIMITIVE elements in a grammar, required for the analysis of linguistic data, e.g. NP, VP, [+grave], [+abstract]. Depending on the COMPONENT of the grammar in which they occur, universals are referred to as 'PHONOLOGICAL universals', 'semantic universals' (cf. 'universal SEMANTICS'), 'SYNTACTIC universals', etc. Some of these categories may actually be found in every language, but it is not crucial to the notion of substantive universal that they should be. All that is required is that they be constructs which need to be defined by linguistic theory to enable cross-language generalisations to be made, i.e. they are not terms established for the analysis of just one language, but are capable of general application. The **universal base** hypothesis in generative linguistics states that all languages can be generated by using the same set of basic rules – though whether these are seen as rules of the BASE syntactic component or as a set of semantic FORMATION-RULES depends on the theory employed (cf. STANDARD THEORY and GENERATIVE SEMANTICS).

Other types of linguistic universal have been suggested. Quantitative studies have introduced the notion of **statistical universals**, i.e. constants of a statistical kind, such as a ratio of use between different structures. **Implicational universals** are generalised statements of the form 'if X, then Y', e.g. if a language has a WORD order of a certain type, it will also have a VERB structure of a certain type. See Lyons 1968: Ch. 8; Huddleston 1976: Ch. 13.

usage The collective term for the speech and writing habits of a community, especially as they are presented DESCRIPTIVELY with information about preferences for alternative linguistic FORMS. LINGUISTS emphasise the importance of describing the facts of usage as a control on the claims made by GRAMMARS, and contrast this emphasis with the PRESCRIPTIVE attitudes of TRADITIONAL grammar, whose RULES often bore no relationship to what people actually did with their language. The many 'LEVELS of usage' which descriptive investigations encounter can be formally taken into account in several ways, such as by adding 'usage labels' (as in dictionary entries, e.g. 'slang', 'nautical'), or by the use of statistical statements about preferences, or (in GENERATIVE contexts) by the notion of VARIABLE rules. See Quirk *et al* 1972: Ch. 1; Bolinger 1975: Ch. 16.

utterance A term used in LINGUISTICS and PHONETICS to refer to a stretch of speech about which no assumptions have been made in terms of linguistic theory (as opposed to the notion of SENTENCE, which receives its definition from a theory of GRAMMAR). In principle, it is a physically definable, behavioural unit, capable of definition in everyday terms. One commonly used definition refers to 'a stretch of speech preceded and followed by silence or a change of speaker'. But it has proved very difficult to construct a satisfactory definition. The definition just given, for instance, applies equally to a one-word response and a sermon, and attempts have been made to produce a more restricted definition, using such features as PAUSE, RHYTHM, breath patterns, PITCH movement, etc. The analogous term in the study of writing is TEXT. See Lyons 1968: Ch. 5.

uvular A term used in the PHONETIC classification of CONSONANT sounds on the basis of their PLACE OF ARTICULATION: it refers to a sound made by the BACK of the tongue against the uvula. The *r* of STANDARD French is uvular, and this quality may be heard in some regional DIALECTS of English, especially in the north-east. It is transcribed as [R]. Uvular PLOSIVE consonants are found in Arabic, for example, and are transcribed [q] and [G] for the VOICELESS and VOICED types respectively. See Gimson 1970: Ch. 2; Catford 1977: Ch. 8.

V

🄢🄢🄢🄢🄢🄢

V forms An abbreviation used in SOCIOLINGUISTICS as part of the study of terms of address in various LANGUAGES. Based on the distinction between *tu* and *vous*, the alternative forms of 'you' in French, and on similar CONTRASTS in many other languages (e.g. German *du/Sie*, Russian *ty/vy*), an OPPOSITION is set up between formal (V) and familiar (T) second PERSON VERB and PRONOUN FORMS. Hypotheses are then developed concerning the system of FORMALITY in use in the language. See Gumperz & Hymes 1971: Ch. 7.

valency A term derived from chemistry and used in some theories of LINGUISTICS to refer to the number and type of bonds which SYNTACTIC ELEMENTS form with each other. As in chemistry, a given element may have different valencies in different CONTEXTS. A **valency grammar** presents a MODEL of a SENTENCE containing a fundamental element (the VERB) and a number of dependent elements whose type is determined by the 'valency' attributed to the verb. 'Valency' was introduced by the French linguist Lucien Tesnière (1893–1954), and has been influential in the development of models of DEPENDENCY GRAMMAR in Europe and the Soviet Union. See Lyons 1977a: Ch. 8.

value (valeur) A term introduced into LINGUISTICS by Ferdinand de SAUSSURE to refer to the FUNCTIONAL identity of an entity when seen in the context of a RULE-governed SYSTEM. In his view, LANGUAGE is a system of independent terms, in which the 'value' of each term results solely from the simultaneous presence of the others, related through the notions of SYNTAGMATIC and PARADIGMATIC association. See Dinneen 1967: Ch. 7.

variable (1) A term sometimes used in the GRAMMATICAL classification of WORDS to refer to one of two postulated major word classes in language, the other being INVARIABLE. 'Variable words' are said to be those which express grammatical relationships through a change of FORM, e.g. *boy/boys, walk/walking, nice/nicer*. Invariable words are unchanging, whatever their distribution, e.g. *in, on, and.* See Robins 1971: Ch. 5.

(2) The term has been introduced into SOCIOLINGUISTICS by the American linguist William Labov (b. 1927) to refer to the UNITS in a language which are most subject to social or STYLISTIC variation, and thus most susceptible to change in the long term. Sets of PHONOLOGICAL, GRAMMATICAL and LEXICAL variables are described quantitatively with reference to such factors as social class, age and sex, and the results of this co-variation are stated in the form of **variable rules**. Variable RULES are GENERATIVE rules which have been modified so as to specify the socio-regional conditions under which they apply. The notion has been developed primarily in relation to hypotheses concerning the relationship between social variation and linguistic evolution. See Gumperz & Hymes 1971: Intro., Ch. 19; Bolinger 1975: Ch. 12.

variant A term used in LINGUISTICS to refer to a linguistic FORM which is one of a set of alternatives in a given CONTEXT. The concept is fundamental to the notion of ALLO- (-PHONE, -MORPH, etc.), as illustrated by the **variant forms** of the past TENSE MORPHEME (/-t/, /-d/, /-ɪd/, etc.). The choice of variants may be subject to contextual constraints (**conditioned variants**) or there may be no stateable CONDITIONS – the cases of **free variants**. See Lyons 1968: Chs. 3, 5; Bolinger 1975: Chs. 2, 4.

variety A term used in SOCIOLINGUISTICS and STYLISTICS to refer to any SYSTEM of LINGUISTIC EXPRESSION whose use is governed by SITUATIONAL VARIABLES. In some cases, the situational DISTINCTIVENESS of the LANGUAGE may be easily stated, as in many regional and occupational varieties (e.g. London English, religious English); in other cases, as in studies of social class, the varieties are more difficult to define, involving the intersection of several variables (e.g. sex, age, occupation). Several classifications of language varieties have been proposed, involving such terms as DIALECT, REGISTER, MEDIUM and FIELD. For some sociolinguists, 'variety' is given a more restricted definition, as one kind of situationally distinctive language – a specialised type of language used within a dialect, e.g. for occupational purposes. See Bolinger 1975: Chs. 11–13; Gumperz & Hymes 1971: Ch. 1.

velar(-ic, -isation, -ise) A term used in the PHONETIC classification of CONSONANT sounds on the basis of their PLACE OF ARTICULATION: it refers to a sound made by the BACK of the tongue against the soft

PALATE, or **velum** (the 'veil' of the palate). Examples in English are [k] and [g], and the *-ng-* sound [ŋ] as in *sing*. Velar FRICATIVE sounds are found in German and Greek, for example, and are transcribed [x] and [ɤ] for the VOICELESS and VOICED types respectively. If the velum is raised to shut off the nasal tract, a 'velic closure' has been made.

Velar sounds are different from **velaric** sounds. The term 'velaric' refers to a quite different mode of speech production: instead of using an AIR-STREAM generated by the lungs, velaric sounds use air generated by a closure in velar position. The back of the tongue is raised against the velum, and articulations are made further forward by the lips or front parts of the tongue. These sounds are usually called CLICKS, and have a distinctive role in some languages, such as Zulu. In English, they may be heard in the 'tut tut' sound, and in a few other contexts.

Velarisation is a general term referring to any SECONDARY ARTICU-LATION involving a movement of the back part of the tongue towards the velum. For a sound to be 'velarised', of course, its primary place of articulation must be elsewhere in the mouth; e.g. a [z] sound, normally made in ALVEOLAR position, is said to be velarised if during its articulation the back of the tongue is raised towards the soft palate; this would give the sound a distinctive back (or 'dark') resonance. The term is usually applied to consonants other than velar consonants; it can be used with reference to VOWELS, but such variations in vowel articulation are usually described in different terms ('centralised', 'retracted', etc.). The velarisation may be an essential feature of the sound's identity, contrasting with other **non-velarised** sounds, as in the distinction between velarised and non-velarised *s* in Arabic (transcribed [ṣ] and [s] respectively). In English, velarisation is dependent on context, as when the *l* in *cool* is given a velar resonance because of the influence of the preceding BACK vowel, [u:]; this can be compared with the *l* of *leap*, which is articulated much further forward in the mouth (towards the palate) because of the influence of the following FRONT vowel [i:]. A loose auditory label for velar resonance sounds is 'dark' (DARK L, etc.), opposed to 'clear', used for the palatal-resonance sounds. The usual symbol for velarised consonants is [~], placed through the letter, as in [t], [d], [ł]. Some English dialects, such as those of the Midlands (Birmingham, Wolverhampton, etc.), have several velarised sounds. See Gimson 1970: Chs. 2, 7, 8; Catford 1977: Ch. 8.

ventricular A term used in PHONETICS to describe a type of sound produced between the ventricular bands, or 'false' VOCAL FOLDS, which lie immediately above and parallel with the true vocal cords. It is not normally used in speech, but ventricular effects involving whisper and VOICE can be heard, the latter sometimes combining with GLOTTAL voice to produce a 'double' or 'diplophonic' voice. See Catford 1977: Ch. 6.

verb(-al) A term used in the GRAMMATICAL classification of words, to refer to a class traditionally defined as 'doing' or 'action' words (a description which has been criticised in LINGUISTICS, largely on the grounds that many verbs do not 'act' in any obvious sense, e.g. *seem*, *be*). The FORMAL definition of a verb refers to an element which can display MORPHOLOGICAL contrasts of TENSE, ASPECT, VOICE, MOOD, PERSON and NUMBER. FUNCTIONALLY, it is the ELEMENT which, singly or in combination with other verbs (i.e. 'verb phrase'), is used as the minimal PREDICATE of a sentence, co-occurring with a SUBJECT, e.g. *he/came*. If the predicate contains other elements (e.g. OBJECT, COMPLEMENT, ADVERBIAL), then it is the verb which more than any other is the unit which influences the choice and extent of these elements, e.g. the verb *put* takes both an object and a LOCATIVE adverbial, as in *he put the book on the table*. In many grammatical theories, accordingly, the verb is considered the most important element in sentence structure.

The term **verb phrase** is used in two senses. Traditionally, it refers to a group of verbs which together have the same syntactic FUNCTION as a single verb, e.g. *is coming, may be coming, get up to*. In such phrases (**verbal groups, verbal clusters**), one verb is the main verb (the **lexical verb**) and the others are subordinate to it (**auxiliary verbs, catenative verbs**). A verb followed by a non-verbal PARTICLE (similar in form to a preposition or adverb) is generally referred to as a **phrasal verb**.

In GENERATIVE grammar, the verb phrase (VP) has a much broader definition, being equivalent to the whole of the predicate of a sentence, as is clear from the expansion of S as NP + VP in PHRASE STRUCTURE grammar.

The adjective from 'verb', **verbal**, is often used in traditional grammatical description (though one must be careful not to confuse it with 'verbal' meaning 'spoken', as in 'verbal skill', 'verbalise', etc.), for instance 'verbal noun' (= a NOUN similar in form or meaning to a verb, e.g. *smoking*), 'verbal adjective' (= an ADJECTIVE similar in form or meaning to a verb, e.g. *interested*). See Lyons 1968: Ch. 7; Quirk *et al* 1972: Ch. 3.

verbless A type of CLAUSE recognised in some MODELS of GRAMMATICAL description, in which the VERB is omitted (and often the SUBJECT as well), e.g. **When ready**, *we waited for the signal, Stay at home **if possible***.

TRANSFORMATIONAL models of analysis would DERIVE such structures using a process of DELETION. See Quirk *et al* 1972: Ch. 11.

vernacular A term used in SOCIOLINGUISTICS to refer to the indigenous LANGUAGE or DIALECT of a SPEECH community, e.g. the vernacular of Liverpool, Berkshire, Jamaica, etc. The study of 'Black English Vernacular' in the United States has been the focus of several linguistic studies since the 1960s. PIDGIN languages are sometimes called **contact vernaculars**. Vernaculars are usually seen in contrast to such notions as STANDARD, LINGUA FRANCA, etc. See Trudgill 1974: Ch. 3.

vocabulary LINGUISTICS uses this term in its everyday sense, reserving for its technical study the use of terms beginning with LEXI- (cf. LEXIS, LEXICON). A distinction is sometimes made between 'active' and 'passive' vocabulary: the former refers to lexical items a person uses; the latter to words which he understands, but does not himself use. See Bolinger 1975: Ch. 5.

vocal-auditory channel A term used in the study of COMMUNICATION to refer to one of the human sensory modes which can be used for the transmission and reception of information. It provides the frame of reference within which the study of PHONETICS proceeds, and constitutes the majority of the subject-matter of LINGUISTICS (which of course is also concerned with the written LANGUAGE). See Lyons 1977b: Ch. 3; Crystal 1969: Ch. 3.

vocal cords/lips/bands/folds Two muscular folds running from a single point inside the front of the thyroid cartilage (Adam's apple) backwards to the front ends of the arytenoid cartilages. The vocal cords are very flexible, being shaped by the combined activities of the associated cartilages and muscles. The space between them is known as the GLOTTIS.

The vocal cords have several functions. Their main role in speech is to vibrate in such a manner as to produce VOICE, a process known as PHONATION. When the cords are not vibrating, two main alternative positions are available. They may be tightly closed, as when the breath is held – a process which produces a GLOTTAL stop upon release. Or they may remain open, so that the breath flowing through the glottis produces audible FRICTION, as in whispering and the [h] sound. Other 'phonation types' are possible, by varying the mode of vibration of the vocal cords in various ways, as in BREATHY and CREAKY voice. Varying the thickness, length and tension of the vocal cords also produces the different REGISTERS in voice production, such as the distinction between 'falsetto' and 'chest' voice. Lastly, by varying the rate and strength of vibration of the vocal cords, variations in PITCH and LOUDNESS can be introduced into speech.

The question of how precisely the vocal cords operate, from a physiological viewpoint, has been the subject of controversy, and is still not wholly understood. The most widely held theory maintains that the cords are set in vibration aerodynamically, solely by a reaction taking place between their elastic properties and the sub-glottal air pressure involved – this is known as the 'myoelastic' theory of voice production. An alternative theory, developed in the 1950s, argued that the cords are set in motion as a result of periodic NEURAL stimulation and contraction of the muscles – this was known as the 'neurochronaxiac' theory. See Catford 1977: Ch. 6; Gimson 1970: Ch. 2.

vocalic One of the MAJOR CLASS FEATURES of sound set up by GENERATIVE phonologists in their DISTINCTIVE FEATURE theory of PHONOLOGY, its opposite being **non-vocalic**. Vocalic sounds may be defined ARTICU-LATORILY or ACOUSTICALLY in this approach: they are sounds where there is a free passage of air through the VOCAL TRACT, the most radical CONSTRICTION in the ORAL CAVITY not exceeding that found in [i] and [u], and the VOCAL CORDS being positioned so as to allow spontaneous VOICING; acoustically, there is a sharply defined FORMANT structure. Non-vocalic sounds lack one or other of these conditions. See Ladefoged 1975: Ch. 9; Hyman 1975: Ch. 2.

vocalisation A general term used in LINGUISTICS and PHONETICS to refer to an UTTERANCE viewed solely as a sequence of sound. No reference is made to its linguistic structure, and indeed, in such phrases as 'infant vocalisation', there may be no such structure. In a somewhat more restricted sense, the term is sometimes used referring to the use of sound involving VOCAL CORD vibration – a vocalisation is then 'any voiced sound'. See Catford 1977: Ch. 1.

vocal organs The collective term for the whole of the anatomical features involved in the production of speech sounds, including the lungs, trachea, oesophagus, LARYNX, PHARYNX, MOUTH and nose. See Catford 1977: Ch. 2; Ladefoged 1975: Ch. 1.

vocal tract A general term used in PHONETICS to refer to the whole of the air passages above the LARYNX, the shape of which is the main factor affecting the QUALITY of speech sounds. It can be divided into the NASAL tract (the air passage above the soft PALATE, within the nose) and the ORAL tract (the mouth and pharyngeal areas, or CAVITIES). In a more general application, the term is used in the sense of VOCAL ORGANS, including all the features of the respiratory tract involved in the production of sounds, i.e. lungs, trachea and LARYNX as well. See Catford 1977: Ch. 2; Ladefoged 1975: Ch. 1.

vocative In LANGUAGES which express GRAMMATICAL relationships by means of INFLECTIONS, this term refers to the CASE FORM taken by a WORD, usually a NOUN or PRONOUN, when it is used in the function of address (including both ANIMATE and inanimate entities). English does not make this distinction inflectionally, but does so using an optional noun PHRASE, in certain positions, and usually with a distinctive INTONATION, as in *John, are you coming?* See Quirk *et al* 1972: Ch. 7; Lyons 1968: Ch. 7.

vocoid A term invented by the American phonetician Kenneth Pike (b. 1912) to help distinguish between the PHONETIC and the PHONOLOGICAL notions of VOWEL. Phonetically, a vowel is defined as a sound lacking any CLOSURE or narrowing sufficient to produce audible FRICTION. Phonologically, it is a unit which functions at the centre of SYLLABLES. In cases such as [l], [r], [w] and [j], however, these criteria do not coincide: these sounds are phonetically vowel-like, but their function is CONSONANTAL. To avoid possible confusion, Pike proposed the term vocoid for sounds which are characterised by a phonetic definition such as the above; the term vowel is then reserved for the phonological sense. Its opposite is CONTOID. See Abercrombie 1967: Ch. 5; Gimson 1970: Ch. 4.

voice (voic-ing, -ed, -eless, de-, un-) (1) A fundamental term used in the PHONETIC classification of speech sounds, referring to the auditory result of the vibration of the VOCAL CORDS. Sounds produced while the vocal cords are vibrating are **voiced** sounds, e.g. [b, z, a, i]; those produced with no such vibration are **voiceless** or **unvoiced**, e.g. [p, s, h]. A sound which is normally voiced, but which in a particular phonetic ENVIRONMENT is produced with less voice than elsewhere, or with no voice at all, is said to be **devoiced** (symbolised by a small circle beneath the symbol) – examples are the reduced voicing on voiced PLOSIVES in a word-final position, as in *bib, bed* [bɪb̥], [bed̥].

This contrast is considered to be of primary significance in phonological analysis, and is used as a main parameter of classification both in PHONEMIC and DISTINCTIVE FEATURE theories of PHONOLOGY. **Voiced**, for example, is one of the SOURCE FEATURES of sound set up by CHOMSKY & Halle in their phonological theory. Voiced sounds are defined ARTICULATORILY, as those where the vocal cords are in a position which will enable them to vibrate in an air flow. Its opposite is **non-voiced** (or 'voiceless'), referring to sounds where vocal cord vibration is impossible, because of the wide gap between them.

Voice onset time (VOT) is a term used in PHONETICS, referring to the point in time at which VOCAL CORD vibration starts, following the release of a CLOSURE. In a fully VOICED PLOSIVE, for example, the vocal cords vibrate throughout; in a voiceless unaspirated plosive, there is a delay before the voicing starts; in a voiceless aspirated plosive, the delay is much longer, depending on the amount of ASPIRATION. The amount of the delay, in relation to the types of plosive, varies from language to language. See Ladefoged 1975: Chs. 6, 11; Hyman 1975: Ch. 2.

(2) A CATEGORY used in the GRAMMATICAL description of SENTENCE or CLAUSE structure, primarily with reference to VERBS, to express the way sentences may alter the relationship between the SUBJECT and OBJECT of a verb, without changing the meaning of the sentence. The main distinction is between ACTIVE and PASSIVE, as illustrated by *The cat bit the dog* and *The dog was bitten by the cat*: in the first sentence, the grammatical subject is also the actor; in the second sentence the grammatical subject is the goal of the action – it is 'acted upon', and thus 'passive'. There will be certain differences in the emphasis or style of these sentences, which will affect the speaker's choice, but the factual content of the two sentences remains the same. In other languages, further contrasts in voice may be encountered, e.g. the 'middle' voice of Greek (which included verbs with a REFLEXIVE meaning, e.g. *He cut himself*), and there are several other types of construction whose role in language is related to that of voice, e.g. 'reflexive', CAUSATIVE, 'impersonal' constructions. Voice contrasts may be formally marked in the verb (e.g. by INFLECTION), WORD order or the use of special AUXILIARIES), or elsewhere in the sentence (e.g. by the use of a passive 'agent'); the English passive can involve all three factors, as in *I was kicked by a bull*. See Lyons 1968: Ch. 8; Quirk *et al* 1972: Ch. 12.

voice dynamics A term used by some PHONETICIANS as a collective term to refer to vocal effects other than VOICE QUALITY and SEGMENTAL features, e.g. LOUDNESS, TEMPO, RHYTHM, REGISTER. These effects are capable of differentiating MEANINGS and SPEECH-communities, and are thus held to be within the purview of LINGUISTICS. See Abercrombie 1967: Ch. 6.

voice-print A display of a person's voice based upon a SPECTROGRAPHIC or similar output. The analogy is with the term 'fingerprint', and the claim is sometimes made that a person's voice is as individual as his fingerprints. Several legal cases have in fact used voiceprints as evidence of speaker identification. But while there are several idiosyncratic features in a spectrogram of a person's voice, it is not the case that such displays are always unequivocal indications of identity. It is often difficult to compare and interpret sets of spectrographic features, and the limitations of the display techniques used must always be borne in mind. See Ladefoged 1975: Ch. 8.

voice/vocal qualifier A term used by some linguists as part of their analysis of the PARALINGUISTIC features of the voice. Examples are the expression of various emotional states, such as anger or sarcasm, by means of vocal effects such as a 'harsh' or 'tense' quality – effects which are sometimes specific to individual languages. The term VOICE QUALITY is sometimes used in a general sense to include these effects. See Crystal 1969: Ch. 3.

voice quality/set A term used in PHONETICS to refer to the permanently present, background, person-identifying feature of speech. All phonetic features contribute to this notion: an individual's voice quality derives from a combination of such factors as PITCH height, LOUDNESS level, TEMPO and TIMBRE of speaking. Labels for the many qualities that can be produced tend to be impressionistic and ambiguous, e.g. a 'cheery', 'haughty', 'sullen' voice. A terminological problem also arises because such labels may be used in both a non-linguistic way (as described above) and in a LINGUISTIC or PARALINGUISTIC context, as when someone who normally does not have a voice one would call 'sullen' deliberately adopts such a voice to communicate a particular emotional state. To classify such latter effects, terms such as VOICE QUALIFIER or paralinguistic feature are available, but 'voice quality' is also commonly used. See Crystal 1969: Ch. 3; Lyons 1977b: Ch. 3.

VOT The usual abbreviation for 'VOICE onset time'.

vowel One of the two general categories used for the classification of speech sounds, the other being CONSONANT. Vowels can be defined in terms of both PHONETICS and PHONOLOGY. Phonetically, they are sounds articulated without a complete CLOSURE in the mouth or a degree of narrowing which would produce audible FRICTION; the air escapes evenly over the centre of the TONGUE. If air escapes solely through the mouth, the vowels are said to be ORAL; if some air is simultaneously released through the nose, the vowels are NASAL. In addition to this, in a phonetic classification of vowels, reference would generally be made to two variables, the first of which is easily describable, the second much less so: (a) the position of the lips – whether rounded, spread, or neutral; (b) which part of the tongue is raised, and the height to which it moves.

Relatively slight movements of the tongue produce quite distinct auditory differences in **vowel quality**. Because it is very difficult to see or feel these movements, classification of vowels is usually carried out using ACOUSTIC or AUDITORY criteria, supplemented by details of lip position. There are several systems for representing vowel position visually, e.g. in terms of a 'vowel triangle', or a 'vowel quadrilateral' such as the CARDINAL VOWEL system.

These sounds are usually voiced, though some languages have been analysed as having 'voiceless' vowels, e.g. Portuguese. From a phonological point of view, vowels are those units which function at the CENTRE of syllables. In some approaches, the term 'vowel' is reserved for the phonological level of analysis; VOCOID is then used for the phonetic level (as opposed to CONTOID, for the phonetic equivalent of a consonant). The usefulness of this distinction is in relation to those sounds which are vowel-like in articulation, but which function as consonants in syllables: [r], for example, is phonetically very similar to a vowel, but it occurs at the margins of syllables, as in *red*, *car*. In such cases, it is sometimes clearer to talk of a 'vocoid with consonantal function'.

In establishing the **vowel system** of a language, several further dimensions of classification may be used. One criterion is in terms of the duration of the vowel (whether relatively 'long' or 'short' vowels are used). Another is whether, during an articulation, there is any detectable change in quality. If the quality of a vowel stays unchanged the term **pure vowel**, or MONOPHTHONG, is used, e.g. the standard British pronunciation of *red*, *car*, *sit*, *seat*. If there is an evident change in quality, one talks instead of a **gliding vowel.** If two auditory elements are involved, the vowel GLIDE is referred to as a DIPHTHONG, e.g. *light*, *say*, *go*; if three elements, as a TRIPHTHONG, e.g. *fire*, *hour* (in some pronunciations).

Yet another way of classifying vowels is in terms of the amount of muscular TENSION required to produce them: vowels articulated in extreme positions are more 'tense' than those articulated nearer the centre of the mouth, which are 'lax': cf. *seat* vs. *sit*, *flute* vs. *foot*.

Vowel harmony is a term used to describe a phonological pattern in some languages, where all the vowels in a word share certain features, e.g. they are all articulated with the front of the tongue, or all are rounded. Turkish illustrates such patterns (though requiring a more complex statement of the relationship between the phonetic variables).

In the DISTINCTIVE FEATURE theory of phonology, the term VOCALIC is used as the main feature in the analysis of vowel sounds. See Gimson 1970: Chs. 4, 5, 7; Robins 1971: Ch. 4; Ladefoged 1975: Ch. 9.

VP The usual abbreviation for VERB PHRASE, and encountered especially in the opening RULES of a GENERATIVE GRAMMAR.

W

wave (1) A term used in HISTORICAL linguistics and SOCIOLINGUISTICS as part of a DYNAMIC MODEL of LANGUAGE change: **wave theory** suggests that speech variations spread from a specific linguistic area, having maximum effect on adjacent languages, and progressively less effect on languages further away – in much the same way that waves in water radiate from a central point of contact. See Bolinger 1975: Ch. 13.

(2) A term used in TAGMEMIC GRAMMAR as one mode of the analysis of linguistic UNITS: in the 'wave' mode, units at any LEVEL are analysed in terms of their status as VARIANTS MANIFESTED in different CONTEXTS, e.g. MORPHEMIC or TRANSFORMATIONAL processes. This mode is contrasted with the analysis of units in terms of PARTICLES and FIELDS. See Bolinger 1975: Ch. 15.

weak form One of two possible pronunciations for a WORD, in the context of CONNECTED SPEECH, the other being STRONG. The weak form is that which is the result of a word being UNSTRESSED as in the normal pronunciation of *of* in *cup of tea*, and in most other GRAMMATICAL WORDS. Several words in English have more than one weak form, e.g. *and* [ænd] can be [ənd], [ən], [n], etc. See Gimson 1970: Ch. 10.

well-formed(-ness) A term used in LINGUISTICS, especially in GENERATIVE grammar, to refer to the GRAMMATICALITY ('well-formedness') of a SENTENCE. A sentence is well-formed if it can be generated by the RULES of a grammar; it is **ill-formed** if it cannot be. The term applies equally to SYNTAX, SEMANTICS and PHONOLOGY. See Lyons 1977a: Ch. 5; Huddleston 1976: Ch. 1.

whistle-speech A term used in LINGUISTICS to refer to a stylised form of COMMUNICATION, in which whistling substitutes for the TONES of normal SPEECH. In some DIALECTS (such as Mazatec, in Mexico), quite sophisticated conversations have been observed to take place using whistle-speech. An analogous system of communication is drum-signalling. See Bolinger 1975: Ch. 3.

whiz-deletion A term sometimes used in GENERATIVE GRAMMAR to refer to a TRANSFORMATIONAL RULE which DELETES a RELATIVE PRONOUN and its associated VERB from a relative CLAUSE to produce a POSTmodifying PHRASE. e.g. *the man **who was** in the street* becoming *the man in the street*. See Huddleston 1976: Ch. 7.

Whorfian Characteristic of, or a follower of, the views of Benjamin Lee Whorf (1897–1941), especially as propounded in the **Whorfian hypothesis** (alternatively, the SAPIR–WHORF HYPOTHESIS), which states that our conceptual categorisation of the world is determined (wholly or partly) by the STRUCTURE of our native LANGUAGE. In its strong form, the hypothesis is not accepted by most LINGUISTS. See Clark & Clark 1977: Ch. 14; Bolinger 1975: Ch. 8.

wh-question A term used in the GRAMMATICAL sub-classification of types of QUESTION to refer to a question beginning with an INTERROGATIVE word, such as *who*, *when* and *what*. These 'particular' or 'question-word' questions are contrasted with YES–NO questions. See Quirk *et al* 1972: Ch. 7.

word A unit of expression which has universal intuitive recognition by NATIVE-SPEAKERS, both in spoken and written language. However, there are several difficulties in arriving at a consistent use of the term in relation to other CATEGORIES of linguistic description, and in the comparison of languages of different structural types. These problems relate mainly to word identification and definition. They include, for example, decisions over word boundaries (e.g. is a unit such as *washing machine* two words, or is it one, to be written *washing-machine*?), as well as decisions over status (e.g. is *the* a word in the same sense as is *chair*?). Regular definitions of words as 'units of meaning' or 'ideas' are of no help, because of the vagueness of such notions as 'idea'. As a result, several theoretical distinctions have been made.

Three main senses of 'word' are usually distinguished (though terminology varies).

(1) Words are the physically definable units which one encounters in a stretch of writing (bounded by spaces) or speech (where identification is more difficult, but where there may be PHONOLOGICAL clues to identify boundaries, such as a PAUSE, or JUNCTURE features). 'Word' in this sense is often referred to as the 'orthographic word'

(for writing) or the 'phonological word' (for speech). A neutral term often used to subsume both is **word-form**.

(2) There is a more abstract sense, referring to the common factor underlying the set of forms which are plainly VARIANTS of the same unit, such as *walk, walks, walking, walked*. The 'underlying' word unit is often referred to as a LEXEME. Lexemes are the units of VOCABULARY, and as such would be listed in a dictionary.

(3) This then leaves the need for a comparably abstract unit to be set up to show how words work in the GRAMMAR of a language, and 'word', without qualification, is usually reserved for this role (alternatively, one may spell out this implication, referring to 'MORPHEMIC/MORPHOSYNTACTIC/GRAMMATICAL' words, though the latter has an alternative sense). A word, then, is a grammatical unit, of the same theoretical kind as MORPHEME and SENTENCE. In a HIERARCHICAL model of analysis, sentences (clauses, etc.) consist of words, and words consist of morphemes (minimally, one free morpheme). **Word order** refers to the sequential arrangement of words in a language. Languages are sometimes classified in terms of whether their word order is relatively 'free' (as in Latin) or 'fixed' (as in English).

Several criteria have been suggested for the identification of words in speech (criteria which would also apply to the written language as well, if they were needed). One is that words are the most stable of all linguistic units, in respect of their internal structure, i.e. the CONSTITUENT parts of a complex word have little potential for rearrangement, compared with the relative POSITIONAL MOBILITY of the constituents of sentences and other grammatical structures (cf. *disestablishment*, where the sequence of *dis-establish-ment* is fixed, and *all boys like girls*, where many alternative sequences are possible, e.g. *boys all like girls*). A second criterion refers to the relative 'uninterruptibility', or COHESIVENESS of words, i.e. new elements (including pauses) cannot usually be inserted within them in normal speech: pauses, by contrast, are always potentially present at word boundaries. A criterion which has influenced linguists' views of the word since it was first suggested by Leonard BLOOMFIELD is the definition of word as a 'minimum free form', i.e. the smallest unit which can constitute, by itself, a complete utterance (it contrasts here with SENTENCE, seen as the maximum free form recognised by most grammars). On this basis, *possibility* is a word, as is *possible* (contexts could be constructed which would enable such units to occur as single-element sentences, e.g. *Is that a probable outcome? Possible.*), but -*ity* is not (nor would any affix be). Not all word-like units satisfy this criterion, however (e.g. *a* and *the* in English), and how to handle these has been the subject of considerable discussion.

Several general sub-classifications of words have been proposed, such as the distinction between VARIABLE and invariable types, GRAMMATICAL (or FUNCTION) words vs. LEXICAL words, CLOSED-CLASS vs. OPEN-CLASS words. At a more specific level, **word classes** can be established, by analysing the various GRAMMATICAL, SEMANTIC and PHONOLOGICAL properties displayed by the words in a language, and grouping words into classes on the basis of formal similarities (e.g. their INFLECTIONS and DISTRIBUTION). The results are analogous to the traditional notion of 'parts of speech', but word classes usually display a wider range of more precisely defined classes, e.g. PARTICLES, AUXILIARIES, etc. alongside NOUNS, VERBS, etc., and lack the vagueness of many of the traditional NOTIONAL definitions (e.g. a noun as the 'name of person, place or thing'). The study of the structure and composition of words (cf. WORD-FORMATION) is carried on by MOR-PHOLOGY. The study of the ARRANGEMENTS of words in sentences is the province of SYNTAX. See Robins 1971: Ch. 5; Matthews 1974: Chs. 2, 9; Lyons 1968: Ch. 5.

word and paradigm (WP) A MORPHOLOGICAL MODEL of description which sees the WORD as the basic UNIT of analysis, operating within a set of variables which constitute a PARADIGM. This is the traditional model of description, as illustrated from Latin GRAMMARS (e.g. *amo, amas, amat,...* constitutes the paradigm of the LEXEME *amo*). WP is seen as a major alternative to the two other main approaches to morphological analysis: ITEM AND PROCESS, and ITEM AND ARRANGE-MENT. In contrast to the traditional use of paradigms in LANGUAGE study, linguistics does not arbitrarily choose one form of a word (the 'leading form') as given, and derive the rest of the paradigm from this (the student usually learning it by rote); rather, the aim is to define a common factor (a ROOT or STEM) within the paradigm, neutral with respect to the variant forms of the paradigm, and to derive the VARIANT forms from this, e.g. using rules. See Matthews 1974: Ch. 4.

word-formation In its most general sense, the term refers to the whole process of MORPHOLOGICAL variation in the constitution of WORDS, i.e. including the two main divisions of INFLECTION (word variations signalling GRAMMATICAL relationships) and DERIVATION (word varia-tions signalling LEXICAL relationships). In a more restricted sense, word-formation refers to the latter processes only, these being sub-classified into such types as 'compositional' or 'compound' (e.g.

blackbird from the free elements *black + bird*), and 'derivational' (e.g. *national, nationalise,* etc. from the addition of the bound elements *-al, -ise,* etc.). Several possibilities of further sub-classification are available in the literature on this subject. See Matthews 1974: Ch. 3; Lyons 1968: Ch. 5; Quirk *et al* 1972: App. 1.

word order A term used in GRAMMATICAL analysis to refer to the SEQUENTIAL arrangement of WORDS in larger linguistic UNITS. Some LANGUAGES (e.g. English) rely on word order as a means of expressing grammatical relationships within CONSTRUCTIONS; in others (e.g. Latin) word order is more flexible, as grammatical relations are signalled by INFLECTIONS. See Robins 1971: Ch. 6.

WP The usual abbreviation for the WORD AND PARADIGM model of description in PHONOLOGY.

wugs A nonsense word invented in the late 1950s for a LANGUAGE ACQUISITION experiment into the learning of MORPHOLOGY. The drawing of a mythical animal (a *wug*) was presented to children, and the child was told: 'This is a wug'. Then the experimenter would point to a second picture, saying 'Now, there's another one. There are two of them. There are two —'. If the child had learned the plural ending, he would say *wugs*; if he had not, he would say *wug*. Using several such NONSENSE words in a range of morphological CONTEXTS, much basic information was obtained concerning the order and timing of the acquisition of GRAMMATICAL MORPHEMES. See Clark & Clark 1977: Ch. 9.

Y

⦿⦿⦿⦿⦿⦿

yes–no question A term used in the GRAMMATICAL sub-classification of types of QUESTION to refer to a question form where a grammatical reply would have to be of the type *yes* or *no*. It is formally marked by INVERTED SUBJECT–VERB order, e.g. *is he coming?* These 'general' or 'inverted order' questions are contrasted with WH-QUESTIONS. See Quirk *et al* 1972: Ch. 7.

Z

⧟⧟⧟⧟⧟⧟

zero A term used in some areas of LINGUISTICS to refer to an abstract unit postulated by an analysis, but which has no physical realisation in the stream of speech. Its symbol is ϕ. In English MORPHOLOGY, for example, the pressure of the grammatical system to analyse plurals as Noun + plural has led some linguists to analyse unchanged nouns, such as *sheep* and *deer* as Noun + plural also, the plurality in these cases being realised as zero (a **zero morph**). A 'zero operation' of this kind is also called an 'identity operation', one where the input and the output of the operation are identical. Similarly, in other grammatical CONTEXTS where a given MORPHEME usually occurs, the absence of that morpheme under certain conditions may be referred to as zero, e.g. **zero-article**, referring to the absence of a definite or indefinite article before a noun; or **zero-connectors**, as in *he said he was coming*, where *that* is omitted. In cases such as *he's laughing, is he*, some linguists analyse the second part of the sentence as a REDUCED form of the verb phrase *is he laughing*, referring to the omitted part by the term **zero anaphora**. Zero is also found in PHONOLOGICAL analysis, e.g. in a conception of some types of JUNCTURE as **zero phonemes**, or to suggest a structural parallelism between SYLLABLE types (a CV sequence being seen as a CVC sequence, with the final C being zero).

Zero is especially encountered in the formulation of GENERATIVE RULES, where the term refers to an item deleted from a given context (a 'DELETION-rule'). Such rules are of the type 'rewrite A as zero, in the CONTEXT X — Y' (A $\rightarrow \phi$/X — Y), and they apply in GRAMMAR, SEMANTICS and PHONOLOGY.

It is plain that the introduction of zero (sometimes referred to as the **null** element, deriving from the use of this term in mathematics) is motivated by the need to maintain a proportionality, or regular pattern, in one's analysis, or in the interests of devising an economical statement. It is also a notion which has to be introduced with careful justification; too many zeros in an analysis weaken its plausibility. See Matthews 1974: Ch. 7; Robins 1971: Ch. 5.

zoösemiotics A branch of SEMIOTICS that studies the features of human COMMUNICATION which, as the end products of an evolutionary series, are shared with animal systems of communication; opposed to 'anthroposemiotic' features, which are exclusively human. Under the heading of 'zoösemiotic features/systems' fall certain features of tone of voice (cf. PARALANGUAGE), facial expression, gesture, etc. (cf. KINESICS, PROXEMICS), as well as several mechanisms of animal communication which seem not to overlap with human signalling systems (e.g. chemical signals (pheromones), echolocation). See Lyons 1977b: Ch. 3.

REFERENCES

Abercrombie, D. 1967. *Elements of general phonetics.* Edinburgh University Press.
Akmajian, A. & Heny, F. 1975. *An introduction to the principles of transformational syntax.* M.I.T. Press.
Bolinger, D. L. 1975. *Aspects of language.* 2nd edn. Harcourt Brace Jovanovich.
Catford, J. C. 1977. *Fundamental problems in phonetics.* Edinburgh University Press.
Clark, H. H. & Clark, E. V. 1977. *Psychology and language.* Harcourt Brace Jovanovich.
Corder, S. P. 1973. *Introducing applied linguistics.* Penguin.
Crystal, D. 1969. *Prosodic systems and intonation in English.* Cambridge University Press.
Dinneen, F. P. 1967. *An introduction to general linguistics.* Holt, Rinehart & Winston.
Gimson, A. C. 1970. *An introduction to the pronunciation of English.* 2nd edn. Longman.
Gumperz, J. J. & Hymes, D. 1972. *Directions in sociolinguistics: the ethnography of communication.* Holt, Rinehart & Winston.
Huddleston, R. 1976. *An introduction to English transformational syntax.* Longman.
Hyman, L. M. 1975. *Phonology, theory and analysis.* Holt, Rinehart & Winston.
Ladefoged, P. 1975. *A course in phonetics.* Harcourt Brace Jovanovich.
Lyons, J. 1968. *Introduction to theoretical linguistics.* Cambridge University Press.
    1977a. *Chomsky.* Fontana.
    1977b. *Semantics.* Vols. I, II. Cambridge University Press.
Matthews, P. H. 1974. *Morphology.* Cambridge University Press.
Palmer, F. R. 1971. *Grammar.* Penguin.
Quirk, R., Greenbaum, S., Leech, G. & Svartvik, J. 1972. *A grammar of contemporary English.* Longman.
Radford, A. 1981. *Generative grammar in the 1970s* (working title). Faber & Faber.
Robins, R. H. 1971. *General linguistics: an introductory survey.* 2nd edn. Longman.
Trudgill, P. 1975. *Sociolinguistics: an introduction.* Penguin.